INTERCULTURAL COMMUNICATION

A TEXT WITH READINGS

PAMELA J. COOPER

UNIVERSITY OF SOUTH CAROLINA BEAUFORT

CAROLYN CALLOWAY-THOMAS

INDIANA UNIVERSITY

CHERI J. SIMONDS

ILLINOIS STATE UNIVERSITY

PEARSON

Boston   New York   San Francisco
Mexico City   Montreal   Toronto   London   Madrid   Munich   Paris
Hong Kong   Singapore   Tokyo   Cape Town   Sydney

Special thanks to J. Richard Hoel, Jr.
for his support of this text/reader—not only his narratives and articles
but also his insights. Rick, you are a prince, not a toad!

Editor-in-Chief, Communication: Karon Bowers
Series Editorial Assistant: Jenny Lupica
Marketing Manager: Suzan Czajkowski
Editorial-Production Service: Omegatype Typography, Inc.
Composition Buyer: Linda Cox
Manufacturing Buyer: JoAnne Sweeney
Electronic Composition: Omegatype Typography, Inc.
Cover Administrator: Joel Gendron

For related titles and support materials, visit our online catalog at www.ablongman.com.

Between the time website information is gathered and then published, it is not unusual for some sites to have closed. Also, the transcription of URLs can result in unintended typographical errors. The publisher would appreciate notification where these errors occur so that they may be corrected in subsequent editions.

ISBN-13:   978-0-205-57946-4
ISBN-10:   0-205-57946-9

Printed in the United States of America

10 9 8 7 6 5 4 3 2 1   11 10 09 08 07

CONTENTS

Preface *xi*

SECTION ONE   Foundations

CHAPTER 1   COMMUNICATION AND CULTURE   1

- A Frog in the Well   1
- Objectives   2

What Is Communication?   3
What Is Culture?   6
What Is Intercultural Communication?   7
A Narrative Approach to Intercultural Communication   7

- Conclusion   10
- For Discussion   10
- References   10

READING

**Coloring Books, Video Recorders, and Sandpaper:
Three Cultural Metaphors** *by Lucy Shahar and David Kurz*   11

- Chapter Activities   17

CHAPTER 2   CULTURAL PATTERNS   19

- Balinese Patterns: Cremations and Villages   19
- Objectives   20

Beliefs, Values, and Norms   20
Approaches to Studying Cultural Patterns   21

Florence Kluckhohn and Frederick Strodtbeck   22
Edward Hall   25
Geert Hofstede   26
Michael Bond   29

- Conclusion   32
- For Discussion   32
- References   32

READING

Cultural Assumptions and Values *by Edward C. Stewart,
Jack Danielian, and Robert J. Foster*   **33**

- Chapter Activities   40

iii

SECTION TWO   Processes

CHAPTER 3   PERCEPTION   42

- We and They *by Rudyard Kipling*   42
- Objectives   42

The Perception Process   42
Components of the Perception Process   43
Culture and Perception   43
Ethnocentrism   43
Cultural Relativism   44
Social Cognition   45
The Situation   45
The People   45
The Relationship   46
The Behavior   47
Making Accurate Attributions   49
Stereotypes   50
Prejudice, Discrimination, and Racism   52
Prejudice   52
Discrimination   53
Racism   53
- Conclusion   53
- For Discussion   54
- References   54

READINGS

The Psychological Process: Perception and Reasoning *by Glen Fisher*   **56**

Communication in Personal Relationships in Iran: A Comparative Analysis *by Fred Zandpour and Golnaz Sadri*   **64**

- Chapter Activities   69

CHAPTER 4   CULTURAL IDENTITY   70

- Spinning Wheels, Bobbins, Wool, and Lace   70
- Objectives   70

Defining Cultural Identity   71
Formation of Cultural Identity   72
Characteristics of Cultural Identity   72
Patriarchy and Gender   73
Ethnicity   74
Regional Factors   78
Religion   79
Class   80
Language, Class, and Cultural Identity   83
Grammar and Class   83
Cultural Identity and Nonverbal Markers   85
Personal Identity   86

- Conclusion   87
- For Discussion   87
- References   87

READINGS

Disgrace, Culture, and Identity Construction in South Africa
by Carolyn Calloway-Thomas and Jack E. Thomas   **89**

**Gender, Masculinities, Identities, and Interpersonal Relationship Systems:
Men in General and Gay Men in Particular** *by James W. Chesebro*   **97**

- Chapter Activities   102

| CHAPTER 5 | VERBAL INTERCULTURAL COMMUNICATION | 103 |

- Frustration, Misunderstanding, Laughter   103
- Objectives   104

What Is Language?   **104**
The Structure of Language   **105**
Semantics   **106**
Pragmatics   **107**
Language and Culture   **108**
Verbal Communication Styles   **109**

Direct versus Indirect Style   *110*
Elaborate versus Succinct Style   *110*
Personal versus Contextual Style   *110*
Instrumental versus Affective Style   *111*

Linguistic Prejudice   **111**

- Conclusion   112
- For Discussion   112
- References   112

READINGS

**Multiple Perspectives: African American Women Conceive
Their Talk** *by Marsha Houston*   **113**

Intercultural Conflict: A Culture-Based Situational Model
by Stella Ting-Toomey and John Oetzel   **121**

- Chapter Activities   131

| CHAPTER 6 | NONVERBAL INTERCULTURAL COMMUNICATION | 132 |

- Shopping with the Bedouins   132
- Objectives   133

Importance of Nonverbal Communication   **133**
Universality of Nonverbal Communication   **133**
Functions of Nonverbal Communication   **134**
Nonverbal Communication Codes   **135**

Kinesics   *135*
Chronemics   *136*
Proxemics   *136*

Haptics   *138*
Artifacts   *139*
Physical Characteristics   *139*
Paralanguage   *140*
- Conclusion   140
- For Discussion   141
- References   141

READINGS

Virtual Grave Sites Play Host to Filial But Busy Chinese *by Matt Forney*   **142**
Bound by Beauty: Narratives of Chinese Footbinding *by Pamela Cooper*   **143**
- Chapter Activities   148

CHAPTER 7   LISTENING   149

- Listening in a Japanese Garden   149
- Objectives   150

Definition of Listening   150
HURIER Model   150

Hearing   *150*
Understanding   *150*
Remembering   *150*
Interpreting   *151*
Evaluating   *151*
Responding   *151*

Importance of Active Listening   151
Levels of Listening   152

Intrapersonal   *152*
Interpersonal   *152*
Intracultural   *152*

Barriers to Effective Listening   153
Effective Listening across Cultures   153
- Conclusion   154
- For Discussion   155
- References   155

READING

Perspectives on Intercultural Listening *by Melissa Beall*   **155**
- Chapter Activities   162

SECTION THREE   Contexts

CHAPTER 8   FAMILY AND FRIENDS   163

- The Spaces in Between *by Laura Elizabeth Pearson Cooper*   163
- Objectives   163

Defining Relationships   163

Universal Dimensions of Relationships   **164**
Relationship Development   **164**

Knapp and Vangelisti's Model of Relationship Development   *164*
Chen's Model of Relationship Development   *165*

Families   **167**
Friends   **169**

■ Conclusion   170
■ For Discussion   170
■ References   171

READINGS

**Mate Selection among Asian Indians Living in America: A Quest
for Traditional Ritual** *by Archana J. Bhatt*   **172**

**It's Not All Blarney: Intergenerational Transmission of Communication Patterns
in Irish American Families** *by Kathleen Galvin*   **181**

■ Chapter Activities   192

CHAPTER 9   **EDUCATION**   **193**

■ Why Can't We Discuss It?   193
■ Objectives   194

Functions of Schools   **194**
Cultural Dimensions   **195**
Recognizing Differences in Learning   **197**
Understanding Cultural Differences   **199**
Communicating Effectively in an Intercultural Classroom   **199**

■ Conclusion   201
■ For Discussion   201
■ References   201

READING

**There's a Lizard in My Living Room and a Pigeon in My Classroom: A Personal
Reflection on What It Takes to Teach in a Different Culture** *by Janet MacLennan*   **203**

■ Chapter Activities   208

CHAPTER 10   **ECONOMICS, BUSINESS,
AND INTERCULTURAL COMMUNICATION**   **209**

■ How Do I Criticize? Let Me Count the Ways *by Rick Hoel*   209
■ Objectives   210

Economic Global Transformations   **210**
New People in the Workplace   **211**
Changing Concept of Global Economic Community   **213**
Uncertainty Reduction   **213**
Using Economic Arrangements to Explain Intercultural Communication   **215**

Values and Lifestyle Patterns   *215*
Information and Decision Making   *215*

Intercultural Communication in the Business Context   216
   Language   216
   Relationships   216
   Evidence, Reasoning, and Persuasive Style   217
Questions to Consider When Doing Business Internationally   218
- Conclusion   219
- For Discussion   220
- References   220

READINGS

The Cultural Practice of Law or How to Successfully Do a Deal in a Foreign Jurisdiction *by J. Richard Hoel, Jr.*   221
"Even the White Ants Confer Before They Scatter": The Use of the Proverb in West African Peacemaking Traditions *by Mary Adams Trujillo*   231
- Chapter Activities   236

CHAPTER 11   HEALTH   238

- The Malaysian Doctor   238
- Objectives   239
Health Belief Systems   240
   Biomedical System   240
   Personalistic System   240
   Naturalistic System   240
Intercultural Barriers of Effective Health Care   240
   Family   242
   Gender   244
   Power   245
   Religion and Spirituality   246
   Ethical Issues   250
- Conclusion   252
- For Discussion   252
- References   252

READINGS

Do Doctors Eat Brains? *by Anne Fadiman*   254
Telling Multicultural Tales in Applied Contexts: Unexpected Journeys into Healing and Interconnectedness in Hospitals and Courtrooms *by Sunwolf*   256
- Chapter Activities   267

CHAPTER 12   MEDIA AND TECHNOLOGY   268

- A Cell Phone on the Great Wall?   268
- Objectives   268
Popular Culture   268
Norms and the Media   272
Gender, Class, Race, and the Media   272
   Gender   272
   Class   273
   Race   274

Media and Power   276
Advertising and the Media   277
Culture and the Internet   278
  Communities of Access and Interaction   279
  Language and Cyberspace   279
International Dimensions and Flow of Information   280
■ Conclusion   281
■ For Discussion   281
■ References   282

READING

Perceived Typicality: American Television as Seen by Mexicans, Turks, and Americans *by Alice Hall, Todd Anten, and Idil Cakim*   **283**
■ Chapter Activities   289

SECTION IV   Intercultural Communication Competence

CHAPTER 13   ETHICS   291

■ Can I Keep the Diamond Bracelet?   291
■ Objectives   291

Ethics Defined   291
Moral Reasoning   292
Principles and Rules of Intercultural Communication   293
  Principles   293
  Rules   294
■ Conclusion   295
■ For Discussion   295
■ References   295

READING

Building on Ethical Conflicts *by J. Richard Hoel, Jr.*   **296**
■ Chapter Activities   297

CHAPTER 14   DEVELOPING INTERCULTURAL COMPETENCE   298

■ Competency Practices *by J. Richard Hoel, Jr.*   298
■ Objectives   299

Factors Shaping Individual Ability   299
  An Appreciative Orientation   300
  Empathy   300
Factors Influencing Intercultural Competence: A Synthesis   300
  Knowledge of Self   300
  Sociocultural Roots   302
  Family   302
  Economics   303
  Political   304
  Stereotypes and Prejudices   305

Religion   305
Language and Context   306
Local and Global Dimensions   307
Improving Intercultural Communication Competence   307
Framing an Approach to Intercultural Competence   307
Ten Basic Rules of Intercultural Effectiveness   310
- Conclusion   310
- For Discussion   311
- References   311

READINGS

Stumbling Blocks in Intercultural Communication *by LaRay M. Barna*   **312**
Communication Competence Problematic in Ethnic Friendships
by Mary Jane Collier   **320**
- Chapter Activities   332

Index   333

PREFACE

We all tell stories. We all listen to stories. As Fisher suggests,* we humans are storytellers. We make sense of others and ourselves through stories. Only when we begin to hear the personal stories of others who have had similar experiences do we begin to be able to make sense of what happens to us as we travel to cultures other than our own.

Thus, this text/reader emphasizes a narrative approach to the study of intercultural communication. Numerous stories and examples are used to explain the concepts of each chapter. Each chapter begins with a narrative. Sometimes these are materials published elsewhere, but most often they are written from one of the authors' own experiences. Readings at the end of each chapter enhance the student's understanding of the material (or story, if you will) covered in the chapter. Each reading is followed by questions about the reading. The narratives, activities, readings, and questions focus on the student making the story of the material her or his own—answering the question, "How does this information fit into my story?"

Why a text/reader combination? If we want our students to understand both the depth and breadth of intercultural communication, we need to expose them to a variety of writings in the field of intercultural communication. The readings introduce students to research and theory as well as practical application of research and theory. However, unlike a text that does not provide full readings, and a reader that too often does not have enough background information to make the readings comprehensive to students, this text/reader combines the best of both a reader and a text. The text material written by the authors presents the foundations of intercultural communication and numerous personal stories and examples to help clarify ideas and principles. The readings provide additional stories to help students answer the question posed above.

We do not propose to be comprehensive in terms of covering all aspects of the field of intercultural communication or to be inclusive of the diversity of those writing in the area of intercultural communication. This is an impossible task for any book. However, this book does include a wide diversity of authors and topics necessary to provide the reader with an understanding of the depth and breadth of intercultural communication theory and practice and to introduce students to research in the field of intercultural communication in a unique and interesting way.

Rick Hoel, former General Counsel for Motorola, discusses the importance of stories in intercultural communication:

> My wife and I lived in Hong Kong in the early 1990s and I did legal work for a large U.S. multi-national company that manufactured and sold electronic and communication equipment. That period was a dynamic one for this industry in Asia particularly in China and as a result I spent a good deal of time negotiating large contracts with representatives of the Chinese government.
>
> My first such experience was both exciting and frustrating. I worked with a company team of six people and we met in Beijing with a similar team of seven from the PRC's Ministry of Posts and Telecommunications. We were there a week and the slow pace of discussions did not surprise me. I had heard repeatedly in my intercultural indoctrination courses back home about the importance that Asian cultures place upon establishing relationships. I could understand this.

*Fisher, W. (1989). *Human communication as narration: Toward a philosophy of reason, value and action.* Columbia: University of South Carolina Press.

Why *would* anyone want to do a deal with someone they did not know well? It became obvious to me that there was going to be a need to develop a certain degree of trust before we even got to the substantive issues we wanted to discuss and I was ready.

I had spent a great deal of time preparing overheads of charts and graphs explaining just what my company did and how successful it had been over the past 10 years in developing and marketing the products we wanted to sell to the Chinese. My entire team worked hard with these tools to impress our hosts with our company and its products. Despite our best efforts that first day however, our presentations simply didn't generate a lot of enthusiasm and I doubted whether or not we had an interested customer.

That evening during a conversation on the phone with my wife Pam, I expressed my frustration that little progress was being made. I told her that I felt like I was speaking often to a stone wall. She said "Tell them a story." I laughed and she said "Tell them about your company with a story and see what happens." I thought about this and agreed to try. I actually was familiar with a story about the struggles and successes of an early founder of the company as he worked to invent an electronic component and I scribbled some notes and went to bed.

The next morning I asked if it would be acceptable to put away our charts and graphs and tell my hosts a story about my company. They shrugged and I started. Within minutes, even through an interpreter, I could see the tension leave my counterparts and the level of interest increase. Fortified I threw a few jokes into the mix and the room unleashed its first decent laugh of the week. We were off and running.

I found that the story form of communication was effective and eventually reciprocated by our hosts. Of course the week had its ups and downs, but as we moved through our discussions I tried as often as I could to communicate in this form in both our formal and informal talks. Over dinner, I told stories about everything from George Washington and the cherry tree to my family cat's struggles with a neighborhood dog. When time came to discuss the relevant legal issues with the Chinese team's lawyer, we broke the ice by exchanging stories of some of the most interesting recent court decisions handed down in our respective countries. They had nothing to do with our deal but helped forge a personal understanding between two lawyers from very different systems.

Today, I always arm myself with as many stories and anecdotes as I can before starting a negotiation.

ACKNOWLEDGMENTS

We would like to thank the reviewers of this text for their helpful comments: Bernardo Attias, California State University at Northridge; Charles A. Braithwaite, University of Nebraska at Lincoln; Victoria Leonard, College of the Canyons; Sheryl D. Lidzy, Murray State University; C. Thomas Preston, University of North Carolina at Chapel Hill; and Ron Robin, Buffalo State University.

CHAPTER 1

COMMUNICATION AND CULTURE

A FROG IN THE WELL

Once upon a time, there was a frog who lived at the bottom of a deep, dark well. It was a very old well filled with shallow water at the bottom. The walls of the well were all covered with wet moss. When the little frog was thirsty, he drank a little bit of the well water, and when he was hungry, he ate some insects. When he was tired, he lay on a little rock at the bottom of the well and looked up at the sky above him. Sometimes he saw passing clouds. He was very happy and satisfied.

Now, the frog had been living at the bottom of this old well since he was born. He had never been to the outside world. Whenever a bird or birds flew by and stopped at the edge of the well, the little frog always looked up and bragged, "Hello! Why don't you come down here and play with me. It's so pleasant down here. Look, I have cool water to drink and countless insects to eat. Come down! At night I can watch the twinkling stars, and sometimes I can see the beautiful moon, too."

Sometimes the birds would tell the little frog, "Hi, Frog! You see, the outside world is much bigger and nicer. It's many times more beautiful than your little well at the bottom." But the frog would not believe them. "Don't lie to me! I don't believe there is any place that could be better than here."

It didn't take long for the birds to get disgusted with the frog's attitude. After all, they thought their world was the best. So, they stopped flying by Frog's well.

One day, a yellow sparrow stopped by at the edge of the well. The little frog was so excited he greeted the sparrow and invited the sparrow eagerly. "Hello, Mr. Yellow Sparrow, how are you? Please come down to my most beautiful house." The yellow sparrow did not say a word and flew away. This continued for several days. Finally, one day, the yellow sparrow said, "Frog, may I show you the outside world?" But the little frog refused the offer.

Now, the yellow sparrow became angry. He flew down to the bottom of the well, picked up the little frog on his back, and flew out of the well.

"Oh!" the little frog exclaimed. "How is it that the outside world is so big and so full of so many interesting things?" He asked the sparrow lots of questions and the sparrow explained to him the mountains, valleys, flowers, trees, rivers, and seas.

"How much bigger your world is than my well. Let me down so I can see better." So the sparrow flew close to the ground and the frog jumped into the grass and began to explore. He left the meadow of flowers and went into a forest. He looked up and saw tall trees; he looked down and found an apple that had fallen to the ground. He picked up an apple and tasted it. "Mmm. That's better than the insects at the bottom of my well!" He listened to the singing birds and watched the squirrels chase one another.

He came to a pond where fish were swimming and the lotus flowers were dancing in the air, and the lotus leaves were floating on the water like umbrellas.

"The outside world is so big, so wonderful, and beautiful!" shouted the frog as he jumped into the pond. He climbed up on a huge lotus leaf and decided to live in the pond instead of at the bottom of his well. One day the yellow sparrow came back and asked, "Frog! How's this outside world?"

"It is wonderful! Thank you! If you had not brought me out to see this world, I would never have known that there are such beautiful things that exist outside my well."

Proverb from the Writings of Zhuangzi

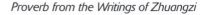

OBJECTIVES

After reading this chapter and completing the readings and activities, you should be able to

- Define communication.
- Explain the transactional model of communication.
- Define culture.
- Explain the relationship between communication and culture.
- Explain the narrative approach to intercultural communication.

The world is small and, in many respects, getting smaller. More than in any era previously, we have the ability, through travel, through the Internet, or by simply staying in our own communities, to come in contact with persons from all over the world. I was reminded of this when I visited my parents in Pelican Rapids, Minnesota. This small midwestern town of around 2,000 people boasts not only the "old-timers" of Western European descent, but in the last 10 years, Vietnamese, Bosnians, and Mexicans.

Often, we have a tendency to think of the entire world as much like the one in which we live. Table 1.1 illustrates what would happen if we could shrink the earth's population

---

TABLE 1.1 If the World Were a Village of 1,000 in the Year 2000

Population		Language	
East Asia & Pacific	354	Chinese, Mandarin	144
South Asia	224	Hindi	60
Sub-Saharan Africa	109	English	56
Latin America & Caribbean	85	Spanish	53
Europe & Central Asia	78	Bengali	34
Middle East & North Africa	49	Portuguese	29
Age & Gender		**Religion**	
Men	506	Christian	330
Women	494	Islam	215
0–14 years old	300	Hinduism	149
16–64 years old	631	Secular/Nonreligious	140
65 and older	69	Buddhism	59
Life expectancy	66	Judaism	2
Health & Education		**Wealth & Work**	
Access to clean water	800	Living in low-income nations	407
Access to sanitation	560	Living in high-income nations	157
Smokers	297	Men in workforce	287
HIV infected	11	Women in workforce	197
Illiterate women	93	Children in workforce	1
Illiterate men	52	Per capita income	$5,107
Land		**Infrastructure**	
Total	5,459	Electricity (KwH/person/year)	2,107
Per person	5.46	Radios	419
Forest area	1,621	Televisions	254
Arable land	573	Automobiles	141
Cropland	55	Telephone lines	136
Other	3,210	Computers	78

Source: Lloyd Russow, http://faculty.philau.ed/russowl/villageof1000.html.

to a village of 1,000 people, with all the existing human ratios remaining the same. In addition (Russow, 2006),

> North America would have 52 people. The population in the five largest countries would be: 208 in China, 168 in India, 47 in the United States, 35 in Indonesia and 28 in Brazil. Seventy-five percent of the population would live in 25 countries, at least 47 of today's nations would not be inhabited at all.
>
> There are 97 pre-school children, 286 between the ages of 5 and 19, and 42 people are over 70 (and of those, 4 men and 5 women are over 80).
>
> There would only be 15 religions in the world (secular/nonreligious is not included as one of these), four of which would have only one follower: Baha'I, Jainism, Shinto, and Cao Dai.
>
> Half the population of the villagers speak one of 20 languages (as opposed to the 6,000+ in the world today). The urban population is 470, the rural is 530, and 50 people are involved in agriculture.
>
> Of the 145 people who are illiterate, 143 live in developing nations and 106 live in Asia (36 men and 70 women). There are 238 men and 60 women who smoke. One new case of tuberculosis diagnosed every year.

When we consider our world from such a compressed perspective, the need for acceptance, understanding, and education becomes glaringly apparent. As the world shrinks, and our contact with people from other cultures expands, the need for competent communication increases. That is what this text/reader will help you do—understand the depth and breadth of intercultural communication. This chapter will define communication, culture, and intercultural communication.

WHAT IS COMMUNICATION?

The world shrinks, and paradoxically, the world expands. As we come in contact with people from cultures other than our own—in our neighborhoods, in our schools, in our churches, and in our workplaces—we begin to understand communication as a transactional process. Viewing communication as a transactional process means that we develop a mutually dependent relationship by exchanging symbols. This definition suggests several axioms or "truths" about communication. First, communication is a process. As such, it is symbolic, continuous, irreversible, and unrepeatable. We'll examine each of these in turn.

Communication is *symbolic*—we use symbols (verbal and nonverbal) to stand for things. General semanticists (people who study how language is used) suggest this idea when they state that the word is not the thing. In other words, the word *chair* stands for, or symbolizes, something we sit on. The word *chair* is not the actual chair. Also, one symbol may have many meanings. For example, when I say, "chair," do I mean a beach chair, or an easy chair, or a rocking chair? I may even mean the head of a committee—the "committee chair." This leads to an important truth about communication: Meanings are in people, not in words. Put another way, words do not have meaning, people do. We communicate via symbols that are arbitrary, abstract, and ambiguous representations of objects and ideas. The words are not the actual objects or ideas. We use these symbols—words and behaviors—to create meaning. In order for us to communicate effectively, we must have common meanings for these symbols. The problem is that meanings are not transferable, only messages are. I can say, "I love you" (that's the message), but I can't control your meaning for those words. As Combs and associates (1971) suggest, "The discovery of meaning . . . can only take place in people" (p. 91). Put another way, meanings are in people, not in words or behaviors. Imagine how difficult communication becomes when two people from two different cultures come together. Not only are their languages different, but the same gesture can mean different things. The meaning of patting a child on the head in the United States (a gesture of affection) is quite different from that same gesture in Thailand (you might damage the spirit of the child, which resides in her or his head).

At the beginning of this section communication was defined. That definition reflects how we—the authors—define communication. But there are numerous ways this word *communication* can be defined. Dance and Larson (1976) list over 125 definitions of this term. Yet despite these different definitions, most theorists agree on the properties of communication. Neuliep (2000) provides a summary of these, along with eight definitions of communication (see Table 1.2). Thus, if we are to communicate more effectively, then we have to come to an agreement about the meaning of words and nonverbal symbols. (We will discuss verbal and nonverbal communication in Chapters 5 and 6.)

Communication is not only symbolic, it is a process. A process has no beginning or end. In other words, it is *continuous*. All the communicating you have done affects the communication you are engaged in right now. Even if you and your instructor have never met prior to the beginning of this course, all your previous communication with other instructors (and your instructor's prior communication with all previous students) affects the communication between the two of you.

This suggests another important idea about communication. Because communication is symbolic and continuous, communication scholars suggest that you cannot not communicate. Anytime you are perceived by another person, you communicate—your clothes,

---

TABLE 1.2 Eight Properties and Definitions of Communication

1. Process	"Communication theory reflects a process point of view . . . you cannot talk about the beginning or the end of communication . . ." (Berlo)[1]
2. Dynamic	"Communication is a transaction among symbol users in which meanings are dynamic, changing as a function of earlier usages and of changes in perceptions and metaperceptions. Common to both meanings is the notion that communication is time-bound and irreversible." (Bowers and Bradac)[2]
3. Interactive/Transactive	"Communication occurs when two or more people interact through the exchange of messages." (Goss)[3]
4. Symbolic	". . . all the symbols of the mind, together with the means of conveying them through space and preserving them in time." (Cooley)[4]
5. Intentional	". . . communication has as its central interest those behavioral situations in which source transmits a message to a receiver(s) with conscious intent to affect the latter's behavior." (Miller)[5]
6. Contextual	"Communication always and inevitably occurs within some context." (Fisher)[6]
7. Ubiquitous	". . . communication is the discriminatory response of an organism to a stimulus." (Stevens)[7]
8. Cultural	". . . culture is communication . . . communication is culture." (Hall)[8]

1. D. K. Berlo, *The Process of Communication* (New York: Holt, Rinehart and Winston, 1960), p. 24.

2. J. W. Bowers and J. J. Bradac, "Issues in Communication Theory: A Metatheoretical Analysis," in *Communication Yearbook*, no. 5, ed. M. Burgoon (New Brunswick: Transaction Books, 1982), p. 3.

3. B. Goss, *Communication in Everyday Life* (Belmont, CA: Wadsworth, 1983).

4. C. Cooley, *Social Organization* (New York: Scribner, 1909), p. 61.

5. G. R. Miller, "On Defining Communication: Another Stab," *Journal of Communication*, 16, nos. 88–89 (1966), 92.

6. B. A. Fisher, *Interpersonal Communication: Pragmatics of Human Relationships* (New York: Random House, 1987), p. 22.

7. S. S. Stevens, "Introduction: A Definition of Communication," *The Journal of the Acoustical Society of America*, 22 (1959), 689.

8. E. T. Hall, *The Silent Language* (New York: Doubleday, 1959).

Source: James Neuliep, *Cultural Communication: A Contextual Approach*, p. 8. Copyright © 2000 by Houghton Mifflin Company. Reprinted with permission.

your hairstyle, your jewelry, your body type, your facial expressions, your body movements, your posture, your tone of voice, and so on, all communicate. Thus, nonverbal symbols as well as verbal symbols communicate.

In addition to being continuous, a process is also *irreversible* and *unrepeatable*. Once you have said or done something, you cannot "take it back." If you hurt your friend's feelings, you can say that you are sorry, but you can't unsay what you said or undo what you did. This fact behooves each of us to think carefully about what we communicate. Because the process is unrepeatable, it logically follows that it is irreversible. You can't "go back." You can say the same thing over and over, but that does not mean communication is repeatable. Time has passed and you have said it before. So saying it again does not repeat the exact same communication.

Referring to communication as a transactional process means that simultaneous role taking exists. Note the transaction model of communication in Figure 1.1. The infinity symbol suggests all that we have discussed about communication thus far. In addition, note that the communicators are designated as "A" and "B" rather than as "source" and "receiver" or "speaker" and "listener." This indicates that neither is only the source of the message nor the receiver of the message. Rather, both participants are simultaneously both source and receiver. As I send messages, I am also receiving them from you and interpreting them and sending messages back to you. You are doing the same. We are not in a ping-pong game in which I sometimes send the ball, wait for you to return it to me, and then hit it back again to you. In essence, I am receiving ping-pong balls from you simultaneously—your voice tone, your words, your facial expression, your stance, and so on. And you, of course, are doing likewise. You don't just stand waiting for the ping-pong ball to reach you. You are sending all the various types of messages to me as you receive them from me.

Communication, as you are no doubt beginning to realize, is quite complex. It has been said that when two people communicate, there are actually six people communicating: my self-perception (all communication begins with self-perception), my perception of you, my perception of your perception of me, your self-perception, your perception of me, and your perception of my perception of you! Suppose you and I are communicating. I have a perception of myself (I am a good conversationalist), a perception of you (you are intelligent), and a perception of how I think you perceive me (I think you also think I am a good conversationalist). You have a perception of yourself, a perception of me, and a perception of how you think I perceive you. (You perceive yourself as intelligent, me as a good conversationalist, and you think I perceive you as intelligent.) In this case, all the perceptions match and communication has a good chance of being effective. But such matching does not often occur. When it does not, communication becomes quite difficult as we try to match these perceptions. In addition to these six "people" (their attitudes, values, beliefs, moods, etc.) there are also factors such as time, place, topic, and circumstances that affect communication and make it complex.

Imagine that three people are engaged in a communication, or four, or five, or an entire classroom! The more people involved in the communication, the more complex the communication becomes because everyone is simultaneously sending and receiving messages from all "participants" in the communication.

FIGURE 1.1 The Transactional Model of Communication

In addition to being a process, communication is also *systemic*. In other words, it takes place within systems. A system consists of entities that interrelate with one another to form a unique whole. When we say a system possesses wholeness, we mean that the whole is more than the sum of its parts. The system possesses a unique quality that cannot be understood by simply summing its parts. For example, every family is unique. Not every four-member family consisting of a mother, father, son, and daughter is the same. Each person within the family is a unique individual and this makes up that family's uniqueness. In the same way, every classroom is different, every corporation is different, every culture is unique. The second characteristic of systems is interdependence. Every part is dependent on every other part. Thus, a change in one part of the system causes a change throughout the system. For example, if a child becomes severely ill in a family, all members of the family will react to that illness. Perhaps each member will have to take on more of the household chores. Perhaps another child will begin to "act out"—attempting to gain more attention in the family. A third characteristic of systems is that they are hierarchical. A family is a subsystem of a community, which is a subsystem of a region, which is a subsystem of a state, which is a subsystem of a nation, and so on. And each subsystem is influenced by other subsystems. For example, a family is influenced by the community in which it lives. What educational facilities, recreational facilities, and religious institutions are available in the community will affect what the family can do. The family in turn can affect change in the community. Perhaps the family desires better recreational facilities and so it begins a campaign to motivate the community to raise money for a new facility. To understand communication we must consider the systems in which it takes place.

The last characteristic of communication is that it has both a content and a relationship component. The content component is the information conveyed; the relationship component suggests how the information should be interpreted in terms of the relationship between the communication participants. If I say, "I love you," in a loving tone, the relationship message of the content is that I care for you. But if I say the same content ("I love you") in a sarcastic tone, the relationship message communicates that I don't really care about you. In general, the content message is the verbal and the relationship message is nonverbal.

WHAT IS CULTURE?

Like the word *communication,* the word *culture* has several different meanings. In 1993, two anthropologists, Alfred Kroeber and Clyde Kluckhorn, examined 300 definitions of culture—none of them the same!

Yet there are some fundamental properties about culture on which most people can agree. Culture is our collective answer to questions such as: Who am I? How should I live my life? Where do I fit in the world? In other words, culture is the set of values and beliefs, norms and customs, and rules and codes that socially defines a group of people, binds them to one another, and gives a sense of commonality (Trenholm and Jensen, 2000).

From this definition flow several important ideas about culture. First, culture affects our perceptions. We'll discuss this more in Chapter 3. Suffice it to say here that perception determines what we see and how we see it—our worldview.

Second, culture also affects our verbal and nonverbal language. The Sapir-Whorf hypothesis suggests that our language affects our worldview. Thus, speakers of different languages view the world differently. In English, we have one word for "you." In German, *du* is the form of "you" used for people you know well; *Sie* (notice the capitalization) is more formal and used for those you do not know well. Nonverbal communication is also affected by culture. For U.S. citizens of European descent, standing close to someone (other than in a crowded elevator or similar situation) signals intimacy. In Middle Eastern cultures, standing close does not necessarily signal intimacy. Rather, Middle Easterners are simply more comfortable with less spatial difference between people when speaking to one another.

Third, culture affects our identity (something we will discuss fully in Chapter 4). Birth order, gender, role of children, and relationships are only a few of the variables that can affect communication. For example, in Chinese culture, the maternal grandmother is *wai zu mu,* and the paternal grandmother is *zu mu;* the maternal grandfather is *wai zu fu,* and the paternal grandfather is *zu fu.* Grandchildren are referred to differently: a son's daughter is *sun nu,* and a daughter's daughter is *wai sun nu.* Uncles and aunts are referred to differently depending on how they are related to the parents of a Chinese child. For example, the father's elder brother is *bo fu;* the mother's brother is *jiu fu.* Because of the importance of relationship in terms of the hierarchy of Chinese culture, each member's name indicates his or her role and status in the family.

As you no doubt have already surmised, the relationship between communication and culture is reciprocal, complex, and interrelated. Indeed, Hall (1959) suggests that communication is culture and culture is communication. As Barnlund (1989) indicates, "The individual and society are antecedent and consequent of each other: Every person is at once a creator of society and its most obvious product" (p. vii). In short, culture and communication act on one another. All communication occurs within some culture.

Communication is the carrier of culture and thus influences the structure of culture. In turn, our culture is manifested in our communication since culture tells us how we should appropriately talk and behave. Thus, culture is affected by and affects communication.

WHAT IS INTERCULTURAL COMMUNICATION?

According to Neuliep (2003), intercultural communication occurs whenever a minimum of two persons from different cultures or microcultures come together and exchange verbal and nonverbal symbols. Microcultures are groups of people that exist within the broader rules and guidelines of the dominant culture, but are distinct in some way: racially, linguistically, occupation, age, or sexual orientation. Often microcultural groups have histories that differ from the dominant cultural group and are subordinate in some way (e.g., economically).

Intercultural communication, like all communication, is contextual. A context is a combination of factors—situation, setting, circumstance, the people involved, the relationship of those people, and so on. In short, context is the overall framework within which communication takes place. Thus, not all communication is appropriate in every context. For example, you communicate differently with your parents than with your teachers. In a given culture, these factors will influence the appropriateness of communication. While living in Hong Kong, I had an *amah*—a full-time, live-in maid—named Nema. The entire flat in which we lived had central air conditioning except Nema's room and the kitchen (where Nema did all the cooking). I wanted to buy window air conditioners for these two rooms. However, my friends who had lived in Hong Kong much longer than I were against it ("We will have to buy the same for our amahs"), nor did Nema want the air conditioners ("The other amahs will think I am acting 'uppity' and won't want to be with me"). The social context, the relationship context, and the microcultural context all determined that buying window air conditioners was unacceptable.

A NARRATIVE APPROACH TO INTERCULTURAL COMMUNICATION

There are numerous approaches to the study of intercultural communication—all of which have their strengths and weaknesses. Based on our own intercultural living experiences, we are convinced that the most effective and insightful approach is the narrative approach. Let's examine why.

Scholars often discuss culture in terms of an iceberg metaphor. What we see in any culture is only the tip of the iceberg. Yet, effective communication occurs only when we begin to understand what is below the water level (see Figure 1.2).

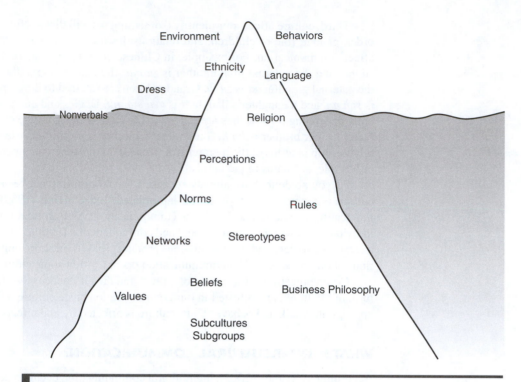

Environment   Behaviors
Ethnicity   Language
Dress
Nonverbals   Religion
Perceptions
Norms   Rules
Networks   Stereotypes
Beliefs   Business Philosophy
Values
Subcultures
Subgroups

FIGURE 1.2   The Iceberg

Another metaphor compares culture to a theatrical production. You see what is on stage, but you don't see all the activity backstage. It is the backstage activity that enables the action on stage to be effective (see Table 1.3).

We suggest a narrative approach to the study of intercultural communication. We are the stories we tell. As Fisher (1987) suggests, we humans are storytellers. We make sense out of others and ourselves through story. As storytellers, our values, emotions, and aesthetic considerations ground our beliefs and behaviors. In his narrative paradigm, Fisher stipulates five postulates:

Fisher's Narrative Paradigm

1. Humans are storytellers.
2. Decision making and communication are based on "good reasons."
3. Good reasons are determined by matters of history, biography, culture, and character.
4. Rationality is based in people's awareness of how internally consistent and truthful to lived experience stories appear.
5. The world is experienced by people as a set of stories from which to choose among. As we choose among these stories, we live life in a process of continual re-creation.

A key concept in the narrative approach is the concept of narrative itself. Often we think of narrative as simply a story. This is a mistake, for as Fisher (1987) indicates, "When I use the term 'narration,' I do not mean a fictive composition whose propositions may be true or false and have no necessary relationship to the message of that composition. By 'narration,' I mean symbolic actions—words and/or deeds—that have sequence and meaning for those who live, create, or interpret them" (p. 58). Fisher (1985a) states it another way: "There is no genre, including technical communication, that is not an episode in the story of life" (p. 347). Thus, for Fisher, all communication is narrative. Narrative is not a specific genre (e.g., stories as opposed to poems), but rather a mode of influence.

TABLE 1.3

On Stage	Backstage	
Music	*Conceptions of:*	*Approaches to:*
Literature	Self	Work
Myths and Legends	Raising Children	Discussing Problems
Theater	Beauty	Problem Solving
Dance	Truth and Goodness	Decision Making
Clothes	Authority	Communication
Food and Drink	Friendship	Social Interaction
Painting and Sculpture	Fairness	Sex
Greetings	Sin	
Outward Behaviors	Time and Space	
Manners	Gender	
Rituals and Ceremonies	Responsibilities	

Thus, listening to a class lecture, talking with your friends, listening to a political speech or the evening news, reading a book—all consist of your hearing and shaping narratives. In Fisher's (1987) thinking, story is imbued in all human communication endeavors, even those involving logic. All arguments include "ideas that cannot be verified or proved in any absolute way. Such ideas arise in metaphor, values, gestures, and so on" (p. 19). In short, Fisher attempts to bridge the divide we often have between logos (rational argument) and mythos (story, or narration).

This concept that humans are essentially storytellers is not unique to the field of communication. It is also found in other disciplines, including anthropology, history, business, philosophy, psychology, theology, education, sociology, and biology (cf., Brown et al., 2004; Denning, 2004; McDrury and Alterio, 2002). There is "the growing belief that narrative represents a universal medium of human consciousness" (Lucaites and Condit, 1985, p. 347). In other words, if story is a universal medium, then story is the key to our understanding of others from cultures unlike our own.

Because our lives are experienced through narratives, some standard for determining which stories to believe and which to disregard is essential. This standard is narrative rationality. It is different from the traditional one in which most Westerners have been trained. *Traditional standards of rationality* ask questions such as:

1. Are the claims supported by the facts?
2. Have all relevant facts been considered?
3. Are the arguments internally consistent?
4. Does the reasoning used conform to the tests of formal and informal logic?

In contrast, *narrative rationality* is concerned with the principle of coherence and fidelity. *Coherence* refers to the internal consistency of the narrative and asks such questions as:

1. Do the elements of the story flow smoothly?
2. Is the story congruent with the stories that seem related to it?
3. Are the characters in the story believable?

Fidelity, the second principle of narrative rationality, concerns truthfulness or reliability of the story. Stories with a high degree of fidelity "ring true" to the listener. When the elements of a story "represent accurate assertions about social reality" (Fisher, 1987, p. 105), they have fidelity. Fisher proposes that we assess narrative fidelity through the logic of good reasons. If a narrative possesses fidelity, it constitutes good reasons for a person to hold a certain belief or act in a certain way. The logic of good reasons enables a person to judge the worth of stories by presenting the listener with a set of values that appeal to her or him and form warrants for accepting or rejecting a certain story.

The logic of good reasons consists of asking two sets of questions. The first set constitutes a logic of reasons:

1. Are the statements that claim to be factual in the narrative really factual?
2. Have any relevant facts been omitted from the narrative or distorted in its telling?
3. What are the patterns of reasoning that exist in the narrative?
4. How relevant are the arguments in the story to any decision the listener may make?
5. How well does the narrative address the important and significant issues of this case?

The second set of questions transforms the logic of reasons into a logic of good reasons by introducing the concept of values into the assessing of practical knowledge. The questions comprising this set are:

1. What are the implicit and explicit values contained in the narrative?
2. Are the values appropriate to the decision that is relevant to the narrative?
3. What would be the effects of adhering to the values embedded in the narrative?
4. Are the values confirmed or validated in lived experience?
5. Are the values of the narrative the basis for ideal human conduct?

We are who we are through the stories we tell. We become who we are because of the stories we listen to with our eyes, ears, and heart. This is true whether we find ourselves in our own culture or one quite different from our own. The point is that communicating interculturally requires us to work harder at hearing and seeing and interpreting those data accurately. This interpretation is most useful to us when it is done from a narrative perspective because story is the crux of our humanness.

CONCLUSION

This chapter presented the foundations for our study of intercultural communication—the definitions and explanations of communication, culture, and intercultural communication. The chapter also outlined the approach to intercultural communication that this text/reader will follow. In the article that follows, this information is further explained. Shahar and Kurz provide three cultural metaphors that help us understand the ways of speaking and behaving that are "Israeli."

FOR DISCUSSION

1. How are communication and culture related?
2. Share an example of when the axiom "Meanings are in people, not in words" caused difficulty when communicating in your own culture. Then share an example when this axiom caused problems in intercultural communication. How was the misunderstanding resolved in each case?
3. Repeat #2 for the axiom "You cannot not communicate."
4. Do you agree with Fisher's concept of the narrative? Why or why not? What approach to the study of intercultural communication do you think would be better? Why?

REFERENCES

Barnlund, D. (1989). *Communication styles of Japanese and Americans: Images and realities.* Belmont, CA: Wadsworth.

Brown, J., Denning, S., Groh, K., and Prusak, L. (2004). *Storytelling in organizations: Why storytelling is transforming 21st century organizations and management.* St. Louis, MO: Butterworth-Heinemann.

Calloway-Thomas, C., Cooper, P., and Blake, C. (1999). *Intercultural communication: Roots to routes.* Boston: Allyn and Bacon.

Combs, A., Avila, D., and Purkey, W. (1971). *Helping relationships: Basic concepts in the helping professions.* Boston: Allyn and Bacon.

Dance, F., and Larson, D. (1976). *The functions of human communication.* New York: Holt, Rinehart and Winston.

Denning, S. (2004). *Squirrel Inc.: A fable of leadership through storytelling.* San Francisco: Jossey Bass.

Fisher, W. (1987). *Human communication as narration: Toward a philosophy of reason, value, and action.* Columbia: University of South Carolina Press.

Fisher, W. (1985a). The narrative paradigm: An elaboration. *Communication Monographs, 52,* 347–367.

Fisher, W. (1985b). The narrative paradigm: In the beginning. *Journal of Communication, 35,* 74–89.

Hall, E. (1959). *The silent language.* Garden City, NJ: Doubleday.

Hill, R. (1997). *WeEuropeans.* Brussels, Belgium: Europublications.

Kroeber, A. I., and Kluckhohn, C. (1954). *Culture: A critical review of concepts and definitions.* New York: Random House.

Lucaites, J. L., and Condit, C. M. (1985). Reconstructing narrative theory: A functional perspective. *Journal of Communication, 35,* 9–108.

McDrury, J., and Alterio, M. (2002). *Learning through storytelling in higher education.* Sterling, VA: Kogan Page.

Neuliep, J. (2000, 2003). *Intercultural communication: A contextual approach.* Boston: Houghton Mifflin.

Russow, L. (2006). Village of 1,000 in the Year 2000. Retrieved from http://faculty.philau.edu/russowl/villageof1000.html.

Seelye, H. N. (1993). *Teaching culture: Strategies for intercultural communication.* Lincolnwood, IL: National Textbook Company.

Something to think about. (2001, May 23). Available online: www.bigfatbaby.com.

Trenholm, S., and Jensen, A. (2000). *Interpersonal communication.* Belmont, CA: Wadsworth.

Coloring Books, Video Recorders, and Sandpaper: Three Cultural Metaphors

Lucy Shahar and David Kurz

. . . We described Israel as a cultural mosaic. At first glance, the many pieces in the mosaic or puzzle fail to form a discernible pattern; that is, there doesn't seem to be a single homogeneous Israeli culture. Israel is both Western and Eastern, secular and religious. . . .

If one studies the puzzle carefully, however, the pieces do fall into place; there is a discernible pattern. Certain behaviors, norms, and attitudes are widely shared among Israelis and are encouraged; others are discouraged. It is into the nexus of these shared values and behaviors that the culture of Israel can be found, and that is what we mean by the term "Israeli culture."

New immigrants pick up the message quite accurately and quite quickly: there are ways of speaking and acting that are "Israeli." If one wants to be included in the society, those ways of speaking and acting must be incorporated into one's repertoire. If one does not take on those attitudes and behaviors, he or she will be "included out."

Three images serve as metaphors for those behaviors and attitudes which we believe are recognizably Israeli. The images are: a page from a coloring book, the "fast-forward" mode on a video recorder, and sandpaper.

THE COLORING BOOK

Take a close look at the pictures from the coloring book. Figure 1 is an exact duplication of a page in a children's coloring book. Figures 2 and 3 reflect the perceptions of Americans and Israelis, respectively. "Israelis can't stay within the lines of the coloring book," Americans frequently say. The fact is that Americans and Israelis have different mental images of the same picture in the coloring book. The American mental image of the coloring book often corresponds to Figure 2. In the American picture, all of the lines are solid and clearly defined. In the Israeli picture—Figure 3—the lines themselves are blurred and even indistinct in places. Whoever has worked on the picture has colored outside the lines. The "artist" was not restrained by the borders, but felt free to create something beyond the defined lines and to make it his or her own. On the other hand, the results give the impression of things being a little out of control. The coloring does not seem to be carefully planned or thought out. The whole picture has an unfinished quality. It may turn out to be a charming example of free-form creativity, or simply a mess.

The coloring book may be seen as an obstacle to creativity or, from another perspective, as a springboard to improvisation. In the workplace, in particular,

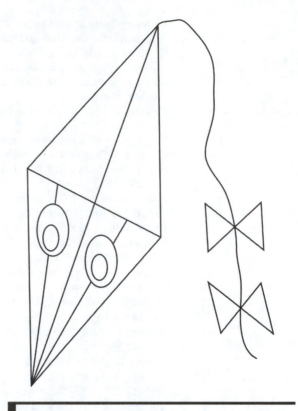

FIGURE 1   Standard Coloring Book Picture

FIGURE 2   American Perception

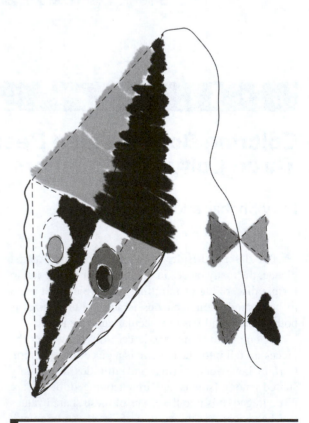

FIGURE 3   Israeli Perception

the *ability* to improvise as well as the *tendency* to do so expresses itself in every area. Israelis cannot be bothered with "doing it by the book." They prefer to take a system apart, to find new or better ways of achieving a goal or solving a problem. Indeed, it is precisely the Israeli capacity for creativity and the ability to improvise which have for many years attracted clients interested in joint ventures in the area of research and development.

Spontaneity

The Israeli communication style is spontaneous, natural, and unrestrained. In the workplace, spontaneity expresses itself in the ability to come up with on-the-spot solutions to problems instead of relying on the book or being limited by it. Staying within the bounds of expected conduct is confining. In a formal meeting, Israeli representatives may offer their views as they come to mind without considering whether they are interrupting, or whether offering an opinion at a particular juncture is appropriate. From an American perspective, that behavior is out of line, that is, aggressive, if not offensive.

Spontaneity in the workplace sometimes expresses itself in a tendency to "wing it." It is not unusual, for example, to witness a staff presentation which seems extemporaneous. It is obvious that the presenter is well grounded in the material and that the presentation has substance, but it clearly has not been thought out systematically in advance. ("I don't prepare ahead of time because it is too confining," many Israelis say.)

In everyday encounters, the inability to stay within the lines is demonstrated literally. Israelis have difficulty waiting in line at banks, movie theaters, health clinics. . . . An Israeli line is amorphous. It is often hard to tell where it begins and where it ends. Sometimes it is even hard to figure out who's in front of whom.

Spontaneity expresses itself in social encounters as a lack of inhibition. If you want to invite someone to your home, you do so. If you are interested in how much someone paid for an apartment or dress, you ask. If you are angry, you show it. If you want to give advice, you give it, even if the advice is unsolicited.

Positive Attitude toward Risk Taking

The readiness to color outside the lines means that the individual working on the picture is willing to take a risk. Maybe the picture will be a mess; maybe it won't. In the workplace this attitude expresses itself in a tendency to try out new approaches even if they have not

been carefully thought through. All of this produces many surprises; but again, surprises are accepted as normal in Israeli life.

In commercial and bureaucratic encounters, the positive attitude toward risk taking expresses itself in a willingness to test the rules: "It's true that the sign says your office is closed, but I'm going to pretend that it is still open. The worst that can happen is that you'll say no and try to throw me out, but even that is negotiable." (Americans also possess a positive approach to risk taking, but the quality expresses itself differently in the two cultures. . . .)

Self-Confidence

Israelis are confident that going out of the lines will work, and even if it doesn't work, they are self-confident enough to take the risk. But, as some outsiders have noticed, there is a thin line between self-confidence and arrogance.

Self-confidence expresses itself in the willingness to improvise, to develop creative solutions for problems in the work environment, to question authority, to make decisions outside the boundaries of one's job description, to risk oneself in a sexual or social encounter. Arrogance expresses itself in a haughty attitude toward those who choose to color inside the lines. The implicit message is: people who stay within the lines of the coloring book (e.g., behave solely according to instructions or established procedures) lack self-confidence. They are rigid, afraid to risk, "square."

A combination of informality, spontaneity, a positive attitude toward risk taking, the improvisational approach to problem solving, and self-confidence explains the easygoing Israeli approach toward planning.

The outline of the picture in the coloring book is a framework providing shape and structure, but Israelis do not view themselves as limited by frameworks. Indeed, few Israelis would expect anyone to color inside the lines. The framework of the picture is analogous to a plan.

Army officers and noncoms are taught to plan. They are taught well. At the same time, they are also taught that *a plan is a basis for change*. The message is drummed into their heads: "Don't be controlled by your plan. Use it to respond to the situation in front of you. Be flexible! Improvise." Most Israelis in senior positions in virtually every civilian field are veterans of the IDF officer corps. They bring to their civilian positions the style of responding and approach to planning that they learned during their army service.

The idea of a plan as a basis for change often finds expression in the workplace. Plans, schedules, and deadlines are viewed as broad guidelines subject to alteration; they are not felt to be binding commitments. (A guideline is simply another line in the drawing.)

Leisure-time activities are also affected by the flexible attitude toward plans and planning. A guide in an organized tour may decide to change the plan and alter the itinerary described in the company brochure.

Individualism

Israelis are highly individualistic, as are Americans, but the trait expresses itself differently in the two cultures. The picture in the coloring book helps us understand what individualism means in Israel. One can almost hear the Israeli who colored the picture saying, "No one is going to tell me how to color the picture. I'll do it my way." Israeli individualism expresses itself in a casual attitude toward rules and regulations, a tendency not to follow instructions, and a resistance to imposed authority. ("Do it because I said so.") Israelis usually have to be convinced that a certain goal should be achieved or a given procedure should be adhered to before they agree to follow orders.

Individualism also expresses itself in self-reliance: "I don't need to ask for help. I can do it myself." Yet Israel's is also a culture in which individualism exists side by side with strong group attachments. Israelis identify themselves as members of groups, are loyal to group members, and are concerned with the well-being and collective interests of the group (e.g., work teams, friendship circles, ethnic organizations, and army units).

Self-reliance is also a strong component of individualism in American culture. Americans believe, as do Israelis, that individuals should be encouraged to solve their own problems and make their own decisions. In other respects, however, the word carries a different meaning. American individualism is expressed in the pursuit of individual rather than common or collective interests. Americans usually view the world from the point of view of the self. One's loyalty is primarily to oneself and one's immediate family, and attachments to groups are relatively loose. American individualism does not appear to conflict with conformity to regulations, going by the rules, or respect for authority.

Many people would argue that Israelis are changing as the country becomes less socialistic and more capitalistic and that, as a result, Israeli individualism is gradually coming to resemble American individualism. The differences remain marked, however. Perhaps the easiest way to understand them is to look at how each group sees the other's behavior. Americans look at behavior which Israelis call "Israeli individualism" and label it childishness, insubordination, disrespect, anarchy, and arrogance. Israelis look at behavior which Americans call "American individualism" and label it selfishness or egotism.

Limited Respect for Authority/Casual Attitude toward Rules and Regulations

By definition, authority implies the existence of limits and constraints: clearly defined rules concerning what is permissible and what is not. Respect for authority means that one stays within the lines, observes the rules. In the Israeli coloring book, however, the lines are either hard to discern or subject to testing.

In everyday life, behavior in the public parking lot is an example of the casual (some would argue indifferent) Israeli attitude toward rules and regulations as well as evidence of their individualism and their improvisations approach to problem solving (see Figure 4). Indeed, the arrangement of cars in the parking lot reveals a great deal about Israeli attitudes toward boundaries and border crossings. Painted demarcation lines, denoting parking spaces, are identical to those in parking lots in all Western countries.

In an Israeli parking lot, however, cars may be parked *on* the line instead of *between* the lines; three cars will be crowded into spaces designed for two. Cars may be parked perpendicular to the cars between

FIGURE 4   Parking Lot

the lines, or they may be parked on the islands separating the lanes. Cars will not only be parked in ingenious ways, they will also be parked in the space in which the sign clearly proclaims "no parking." (Some people think that the way Israelis park can be explained by the fact that there are too many cars and too few parking lots in Israeli cities. But even when there is plenty of space, the parking-lot picture tends to look the same.)

Somehow, Israelis devise ingenious ways of solving their parking problems, even if doing so means that the overall result is extremely disorderly. In fact, one person's solution to the parking problem may in turn create difficulties for other drivers who discover that it is almost impossible to move into or out of a space, or into or out of the parking lot itself. That becomes a problem-solving challenge for those drivers, often leading to a higher order of ingenuity and improvisation.

If one has parked in a tow-away zone and been graced with a boot on one's car (Israelis *do* receive parking tickets for violations and *do* pay heavy fines), one feels free to argue with the officer in charge, to "step out of line." Consider the following scene:

A newcomer to the city is driving on a busy street looking for a place to park. He sees cars parked on the sidewalk or with the side wheels up on the curb. Where he comes from, sidewalks are for pedestrians. Uncertain whether parking on the sidewalk is permissible in Israel, he stops a policeman.

Newcomer: "Is it OK if I park my car on the sidewalk?"
Policeman: "Of course not. It's illegal."
Newcomer: "What about all of these cars?"
Policeman: "Their drivers didn't ask!"

THE FAST-FORWARD MODE ON THE VIDEOCASSETTE RECORDER

Our second metaphorical image is the fast-forward mode of a video cassette recorder (see Figure 5). On "play," everything is as it should be, moving at a normal pace and rhythm. When one presses the fast-forward button, the pictures on the television screen flash by in rapid succession. It is difficult for the viewer to keep track of the movements of arms, legs, and "talking heads." All the figures appear to be very animated, like characters in a cartoon. Everything is hurried and nothing stays on the screen for more than a moment.

The fast-forward analogy sheds additional light on informality as an Israeli cultural trait. In an infor-

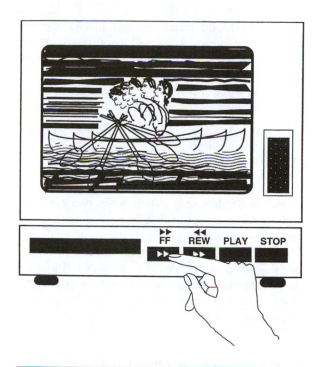

FIGURE 5   The Fast-Foward Mode on the Video Cassette Recorder

mal culture, the transition from stranger to acquaintance occurs at a rapid pace; people get to know each other quickly and feel free to shift into a closer personal relationship at a relatively early point. Since Israeli culture is more informal than American culture, or almost any other, it often seems that Israelis operate on the fast-forward mode while Americans operate on "play."

Fast-forward expresses itself in both business and social settings. An Israeli who is a guest or stranger at a formal meeting in the workplace may behave as if he or she has known the other participants for years. This will usually include shifting into a direct mode of communication at a surprisingly early and, from an American point of view, sometimes inappropriate juncture: "Let's forget all these welcoming speeches and get down to work!"

In social encounters, distances are bridged quickly. There are few social barriers, and those that exist disintegrate rapidly. Israelis feel uncomfortable standing on ceremony. Small talk, for example, may be short-lived or nonexistent. "Hello. Nice to have you as a guest in our home. How was your trip? So you work for the Atomic Energy Commission. How did you ever allow Three-Mile Island to happen?" From the American perspective, all of this occurs in fast-forward. Messages may be garbled, the picture unclear. Indeed, fast-forward often induces sensory and emotional overload. Foreigners feel uneasy as they try to manage, or at least respond properly to, a barrage of demands normally spread over a longer period of time at a more leisurely, controllable pace.

SANDPAPER

Our third metaphor—visual, aural, and tactile—is sandpaper. Sandpaper is rough. When two pieces of sandpaper are rubbed together, they cause friction. The sound may be grating, jarring, irritating. If sandpaper gets rubbed on skin, it hurts. But used to smooth out rough surfaces and paper [it] is an essential tool for every carpenter, professional or amateur. It gets the job done. Of course, sandpaper comes in grades, from extra-rough to extra-fine.

Direct Israeli Communication Style

The direct Israeli communication style, verbal and nonverbal, is analogous to sandpaper. It is often rough, grating, devoid of a smooth finish. To a considerable extent, Israel retains the unpolished communication style of the frontier. In its extra-rough mode, this style is aggressive; in its extra-fine mode, it is simple and straightforward. Consider the following scenes:

- You are in a crowded shopping mall. People jostle, push, and bump. There is a great deal of physical contact. The friction of contact in passing is considered normal and does not call for an "excuse me."
- You are conducting a workshop. The Israeli participants tell you that they want feedback on their presentations. Translation: "Never mind the compliments. Lay on the criticism and forget the frills."
- You've just presented your point of view on an important and controversial issue. As an American, chances are that you expect to hear disagreement in the form of: "Excuse me, I have a problem with what you've just said." In Israel you are likely to hear, "You're wrong!"

These experiences are upsetting to the uninitiated. They grate on the senses, rub against the grain.

Sandpaper is rough. The opposite of rough, or coarse, is smooth. In more formal cultures, high priority is given to teaching children manners—the norms of acceptable speech and behavior. These are viewed as the lubricating niceties that facilitate social interactions. "Lucy, Lucy, if you're able, take your elbows off the table." By the age of seven, children have learned the magic words: please, thank you, excuse me, and such basic formulas as "Mom, this is my friend David. David, I would like you to meet my mom."

Many Americans are convinced that Israelis *never* say please, thank you, or excuse me. The truth is that Israelis do use these polite forms. They are employed much less frequently, however; and Americans, who are accustomed to using and hearing a greater number them, come away convinced that the words have not been uttered at all!

In many cultures, this kind of rough behavior is avoided at all costs. Filipinos, for instance, place an overriding importance on what is universally called "smooth interpersonal relations." In informal Israel, "smooth" is often suspect. It is equated with being artificial, insincere, hypocritical. Rough is real; it is honest, authentic. Rough hurts, but in Israel, it is assumed that you are able to "dish it out and take it too." Rough works.

Americans will frequently use the phrase: "I'm going to tell you the unvarnished truth" when they are about to communicate something potentially painful. Most do-it-yourselfers know that varnish is put on wood that has already been sandpapered. Wood that is unvarnished is simply unpolished. The American unvarnished truth is considerably smoother than Israeli truth is delivered sandpaper style.

If asked (and they have been), Israelis overwhelmingly express preference for directness, however painful, over indirection—messages padded for politeness' sake.

The direct, confrontational, no-frills style is known as "dugri talk" in Israeli slang. The word *dugri* comes from the Arabic where it has a similar, but not identical meaning. The dugri style of speaking characterizes sabra communication style. Part of being an Israeli is "speaking dugri." Dugri, in the minds of many Israelis, is contrasted with more diplomatic, less direct, less confrontational communication styles, which are often perceived by Israelis as insincere and artificial. Dugri speech, on the other hand, is equated with sincerity and integrity.[1]

NOTE

1. For a fascinating discussion of dugri speech, see Tamar Katriel, *Talking Straight: Dugri Speech in Israeli Sabra Culture* (Cambridge: Cambridge University Press, 1986).

CHECK YOUR UNDERSTANDING

1. Describe the Israeli communication style.
2. How do the three metaphors help us understand this style?
3. What metaphors could you use to describe your own culture's communication style?

4. Given your own cultural background, what will be the most important idea for you to remember about Israeli communication style if you are to be an effective communicator in that culture?

CHAPTER ACTIVITIES

1. Joseph Campbell has said that the myths of every culture provide answers to four questions: Who am I? Who are we? What is the nature of the world in which we live? and What is the nature of the answers to these questions? Think of a myth of your culture. How does that myth answer these four questions? How does answering those four questions help us be better intercultural communicators?

2. Read the materials on journals, personal narratives, and autobiographies and autobiographical literature that follow. Begin the work on these term projects.

Activities for the Term

Journals

During this term, keep a personal narrative journal. Jot down your ideas about travel and intercultural communication. Write quotes that are meaningful to you. Clip news articles related to intercultural communication and place these in your journal. Add postcards, photos, cartoons—anything that "speaks" to you about intercultural communication. Use this journal to help you clarify your thinking about intercultural communication and make sense of your intercultural experience. In this journal write about your reaction to these readings, class discussions, media discussion related to international relations, movies, music, art, proverbs, folktales, poetry, and quotations about travel, other cultures, and your own culture that spark your thinking about intercultural communication.

Personal Narratives

McAdams (1993) suggests the importance of personal narratives: "Human beings are storytellers by nature. In many guises, as folktale, legend, myth, epic, history, motion picture and television program, the story appears in every known human culture. The story is a natural package for organizing many different kinds of information. Storytelling appears to be a fundamental

way of expressing ourselves and our world to others" (p. 27).

The psychologist Jerome Bruner (1990) argues that human beings understand the world in two very different ways. The first he calls the "paradigmatic mode" of thought. In this mode, we try to comprehend our experience in terms of tightly reasoned analyses, logical proof, and empirical observation. In the second mode, the "narrative mode" of thought, we are concerned with human wants, needs, and goals. This is the mode of stories wherein we deal with "the vicissitudes of human intention" organized in time.

Several writers in communication have suggested that humans are essentially storytellers. As we have already discussed, Fisher (1987) suggests that human beings are inherently storytellers. They experience and understand life as a "series of ongoing narratives, as conflicts, characters, beginnings, middles, and ends." Thus, all forms of communication can be viewed fundamentally as stories, as narratives—symbolic interpretations of aspects of the world occurring in time and shaped by history, culture, and character.

Our stories affect how we "hear" the stories of other cultures. Howard (1991) suggests that cultures organized around the wisdom of a set of stories that are quite different from our (i.e., Western) dominant cultural tales are often labeled as *backward* or *primitive* cultures. Such a label certainly affects the way we would communicate with people from these cultures.

In sum, the stories we create influence the stories of other people, those stories give rise to still others, and soon we find meaning and connection within a web of story making and story living. Through our personal stories, we help create the world we live in, at the same time it is creating us.

For each section of this text/reader write a personal narrative about your experiences in and thinking about intercultural communication. Using the material in this first section, write a personal narrative describing how the information in this section fits into your personal story.

Autobiographies and Autobiographical Fiction

Finkelstein and Traubitz (1998) view autobiography and autobiographical fiction as vehicles for cultural understanding:

> There are few types of literature that illuminate culture as poignantly or as provocatively as works of autobiography and autobiographical fiction. Through personal recollection and lived experience, writers of autobiography and autobiographical fiction give readers uncommonly powerful lenses through which to view their own experiences, communicate and share those experiences with others, and ultimately reflect on their own habits of heart, mind, and association. Works of autobiography and autobiographical fiction reveal ways in which individuals experience the power of economic and political circumstance. They expose the ofttimes hidden dimensions of inhumanity by rendering the impersonal, personal; the abstract, concrete; the hidden, visible. They give personal meaning to abstract concepts like *prejudice* and *discrimination* . . . The genre provides a realistic context . . . to discover the voices of cultural others; reflect on different ways of knowing, being, and doing; and, through this process, begin to substitute understanding for prejudice. (p. 39)

During this term, choose two autobiographies and two books of autobiographical fiction and read them. What do these pieces of literature tell you about the culture of the person who wrote them? What do they tell you about being an effective communicator with people from that culture?

REFERENCES

Bruner, Jerome. (1990). *Acts of meaning.* Cambridge, MA: Harvard University Press.

Finkelstein, B., and Traubitz, N. (1998). Seeing through words: Autobiography and autobiographical fiction as vehicles for cultural understanding. In B. Finkelstein and E. Eder (Eds.), *Hidden messages: Instructional materials for investigating culture.* Yarmouth, ME: Intercultural Press.

Fisher, W. (1987). *Human communication as narration: Toward a philosophy of reason, value, and action.* Columbia: University of South Carolina Press.

Howard, G. (1991). Culture tales: A narrative approach to thinking, cross-cultural psychology, and psychotherapy. *American Psychologist, 46* (3), 187–197.

McAdams, D. (1993). *The stories we live by: Personal myths and the making of the self.* New York: Guilford.

CHAPTER 2

CULTURAL PATTERNS

BALINESE PATTERNS: CREMATIONS AND VILLAGES

My family was less than excited when I suggested that we should attend the Balinese cremation ceremony. We had been traveling for several weeks, and they were tired of doing anything "cultural." Their wish was to relax on the beach. But finally, after much begging (and, I am sorry to say, guilt-inducing communication), they reluctantly agreed.

We were taken to the village of the deceased, where much celebration was already in progress. The villagers and relatives had feasted for days and were now lined up in a processional. All is loud and luxurious. Orchestras, dancers, scores of boys carrying spears, banners, and flags, followed by long lines of female offering bearers, girls in full ceremonial dress all precede the casket. The casket sits precariously on top of a tower—each level symbolic of the status of the deceased. The tower sits on a wagon. The casket sways as the men pull the wagon and swing it around and around.

Soon we are at the place of the cremation. The casket is taken from the tower and placed on a wooden pier. The priest and the offering bearers approach the casket, into which they place the items they have carried. Then the flame is lit.

As the ashes fall into the container under the pier and the flames die down, people begin to walk back into the village—singing and dancing as they go. The family members remain. They will gather the ashes and take them out to sea. This pattern is followed, with little change, for every funeral.

After the cremation, we visited the Balinese village in which the deceased's family lived. The Balinese village is a place of communal order. It is a closely knit network of social, religious, and economic institutions to which every Balinese belongs. Every village has the same spatial arrangement. The most important points of reference are *kaja* ("toward the mountain"; in south Bali this is to the north, and in north Bali, it is to the south) and *kelod* ("downstream" or "seawards"). *Kangin* (east) and *kauh* (west) and intermediary compass points are of equal importance. Thus, the Temple of Origin lies nearest the mountain and the Temple of the Great Meeting Hall lies in the center of the village. Clustered around the Temple of Origin are the residential sections of the village called *Banjars*. Each *banjar* has its own meeting hall, which is the center of the community. Each *banjar* also is surrounded by rice fields and gardens. The outer boundaries of the village are usually clearly marked by hedges, forests, valleys, streams, or other natural boundaries. Although there are local and regional variations in village layout, there is this common pattern.

The family compound, like the village, consists of several buildings whose location and function are strictly defined and spatially determined. In the mountain corner is the family's temple. Also toward the mountain are the quarters for the parents and grandparents. The east pavilion is where family ceremonies such as tooth-filings and weddings are held. The children sleep in the west pavilion In the seaward section of the compound are the kitchen, rice granary, pigsty, and bathroom (if there is one). Upon marriage, a girl moves to the compound of her in-laws. She has little to learn about "where things are," for the pattern of her new home is the same as the home in which she grew up.

OBJECTIVES

After reading this chapter and completing the readings and activities, you should be able to

- Describe the cultural patterns proposed by Kluckhohn and Strodtbeck, Hall, Hofstede, and Bond.
- Describe the cultural patterns of your own culture.
- Describe how cultural patterns relate to communication.

As the previous narrative indicates, patterns appear in culture. These patterns help us predict what comes next and what is appropriate. Patterns—whether for sewing a dress, embroidering a tapestry, or building a house—provide us with expectations and an ability to plan. Cultural patterns are shared beliefs, values, and norms that are stable over time and that lead to similar behaviors across similar situations. These cultural patterns allow us to make predictions about a culture and adapt our communication accordingly. Fisher (1989) describes these patterns as a mindset that provides ways of thinking about the world and one's place in it. In short, cultural patterns are shared mental programs that govern behavior.

Since no two people are exactly alike, certain aspects of these mental programs are unique to each individual. Some of these mental patterns are universal, such as communicating with a verbal language, raising children in some sort of a family setting, having rules to regulate sexual behavior, and having art, to name a few. Most of these core assumptions are programmed at an early age and are reinforced constantly. However, different cultures have developed their own specific ways of expressing these aspects. For example, in terms of the rules of sexual behavior, conservative Muslim societies view European women as highly immoral and immodest for going out in public without a male relative and without their bodies covered from head to toe.

BELIEFS, VALUES, AND NORMS

Regardless of the culture, all cultural patterns have basic components: beliefs, values, and norms. Beliefs are ideas about the world that people assume are true. For example, the people of Thailand believe that spirits reside in all things—both animate and inanimate. As a result, the countryside is scattered with spirit houses and the Thai people place daily offerings in these spirit houses. Chinese people believe the number 14 is unlucky. The Vietnamese believe the head is a sensitive spiritual part of the body.

Values are things we hold dear—those things we consider worthwhile or desirable. These values guide human behavior toward others, our culture, and ourselves. Sitaram and Haapanen (1979) suggest two important propositions about values:

1. Values are communicated explicitly and implicitly through symbolic behavior.
2. The way people communicate is influenced by the values people hold.

Problems occur when we judge others by using our personal set of values as a standard. This is termed *ethnocentrism*—believing our way of doing things and of believing is best. The opposite of ethnocentrism is *cultural relativity*—studying the cultural values of others with the framework of that culture rather than through a comparison with our own values.

Values can be different in both valence (whether the value is positive or negative) and in intensity (importance of the value). In the United States, ensuring equal opportunities for women has a positive valence and a high degree of intensity. In some Arab countries, equal opportunities for women has a negative valence and a high degree of intensity. A comparison of the top 10 cultural values of U.S. Americans, Japanese, and Arabs appears in Table 2.1.

TABLE 2.1 A Comparison of Values of U.S. Americans, Japanese, and Arabs		
U.S. Americans	**Japanese**	**Arabs**
1. Freedom	1. Belonging	1. Family security
2. Independence	2. Group harmony	2. Family harmony
3. Self-reliance	3. Collectiveness	3. Parental guidance
4. Equality	4. Age/seniority	4. Age
5. Individualism	5. Group consensus	5. Authority
6. Competition	6. Cooperation	6. Compromise
7. Efficiency	7. Quality	7. Devotion
8. Time	8. Patience	8. Patience
9. Directness	9. Indirectness	9. Indirectness
10. Openness	10. Go between	10. Hospitality

Source: Reprinted from *Multicultural Management 2000: Essential Cultural Insights for Global Business Success,* F. Elashmawi and P. Harris, p. 196, 198, copyright ©1998, with permission from Elsevier.

Norms are rules that are socially enforced. In short, norms are a code of conduct. They define what is appropriate in a given culture. If I am the teacher, I stand at the front of the room, I grade exams and papers, and I prepare and teach the curriculum. The norms for students are different. You sit at your desks, you do homework, and you answer questions that, generally, I ask. Norms are the outward manifestations of beliefs and values. Like values, norms can vary within a culture in terms of their importance and intensity. U.S. Americans of African descent view time a bit differently than those of Western Europe descent. Daniel and Smitherman (1976) describe the view of time in African American culture:

> Being on time has to do with participating in the fulfillment of an activity that is vital to the sustenance of a basic rhythm, rather than with appearing on the scene at, say, "twelve o'clock sharp." The key is not to be "on time" but "in" time. For people of Western Europe descent, time is oriented more towards being "on time" than "in time." (p. 29)

What do cultural patterns of beliefs, values, and norms do in terms of communication in a culture? The patterns are the filter through which all verbal and nonverbal symbols are interpreted. In a sense, the relationship between patterns and communication is reciprocal. We communicate on the basis of the cultural patterns we have learned; we learn these cultural patterns through communication with others in our culture. For example, how do we treat children? Do we believe they are to be "seen and not heard" and so never ask their opinions or help in making decisions? Or, do we see them as individuals who require our guidance, but also deserve their independence? My daughter had major conflicts about how our *amah*, Nema, treated her. Nema came from a culture that allowed children little independence. Jamie did not want help getting dressed or brushing her teeth. Yet, from Nema's perspective, these were things that should be done for children—even those in third grade.

APPROACHES TO STUDYING CULTURAL PATTERNS

There are several approaches to studying cultural patterns. All are valuable for their contribution to the study of intercultural communication. We will discuss four that have most affected our study of intercultural communication and are the major ones used by intercultural researchers and scholars: Kluckhohn and Strodtbeck (1961), Hall (1976), Hofstede (1997), and Bond (1987). Although there are many approaches, these four are the major ones used by intercultural communication researchers and scholars.

Florence Kluckhohn and Frederick Strodtbeck

Kluckhohn and Strodtbeck (1961) suggest five conclusions about the functions of cultural patterns. First, these researchers suggest that people in all cultures face common human problems for which they must find answers and that these questions could be answered with three possible variations:

1. What is the character of innate human nature? Are humans basically bad, good, or a mixture of good and bad? (Human nature orientation)
2. What is the relationship of people to nature? Are humans controlled by nature, control nature, or live in balance with nature? (Man–nature relationship)
3. What is the time sense of human life? Do they emphasize the past, present, or future? (Time orientation)
4. What is the culture's activity orientation? Are humans being, being-in-becoming, or doing? (Activity orientation)
5. What is the social relationship of humans to one another? Is it authorization, group, or individual? (Relational orientation)

Second, the range of alternative solutions is limited. Each of these five orientations can be put on a continuum. For example, a culture's orientation to activity can range from passive acceptance of the world, to preference for a gradual transformation of the human condition, to a more direct intervention. This idea is depicted in Table 2.2.

If we plot cultures on the continuums, the U.S. American culture, Arab culture, and Japanese culture would be plotted as indicated in Tables 2.3, 2.4, and 2.5, respectively. Here is a comparison of each culture's answers to the five questions:

1. What is the character of innate human nature? U.S. Americans would answer basically good and changeable; Arabs would answer neutral and unchangeable; and Japanese would answer a mixture of good and evil and unchangeable.
2. What is the relationship of humans to nature? U.S. Americans would answer that humans are the masters of nature; Arabs, humans are subjugated by or live in harmony with nature; and Japanese, humans live in harmony with nature.
3. What is the time sense of human life? U.S. Americans would answer future oriented; Arabs, past oriented; and Japanese, past oriented and future oriented.
4. What is the culture's activity orientation? U.S. Americans would answer doing; Arabs, being; and Japanese, growing and doing.

TABLE 2.2 Possible Responses to Kluckholm and Strodbeck's Value Orientations

ORIENTATION	BELIEFS AND BEHAVIORS		
Human Nature	Basically evil	Mixture of good and evil	Basically good
Relationship to Nature	Humans subjugated by nature	Humans in harmony with nature	Humans the masters of nature
Sense of Time	Past-oriented	Present-oriented	Future-oriented
Activity	Being (stress on who you are)	Growing (stress on self-development)	Doing (stress on action)
Social Relationships	Authoritarian	Group-oriented	Individualistic

Source: Kohls (1996, p. 30).

TABLE 2.3   U.S. American Value System

ORIENTATION	BELIEFS AND BEHAVIORS		
Human Nature	Basically evil	Mixture of good and evil	Basically good (changeable)
Relationship to Nature			Humans the masters of nature
Sense of Time			Future-oriented
Activity			Doing (stress on action)
Social Relationships			Individualistic

Source: Kohls (1996, p. 33).

TABLE 2.4   How U.S. Americans See the Arab Culture

There would be important variations from one specific culture to another—Egyptian, Saudi, Lebanese, and so on. Notice that in one category (Relationship to Nature) Arabs seem to fall more or less equally into two of the classifications.

ORIENTATION	BELIEFS AND BEHAVIORS		
Human Nature		Neutral Unchangeable	Basically good (changeable)
Relationship to Nature	Humans subjugated by nature	Humans in harmony with nature	
Sense of Time	Past-oriented		
Activity	Being (stress on who you are)		
Social Relationships	Authoritarian		

Source: Kohls (1996, p. 34).

TABLE 2.5   How U.S. Americans See the Japanese Culture

The Japanese culture is very complex and even more "contradictory" than the Arab culture.

ORIENTATION	BELIEFS AND BEHAVIORS		
Human Nature		Mixture of good and evil Unchangeable	Basically good (changeable)
Relationship to Nature		Humans in harmony with nature	
Sense of Time	Past-oriented		Future-oriented
Activity		Growing	Doing (stress on action)
Social Relationships	Authoritarian	Group-oriented	

Source: Kohls (1996, p. 35).

TABLE 2.6 The Kluckhohn Model

ORIENTATION	BELIEFS AND BEHAVIORS					
	Basically evil		Neutral	Mixture of good and evil	Basically good	
Human Nature	*Mutable*	*Immutable*	*Mutable*	*Immutable*	*Mutable*	*Immutable*
Relationship to Nature	Subjugation with nature		Harmony with nature			
Sense of Time	Past-oriented (tradition-bound)		Present-oriented (situational)		Future-oriented (goal-oriented)	
Activity	Being (expressive/emotional)		Being-in-becoming* (inner development)		Doing (action-oriented)	
Social Relationships	Lineality** (authoritarian)		Collaterality*** (collective decisions)		Individualism**** (equal rights)	

Explanation of Terms Used Above

*Being-in-Becoming—The personality is given to containment and control by means of such activities as meditation and detachment, for the purpose of the development of the self as a unified whole.

**Lineality—Lines of authority clearly established and dominant-subordinate relationships clearly defined and respected.

***Collaterality—A human being is an individual and also a member of many groups and subgroups; he/she is independent and dependent.

****Individualism—Autonomy of the individual.

Source: Florence Kluckhohn and Frederick Strodtbeck, *Variations in Value Orientations* (Evanston, IL: Row, Peterson, 1961). (See especially Chapter 1.)

In terms of the *values* they represent, the Kluckhohn Model would look like this:

ORIENTATION	RANGE		
Human Nature	Most people can't be trusted.	There are both evil people and good people in the world, and you have to check people out to find out which they are.	Most people are basically pretty good at heart.
Relationship to Nature	Life is largely determined by external forces, such as God, fate, or genetics. A person can't surpass the conditions life has set.	Humans should, in every way, live in complete harmony with nature.	Humans' challenge is to conquer and control nature. Everything from air conditioning to the "green revolution" has resulted from having met this challenge.
Sense of Time	Humans should learn from history and attempt to emulate the glorious ages of the past.	The present moment is everything. Let's make the most of it. Don't worry about tomorrow, enjoy today.	Planning and goal setting make it possible to accomplish miracles. A little sacrifice today will bring a better tomorrow.
Activity	It's enough to just "be." It's not necessary to accomplish great things in life to feel your life has been worthwhile.	Humans' main purpose for being placed on this earth is for their own inner development.	If people work hard and apply themselves fully, their efforts will be rewarded.
Social Relationships	Some people are born to lead others. There are leaders and there are followers.	Whenever I have a serious problem, I like to get the advice of my family or close friends on how best to solve it.	All people should have equal rights and complete control over their own destiny.

Source: Kohls (1996, pp. 134–135).

5. What is the social relationship of humans to one another? U.S. Americans would answer individualistic; Arabs, authoritarian; and Japanese, authoritarian and group oriented.

You might ask why there can be two answers by a culture to the questions. The Arab culture is vast, including Egyptian, Saudi, Lebanese, and others. These specific cultures account for the variations in some of the categories. In the case of Japanese culture, the answers indicate that Japan, although it maintains very traditional values in certain areas, is moving toward a more Western perspective.

The third conclusion about the functions of cultural patterns is that, within a given culture, there are preferred solutions. In other words, most people within the culture will select the preferred solution. However, there will also be people who choose other solutions. For example, members of U.S. American minority groups might find their orientations divergent from those of the Western European U.S. American culture.

Fourth, over time, the preferred solutions shape the culture's basic assumptions about beliefs, values, and norms. In other words, the preferred solutions comprise the culture's cultural patterns. Table 2.6 summarizes the approach of Kluckhohn and Strodtbeck and indicates the values each orientation represents.

Edward Hall

Hall (1976) divided culture into two dimensions: low-context cultures and high-context cultures. Like Kluckhohn and Strodtbeck, Hall placed these two dimensions on a continuum and suggested that all cultures could be plotted along the continuum. According to Hall and Hall (1990), low-context and high-context communication refers

> to the fact that when people communicate, they take for granted how much the listener knows about the subject under discussion. In low-context communication, the listener knows very little and must be told practically everything. In high-context communication, the listener is already "contexted" and does not need to be given much background information. (pp. 183–184)

A communication context includes not only the communicators and the verbal and nonverbal codes exchanged. Important features of the communication context include the cultural, physical, sociorelational, and perceptual environments. All of these provide the communicator with knowledge as to how to communicate appropriately in a given situation. In high-context cultures, these contexts are the major focus. In low-context cultures, the focus is more on the verbal codes than the nonverbal elements of context.

Hall (1976) suggests:

> [High-context] communication transactions feature programmed information that is in the receiver and in the setting, with only minimal information in the transmitted message. [Low-context] transactions are the reverse. Most of the information must be in the transmitted message in order to make up for what is missing in the context (both internal and external). (p. 101)

In short, in a high-context culture, most of the information is either in the physical setting or is internalized in the person; very little is in the coded, explicit, transmitted part of the message. In contrast, in a low-context culture, the mass of information is vested in the explicit code. Thus, high-context cultures prefer messages in which most of the meaning is either implicit in the physical setting or in the individual's beliefs, values, and norms. In low-context cultures, people prefer to use messages in which the majority of the information is in the verbal code, and not in the physical setting or in the individual.

High-context cultures focus on the nonverbal context; low-context cultures focus on the verbal context. Chinese, Japanese, Korean, Vietnamese, Greek, and Arab cultures orient mainly to the high-context end of the continuum. German, Scandinavian, U.S. American, and Swiss cultures orient mainly toward the low-context end of the continuum.

What does the difference in context mean in terms of communication? The style of communication in each of the two contexts differs greatly. Table 2.7 indicates the major differences between these two contexts. As you might guess, such differences can cause difficulty in communication. To members of a high-context culture, members of a low-context culture often appear overly talkative, lacking in subtlety, and redundant to those in a high-context culture. To members of a low-context culture, high-context communicators often appear unexpressive or even dishonest. Remember, in a high-context culture communication is viewed as intrinsic to the individual. If an issue is attacked, so is the person. In a low-context culture, people often say, "That was a terrible idea, but don't take it personally." Such a statement indicates that in low-context cultures, the issue can be separated from the person.

A simple example of high-context communication occurs in families. Much of the information is implicit and covert. For example, we know what "the look" from Mom means, or the reasons for the formal table settings when company comes to dinner, or what the statement "I hope you can get home this year for the holidays" really means without being told explicitly. In contrast, consider the communication you do with a computer. Every message must be very explicit and overt for the computer to perform the functions you require.

Geert Hofstede

A third approach to the study of cultural patterns is that of Geert Hofstede (1997). In the late 1960s and early 1970s Hofstede surveyed over 100,000 employees of IBM, a large multinational business organization with branches in 72 countries. Hofstede obtained information in 50 countries and three regions. He compared work-related attitudes across the countries and found four dimensions of cultural values held by both employees and managers: individualism/collectivism, power distance, uncertainty avoidance, and masculinity/femininity.

Individualism/Collectivism   The dimension of individualism and collectivism describes the relationship between the individual and the groups to which she or he belongs. This dimension relates to the question of what a culture values in terms of individual achievement or collective group accomplishments. In individualist cultures, the individual is the most

---

TABLE 2.7   Comparison of Low- and High-Context Cultures

Low Context	High Context
1. Communication is overt and explicit.	1. Communication is covert and implicit.
2. Individualism is valued.	2. Group is valued.
3. Interpersonal bonds are fragile.	3. Interpersonal bonds are strong.
4. Linear logic is emphasized.	4. Spiral logic is emphasized.
5. Direct verbal interaction is valued and one is less able to read nonverbal expressions.	5. Indirect verbal interaction is valued and one is more able to read nonverbal expressions.
6. More "logic" is used to present ideas.	6. More "feeling" is used in expression.
7. Highly structured messages, with many details, are emphasized.	7. Simple, ambiguous messages are used.
8. Self-expression is valued, opinions and desires are stated directly, and the individual tries to persuade others to his or her viewpoint.	8. Harmony is valued, so language is ambiguous and silence is often used to avoid confrontation. Saying "no" directly is avoided.
9. Clear, eloquent speech and verbal fluency is praiseworthy and admired.	9. Ambiguity and use of silence is admired. Communicators "talk around" the point, allowing each other to fill in the missing pieces
10. Time is highly organized and structured, less responsive to people's needs.	10. Time is open and flexible, more responsive to people's needs.

important element in any social setting. The individual and achievement are prominent. Personal goals override group goals and competition is encouraged. An individual's self-concept is accentuated. More dating, flirting, and small talk in social interactions are emphasized. Countries such as the United States, Australia, Great Britain, Canada, the Netherlands, New Zealand, Italy, Belgium, and Denmark are examples of individualistic cultures.

In contrast, in collectivist cultures the group is the major element. Needs and views of the person's in-groups (the immediate and extended family) override the needs and desires of the individual. Self-concept does not play as important a role as it does in individualistic cultures. People are expected to conform to the group's norms and values. Thus, the social networks are more fixed and less reliant on individual initiative. Columbia, Venezuela, Pakistan, Peru, Taiwan, Thailand, Singapore, Chile, and Hong Kong are collectivist countries. In general, collectivist countries tend to be high context in their orientation to communication, whereas individualistic countries tend to be low context in their orientation to communication (see Table 2.8).

The individualistic/collectivist dimension has been studied extensively by scholars and researchers. Triandis (1990, 1995) suggests that not only do individualistic cultures differ from collectivist cultures but they also differ within each dimension. In other words, some individualistic cultures differ from other individualistic cultures. Similarly, not all collectivist cultures are alike. Triandis sought to clarify the individualistic and collectivist dimensions by introducing the concepts of horizontal and vertical individualism and collectivism. In *horizontal individualism,* the self is valued, but the individual is more or less equal in status to others. Thus, the self is independent, but the same as others. In *vertical individualism,* the self is valued, but is viewed as different from and perhaps unequal in status to others. Status and competition are important in vertical individualism. France and the United States are oriented toward vertical individualism, whereas Austria and Sweden are examples of countries oriented toward horizontal individualism.

In horizontal collectivism, the self is viewed as a part of an in-group whose members are similar to one another. Equality is important in this orientation since the self is interdependent and the same as the self of others. The individual in a vertical collectivism orientation views self as part of an in-group in which the members are different from one another in terms of status. The self is interdependent and inequality within the group is valued. Sacrifice and serving are important in this orientation. China is an example of a country oriented toward horizontal collectivism; India is an example of a vertical collectivism orientation. Triandis's work suggests that we need to understand the differences in cultures even within each dimension.

Power Distance   Power distance is the degree to which a culture tolerates inequality in power distribution in relationships and organizations. Does the culture favor hierarchical

TABLE 2.8   Differences between Collectivist and Individualistic Cultures

Collectivist	Individualistic
Identity is based on the social network.	Identity is based on the individual.
Children think in terms of "we."	Children think in terms of "I."
Harmony should always be maintained and direct communication avoided.	Speaking one's mind is important.
At work, relationship prevails over task.	Task prevails over relationship.
Ideologies of equality prevail over ideologies of individual freedom.	Ideologies of individual freedom prevail over ideologies of equality.
Harmony and consensus in society are the ultimate goals.	Self-actualization of every individual is the ultimate goal.

Source: Adapted from Hofstede (1997).

power structures or does it favor a more equal distribution of power? High-power distance cultures tend to be authoritarian, with a hierarchical or vertical structure of social relationships. People are assumed to be unequal. Differences in age, sex, generation, and status are maximized. Relationships in a high-power distance culture are based on levels of hierarchy. France, Brazil, Hong Kong, Colombia, Mexico, Venezuela, India, the Philippines, and Singapore are representative of the high-power distance countries.

Low-power distance cultures are characterized by an emphasis on horizontal relationships rather than vertical ones. Differences in age, sex, generation, status, roles, and so on, are minimized and individual differences are encouraged. These countries tend to be less formal and more direct in their communication. Examples of low-power distance countries are Australia, Israel, Denmark, Norway, Sweden, Finland, Switzerland, New Zealand, and Ireland (see Table 2.9).

Uncertainty Avoidance   The dimension of uncertainty avoidance measures the degree to which a culture can tolerate uncertainty and ambiguous situations. Does the culture hold rigid and explicit behavioral expectations or does it appreciate ambiguity and uncertainty? Members of high-uncertainty avoidance countries (e.g., Greece, Portugal, Belgium, Argentina, Chile, Peru, Spain, France, and Japan) try to reduce the level of ambiguity and uncertainty in social and organizational life. They resist change, fear failure, avoid risk taking, pursue life and job security, and desire behavioral rules that can be followed in interactions with others. As a result of this orientation, they also use fewer oral cues and are more able to predict the behavior of others.

Low-uncertainty avoidance cultures are more comfortable with ambiguity and uncertainty. Their members are able to cope with the stress and anxiety that uncertainty causes. As a result, they are better able to tolerate deviant behaviors. They take more initiative, exhibit greater flexibility, and feel more relaxed in social situations. Denmark, Norway, Sweden, Finland, Ireland, Great Britain, the Netherlands, the Philippines, and the United States are examples of countries with low-uncertainty avoidance (see Table 2.10).

Masculinity/Femininity   Hofstede's last dimension, masculinity/femininity, is the degree to which stereotypically masculine and feminine traits prevail in a culture. Does the culture place the highest value on assertiveness, wealth, and achievement, or on relationships, caring for others, and the overall quality of life? In a masculine culture, men are dominant. They should be ambitious, assertive, strong, competitive, and strive for success and achievement. As a result, communication style tends to be aggressive. Women are to be nurturing. Japan, Australia, Germany, Great Britain, Mexico, Ireland, Switzerland, and Venezuela are masculine countries.

TABLE 2.9   Key Differences between Small- and Large-Power Distance Cultures

Small-Power Distance	Large-Power Distance
Inequalities among people should be minimized.	Inequalities among people are both expected and desired.
Subordinates expect to be consulted.	Subordinates expect to be told what to do.
Privileges and status symbols are frowned on.	Privileges and status symbols for managers are both expected and popular.
Power is based on formal position, expertise, and the ability to give rewards.	Power is based on family or friends, charisma, and the ability to use force.
The use of power should be legitimate and is subject to the criteria of good and evil.	Might prevails over right; whoever holds the power is right and good.

Source: Adapted from Hofstede (1997).

TABLE 2.10 Differences between Weak and Strong Uncertainty Avoidance Cultures

Weak Uncertainty Avoidance	**Strong Uncertainty Avoidance**
Uncertainty is a normal feature of life and each day is accepted as it comes.	Uncertainty in life is felt as a continuous threat that must be fought.
Stress is low.	Stress is high.
Aggression and emotions should not be shown.	Aggression and emotions may be shown at the appropriate time and place.
Deviant behaviors and ideas are tolerated.	Deviant behaviors and ideas are suppressed.
There are few and general laws and rules.	There are numerous and precise laws and rules.
Tolerance and moderation are practiced.	Conservatism, extremism, and law and order are practiced.
Citizen protest is acceptable.	Citizen protest should be repressed.

Source: Adapted from Hofstede (1997).

Members of feminine cultures emphasize compassion, emotion, nurturing, affection, and sensitivity. Men are not expected to be assertive. Gender roles are more equal. Thus, people are more tolerant of ambiguous situations and more capable of reading nonverbal cues. Sweden, Norway, the Netherlands, Denmark, Finland, Chile, Portugal, and Thailand represent feminine cultures. Table 2.11 summarizes the differences between masculine and feminine cultures.

Tables 2.8 through 2.11 will help you understand the differences in each of Hofstede's four dimensions. No doubt you have begun to see some similarities between Hall's concept of context and Hofstede's four dimensions. Table 2.12 lists 10 countries and how they compare on Hall's and Hofstede's dimensions.

Michael Bond

Several researchers (e.g., Kim, 2002) have suggested that all of the previous approaches we have discussed are biased in that they present a Western perspective. Indeed, most claims of intercultural communication have been made on the basis of data obtained from persons

TABLE 2.11 Differences between Feminine and Masculine Cultures

Feminine	**Masculine**
Dominant values are caring for others and preservation.	Dominant values are material success and progress.
People and warm relationships are important.	Money and things are important.
Everyone should be modest.	Males are to be assertive, ambitious, and tough.
Men and women are allowed to be tender and concerned with relationships.	Women are to be tender and take care of relationships.
Both fathers and mothers deal with facts and feelings.	Fathers deal with facts; mothers deal with feelings.
Equality, solidarity, and quality of work life are stressed.	Equity, competition among colleagues, and performance are stressed.
Preservation of the environment is a high priority.	Maintenance of economic growth is a high priority.

Source: Adapted from Hofstede (1997).

TABLE 2.12 Comparison of Hofstede and Hall					
Location	**Masculinity/ Feminity**	**Uncertainty/ Avoidance**	**Power Distance**	**Individualism/ Collectivism**	**Context**
Areas					
Africa	M	M	H	L	H
Arab	M	M	H	M	H
Countries					
China	M	M	H	L	H
France	M	H	H	H	L
Germany	H	M	L	H	L
Great Britain	H	L	L	H	L
Indonesia	M	L	H	L	H
Japan	H	H	M	M	H
Netherlands	L	M	L	H	L
United States	H	L	L	H	L

L = low; M = medium; H = high

from the Anglo ethnic group in the United States. Thus, researchers are calling for an understanding of communication from a multicultural perspective. Michael Bond, a Canadian who has lived in Asia for 40 years, believes that the much of the work in intercultural communication has derived from a Western bias. Since most scholars have been Westerners from Europe or the United States, they studied culture from their Western assumptions. To remedy this situation, Bond assembled a team of researchers from China and Taiwan and developed and administered the Chinese Value Survey to university students in 23 countries (Bond, 1987). Bond and his team found four dimensions of cultural patterns: integration, human-heartedness, moral discipline, and Confucian work dynamism. The first three correspond to three of the dimensions of cultural patterns that Hofstede found.

Integration   Integration is closely related to the individualism/collectivism dimension. Integration refers to a sense of social stability. Those individuals in high-integration cultures value tolerance, noncompetitiveness, interpersonal harmony, and group solidarity.

Human-Heartedness   Human-heartedness refers to a sense of gentleness and compassion. As you might guess, this dimension is closely related to Hofstede's masculinity/femininity dimension. Those individuals living in cultures that rated high on this dimension value patience, courtesy, and kindness toward others.

Moral Discipline   The third dimension, moral discipline, refers to a sense of moderation and restraint in daily activities. Moral discipline relates closely to Hofstede's power distance dimension. People living in cultures high on moral discipline prefer to follow the middle-of-the-road path, attempt to keep themselves disinterested and pure in their relationships and activities, and regard personal desires as negative.

Confucian Work Dynamism   Bond's fourth dimension, Confucian work dynamism, refers to a person's orientation toward life and work. Bond terms this "Confucian" because the values, at both extremes of the dimension, seem to be taken straight from the teachings of Confucius. At one extreme on this dimension are cultures that value thriftiness, persistence, status differences within relationships, and a sense of shame. Hofstede (1991) suggests that this dimension is a long-term orientation toward life. Examples of countries that prefer the Confucian value of long-term orientation are China, Taiwan, Japan, South Korea, Brazil, and India. On the other extreme of this dimension is what Hofstede termed a short-term orientation to life. Cultures at this extreme value following and maintaining traditions, practicing personal steadiness and stability, acknowledging balance or reciprocity when greeting others, giving gifts, giving and receiving favors, and maintaining the "face" of self and others. Examples of countries that prefer a short-term orientation are Pakistan, Nigeria, the Philippines, Canada, Great Britain, and the United States.

What are Confucian values? Before explaining those, it is important to remember that Confucianism is not a religion. Rather, it is a set of practical principles and ethical rules for daily life. Four key principles of Confucian teaching will aid your understanding of the Confucian work dynamism dimension of Bond's work.

The first principle is the idea that social order and stability are based on unequal relationships between people. Following are the five basic relationships and the social virtues inherent in each:

1. Leader and follower (justice and loyalty)
2. Father and son (love and closeness)
3. Husband and wife (initiative and obedience)
4. Older brother and younger brother (friendliness and reverence)
5. Friends (mutual faithfulness)

The higher-status person in each relationship is obligated to provide protection and consideration; the lower-status person reciprocates by showing respect and obedience.

The second principle is that the family is the prototype for all social relationships. The virtues and values learned in the family extend to all social relationships. Thus, elders are treated with respect, harmony is important in all relationships, and the rules set forth in the first principle are to be followed at all times.

Third, do not treat others as you would not like to be treated yourself. This negatively phrased Golden Rule has some limitations to the Golden Rule with which some of you may be familiar. In Confucian teachings, this rule applies only in the context of a reciprocal relationship in which there are shared expectations about social obligations and responsibilities. In other words, Confucius was not suggesting that we love our enemy. Rather, the principle implies that we should surround ourselves with those people who are devoted, learned, and moral and avoid those who are not worthy to be treated like ourselves—those who use flattery, are too eloquent, and are fawning.

The final principle is that people should be skilled, thrifty, modest, patient, persevering, hard working, and educated. Moderation in all things is preferred. Teaching and learning are highly valued. Conspicuous consumption is to be avoided. Losing one's temper is unacceptable. Each individual has a responsibility to meet these standards of behavior.

How does Hofstede's uncertainty avoidance dimension relate to the work of Bond and vice versa? According to Hofstede, the reason this dimension does not correlate to any of Bond's dimensions is that uncertainty avoidance refers to people's search for truth. This dimension was found by researchers with a Western perspective—a perspective to which one essential truth is important. The search for one essential truth appears not to be as important to Chinese and other Asian cultures. Similarly, the dimension of Confucian dynamism was found only when culture was investigated by researchers with an Asian perspective. This dimension relates not to truth, but to virtue. Hofstede and Bond (1984) believe that this difference in findings between European and Asian perspectives suggests a

> powerful illustration of how fundamental a phenomenon culture really is. It not only affects our daily practices (the way we live, the way we are brought up, the way we manage, the way we are managed); it also affects the theories we are able to develop to explain our practices. Culture's grip on us is complete.

CONCLUSION

This chapter discussed cultural patterns—the shared beliefs, values, and norms that are stable over time and that lead to similar behaviors across cultures. Each culture has its own unique characteristics. Yet each culture shares the same basic problems. Several researchers have examined how cultures solve these shared problems. The chapter also focused on the approaches of Kluckhohn and Strodbeck, Hall, Hofstede, and Bond. Using the cultural patterns described in this chapter, you can describe the cultural patterns of a country. Being able to describe these patterns is the first step in understanding communication within a culture. The reading that follows will enhance your understanding of cultural patterns. Stewart and associates discuss the values, behaviors, assumptions, and cultural forms of Americans and compare these to those of other cultures.

FOR DISCUSSION

1. Compare and contrast the patterns developed by Kluckhohn and Strodtbeck, Hall, Hofstede, and Bond.
2. Which of the patterns discussed coincide with your own experience in intercultural communication? Explain.
3. Describe how each of Hofstede's dimensions of cultural patterns is displayed in your own culture.
4. In what ways are your own values similar to those of Bond's Confucian work dynamism dimension? How are they different? How do these affect your communication?

REFERENCES

Bond, M. (1987). Chinese values and the search for culture-free dimensions of culture. *Journal of Cross-Cultural Psychology, 18,* 143–164.

Daniel, J., and Smitherman, G. (1976). How I got over: Communication dynamics in the Black community. *Quarterly Journal of Speech, 62,* 22–30.

Elashmawi, F., and Harris, P. (1993). *Multicultural management.* Houston: Gulf Publishing.

Fisher, G. (1989). *Mindsets: The role of culture and perception in international relations,* 2nd ed. Yarmouth, ME: Intercultural Press.

Hall, E. T. (1976). *Beyond culture.* New York: Anchor Books/Doubleday.

Hall, E. T., and Hall, M. R. (1990). *Understanding cultural differences: Germans, French and Americans.* Yarmouth, ME: Intercultural Press.

Hofstede, G. (2001). *Culture's consequences: Comparing values, behaviors, institutions, and organizations across nations,* 2nd ed. Thousand Oaks, CA: Sage.

Hofstede, G. (1997). *Culture and organizations: Software of the mind.* New York: McGraw Hill.

Hofstede, G., and Bond, M. (1984). Hofstede's culture dimensions. *Journal of Cross-Cultural Psychology, 15,* 417–433.

Kim, Min-Sun. (2002). *Non-western perspectives on human communication.* Thousand Oaks, CA: Sage.

Kluckhohn, F., and Strodtbeck, F. (1961). *Variations in value orientations.* Evanston, IL: Row, Peterson.

Kohls, L. R. (1996). *Survival kit for overseas living.* Yarmouth, ME: Intercultural Press.

Sitaram, K. S., and Haapanen, L. W. (1979). The role of values in intercultural communication. In M. K. Asante and C. A. Blake (Eds.), *The handbook of intercultural communication* (pp. 147–160). Beverly Hills, CA: Sage.

Stewart, E. C., and Bennett, M. J. (1991). *American cultural patterns: A cross-cultural perspective.* Yarmouth, ME: Intercultural Press.

Triandis, H.C. (1995). *Individualism and collectivism.* Boulder, CO: Westview Press.

Triandis, H. C. (1990). Cross-cultural studies in individualism and collectivism. In J. J. Berman (Ed.), *Cross-cultural perspective* (pp. 41–133). Lincoln: University of Nebraska Press.

Ting-Toomey, S. (1999). *Communicating across cultures.* New York: Guilford.

Cultural Assumptions and Values

Edward C. Stewart, Jack Danielian, and Robert J. Foster

For purposes of analysis, culture may be examined at four levels: concrete *behavior, values, assumptions,* and generalized *cultural forms.* The last three are necessarily derived from observations of behavior but can be usefully treated as a motivational explanation underlying most human behavior. Viewed at the individual level they are, in effect, internalized components of personality that are generally shared with other members of the cultural group.

> Values are relatively concrete, discrete, and specific; for instance, typical American values are the sanctity of private property, and desirability of physical comfort, and the need for tangible measures of success. Values also have a quality of "oughtness" and are relatively available to individual awareness. (Kluckhohn et al., 1951). A person will often discuss values when explaining his or her own or others' feelings or behavior.

Assumptions, on the other hand, are more abstract and more outside of conscious awareness. They represent the predispositions the individual employs to pattern the world and are usually felt by the individual to be an aspect of the world itself and not simply his or her perception of it. Examples of American assumptions are a predisposition to see the self as separate from the world and the usual endorsement of "doing" as the preferred means of self-expression (Kluckhohn and Strodtbeck, 1963).

Assumptions provide a person with a sense of reality—which is only one of several possible realities—and values provide a basis for choice and evaluation. However, assumptions and values merge into one another. What is an assumption for one individual, or for one culture, may be a value for another individual or for another culture. Any one concept held by a person is likely to combine aspects of both assumptions and values; hence it is difficult, and often unimportant, to determine whether it is one or the other.

In some cases the cognitive processes underlying cultural thinking are so abstract and lacking in substantive reference that they are probably best distinguished from assumptions and called *cultural forms.* Examples include assumptions about time, space, essence, energy, and logical process. Cultural forms tend to overlap with assumptions and, to a lesser degree, values. . . .

A frequent objection made to efforts to analyze any culture is that people differ from one another in many ways, even within a culture, and any attempt to describe a people according to broad generalizations, such as cultural characteristics, results in stereotypes. It is clear that people differ widely with respect to any particular behavior or value. Nevertheless, certain values and assumptions are dominant in, for example, American culture and are shared to one degree or another by most members. Thus, when we speak of an American value (or assumption), we refer to a peak or modal tendency for a range (distribution) of that value in the culture. All points on the distribution can be found in any society; thus, when two cultures are compared on a given dimension, there is overlap (i.e., some members of Culture A will be more typical of Culture B than many members of Culture C who may be far from the modal point of their culture).

In addition, an individual's reactions will vary from situation to situation and from time to time in the same situation. However, there is a relative internal integration and stability in behavior over time and situation. Variations, thus, should not obscure systematic differences which do exist or the validity of stereotypes (modal tendencies) in understanding intercultural phenomena.

Culture patterns, including their variations, may be seen as guides to "a limited number of common human problems for which all peoples at all times must find some solution" (Kluckhohn, 1963, 221). These problem areas can be used as a framework for identifying inclusive cultural dimensions on which all cultures can be plotted (Kluckhohn, 1963). The common human problems covered by such a system of assumptions and values can be classified under five categories: activity, social relations, motivation, perception of the world, and perception of the self and of the individual. Each category is briefly identified by describing *some* American values and assumptions, together with non-Western alternatives, which fall within each category. Their identification follows the work of Florence R. Kluckhohn, with a few divergences.

ACTIVITY

Self-expression is a problem common to all humans; Kluckhohn refers to this as the activity modality (Kluckhohn and Strodtbeck, 1963). In American society, the dominant mode of activity is *doing*. Doing refers to the assumption that activity should result in externalized, visible accomplishment as exemplified by the stock American phrase, "getting things done." The contrasting mode is *being,* which, however, does not connote passivity, since a person with a being orientation can be very active. The being orientation refers to the spontaneous expression of what is regarded as the given nature of human personality. It values the phenomenological experience of humanity rather than tangible accomplishments and is associated with the notion of having a natural and given position in society. A third possible orientation to activity, which stresses development of all aspects of the integrated person—*being-in-becoming*—is similar to being in its stress on experience rather than accomplishment, but it is dynamic.

Another area of activity that can be analyzed according to several dimensions is problem-solving decision making. In some cultures, decisions are more likely to be made by an individual because of the role he or she occupies; under this condition, decisions are much more likely to be influenced by the characteristics of the role than by the preferences or commitments of the individual. Another possibility is for decision making to be a function of a group, and for no one individual or role occupant to assume responsibility for it. This last alternative, for example, is more typical of Japanese culture than of American culture (Kerlinger, 1951).

The concept of what constitutes decision making varies from culture to culture and thus requires some alteration when examined within different cultural frameworks. In American society the process of decision making unfolds primarily through the anticipation of the consequences of alternative courses of action. In some other cultures, however, the function of the decision maker or makers is to evaluate a situation by classifying it according to pre-established categories. Whatever action ensues, or whatever decisions are made, will follow automatically from this traditional classifying activity (Silvert, 1963). Perhaps it is such a process of classification that leads some Western observers to conclude that in the underdeveloped world few decisions are required. This example illustrates the difficulty of getting outside of one's own cultural framework when one is required to examine parallel processes from culture to culture.

The distinctions between different ways of organizing activity also have important implications for learning or teaching (Bateson, 1947). For example, Americans implicitly assume that learning is an *active* process requiring performance by the learner, whose incentive to learn is either a future reward or the avoidance of punishment; thus, learning is regarded as a process of shaping the responses of the learner and building upon them. In some cultures the learner is assumed to be passive and the chief technique used is serial rote learning (Reichel-Dolmatoff and Reichel-Dolmatoff, 1961); learning is assumed to be an automatic process occurring in a highly structured situation. From this perspective, events in the natural and social world of the learner occur automatically in response to his or her actions. Since the world is considered as overwhelming, highly structured, and impervious to the initiative of the individual, no stress is put on spontaneity or upon the characteristics of the learner. This kind of learning corresponds to a Pavlovian situation, and is more prevalent in Bali, for example, than in the United States (Bateson, 1947).

These brief descriptions of some possible alternative values and assumptions underlying different expressions of activity call attention to the necessity for using several dimensions to explain any specific behavior. In speaking of decision making and learning, for instance, allusions to perception of the self, perception of the world, and motivation are required.

SOCIAL RELATIONSHIPS

A chief characteristic of social relationships among Americans of the middle class is equality (Williams, 1961). Its ramifications are so profound that it should be considered an assumption of American culture, even though as an expressed value there is no uniform application to all segments of the society. In nearly every other culture there is a much greater emphasis on inequality of persons (Arensberg and Niehoff, 1964). To assume that everyone is equal and should be treated alike is considered, in some cultures, to be demeaning to the individuality of the person. Inequality underlies social conventions and etiquette and clearly defined reciprocity among persons engaged in social interactions.

In American culture social conventions tend to be more informal and social reciprocities much less clearly defined. For example, equality removes the need for elaborate forms of social address, since one of the functions of formality is to call attention to the participants' respective status and ascriptions. Americans usually tend to ignore these qualities of social intercourse, quickly achieve a first-name basis with others, and conduct both business and social intercourse with directness and informality. Unlike members of other cultures such as the Thai, Americans prefer direct contact with others in either business or social affairs and hence seldom have need of a third person, an intermediary, as do the Thai.

Despite the emphasis on equality and informality, there is an element of depersonalization in relationships between Americans. Americans have many friends, but these are often associated with a given situation or time (Kluckhohn, 1957). Furthermore, the word *friend* may serve to describe anyone from a passing acquaintance to a lifetime associate. American friendship differs from that found in many parts of the world, where an individual may have few friends but is likely to have a total, rather than a selective, commitment to them. Individuals may be disinclined to share friends with other friends, since both the quality of friendship and the number of friends are considered limited and hence not to be squandered (Foster, 1965).

Americans tend to be relatively impartial and objective in the conduct of social relations, compared to the personalized interactions found in many parts of the world. Examples of the former are large charitable fund-raising efforts, objective standards of promotion, and the uneasiness about gift giving in business. Examples of personalized interaction are found in the paternal benevolence of the Japanese and Latin Americans, personal leadership of the Latin *caudillos,* and the nepotism endemic to Asia, Africa, and Latin America.[1]

The depersonalized predisposition of Americans combines with other values to nurture competition in which each individual strives for his or her own personal goals. For example, "joshing," "one-upmanship," "repartee," and a "friendly suggestion" are subtle forms of competition. Although this sort of behavior in interpersonal relations usually seems innocuous to Americans, such actions are perceived as subtle coercion in many other cultures (Wax and Thomas, 1961).

MOTIVATION

A third category of assumptions and values is motivation. Achievement is generally agreed to be a chief motivating force in American culture. It is the force which gives the culture its quality of "drivenness" (Henry, 1963). An American's identity and, to a large

degree, worth are established by accomplishments; an American *is* what an American achieves. Furthermore, accomplishments should be objective, visible, and measurable, since the culture does not readily provide a means of evaluating and knowing the self except through external performance.

Relative to members of many other societies, Americans do not attribute particular meaning to place of birth, family, heritage, traditional status, or other prescriptive considerations which can be used to define the self. American culture, then, emphasizes personal achievement through externally documented accomplishments while many other societies emphasize ascription with its attendant concern for the traditionally fixed status of the individual (Potter, 1954).

An American's investment in material and visible signs of success leads one to inquire about American notions about failure. For Americans the concept is difficult to accept and hence is usually avoided or rationalized. A typical response is to rationalize the failure as an inevitable part of the learning process leading to future accomplishment or to regard the situation as the fault of others.

PERCEPTION OF THE WORLD

A dominant perception in American culture assumes that the world is material rather than spirit (or idea, essence, will, or process), and should be exploited for the material benefit of humanity. This perception implies a clear separation between humans and all other forms of life and nature. Men's and women's quality of humanness endows them with a value absent in other forms of life; they are unique because of their souls. Nature and the physical world, although often referred to as living, are conceived of as material and mechanistic.

This perspective is distinct from assumptions held in some other parts of the world (and variant assumptions in American culture) that humanity is inseparable from the environment and should strive for harmony with it (Arensberg and Niehoff, 1964). Nature is perceived as alive and animistic; animals and even inanimate objects have their own essence. Hence, no clear dividing line separates plants, rocks, rivers, and mountains from humans. Consequently, they should strive for unity and integration with nature and the physical world rather than attempt to control these forces.

Control and exploitation of the environment are closely associated with the concept of progress, a notion relatively absent in many parts of the world. There is a prevalent notion among Americans that a person and especially an organization must progress or cease to exist; one cannot stand still and continue to function.

Bound up with the idea of progress and achievement, motivation in American culture is a feeling of general optimism toward the future. Most Americans feel that through their efforts a better future can be brought about which will not compromise the welfare and progress of others (Kluckhohn and Kluckhohn, 1947). There is enough for everyone. Such a system of values and assumptions, of course, receives repeated reinforcement, since Americans live in a country with an expanding economy and resources. These assumption contrast with the concept of "limited good" and fatalism found in many parts of the world (Foster, 1965).

PERCEPTION OF SELF AND THE INDIVIDUAL

The concept of an individualistic self is an integral assumption of American culture so deeply ingrained that Americans ordinarily do not question it. They naturally assume that each person has his or her own separate identity. However, since this cultural assumption is implicit and generally outside the awareness of the American, the nature of self-identity is somewhat elusive. An individual's relatively diffuse identity is, in part, a consequence of the absence of clear ascriptive classifications such as *caste* and *class* found in other cultures (Mead, 1963).

Stress on the individual begins at a very early age when the American child is encouraged to be autonomous. It is an accepted value that children (and adults) should be encouraged to make decisions for themselves, develop their own opinions, solve their own problems, have their own possessions. The concepts of freedom of choice and self-autonomy are, however, moderated by social control mechanisms in the form of expectations that the individual will choose according to the wishes of others.

An important consequence of this emphasis on the individual is that the American tends to resist formal authoritative control (Gorer, 1948). The concept of ideal authority for the American is one that is minimal and exercised informally by means of persuasion and appeals to the individual, rather than by coercion or by expectation of compliance to tradition, as is the case in many other cultures.

Another consequence of the American's individuality is that his or her self-concept is not easily merged with a group, ranging from a small one to the nation, and is conceived as a collection of individuals. The American resists becoming lost in a group or expresses concern about the nonperson emphasis of a cause or abstract ideology.

This avoidance of nonperson is tied to the fact that in the American culture ideas and concepts are typically made meaningful by using the individual as a point of reference. For example, concepts of dignity and human nature most likely take the form of self-respect, personal needs, and individual goals. With emphasis on concrete and self-referring terms, Americans are uncomfortable when referring to concepts that do not have clear reference to the individual.

Another dimension of the perception of self and others revolves around the wholeness-divisibility of the person and is closely related to the American's emphasis on objectives rather than personal relationships. Americans tend to fragment personalities. They do not have to accept other people in totality to be able to work with them; an American may disapprove of the politics, hobbies, or personal life of an associate and still work effectively with him or her. An individual with ascriptive motivation, however, tends to react to others as total or whole persons and, consequently, often cannot work or cooperate with a person of different religion, belief system, or ethical code.

Action, thoughts, and intent are separately evaluated in American culture. For example, the individual cannot be held legally liable for harboring undesirable thoughts. In parts of the non-West (perhaps China is the best example), there is not such clear differentiation. Instead, action, thoughts, feelings, and intents are synthesized in a total assessment of the person. Thus, an indication of "wrong thoughts" would be grounds for censure even though undesirable action did not actually occur. When the assumptions underlying cultural thinking are pervasive and lack substantive reference, they are probably best called cultural forms or form cognitions . . . .

For Americans, the cultural form of *time* may usually be regarded as lineal. American concepts of planning, progress, preventive measures in health and technology, and orientation to the future may be seen to be associated with a lineal concept of time. Progress, for example, is closely associated with the view that time flows in one direction, toward the future. "You've got to keep up with the times" is an American expression which illustrates this association. This concept of time is eminently suited to a rational view of the world. One can distinguish various events in time and note their relationship by calling the preceding moment "the cause" and the next one "an effect." Although this description is oversimplified, it identifies the American predilection for seeing the world in concrete and delimited cause-and-effect sequences and provides a firm foundation on which to base the dominant American beliefs in accomplishment, in one's ability to master one's environment.

Concepts concerning contiguity and location may be regarded as aspects of *space,* a second kind of cultural form. Concepts of using space show important cultural differences. It is clear that different cultures deploy living and working areas in different patterns. Some cultures, such as Chinese, have a strong sense of territorialism; in other cultures, American for instance, territorialism is less highly developed, and one might expect it to be nearly absent in some nomadic cultures. Spatial displacements of persons in face-to-face interactions are also noticeably and measurably different from culture to culture (Hall, 1966). At the most abstract level, formal causes and correctional thinking may be considered expressions of spatial relations. Although they occur in American culture, they are not nearly so frequent as, for example, in Chinese culture (Nakamura, 1964). Temporal concepts, and efficient and material causes, are usually preferred by Americans.

A third kind of cultural form refers to the definitions of *essence* and *energy.* Primarily, for Americans, the universe is conceived as matter, or as things; in contrast, some people from sub-Saharan Africa view the universe as consisting of a network of living forces. In their perspective, force is synonymous with being (John, 1964).

The *relational* form, a fourth possible kind of form cognition, is the one which perhaps most clearly refers to process rather than to structure. A basic issue underlying human behavior is the relationship between the empirical world and the cognitive world. If the relationship is isometric, the empirical world can be apprehended directly. Americans tend to comprehend what they observe through intermediate explanatory concepts, whereas many non-Western people are more likely to apprehend experience directly through intuition and spontaneous reaction, without a need for "explanation" in the Western sense of the word.

The American is more likely to take a relativistic and pragmatic position than to assume the existence of a directly knowable reality. Another aspect of this contrast in relational forms is manifest in the American emphasis on analysis and logic as modes of expression rather than esthetic appreciation or sensitivity.

Other cultural forms are related to those described above: for example, the American tendency toward inductive thinking about quantification in contrast to deduction and inherent qualities. Another important contrast is that between comparative judgment, which is typically American, and absolute judgment (i.e., comparison against an abstract standard).

A final additional example, the concept of limits, should be mentioned. George M. Foster has described a chief distinction between peasant and Western societies in terms of the concept of "limited good" (1965). The concept, in the most general sense of a cultural form, refers to the tendency to conceive of the world in limited rather than expansive terms. The assumption of "unlimited good," in American culture, underlies achievement motivation, in which individuals see their opportunities and achievements as relatively unlimited and at least partly determined by their efforts. The value configuration is frequently referred to as "effort-optimism," as a key concept in understanding American behavior. In peasant societies the basic motivation is ascription, maintenance and entrenchment of status, privileges, and prerogatives (Foster, 1965; Potter, 1954). Underlying this value is the concept that the good in the world is limited and that gains for one individual are necessarily obtained at the expense of others. Foster describes the "image of the limited good" as

> one in which all of the desired things in life such as land, wealth, health, friendship and love, manliness and honor, respect and status, power and influence, security and safety, *exist in finite quantity,* and *are always in short supply . . .* Not only do these and other "good things" exist in finite and limited quantities, but in addition *there is no way directly within peasant power to increase the available quantities.* It is as if the obvious fact of land shortage in a densely populated area applied to all other desired things: not enough to go around. "Good," like land, is seen as inherent in nature, there to be divided and redivided, if necessary, but not to be augmented. (p. 296)

This concept of limits has far-reaching consequences in all aspects of the cultural pattern.

TABLE 1 Summary of Cultural Assumptions and Values

American	Contrast-American

1. Definition of Activity
    a. How do people approach activity?
        (1) concern with "doing," progress, change . . . . "being"
        (2) external achievement . . . . spontaneous expression
        (3) optimistic, striving . . . . fatalistic
    b. What is the desirable pace of life?
        (1) fast, busy . . . . steady, rhythmic
        (2) driving . . . . noncompulsive
    c. How important are goals in life?
        (1) stress means, procedures, techniques . . . . stress final goals
    d. What are important goals in life?
        (1) material . . . . spiritual
        (2) comfort and absence of pain . . . . fullness of pleasure and pain
        (3) activity . . . . experience
    e. Where does responsibility for decisions lie?
        (1) responsibility lies with each individual . . . . function of a group or resides
        in a role *(dual contrast)*
    f. At what level do people live?
        (1) operational, goals evaluated in terms of consequence . . . . experiential truth
    g. How do people assign value?
        (1) utility (does it work?) . . . . essence (ideal)
    h. Who should make decisions?
        (1) the people affected . . . . those with proper authority
    i. How do people solve problems?
        (1) planning outcomes . . . . coping with outcomes
        (2) anticipating consequences . . . . classifying the situation
    j. How do people learn?
        (1) actively (student-centered learning) . . . . passively (serial rote learning)
2. Definition of Social Relations
    a. How are roles defined?
        (1) attained . . . . ascribed
        (2) loosely . . . . tightly
        (3) generally . . . . specifically
    b. How do people relate to others whose status is different?
        (1) stress equality, minimize differences . . . . stress hierarchical ranks, stress differences
        (2) stress informality and spontaneity . . . . stress formality, behavior more easily anticipated
    c. How are sex roles defined?
        (1) similar, overlapping . . . . distinct
        (2) sex equality . . . . male superiority
        (3) friends of both sexes . . . . friends of same sex only
        (4) less legitimized . . . . legitimized
    d. What are members' rights and duties in a group?
        (1) assume limited responsibility . . . . assume unlimited responsibility
        (2) join group to seek own goals . . . . accept constraint by group
        (3) active members can influence group . . . . leader runs group, members do not
    e. How do people judge and relate to others?
        (1) specific abilities or interests . . . . overall individuality of person and his/her status
        (2) task-centered . . . . person-centered
        (3) limited involvement . . . . total involvement
    f. What is the meaning of friendship?
        (1) social friendship (short-term commitment, friends shared) . . . . intense friendship (long-term commitment
        friends are exclusive)
    g. How do people regard friendly aggression in social interaction?
        (1) acceptable, interesting, fun . . . . not acceptable, embarrassing
3. Motivation
    a. What is the motivating force?
        (1) achievement . . . . ascription
    b. How is competition among humans evaluated?
        (1) as constructive, healthy . . . . as destructive, antisocial

TABLE 1 Summary of Cultural Assumptions and Values* (Continued)

American   **Contrast-American**

4. Perception of the World (Worldview)
   a. What is the (natural) world like?
      (1) physical . . . . spiritual
      (2) mechanical . . . . organic
      (3) subject to control by machines. . . . . not subject to control by machines
   b. How does the world operate?
      (1) in a rational, learnable, controllable manner . . . . in a mystically ordered, spiritually conceived
                                                                                              manner (fate, divination)
      (2) through chance and probability. . . . . through fate
   c. Where do humans stand in nature?
      (1) apart from nature or any hierarchy . . . . .part of nature or of some
                                                                                              hierarchy (dual contrast)
      (2) things are impermanent, not fixed, changeable . . . . things are permanent,
                                                                                              fixed, not changeable
   d. What are the relationships between people and nature?
      (1) good is unlimited . . . . good is limited
      (2) humanity should modify nature for its ends . . . . humanity should accept the natural order
      (3) good health and material comforts expected and desired . . . . .some disease and material
                                                                                              deprivation are natural, expected
   e. What is truth? goodness?
      (1) tentative. . . . . definite
      (2) relative to circumstances. . . . . .absolute
      (3) experience analyzed in separate components, dichotomies. . . . . .experience apprehended as a whole
   f. How is time defined? valued?
      (1) future (anticipation) . . . . .past (remembrance) or present experience (dual contrast)
      (2) precise units . . . . undifferentiated
      (3) limited resource . . . . limitless resource
      (4) lineal . . . . circular undifferentiated
   g. What is the nature of property?
      (1) private ownership important as extension of self . . . . .use for "natural" purpose regardless of ownership
5. Perception of the Self and the Individual
   a. How is the self defined?
      (1) diffuse, changing. . . . . fixed, clearly defined
      (2) flexible behavior . . . . .person located in a social system
   b. Where does a person's identity seem to be?
      (1) within the self (achievement) . . . . outside the self in roles, groups, family, clan, caste, society
   c. Nature of the individual
      (1) characteristics separable . . . . perceived as totality
   d. On whom should one rely?
      (1) self. . . . . .superiors, patrons, others
      (2) impersonal organizations, abstract principles. . . . . .people
   e. What are the qualities of a person who is valued and respected?
      (1) youthful (vigorous) . . . . aged (wise, experienced)
   f. What is the basis of social control?
      (1) persuasion, appeal to the individual. . . . . .formal, authoritative
      (2) guilt . . . . shame
Generalized Forms
   a. linear (time). . . . . .nonlinear
   b. efficient and material, cause-and-effect thinking (space). . . . . .formal causes, correlative thinking
   c. materials substantive (essence and energy). . . . . .spirit, energy
   d. operationalism (implied observer) . . . . direct apprehension or formalism (dual contrast)
   e. induction . . . . deduction or transduction (dual contrast)
   f. judgment by comparison . . . . judgment against an absolute standard

The authors wish to acknowledge the contribution of Dr. Jasper Ingersoll, Department of Anthropology, Catholic University, to the development of this table.

NOTE

1. In describing American social relations as "depersonalized" and those of others as "personalized," no invidious comparison is intended. Trust, goodwill, and acceptance of other people for what they are, for example, are American characteristics but they need not be personalized in their expression. Distrust and suspicion are quite personal and more common in many other parts of the world than in the United States.

REFERENCES

Arensberg, C. and Niehoff, A. (1964). *Introducing social change.* Chicago: Aldine.

Bateson, G. (1947). Social planning and the concept of deuteron-learning. In T. Newcombe and E. Hartley (Eds.). *Readings in social psychology* (pp. 121–128). Troy, MO: Holt, Rinehart and Winston.

Foster, G. (1965). Peasant society and the image of limited good. *American Anthropologist, 67,* 293–315.

Gorer, G. (1948). *The American people: A study in national character.* New York: W. W. Norton.

Hall, E. (1966). *The hidden dimension.* New York: Anchor.

Henry, J. (1963). *Culture against man.* New York: Random House.

John, J. (1964). Value conceptions in sub-Saharan Africa. In F. Northrop and H. Livingston (Eds.). *Cross-cultural understanding: Epistemology in anthropology.* New York: Macmillan.

Kerlinger, F. (1951). *Decision making in Japan. Social Forces, 30,* 36–41.

Kluckhohn, C. (1957). American culture-a general description. In R. Williams (Ed.). *Human factors in military operations* (pp. 94–111). Chevey Chase, MD: Johns Hopkins University.

Kluckhohn, C. et al. (1951). Values and value orientations in the theory of action. In T. Parsons and E. Shils (Eds.). *Toward a theory of action* (pp. 388–433). Cambridge: Harvard University Press.

Kluckhohn, C., and Kluckhohn, F. (1947). American culture: Generalized orientations and class patterns. In L. Bryson (Ed.). *Conflicts of power in modern culture: Seventh symposium.* New York: Harper and Row.

Kluckhohn, F. (1963). Some reflections on the nature of cultural integration and change. In E. Tinyakian (Ed.). *Sociological theory, values and sociocultural change: Essays in honor of P. A. Sorokin* (pp. 215–225). New York: Free Press.

Kluckhohn, F. and Strodtbeck, F. (1963). *Variations in value orientations.* Westport, CT: Greenwood Press.

Mead, M. (1963). The factor of culture. In M. Torre (Ed.). *The selection of personnel for international services* (pp. 3–22). Geneva: Federation for Mental Health.

Nakamura, H. (1964). *Ways of thinking of Eastern peoples: India, China, Tibet, Japan.* Honolulu: East-West Center Press.

Potter, D. (1954). *People of plenty: Economic abundance and the American character.* Chicago: University of Chicago Press.

Reichel-Dolmatoff, G. and Reichel-Dolmatoff, A. (1961). *The people of Anitama: The cultural personality of a Colombian Mestizo Village.* Chicago: Chicago University Press.

Silvert, K. (1963). National values, development, and leaders and followers. UNESCO *International Social Science Journal, 15,* 560–570.

Wax, R., and Thomas, R. (1961). American Indians and Whites. *Phylon, 22,* 305–17.

Williams, R. (1961). *American society: A sociological interpretation.* New York: Alfred A. Knopf.

CHECK YOUR UNDERSTANDING

1. What are the differences between values and assumptions?
2. What are cultural patterns?
3. Consider your own culture. What is your culture's orientation to decision making, motivation, social relationships, and perception of the world? Write a paragraph in which you describe how you personally view each of these. Are your perceptions consistent with the authors' description of your culture?
4. Create a visual description of yourself—a self-portrait, collage, or abstract painting. How will your self-perception affect your intercultural communication?
5. Explain the concept of "limited good." Write a scenario in which this concept could cause problems in intercultural communication. Ask your classmates to role play the scenario.

CHAPTER ACTIVITIES

1. Write a personal narrative in which you describe an incident of perceptual differences between you and a person from another culture. What problems were created? How was the communication affected? What did you do to help alleviate the problems?

2. In your journal write an "I Am" poem. Begin each line of the poem with "I am from . . ." describing in your own words who you are and what is important to your identity. Here is an example:

I AM FROM

I am from being the second of five, the oldest girl

I am from things my mother taught me—to dream, to dare, to dance, to believe in myself

I am from things my father taught me—to dance on roller skates in his strong arms; to understand that the journey, not the destination, is most important

I am from parents who believed that "different from" is not "better than"

I am from siblings who each gave me the gift of love and numerous opportunities to test my sense of humor

I am from a grandmother I never knew, but whose legacy lives in me

I am from rolling down Grandpa's hill in a cardboard box

I am from a grandmother whose joy and love of life knew no bounds

I am from stealing candy and bubble gum from Grandfather's general store

I am from building leaf houses, roller skating, ice-skating, and sledding with cousins

I am from a husband who is my soul mate

I am from children and grandchildren who teach me that life is sacred

I am from friends who tell me when I am right, but more importantly, when I am wrong

I am from debate and speech teams and theater

I am from cheerleading

I am from tap and ballet, jazz and ballroom dance

I am from storytelling

I am from singing in choirs

I am from teaching Sunday School, from church picnics and Christmas pageants

I am from an Iowa farm

I am from crisp fall nights with full moons and the sound of leaves beneath my feet

I am from springs filled with new life and promise

I am from winters of snow and ice-covered trees

I am from summers at the lake

I am from moonlight walks and sun-filled days on the beach

I am from swinging on ropes from the barn roof

I am from trips to the state fair

I am from dogs, and kittens, and frogs

I am from the smell of God's green fields and rich harvests

I from 4-H and Girl Scouts

I am from spinning and carding wool

I am from sewing and embroidery

I am from a first kiss from the boy of my dreams

I am from a love of teaching and learning

I am from traveling around the world

I am from dreams that didn't come true as well as dreams that did

I am from closed doors leading away from and, simultaneously, leading to

I am from an abiding faith and more blessings than I deserve

What does your poem tell you about who you are and how this might affect your perceptions? What affect will your image of self have on your intercultural communication?

3. Think of a myth, folktale, or legend of your campus. What does this tell you about the culture of your campus?

CHAPTER 3

PERCEPTION

WE AND THEY

Rudyard Kipling

Father, Mother, and Me,
Sister and Auntie say
All the people like us are We,
And everyone else is They.
And They live over the sea,
While We live over the way,
But—would you believe it?—They look upon We
As only a sort of They!
All good people agree,
And all good people say,
All nice people, like Us, are We
And everyone else is They:
But if you cross over the sea,
Instead of over the way,
You may end by (think of it!) looking on We
As only a sort of They!

OBJECTIVES

After reading this chapter and completing the readings and activities, you should be able to

- List the five steps in the perception process.
- Explain ethnocentrism and cultural relativism and their relationship to perception.
- Explain the social cognition process.
- Give an example of the self-fulfilling prophecy.
- Define five types of attribution error.
- Explain techniques used to help make accurate attributions.
- Explain the relationship between stereotypes and prejudice and how they affect intercultural communication.

Why might two people have different views of the same situation? The answer is that we select, organize, and interpret the stimuli we receive through our senses into a meaningful picture of the world around us. This process is called *perception* and it is the basis of our communication with others. However, as Singer (1987) indicates, "We experience everything in the world not as it is—but only as the world comes to us through our sensory receptors" (p. 9). In other words, we each construct our own reality. Thus, my reality may not be the same as yours.

THE PERCEPTION PROCESS

Each of us goes through the process of perception as we come into contact with others:

- We observe the available data in our environment.
- We choose what data we see/hear/feel/smell/taste and process it (selective perception).

- We define the person or event and build expectations of future behavior.
- Our expectations help determine our behavior toward the person.
- Our behavior affects the other person's perceptions.

Obviously, the data we select from all the available data is affected by our personal experiences, our psychological states, our values, our culture, and many other factors. Perception affects our communication. We make judgments of others based on those perceptions, and we communicate accordingly. If people interpret reality differently, communication problems may result. For example, in the United States, a firm handshake is considered proper. But in the Middle East, shaking hands too firmly or pumping is to be avoided; rather, a gentle or limp handshake is preferred. If I am meeting a person in a business setting, I first observe the data (e.g., the people, the environment, etc.). I select data to process—in this case, I might select to focus on who is at the meeting and who is talking. I approach the persons from the Middle East and give a good old-fashioned firm handshake, but the one returned is limp. I perceive this as rude and unfriendly and expect the business negotiation to be adversarial. So, I then behave in a somewhat adversarial manner. And, the Middle Eastern person may in turn perceive my behavior as adversarial and we are off and running toward a failed intercultural communication event.

Components of the Perception Process

Three components are involved in our interpretation of our reality: the attributive, the expectative, and the affective. The *attributive* component consists of those characteristics we attribute to the person or object or event. These characteristics may or may not be present. However, based on our experiences, we perceive them as being there. We may view foreigners as hard-working, eager, and intelligent. Or we may view them as lazy, unmotivated, and unintelligent.

The *expectative* component consists of the expectations we have of the things we perceive. In U.S. culture, we expect a college professor to read different kinds of books than a construction worker might read. We also expect them to dress differently. Based on the characteristics you attribute to others, you will expect certain behaviors. For example, if you view foreigners as hard-working, eager, and intelligent, you will expect them to be good employees.

Finally, we have feelings about the objects and people we perceive—the *affective* component of perception. The feelings are derived from our experiences with whatever we are perceiving, the characteristics we attribute to whatever we are perceiving, and our expectations concerning whatever we are perceiving. For instance, if your first view of foreigners is a positive experience, you will probably feel positively toward them. If you first impression of foreigners is a negative experience, you will no doubt dislike foreigners.

This whole process is, of course, reciprocal. For example, Americans tend to believe that opinions should be stated clearly and forcefully. Japanese tend to believe that opinions should be stated more indirectly and humbly. Thus, Americans might perceive Japanese as "wishy-washy," while Japanese might perceive Americans as "pushy."

CULTURE AND PERCEPTION

Ethnocentrism

Our culture plays a key role in structuring our perceptions. We are all taught ways of perceiving people, objects, and events. As the song from the musical *South Pacific* so aptly states, "You have to be carefully taught." This teaching may lead to ethnocentrism. Summer (1950) defines *ethnocentrism* as "the view of things in which one's own group is the center of everything, and all others are scaled and rated with reference to it" (p. 13).

Everyone is ethnocentric to some degree. Since our culture teaches us what the world is "really like," we believe that the values of our culture are the best. Thus, we may consider people from other cultures who do things differently—"wrong," "odd," or "strange." If we are highly ethnocentric, we see our in-group (our culture, our family, our friends—people we perceive as like us) as virtuous and superior and our values as universals (applying to everyone). We see out-groups (those outside of our in-group who we perceive as unlike us) as contemptible and inferior and we reject their values. Thus, our tendency is to evaluate the patterns of out-group behavior negatively rather than try to understand the behavior of out-group members.

Cultural Relativism

The opposite of ethnocentrism is *cultural relativism*—trying to understand others' behavior in the context of the culture or group of the person engaging in the behavior (Gudykunst, 1994, p. 78). If we try to interpret a person's behaviors from her or his own cultural frame of reference, we have a better chance of communicating effectively. For example, while interviewing women with bound feet in China, Cooper (2005) tried to put the practice in the context of Western beauty practices (e.g., plastic surgery and breast implants) as well as the historical times and women's roles in China to understand the footbinding process (see the reading in Chapter 6).

So, how might ethnocentrism and cultural relativism relate to communication? In 1978 Lukens wrote about the concept of ethnocentric speech in which we use our speech patterns to create a feeling of communication distance between us and the people with whom we communicate. Using Lukens's analysis, Gudykunst and Kim (1997) extended Lukens's idea of ethnocentric speech to include cultural relativism. If we combine these two concepts, we can place them on five positions on a continuum: very low cultural relativism/very high ethnocentrism, high ethnocentrism/low cultural relativism, moderate ethnocentrism/ moderate cultural relativism, low ethnocentrism/high cultural relativism, and very high cultural relativism/very low ethnocentrism.

What happens to communication as we move along this continuum? Communication distances are created by the distances between these positions. For example, the distance of disparagement involves very high levels of ethnocentrism and very low levels of cultural relativism. The in-group has animosity toward the out-group. This level of communication is characterized by the use of pejorative expressions about the out-group and the use of name-calling. Imitation and mockery of speech styles are also frequent.

The distance of avoidance minimizes contact with members of an out-group. A technique often used to accomplish this is an in-group dialect. For example, the use of "Black pride" or other in-group jargon might be used to show solidarity of the in-group and exclusion of the out-group.

The distance of indifference is the speech form used to "reflect the view that one's own [group] is the center of everything" (Lukens, 1978, p. 42). This distance reflects an insensitivity to the other group's perspective. As Gudykunst (1994) suggests, "One example of the speech use at this distance is 'foreigner talk,' the form of speech used when talking to people who are not native speakers of a language. It usually takes the form of loud and slow speech patterns, exaggerated pronunciation, and simplification (e.g., deletion of articles)" (p. 79).

The distance of sensitivity reveals, as its name implies, a sensitivity to group differences and reflects a desire to decrease communicative distance between people. When communicating at this level, we would, for example, use the term for the other person's ethnic group that she or he prefers (e.g., African American rather than Black American or Negro).

Finally, the distance of equality reflects our desire to minimize the distance between ourselves and others. We have an attitude of equality. At this level we strive to avoid evaluations of the other. We use speech that reflects our desire for equality. For example, we would not use the generic pronoun *he,* but rather the more reflective term of equality, *he or she.*

SOCIAL COGNITION

Social cognition concerns the way we make a coherent "picture" of any event. The process of social cognition involves the situation, the people involved, the relationship of the people, and the behavior we perceive.

The Situation

First, we "size up" the situation: What is going on? In order to communicate effectively, we need to understand "where we are"—the physical setting as well as the social setting. The social setting involves social episodes, or the "internal cognitive representations about common, recurring interaction routines within a defined cultural milieu" (Forgas, 1981). In other words, each culture has its own social episodes. Thus, the social episode of Chinese New Year celebrations differ from our U.S. American New Year celebration. Although both cultures celebrate the new year, we do so in different ways. For example, in the United States, the new year begins on the first day of January. The beginning of the Chinese New Year varies from year to year. In addition, Chinese traditions include paying off all debts (financial and moral) incurred in the previous year, putting up good-luck papers, buying flowers and plants (the favorite plant is the peach tree just coming into bloom, because the wood is a potent enemy of demons and the peach itself is symbolic of longevity), feeding the Kitchen God sweets before he ascends to heaven to report to the Jade Emperor about the family's activities during the previous year, and giving children bright red "lucky money" envelopes with money inside. The celebrations last for two weeks and the focus of activities is the family.

The People

We also need to size up the other individuals in the social episode. Trenholm and Jensen (1996) suggest four factors to consider: personal constructs, implicit personality theory, self-fulfilling prophecies, and cognitive complexity. Let's briefly examine each one.

Personal constructs are the mental yardsticks for evaluating objects, events, and people. These constructs are of four types (Duck, 1976):

1. *Physical constructs (tall–short, ugly–beautiful).*   These are generally the constructs we use to form first impressions.
2. *Role constructs (buyer–seller, student–teacher).*   We try to understand each person's position in the social situation.
3. *Interaction constructs (friendly–hostile, polite–rude).*   We try to understand the other person's style of communication.
4. *Psychological constructs (motivated–lazy, kind–cruel).*   We use the three other constructs to understand what kind of people the other interactants are.

Implicit personality theory suggests that we organize our individual perceptions into a cluster, filling in missing data. Thus, individual traits are related to other traits, and when we "see" an individual trait, we assume the person possesses the other traits in the cluster. For example, Kelley (1950) conducted research that suggests that "intelligent," "quiet," and "friendly" cluster together. So, if we view someone as friendly, we also view them as quiet and intelligent. Interestingly, once we have formed an impression of someone (which is formed during the first four minutes of interaction [Zunin, 1972]), we ignore other cues that are not consistent with our original first impression.

This relates to another perceptual tendency—the self-fulfilling prophecy. A *self-fulfilling prophecy* occurs when one person (the observer) believes something to be true about another person (the target). The observer behaves toward the target as if the belief is fact. This behavior prompts the target to behave as the observer expected. For example, if a teacher believes all Japanese people are hardworking and studious, he or she will treat the

Japanese students as such (call on them more often, ask them higher-level questions), and they will behave intelligently in that classroom. The Japanese students will self-fulfill the teacher's prophecy for them.

Finally, we differ in the *complexity of our cognitions*. We differ in both the number (differentiation) and quality (abstraction) as well as the ways we integrate these cognitions when evaluating others. If we are cognitively complex, we use a larger number of personal constructs, use more abstract psychological constructs, and have more elaborate ways of relating these constructs. In contrast, if we are less cognitively complex, we use fewer constructs, use less abstract constructs, and see the constructs more as isolated impressions (Delia, 1977).

So what does this mean in terms of intercultural communication? In general, less cognitively complex people are unable to integrate the constructs they use to form a more complete image. Thus, they ignore contradictory information or are unable to use new information to change their initial impression (Delia et al., 1979). More cognitively complex people are more accurate in processing information about others, probably because they weigh more evidence before formulating a complete impression. In addition, they are better able to put themselves in the role of the other person. It is likely that people who are more cognitively complex are better able to adapt to cultures different from their own than are less cognitively complex people.

Culture affects the variables that people use to explain the behavior of others. Collectivist cultures make greater references to situational factors and less references to personality factors than individualistic cultures (Gudykunst and Ting-Toomey, 1988).

In addition, culture seems to affect what information people emphasize when making attributions. Okabe (1983) indicates that verbal skills are more necessary and more prized in low-context, individualistic cultures than in high-context, collectivist cultures. In high-context cultures, verbal skills are considered suspect. Thus, confidence is placed in the nonverbal aspects of the interaction. For example, Tsujimura (1987) examines four characteristics of Japanese communication: (1) *ishin-denshin* (traditional mental telepathy), (2) taciturnity, (3) *kuki* (mood or atmosphere), and (4) respect for indirect communication. Notice that the emphasis for Japanese people is primarily on nonverbal communication.

The Relationship

After sizing up the people and the situation, we size up the relationship. In order to do this, we label the relationship—parent/child, spouse, friend, acquaintance, co-worker, business partner, and so on. Whatever level we assign determines our perception of the appropriate behavior in the relationship. As the relationship develops, we will develop a master contract with the other person that guides our recurring interaction.

One variable that governs how we do this is *self*—determining what aspects of our self-perception fit into the relationship. Our ability to be aware of and adapt our self-image to the current situation is referred to as a *self-monitoring* (Snyder, 1974). Snyder suggests that, in a given situation,

> The high self-monitor asks, "Who does this situation want me to be and how can I be that person?" In so doing, the high self-monitoring individual reads the character of the situation to identify the type of person called for by that type of situation, constructs a mental image or representation of a person who best exemplifies that type of person, and uses the prototypic person's self-presentation and expressive behavior as a set of guidelines for monitoring his or her own verbal and nonverbal actions. [The low self-monitor asks,] "Who am I and how can I be in this situation?" (p. 89)

Thus, the low self-monitor presents a consistent image regardless of the situation, whereas the high self-monitor "reads" the situation and adapts his or her self-image appropriately (Snyder, 1979). In terms of intercultural communication, this awareness and adaptation become extremely important. If we cannot "read" the new situation and adapt to it, we will not be effective in our intercultural interactions.

The Behavior

Finally, we explain the behavior in which both we and the other individuals in the situation have engaged. Theories that deal with the ways people infer the causes of behavior are called *attribution theories*. Attribution has three general principles:

1. People attempt to determine the causes of behavior.
2. People assign causes systematically.
3. The attributed cause affects our perception and our behavior.

We'll discuss each of these briefly.

Heider (1958) suggests that people try to figure out whether an observed behavior has been caused by personal or situational factors. Whenever we explain someone's behavior in terms of her or his personality, motivation, or personal preferences, we are using personal attributes. When we explain someone's behavior in terms of unusual circumstances, social pressure, or physical forces beyond the person's control, we are using situational attributes.

Kelley (1967) presents covariance theory—another theory that attempts to explain the types of information we use to make our attributions. According to Kelley, we attribute another's behavior to one of four variables:

1. The actor (the person who performed the behavior).
2. The target (the stimulus object or person the behavior is aimed at).
3. The circumstances (the physical setting or social context).
4. The relationship (the master contract governing actor and target when they interact).

We make our attributions to one of these variables based on three types of information:

1. Consensus.   Does the actor typically behave the same way in similar situations? If so, we have information leading to high consensus.
2. Consistency.   Does the actor behave the same way across a wide range of situations? If so, we have information leading to high consistency.
3. Distinctiveness.   Does the actor behave this way only toward the target? If so, we have information leading to high distinctiveness.

Table 3.1 outlines how we use consensus, consistency, and distinctiveness to make our attributions.

TABLE 3.1   A Model of Attribution Theory Outcomes, Based on the Work of Harold H. Kelley

When	We are most likely to attribute responsibility to
CONSENSUS is low CONSISTENCY is high DISTINCTIVENESS is low	THE ACTOR: The person who performed the behavior
CONSENSUS is high CONSISTENCY is high DISTINCTIVENESS is high	THE TARGET: The person toward whom the behavior is directed
CONSENSUS is high CONSISTENCY is low DISTINCTIVENESS is low	THE SITUATION: The setting or circumstances outside the control of either person
CONSENSUS is low CONSISTENCY is low DISTINCTIVENESS is high	THE RELATIONSHIP: Behavior pattern negotiated implicitly or explicitly by both parties

Source: Sarah Trenholm and Arthur Jensen, *Interpersonal Communication,* Second Edition, p. 82. © 1992 by Wadworth Publishing Co., Belmont, CA. Used by permission.

When we make our attributions, we are prone to several biases. The first of these is *personality error*. When we explain another's behavior in terms of personality and underestimate the influence of situational factors, we engage in personality error. As Littlejohn (1996) suggests,

> One of the most persistent findings in attribution research is the fundamental attribution error. This is the tendency to attribute the cause of events to personal action, the feeling that people are personally to blame for what happens to them. This tendency results from the insensitivity to many circumstantial factors causing events. Many of us tend to overlook causes of behavior that may not be the person's fault. This tendency, however, is reduced in the case of one's own responsibility. In other words, you tend to blame other people for what happens to them, but you blame the situation for what happens to you. If your roommate fails a test, you are apt to claim that he did not study hard enough, but if you fail the test, you will probably say that the test was too hard. (p. 137)

Second, we also might engage in *group bias*. We tend to attribute positive behavior by in-group members to their personality and their negative behavior to situational variables. In contrast, we tend to attribute positive behavior by out-group members to situational variables and negative behavior to personality variables (Jaspers and Hewstone, 1982).

Differences in cultural attributions can create misunderstanding. For example, Yum (1988) contends that silence and the use of indirect forms of communication are used widely in Korean cultures. Hall (1976), Hsu (1981), and Bond (1994) make similar observations about Chinese culture. If we come from a culture in which those behaviors are not used widely, we may attribute the wrong reasons to a behavior.

For example, the Chinese are reluctant to say "no," especially to a foreigner, because this might upset harmony. Thus, they are more indirect. When asked a question to which the answer is "no," they might say, "maybe." A Westerner assumes that this "maybe" means that there is a possibility of "yes." When the Westerner finds out the answer is, and always was, "no," she or he may think the Chinese person is a liar, unethical, or even immoral. However, the fact is that the Chinese person's response was entirely appropriate within his or her culture. Another Chinese person would realize that "maybe" is an indirect way of saying "no."

Triandis and colleagues (1994) suggest we use *isomorphic* attributions. These are shared attributions about people or events that take cultural differences into account. How do we do this? Bond (1994) indicates that vivid, personalized incidents overwhelm our attention and therefore carry more weight than they should in our final attributions. Cushner and Brislin (1996) provide the following example and solution to the problem Bond cites:

> John is searching for housing in the country to which he has been assigned. He buys a guidebook put out by a group of concerned sojourners who want to help newcomers make their way in the host country. The developers of the guide sampled the opinions of 200 sojourners concerning good housing possibilities, and the book specifies several good neighborhoods. John then happens to name one of these neighborhoods to a person he has recently met and who has been helpful in John's adjustment. The friend says: "I know that area. My wife's cousin lived there and didn't like it. This person found that it had poor bus service and was too far from stores." What does John do?
>
> There is a strong tendency, which all of us have, to place a great deal of weight on personal input. This input is given to John orally, probably with some colorful gestures, in contrast to the dull manner in which information is presented in the guidebook. But examine the situation more closely. The cousin is 1 person, and the guidebook was developed based on a survey of 200 people. So John now has input from 201 people, and the weight of the evidence is still strongly in favor of the neighborhood he was considering. However, the vivid, personalized input is likely to have more impact than simply 1 of 201 pieces of information. This tendency to react to vivid events is especially common among sojourners because they are exposed to many new and exciting events, but what is new and exciting is not necessarily important. Sojourners should

keep this point in mind and ask themselves, am I overacting to a vivid incident directed at me, personally? Is there other information I might use before coming to a conclusion? (p. 345)

In addition to personality and group bias error, three other attribution errors are possible: *egocentric bias*—the tendency to see our own behavior as normal and appropriate (Kelley, 1967), *premature closure*—the tendency to stop searching for explanations of behavior once we have a reasonable and relevant explanation (Taylor and Fiske, 1978), and the principle of *negativity*—the tendency to overemphasize negative information about others' behavior (Kanhouse and Hanson, 1972). If we engage in any of these, our intercultural communication will probably not be as effective as it would be if we did not engage in them.

Our own personalities influence our attributions. Gudykunst (1994) suggests two of these personality factors: category width and uncertainty orientation. Remember: When we perceive, we place our perceptions into categories. Category width is "the range of instances included in a cognitive category" (Pettigrew, 1982, p. 200).

Detweiler (1975) studied how category width influences the attributions European Americans use about people who are culturally similar and those who are culturally different (a person from Haiti). He found that, in general, wide categorizers are more likely to search for appropriate interpretations of a culturally dissimilar person's behavior than are narrow categorizers.

Sorrentino and Short (1986) explain the second personality factor that affects our perceptions: uncertainty orientation. In general, uncertainty-oriented people evaluate ideas on their own merit and do not necessarily compare them with others, want to understand themselves and their environment, are more likely to question their own behavior and its appropriateness when communicating with strangers, and are likely to try to gather information about strangers so they can communicate more effectively with them. In contrast, certainty-oriented people hold onto traditional beliefs, have a tendency to reject ideas that are different from their own, and do not examine themselves or their behavior. Thus, certainty-oriented people have more difficulty communicating effectively in intercultural communication situations.

Making Accurate Attributions

If we want to improve the accuracy of our attributions in order to be more effective intercultural communicators, we can use three techniques: perception checking, active listening, and feedback. *Perception checking* helps us make sure that our interpretation of another's behavior is what she or he meant. A perception check consists of stating three things: (1) a description of what you have heard and seen, (2) the conclusion you have drawn, and (3) a question that asks the other person whether your perception is accurate. For example, you might say, "I saw you are frowning and your eyes are red. You look like you were crying. Were you?" Note that the perception check has no evaluative element to it. In other words, you aren't saying, "You're always crying." That would be passing judgment, and perception checks are void of judgment. One note of caution is warranted here. As Gudykunst (1994) suggests, if you are an individualist communicating with a collectivist, it is important to keep in mind that collectivists may not feel comfortable answering direct questions. In that case, you have to ask your perception-checking questions indirectly.

A second technique for improving the accuracy of attributions is *active listening*. We will discuss this concept more fully in Chapter 7. Suffice it to say here that active listening assumes that listening is an active, not a passive, activity. We need to become actively involved in the listening process. We can do this by attending to the other person (leaning forward and facing the speaker, maintaining eye contact, giving the other person our undivided attention) and using perception checking. We also can use paraphrasing to make sure we understand the other person's ideas and perspective. Paraphrasing is restating in our own words what the other person says to make sure we have interpreted the person's ideas as he or she intended.

Finally, we can seek feedback from others and provide feedback on their communication. *Feedback* is "the response listeners give to others about their behavior . . . Feedback from others enables us to understand how our behavior affects them, and allows us to modify our behavior to achieve our desired goals" (Haslett and Ogilvie, 1988, p. 385). When we give feedback, we need to use "I" statements, which give our thoughts and feelings, and avoid "you" statements, which can only be our perceptions of another's thoughts and feelings. We need also to keep in the "here and now." Bringing up old issues, resentments, or concerns can only cloud the issue presently being discussed. In terms of intercultural communication, we need also to consider how feedback is given in the other person's culture. As Gudykunst (1994) suggests:

> To illustrate, assume that I (a European American male) want to present feedback to a Japanese male friend with whom I am communicating in Japan. If I am direct in the feedback that I give my friend, he may perceive my feedback as a threat to his public image (i.e., it may threaten his face). The reason for this is that Japanese try to preserve harmony in relations with friends. To accomplish this, they use an indirect style of communication. If I am direct and he perceives this as a threat, my feedback will be ineffective. To provide culturally sensitive feedback, I have to be indirect in the way I give it. If we are in the United States speaking English, I can be more direct than if we are in Japan speaking Japanese. (p. 236)

STEREOTYPES

Stereotypes influence the way we process information. A *stereotype* is a generalization about a group of people and can be positive or negative. When we stereotype, we make assertions about the characteristics of all people who belong to a particular category, such as women, African Americans, Asians, and so on. However, the problem is that members of a social group never all share a particular characteristic. For example, "Women are nurturing" is a stereotype, because not all women are nurturing. Hamilton and colleagues (1992) write that we need to remember that

> stereotypes are certain generalizations reached by individuals. They derive in large measure from, or are an instance of, the general cognitive process of categorizing. The main function of the process is to simplify or systematize, for purposes of cognitive and behavioral adaptation, the abundance and complexity of the information received from its environment by the human organism. . . . But such stereotypes can become social only when they are shared by large numbers of people within social groups. (pp. 146–147)

Stereotypes involve three essential aspects:

1. We categorize others based on easily identifiable characteristics.
2. We assume that certain attributes apply to most or all of the people in the category.
3. We assume that individual members of the category have the attributes associated with the group.

Stereotypes can be individual or social. In other words, we have stereotypes that

> operate as a source of expectancies about what a group as a whole is like (e.g., Hispanics) as well as about what attributes individual group members are likely to possess (e.g., Juan Garcia). Their influence can be pervasive, affecting the perceiver's attention to, encoding of, inferences about, and judgments based on that information. And the resulting interpretations, inferences, and judgments typically are made so as to be consistent with preexistent beliefs that guided them. (Taijfel, 1981, p. 142)

Often stereotypes serve as self-fulfilling prophecies—the tendency to see behavior that confirms our expectations, even when the behavior is absent. Hamilton and colleagues (1992) explain that

> perceivers can influence a person with whom they interact by constraining the person's behavior. However, perceivers typically do not recognize this influence or take it into consideration

when interpreting the target's behavior. Although a target person's behavior may be affected by perceiver-induced constraints, it is often interpreted by the perceiver as a manifestation of the target's personality. (p. 149)

How do stereotypes affect our intercultural communication? When we stereotype, we often make errors in the interpretation of others' behavior. We also make assumptions about how these people will behave and we make judgments about that behavior. Kunta and Sherman-Williams (1993) write:

> Consider, for example, the unambiguous act of failing a test. Ethnic stereotypes may lead perceivers to attribute such failure to laziness if the actor is Asian but to low ability if the actor is Black. Thus stereotypes will affect judgments of the targets' ability even if subjects base these judgments only on the act, because the stereotypes will determine the meaning of the act. (p. 97)

If we are to be more effective intercultural communicators, we need to focus on three key behaviors. First, we need to increase the complexity of our stereotypes (i.e., we need to include a large number of traits in the stereotype and differentiate subgroups within the group being stereotyped). Second, we need to question our unconscious assumption that most, if not all, members of a group fit a single stereotype. Third, we should cultivate what psychologist Ellen Langer (1989) calls mindfulness, a state of "alert and lively awareness" (p. 140), and avoid mindlessness, a state of reduced attention. Langer outlines three characteristics of mindfulness. The first of these is the creation of new categories. According to Langer, we need to create more, not fewer, distinctions (categories). Langer uses the example in the category "cripple." If we treat all people in this category the same, we begin to treat the category in which we place a person (in this case, "cripple") as her or his identity. If, on the other hand, we make more distinctions within this category (create new categories), we stop treating the person as a category. If we see someone with a broken leg, or a broken arm, or on crutches, we do not necessarily treat that person as a "cripple."

In addition to the creation of new categories, Langer (1989) suggests that mindfulness involves openness to new information and awareness of more than one perspective. These two characteristics are related to the third characteristic—that is, to focus on the process of communication, not the outcome. Langer explains:

> An outcome orientation in social situations can induce mindlessness. If we think we know how to handle a situation, we don't feel a need to pay attention. If we respond to the situation as very familiar (as a result, for example, of over-learning), we notice only minimal cues necessary to carry out the proper scenarios. If, on the other hand, the situation is strange, we might be so preoccupied with the thought of failure ("What if I make a fool of myself?") that we miss nuances of our own and others' behavior. In this sense, we are mindless with respect to the immediate situation, although we may be thinking quite actively about outcome related issues. (p. 34)

Thus, according to Langer, focusing on the process of communication (i.e., how we communicate) forces us to be mindful of our behavior in the situations in which we find ourselves.

Before we leave the discussion of stereotyping, it is important to point out that we all have stereotypes. It is a part of human interaction—a way we categorize data in order to communicate. However, we need to be aware of and move beyond our stereotypes to communicate with each individual as an individual, not as a group member.

It is also important to remember that all cultures stereotype people from other cultures. Kohls (1996) provides some examples of how people from other cultures stereotype Americans:

1. *India:*

   Americans seem to be in a perpetual hurry. Just watch the way they walk down the street. They never allow themselves the leisure to enjoy life; there are too many things to do. . . .

2. *Japan:*

   Americans seem to feel like they have to say something instead of having silence—even when what they say is so well known that it sounds stupid. They say things that are so obvious. Japanese people realize that we have all observed these things so it is unnecessary to talk about them.

3. *Iran:*

   The first time . . . my [American] professor told me, "I don't know the answer, I will have to look it up," I was shocked. I asked myself, "Why is he teaching me?" In my country a professor would give a wrong answer rather than admit ignorance.

4. *Colombia:*

   I was surprised in the United States to find so many young people who were not living with their parents, although they were not yet married. Also, I was surprised to see so many single people of all ages living alone, eating alone, and walking the streets alone. The United States must be the loneliest country in the world. (pp. 43–45)

PREJUDICE, DISCRIMINATION, AND RACISM

Prejudice

Prejudice is a negative attitude toward individuals resulting from stereotypes. It is helpful to break down the term. *Pre* means beforehand; *judice* comes from the same root as *judge*. Thus, prejudice is a form of prejudgment, or judging based on particular knowledge, without any previous thought or concern (Cushner and Brislin, 1996). Allport (1954) suggests that prejudiced people (1) ignore evidence that is inconsistent with their biased viewpoint or (2) distort the evidence to fit their prejudice.

In his analysis of prejudices, Van Dijk (1987) suggests several characteristics. According to Van Dijk,

- Prejudices are attitudes—generalized evaluations about a person, object, or action that are the result of individual experience, interpersonal communication, or media influence.
- Prejudices are group based—developed through communication with in-group members and used to describe out-group members.
- Prejudices fulfill social functions for in-groups—support the power and dominance of in-group members.
- Prejudices are negative evaluations—we devalue others for not being like us, for competing for scarce resources, and for threatening the in-group's way of life.
- Prejudices are based on cognitive models. (When in-group members interpret "ethnic encounters," their goal is not primarily to establish a truthful and reliable representation of "what is really going on." Instead, as in the interpretation of most encounters, people construct a model that is coherent with previous models of ethnic encounters.)

It is possible that the cognitive model is biased. Table 3.2 outlines the major types of cognitive bias.

TABLE 3.2   Major Types of Cognitive Bias

Cognitive Bias	Definition
Negative interpretations	Interpreting everything the out-group does as negative
Discounting	Dismissing information that doesn't fit the preconceived schemeta
Fundamental attribution error	Interpreting another's negative behavior as dispositional (personality) rather than situational
Exaggeration	Exaggerating negative character of out-group actions
Polarization	Tendency to perceive minor differences between in-group and out-groups as major

If prejudice is destructive, why do people have prejudices? Brislin (1991) suggests that prejudice serves several functions, and he outlines four. The first is the utilitarian function. Our prejudices may be rewarded—either economically or socially. When this is the case, we maintain these prejudices. The second function is the ego-defensive function, which allows us to avoid admitting certain things about ourselves. If I have been unsuccessful in any kind of endeavor, I can blame those who are successful and avoid examining the reasons for my own failure. In this way I can protect my own self-esteem. The third function is the value-expressive function. Prejudices can be held because they allow people to highlight certain aspects of life that they value highly, including such basic values as religion, government, aesthetics, relationships, and so on. For example, I may value my religion above all others, believing if you are not a member of my religion you are "wrong" or "heathen." The fourth function is the knowledge function. This function allows us to organize and structure our world in ways that make sense and are relatively convenient. We can avoid dealing with individuals on an individual level, thus making many social decisions quick and easy. Based on the other's group membership, we know whether or not to interact with that person.

Discrimination

Prejudice leads to discrimination—the unequal treatment of certain individuals based on their membership in a certain group, whether defined by race, ethnicity, age, religion, or some other characteristic.

Van Dijk (1987) studied people's everyday conversations as they discussed different racial and cultural groups. Based on these studies, Van Dijk suggests that when people make prejudiced comments, share negative stereotypes about others, and/or tell jokes that belittle and dehumanize others, they establish and legitimize the existence of their prejudices. This laying of "communication groundwork" makes it acceptable for people to perform discriminatory acts.

Racism

Prejudice can lead to discrimination and discrimination often leads to racism. Racism is distinguished from prejudice and discrimination by oppression and power. Thus, *racism* is the tendency by groups with institutional and cultural power to use that power to oppress members of groups who do not have access to the same kinds of power. Racism oppresses groups of people and makes it difficult, if not impossible, for their members to have political, economic, and social power.

CONCLUSION

This chapter discussed the perception process and its relationship to the intercultural communication process—particularly in terms of stereotypes and prejudices. In 1935, Burke wrote, "A way of seeing is also a way of not seeing—a focus on object A involves a neglect of object B" (p. 70). When we focus on one variable in a communication situation—for example, the person—and ignore other variables, such as the situation or the relationship, our perceptions will be skewed. As a result, what we perceive and what is "real" may not be the same at all. In the first reading, Fisher introduces the concept of "mindsets"—a way to think about perception and reasoning. In the reading, Zandpour and Sadri provide a theoretical framework through which communication patterns in Iran can be explained and predicted.

FOR DISCUSSION

1. We all have prejudices and stereotypes. Think about yours and how they will affect your intercultural communication effectiveness.
2. Describe an incident in which your ethnocentrism caused an intercultural misunderstanding.
3. Are you a high self-monitor or a low self-monitor? How do these two affect intercultural communication?

REFERENCES

Allport, G. (1954). *The nature of prejudice.* New York: Macmillan.

Bond, M. H. (1994). Continuing encounters with Hong Kong. In D. Sloan (Ed.), *Education and values.* New York: Teachers College Press.

Brislin, R. (1991). *Cross-cultural encounters: Face-to-face interaction.* New York: Pergamon.

Burke, K. (1935). *Permanence and change.* New Republic (p. 70).

Cooper, H., and Tom, D. (1984). Teacher expectation research: A review with implications for classroom instruction. *The Elementary School Journal, 85,* 77–89.

Cooper, P. (2005). *Bound for beauty: Narratives of Chinese footbinding.* Bloomington, IN: Tichenor Publishing.

Cooper, P., and Simonds, C. (2003). *Communication for the classroom teacher,* 7th ed. Boston: Allyn and Bacon.

Crockett, W. (1985). Cognitive complexity and impression formation. In B. A. Mather (Ed.), *Progress in experimental psychology research,* 2nd ed. New York: Academic Press.

Cushner, K., and Brislin, R. (1996). *Intercultural interactions: A practical guide,* 2nd ed. Thousand Oaks, CA: Sage.

Delia, J. (1977). Constructivism and the study of human communication. *Quarterly Journal of Speech, 63,* 68–83.

Delia, J., Clark, R., and Switzer, D. (1979). Cognitive complexity and impression formation in informal social interaction. *Speech Monographs, 41,* 299–308.

Detweiler, R. (1975). On inferring the intentions of a person from another culture. *Journal of Personality, 43,* 591–611.

Detweiler, R. (1978). Culture, category width, and attributions. *Journal of Cross-Cultural Psychology, 11,* 101–124.

Duck, S. (1976). Interpersonal communication in developing acquaintances. In G. R. Miller (Ed.), *Explorations in interpersonal communication* (pp. 127–147). Beverly Hills, CA: Sage.

Forgas, J. (1981). Affective and emotional influences on episode representations. In J. Forgas (Ed.), *Social cognition: Perspectives on everyday understanding* (pp. 165–180). London: Academic Press.

Gudykunst, W. B. (1988). Uncertainty and anxiety. In Y. Kim and W. Gudykunst (Eds.), *Theories in intercultural communication.* Newbury Park, CA: Sage.

Gudykunst, W. B. (1994). *Bridging differences: Effective intergroup communication,* 2nd ed. Thousand Oaks, CA: Sage.

Gudykunst, W. B., and Kim, Y. Y. (1984). *Communicating with strangers: An approach to intercultural communication.* New York: McGraw-Hill.

Gudykunst, W. B., and Kim, Y. Y. (1997). *Communicating with strangers: An approach to intercultural communication,* 3rd ed. New York: McGraw-Hill.

Gudykunst, W. B., and Ting-Toomey, S., with Chua, E. (1988). *Culture and interpersonal communication.* Newbury Park, CA: Sage.

Hall, E. T. (1976). *Beyond culture.* New York: Doubleday.

Hamilton, D., Sherman, S., and Ruvolo, C. (1992). Stereotyped based expectancies. In W. B. Gudykunst and Y. Y. Kim (Eds.), *Readings on communicating with strangers.* New York: McGraw-Hill. (Originally published in *Journal of Social Issues,* 1990, *46 [2],* 35–60.)

Haslett, B., and Ogilvie, J. (1988). Feedback processes in small groups. In R. Cathcart and L. Samovar (Eds.), *Small group communication: A reader,* 5th ed. Dubuque, IA: William C. Brown.

Heider, F. (1958). *The psychology of interpersonal relations.* New York: John Wiley & Sons.

Hewstone, M., and Brown, R. (1986). Contact is not enough. In M. Hewstone and R. Brown (Eds.), *Contact and conflict in intergroup encounters.* Oxford, United Kingdom: Blackwell.

Hsu, F. (1981). *Americans and Chinese,* 3rd ed. Honolulu: University of Hawaii Press.

Jaspers, J., and Hewstone, M. (1982). Cross-cultural interaction, social attribution, and intergroup relations. In S. Bochner (Ed.), *Cultures in contact.* Elmsford, NY: Pergamon.

Kanhouse, D., and Hanson, L. (1972). Negativity in evaluations. In E. Jonmes, D. Kanouse, H. H. Kelley, R. Nisbett, S. Valins, and L. Petrullo (Eds.), *Attribution: Perceiving the causes of behavior.* Morristown, NJ: General Learning Press.

Kelley, H. H. (1950). The warm-cold variable in first impressions of persons. *Journal of Personality, 18,* 431–439.

Kelley, H. H. (1967). Attribution theory in social psychology. *Nebraska Symposium on Motivation, 15,* 192–238.

Kohls, L. R. (1996). *Survival kit for overseas living,* 3rd ed. Yarmouth, ME: Intercultural Press.

Kohls, L. R., and Knight, J. M. (1994). *Developing intercultural awareness.* Yarmouth, ME: Intercultural Press.

Kunta, Q., and Sherman-Williams, B. (1993). Stereotypes and the construal of individuating information. *Personality and Social Psychology Bulletin, 19,* 12–17.

Langer, E. (1989). *Mindfulness.* Reading, MA: Addison-Wesley.

Littlejohn, S. (1996). *Theories of human communication,* 5th ed. Belmont, CA: Wadsworth.

Loveday, L. (1982). Communicative interference. *International Review of Applied Linguistics in Language Teaching, 20,* 1–16.

Lukens, J. (1978). Ethnocentric speech. *Ethnic Groups, 2,* 35–53.

Lustig, M., and Koester, J. (1996). *Intercultural competence: Interpersonal communication across cultures.* New York: HarperCollins.

Okabe, R. (1983). Cultural assumptions of east and west: Japan and the United States. In W. B. Gundykunst (Ed.), *Intercultural communication theory.* Beverly Hills, CA: Sage.

Pettigrew, T. F. (1982). Cognitive styles and social behavior. In L. Wheeler (Ed.), *Review of personality and social psychology* (vol. 3). Beverly Hills, CA: Sage.

Rosenthal, R., and Jacobson, L. (1968). *Pygmalion in the classroom.* New York: Holt, Rinehart and Winston.

Singer, M. (1987). *Intercultural communication: A perceptual approach.* Englewood Cliffs, NJ: Prentice Hall.

Snyder, M. (1974). Self-monitoring of expressive behavior. *Journal of Personality and Social Psychology, 30,* 526–537.

Snyder, M. (1979). Self-monitoring processes. In L. Berkowitz (Ed.), *Advances in experimental social psychology* (pp. 86–131). New York: Academic Press.

Sorrentino, R. M., and Short, J. A. (1986). Uncertainty orientation, motivation, and cognition. In E. T. Higgins and L. M. Sorrentino (Eds.), *Handbook of motivation and cognition.* New York: Guilford.

Stephan, W. G., and Rosenfield, D. (1982). Racial and ethnic stereotyping. In A. Millar (Ed.), *In the eye of the beholder.* New York: Praeger.

Summer, W. G. (1950). *Folkways.* Boston: Ginn.

Taijfel, H. (1978). Social categorization, social identity, and social comparisons. In H. Taijfel (Ed.), *Differentiation between social groups.* London: Academic Press.

Taijfel, H. (1981). Social stereotypes and social groups. In J. Turner and H. Giles (Eds.), *Intergroup behavior.* Chicago: University of Chicago Press.

Taylor, S., and Fiske, S. (1978). Salience, attention, and attribution. In L. Berkowitz (Ed.), *Advances in experimental social psychology* (vol. 11). New York: Academic Press.

Ting-Toomey, S. (1988). A face negotiation theory. In Y. Kim and W. Gudykunst (Eds.), *Theories in intercultural communication.* Newbury Park, CA: Sage.

Trenholm, S., and Jensen, A. (1993). *Interpersonal communication,* 2nd ed. Belmont, CA: Wadsworth.

Trenholm, S., and Jensen, A. (1996). *Interpersonal communication,* 3rd ed. Belmont, CA: Wadsworth.

Triandis, H. C., Kurowski, L., and Gelfand, M. (1994). Workplace diversity. In H. C. Triandis, M. Dunnette, and L. Hough (Eds.), *Handbook of industrial and organizational psychology,* 2nd ed. (vol. 4, pp. 769–827). Palo Alto, CA: Consulting Psychologists Press.

Tsujimura, A. (1987). Some characteristics of the Japanese way of communication. In D. Kinkaid (Ed.), *Communication theory from Eastern and Western perspectives.* New York: Academic Press.

Van Dijk, T. (1987). *Communicating racism: Ethnic prejudice in thought and talk.* Newbury Park, CA: Sage.

Yum, J. O. (1988). The impact of Confucianism in interpersonal relationships and communication in East Asia. *Communication Monographs, 55,* 374–388.

Zunin, L. (1972). *Contact: The first four minutes.* Los Angeles: Nash.

The Psychological Process: Perception and Reasoning

Glen Fisher

Mindsets[1] is more a popular than a technical word for discussing how contrasts in habits of perception and patterns of reasoning affect give-and-take on the international scene. Yet we propose using it, for although it covers a rather diffuse range of psychological considerations, its popular meaning and usage give a good initial idea of the difficulties we wish to address and the international communication problem that needs to be understood better. Also, it is easy to apply the mindset idea to the everyday subject matter with which we deal. People do draw on differing mindsets when thinking about how an economy should work, how young people should be educated, the way that U.S. actions affect the rest of the world, or even what constitutes the good life.

But we need to flesh out just what we mean by mindsets and think through what they are and how they work. So this reading invites readers to review the fundamentals of social psychology and consider how principles of perception and reasoning apply to international interaction problems.[2] The prospect of everyone playing amateur psychologist may be a little frightening, yet we all do make psychological judgments when engaged in international activities, whether naively or with some notion of what we are doing.

The psychological phenomena we are trying to identify when we talk about mindsets will stand out more clearly if we note other terms which the reader may have encountered or used before to refer to some aspect of the process by which a person invokes a preset formula for thinking about a subject. A common thread runs through the following:

Attitude	Image
Stereotype	Cognitive set
Idée fixe	Cognitive map
Prejudice	Operational code
Worldview	Perception habit
Definition of the situation	Mental construct
Thought pattern	"Where a person is coming from"

If we put all these together and come back to mindsets, we see that we are concerned with predispositions to perceive and reason in certain ways. If one of the core difficulties in dealing with international issues derives from this kind of preprogramming, then some of the psychologist's basic ideas regarding perception and reasoning need to be applied.

Happily, this is a reasonably straightforward exercise. Whether one has gone over this ground in introductory psychology classes or not, these ideas are congenial to common vocabulary and usage. When we use expressions like, "The way the senator perceived the problem . . ." or "What a strange line of reasoning!" our psychological vocabulary is adequate, at least for a start.

So the question now is, what are the points that psychologists would make for our consideration?

1. *Some kind of design for perceiving and reasoning is indispensable.* In pursuing problems created by misperception in international affairs, it is easy to think of mindsets as barriers to appropriate reactions to reality and, therefore, as something to deplore and remedy. But the ability to develop an efficient and coherent mental cross-referencing system is not only constructive, it is phenomenally productive when viewed from the perspective of human evolution. It would be a limited psyche indeed that would have to process each new stimulus as it came along without reference to past experience. The human mind simply cannot encompass the full complexity of all the events and stimuli which press upon it from even its own immediate, everyday environment, much less a radically expanded international environment. It must therefore have a means of efficiently screening, sorting, coding, and storing sensory data. This need is met by structuring experience, for example, by establishing categories within which we can pigeonhole given ranges of phenomena which concern us. Thus, we have ways of interrelating experience and giving it meaning. At one level we adopt words and phrases to designate given slices of our experience or our physical surroundings: for growing plants (trees, grass, shrubs); for power-wheeled vehicles (automobiles, trucks, busses); for people engaged in government (politicians, senators, civil servants).

Mindsets, then, are to larger issues what words are to the specifics—a means of simplifying the environment and bringing to each new experience or event a preestablished frame of reference for understanding it.

Because this environment includes other people and because any infant has to learn from other people how to survive, there is both a need and a basis for similarity in the cognitive structures adopted by members of a group, so that everyone who has to cooperate "simplifies" the environment in the same way. Consequently, we have culture.

Without a system of cognitive structures defined and shared by their group, parents probably would not have acquired enough knowledge to do what was necessary to nurture children until they were able to fend for themselves. The species would have disappeared, for this ability to program minds in shared and cumulative ways, rather than trust to mere instinct, is the human's means of survival. In sum, the human mind becomes a *cognitive system,* that is, a framework of mental constructs of the external world and of beliefs, images, assumptions, habits of reasoning, and so forth, by which the continuing barrage of stimuli a person receives can be sorted out and given meaning. Even beliefs that do not have a basis in reality can be useful in this regard. Whether they are fully accurate or not, stereotypes too have a function, providing a way to make sense of one's environment with the speed necessary to produce a response when urgently needed. It is within this psychological reality that we must, in

the final analysis, expect to manage our international problem solving. These processes are not subject to fundamental change.

If one's overall cognitive system is to serve its purpose, it must have a substantial degree of stability over time. Its component elements have to be mutually compatible, at least in large degree, and it has to be enough in tune with the real world and with the cognitive systems of other people to allow the individual to meet basic physical and social needs; hence, the following:

We perceive very selectively in accordance with the structure of cognitive systems, as will be discussed further below. It would be inefficient, even counterproductive, to notice everything there is to notice, so our cognitive system allows us to perceive selectively without conscious effort, without having to decide in each case. Thus, a casual American newspaper reader might come to a page with, among other items, two stories with equally prominent headlines. One is headed "Attempt to Hijack American Aircraft Foiled by Alert Security Guard" and another headed "Government of Country X Resigns after Parliament Votes No Confidence." The reader may notice and read the first, then go on to the next page without even seeing the second item or any others on the page. It is not a matter of which is actually more important, but what the reader is tuned by experience and interest to notice.

We tend to perceive in a way that will disturb our established cognitive system as little as possible and to interpret what we perceive in a manner consistent with our own particular mindset. We do not easily accommodate discordant facts if our cognitive systems are doing the jobs they are supposed to. Thus, while the news item above might identify the hijacker as, let us say, a distraught rejected lover, the average reader would probably conclude simply that terrorists are striking again. A teenager or a more intensely romantic person might, on the other hand, perceive the event as a vivid life drama with no relation to international politics.

This is not to say that cognitive systems never change. However, in changing, the mind still seeks consistency. Its changes are made up of ongoing adjustments. When the parts do lose their internal consistency or when new information or experience cannot be interpreted satisfactorily—when there is *cognitive dissonance,* to use standard terminology—the change for seeking alternative explanations is greatest. Ironically, a mind at peace is a mind that is closed.

2. *The way we perceive is much more locked in than we realize.* In perceiving the world and what happens in it, we think that we are in charge. Sometimes we are, but the evidence indicates that our internal computers are rather rigidly programmed as to what incoming data will be accepted and how it will be processed. It takes considerable effort to override our habitual ways of perceiving and reasoning, to break out of habitual ways of perceiving and reasoning to break out of established mindsets. We (our conscious selves) are thus not so much in charge as we think.

The reason for this is that what we end up perceiving is actually much more than meets the eye. That is, most perception starts with some kind of limited stimulus that, in effect, triggers a release of previous experience to round out the whole picture. The stimulus may be a word, a symbol, a picture, a scene from one vantage point, but rarely will a stimulus carry so complete a meaning as to be sufficient in itself. The mind must still add pieces to complete the picture.

Hence, we can say that people are very selective in what they perceive directly through their senses. Then, what is perceived through the senses is enlarged upon as the incoming data is entered into the existing cognitive system and assigned its meaning. Consequently, for better or worse, we can perceive the item or event without necessarily seeing the whole; or we can perceive what probably is there, or . . . perceive that which is not there at all! Thus the potential for misperception.

This leap from stimulus to a fuller-blown idea is amply demonstrated in the process of visual perception. In a civilization where we are surrounded by right angles in windows and walls and a multitude of daily objects, we expect to "see" rectangles where rectangles are supposed to be. Thus, if asked about the shape of a desk top table in a room, one would not hesitate to report that it is rectangular; a group of people looking at the same desk top would also agree. Yet it would be highly unlikely any of the observers would be looking at the desk from directly above or below it, the only angles where an image of a perfect rectangle can be projected onto the retina of the eye. Thus, no one present actually physically observes a rectangle where he or she perceives one. What happens is that each pair of eyes in the assembled group picks up stimuli that fit into what is already known about tables, desks, windows, and room corners, and the computer banks of the several minds present supply something in *addition* to what is actually received through the senses. The importance of the "something supplied in addition" can hardly be overestimated in our discussion of the effect of mindsets.

As psychologists can demonstrate, this additional input can be so strong that it becomes very difficult to perceive variations from what is expected because they would conflict with the cognitive system as established. This is the basis for optical illusions.

The classic example is the experimental distorted room developed in early studies of perception psychology by Hadley Cantril and colleagues in their Princeton research facilities. A full-sized room is constructed, but the floor and ceiling are not level, the windows are not quite rectangular, and corners are distorted. All this is done so cleverly that from a certain observation point at one end of the room, all appears normally proportioned. Then, in experiments, identical objects—even people—are placed in the corners of the room. But instead of causing us as observers to see that the room is in fact distorted, our perceptions are adjusted to fit our belief in the normality of the room. We perceive the two identical objects as being different sizes, one large and one small. When the objects are reversed in position, they grow or shrink accordingly. Interestingly, even when the observer knows intellectually the true nature of the room or has been allowed to enter and examine it, it is still nearly impossible for the observer to perceive the sizes of the objects correctly—impossible, in other words, to visually perceive reality as it is. What one's cognitive system imposes on one's visual perception is too strong.[3]

The reader is familiar enough with optical illusions and needs only extend the example a little to see that the same process is at work when a foreign mindset, suspicious of U.S. intentions, leads its owner to "see" a CIA agent in a Peace Corps volunteer or leads many a thoroughly programmed mind to jump to conclusions at one level or another of international affairs.

Moving from psychology to social psychological carries our examination of this subject to its next level of complexity—that of programmed perception and reasoning as a function of interaction with other people. One's cognitive system is molded by society and culture, by education and the socialization process, social experience, information and knowledge transmitted from other people, and in specific situations, by suggestion and a sense of group sanction or censure. Through social experience, habits of perceiving and reasoning become, in large degree, those of the groups to which we as individuals belong. Such commonality provides the shared outlooks that make social life possible . . .

The point is that the way a person perceives other people, interprets what they are doing and why, and chooses how to respond to them is also locked in by sociocultural circumstances. This phenomenon eventually extends to the way one society perceives another.

Social psychologists spend many of their waking hours studying regularities in the social perception process, and their introductory texts are concerned with the effects of stereotyping, interpersonal perceptions, attitudes and attitude change, persuasion, and much more that need not be repeated here. But their study and their experimental evidence all support the idea that in social as in physical reality, people perceive, reason, and respond not necessarily according to the facts but according to *the image they have of the facts*. They also stress that social images or mindsets regarding people, as in the case of rectangles and optical illusions, tend to purposefully channel the range of perception alternatives, generally making it highly improbable that one can override all one's mental habits in the interest of objectivity. Thus, as in our interactions with the physical world, we have developed social "optical illusions" in interacting with people—and probably with much greater frequency.

One further facet of the locked-in perception phenomenon needs to be considered at this point. The more abstract the subject to be perceived—a point, a law, a development plan, a religious tenet, a work of art—the more one will necessarily draw on the resources of the cognitive system to establish substance and meaning. That is, in constructing a picture of an intangible issue, the proportion of information that comes from previous experience and knowledge (in contrast to that which is available from the actual stimulus) is going to be higher than if the subject were more concrete. While you may "see" a production plan, for example, as words or flow charts on paper, you cannot actually see it until it is executed, and then probably not as one entity.

Hence, the potential for variation in the way that abstract subjects are perceived and reasoned about is very substantial, especially when perceptions are made from the vantage points of differing societies or positions within societies. And in international professional level activities, abstract subjects are of constant concern. For example, the following are all very abstract concepts as far as our perception of them is concerned: capitalism, political ideologies, contractual obligations, cultural exchange, educational philosophy, or advertising appeals. But the psychological principle still applies. Perception and reasoning are programmed, even locked in, unless a very concerted intellectual effort is made to open up the process.

Or, turned the other way around, perceiving abstract subjects *requires* the help of a supporting cognitive system. If the subject that is called to one's attention is entirely foreign, that is, completely outside one's experience, it will be difficult to assign even a distorted meaning to it. An example for Westerners might be Buddhist theology. Although it may be explained repeatedly, it resists comprehension by Westerners, who have to acquire a complex new frame of reference in order to understand it. For most, the same would apply to the theory of relativity. The appropriate "software" for one's mental computer is missing. In these cases, perception is "locked out" rather than "locked in."

It is apparent that in seeking an applied social psychology for international practice, the objective often will be to capture a workable understanding of the various cognitive systems—of individuals or of groups—that may come into play relative to a given issue or problem. . . .

3. *There are fewer universal commonalties in human thought processes than most people think.* One of the threads that will run through our argument will be the need to be wary of those who claim universality for certain beliefs or for particular ways human beings think or express emotion. While all human beings are essentially alike in physical composition, share certain fundamental needs and potentials, and are sentimentally "brothers under the skin," the supposed commonalties of human nature prove evanescent where mindsets and perception habits are concerned. In fact, the range of what can be considered normal across the world's cultures is very broad. Even someone who might be judged as needing psychiatric help in one society may be considered quite sane in another. Culture and personality studies conducted by anthropologists have documented stark contrasts in the most fundamental aspects of human existence: cosmology, ethics, meaning of death, family roles, governance.

These kinds of contrasts were highlighted during World War II when Americans, in an effort to predict Japanese actions, were brought face to face with, to them, incomprehensible behaviors: suicide bombing, for instance, or unexpectedly cooperative prisoner behavior immediately after what was considered by Americans to be irrational attempts to avoid capture—including suicide. Twenty-eight years after the war ended, one Lieutenant Onoda gained international attention when he was discovered still hiding out on Lubang Island in the Philippines. He had never surrendered; he had never been ordered to do so and had spent all those years honorably surviving in the Philippine jungle until a change in his duty was defined by acceptable authority. After his eventual return to Japan, there was a wave of approbation for his exemplary behavior and the degree to which it accorded with Japanese values, although some thought it a bit overdone.[4]

The importance of this kind of radical variation in values and behavior can hardly be overstated. After all, it is the enduring mindsets of both the general public and their leaders, exemplified in the extreme by Lieutenant Onoda, that plague our efforts to find solutions to the highest order of world problems.

4. *How one perceives events, issues, or policies depends on how they are presented.* . . . Psychologists stress the need to study the nature of the stimulus. This is also the concern of artists, advertisers, propagandists, and psychological warfare specialists, all of whom are practicing applied psychology in their specialized fields. Again, there are basics to consider. Stimuli can vary in intensity, strength, duration, and repetition, and in the way they are tuned to fit into the needs and interests of the perceiver.

Perhaps the most important consideration for foreign affairs applications is that perception is affected by the context in which a specific stimulus is presented and by the way that the context itself is perceived and understood. A military exercise may be perceived as threatening or defensive, depending on what else is going on at the same time. For example, during the Cold War the continuing state of tension between the United States and the USSR supplied the context for interpreting almost any action or statement by the other as a devious plot or aggressive strategy.

International news stories carried on evening television may be interpreted in entirely different ways, depending on contextual factors that affect perception—what else is going on at the time, whether the story is placed at the beginning or end of the program, how dramatic the film footage is, and what tone of voice the reporter uses. Conversely, meaning can be changed by leaving out the context. A street demonstration photographed by a narrow-angle lens to cut out the bemused and peaceful onlookers may appear far more significant to the TV viewer than to someone at the scene. . . .

5. *The naive but normal practice is to project one's own mindset onto other people.* . . . If I see something in a given way, others must see it that way too. Even more, the normal and unconscious assumption is that the habitual ways of thinking of one's own society are a matter of human nature and therefore have universal application.

There is much to be gained by the direct application to foreign affairs of "projection theory." For example, during the Vietnam conflict Marc Lewis reported a tendency among Central Intelligence Agency analysts to interpret developments there by projecting much more of an American frame of reference onto events than they were aware of. This led to seriously distorted interpretations when they tried to explain and predict political developments in a foreign and very different Vietnamese society and culture.[5] Many years later, Robert McNamara, who was Secretary of Defense at the time, came to acknowledge this projection problem almost as a theme in his review of where judgments went wrong.

When he was a congressman, Les Aspin suggested somewhat the same thing in an article in *Foreign Policy*.[6] He noted that distortions may have been introduced in U.S. intelligence estimates of Soviet military threats because analysts tended to focus mainly on hard evidence of technical capabilities rather than on intentions or Soviet conceptions of how hardware would be used—that is, on knowing "what is going on inside Soviet heads." He argued that Americans saw mirror images in judging future Soviet offensive capabilities by projecting onto the Soviets their own assumptions as to how resources, including nuclear weapons, would be deployed and used. Now that the Soviet Union has collapsed, it has become apparent that this mindset prevented attention to a wide range of critical social and economic developments and that, in the process, the threat posed by Soviet power was exaggerated.

This tendency to project is normal for people in any society, of course, for culture's function is to establish a more or less homogeneous set of beliefs and assumptions by which everyone can project their perception expectations onto other people without thinking about it. This provides the sense of security that comes with predictability; it is the cement that holds societies together; it vastly facilitates interaction and cooperation. At home it is best if everyone does internalize the society's common sense beliefs and attitudes, even though they inevitably mistake them for human nature. But when interaction crosses national lines, naive projection is not supportable. Therefore, judgments are often off the mark and responses become unpredictable.

This problem has been a continuing one for the United States Information Agency and the Voice of America, whose task it is to explain to the world the nature of American society and the intent of U.S. policies and actions in world affairs. Especially during the peak of ideological competition, Washington administrators tended to project what they had learned about communication at home onto programs and materials prepared for foreign audiences. Accordingly, they were prone to use the kind of people, methods, and procedures found successful in American advertising, and, for efficiency, they developed standard packages of information to be used in all countries with, at most, the translation that was required to adapt it to specific language "targets." Overseas, more experienced career professionals were in a constant state of frustration. They knew international communication did not work that way. They wanted materials designed to communicate a message in their particular country of assignment, one that took into account the way that their audience would actually see and comprehend what USIA was trying to say.

6. *Attribution of motive is a form of projection that is particularly important in foreign affairs.* This is a spin-off from attribution theory in social psychology. The idea is that in order to interpret what people are doing, we normally and consistently *attribute motives* to them and usually do so unconsciously. The motives attributed are those common to one's experience as related to the situation of the moment, the category of person, and the expected role.

The following is an illustration. In one of my early ventures abroad, I was part of a group of American students working as volunteers in public health projects in rural Mexico, rather like the later Peace Corps. We did a lot of physical labor, especially digging drainage ditches and pits for latrines, as part of an effort to control malaria and improve sanitation. To the local community we explained our volunteer work in terms of working for better international understanding, of humanitarian service, and of any number of other cliches that go with "doing good." All this was rather far removed from local experience, and people were not convinced. Instead, they attributed motives to us that did make sense based on their experience with foreigners and strangers: we were looking for oil or digging for gold. Perhaps the "attribution of motive" that satisfied them most was that we were doing penance!

This kind of experience is familiar to those who have lived abroad; it seems that others are constantly misattributing motives to us, either naively or perversely. What we fail to see is that we too misattribute motives. Combine the error on both sides and it can be argued that nothing obstructs international interchange as much as this psychological mechanism running amok in a cross-cultural situation. Misattributing motives and intentions is a central thread that potentially

runs through all international relations calculations, from those of policymakers to those propounded by self-styled experts in the neighborhood bar. And the most intractable misattributions are the products of mindsets of which the actors are unaware; they may even fail to perceive subsequent evidence that motives have been misattributed.

One of the more dramatic cases occurred when a Soviet fighter plane shot down Korean Airlines Flight 007, an unarmed passenger jet, in Soviet air space over a sensitive area near Sakhalin Island in 1983. Americans, with the president and the press in the lead, immediately attributed the motive to a trigger-happy and callous Soviet disregard for human life, assuming that the action was taken with full knowledge that the plane being attacked was a passenger aircraft. As it turned out, according to later analysis and especially after the Cold War ended and previously secret Soviet files would be reviewed, this was not quite what happened. When the Korean aircraft strayed from its flight path, the Soviets also misattributed motives. In fact, the pilot who downed the passenger plane apparently never imagined that it was not a foreign reconnaissance military plane. The attack was something of a trigger-happy response, complicated by chain-of-command problems, but the point is that the damage was compounded and decision making confused by this form of jumping to conclusions. The problem does not seem to be eliminated by computer technology; during the Gulf War era, an Iranian passenger plane whose flight path was misinterpreted was shot down by U.S. fliers.

7. *Institutionalized information processing is also a study in perception and reasoning.* A predominant part of international activity revolves around formally processing information in institutional settings—selecting, storing, recalling, and transmitting it by ever more sophisticated means, and using it in solving problems. Increasingly, we refer to some of the technologically advanced countries as "information societies" because producing and using information tends to surpass agriculture or industrial production as a mainstream activity. It follows that the functioning of the international community itself is also based to an ever larger extent on the flow and use of information. Therefore, along with taking individual perception and reasoning into account, psychological factors affecting information processing in more institutional contexts becomes an important consideration.

When we think of handling "information," we tend to assume a distinctly rational or objective level of mental activity by educated and experienced people.

There is a tendency to expect that formal information processing will be carried out above the level of mindset complications, that all educated people will be led by the same information and evidence to the same conclusions, more or less as Aristotle argued. Yet, for the purposes of our discussion here, the question still persists: how subjective is this process? Is it a function of all the perception and reasoning factors set forth above, or can people rise above the psychological forces that distort reality and thereby take control of the information processing that is required of humans as problem solvers and shapers of their own environment?

This question goes quickly to the heart of the philosophy of scientific methodology. In fact, psychological theory does see human thinking as being far from passive in its decision-making mode.[7] Even in pursuing the subject matter of this book, our attempt to "think about thought" represents a mental activity of a high order. Yet, both cross-cultural evidence and the problems encountered in the pursuit of true scientific objectivity indicate that a full escape from subjectivity is rare if not nonexistent. Values, implicit assumptions that are not easily recognized and controlled, styles of reasoning, possibly an epistemology that is tied to language and its structure all stand out as the uncontrolled variables in information processing. In any case, most of the time in international relations activities, people are at best amateur scientists in their quest for gaining and using information, sifting evidence, and relating cause and effect. Adding research staffs and computer technology does not necessarily improve the quality of information processing, although such does add to a capacity to expand information resources and test out conclusions.

Part of the difficulty, psychologists warn, is that in institutions information is produced and used in group settings, that is, in the context of group processes and collective decision making in staff meetings, through multiple copies of interoffice memos, in board reviews, sign-off procedures, interagency or interdepartmental panels, and a maze of informal consulting. This tends to fortify the effect of conventional wisdom and the subjective meaning and interpretation that goes with the group's larger social experience and intellectual moorings. In other words, the group setting draws the net of culture or subculture tighter and restrains such individual creativity as might conflict with the larger prescriptions of the society. The interaction in such information processing and decision making brings into play the psychological principles of group dynamics. . . . Irving Janis has produced a clear reminder of this in his book *Victims of Group Think*.[8] In it he examines the ways in which conflicting interpretations of information are compromised, how subjective common sense is reinforced, and how even conclusions that individual members of the group might doubt if working alone are reinforced by group consensus.

The psychologists counsel, then, is that quality can be achieved in information processing and decision making only by confronting this situational potential for misperception which fortifies subjective and erroneous interpretations. Methods have to be adopted by decision makers which enable them to review context, develop alternative explanations, and uncover the patterns of belief by which naive diagnoses are made. This is especially needed when decision makers are fatigued or under stress, or are working under severe time constraints.

The "group think" problem is particularly apropos in examining the decision-making process in international affairs, for each national group involved has to be able to consider in some detail the lens through which its own culture views the world. As the preceding discussion should have made clear, decision makers are not easily prepared to do so.

8. *Language differences are more significant as factors in perception and reasoning than one expects.* As noted at the beginning of the chapter, the words we use to express ideas and communicate experience are themselves ways of categorizing and simplifying the environment, ways of helping the mind get organized.

The importance of this point in practical application needs emphasis. Words can become in effect, mini-mindsets. As we know from the study of semantics, by choosing one word over another we supply different programming for treating the subject at hand. When a press report chooses between *terrorists* and *freedom fighters,* the perception and reasoning that follow have been channeled at the outset. This is why official announcements and news reports are so important and can have such an impact. Whatever the subject, the writer has the opportunity to code the action, to choose the category to be used in thinking abut it, and to predispose listeners or readers to desired conclusions. Alternative consultations can also be cut off. Hence, a bank loan in default looks better from the start if it is labeled a "nonperforming" loan. Civilians killed in a bombing raid are not anyone's responsibility, really; they are part of "collateral damage." Political leaders do not lie, they "misspeak." A strategist does not take a gamble, but a "calculated risk." Our community does not have a garbage dump, but a "landfill."

All this has significance enough for understanding perception and reasoning when just one language is involved. The question raised in going from one language to another is whether words used in translation bring to bear equivalent mini-mindsets. The question becomes even more important where abstract ideas are concerned. Consider concepts like capitalism, socialism, public interest, corporate responsibility, human rights. *Complete* translation into other languages is unlikely when the problem of equating the mini-mindsets that go with the words is taken into account. . . . However, we should point out here that if a mini-mindset exists for speakers of one language and not another, the problem cannot be met by ordinary translation. One of my favorite examples is the outlook on life and on relations among people that we incorporate into the English term *fair play.* I invite the reader to try translating this—both the word and the mini-mindset that goes with it—into any other language. . . .

This raises the further question of what happens in the conduct of international business when translation and interpretation are used, or when one side is speaking in a second language. How much does one switch from one pattern of perceiving and reasoning to another when speaking a foreign language? Language and culture are so closely related that an answer to this will require thinking through the effect of culture on language. . . .

But there is another aspect of language, perception, and reasoning which, according to specialists in psychocultural studies, causes even more difficulties in international communication. They argue that beyond words and choice of phrases, the basic grammar and fundamental structure of a language presents a model or master framework for channeling cognitive processes, for conceptualizing the environment and the manner in which its elements interrelate, and for choosing the way that one idea leads to the next. In short, is one likely to think the same way in all languages? Benjamin Lee Whorf thought not. His "Whorfian hypothesis" proposed that "the structure of the language one habitually uses influences the manner in which one understand his environment"; that is, "the picture of the universe shifts from tongue to tongue." Whorf argued that "we are thus introduced to a new principle of relativity, which holds that all observers are not led by the same physical evidence to the same picture of the universe, unless their linguistic backgrounds are similar, or can in some way be calibrated."[9]

While the Whorfian hypothesis has been disputed by some linguists, it is nevertheless highly suggestive for the analysis of cross-cultural interaction, and attention keeps coming back to it. If different languages represent differing psychological words, people working internationally have to wonder if their own thoughts and usual patterns of reasoning are really striking responsible chords in the thinking of speakers of another language. While the hypothesis may not be as significantly consequential when language structures are relatively similar, as in the case of European languages, anthropologists tend to line up with Whorf when the contrasts are across language families—English and Chinese, for example, or English and Arabic. . . .

When we say that "it loses something in translation," finding out what that something is may be the most important element in bridging mindsets. . . .

NOTES

1. A mindset is a fixed mental attitude formed by experience, education, prejudice, etc.
2. For one introductory summary of perception and the way it relates to culture, see the first three chapters of Marshall R. Singer, *Intercultural Communication: A Perceptual Approach* (Englewood Cliffs, NJ: Prentice Hall, 1986).
3. The Exploratorium Science Museum in San Francisco contains a version of the Cantril room.
4. His story is available in Hiroo Onoda's *My Thirty-year War,* trans. by Charles S. Terry (Tokyo: Kodansha International, 1974), distributed by Harper and Row in the U.S. A classic study that explored such facets of Japanese personality was Ruth Benedict's *The Chrysanthemum and the Sword* (Boston: Houghton Mifflin, 1946), which is still read with interest by both Americans and Japanese despite the fact that the entire study was done from the distant vantage point of the United States during wartime. For a more recent source that tried to cover Japanese characters see Takie Sugiyama Lebra, *Japanese Patterns of Behavior* (Honolulu: University of Hawaii Press, 1976).
5. Anthony Marc Lewis, "The Blind Spot of U.S. Foreign Intelligence," *Journal of Communication, 26,* no. 1 (Winter 1976): 44–54.
6. Les Aspin, "Misreading Intelligence," *Foreign Policy* no. 43 (Summer 1981): 166–72.
7. For a review of this problem and current theory as related to decision making, see George, *Presidential Decision-making,* chapters 2 and 3.
8. Irving Janis, *Victims of Group Think* (Boston: Houghton Mifflin, 1972).
9. For my own more extended review of the relationship between language and culture, see Fisher, *Public Diplomacy,* chapter 5. The references to Whorf come from Benjamin Lee.

CHECK YOUR UNDERSTANDING

1. Define *mindsets*. How does this concept relate to culture?
2. What is cognitive dissonance and why does it occur? Give an example of when you have experienced cognitive dissonance.
3. Bring an international news story to class. Share the story with your classmates. How do you interpret the event described? How do your classmates interpret it? How do these differences affect communication?
4. What happens to communication when we project our mindsets onto the behaviors of other people?

Communication in Personal Relationships in Iran: A Comparative Analysis

Fred Zandpour and Golnaz Sadri

Communication may be defined as the process by which we understand others and, in turn, try to be understood by them. Accordingly, it is a dynamic process, constantly changing and shifting in response to the total situation. In addition, communication involves sharing and interchange; transmission of information, ideas, emotions, skills; and so on, through the use of verbal and visual symbols. It also serves to reduce uncertainty (see Littlejohn, 1983, p. 7) and to satisfy needs (Katz, 1974). Based upon the discussion of differences across cultures, it is possible to provide a number of theoretical generalizations about patterns of communication in Iran.

IRANIANS DO NOT STRESS SELF-ASSERTION AND INDIVIDUAL EXPRESSIVENESS

Gudykunst, Yoon, and Nishida (1987) point out that in collectivistic cultures communication with outgroup members is more synchronized, and behavior is governed by situational norms, not individual needs. In individualistic cultures, the level of intimacy and self-disclosure is a result of a person's desire to form a relationship with others. One would therefore expect lower levels of affection and inclusion motives (Rubin, 1992) for Iranian people than for individualistic people.

Iranians emphasize adherence to culturally defined social expectations and rules rather than encouraging the expression of individuality through the articulation of words. Much emphasis is placed on conformity to the already established social relationships defined by the position in society of the individual speaker. For example, Iranian women can freely talk as sisters, mothers, wives, or neighbors, but they are seldom expected to discuss their feelings as an individual.

In addition, Iranians place less emphasis on the use of the name of a person with whom they are communicating. They are also less likely to use first-person or second-person pronouns during a typical conversation (see "Human Interest," Carbone, 1975) as compared with most Western cultures.

Humility is very characteristic of the communication patterns of most Iranians. They seldom feel comfortable in taking credit for their achievements, good taste, or choice and tend to become embarrassed as a result of excessive praise. If you compliment Iranians on a gift they have given you, they will tend to downplay the gesture by remarking that the gift is unworthy of the recipient. There are a number of other expressions of humility that Iranians typically adopt to express their affection for another person; for example, "I would die for you."

IRANIANS RELY MORE ON NONVERBAL COMMUNICATION THAN ON THE ARTICULATION OF WORDS

The people of Iran, like those of Asia (Hecht et al., 1989), expect communicators to understand inarticulate moods, subtle gestures, and environmental cues that people from low-context cultures simply do not process. In this respect, Iranian communication is receiver-centered (Yum, 1991). That is to say, the task of understanding is placed on the listener and his or her interpretation, in contrast to the Western cultures that place emphasis on the message sender's delivery skills and so forth.

Iranians' attitude toward speech and rhetoric, like that of Asians (Gudykunst & Kim, 1984; Oliver, 1971), is characteristically a holistic one—words are perceived as part of and inseparable from the total communication context. Consequently, even periods of silence embedded between words carry meaning. Verbal individuals are perceived as attractive in Western cultures, but in Iran, less verbal people are perceived as more attractive. In fact, Iranians border on having a mistrust of words, like Asian cultures (Oliver, 1971); they prefer silence to improper words that might offend the other party (Hall, 1983). As an illustration of the differences attached to the importance of speech across cultures, research conducted in the United States has shown that speaking fast enhances the speaker's credibility (MacLachlan, 1982; Miller, Maruyama, Beaber, & Valone, 1976; Petrie, 1963). By contrast, in Iran, slow speakers are likely to be perceived as more competent than fast speakers because the deliberate nature of their speech suggests they are taking more care in the preparation and production of their message. This preference for slower rates of communication is similar to that of Asian cultures (Lee & Boster, 1992). This may explain why Iranians are more likely to use complex and longer sentences than Americans (see "Listenability," Carbone, 1975).

Because words are not relied upon heavily, we would also expect Iranian people to use more nonverbal communications such as head nodding, bowing, hugging, and kissing (see "Alertness" and Haptics" in Sillars, Pike, Jones, & Murphy, 1984). As an example, in Iran it is customary to greet friends and family with a kiss on each cheek.

Showing affection may also be expressed through symbolic means. If an Iranian person invites you to his or her home and wishes to show how important you are, this will be expressed through the means of hospitality. There will, as mentioned previously, be a great deal of attention paid to elaborately prepared foods and lavish service. Gifts also play an important nonverbal role in Iranian society, in the expression of warmth, affection, and even respect. Gifts are exchanged on birthdays, and the first visit to someone's home is usually accompanied by the giving of a very elaborate gift. At the new year, *Nowruz,* which is the first day of spring, it is customary for the older members of a family to give gifts in the form of cash to younger members.

Expressions of anger and discontent are also expressed nonverbally through the process of ignoring the object of the hostility. Silence becomes an important tool for younger and less respected members of society who, by society's standards, are not in the position of talking to their seniors as equals. Such behavior would be considered a transgression against the expected normative standards.

IRANIANS ARE NOT DIRECT AND ASSERTIVE

An important communication goal in Iran, as in most collectivistic societies, is to avoid being embarrassed or embarrassing members of your ingroup in the course of symbolic exchanges. Eventual face-honoring and face-compensating is important for the maintenance of both social and personal relationship developments (Gudykunst, 1988). This is attained by being indirect and ambiguous in communications (Lee & Boster, 1992). Like the French and Asians (Hall, 1983), Iranians often do not spell out the details. They will often talk around the point they wish to make and expect the listener to be intuitive enough to discover the hidden message being communicated. For example, the use of metaphor and satire *(Tanz)* is very prevalent in Iranian arts and literature. Furthermore, by being deliberate in one's speech, additional time is available to qualify potentially face-threatening messages nonverbally (Lee & Boster, 1992).

Iranians are more likely to use abstract (Carbone, 1975) ideas as opposed to concrete facts in their communication as compared with Americans and Northern Europeans. Iranians often tend to speak in general terms and to make statements with implicit meanings as opposed to being explicit, which is a common practice among Americans and Northern Europeans. As a result, in a typical Iranian conversation a great deal of background information will be provided about the topic, which may appear to be more than that needed by Western standards.

Considering the structure of messages (McGuire, 1957), Iranians invariably present the more pleasant aspects prior to the less pleasant parts of an issue. There is also a tendency to avoid the presentation of bad news where possible. Doctors may attempt to avoid giving very negative pieces of information to their patients. In some instances in which a close family member dies, the communication of this information may be postponed for months and even years.

The Iranian use of subdued and ambiguous verbal expressions is not limited to situations in which one might express negative emotions such as disagreement, embarrassment, doubt, or anger. Even when expressing strong personal affection, a style of hesitancy and indirectness (Sillars et al., 1984) is commonly preferred. As mentioned previously, like Asians (Gudykunst & Kim, 1984), Iranians communicate excessive verbal praise or compliments with feelings of embarrassment.

IRANIANS DEMONSTRATE ANXIETY WHEN CONFRONTED WITH UNCERTAINTY

In order to remove the uncertainty in a given communication episode, Iranians often resort to intuitive explanations of events and speculations, sometimes on the basis of little factual information. Like most Asian cultures (Gudykunst, 1988), they have a need for formal rules and a low tolerance for deviant groups or inconsistent beliefs. Iranians are less likely to present all sides of an issue and often use one-sided arguments (Zandpour, 1990).

Observance of typical communication patterns among Iranians might reveal this greater desire to reduce uncertainty by the manner in which communication tends to be very ritualistic. Iranians have a pattern of communication referred to as *taarof,* which essentially prescribes certain responses to various comments. For example, in many instances if Iranian individuals receive a compliment on some aspect of their appearance, they will respond by suggesting that beauty is in the eyes of the beholder. Such prescribed patterns of communication are observed much less frequently in U.S. communications.

IRANIANS RESPECT AUTHORITY

In Iranian institutions there is a highly centralized authority structure. In Iran, it is considered inappropriate to downplay status differences in ways that are considered highly appropriate in the United States. For example, Iranians do not generally call their instructors, supervisors, or elders by their first names. Moreover, in the official Iranian language (Farsi), the second person has two forms, similar to the *you* and *thou* as previously used in the English language. Persons in positions of higher status and authority should be referred to using only the *thou* form. Further, older people are referred to by younger members of society in terms of *thou;* they are relied upon to give advice and implicitly take on this role. It would be considered rude for a younger person to challenge directly the view of an older Iranian person.

As in other Asian countries, in Iran the individual in a public forum is somewhat cold, formal, ritualistic, and preoccupied with status. An Iranian person will generally pay a great deal of attention to who you are and not necessarily to what you are saying. As an illustration, a person with a title such as doctor or general will probably be listened to more carefully than a person without such a qualification or status. However, there is also a private self that is observed in an informal world that is warm, close, friendly, and egalitarian. Iranians seem to have no trouble shifting from one world to the other, which is similar to individuals from Asian cultures (Hall, 1983).

In power-discrepant circumstances, Iranians show more bodily tension and smile in an effort to appease superiors and to appear polite. Again, this pattern is replicated in most of the Asian cultures (Andersen & Bowman, 1985; Hecht et al., 1989). In such situations, individuals remain alert and polite by being quiet and supporting the speaker with frequent nodding and other affirmative gestures.

As a result of this respect for authority, we would expect powerful and credible sources of information to be more effective in Iran than in Western cultures. The Iranians' love for authority and social approval may also be observed by a slight and indirect exaggeration of their credentials in some instances, by the person him- or herself or by another person. Iranians also like to be told in public that they are right about a particular issue. To improve the chances of this occurring, the dominant or most accepted position on a particular issue is usually adopted.

In social interaction, we expect to observe more frequent use of asymmetrical or superior–subordinate relationships (Watzlawick, Beavin, & Jackson, 1967) among Iranians than among Westerners. Asymmetric interaction serves the dual purpose of maintaining one's status and conferring status and respect on another person.

IRANIANS TEND TO AVOID DEALING DIRECTLY WITH CONFLICT

Iranians value harmony: A fundamental communication goal in Iran, as in other collectivistic societies, is to avoid being embarrassed and embarrassing others in the course of symbolic exchanges. A premium is placed on the maintenance of personal relationships (Triandis, Bontempo, Villareal, Asai, & Lucca, 1988; Wheeler, Reis, & Bond, 1989). In individualistic societies, face-threatening remarks are not considered as detrimental as they are in collectivistic societies, because the maintenance of ingroup relations is less important (Triandis et al., 1988). Iranians, like other collectivistic (Lee & Boster, 1992) cultures, sometimes avoid making face-threatening comments by being indirect and ambiguous in their communications. In general, Iranians greatly enjoy being approved and praised by others.

When dealing with members of their ingroups, Iranians prefer indirect styles of dealing with conflict, like the Asian cultures (Gudykunst, 1991). This allows all those involved in the communication to save face. Iranians tend to perceive conflict as expressive-oriented in focus. As for Asians (Ting-Toomey, 1985), for Iranians the conflict issue and the conflict person tend to be the same. In Iran, one tool that is sometimes adopted in avoiding a conflict episode is to pay attention to only certain pieces of information, which appear favorable, and to ignore all other pieces of data. The listener may thus remain comfortable and avoid direct conflict.

This is in sharp contrast to the Western cultures, which are more likely to view the world in analytic, linear, logical terms. Because issues and persons are commonly perceived as dichotomous concepts in the West, individuals from such cultures are more likely to perceive a conflict event as primarily instrumental-oriented. Hence Americans and Europeans prefer a direct mode of resolving conflict, such as the use of confrontational strategies or solution-oriented strategies (Gudykunst, 1988). In a low-context culture, such as the United States, individuals are better able to separate the conflict issue from the person involved in the conflict. In these cultures individuals can fight over an issue and yet be able to remain friends afterwards (Gudykunst, 1991), something that is very unlikely in Iran.

IRANIANS ARE ORIENTED TO THE PAST

In terms of time orientation or *chronemics* (Williams, 1989), Iranians tend to focus on the past. They give more attention to causes, and, like Asians (Jung-Sun, 1962), they perceive events or objects that have similar signs or symbols as sharing a common relationship. Similarly, their causal pattern of thought does not build on linear time, but instead uses visual space and relies on analogies and associations (Ting-Toomey, 1985) with the past, which is used to speculate about the future. Unlike Americans, Iranians are very interested in general background information and historical antecedents regarding the issue they are dealing with. The Western cultures (such as the United States, Great Britain, and Germany), by contrast, have present-orientations that pay relatively little attention to either traditions or speculation (Gudykunst & Ting-Toomey, 1988).

The Western communication style is typically short and concise. Americans, for example, have a narrow focus when eliciting information and show little interest in general background information but prefer to obtain the information that they need to know promptly (Hall, 1983). Again, stylistically, we expect Iranians to be more abstract and general (Carbone, 1975) in their communications than people from the United States and Northern Europe.

There are a number of manifestations in Iranian culture of this attention to the past. Iranians value and respect their traditions and cultural heritage. Like people of many other cultures, Iranians who emigrate to other countries like to maintain their traditions and pass these on to their children. As part of their respect for tradition, Iranians also respect and pay attention to history and historic events. Whereas in the West old ideas are sometimes viewed negatively because of their lack of perceived currency, in Iran old fables and stories are abundant and relied upon in the explanation of current issues and events.

IRANIANS DEMONSTRATE THEIR EMOTIONS

Iranians may be seen to be highly demonstrative of their emotions. They tend to create a sense of immediacy by increasing the level of sensory input in a communication situation, as opposed to communicators from North America, Northern Europe, and Asia (Sussman & Rosenfeld, 1982), who tend to prefer less sensory involvement. Iranians use all of their senses and talk and communicate with their whole bodies. Their faces and gestures are expressive and reflect the intensity of their involvement with each other. When observing a typical Iranian conversation, it would be normal to observe elevated volume or even shouting when important or interesting points are being conveyed.

In emotional situations Iranians are more likely to use vocal language to substitute for words, such as crying in the course of a conversation; it is considered acceptable for Iranian men to cry. Iranians communicate their emotions nonverbally through the use of their hands and animated facial expressions. We expect to see higher frequencies of movement of hands and arms, nodding or shaking of the head, leaning toward the communication source, and occasional interruptions of the speaker among Iranians. In addition, Iranians may express their emotions through repetition (Carbone, 1975) of words or sentences.

Unlike the Asian and Western cultures (Patterson, 1983), when friends meet or part in Iran, they shake hands, embrace, and sometimes kiss each other.

Similarly, we expect to see more frequent use of emotional appeals attempting to entice the receiver's values and feelings, as opposed to rational appeals with empirical and logical evidence (McGuire, 1969) in communications by Iranians. In addition, like the traditional Japanese culture (Chu, 1991), we expect the Iranian communication themes to center on sadness and sometime fear.

IRANIANS COMMUNICATE FROM A CLOSE DISTANCE

Iranians tend to stand and sit closer to each other than do most Americans. In their interactions, they are totally engrossed in their discussions. Typically, Iranians have a smaller zone of interpersonal space than Americans do and are not highly territorial; instead, they thrive on constant interaction and high information flow. In addition, Iranians rely more heavily on personal communication whenever possible, as opposed to more formal methods of communication such as letters or telephone calls. Examples of high-contact interactions and communications in Iran include holding hands, whispering, and sitting close to one another.

CONCLUSION

In summary, we can classify Iranian communication patterns into six groups: style, interaction, message structure, context, type of appeal, and nonverbal. In terms of style, Iranians are more likely to provide abstract and general information as opposed to detailed facts. They are less likely to provide or be interested in expressions of individuality. We expect them to use less vocabulary diversity and more repetition of words and sentences. In addition, Iranians prefer to communicate from a close distance.

In terms of interactive variables, Iranians are expected to place emphasis on the credibility of the communication source, as opposed to the message content and the evidence that is presented. They tend to utilize asymmetrical communication, taking a superior–subordinate position such as in parent–child or teacher–student relationships. Further, communication in Iran tends to be receiver centered, placing emphasis on the receiver's interpretation and understanding, as opposed to emphasizing delivery skills.

Considering message structures, Iranians are less likely to be explicit, letting the receiver draw his or her own conclusions. They are more likely to present pleasant and agreeable information first and even to withhold threatening and negative information. Irani-

ans tend to focus on the side of an issue that is more consistent with their group's thinking and are less likely to deal with the opposing sides of the issue.

As far as context is concerned, Iranians are past oriented; they tend to provide extensive background information. They are receiver centered in the sense that the receiver must use contextual cues in order to interpret the information, because he or she tends to be provided with very little detailed and concrete information.

Iranians often resort to emotional and fear appeals to change the attitudes and behavior of others. It is common to focus on sadness and tragedy. They tend to display their emotions through their body movements, facial expressions, and the tone and volume of their voice. Iranians rely heavily on nonverbal communication, use vocal variety, touch, and communicate from a close distance.

REFERENCES

Andersen, P. A., & Bowman, L. (1985). *Positions of power: Nonverbal cues of status and dominance in organizational communication.* Paper presented at the International Communication Association, Honolulu, HI.

Carbone, T. (1975). Stylistic variables as related to source credibility: A content analysis approach. *Speech Monographs, 42,* 99–106.

Chu, C.-N. (1991). *The Asian mind game.* New York: Maxwell Macmillan International.

Gudykunst, W. B. (1988). Uncertainty and anxiety. In Y. Y. Kim & W. B. Gudykunst (Eds.), *Theories in intercultural communication* (pp. 123–156). Newbury Park, CA: Sage.

Gudykunst, W. B. (1991). *Bridging differences.* Newbury Park, CA: Sage.

Gudykunst, W. B., & Kim, Y. Y. (1984). *Communicating with strangers: An approach to intercultural communication.* Reading, MA: Addison-Wesley.

Gudykunst, W. B., Yoon, Y., & Nishida, T. (1987). The influence of individualism-collectivism on perceptions of communication ingroup and outgroup relationships. *Communication Monographs, 54,* 295–306.

Hall, E. T. (1983). *The dance of life: The other dimension of time.* Garden City, NY: Anchor/Doubleday.

Hecht, M., Andersen, P., & Ribeau, S. (1989). Cultural dimensions of nonverbal communication. In M. Asante & W. B. Gudykunst (Eds.), *Handbook of international and intercutural communication.* Newbury Park, CA: Sage.

Jung-Sun, C. (1962). A Chinese philosopher's theory of knowledge. *A Review of General Semantics, 9,* 215–232.

Katz, P. (1974). *Acculturation and social networks of American immigrants in Israel.* Unpublished doctoral dissertation, State University of New York at Buffalo.

Lee, H. O., & Boster, F. (1992). Collectivism-individualism in perceptions of speech rate. *Journal of Cross-Cultural Psychology, 23,* 377–388.

Littlejohn, S. W. (1983). *Theories of human communication.* Belmont, CA: Wadsworth.

MacLachlan, J. (1982). Listener perception of time compressed spokespersons. *Journal of Advertising Research, 22,* 47–51.

McGuire, J. W. (1969). The nature of attitude and attitude change. In G. Lindzey & E. Aronson (Eds.), *Handbook of social psychology,* 2nd ed. (vol. 3). New York: Random House.

McGuire, W. (1957). Order of presentation as a factor in conditioning persuasiveness. In C. I. Hovland (Ed.), *Order of presentation in persuasion.* New Haven, CT: Yale University Press.

Miller, N., Maruyama, G., Beaber, R., & Valone, K. (1976). Speed of speech and persuasion. *Journal of Personality and Social Psychology, 34,* 615–624.

Oliver, R. (1971). *Communication and culture in ancient India and China.* Syracuse, NY: Syracuse University Press.

Patterson, M. L. (1983). *Nonverbal behavior: A functional perspective.* New York: Springer.

Petrie, C. R. (1963). Informative speaking. *Speech Monographs, 30,* 79–91.

Rubin, R. B. (1992). A cross-cultural examination of interpersonal communication motives in Mexico and the United States. *International Journal of Intercultural Relations, 16,* 145–157.

Sillars, A. L., Pike, G., Jones, T., & Murphy, M. (1984). Communication and understanding in marriage. *Human Communication Research, 10,* 317–350.

Sussman, N. M., & Rosenfeld, H. (1982). Influence of culture, language, and sex on conversational distance. *Journal of Personality and Social Psychology, 42,* 66–74.

Ting-Toomey, S. (1985). Toward a theory of conflict and culture. In W. B. Gudykunst, L. P. Stewart, & S. Ting-Toomey (Eds.), *Communication, culture, and organizational processes.* Beverly Hills, CA: Sage.

Ting-Toomey, S. (1988). Intercultural conflict styles: A face-negotiation theory. In Y. Y. Kim & W. B. Gudykunst (Eds.), *Theories in intercultural communication.* Newbury Park, CA: Sage.

Triandis, H. C., Bontempo, R., Villareal, M., Asai, M., & Lucca, N. (1988). Individualism and collectivism. *Journal of Personality and Social Psychology, 54,* 323–338.

Watzlawick, P., Beavin, J. H., & Jackson, D. (1967). *Pragmatics of human communication.* New York: Norton.

Wheeler, L., Reis, H., & Bond, M. (1989). Collectivism—individualism in everyday social life. *Journal of Personality and Social Psychology, 57,* 79–86.

Williams, F. (1989). *The new communications.* Belmont, CA: Wadsworth.

Yum, J. O. (1991). The impact of Confucianism on interpersonal relationships and communication patterns in East Asia. In L. Samovar & R. Porter (Eds.), *Intercultural communication.* Belmont, CA: Wadsworth.

Zandpour, F. (1990). Candidate evaluation: Selectives versus comparatives. *Mass Communication Review, 17,* 34–46.

CHECK YOUR UNDERSTANDING

1. Describe the Iranian style of communication. Consider variables such as directness, amount of reliance on nonverbal communication, personal space, and demonstration of emotions.

2. How does the U.S. style of communication compare to that of the Iranian? What effect will such differences have as persons from Iran communicate with persons from the United States?

3. How might a classroom in Iran differ from one in the United States? Consider respect for authority, directness, conflict, individual expressiveness, and chronemics.

4. Given the description of Iranian communication in this reading, is Iran a high- or low-contact culture? A high- or low-context culture? A high- or low-power distance culture? A high- or low-uncertainty avoidance culture? A masculine or feminine culture?

CHAPTER ACTIVITIES

1. Try perception checking for a week. Report to the class how this technique affected your communication effectiveness.

2. With two to three classmates, attend a foreign film or cultural activity. Observe people and events closely. Discuss with one another what you saw and heard. What attributions did you make? What was the effect of these attributions?

3. Remember to continue working on your term projects.

CHAPTER 4

CULTURAL IDENTITY

SPINNING WHEELS, BOBBINS, WOOL, AND LACE

The carved picture hung in my Grandmother Pearson's living room—just to the right of the front door. It was an intricate carving of two old women sitting on either side of a large fireplace. Hanging in the fireplace was a large pot. On one side of the fireplace sat an old woman spinning. Across from her sat another old woman with a cup of tea in her hand. They were obviously having a wonderful visit.

I loved this picture. As a child I made up stories about it. After my grandmother's death, the carving came to me, and now it is in my living room. What I loved most about the carving was the old woman spinning. I was fascinated by that. I always wanted to learn to spin and when I was in graduate school, to ease the stress, I joined a spinning guild and learned to spin wool, which I then crocheted into various items.

Our childhoods follow us, and that fascination with spinning led to fascination with handcrafted items. So, when I travel, that carving follows me and I want to examine the local handicrafts. The first place this idea of how important that carving was and is to me came in Ireland. I watched the sheep in the fields, watched a man sheer sheep, and bought a beautiful hand-knit sweater.

In China I visited a silk factory. In large bins were bobbins of silk from the spinning machines. I asked the factory manager if I could buy one of the bobbins. My request caused quite a bit of laughter. After all, why would anyone want such an item? Through my interpreter I explained the carving and my fascination with spinning. I described my own spinning wheel and its similarities to the large machines in the factory. I left with a bobbin.

My daughter and I traveled to Bruges Belgium, in the mid-1990s. Not only in Bruges but in other cities of Belgium we saw beautiful, intricate lace. I spent several hours in Bruges talking to the women as they maneuvered the tiny lace bobbins into intricate patterns. And I bought a piece of hand-made lace, in the middle of which was a woman spinning. Again, I was reminded of the old woman at the fireplace and how my childhood identity is always with me.

OBJECTIVES

After reading this chapter and completing the readings and activities, you should be able to

- Define cultural identity.
- Describe the formation of cultural identity.
- Explain the role of identity in intercultural communication.
- Explain the sources and characteristics of cultural identity.

In 1996 Samuel P. Huntington published a book titled *The Clash of Civilizations and the Remaking of World Order*, which generated much discussion about the direction of global culture. He argues that the clash of civilizations is the greatest threat to world peace and that universal order is based on the way in which civilizations arrange themselves. He also claims that in our post–Cold War world, identities would solidify around one basic, compelling question: Who are we? Huntington said that humans are not only answering the question in traditional ways but also "by reference to the things that mean most to them" in terms of ancestry, religion, language, history, values, customs, and institutions (Huntington, 1996, p. 21). The book raises crucial questions about the role of cultural identity in human communication. Why, for example, are people moved to rally around cultural identity? What roles do ethnic, gender, and class identities play in intercultural communication?

In this section we will discuss several aspects of cultural identity: definition and formation of cultural identity as well as several characteristics of cultural identity. An understanding of each component is central to the development of our abilities to perceive other people accurately.

DEFINING CULTURAL IDENTITY

There are many ways of viewing cultural identity. For our purposes, however, cultural identity is a broad way of looking at cultural groups at various levels, including assumptions, underlying values, social relations, customs, and overall outlook on life that differ significantly among groups (Huntington, 1996, p. 28). When we say that cultural identity is broad, we mean that we can classify people according to whether they are Egyptian, Cambodian, Chinese, Japanese, Malay, and so on. For example, this means that a village in southern Iran may be different from a village in northern Iran, but both will share a common Iranian culture that distinguishes them from Iraq. As early as the fifth century B.C., Greeks identified what they shared in common and what distinguished them from the Persians and other non-Greeks: blood, language, religion, and way of life. And the list has not changed considerably since the time of the ancient Greeks. Cultural identity, then, is concerned with characteristics that people use to distinguish their ways of thinking and behaving from those of others. For example, the world's great religions, including Islam, Buddhism, and Christianity, are often used as marks of cultural distinction with regard to values, beliefs, and the like.

When people proclaim fidelity to specific customs, traditions, language, and religion, they can and do define their identity as a result of such composition and shapes. This way of marking boundaries between oneself and others explains a great deal about why people think and act as they do. It explains why one says with such firmness and commitment, "I am Russian," "I am African," or "I am Middle Eastern." Furthermore, as Gilroy (2000) notes, such markings of cultural identity give people "an obvious, common-sense way of talking about their individuality, community, and solidarity." (p. 98). Even more critically, such boundaries help people understand the role that subjective experiences play in their lives and the historical context in which experiences are played out.

Another way of looking at cultural identity is to say that it helps people to "comprehend the formation of that perilous pronoun 'we' and to reckon with the patterns of inclusion and exclusion that it cannot help creating" (Gilroy, 2000, p. 99). Put another way, cultural identity helps people reckon with who belongs to their group and who does not belong. For example, in the process of proclaiming who is Indonesian as opposed to who is Italian, patterns of inclusion and exclusion are formed and intensified. Thus, when people define themselves as belonging to cultural group A and not B, they are also transformed into solidarity groups and cultural entities. In 1994, for example, over 2,000 people rallied in Sarajevo and hoisted the flags of Saudi Arabia and Turkey and not the banners of the North Atlantic Treaty Organization (NATO) or the United Nations. Symbolically, by flying the banners of Saudi Arabia and Turkey, Sarajevans identified themselves with their fellow Muslims and announced to the world who was friend and not friend (Huntington, 1996, p. 19). This example illustrates another important component of cultural identity and that is the role of symbols in mapping where one belongs and how.

Although we are talking about cultural identities, we are not attempting here to explain *how* cultural identities evolve, because the story is as old as humankind and would require reams of paper to explicate such a complex phenomenon. It is significant to note, however, that once humans define themselves as belonging to one cultural group as opposed to another, they attach huge importance to such belonging. Of course these definitions change over time. During the heyday of the Roman Empire, Egyptian soldiers reportedly pleaded to become Roman citizens because at the time men all over the world, according to Van Doren (1991, p. 69), aspired to become Roman citizens. Today, however, things are very different and it is highly unlikely that Egyptian soldiers *en masse* would yearn to become citizens of Italy. This example reveals a component of cultural identity that is noteworthy: Cultural identities evolve and change, creating new associations and modes of identification.

Finally, cultural identity serves as an interpretive device. It helps us see ourselves along such dimensions as race, ethnicity, kinship, soil, region, gender, and religion. The categories, in turn, help us know who we are, what we want, and where we wish to go. Cultural identity as an "interpretive device" is similar to human perception in the sense that the information we select from all the available data around us is shaped by our cultural group, personal experiences, values, and many other factors. Interpretation affects our communication and the stories we tell. Gilroy (2000, p. 98) sees the interpretive dimension of identity as "bounded and particular," and as a way of making sense of the world.

FORMATION OF CULTURAL IDENTITY

Although the formation of cultural identity is a complex process, it involves a three-stage process (Phinney, 1993; Lustig and Koester, 1999): unexamined cultural identity, cultural identity search, and cultural identity achievement. In *unexamined cultural identity,* one has little interest in exploring matters of culture because it exists at the "taken-for-granted" level of consciousness. Young children, for example, are unaware of the characteristics that distinguish one culture from another. As children grow older, however, they become mindful of categories and who belongs to a particular culture. Parents, the media, social memberships, and other sources play a role in helping individuals understand what is meant by cultural identity.

The second stage, *cultural identity search,* is process oriented and involves a questioning mode about one's culture. During this stage the individual is keen to understand cultural memberships and the implications of such memberships. Activities that help the individual move toward cultural identity include chatting with family and friends, attending festivals, going to museums, watching films and television, and so on. As a result of the search, the individual comes to know that he or she belongs to cultural group "A" as opposed to cultural group "B." As individuals become more aware of their culture, they develop an emotional attachment to their own cultural group. This means that individuals are beginning to take their cultural identity very seriously. *Emotional intensity* is a term that captures this type of behavior.

Cultural identity achievement completes the process and involves an internalization of individuals' attachment to their group. In this stage people are clear and confident about personal meanings of their culture and can deal with such matters as stereotypes and discrimination without internalizing others' negative perceptions. The words *clear and confident* are key to understanding the formation of cultural identity because of their directional qualities. By being clear and confident about their culture, people can use the qualities of their culture to guide their future actions. Such guides can and do go a long way in determining the extent to which one identifies with a range of behaviors.

CHARACTERISTICS OF CULTURAL IDENTITY

As shown in the preceding section, cultural identity orchestrates our lives. To this notion it is useful for our purposes to add several characteristics of cultural identity, including gender. To understand fully the implications of gender's role in constructing identity, we need to consider for a moment the importance of gender in culture.

Women traditionally have had a historical and cultural identity significantly different from that of men. Until recently men argued that such differences were based on biologically determined characteristics of women. Women were considered, for example, to be both emotional and nurturing, whereas men were considered to be rational and strong. Based on these differences, men assumed roles of ruler and protector and developed a family organizational structure known as *patriarchy* (Lerner, 1986).

Patriarchy and Gender

Patriarchy refers to a system of rule by men in which many of the groups they dominate exchange responsibilities and obligations for their protection. For example, men have historically dominated women in exchange for the responsibility of their economic support and protection. In some cultures, patriarchal structures have led women to be exchanged in marriage among tribes, denied an education, and excluded from participating in public talk.

Once men's dominance was established largely on the basis of sexual dominance, it lasted for nearly 2,500 years and was incorporated into most cultures, including the Near East, Asia, Europe, Africa, and the United States. Thus, in patriarchal societies, as some scholars argue, women's identities were intricately interwoven with that of men. For instance, the title "Mrs." reveals the identity of the husband but conceals the identity of the wife. Today, however, women are free to be called "Mrs." or "Miss" or "Ms."

Gender and Gender Formation   We define *gender formation* as the sociocultural process by which female and male identities are created and transformed. From a gender identity-formation perspective, our conceptions of gender are influenced by both social structure and cultural development. All cultures differentiate between male and female behavior; once these behaviors are learned and categorized, they become associated with the identity characteristics of a specific sex. For example, in North America, the prevailing cultural view based on gender is that little girls play with dolls and little boys play with trucks. In playing with dolls, little girls begin to identify with role characteristics such as nurturing, caring, and childcare. Thus, by internalizing the characteristics of these roles, men and women begin to accept specific roles, causing them to become *natural* or *commonsensical* to both men and women.

Social construction is a term that refers to the way that gender identification develops. Wood (2000) notes that "throughout our interaction with others, we receive constant messages that reinforce females' conformity to femininity and males' to masculinity. This reveals gender identity as a social creation, not an individual characteristic" (p. 1997). In the previous example of little girls playing with dolls and little boys playing with trucks, gender identity is reinforced when parents and others teach children to associate one practice (playing with dolls) with girls and the other practice (playing with trucks) with boys. Soon, children learn that they should behave according to the norms prescribed by people in their group. In this way, one's cultural identity is seen as natural and therefore promotes gender identity construction. Our gender identity tells us how to be and act with others.

Forms of persuasion outside the home also influence gender identity. Think of television programs, movies, and other media activities that reinforce daily how women and men identify with each other. In those media cases that you can think of, how are men and women perceived? Note the relationship that exists between gender and media structures and practices.

Thus, we are not born with a tendency toward masculine or feminine identity. We are taught, and the lessons that we learn are internalized. This means that such lessons become a crucial part of our socialization and communication processes. Another way of stating this is to say that a child who is constantly reinforced for playing with dolls will soon believe that such identity behavior is not only appropriate but desirable. These social roles then lead men and women to view themselves as "different in their essence and their function" (Lerner, 1986). In this way, set ideas of gender identity are formed and normalized.

Gender and Culture   Cultures normalize gender norms in different ways and in different places, however. Lewis (2002) argues that the status of women is probably "the most profound difference" between Christendom and Islam (p. 67). In Saudia Arabia, according to Carmen Bin Ladin (2004), women and men must observe "polite rituals of segregation" (p. 158). In some instances women cannot speak the name of a friend's husband in conversation, because to do so out loud or inquire about his health would suggest a measure of intimacy. Princes and princesses in the Saudi Kingdom are allocated income from the Treasury based on age, rank, power, and gender (Bin Ladin, 2004, p. 171). Girls receive half as much money as boys.

In Iran, although gender roles are changing, some women still wear the traditional Muslim *hijab*, long, loose clothing that reaches the ankles. To ensure that women observed the codes of dress behavior, the hijab law was written into Iran's constitution after the Islamic Republic's victory in 1979 (Fassihi, 2003, p. 1). The purpose of such dress is to hide the shape of the female form and other aspects of sexuality. Increasingly, in such countries, women are seeking new and different modes of dress, however. For example, women in Iran have begun to wear "illegal designs," which are more tailored to the female physical form (Fassihi, 2003, p. 1). Note the symbolic and real way in which social and political factors are intertwined with women's clothing. Despite the fact that some Muslim women still choose to wear religiously dictated clothing, others, according to Fassihi, "chafe at government-dictated religious rules" and have begun to stretch the dress codes passionately (Fassihi, 2003, p. 1).

In some instances, however, dress codes can influence the social behavior of women who have left the land of the Middle East and settled elsewhere. In 2003 "all-girl Muslim proms" were held in California because "a lot of Muslim girls don't go to proms" in keeping with gender norms of the culture (Brown, 2003, p. 3). At the proms, hijabs were removed, since no men were present. This story also illustrates the power of gender roles to transcend national boundaries.

Today, in Japan, businesswomen's competence is questioned because they have stepped outside the bounds of what is considered to be feminine behavior. One woman said that "as an independent saleswoman, she found that customers merely pretended to listen to her" (French, 2003, p. 3). In fact, according to her testimony, "Time and again when she finished a presentation men would ask who her boss was" (p. 3). The significance of gender identity formation to intercultural communication is that it influences our feelings, beliefs, and behaviors in our relations to people unlike ourselves.

Ethnicity

In 1992 the *New York Times* ("Ethnic Cleansing," p. 4E) reported that over two million people had been "driven from their homes or fled in fear" as a result of the fighting in the former Republic of Yugoslavia. Groups such as Croats, Serbs, and Macedonians struggled in bitter antagonism over the issue of ethnicity. Atrocities, attacks, mortar shellings, and maiming all occurred in the name of "ethnic cleansing." *Ethnic cleansing* refers to one group's systematic attempts to eliminate another group through intimidation, war, and physical violence. Yugoslavian neighbors who had once visited with each other, shared bread, and played games in the same community hall began to perceive themselves differently. One soldier in the Muslim territory of former Yugoslavia noted that "for the Serbs, for the Croats and for Europe Muslim people are nothing; Muslim people are just dirt" (*New York Times,* 1992, p. 4E).

The war that took place among ethnic Yugoslavians who had once lived in relative harmony with each other raises key questions about the role of ethnicity in human communication. Why, for example, are people moved to commit heinous crimes in the name of a particular group? What role does ethnicity play in intercultural communication? In this section we will discuss several aspects of ethnicity, conceptions of ethnicity, and ethnic identity. An understanding of each component is central to the development of our abilities to perceive other people accurately.

Conceptions of Ethnicity   There are many definitions of ethnicity. For our purposes, however, an *ethnic group* is one whose members "entertain a subjective belief in their common descent because of similarities of physical type or of customs or both, or because of blood relationship" (Alba, 1990) is not as important as issues of rootedness and ancestry. Ethnicity is concerned with "real" or "presumed" ancestry, a common history that is apart from others, interaction among members who share a consciousness of kind, and an important attachment to the past.

A practical way of looking at ethnicity is to say that it involves a linguistic construction such as "I am Polish American" (or "Italian American," "Mexican American," etc.), with an accompanying tie to the country of one's roots or origins. References to one's country of origin, as well as ethnic markers, serve as powerful ways of forging group identity. Later we will discuss how ethnic identity influences the nature of intercultural communication.

At this point, it is useful to note that there are basically two ways of viewing ethnicity: social allocation and social solidarity. *Social allocation* (Alba, 1990; Wilson, 1987; Yinger, 1981) holds that individuals are situated in the social structure based on their ethnic characteristics (groups distinguished by occupation, educational level, and residence). *Social solidarity* provides keys for identifying people who interact with each other to achieve common purposes (e.g., Asians who are members of the Asian American Center for Justice). Some scholars note that social allocation is losing strength as a way of measuring or explaining ethnicity (Alba, 1990). Social solidarity, however, is gaining ground as a way of looking at ethnic membership.

There are three major sources of social solidarity. First, social solidarity signals a consciousness of kind. Individuals may, for example, interact with others because they are conscious of something such as distinctions between in-groups and out-groups. Social solidarity also may signal a consciousness that individuals share a common fate. For example, for years Jews in Europe maintained a common bond because of the virulent forms of discrimination leveled against them. Based on unpleasant experiences, Jews inferred that they could advance their mutual interest by banding together. The notion of a common fate, however, is not characteristic of Jews exclusively. This type of behavior is evident among African Americans, Hispanics, and the male-dominated organization, Promise Keepers, which held a rally in Washington, DC, in October 1997.

A third way that groups signal social solidarity is through a *valued* heritage. Here, the past assumes importance. Group solidarity is built around one's roots, ancestry, or descent. Notice that ancestry forces to the foreground one's background and the things that that background summons or evokes. For example, to say that one is Thai American is to declare that one shares with other like-minded individuals a series of activities, beliefs, and values that are *Thai-like.* These might include eating Thai food, visiting the graves of one's ancestors frequently, or wearing a special kind of jewelry. In these instances, the specific ethnic strands are rooted in ancestry, which, of course, is not the entire story of ethnic identity. We will now discuss ethnic identity, demonstrating its relevance to our multiethnic and multiracial world.

Ethnic Identity   In the Texas town of Amarillo, two women, fluent in both Spanish and English, lost their jobs because they chatted in Spanish (Verhovek, 1997, p. A10). Rosa Gonzales and Ester Hernandez were hired by an insurance company because they spoke Spanish. Later, the owner of the company asked that Gonzales and Hernandez speak only English while at work. In fact, he allegedly demanded that the women sign a pledge that they would not speak Spanish in the workplace, except to service their Hispanic customers. When Gonzales and Hernandez refused to sign a written agreement, expressing their intent to honor their owner's request, they were fired.

In refusing to sign the agreement, Mrs. Gonzales said, "I told him (the owner of the company) no. This is what I am; this is what I do. This is normal to me. I'm not doing it to offend anybody" (Verhovek, 1997, p. A10). As this story suggests, some people uphold their ethnic identity, whether the identity is expressed through language or customs. As

Alba (1990), Taylor (1992), and others indicate, ethnic identity is increasingly becoming an important dimension of intercultural interactions.

Scholars who study ethnic identity posit two alternative points of view about the concept. Ethnic identity is grounded in theories first developed by the noted psychoanalyst, Erick Erikson. Erikson (1980) observes that identity rests heavily on what he terms the *prototypes* that are available to individuals, based on their history and location. Erikson argues that we form our identity because we find within our environment models (prototypes) of "good and evil." This means that during our formative years, our parents, extended family members, and significant others exhibit modes of behavior (good and bad) that serve as frameworks for how we subsequently behave. These models, in turn, become linked to who we are, as well as to our membership in particular ethnic groups.

For example, children who grow up in Greek households learn early that their identity is formed on the basis of what Holden (quoted in Broome, 1997, p. 117) terms "truly double-born souls." The Greeks' struggle between opposites "spirit and flesh," "ideal and reality," "triumph and despair," according to this view, leads Greeks to perceive themselves to be constantly in a struggle between opposites. For this reason, Greeks see aspects of their universe in terms of the in-group over the out-group. This view, in turn, affects their intercultural interactions with others. Out-group members are viewed more with suspicion and mistrust. In Greek society, therefore, family members, friends, and friends of friends form tight identification circles. Using this model (prototype) of good and evil, Greeks develop an identity that is akin to something like the following: "Our sense of responsibility and obligation is to our family," "This is how we see ourselves," and "This is a good thing." Taken together, the communication activities we have outlined influence Greek's perceptions of self and their ethnic identity.

Another example of how our cultural collective stories (ethnic identities) influence the way in which we communicate is found in the 1996 protests that accompanied the selection of a Black Caribbean immigrant as Miss Italy (*New York Times,* "Italians Contemplate Beauty," September 10, 1996, p. 3). The controversy centered on the issue of whether Miss Denny Mendez, a non-European Italian, could accurately represent Italy in a beauty pageant. Some Italians claimed that she did not have the physical features characteristic of Italian female beauty. Other Italians, however, recognized Italy's changing identity from a relatively homogenous culture to a more cosmopolitan one. Italy, like many countries worldwide, is increasingly becoming a place of immigrants. Along with these changing demographics should come a more heightened awareness of the tensions that can exist between people based on their physical attributes as well.

One must be careful, however, not to imply that membership in an ethnic group automatically promotes conscious identity. As Alba (1990) notes, "Individuals may be ethnic in their 'identities' and still consciously reject their ethnic backgrounds" (p. 22). This view suggests that sometimes we unconsciously hold fast to our ethnic roots because they have become "impregnated with influence." For example, one can exhibit traits of an Irish American even if one no longer consciously identifies as Irish. Another way of looking at this point is to say that one can publicly and privately deny one's Irish roots and yet cling to forms of storytelling, which are manifestations of being Irish.

Another aspect of ethnic identity rests in the notion of self-concept and social recognition. This view holds that we gain a sense of who we are based not only on how we see ourselves but also on how others see us. This conception of ethnic identity is often described as the *image* or *looking-glass theory.* The image theory also suggests that our membership categories help to define who we are. For example, to say that Idell is "female, white, a mother, and an author" is to suggest that these categories help to define who Idell is.

Subsumed under the conception of ethnic identity are two elements that are crucial: commitment and salience. *Commitment* refers to "the degree of investment in relationships to others that is premised on a specific identity, and thus the social cost of renouncing it," and *salience* is the "probability for a given person, of a given identity being invoked in a variety of situations" (Alba, 1990, p. 23). Put another way, commitment refers to how faithful one is to a specific ethnic identity and what could happen if one ceased to be faithful to social relations that are based on ethnic identity. For example, if you live in Rwanda, East Africa, and you are a member of the Hutu ethnic group, to what extent might you broadcast your friendship with a Tutsi? And what harm would come to you were you to give up membership in the Hutu group? What would your ethnic membership cost you? Would the friendship leave you isolated and without Hutu friends?

Salience, in contrast, refers to the likelihood or chance that one will use or mention one's identity in a given social situation, whether that situation is in a classroom or church. In other words, salience is probability driven because it invites odds as to whether one will acknowledge one's ancestry or identity. For example, a woman might identify herself as Chinese American simply as a way of noting that she has roots in China without making an issue of her ancestry. This means that Chinese ancestry does not have *high salience* for the Chinese woman in our example. For this reason, the odds of her invoking or using her Chinese ancestry in social situations are not very good.

In the context of intercultural communication, however, Taylor (1992, p. 25) locates a central reason why there is tension and conflict among groups based on ethnic identity. Our "identity," Taylor argues, "is partly shaped by recognition or its absence." This suggests "that a person or group of people or society around them mirror back to them a confining or contemptible picture of themselves" (p. 25). Herein lie the roots of some difficulty in the United States among ethnic groups and women. Women in the United States, for instance, maintain that a male-oriented (patriarchy) society has contributed to women's depreciatory image of themselves. Similarly, African Americans, Hispanics, and other ethnic groups claim that they are not being taken seriously by members of the larger society. Furthermore, the narratives that members of the larger society tell themselves are entirely different from the stories that ethnic groups tell.

Asante (1987) and Dates and Barlow (1990) maintain that a negative portraiture derides, belittles, and robs African Americans of public virtue. Thus, minority group demands for recognition are deeply rooted in their claims to public virtue. The search for recognition by women and minorities clearly undergird the cultural clash over ethnicity. The debate over the representation of women and ethnic groups in literary and historical texts is an example of individuals' search for identity and meaning.

The following example should give us a sense of the deep intersection between stories and identity. The debate over the Western canon once moved author Saul Bellow to say, "When the Zulus produce a Tolstoy we will read him," and Houston Baker to say that choosing between Pearl Buck and Virginia Woolf is "no different from choosing between a hoagy and a pizza" (quoted in Kimball, 1990). By *Western canon* we mean "the unofficial, shifting . . . generally recognized body of great works that have stood the test of time and are acknowledged to be central to a complete liberal arts education" (Kimball, 1990, p. 1). The Western canon is being contested today because it raises such questions as: Who has a right to decide what is taught or not taught in universities? And what should or should not be included? Such questions can and do generate tensions over whether, for example, Toni Morrison's book, *The Song of Solomon*, should be given priority over Tolstoy's book, *War and Peace*.

These cultural tensions arise not from small disagreements or mundane matters. Rather, they arise from strong notions (commitment) of who individuals are, as well as from one side's claim that recognition should not be based on ethnic identity but on individual achievement in keeping with the ideals of democracy. The other side argues for recognition, elevating (implicitly and/or explicitly) ethnic origins and identity. We saw evidence of the importance of identity in our earlier example of the Hernandez and Gonzales case.

Some critical questions that you should grapple with are the following: To what extent do claims to ethnic identity foster divisions among different groups? What is the relationship between ethnic identities and the building of intercultural community? How important is ethnic identity to democracy? How will ethnicity influence intercultural communication in this century? However you answer these questions, it is important to remember that our ancestry, our claims to ethnic identity, and the way our cultural stories shape who we are in relation to others profoundly influence our perceptions of others.

For example, a professor at a major university presented a lively seminar presentation titled "Under Cherry Trees There Are No Strangers: Communicating Interculturally." Following the presentation, the professor invited her delightfully attentive audience to ask questions and make comments. Things proceeded as expected until a gentleman made an observation that is of the greatest pertinence today: "I don't understand why people refer to themselves as African American, Asian American, or Hispanic American. We are all Americans!" The man's implied suggestion is that recognition of a person's ethnic identity is irrelevant to who we are as Americans. Is ethnicity irrelevant to improving intercultural communication?

Regional Factors

"My uncle's body was taken from Beirut back to Palestine and to the town of Tulkarm for burial," writes Ghada Karmi in her book, *In Search of Fatima: A Palestinian Story* (2002, p. 14). She explains that "this was because our family originates from Tulkarm." Karmi notes further that her uncle's body was carried back to the region in which he was born "because our family originates from Tulkarm, hence our name of Karmi (Arabic surnames often derive from their place of origin)" (p. 14). We learn from Karmi's story that territory meant a great deal to her family and that there was an intimate association between the region in which they lived and their sense of who they were. Regional associations have the power to invoke in humans fond memories of where they have been and where they are going because territory often serves as landmarks on which a person can base his or her stories. In this section we discuss how identity and territory are associated in humans' minds and, by extension, how the two influence intercultural interactions.

The concept of *region* carries with it ideas about the interplay of territory and place. And it is just not any place; rather, like an old armchair, people tend to imbue their regions with meaning, which derives specifically from what takes place there. For example, Karmi reveals that even when her family immigrated to England, her mother remained faithful to Palestine—her place of origin, her territory. In one portion of the book, Karmi (2002) writes poignantly, "Our mother had little interest in places which had no relation to what was familiar to her, like many Arabs, her concept of enjoyment was being with other people, not gazing at historical monuments which she scornfully referred to as 'piles of stones'" (p. 258). Later, however, when Karmi's mother had an opportunity to visit Spain—a region that was suffused with Arab culture—the mother's orientation to "piles of stones" changed dramatically.

Karmi (2002) writes, "The only exception to this position she ever encountered in her life was when once, long after we were grown up, our father took her to southern Spain. There, agog at the splendid Islamic buildings of Cordova and Granada, where she could see the grand legacy of Spain's Arab past, she felt the thrill that piles of stones could import. 'What colour, what lightness!' she enthused, 'how marvelous the Arabs were!'"(p. 263).

Karmi's story reveals another powerful dimension of regional identity: the generative and sustaining way that region evokes memories of what is done where, with whom, and with what effect. The story illustrates further how sameness and difference play out under the rubric of identity. In the Karmi narrative, her mother not only reverenced the soil of her birth but also what that soil represented: dynamism and warm memories—interacting with people in a Palestinian village. Karmi's mother defined her very existence by what emanated from the soil in terms of identification and its counterparts: ethnicity, roots, and shared humanity.

Hannerz (1992) reminds us that "what revolves around the village square is a face-to-face society. Its members stay within the same geographical territory and on the whole interact only with one another, but do a great deal of that" (p. 41). Karmi's mother missed such village interactions. Building on this insight, Tuan (1977), in describing the significance of land for the Maori in New Zealand, says that they "had a great respect for land per se, and an exceedingly strong affection for ancestral soil" (p. 155). Historically, nowhere was the Maori's profound attachment to territory greater than in how they treated prisoners. According to Tuan (1977), "A prisoner before being put to death could be given permission to return to his tribal territory," or "he might ask that he should be allowed to drink of the waters of some stream which flowed through the borders of his home" (p. 155). Such stories are emotionally moving and reveal the intense attachment that people have to their home-land or region. Thus, flow of meanings and the personal nature of landscapes associated with such "high visibility signs as monuments, shrines, a hallowed battlefield or cemetery" serve, as Tuan (1977) aptly notes, to "enhance a people's sense of identity" (p. 159).

Another point that you should remember about culture and region is that regional factors do not operate in isolation from political, cultural, and psychological components and other concerns (Gilroy, 2000, p. 101). For example, when Nelson Mandela—the first Black president of South Africa—after having spent 27 years in prison, gave his inaugural address, he strategically used the "common ground symbol" of home and citizenship as a way of reaching the people. In other words, Mandela crafted his speech based on shared symbols and relationships between region and identity, defined in terms of "claims of soil, roots, and territory" (p. 111). Gilroy notes that Mandela spoke "not only of the soil but of the beauty of the country and offered the idea of a common relationship to both the culti-vated and the natural beauty of the land as elements of a new beginning" (p. 110). In this way, Mandela took the notion of sentiment for land and region and turned it to his advan-tage, creating in many of the people warm positive feelings about the new South Africa.

In our relationships with others, we must keep in mind that the stories we learn in specific spaces and places reside deep within us!

Religion

Another major component of identity is religion. Daily, we are bombarded with stories of the power of religion, from former Supreme Court Justice Roy Moore, who, in 2003, worked vigorously to exhibit the Ten Commandments in front of the rotunda of the Ala-bama Supreme Court building in Montgomery, to the young Swedish Islamic woman who was murdered by her father because she did not, to her father's way of thinking, follow the tenets of Islam (Lyall, 2002).

In the literature, religion is defined both widely and narrowly, and much scholarly debate surrounds the meaning of the term. According to the *HarperCollins Dictionary of Religion* (1995), religion is "a system of beliefs and practices that are relative to super-human being" (p. 893). This definition of religion "moves away from defining religion as some special kind of experience or worldview" (p. 892). Smith (1991), however, writes that if religion is taken broadly, it means "a life woven around a people's ultimate concerns." If narrowly, it means "concern to align humanity with the transcendental ground of existence" (p. 183).

Some religions, as Smith (1991, p. 85) observes, are questioned on the grounds of eth-ics or religion, such as Confucianism. Is it ethics or religion? Although these are thorny and significant questions, we will not focus here on the freighted debate. Rather, we underline the point that the practice of religion is tied to the relationship that exists among cults, sects, denominations, synagogues, churches, temples, and culture.

Culture and religion are intimately linked. For example, much of the present-day tur-moil in the Middle East is centered on the controversy between Islam and Christianity. In fact, Huntington (1996) argues that religion is "a central defining characteristic of civiliza-tions" and that the four major religions (Christianity, Islam, Hinduism, and Confucianism) are associated with major civilizations. This means that religion is a crucible out of which values, beliefs, norms, and ethics are formed. Furthermore, religion acts as a scaffolding for framing humans' perspectives on the world; religion also helps people structure their thoughts as well as align their behavior. In the earlier example, Judge Roy Moore defended placing the Ten Commandments on the secular courthouse square because he believed that the 10 tenets, if adhered to, should order how people respond to other human beings in keeping with his religious beliefs.

Of course, in the realm of intercultural communication such principles are rarely so simple. Since adherence to codes of conduct is very much religiously based, we sometimes find ourselves at odds with others simply because their religious views differ from our own value orientations. For example, religious beliefs order when, where, and how we practice such cultural activities as festivals and holidays; even the clothes we wear are delicately tied to our religion.

In Indian Hindu culture the Dance of Shiva has been described as the "clearest image of the activity of God which any art or religion can boast of" (Gannon, 2003, p. 65). In this regard, according to religion credo, every facet of nature—man, bird, beast, insect, trees, wind, waves, stars—all display a dance pattern; hence, we see the interrelatedness of dance and culture in India. In contrast, in traditional African religions (Van Der Veur, 2003, pp. 81–82), God is worshiped through ancestors and the dead can come back to haunt one! One of the authors of this book remembers a food-gathering event at the home of one of her Gambian friends that resulted in the friend dropping a pot on the floor and exclaiming, "Stop it, Binta!" (the name of the author's friend's ancestral grandmother). When the author asked what was the matter, the friend replied, "Binta is speaking to me." It was the friend's way of demonstrating that the dead can indeed speak from the grave! In this example, notice the unending resonance of stories and their power literally to govern the lives of individuals.

Stories about the link between religion and culture abound, and we offer additional examples to illustrate the principle. In Egyptian and other Islamic cultures, at least once during a person's lifetime he or she must say the *Shahadah* "correctly, slowly, thoughtfully, aloud, with full understanding and with heartfelt conviction" (Smith, 1991, p. 244). The *Shahadah* is Islam's creed, or confession of faith. It is important to note that the *Shahadah* can influence almost every aspect of a Muslim's being. The Muslim religion encourages individuals to sprinkle their everyday speech with such sayings as "There is no god but God," especially in the midst of such human moments as death, birth, learning, and giving. Remember that some people do not "just mouth" such principles; they also live the principles. This is an important distinction to make about religion and culture. In a manner of speaking, religion is culture and culture is religion. By this tautology we mean that it is almost impossible to reference one without the other.

By this tautology we also mean to convey the idea that the principles of religion are designed to regulate the way people think and behave, whether those ways are steeped in Islam, Hinduism, or Confucianism. In the countries of Korea, China, and Japan, as Ishii, Klopf, and Cook (2003) observe, because "deity is in every place in every form, rather than a single place or form" (p. 32), the concept influences everyday interactions in such countries. For example, as a result of such principles, people believe that "everything is benign, nothing is worth worrying about" (p. 32); therefore, one finds a great emphasis on being pleasant in interpersonal relations. The logical conclusion of the principle is that one might as well smile because in the long haul nothing is going to mean much anyhow. In intercultural interactions, if one is unfamiliar with such religious beliefs, tenets can invite incorrect and harsh judgments, such as Easterners are "easygoing and uncaring." However, upon closer scrutiny, if one is mindful of the tight association between religion and culture, one can become a more effective intercultural communicator.

Class

Religion, race, ethnicity, and region are not the only factors that matter in significant ways. Class is also arguably an intriguing cultural concept despite its murky and sometimes touchy qualities. Of all the factors that we are considering in this chapter, the word *class* is fraught with the most unpleasant associations in some parts of the world, especially in the United States.

As long ago as 800 years before Christ, during the times of early Hebrew prophets Amos, Micah, and Isaiah, we find "repeated denunciations of the rich and powerful members of society" (Lenski, quoted in Kerbo, 1996, p. 83). In fact, throughout history, especially during the seventeenth and eighteenth centuries, the subject of who got what and why was the subject of much discussion and debate. It was not until the Age of Enlightenment that feudal arrangements between serf and lord were attacked by such philosophers as Locke, Rousseau, and Montesquieu. By the end of the nineteenth century, it seemed possible to attack wealth and class more easily than ever before. The century also saw the rise of theories to explain notions of class and inequalities among social groups.

In this section we will define class, briefly consider the nature of class, and explain some of the factors that create inequalities among human beings. For our purpose—which is to understand the relationship between class and cultural identity—the work of Hofstede (2001) will be important. By *class*, we mean "a group of people who share common objective interests in the system of social stratification" (Kerbo, 1996, p. 146). Although this definition of class does not capture all of its many complexities, it does serve to highlight various dimensions of the concept. As Kerbo observes, class carries with it the convergence of three major divisions: occupational class, bureaucratic power, and property divisions based on owner and nonowner categories of property (pp. 146–147) (see Figure 4.1).

Occupational class refers to groupings around education, professions, jobs, and what people do to earn a living. This creates distinctions among, say, doctors, lawyers, kings, queens, factory workers, and taxi drivers. In Monica Ali's novel, *Brick Lane* (2003), for example, one of the characters, Chanu, an immigrant from Bangladesh living in London, constantly reminded his wife and friends of his high educational status, despite the fact that he had become a taxi driver. While driving throughout the city of London, he repeatedly referred to his passengers as "ignorant type people," making a conscious effort to distinguish himself from the unlearned (p. 232). Because Chanu had been educated at the top university in Bangladesh and because he loved books, he identified himself as a member of the educated class, although he was pursuing a line of work that is typically associated with the working class. In one scene in Ali's book, Chanu has been summoned to traffic court for speeding, as we detail here.

While reading the passage, note Chanu's references to class identification. "Though Chanu was a very careful and able driver, it seemed that the Authorities conspired against him . . . On one occasion Chanu had to attend court over some fabricated indictment. He put on his suit and he rehearsed his speech in front of the mirror. "They don't know who they are dealing with," he told Nazneed, his wife. "They think it is some peasant-type person who will tremble at their gowns and wigs" (Ali, p. 232).

The passage contains important information about the nature of class and how it places people in various camps, based on their occupation. This means that occupation acts in divisive ways to separate one person from another. In the novel, Chanu is careful to rehearse his speech so that he could send the correct linguistic and nonverbal signals, aspects of class that we will discuss later. Meanwhile, it is worth noting that Chanu was signifying his own class position with reference to occupation, but clearly not with reference to income. This shows that notions of class and identity are multilayered.

█ FIGURE 4.1   Dimensions of Class, Power, and Status

Occupational class: Education, profession, jobs
Bureaucratic power: Upper class, middle class, working class, lower class
Property dimensions: Ownership of land and material things

A second dimension of class or inequality is *bureaucratic power*. This means that people are divided "with respect to positions within bureaucratic authority structures" (Kerbo, 1996, p. 220). Such structures are typically associated with four broad general classes: upper class, middle class, working class, and lower class. Each position within the class structure carries with it such forms of cultural identification as skills, job complexity, design or furnishings, automobiles, what one drinks (mineral waters, wine, beer, or aperitifs), where one vacations, and what one wears. For example, although in the United States there has been a movement away from formal dress in the workplace, and although there is increasingly a shift back to more formal modes of dress, middle-class people are usually identified by what they wear to work (e.g., a suit, overalls, "work clothes"). It is important to underline that status markers, what Bourdieu (1984) terms "distinctive features," function cooperatively as a "system of differences" (p. 226).

In other words, by consciously or unconsciously choosing to identify with class marker "A" as opposed to class marker "B," one necessarily signals a choice of cultural worlds. Our point is that material goods or property serve as markers of class and in turn carry with them preferred notions of taste—whether implicit or explicit.

In terms of Hofstede's research (2001) that we discussed earlier regarding the four dimensions of culture, it can be seen that the power dimension is an integral part of class and cultural identity. Typically, as we explained in Chapter 2, some cultures are very vertical and people expect to boss and be bossed, whereas in other more horizontal cultures people are less organized around hierarchical relationships. In the United States, for example, although one may be the president of Scholar Accounting Firm, it is likely that he or she still can be addressed by his or her first name. It is significant for you to remember that the very act of placing oneself in middle versus working class carries with it forms of cultural identification that are based on status markers such as office size, food, or favored restaurant.

In Amy Chua's book, *World on Fire* (2003), which describes the cultural tensions that exist among market-dominant immigrants and indigenous people worldwide, she writes, "The extremely wealthy stick out—whether because of their origins, skin color, language, or 'blood ties'—from the impoverished masses around them, and they are seen by these majorities as belonging to a different ethnicity or people—as 'outsiders' who look different, speak differently, or as Fiji's nationalist leader George Speight recently said of his country's market-dominant Indiana minority 'smell different'"(p. 20).

It is worth remembering that ethnic conflict stems from "the overlap of class and ethnic division" (Chua, p. 20). In Rwanda, class was often associated with physical type, which even led to genocide. Some Hutus, absent "being tall and having a straight nose," were murdered alongside the Tutsis because their crime was "being too tall for a Hutu" (Gilroy, 2000, p. 104.). Although this is an extreme example, it reveals a great deal about what can and does happen when stories about class, identity, and belonging are taken very seriously indeed.

A final category that converges to form class categories is *property*—that is, the ownership of land and material things and their consequences for identity and belonging. One thousand years ago, a man named Machmud of Gjarzni, and 650 years ago, an African king named Mansa Musa created large sums of wealth, according to Crossen (2000, pp. xii and 3). In each instance, gold, silver, jewels, land, little statues, and even a box of pepper were used as markers of power. Unquestionably, there are associations between wealth, status, and power.

In his book, *The Noblest Triumph: Property and Prosperity through the Ages,* Bethell (1998, p. 11), argues that a strong emphasis on the institution of private property helps to explain the cultural preeminence of the West. In this way, we add another dimension to our understanding of the complexity of culture and identity. Nation-states also serve as modes of cultural and class identity. According to the 2000 census, Microsoft owner, Bill Gates, owns 40 percent of the world's wealth. And according to Joseph Stiglitz, the 2001 winner of the Nobel Prize in economics, ownership of property and other goods can have devastating effects on developing countries and especially the poor within those countries" (2002, p. ix).

So far, we have discussed the nature of class. Now, we turn our attention to language, class, and cultural identity.

LANGUAGE, CLASS, AND CULTURAL IDENTITY

In his work on discriminating attitudes toward speech, Cargile (2003) asks his readers to ponder the following scenario:

> Consider, for example, a New York business woman interviewing a West Virginia job candidate who answers questions with an Appalachian drawl. She may comprehend with little, if any difficulty what is being said; however, she may not feel completely at ease during the interaction or afterward if she decides the person's fate of employment. (p. 216)

Why? Because the New York business woman knows that language and accent are used as indicators of class and background, although such views might, in fact, be biased ways of viewing the other. This is what Ben Johnson had in mind in the seventeenth century when he said, "Language most shows a man. Speak, that I may see thee" (quoted in Fussel, 1983, p. 151). It must be borne in mind, however, that we are talking about perceptions that people have of the other that grow out of stereotypes and prejudices and *not* the quality of mind of a West Virginia speaker.

Interculturally, humans are constantly announcing who they are, and such announcements are intimately interwoven with notions of identity and belonging. One's social class influences whether one speaks an elaborated or a restricted linguistic code (Bernstein, 1971). Restricted codes have fewer ways to say things. These codes don't allow speakers to expand on (elaborate) what they mean. The elaborated code provides a wide range of different ways to say something. This code is used by a group when common perspectives are not shared. Thus, people have to explain a great deal of what they mean.

What is more significant in this section is that human beings use grammar, phonology (sound), and vocabulary as ways of directing attention to social background and other cultural factors that demonstrate their class. The words you choose, common expressions you use, as well as your accent are not necessarily accidental. Let us focus for a moment on one domain of experience: vocabulary. Fussell (1983) argues that because of middle-class U.S. Americans' need for "the illusion of power and success," members of the middle class tend to multiply syllables. For example, in the United States, the middle class typically say *cocktails, position, albeit, roadway*, and *purchase* rather than *drinks, job, although, road*, and *buy*, respectively (Fussell, p. 162). Middle-class people in North America are also inclined to "adopt advertisers' *wear* compounds," such as *footwear, nightwear* (or *sleepware*), *leisurewear, stormwear*, and *citywear*. Words, then, are useful reminders of the class to which one belongs. Once such linguistic markers are established as custom, they can draw very distinct boundaries between classes.

For example, upper-class U.S. Americans typically use the word *car* instead of *limousine*, which is used by middle-class people. Notice the power of two words to instantly indicate class! This means that in an ordinary conversation between a middle-class person and an upper-middle-class person that two words used differently can signal class straight away despite other seemingly equal symbols that might seem equal, such as, for example, clothes and jewelry.

Grammar and Class

Trudgill (1974) writes the following about grammar and class: "If you are an English-speaker you will be able to estimate the relative social status of the following speakers solely on the basis of the linguistic evidence given here: Speaker A: *I done it yesterday* and speaker B: *I did it yesterday*" (p. 34). Trudgill's example, which reveals that people would guess that speaker B was of higher social status than speaker A leads us to a second way that language solicits identification. Grammatical differences between speakers also give us clues about their social backgrounds. Different social groups use different grammatical forms. Scholars have found, for example, that African American Language (AAL), the speech of the Hip Hop Nation, "is embodied in the communicative practices of the larger Black speech community" (Smitherman, 1999, p. 271).

The previous example reveals the complexities of language and class as well as teaches the following valuable lesson: Even though aspects of language and class are separated for purposes of analysis, at a fundamental level, language and class are both integrative and additive. By *integrative and additive*, we mean that relationships of inclusion, exclusion, resistance, and conflict can and do inhabit our linguistic worlds and contribute to how we behave toward others.

We began the section on language and class with an example of Appalachian speech. We end this section with a discussion of the role of accent—that is, how people say words or phonetic and phonological features of language form bonds of identification and belonging. Of the many forms of social-class differentiation, none is perhaps more powerful than accent. The working-class accents of Birmingham and Liverpool in England versus the British Broadcasting Company (BBC) accent, African American Language versus European American Language, Serb versus Croat, all contain linguistic clues that may act as *defining* characteristics of class. In England, for example, working-class accents of Birmingham, Liverpool, and Norwich all have patterns of intonation that distinguish them from middle-class speakers in the same region. The extent to which working-class speakers in Norwich pronounce *n'* as opposed to *ing* in words such as *walking, running,* and so on, as opposed to their middle-class counterpart is revealing.

It is the case that these very distinctions based on how one says a word can have profound implications for how we view the "other." The language that others use and that is used to describe them can affect our perceptions of them. The concept that is used to describe such attitudes and behavior is linguistic prejudice (Spender, 1985; Hudson, 1980). Hudson (1980) defines *linguistic prejudice* as the "habit of using social signals as sources of information" (p. 195). As Figure 4.2 illustrates, linguistic prejudice derives from such stereotypes as accent, clothing, speech patterns, education, class, and occupation. Stereotypes are rigid preconceptions that are applied to all members of a group or to an individual over time, regardless of individual variations.

In terms of linguistic prejudice, people attach values to speech, resulting in a prototype (model) that works this way: A person who has "highly valued characteristics (class, education) will naturally be highly valued, and conversely for characteristics which are held in low esteem" (Hudson, 1980, p. 197). If, for example, Prince Harry of England has a highly valued accent (BBC), it is likely that he will be highly valued. Cockney speech of England is not as highly valued, however. A similar valence prevails for some African Americans who speak Black English or Ebonics.

It follows, therefore, that if people have prejudiced attitudes toward the accents of certain users, the users can be disadvantaged in terms of how they are seen, the language they use, and the extent to which they are taken seriously. Research reveals, for example, that on first hearing an instructor's accent, students will often "unknowingly" make judgments about the instructor's personality based solely on their own attitudes toward foreign-

▌ FIGURE 4.2 Linguistic Prototype

Highly valued characteristics (class, clothes, occupation, education, money)
= A highly valued accent (e.g., British, BBC, educated speech)
= Highly valued users of such speech (e.g., Prince Charles)

accented speakers (Cargile and Giles, 1998). The judgment, in turn, is often accompanied by such statements as "The person is not too friendly" or "The person is not too intelligent." Although it is sometimes difficult to rid oneself of traits that have been internalized over many years, Cargile (2003, pp. 220–221) suggests the following things that people can do to rid themselves of discriminating attitudes toward speech. First, we can manage our attitudes toward the users of speech by asking the following question: "Am I thinking this about the person only because of the way that he or she speaks?" If you answer no to this question, Cargile argues that the role that attitudes are playing is minimal. If you answer yes to the question, it may mean that your attitudes are playing a major role.

Second, once you are mindful of the role that attitudes play in your responses to speech, it is possible to move to the next level of the evaluation process. This level involves seeking out integrating additional information into the evaluation process. For example, if you are a student enrolled in a mathematics class at Pine Lilly University taught by a non-native English speaker, you may wish to secure as much information as possible about the instructor's educational background and prior teaching experience. You may also listen to the instructor as attentively as possible before concluding that the person is unintelligent and lacks an ability to be a successful teacher. Our point is that "fact finding" is one central way of correcting assumptions about attitudes toward speech.

CULTURAL IDENTITY AND NONVERBAL MARKERS

Stories tell us who we are, how we should dress, what household furnishings, jewelry, and cars to buy—all are powerful ways of revealing class differences. Such external characteristics are referred to as *markers* because they serve as visible indicators of who and what we are. In other words, social-class characteristics generally "mark" who we are. Of course nonverbal markers can be incorrectly perceived by others. Fussell (1983) argues that although we may not know what really goes on inside people's heads, we can infer "from their looks, figures, clothing, speech, and gestures . . . what's happening on their outsides." Bourdieu (1984) maintains that aesthetics about what we wear and the food we eat can be classified in terms of distinctions that people make between the visible and the invisible or the inside versus the outside. He notes further that such distinctions can be divided into form and appearance, as evident by the working class who make "a realistic . . . or functionalist use of clothing" (p. 200). Because members of the working class are keen to the functionalist aspects of clothing, they tend to prefer substance over form and thus seek "value for money." Middle classes are just the opposite, in Bourdieu's view. They place undue emphasis on external appearances, in terms of both clothing and cosmetics.

In his study, for example, Bourdieu (1984) found that men's clothing is more socially distinctive or marked than women's clothing. This can be seen keenly in the stories that uniforms tell about manual workers who wear blue dungarees or boiler-suits and relaxed moccasins. In terms of gender, women's stories are equally compelling. According to Bourdieu's study, clothing purchases by French women increase as they move up the social hierarchy, with a marked preference for suits and costumes (i.e., expensive garments). Working-class women show a preference for the smock and the apron; Bourdieu refers to this as "virtually the housewife's uniform" (p. 201).

Although indicators of class are changing, Bourdieu's (1984) study reveals an important point that we must bear in mind as we discuss class and that is that self-presentation is a crucial indicator of identity and belonging. Recall our previous statement in the opening section of this chapter about the role that identity plays in interpreting who we are and what stories we prefer. Clothing and food also help individuals understand who belongs to a particular group and who does not, and uniforms can in some instances even promote confidence. General George S. Patton, a decorated general of World War II, confided in his diary that "a little fancy dress" elevates the morale of those who witness it. At the height of his battle campaign in North Africa in 1943, General Patton said that his courage was not always as high as it seemed and that he relied on his dress—his military uniform—to give him courage (quoted in Fussell, 1983, p. 38).

On the face of it, this might seem like an audacious statement; however, upon closer reflection, it is probably the case that at some time in our lives, we all have relied on dress to get us through the day—to note our identity. Today, for example, young women wear pajama bottoms in public, the workplace has embraced khakis, and casual clothes such as sweats, sneakers, and T-shirts; jeans are basically the norm in the United States. These forms of dress point toward a more casual approach to social class in North America, according to business columnist and novelist Daniel Akst. Hip-hop culture is also gaining popularity nationwide through the distribution of the Phat Fashions clothing company, which is owned by hip-hop impresario Russell Simmons. According to Tracie Rozhon (2003), Simmons markets clothing from baggy jeans to "nylon basketball shirts to zebra-printed bustiers to baby clothing." Nylon basketball shirts, for example, help to identify class. As Rozhon notes, "What Mr. Simmons strives for . . . is what those in hip-hop culture strive for: Class."

PERSONAL IDENTITY

Cultural identities are also anchored in the individual. Alba (1990) uses the term "privatization of ethnic identity" to signify a "reduction of its expression to largely personal and family terms" (p. 300). This means that we have identity zones that are clearly reserved for the group and family and some zones that are clearly reserved for the individual. This means further that a type of "privatization" occurs when the individual establishes what belongs to his or her ethnic group and what identity behaviors are the province of the personal (Gans, 1988; Alba, 1990). Personal identity consists of several aspects, including such factors as what makes one unique as an individual, the way a person sees himself or herself, and the way a person defines himself or herself. Fisher says that "every person has life experiences that become his/her story" (quoted in Tanno, 2000, p. 25).

In practical terms, self-identity is the answer that one gives to the question, Who am I? English philosopher John Locke says that one special property of personal identity is "self-consciousness"—that is, the ability to conceive of yourself as a self (in other words, as an abstract entity called "I"). Once a person views herself or himself in this manner, he or she can then think about the image that he or she has created. The crucial point is that the individual then responds to the image he or she has constructed. Personal identity is not created in a vacuum, however. Rather, it grows out of the ethnic and familiar communities that make up the person's culture or worldview. For this reason, a person can define herself in multiple ways, such as female, Malay, mother, and doctor, all intertwined in one body!

We must remember, however, that although the individual may constitute all these factors, they are usually *not* expressed simultaneously in one setting. Knowing this, it is possible for an individual to identify himself as a father in one setting and a college president in another. Our point is that people's complex social lives and context order the part of self that finds expression in any given setting. For example, in a setting of Irish Americans at a St. Patrick's Day parade in downtown Chicago, it is likely that some individuals will see themselves as Irish American. In a word, there are ethnic models of self that may well lie below the surface (Alba, 1990, p. 23). Tanno (2000, p. 26), in telling of her encounters with individuals who consistently ask, *"What are you?"* reveals the complexities of cultural identity as well as the intricate relationship between personal identity and ethnic identity. According to Tanno, when she was first asked, "What are you?" she at first replied, "I am human." However, upon reflection, she realized that the response hurt others. Now, she answers, "I am Spanish," but she has gone in many directions in terms of her personal identity, from "I am Mexican American," to "I am Latina," to "I am Chicana" (p. 26). In some sense, when one uses the perilous pronoun *I,* there is also the likelihood that the equally perilous pronoun *we* is attached in some way.

CONCLUSION

This chapter considered several important characteristics of cultural identity that play a major role in human interaction and have played a major role in the history of humankind: gender, race, ethnicity, regional factors, religion, and class. Because groups interact on the basis of cultural categories—through judgment-making behavior—we tend to be greatly influenced by such categories. These cultural emphases often become enormously important, sometimes disturbing normal communication with others. In the twenty-first century, we must search for a way out of the limiting and confining aspects of cultural identity.

In Calloway-Thomas and Thomas's reading on identity and belonging in South Africa and Chesebro's reading on gender, masculinities, and identities, you should learn a great deal about the tension that exists between traditional and new values. You should also take note of what happens when individuals long accustomed to one way of acting are suddenly forced to confront a different reality.

FOR DISCUSSION

1. In what sense can one say that humans live in different worlds?
2. What does the following statement by Huntington (1996, p. 21) reveal about the nature of identity and belonging: "We know who we are only when we know who we are not and often only when we know whom we are against." What evidence can you cite to support the statement?
3. How do perceptions of religion, class, and ethnicity hinder effective intercultural communication?

REFERENCES

Akst, D. (2003, September 19). Casualties. *The Wall Street Journal,* p. W21.

Alba, R. (1990). *Ethnic identity: The transformation of white America.* New Haven, CT: Yale University Press.

Ali, M. (2003). *Brick lane: A novel.* New York: Scribner.

Asante, M. (1987). *The Afrocentric idea.* Philadelphia: Temple University Press.

Bernstein, B. (1971). *Class, codes and control: Theoretical studies toward a sociology of language.* London: Routledge & Keegan Paul.

Bethell, T. (1998). *The noblest triumph: Property and prosperity through the ages.* New York: St. Martin's Griffin.

Bin Ladin. C. (2004). *Inside the Kingdom: My life in Saudi Arabia.* New York: Warner Brothers.

Bourdieu, P. (1984). *Distinction: A social critique of the judgment of taste.* Cambridge, MA: Harvard University Press.

Broome, B. (1997). Pavelone: Foundations of struggle and conflict in Greek interpersonal communication. In L. Samavor and R. Porter (Eds.), *Intercultural communication: A reader* (pp. 116–124). Belmont, CA: Wadsworth.

Brown, P. (2003, June 9). At Muslim prom, it's a girls-only night out. *The New York Times,* p. 3.

Cargile, A. (2003). Discriminating attitudes toward speech. In L. Samovar and R. Porter (Eds.), *Intercultural communication: A reader* (pp. 216–223). Belmont, CA: Wadsworth.

Cargile, A. C., and Giles, H. (1998). Language attitudes toward varieties of English: An American-Japanese context. *Journal of Applied Communication Research, 26,* 338–356.

Chi, L. (1967). *Book of rites: An encyclopedia of ancient ceremonial usages, religious creeds, and social institutions.* (J. Legge, Trans.). New Hyde Park, NY: University Books.

Chua, A. (2003). *World on fire: How exploring free market democracy breeds ethnic hatred and global instability.* New York: Doubleday.

Crossen, C. (2000). *The rich and how they got that way.* New York: Crown Business.

Dates, J., and Barlow, W. (Eds.). (1990). *Split image: African Americans in the mass media.* Washington, DC: Howard University Press.

Erickson, E. (1980). *Identity and the life cycle.* New York: W. W. Norton.

"Ethnic cleansing," Europe's old horror, with new victims. (1992, August 2). *The New York Times,* p. 4E.

Fassihi, F. (2003, July 28). In Tehran, boutiques stock hot outerwear under the counter. *The Wall Street Journal,* p. 1.

French, H. (2003, July 25). Japan's neglected resource: Female workers. *The New York Times,* p. 3.

Fussell, P. (1983). *Class: A guide through the American status system.* New York: Simon and Schuster.

Gannon, M. (2003). India: The dance of shiva. In L. Samavor and R. Porter (Eds.), *Intercultural communication: A reader* (pp. 65–77). Belmont, CA: Wadsworth.

Gans, H. (1988). *Middle American individualism: The future of liberal democracy.* New York: Free Press.

Gilroy, P. (2000). *Against race: Imagining political culture beyond the color line.* Cambridge, MA: The Belknap Press of Harvard University Press.

Hannerz, U. (1992). *Cultural complexity: Studies in the social organization of meaning.* New York: Columbia University Press.

Hofstede, G. (2001). *Culture's consequences: Comparing values, behaviors, institutions, and organization across nations,* 2nd ed. Thousand Oaks, CA: Sage.

Hudson, R. A. (1980). *Sociolinguistics.* New York: Cambridge University Press.

Huntington, S. P. (1996). *The clash of civilizations and the remaking of world order.* New York: Simon and Schuster.

Ishii, S., Cooke, D., and Klopf, D. (2003). Our locus in the universe: Worldview and intercultural communication. In L. Samavor and R. Porter (eds.), *Intercultural communication: A reader* (pp. 28–35). Belmont, CA: Wadsworth.

Italians contemplate beauty in a Caribbean brow. (1996, September 10). *The New York Times,* p. A3.

Karmi, G. (2002). *In search of Fatima: A Palestinian story.* London: Verso.

Kerbo, H. R. (1996). *Social stratification and inequality: Class conflict in historical and comparative perspective.* New York: McGraw-Hill.

Kimball, R. (1990). *Tenured radicals: How politics has corrupted our higher education.* New York: Harper and Row.

Lerner, G. (1986). *The creation of patriarchy.* New York: Oxford University Press.

Lewis, B. (2002). *What went wrong? Western impact and Middle Eastern response.* New York: Oxford University Press.

Lustig, M., and Koester, J. (1999). *Intercultural competence: Interpersonal communication across cultures.* New York: Longman.

Lyall, S. (2002, July 23). Lost in Sweden: A Kurdish daughter is sacrificed. *The New York Times.*

Phinney, J. (1993). A three stage model of ethnic identity development in adolescence. In M. Bernal and G. Knight (Eds.), *Ethnic identity formation and transformation among Hispanics and other minorities.* Albany, New York: State University of New York Press.

Rozhon, T. (2003, August 24). Can urban fashion be def in Des Moines? *The New York Times,* section 3, p. 1.

Smith, J. S. (Ed.). (1995). *The HarperCollins Dictionary of Religion.* San Francisco: Harper San Francisco.

Smith, H. (1991). *The world's religions.* San Franciso: Harper San Francisco.

Smitherman, G. (1999). *Talkin that talk: Language, culture, and education in African America.* London: Routledge.

Spender, D. (1985). *Man made language,* 2nd ed. London: Routledge and Kean Paul.

Stiglitz, J. E. (2002). *Globalization and its discontents.* New York: Norton.

Tanno, D. V. (2000). Names, narratives, and the evolution of ethnic identity. In A. Gonzalez, M. Houston, and V. Chen (Eds.), *Our voices.* Los Angeles: Roxbury.

Taylor, C. (1992). *Multiculturalism and "the politics of recognition."* Princeton, NJ: Princeton University Press.

Trudgill, P. (1974). *Sociolinguistics: An introduction.* New York: Penguin Books.

Tuan, Y-F. (1977). *Space and place: The perspectives of experience.* Minneapolis: University of Minnesota.

Van Der Veur, S. (2003). Africa: Communication and cultural patterns. In L. Samavor and R. Porter (Eds.), *Intercultural communication: A reader* (pp. 78–86). Belmont, CA: Wadsworth.

Van Doren, C. (1991). *A history of knowledge past, present, and future.* New York: Ballantine Books.

Verhovek, S. H. (1997, September 30). Clash of culture tears Texas city. *The New York Times,* p. A10.

Wilson, J. (1987). *The truly disadvantaged: The inner city, the underclass, and public policy.* Chicago: University of Chicago Press.

Wood, J. T. (2000). *Communication in our lives.* Australia: Wadsworth.

Yinger, M. (1981). Towards a theory of assimilation and dissimilation. *Ethnic and Racial Studies, 4* (July), 249–264.

Disgrace, Culture, and Identity Construction in South Africa

Carolyn Calloway-Thomas and Jack E. Thomas

If he wants me to be known as his third wife, so be it. As his concubine, ditto. But then the child becomes his too. The child becomes part of his family. As for the land, say I will sign the land over to him as long as the house remains mine. I will become a tenant on his land. (Coetzee, 1999)

In J. M. Coetzee's (1999) eighth novel, *Disgrace,* winner of the 1999 prestigious literary Booker Prize in Britain, Lucy Lurie, a white South African woman, and one of the main characters in the novel, utters the above sociologically bizarre words. The unlikely situation that Coetzee describes is hauntingly strange and shocking for what it reveals about the cultural, personal, and political aspects of the new, post-apartheid South Africa. In the chapter in which the scenario occurs, Lucy has been gang raped by three black men (actually one boy and two men), and considers giving birth to the ill-conceived child and marrying the very man who is allegedly behind the rape.

Why would a white South African novelist at the beginning of the twenty-first century create such an unlikely scenario? Is he predicting the doom of the new South Africa? Detailing the degradation of the white race? Painting a horrifying picture of the inevitable demise of South African civilization? Insulting black South Africans? What? What is his rhetorical mission?

The questions that we pose, although fascinating, are difficult to answer fully and without some intellectual hesitation because of the spare and multifaceted way that Coetzee manipulates language, characters, and identity, which we will detail later. Throughout this highly rated novel, Coetzee, the first author in the 32-year history of the Booker Prize to win twice, weaves several themes in one slim book, which consists of 220 pages. Some of the themes advanced in the novel include the following: (1) an allegory about racial identity, (2) the dichotomies both in personal relations and the uncertainties of cultural change, (3) fear and loathing, (4) an apocalyptic vision of post-apartheid South Africa, (5) political correctness, and (6) gender relations. Although all of these topics are meaningful, and in some way shed light on the question of racial adjustment and identity in South Africa, in this article, we are especially interested in the persuasive techniques

that Coetzee employs in promoting white identities in post-apartheid South Africa through the symbolic vehicle of rape and its aftermath.

Understanding Coetzee's narrative should tell us a great deal about how culture and memory intersect with identity in forging the dynamics on which intercultural interactions can be based. Moreover, Coetzee's story reveals much about the nature of issues and conflicts that must be worked through when cultures are in transition. In this instance, the cultural change occurred in South Africa. But does Coetzee's tale contain within it seeds for understanding how other cultures respond when their accustomed ways of thinking, acting and being are challenged, and in some instances, even uprooted?

Our fundamental argument is that Coetzee offers an apocalyptic vision of the new South Africa as he and other whites try to find their place and space in the world of black majority rule. By apocalyptic, we mean a revelation or prophecy about the way things will be culturally, socially, politically, and otherwise. Coetzee, we argue, uses the metaphorical device of black on white rape as an apocalyptic instrument for problematizing the cultural and social mechanics of belonging and racial solidarity in South Africa. Through the enthymeme, Coetzee pits white identity against the warring domains of black male perversion. Exactly what an enthymeme is has been a subject of much discussion by philosophers and rhetorical scholars. Aristotle, who coined the term, defined an enthymeme as "the substance of rhetorical persuasion" (Aristotle, p. 26). Enthymemes rely for their effect on logical reasoning in the form of "a rhetorical syllogism" (Aristotle, p. 26). One of the most common examples of a syllogism is the following construction: All men are mortal (major premise), Socrates is a man (minor premise). Therefore, Socrates is mortal (conclusion). Within this example, three crucial terms (men, mortal, and Socrates) are related to one another such that listeners or readers can draw a conclusion about Socrates.

For our purposes, it is important to note that the reader helps to construct the rhetorical syllogisms in *Disgrace* by supplying some part of Coetzee's powerfully appealing argument. We claim, therefore, that

Coetzee strategically encourages, indeed, programs his readers to participate in the construction of his argument, because he intuits that they can provide materials of proof as readily as he can. We do not mean to suggest that Coetzee and his target audience explicitly recount each step of a formal syllogism. Rather, we mean that by linguistically goading his readers to participate in the construction of enthymemes, Coetzee taps into beliefs and values already held by white South Africans. Coetzee's employment of enthymemes works well precisely because of the way he reorients his readers toward the concept of white identity.

The article is divided into four overlapping sections. The first part provides some definitions of identity, which frame the argument. The second part deals with a brief description of the novel, which organizes the argument of the book as a whole. It contains several dimensions of Coetzee's overall treatment of the several themes that we outlined earlier. In part three attention turns toward the cultural and identity aspects of Lucy's rape. It tries to explain that even though Coetzee's ultimate motive for writing *Disgrace* is fraught with moral and cultural complexities, that the rape scene does indeed convey an apocalyptic vision of the new South Africa. Part four offers a summary and conclusions.

A GLANCE AT IDENTITY

In his recent book, *Against Race: Imagining Political Culture Beyond the Color Line,* Paul Gilroy (2000) writes "We have seen that the uncertain and divided world we inhabit has made racial identity matter in novel and powerful ways" (p. 97). Indeed, the word, "identity" does matter in many different ways, including cultural, social, political, and personal (Turkle, 1995; Connolly, 1991). Gilroy adds a cautionary note about the term, indicating that we

> should not take the concept of identity and its multiple associations with "race" and raciology for granted. The term identity has recently acquired great resonance both inside and outside the academic world. It offers far more than an obvious, common-sense way of talking about individuality, community, and solidarity and has provided means to understand the interplay between subjective experiences of the world and the cultural and historical settings in which those fragile, meaningful subjectivities are formed. (pp. 97–98)

Other scholars have also tried to make sense of the multiple meanings of the term identity. Richard Alba (1990), for example, argues that ethnic identity is "a person's subjective orientation toward his or her ethnic

origins" (p. 25), while Charles Taylor views it (1992) as "something like a person's understanding of who they are, of their fundamental defining characteristics as a human being" (p. 25). Fused with identity, according to Taylor, is recognition (or its absence), which is partly shaped by identity. Ronald Jackson (1999, p. 8) argues that "identity is that which confers a sense of self or personhood. It also refers to self-definition." Jackson claims further that "there is a direct relationship between identity and one's ability to define self" (p. 8).

Thus, however one defines identity, it appears to have the following characteristics: (1) it is a complex term, (2) it is related to a number of "urgent theoretical and political issues, not least belonging, ethnicity, and nationality" (Gilroy, 2000, p. 98), (3) it is usually bounded and particular, (4) it delineates separateness and subsidiary points in our social world, and (5) it employs a specific language to demarcate self, belonging, ethnicity, nationality, solidarity, and other characteristics. Rather than detailing the piles of facts and information about this nettlesome term, its causes and consequences, we will emphasize the techniques that Coetzee employs in his novel to reframe white South African identity.

DISGRACE: A SHORT DESCRIPTION

Disgrace is about fifty-two-year-old David Lurie who teaches communications at Cape Technical University, formerly Cape Town University. David is disdainful of the name change of the university, which symbolically suggests the pitiful state of affairs in South Africa. At Cape Technical University, both the classics and modern language departments have been eliminated as a result of what David Lurie calls "rationalization." Lurie's dismissive and disdainful attitude toward the discipline of communication is evident in the term that he uses to describe it; communication is inherently "preposterous." "Because he has no respect for the material he teaches, he makes no impression on his students" (Coetzee, 1999, p. 4). "He continues to teach because it provides him with a livelihood; also because it teaches him humility, brings it home to him who he is in the world" (Coetzee, p. 5). Consequently, very early in the novel, the reader has some inkling of David Lurie's existential anguish and his search for identity.

Soon after we meet David Lurie we know that he is having a relationship with a prostitute, Soraya, which sours when he discovers that she is not only married, but also has two children. Sometime later David has an unsanctioned physical relationship with one of his students, Melanie Issacs, which ultimately leads to his dismissal from Cape Technical University. He is reported by her to the vice rector and dismissed because he refuses to apologize for his behavior.

This is his first "disgrace," which leads to a type of exile at his daughter's place in the country in the Eastern Cape, on a smallholding. His daughter, Lucy, is an ex-hippie lesbian, "in flowered dress, bare feet and all, in a house full of the smell of baking, no longer a child playing at farming but a solid countrywoman, a *boevrou"* (Coetzee, 1999, p. 60).

Lucy (her lesbian mate, Helen, having returned to Johannesburg) spends her time caring for dogs, raising flowers, and selling local produce at the farmers' market. Lucy's tranquil agrarian lifestyle stands in contradistinction to David's appetite for sensual pleasure. David busies himself by helping out at a local dog pound where slowly he recovers some of his sensibilities.

The Rape

It is significant that Coetzee introduces rape into a remote country place, which functions not only as an agrarian symbol, but also as a political struggle for land, which is a linchpin of tensions in South Africa (Thompson, 1995). It is significant as well that at the very moment that David Lurie is in a rehabilitative mode, adjusting to his reduced circumstances, an event of even greater proportion occurs, the rape! To understand the nuances of the rape scene and its apocalyptic sense of identity gone haywire, we should note that Lucy has a former assistant, a black man by the name of Petrus, who is in post-apartheid South Africa, her co-proprietor. It should not go unnoticed that Coetzee chooses a diseased-ridden name for Petrus and the men who attack Lucy.

Lucy's first moment of disgrace and David's second or third, begins on page 88, in chapter 11, in an idyllic and serene setting. "It is WEDNESDAY. He [David] gets up early, but Lucy is up before him. He finds her watching the wild geese on the dam," the very dam that separates Lucy's property from Petrus, her co-proprietor. "'Aren't they lovely,' she says. 'They come back every year. The same three. I feel so lucky to be visited. To be the one chosen.'" (Coetzee, p. 88). The phrase, "To be the one chosen" is powerful in its twin apocalyptic meaning, and for its later joining of the beautiful and the wretched. David and Lucy carry on a decent conversation about scandal-mongering, "the dogs, the gardening, the astrology books, the asexual clothes: in each, he [David] recognizes a statement of independence, considered, purposeful" (Coetzee, p. 89).

Lucy and David's chit chat is interrupted when they see "three men coming toward them on the path,

or two men and a boy. They are walking fast, with countrymen's long strides. The dog at Lucy's side slows down, bristles. 'Should we be nervous?' he murmurs. 'I don't know,' she murmurs as she shortens the Dobermans' leashes. The men are upon them. A nod, a greeting, and they have passed" (Coetzee, 1999, p. 91). We have cited some paragraphs to illustrate the spatial precursor to the rape scene, and to underline as well the spareness of Lucy's and David's utterances because these factors have a central bearing on the political language of identity that Coetzee creates.

LANGUAGE, CULTURE, AND IDENTITY

In one compact interrogative, "Should we be nervous?" Coetzee summons to the foreground the cultural and ethnic identities of black vs. white South Africans and the tension that that summoning signifies. It is important to note, for example, that there is no specific, defining reference to ethnicity in the interrogative, "Should we be nervous?" and yet the reader knows straight away to whom the reference refers. Coetzee achieves much of his linguistic bridge work through enthymemes which rely on implicit arguments where the audience must provide one of the premises. Employing the interrogative, Coetzee never, at the outset, articulates his major premise. However, the idea that he is referring to black South Africans only makes sense if the reader provides the information. One of the reasons that it is a powerful interrogative is because the missing premise is so clearly understood to the reader. Aristotle called the rhetorical technique of the enthymeme the "most effective of all forms of persuasion" (Aristotle, p. 26).

We also find in the "interrogative scene" a parallel with racial profiling in the United States where African-American men are 75 times more likely to be stopped by the police while driving than white American men (*The New Republic,* 2000). Coetzee's question, "Should we be nervous?" is the type of interrogative that some North Americans act on when they encounter black men in department stores and on elevators. Since Coetzee received his Ph.D. at University of Texas at Austin, and has lectured at Harvard, University of California, Berkeley, and other universities in North America, he had to be mindful of the inherent power of his interrogative, "Should we be nervous?" and especially in the context in which the novel is set. For Coetzee, the interrogative is not only a linguistic foreshadowing of things to come, but also a question that engenders discomfort after many years of white South African rule where few whites would bother to utter such a question. The situation simply did not demand it, because blacks clearly knew their place in pre-apartheid South Africa.

To continue with the foreshadowing scene, by the time that Lucy and her father reach the "plantation boundary," and "turn back," "the strangers are out of sight." Coetzee's invocation of silence and calm with its guerilla-like simplicity, is emblematic of the way that his meager words create modes of identification and their absence. By the time the rape occurs it seems outside of sequential causality and part of a larger scheme of forging cultural and ancestral identification. "As they near the house they hear the caged dogs in an uproar. Lucy quickens her pace. The three are there waiting for them. The two men stand at a remove while the boy, beside the cages, hisses at the dogs and makes sudden, threatening gestures. The dogs, in a rage, bark and snap" (Coetzee, 1999, p. 92).

The initial movement closer to the rape is notable for its animality and quasi-violent actions: hissing and quickness frame the rape and provide a guide to its meaning. The killing of the dogs, which occurs later, pits a brutal act of violence against two helpless white South Africans, a man and a woman, a father and daughter. " 'Petrus!' calls Lucy. But there is no sign of Petrus. 'Get away from the dogs!' she shouts. *Hamba!'* (Coetzee, 1999, p. 92). As Lucy moves closer to the dogs they calm down and she "releases the two Dobermans into it," which leads her father to think, "A brave gesture . . . but is it wise?" (Coetzee, p. 92).

Next, Coetzee details the processes involved in the bestial deed. Up to this point, there merely has been a foreshadowing to the real, specific event. To gain access to the house, the two men and a boy pretend that they want to use the telephone, in response to Lucy's sensible and rational question, "What do you want?" The men inform her that there has been an "accident," meaning that one of the rapists' sisters "is having a baby." Not quite buying this, Lucy reasons that if the men are from Erasmuskraal, a heavily forested area, that there was no telephone there "inside the forestry concession," because it is a hamlet with no electricity, no telephone. The story makes sense (Coetzee, 1999, pp. 92–93).

Once the first man is inside the house, the second man "pushes pass him [David] and enters the house too" (Coetzee, 1999, p. 93). "Something is wrong, he knows at once. 'Lucy, come out here!'" David shouts; however, all is silent. Here again, is where Coetzee's use of the enthymeme and projection come to the fore. Hence the emphasis on silence. Hence the ability of the reader to fill in the empty spaces with a series of questions, such as: What is going on? Where is Lucy? What is happening to her? This is an enterprising technique,

and Coetzee's methods of identification are especially significant because he begins the rape sequence by seeming to turn over the scene to the reader. Coetzee then shifts to the boy who "turns and sprints, heading for the front door. He lets go the bulldog's leash. 'Get him,' he [David] shouts," and "the dog trots heavily after the boy" (Coetzee, p. 93).

By this time the boy has picked up a stick and is using it to keep the dog at bay. Realizing more intensely now Lucy's apparent plight, David abandons the dog and the boy and "rushes back to the kitchen door" (where he finds the "bottom leaf is not bolted, gives a few heavy kicks and it swings open). On all fours he creeps into the kitchen" (Coetzee, 1999, p. 93). It is noteworthy, we think, that the attackers have reduced David to a dog-like posture as he attempts to find out what is happening to his daughter, Lucy. Before David can process his state of semi-consciousness "a blow catches him on the crown of his head," and he has time to think, " 'If I am still conscious then I am all right,' before his limbs turn to water and he crumples" (Coetzee, p. 93).

The intruders struck a severe blow, taking David's consciousness from him, giving the appearance, at least symbolically so, of white men's inability to protect their daughters and wives in the new South Africa. And is it just possible that an equally important feature of this part of the rape scene is not so much in David's "crumpling," lying prostrate, being dragged across the kitchen floor and blacking out, per se, but in the fact that by means of these physical bodily processes of inaction on David's part Coetzee provides a "mode of identification," a world view for white South Africans who are fearful of their role in the new order of things. Are these compelling glimpses of menacing things to come in the future?

In the rape scene, we see in Coetzee's novel a compelling tension between what was (a serene white South Africa) that he and whites controlled and the brutality of the new South Africa, which is, nominally at least, controlled by blacks. Moreover, the complexities of race, sex, culture, identity and nationality all are embodied in the activity of rape. The absence of concreteness in the rape scene "matters in novel and powerful ways."

Leonard Thompson (1999), a foremost authority on South Africa, reports, for example, that "murders, rapes, assaults, and violent robberies have reportedly risen dramatically" in South Africa, and that "surveys reveal that more than half the population feels unsafe, and 83 percent believe that the government has little or no control over crime" (p. 87). Given these dreadful statistics, it is perhaps unsurprising that in *Disgrace*

Coetzee works to produce the idea that the tranquil life of white South Africans is being hijacked because of the dynamics of black on white rape, despite the fact that in South Africa many black women are also raped. Our purpose here, of course, is to *unpack* how words work in Coetzee's novel rather than to offer a confrontation with the harsh realities of crime in South Africa.

Finally, to return to the rape, David comes to, hears footsteps along the passage, and sees the opening of the door to the toilet, where he has been exiled physically and metaphorically. At this moment, David is able to witness some behavioral actions of the attackers that tell us much about how Coetzee works his story of identification, albeit using frugal and less intense language. David observes, for example, "the boy in the flowered shirt, eating from a tub of ice cream" (Coetzee, 1999, p. 96). Coetzee's description of the boy "eating from a tub of ice cream" is a succinct sentence, and yet it pushes the outer limits of the grotesque and the cruel.

What could be more senseless, vulgar, and cold-hearted than a black boy eating ice cream (stolen ice cream!) while a white South African woman is being violated by two black men! Here, we see the distinguishing quality of Coetzee's method as an instrument of persuasion, in all of its linguistic spareness. Noteworthy also is the fact that Coetzee refrains from superfluous affect; the passage is void of linguistic, raw intensity. Although Coetzee presents the sentence in a matter of fact manner, the associations between traditional virtues of good living and disturbance of such virtues are constructed in the reader's mind. This is a superb enthymematic technique that undoubtedly created loathing in the minds of white South Africans. At least, that is the potential effect of such linguistic constructions.

Momentarily, David thinks that he and Lucy are "being let off lightly"; he was wrong! Had Alan Paton's words in *Cry the Beloved Country* (1948) about white South Africans occupied David's brain: "I have one great fear in my heart, that one day when they [whites] turn to loving they will find we [blacks] are turned to hating." In any case, the men torch David's body, his "hair crackles as it catches alight," he "tries to stand up and is forced down again," he "hangs his head over the toilet bowl," splashes "water over his face, dousing his head. There is a nasty smell of singed hair" (Coetzee, 1999, p. 96). When the men are finished with David, he presents a pitiful picture: "His eyes are stinging, one eyelid is already closing. He runs a hand over his head and his fingertips come away black with soot. Save for a patch over one ear, he seems to have no

hair; his whole scalp is tender. Everything is tender, everything is burned. Burned, burnt."

This fiery image is one terrifically effective weapon in a period where the tire burnings of black South Africans still are vivid in the public's mind. Coetzee repeats the word "burned" three times, and the terms are important to persuasion and identity making, because they offer the raw materials to help white South Africans understand the relations between brutal acts and the coming apocalyptic storm of discontent. Later, in revisiting the scene Lucy also will observe that the animalistic nature of the men who raped her was such that they spurred each other on, "together," "like dogs in a pack." (Coetzee, 1999, p. 159).

To continue with our description of the rape scene, when David finally reaches Lucy, she is so embarrassed, humiliated, and devastated that she turns her back on him, while dressed in her house coat, in bare feet, and wet. When they survey the house, they find that their clothing, "his jacket, his good shoes, and that is only the beginning of it," are gone! And six dogs have been murdered. When David finally has a chance to view himself in the mirror, he sees "brown ash, all that is left of his hair, coats his scalp and forehead. Underneath it the scalp is an angry pink." For Coetzee, the rape scene only makes sense if it is examined in the light of the word, "angry," because he is able to identify with white South Africans. This is perhaps what he believes many are feeling at this time. In this way, Coetzee fuses thought and action, relying very heavily upon a few well-chosen specifics to separate the behavior of blacks from the behavior of whites. If words work in the novel the way they are supposed to, then symbolically, the rape is serving as a mode of building and maintaining solidarity for white South Africans.

As mentioned earlier, according to Aristotle, arguments can be made using the technique of enthymeme or example. An enthymeme is a syllogism in which one of the premises is left out. In order to make sense of the argument, the reader or the listener must supply the missing premise.

Coetzee relies on this technique because he is able to highlight the misdeeds of black South Africans. It is telling that Coetzee pulls from his identity pouch a series of phrases that clearly must be evocative for white South Africans. A few temporally specific and concrete sentences that pertain to the rape scene include the following: "It happens every day, every hour, every minute. . . . A risk to own anything: a car, a pair of shoes, a packet of cigarettes. Not enough to go around, not enough cars, shoes, cigarettes. Too many people, too few things. What there is must go into circulation, so that everyone can have a chance to be happy for a day. . . . No human evil, just a vast circulatory system, to whose workings pity and terror are irrelevant" (Coetzee, 1999, p. 98). Although Coetzee uses the economics of the marketplace, one can see in the previous quotation a commentary on black theft and the structure of the minds of black South Africans.

In David's comments, one notices identity markers that locate deeper conflicts between black and white South Africans and civilization. Coetzee's ideological diagnosis sets up or perhaps confirms the even more widespread belief that the lives and livelihood of white South Africans are in jeopardy. The distinctive political language of identity with its reliance on the enthymeme, suggests how the barbaric act of rape and thievery can be transformed into more active styles of solidarity among white South Africans. In this way, Coetzee's language functions as space and place metaphors for where the boundaries around white South Africans should be constituted. Limits are drawn and they are, to borrow Gilroy's words, "bounded and particular" (Gilroy, 2000, p. 98; Yi-Fu, 1977).

Gilroy, quoting Rousseau, notes how Moses created a "unifying common identity" among the Children of Israel. Rousseau claims that "to prevent his people from melting away among foreign peoples, he [Moses] gave them customs and usages incompatible with those of other nations; he over-burdened them with peculiar rites and ceremonies; he inconvenienced them in a thousand ways in order to keep them constantly on the alert and to make them forever strangers among other men" (quoted in Gilroy, 2000, p. 100). There is a parallel between Rousseau's conclusions about the Children of Israel and Coetzee's conclusions about the white Children of South Africa. In the passages cited above, for example, one sees that Coetzee is also implicitly outlining the boundaries that ought to obtain between white and black South Africans.

Coetzee (1999) knows that work must be done to summon the feelings of white South Africans and to make them conscious of their identity in a land of black majority rule. Coetzee does not stop with the aforementioned words, however. Rather, he taps deeper and deeper into the soul of white South Africans by reminding them of the links between their political, cultural and social identity. For example, the rape, "the events of yesterday . . . shocked him [David] to the depths." Existentially, "for the first time he has a taste of what it will be like to be an old man, tired to the bone, without hopes, without desires, indifferent to the future" in "an after-effect of the invasion," a "massacre."

The words are sharp, dramatic and full of misery. And they signify a striking contrast between what David used to be and what he has become.

SAMENESS AND DIFFERENCE

Coetzee clearly draws a distinction between sameness and difference, between moral and political consequences. Is Coetzee being prophetic here? Will the new South Africa function as a series of shocks and aftershocks which David calls "an invasion?" Notice, as well, that the term "invasion" suggests forced conflict and bitterness, and it is directional. Prophetically, the invasion reveals to white South Africans where their future identity and place likely will be. Will white South Africans emerge impotent as a result of tools of violence such as rape? Implicitly, Coetzee plants the seed bed for the germination of such ideas. Hannah Arendt (1970) maintains that violence "is distinguished by its instrumental character. Phenomenologically, it is close to strength, since the implements of violence, like all other tools, are designed and used for the purpose of multiplying natural strength until, in the last stage of their development, they can substitute for it" (p. 46).

The use of additional symbols to create a sameness of identity among white South Africans is seen in other utterances as well. "Like a leaf on a stream, like a puffball on a breeze," David "has begun to float toward his end." Although Lucy is more sanguine and resigned about her role in the new South Africa than her father, David, she too wonders whether, despite her love of the land, "if that way of life is doomed." Lucy's comment is all the more urgent because of the context in which it is uttered. She, after all, is sharing her land with Petrus, whom she and David suspect knew all about the rapists' mission, and yet chose inaction and rhetorical silence. As David observes, "It is a new world they live in, he and Lucy and Petrus. Petrus knows it, and he knows it, and Petrus knows that he knows it" (Coetzee, 1999, p. 117). There is no ambiguity here about identity and consciousness!

MOVING CLOSER TOWARD THE APOCALYPSE

David's sobering words signify forms of rootedness that are diverging politically, socially, and culturally in post-apartheid South Africa. On September 12, 2000, the *New York Times,* under a heading titled, "South Africa's New Poor: White and Bewildered," described the changing social and cultural life styles of white South Africans. In the article, Swarns (2000) quotes one white South African, Mr. Van Niekerk, as saying, "This new South Africa is a very difficult place. . . . I used to feel different. I used to feel like it was my country. You can't say it's your country anymore" (p. A4).

In *Disgrace,* David notes, for example, that "Petrus has a vision of the future in which people like

Lucy have no place" (Coetzee, 1999, p 118). This is a very specific, explicit example of Coetzee's apocalyptic notions of the nature of whites' primordial kinship and belonging in the new South Africa. The sentence, "Petrus has a vision of the future in which people like Lucy have no place," rhetorically, is meant to signify the thinking of most (all?) blacks toward the space and place of whites in post-apartheid South Africa. Of course, David quickly adds, "But that need not make an enemy of Petrus." What does Coetzee mean by "need not make an enemy of Petrus"? But clearly it does. This is what we meant previously about the slippery nature of Coetzee's use of words. Here it would appear that David will be somewhat at ease in the new South Africa, with his identity at least left halfway intact. However, when one reads the moundings in the novel and the sheer quantity of terms that bespeak a menaced white South African existence in the twenty-first century, Coetzee's ambiguity quickly fades into the background, and his philosophical and linguistic subversions become more apparent.

Even the language in which David and Lucy have deposited their hopes and dreams is "arthritic, bygone"; the language does not function wholly and beautifully in the new South Africa where the emotional and affective bonds are becoming unraveled. "Stretches of English code whole sentences long have thickened, lost their articulations, their articulateness, their articulatedness. Like a dinosaur expiring and settling in the mud, the language has stiffened" (Coetzee, 1999, p. 117).

In this way, Coetzee uses language as a mechanism for crafting white South African racial and social solidarity. In this light, language becomes a way of yielding to change and outlook in the new South Africa, where whites are threatened. It is significant that Lucy's tongue cannot bring itself to "speak of," or even "talk about" the particulars of her rape. Indeed, Coetzee paints no picture of it, disallows his reader even a concrete glimpse of what might have happened, could have happened, or did happen. Instead, the reader is free to write on his/her own Lockean and Roussean blank slate! But notice what it is possible to etch there. Coetzee's very linguistic restraint is powerfully persuasive precisely because he does not fill in the terrain with trees, thistles, and thorns. This is Lucy's disgrace. And it is the "disgrace" of the new South Africa!

CONFRONTATION, CULTURE, AND IDENTITY

The reader comes close to the imagery that he/she could or should summon about the rape scene when

David interrogates Petrus about the latter's knowledge of the men who assaulted Lucy. "At this moment he would like to take Petrus by the throat. *If it had been your wife instead of my daughter,* he would like to say to Petrus, *you would not be tapping your pipe and weighing your words so judiciously.* Violation: that is the word he would like to force out of Petrus. Yes, *it was a violation,* he would like to hear Petrus say; *yes it was an outrage"* (Coetzee, 1999, p. 119). Petrus, however, does not speak the words. By not allowing Petrus to say the egregious words, the reader is free to conclude that Petrus is a hard-hearted, nasty and brutish fellow.

By privileging the words, "If it had been your wife instead of my daughter" Petrus "would not be tapping [his] pipe and weighing [his] words so judiciously," Coetzee invites the reader to view Petrus's words against the "us vs. them" framework, and as new bases for solidarity and identity with white South Africans. Petrus's refusal even to talk about the matter directly is cool and calculated, and dramatically highlights what is present and what is absent in South Africa. In a way, Petrus's absent linguistic utterances stand for a special type of bestiality. Is it the case that Petrus instigated the attack to scare Lucy off the land so that he can claim it? Obviously, land reclamation is and was an issue of concern to the founders of the Union of South Africa (Thompson, 1995). In his book, *A History of South Africa* (1995), Thompson discusses the role of land in South Africa during both the segregation era (1910–1948), and portions of the apartheid era (1948–1978).

Even before Coetzee puts the aforementioned words in David's mouth, David had already, on page 117, defined Petrus as "a peasant, a *paysan,* a man of the country. A plotter and a schemer and no doubt a liar too, like peasants everywhere. Honest toil and cunning" (Coetzee, 1999, p. 117). In fairness to Coetzee, he does take a rather jaundiced view of all peasants, regardless of racial identify. However, it is the context in which the words under scrutiny are made that gives our interpretation greater resonance.

Coetzee's words are powerful because they give white South Africans something to work with when they consider their space and place in a country where majority rule is the law of the land. And for Coetzee to construct a scenario where Lucy is not only impregnated by her rapists, but is also put at risk because of rampant AIDS in South Africa, and for Coetzee to construct a scenario in which Lucy considers submitting entirely to her pragmatic impulse (becoming the third wife of a black South African man!), raise serious questions about identity construction in South Africa and the demands of the historical moment. Will the new South Africa be one that Lucy constructs or one that her father, the exiled professor of Cape Technical University, constructs?

SUMMARY AND CONCLUSIONS

In this novel, *Disgrace,* Coetzee tells a story with the following points of intersection: (1) a white South African woman is gang raped, (2) her dogs are murdered, (3) her father is burned and their house is ramshackled. These three acts, we argue, signify Coetzee's attempts to paint an apocalyptic view of the new South Africa in the following ways.

First, Coeetze uses the rape scene to dramatize the most alarming sign that majority rule in South Africa is fraught with peril. The prominence of sex and rape in the novel, the subtle and implicit references to the possibility of a land-grab on the part of black South Africans, and the "shameless," implicitly sensational narrative that a white woman is driven to considering becoming the third wife of a black South African male, emerge as a compelling vehicle for Coetzee to promote white South African's critical reflection upon who they are, where they have been, and where they are going. Coettzee's stance notwithstanding, "If human beings are to cohere, they are required at least to have common threads out of which to craft such coherence" (Calloway-Thomas and Garner, 2000). Crafting common ground is a core concept for formulating arguments that are designed to move and influence human beings in the public square, especially under a heightened sense of identity construction. And, yet, in one sense, it appears "as if" Coetzee is moving in the opposite, bi-polar direction, making it extremely difficult to resolve the cultural and social tensions that exist between black and white South Africans.

Second, Coetzee uses the enthymeme and apocalyptic storytelling as key rhetorical instruments for white South Africans to comprehend their kinship. Throughout the novel there is a distinctive language of identity, however subtle, that helps white South Africans to draw boundaries between their social and cultural life and the social and cultural life of black South Africans. Cross culturally, if one is to expect anything bordering on congeniality, then we must find some way of checking our polarizing impulses or tendencies (Calloway-Thomas and Garner, 2000, p. 149). Because history depends upon memory, experience, and powerful cultural, political and economic legacies, the very arguments over ethnicity is presumed to grow out of—at least in some measure—the question of "iden-

tity," a major crucible in cross-cultural interactions. We learn from Coetzee that some intercultural interactions are indeed tenuous! In fact, his novel brings to the foreground the absence of one of the foundational principles of human cooperation—trust. Francis Fukuyama (1995) reminds us that individuals "who do not trust one another will end up cooperating only under a system of formal rules and regulations, which have to be negotiated, agreed to, litigated, and enforced, sometimes by coercive means" (p. 27).

Third, Coetzee interrogates the uncomfortable and awful tension that can occur when cultures are in transition from minority to majority rule. Although readers may disagree on the persuasive techniques that Coetzee uses to highlight such tension, he does make us mindful of the peculiar anguish that change engenders in humans. And he does, in effect, attempt in some places in the novel to provide a balanced view, however subversive, of post-apartheid South Africa. Lucy, who symbolizes a new generation in South Africa, is his model, and we will end with a comment about her overarching role in the novel.

Finally, Coetzee implicitly constructs social boundaries between blacks and whites, despite the fact that he uses Lucy's voice as an appositional one. Despite the fact that Coetzee paints Lucy as a yielding, tragic figure who seems to accept what *might be* in post-apartheid South Africa, even her tentative yielding bodes ill for white South Africans. Indeed, through Lucy's cultural and social stance, Coetzee makes one ever mindful of what he perceives to be the coming fragility of white South African culture and identity!

REFERENCES

Alba, R. D. (1990). *Ethnic Identity: The Transformation of White America.* New Haven, CT: Yale University Press.

Arendt, H. (1970). *On Violence.* New York: Harcourt Brace Jovanovich, Inc.

Aristotle. *Rhetoric.* Trans. and ed. J. S. Watson. New York: The Modern Library.

Calloway-Thomas, C., Pamela J. Cooper and Cecil Blake. (1999). *Intercultural Communication: Roots and Routes.* Boston, MA: Allyn & Bacon.

Calloway-Thomas, C. and Thurmon Garner. (2000). A Confrontation with Diversity: Communication and Culture in the 21st Century. *Journal of the Association for Communication Administration, 29,* 145–154.

Coetzee, J. M. (1999). *Disgrace.* New York: Penguin Group.

Connolly, W. (1991). *Identity/Difference.* Ithaca, NY: Cornell University Press.

Fukuyama. F. (1995). *Trust, The Social Virtues and the Creation of Prosperity.* New York: Free Press Paperbacks.

Gilroy, P. (2000). *Against Race: Imagining Political Culture Beyond the Color Line.* Cambridge, MA: Harvard University Press.

Jackson, R. (1999). *The Negotiation of Cultural Identity, Perceptions of European Americans and African Americans.* Westport, CT: Praeger Publishers.

Lewis, A. (1999, August 16). A Lucky Country. *The New York Times,* p. A23.

Lewis, A. (1999, August 9). South African Reality. *The New York Times,* p. A19.

Paton, A. (1948). *Cry the Beloved Country.* New York: Charles Scribner & Sons.

Swarns, R. L. (2000, September 12). South Africa's New Poor: White and Bewildered. *The New York Times,* p. 4.

Taylor, C. (1992). *Multiculturalism and "The Politics of Recognition."* Princeton, NJ: Princeton University Press.

Thompson, L. (1999, November–December). Mbeki's Uphill Challenge. *Foreign Affairs.*

Thompson, L. (1995). A *History of South Africa.* New Haven, CT: Yale University Press.

The New Republic. (July, 2000).

Turkle, S. (1995). *Life on the Screen: Identity in the Age of the Internet.* New York: Simon and Schuster.

Yi-Fu, T. (1977). *Space and Place: The Perspective of Experience.* Minneapolis, MN: University of Minnesota Press.

CHECK YOUR UNDERSTANDING

1. How does Coetzee's novel, as described and analyzed by the authors, help us understand how cultures respond when their accustomed ways of thinking, behaving, and being are challenged?

2. What are the characteristics of identity? What is your identity as defined by the groups to which you belong, your ethnicity, the political–social issues of your culture, and the language you use to define yourself?

3. How can the analysis of a piece of literature help us understand culture? What did this analysis reveal to you about South African culture?

4. Read and analyze a children's picture book about another culture. In your analysis consider how the characters define their own identity. What role does language have in terms of defining the character's identity? In other words, how do the characters talk about themselves? How do others talk about them? How do the characters' identities differ from yours?

Gender, Masculinities, Identities, and Interpersonal Relationship Systems: Men in General and Gay Men in Particular

James W. Chesebro

INTERPERSONAL RELATIONSHIP SYSTEMS

Interpersonal relationship systems are ultimately a function of or are derived from the sense of identity men have of themselves . . . We are particularly concerned with gay men and the ways in which their sense of masculinity affects how they perceive and understand themselves. In this regard, we begin with the premise that the factors determining masculinity are many rather than few. Accordingly, because these factors can interact in any number of ways, they create many rather than one form of masculinity. In this sense, the term *masculinities,* in its plural form, rather than *masculinity,* in its singular form, more accurately reflects the understandings conveyed in this [reading]. And, as you know, men prefer to participate and function in social groupings or interpersonal relationship systems and reflect their own style of masculinity. Our attention thus turns to one central question: *What kinds of interpersonal relationship systems do gay men employ?*

Interpersonal relationship systems continually change and adjust to the changing sociocultural organizations (for details regarding these specific changes that follow here, see: Chesebro, 1981). In the 1950s, homosexual or homophile organizations were private, "closeted," high-risk environments, designed only for gay men who were particularly brave and willing to handle tremendously negative social consequences if they were even identified as gay. After the Stonewall riots of 1969, which created the gay liberation movement, new kinds of social organizations developed and emerged, far more public and political, involving the parents and straight friends of gay men, and ultimately even transformations in the political, social, and cultural systems of the United States. After the outbreak of AIDS in 1982, again the interpersonal relationship systems of gay men necessarily underwent dramatic and profound transformations when young men unexpectedly began to die, affecting the personal lives of virtually all Americans. And, as gay men began to recover from the disastrous and devastating effects of AIDS, insofar as that was possible, new interpersonal relationship systems also emerged (see, e.g., Chesebro, 1994 and 1997).

Accordingly, several kinds of specific interpersonal relationship systems were identified. Three of these systems are considered here. Each of these systems is intentionally selected, because each reflects a different way of thinking about interpersonal relationships at a different sociocultural historical point in time as well as a different understanding of the lifestyles and social organization of gay men. Of course, given the perspective of this [reading], what is most intriguing about these systems is the assumption each makes about how gender, masculinity, and identity affect how gay men are defined, organized, and understood.

In 1976, Joseph J. Hayes proposed to examine "gayspeak," the "language" of "America's largest subculture, homosexuals" (256). To "account for some specific behavior patterns" and the "contextual framework" of gay men, he identified three different "settings" within the gay community, the "secret," the "social," and the "radical activist" settings. Each deserves special mention for the ways in which Hayes understood the organization system, types of interpersonal relationship styles, and types of masculinity that dominated the gay community in the 1970s.

In the secret setting, gay men are "covert in expressing their gay identity, separatists (from the straight world specifically but often from the gay community as well), apolitical, and conservative.... [These men take] great pains to avoid any mannerisms or language which would stereotype them" (Hayes, 1976: 257). In this setting, men not only avoid the use of gay-identifying language, they avoid, according to Hayes, the use of any kind of "specific gender reference" or they become "adept at switching gender references when there is a perceived threat" of "exposure" as gay men (257–258). For this group, then, being publicly identified as gay is a denial of masculinity, for masculinity is perceived.

In the social setting, gay men are gathered predominantly in the "gay bar or club" (Hayes, 1976: 258). The men who gather in this setting, according to Hayes, "may be open about their subcultural identity with friends or fellow workers in the straight world" (257). More particularly, Hayes believed that a "vast metaphor of theatre" dominates this setting. The social setting includes:

> role stereotypes, clear notions of approved sexual behavior and the rewards and punishments that are assigned according to one's ability or failure to use the symbols assigned by sex role.... Thus, the humor in Gayspeak, especially camp, is often cynical because it is based on a serious relation to the world. In the social setting, Gayspeak suggests that there is always a vast gulf between what people pretend to be and what they are. (1976: 258)

In this social setting, at least two types of masculinity exist, one that is appropriate for heterosexual men and another that is appropriate for gay men. However, the cynicism that dominates camp as well as the "irony" used to deny masculine imagery whenever it emerges (Hayes, 1976: 261) suggest that gay masculinity is, at least, extremely flexible. A harsher judgment of the language choices made in such social settings might suggest that these gay men ultimately deny that they possess any meaningful sense of identity as men and that they predominantly dehumanized themselves with the language choices they make, for they define "gays largely in terms of specific sexual practices" (Hayes, 1976: 259).

In the radical-activists setting, "although they may not have formal ties with the gay liberation movement, they are usually highly political and freely expressive about their identity. . . . Because of their association with the counterculture, [they are] sometimes alienated from people who move only in secret and social settings" (Hayes, 1976: 257). At the same time, in Hayes's view, this group seeks to "stop both the process of alienation and ghettoization and to reject the value system Gayspeak has incorporated from the mainstream culture" (262). In all, according to Hayes, the language choices of the radical-activist seek to "dramatize and intensify rather than trivialize," for the radical-activist must often verbally and physically confront, challenge, and deny the conceptions offered by gay men in the larger established society. As Hayes himself has concluded, "Radical-activist rhetoric or discourse reflects a more traditionally 'masculine' tone" (263).

In sharp contrast to the interpersonal relationship systems described by Hayes, Alan P. Bell and Martin S. Weinberg (1978), two researchers from the Kinsey Institute, sought to describe the interpersonal relationship systems of gay men in terms of six criteria: (1) the degree to which gay men are involved in a "quasi-marriage"; (2) how much they regret being homosexual; (3) the number of sexual problems they have; (4) how many sexual partners they report having over the past year; (5) the amount of "cruising" they do; and (6) the "level of their sexual activity."

While the criteria used by Bell and Weinberg would clearly seem to reflect an explicit bias against homosexual men, the criteria generated a set of five categories or lifestyles designed to reflect the interpersonal relationship systems of gay men. In this scheme *closed couples* were defined as those in quasi-marriage, with few sexual problems, few partners other than their "mates," and who engage in little cruising. Open couples were defined as those in a quasi-marriage who are high on one of the following variables: number of sexual partners, number of sexual problems, or amount of cruising. *Functional* were defined as those who are not in a quasi-marriage and who also reported a large number of sexual partners, a high level of sexual activity during the year, and little regret over being homosexual. *Dysfunctionals* reported regret over being homosexual although they also reported having a large number of sexual partners and are extremely active sexually. Finally, *asexuals* reported having a few sexual partners during the previous year, had a low level of sexual activity, and possessed a great deal of regret over being homosexual. While 29.7 percent

of those they interviewed could not be classified into their five-part category system, in terms of specific numbers and the relative significance of each of these categories, Bell and Weinberg (1978) reported the following categories and statistics:

Style	Gay Men		Lesbians		Gay Men and Lesbians	
	N	%	N	%	N	%
Closed Couples	67	13.8	81	38.0	148	21.0
Open Couples	120	24.7	51	24.0	171	24.5
Functional	102	21.0	30	14.0	132	18.9
Dysfunctional	86	17.7	16	7.5	102	14.6
Asexual	110	22.0	33	15.6	143	20.5

Bell and Weinberg (1978: 23) concluded, "Our hope is that, at the very least, it will become increasingly clear to the reader that there is no such thing as the homosexual (or the heterosexual, for that matter) and that statements of any kind which are made about human beings on the basis of their sexual orientation must always be highly qualified."

For many, the category system itself seems unduly restrictive in terms of reflecting "lifestyle" preferences of gay men. For one thing, many gay men believe they have been legally, institutionally, and psychologically restricted or discouraged from participating in a quasi-marriage, which would suggest that participation in a quasi-marriage is an externally derived heterosexual standard for measuring the lifestyles of gay men. Additionally, it is unclear that the number of sexual acts, sexual partners, and sexual problems is an appropriate standard for identifying lifestyles, especially if some 15 to 20 percent of men identifying themselves as homosexual have never had a sexual experience (see, e.g., Task Force on Homosexuality, 1971: 48), some 25 percent of men engaging in sex with other men in quasi-public arenas such as men's rooms espouse some of the most oppressive condemnations of homosexuality (Humphrey, 1970), and "only 1 percent of the behavior of those classified as 'exclusively homosexual' involves any kind of sexual release with another person of the same sex" (Karlen, 1971: 525). In all, then, actual sexual behavior constitutes a relatively small percentage of total human behavior.

Nonetheless, if a quasi-marriage and sexual behavior are used as the constitutional elements and measures of lifestyles, then concomitantly conceptions of masculinity are necessarily derived from these measures. Accordingly, among gay men, one would expect that one of the partners is the "active," "top," "inserter," or "penetrator" and therefore the "male" and "masculine," while the other partner is "passive," the "bottom," the "insertee," or "penetratee" and therefore the "female" and "feminine."

Ultimately, while Bell and Weinberg's system provides one view of how the interpersonal relationship systems of gay men might be viewed if gay men were more like heterosexuals, the scheme appears to have severe limitations. Of the many hesitations one might have about Bell and Weinberg's findings, at a minimum it would seem appropriate to note that sexual activity is now far more varied and diverse in its engagements than the two roles suggested here.

Finally, we might consider an interpersonal relationship system of gay men that is based upon their sexual fantasies. Needless to say, such a scheme does not rely upon what is, but rather it presumes that because of the restrictions of society, gay men have been unable to construct the kind of social system they truly desire. Additionally, fantasy presumes an almost unrestricted set of choices in how life might be organized, when total freedom is seldom an option. Accordingly, we are exploring what a system of relationships might look like if it could be built solely upon one's pleasure principles, a system that emphasizes the "culture of desire" that Browning (1996) has maintained constitutes the core of "gay lives today."

In a series of papers presented in 1999 and 2000, I began to work out a scheme for describing gay men's idealized or fantasized interpersonal relationship systems based upon a textual reading of gay pornography (Chesebro, 1999, 2000a, 2000b, 2000c). Among several other objectives, a content analysis of gay pornography should reveal the idealized relationships as well as the idealized conceptions of manliness of gay men.

As a point of departure for such an analysis, it should be noted that gay pornography plays a central role in organizational, social, and symbolic environments of gay men. As I (Chesebro, 2000c: 38) have previously argued:

> First, these videos create and unify the gay community. . . . Gay pornographic videos provide part of the verbal and nonverbal symbols that constitute and define the gay community. . . . for they serve as a unifying set of verbal and nonverbal symbols proclaiming homosexuality, confronting those who would silence and shame gay men, and ultimately reconstructing the relationships between public and private spheres . . .
>
> For gay men, a second function of gay pornographic videos is its ability to more fully and completely represent the nature, emotional meaning, culture, and idealized views of "male homosexual sex." . . .

> Third, for gay men, gay pornographic videos also serve . . . to "validate and legitimate homosexuality to its viewers."
>
> Fourth, these videos are "educational" in the most basic sense of sex education. . . .
>
> Fifth, gay pornographic videos literally show gay men various styles of masculinity, and they frequently "recommend" one style as more appropriate than another. . . .
>
> Sixth, and perhaps paradoxically, gay men use gay pornographic videos as a way of confronting the reality created by and adjusting to the heterosexual world.

Given the central functions that gay pornographic videos play for gay men, especially because they "show gay men various styles of masculinity and . . . frequently 'recommend' one style as more appropriate than another," I examined 242 summaries of gay pornographic videos provided in the *Adam Gay Video 1999 Directory*. These summaries identify the content themes of these videos in several different ways (see Chesebro, 2000c: p. 42). Ultimately, 640 themes from these videos were extracted and coded into a system emphasizing idealized age, sexual acts, number of partners, personality types and images of sexual partners, race and nationality of partners, and "miscellaneous."

Two major conclusions from this study regarding masculinity are particularly relevant here. First, traditional concepts of masculinity, as reflected in the images of the "bodybuilder," "jocks and sports," "straight men," and "motorcyclists" constituted . . . "a relatively small percentage of 1999 gay pornographic feature videos" (Chesebro, 2000c: 43). Second, as I have previously argued,

> the data derived from this content analysis of 1999 gay pornographic feature videos provides a tentative warrant for the growing importance of the concept of masculinities or multiple standards and lifestyles when defining what masculine is. . . . In this sense, 'straight men' are no longer the ideal type. The diversity of occupational differences associated with 'personality type and image' suggests men in all social strata from 'blue collar' to 'bears' are being cast as objects of desire. . . . [Additionally], Asian, Black, European, and Latin men are cast as desired types or classes of men and perhaps even as cultural alternatives to the culture created by white people." In this regard, interracial interactions and sexual acts constituted 22 percent of the themes in this category.

In all, while we are dealing with fantasies about idealized forms of masculinities, the examination of these gay pornographic videos suggests that "a transformation has been occurring in the self-conception gay males possess. . . . Many, rather than one, forms of masculinity are emerging" (Chesebro, 2000c: 47).

CONCLUSION

I suggest that men—straight or gay—are more likely to respond humanely to others and to themselves if the notion of masculinities, in its *plural* form, displaces masculinity, as a *singular* noun. Masculinities, as a concept, is a flagrantly open-ended concept, and this flexibility is exactly why the concept can be so useful and powerful in today's society. For some, masculinities refers to the changing goals and styles of manliness across historical eras (see, e.g., Breitenberg, 1996; Hitchcock and Cohen, 1999; Lees, 1994). For others, masculinities characterizes the different social groupings and regroupings that emerge within contemporary societies (see, e.g., Connell, 1995; Pringle, 1995). For another group, masculinities refers to the different goals, self-conceptions, and styles of men of different races and nationalities (see, e.g., Molloy and Irwin, 1998; Conway-Long, 1994). And, perhaps most usefully for researchers, masculinities has been viewed as a concept that crosses all demographic categorizations or can arise from any one demographic category (see, e.g., Hearn and Collinson, 1994). Indeed, Messner (1991) and Brod and Kaufman (1994) have suggested that the notion of masculinities can be employed usefully when linked to demographic categories in a variety of different ways.

From my perspective as a communication critic, masculinities is a way of equalizing or leveling the playing field, of creating a social and symbolic enclave in which men of all types are appreciated as masculine regardless of the specific groups they are part of or the unique form of masculine identity each might formulate and enact as an individual. Certainly, not each form of masculinity promotes civility and solace, nor can each be said to work toward humane needs. But, the notion of masculinities asks us to avoid predeterminations and traditional understandings about what masculinity is and means and to be open to fresh and new interpretations about the meaning of different men's motivations, understandings, and behaviors when they define themselves and act as men.

REFERENCES

Bell, A. P., and M. S. Weinberg. 1978. *Homosexualities: A Study of Diversity among Men and Women.* New York: Simon and Schuster.

Breitenberg, M. 1996. *Anxious Masculinity in Early Modern England.* New York: Cambridge University Press.

Brod, H., and M. Kaufman, eds. 1994. *Theorizing Masculinities.* Thousand Oaks, CA: Sage.

Browning, F. 1996. *A Queer Geography: Journeys toward a Sexual Self* (rev. ed.). New York: Farrar, Straus and Giroux.

Chesebro, J. W., ed. 1981. *Gayspeak: Gay Males and Lesbian Communication.* New York: The Pilgrim Press.

———. 1994. Reflections on gay and lesbian rhetoric. In R. J. Ringer, ed., *Queer Words, Queer Images: Communication and the Construction of Homosexuality.* New York: New York University Press, 77–88.

———. 1997. Ethical communication and sexual orientation. In J. M. Makau and R. C. Arnett, eds., *Communication Ethics in an Age of Diversity.* Urbana and Chicago: University of Illinois Press, 126–151.

———. 1999, December. *Masculinity as a Symbolic and Social Construction in Pornography.* Paper read at the annual meeting of the Speech Communication Association of Puerto Rico, San Juan, PR.

———. 2000a, March 27. *Social and Symbolic Constructions of Masculinity.* Paper read at New York University, New York, NY.

———. 2000b, April 5. *Social and Symbolic Constructions of Masculinity.* Paper read at the University of Minnesota, Minneapolis, MN.

———. 2000c, April 28. *Exploring the Symbolic and Social Construction of Masculinity and Sexual Preference in Pornography.* Paper read at the annual meeting of the Eastern Communication Association, Pittsburgh, PA.

Connell, R. W. 1995. *Masculinities.* Berkeley: University of California Press.

Conway-Long, D. 1994. Ethnographies and masculinities. In H. Brod and M. Kaufman, eds., *Theorizing Masculinities.* Thousand Oaks, CA: Sage, 61–81.

Hayes, J. J. 1976, October. Gayspeak. *Quarterly Journal of Speech 62:* 256–266.

Hearn, J., and D. L. Collinson. 1994. Theorizing unities and differences between men and between masculinities. In H. Brod and M. Kaufman, eds., *Theorizing Masculinities.* Thousand Oaks, CA: Sage, 97–118.

Hitchcock, T., and M. Cohen, eds. 1999. *English Masculinities, 1660–1800.* New York: Longman.

Humphrey, L. 1970. *Tearoom Trade: Impersonal Sex in Public Places.* Chicago: Aldine.

Jagose, A. 1996. *Queer Theory: An Introduction.* Washington Square: New York University Press.

Karlen, A. 1971. *Sexuality and Homosexuality: A New View.* New York: Norton.

Lees, C. A., ed. 1994. *Medieval Masculinities: Regarding Men in the Middle Ages.* Minneapolis: University of Minnesota Press.

Messner, M. A. 1991. Masculinities and athletic careers. In J. Lorber and S. A. Farrell, eds., *The Social Construction of Gender.* Newbury Park, CA: Sage, 60–75.

Molloy, S., and R. M. Irwin, eds. 1998. *Hispanisms and Homosexualities.* Durham, NC: Duke University Press.

Pringle, K. 1995. *Men, Masculinities, and Social Welfare.* London: UCL Press.

Task Force on Homosexuality of the Human Rights Commission. 1971. *The Isolation Sex Life, Discrimination,* *and Liberation of the Homosexual.* St. Paul: Human Rights Commission of the State of Minnesota.

CHECK YOUR UNDERSTANDING

1. What is your definition of masculinity?
2. Where did you learn about what masculinity and femininity are? Your parents? Your church? Your educational system? Media?
3. Examine advertisements on television and magazines. What percentage of the men is Caucasian? African American? North American Indian? Asian American? Latino? Are the images of masculinity different for different groups?
4. Chesebro suggests we can view relationship systems of gay men in terms of language use, quasi-marriage, and fantasized relationships. How do each of these relate to the concept of "masculinities"?
5. Why does Chesebro suggest that we should talk in terms of "masculinities" rather than "masculinity"? What effect does this distinction have on communication between homosexuals and heterosexuals?

CHAPTER ACTIVITIES

1. Analyze the popular film *My Big Fat Greek Wedding* for what it reveals about identity and belonging. How do the characters use both language and nonverbal behavior to signal modes of identification?
2. Collect a list of terms from representative intercultural novels or films that authors and producers use to define *class*. What do such terms indicate about the nature of class relations? How do the words put in the mouths of middle-class characters differ from the ones put in the mouths of working-class characters? To what extent are such descriptions accurate or inaccurate?
3. Find the best article that you can on culture, identity, and belonging in a representative newspaper such as the *New York Times* or the *Wall Street Journal*. Then be prepared to share the article with your classmates, paying attention to such questions as: What culture is the subject of discussion? What is the content of the article? What does the article reveal about the nature of human affairs in the twenty-first century? Do you agree or disagree with the author's point of view? Why or why not?

CHAPTER 5

VERBAL INTERCULTURAL COMMUNICATION

FRUSTRATION, MISUNDERSTANDING, LAUGHTER

Verbal communication in one's own culture often leads to frustration, misunderstanding, and even laughter. But the problem of verbal communication becomes extremely tricky when one is from another culture. The following examples demonstrate the problem.

- I received a message from a friend of mine who was studying in Thailand. She was preparing for a university exam in second-year Thai. She emailed:

  I am a little worried about tones. On Monday I went into a store to buy envelopes. I got a strange look. If I said the word in the wrong tone, I asked the shopkeeper "Do you have a brothel?" instead of "Do you have an envelope?" It is a dangerous language!

- Soon after arriving in Hong Kong, I joined an orientation group sponsored by the YWCA. On a tour of various temples, we stopped at a tea-seller's stall to sample various Chinese teas. We Westerners wanted to show the tea seller how much we liked the tea. We looked at him and said, "Mmmm." Our orientation leader quickly told us that in Cantonese, "Mmmmm" means "No."

- The following is an excerpt from my journal. I was living in Hong Kong at the time this was written.

  I awaken to the sound of running water. In my semi-sleep state, I vaguely remember my husband is to leave early this morning for Pakistan. It is not yet light so I turn over to fall back asleep. Then it dawns on me—my husband left in the wee hours of the morning, so there should be no running water in the bathroom next to our bedroom. I am immediately awake.

  I walk into the bathroom and water is indeed running. But not from faucets. A steady flow falls from the ceiling. The flow is heaviest into my shower, but the entire room appears to be experiencing a sudden downpour so common in the tropics. Generally, however, these downpours occur outside my flat, not inside my bathroom!

  I run up to the flat above ours and knock loudly on the door. My neighbor appears, clad in a bath towel. I explain to him what is happening in my flat and he rushes to turn off his shower. Indeed, we agree he should run no more water or even flush his toilet.

  I return to my flat and, because it is too early for the maintenance man to be on duty, I cover the bathroom floor and countertops with towels to soak the excess water.

  As soon as 8:00 A.M. arrives, I call the maintenance office. As I struggle to explain (in broken Cantonese) my problem, the person on the other end of the line (who speaks broken English) seeks to understand:

  I have water in my bathroom.

  Yes.

  I have lots of water in my bathroom.

  Yes, that is good. The water pressure is OK now. (We had had problems with this earlier.)

It is becoming rapidly apparent that this line of conversation will get me nowhere.
So, I try another approach:
I want it fixed.
You don't want the water?
I want the water. I don't want too much water. I think the pipes broke.
In your bathroom?
No, in my neighbor's bathroom. I need you to fix my neighbor's bathroom.
He has too much water?
No, his water is fine. I have too much water. His water leaks.
Leaks?
Yes, leaks into my bathroom. Water is all over.
All over your bathroom?
Yes.
I will come.
I hang up the phone, exhausted! Oh, to say what I mean in clear, concrete language is a skill I must learn here!

- Translations from one language to another lead to some interesting problems. Several years ago Coca Cola had a million-dollar campaign to introduce Coca Cola into China. Its slogan, "Bite the wax tadpole," was set in bright lights in all the large cities. Similarly, when Gerber started selling baby food in Africa, they used the same packaging as in the United States, with an adorable baby on the label. Later the company learned that in Africa, since most people can't read English, companies routinely put pictures on the label of what is inside.

These episodes suggest the difficulty of using language effectively. One of the roots of our culture is our language. We learn the syntax, semantics, and pragmatics of our language. As long as we remain in our own culture, our ability to use language to communicate is fairly high. However, when we enter a culture with a language different from our native language, our communication ability lessens. In this chapter we will suggest some reasons why this is so.

OBJECTIVES

After reading the chapter and completing the readings and the activities, you should be able to

- Explain the relationship of the triangle of meaning to intercultural communication.
- Define semantics and pragmatics.
- Explain how languages differ in their structures.
- Explain the concept of general semantics and its relationship to intercultural communication.
- Define speech acts and give an example.
- Using the Sapir-Whorf hypothesis, explain how language relates to culture.
- Explain how differences in verbal style can lead to misunderstanding.
- Define linguistic prejudice.

WHAT IS LANGUAGE?

Language is a code. In other words, meaning is conveyed symbolically. Symbols are units of meaning that are conventional (based on social agreement) and arbitrary. As we discussed in Chapter 1, words are symbols. As such, their meaning is arbitrary and conventional. For example, consider the word *cat*. The word is a symbol that refers to or "stands for" the actual furry, four-footed animal we have as a pet. We could have agreed (convention) to call this animal *tac* or anything else. In other words, the word *cat* is arbitrary. This symbolic, arbitrary nature of language can be diagrammed as in Figure 5.1. This is called the *triangle of meaning* (Ogden and Richards, 1927). The word you speak (*cat*) is the

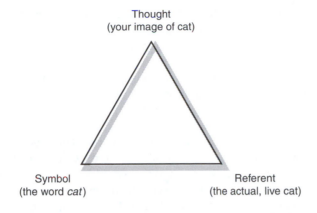

FIGURE 5.1   Triangle of Meaning

Source: C. K. Ogden and I. A. Richards, *The Meaning of Meaning: A Study of the Influence of Language upon Thought and the Science of Symbolisms,* 1927, p. 11. New York: Harcourt Brace. Used with permission.

symbol, the thought is the image in your mind of a cat, and the referent is the actual, live cat. Notice that the line connecting the symbol and the referent is broken. This indicates that the symbol and the referent have no connection except that which you make in your mind—in your thoughts. This causes particular problems when the referent is not concrete, but abstract—such as freedom, family, and beauty.

This symbolic, arbitrary nature of language suggests that words don't mean, people do. Put another way, meanings are in people, not in words. What I think of when I hear the word *cat* may not be what you think of. Our attributions, expectancies, and feelings about the referent may differ. Thus, our meanings differ.

Imagine the difficulty this idea of "meanings are in people" has as we move from our own language to that of another culture. For example, as Lewis (1996) suggests:

> As the globalisation of business brings executives more frequently together, there is a growing realization that if we examine concepts and values, we can take almost nothing for granted. The word "contract" translates easily from language to language, but nationally it has many interpretations. To a Swiss, German, Scandinavian, American or British person it is something that has been signed in order to be adhered to. Signatures give it a sense of finality. But a Japanese regards a contract as a starting document to be rewritten and modified as circumstances require. A South American sees it as an ideal which is unlikely to be achieved, but which is signed to avoid argument. (p. 11)

THE STRUCTURE OF LANGUAGE

Although symbols are arbitrary, language is rule governed. These rules are the syntax and grammar of a language. The rules have to do with what letters or symbols can be combined with others to form words and what words can be combined, and in what order, to form sentences. For example, the sentence "Communication is the process of creating meaning" makes sense to English speakers. However, "Creating meaning communication the process is of" does not because the word order makes no sense to English speakers.

Sentence order can differ across cultures. In Japanese the verb comes at the end of the sentence, making it difficult for English speakers to understand what is being said until the entire sentence has been uttered. Americans say, "How are you?" Chinese say, "Nie hau ma?" (*ma* at the end of a declarative sentence changes that sentence to an interrogative), meaning "You good?" Germans say, "Wie geht es Ihnen?" meaning "How goes it with you?" In Vietnamese the verb is followed by the subject of the sentence—the reverse of the English language. Some languages are tonal and the meaning differs depending on the tone. Chinese, for example, is a tonal language, and different tones or intonations distinguish words that are otherwise pronounced identically. For example, *ma* with a high-level tone means mother; in a low-rising tone, horse; in a high-rising tone, hemp; and in a high-falling to low tone, to curse. To confuse matters even more, each tone usually offers a large number of homonyms. For example, *yi* in a high-level tone can mean, among other things, one, clothes, doctor, and to cure.

Plurals differ in the way they are formed in various languages. In the United States we generally form the plural of a word by adding *s* to the end of the word. In the Indonesian language plurals are formed by repeating the word—for example, *angan* means fantasy, *angan-angan* means fantasies. In Korean "the distinction between singular and plural is made by the context of the sentence" (Honig, 1992, p. 66). Some languages have no plurals, such as the Chinese language. Nor does it have cases, tenses, prefixes, or suffixes. In addition, Chinese sentences do not need a verb and there is no verb "to be" in Chinese.

Languages also "look" different. The English alphabet consists of 26 letters; the Italian alphabet has 21 letters. Some languages, like Russian, Chinese, Persian, Hebrew, Gaelic, and Thai, have alphabets that do not look like the letters of the English alphabet. Although a Thai alphabet may look "strange" to English speakers, remember that the English alphabet looks "strange" to a Thai speaker!

Finally, language structure affects what speakers focus on in their communication. In Asian languages the language forces the speaker to focus primarily on human relationships. In Western languages the focus is on objects or referents and their logical relationships. For example, for Japanese, communication is meant to promote and maintain harmony. Thus, the *way* something is said is as important as *how* something is said. Threatening tones are avoided and the emphasis is on politeness and respect. The information that surrounds the words—the voice tone, the gestures, even the words that are not said—are extremely important. Thus, language should be as clear and precise as possible. North Americans tend to ask a lot of questions so that they have as much information as possible before making a decision. They generally pay less attention to factors such as voice tone and gestures than Japanese.

SEMANTICS

It is not enough to know the structure of a language. To communicate effectively, one needs to understand the meaning of words. Semantics is the study of meaning. At the simplest level, a meaning is denotative or connotative. The *denotative meaning* is the conventional meaning—the meaning that was agreed on when the language code was constructed. In other words, we can find the denotative meaning of a word in a dictionary.

The *connotative meaning* is private and often emotionally charged. Connotative meaning becomes attached to words through our experiences and associations. For example, in our earlier example of the word *cat,* the denotative meaning is a small furry domesticated animal often kept as a pet. My personal definition depends on my experience with cats. If I have had positive experiences, my emotional attachment to the word *cat* will be positive and a positive emotion will result. I will be happy. However, if my experience has been negative, a negative emotion will result. Perhaps I will fear cats.

General semanticists (people interested in how humans use their language and how language relates to behavior) suggest that words are at various levels of abstraction. We organize and order our world by using language to classify things into general categories, thus helping make our world more predictable. For example, we classify some people into the category of *foreigner.* We abstract from each of these people the characteristics they have in common. This abstraction notes the similarities and overlooks the differences among foreigners. Based on this abstraction of foreigners, we make predictions about what foreigners will say and do.

However, abstractions can cause problems in intercultural communication. We often overlook the differences in people and things simply because they fall into the same category. If we respond to the stereotypes or the abstraction rather than to the person with whom we are trying to communicate, we will not be effective communicators.

General semanticists provide devices to aid us in avoiding the dangers inherent in abstraction. The first device is called *dating*. People, objects, events—everything—is in constant flux. Thus, you in 1998 is not the same as you in 1970 or 2001. If you mentally attach a date to such statements as "That foreigner is rude" (by saying "That foreigner is rude now") you'll keep from assuming that the particular foreigner is always rude. You'll refrain from communicating as if people and events are static. Remember that one thing is different at two different times.

Indexing is closely related to dating. Indexing helps us account for individual differences. People, as well as objects and events, differ from one another. Thus, foreigner 1 is not foreigner 2. If we index, we keep from making such generalizations as, "All foreigners are rude." If you've seen one, you haven't seen them all!

Both indexing and dating point to the fact that the verb *is* should be used with caution. When we say *is,* we imply a static, unchanging phenomenon. This negates the concept that communication is a dynamic, continuous, and ever-changing process. There's a difference between saying, "That foreigner is rude" and "That foreigner appears to be rude." When we say, "That foreigner is rude," we leave ourselves open for misevaluation.

Finally, the use of *mental quotation marks* reminds us that meanings are in people, not in words. When you say, "That foreigner is rude," you may mean that the person did not say "Excuse me" when bumping into you. Your friend might consider "rude" to mean that the foreigner failed to speak English. If you use mental quotation marks—"rude"—you'll be reminded that the term has different meanings to different people.

These principles of general semantics can help us be more competent communicators. As we travel the routes of other cultures, we need to remember that words are abstract and, as such, can limit our understanding in numerous ways. One student writes, for example: "If I had known about general semantics when I went to study in France, I think my communication would have been more effective. I think it would have helped me avoid as much stereotyping as I did."

PRAGMATICS

Knowing the rules of a language and possessing a large vocabulary will not guarantee effective communication. We have to know how to use the language in actual conversation. As anyone who has taken a foreign language knows, using a language in its native country with native speakers is very different from using it in a classroom! Pragmatics examines language as it is used in actual, everyday interactions. For example, Iraqis who speak English use the word "hello" when they mean "goodbye." This can be very confusing to Western visitors who use "hello" to begin a conversation, not end it.

When we use language, we use it to reach specific goals. These goals are called *speech acts*. Examples of speech acts are threats, jokes, questions, requests, and praise. Assume you are taking an art class. You've finished an abstract painting and you show it to your friend. Your friend looks at the painting, pauses, and says, "That's very unusual." What does your friend mean? Does your friend like your painting? Thinking about the syntax and the semantics of the sentence your friend uttered will not be much help. In order to understand what your friend actually means, you have to know what your friend was trying to do—compliment you, criticize you, or remain neutral.

How do we know how to interpret a speech act? A theory called the *coordinated management of meaning (CMM)* helps answer this question (Cronen et al., 1982). This theory suggests that we know how to use language because we follow rules that tell us how to understand and produce speech acts. Constitutive rules tell us how to recognize speech acts.

Regulative rules identify, in a given context, the speech acts that are appropriate or inappropriate for the context. In other words, communication makes sense only in the context in which it occurs.

To interpret a speaker's intended speech act, you have to consult constitutive rules. Because words have different meanings in different contexts, to choose the right rule, you need to examine the context. If a professor says "You're in serious trouble," you will no doubt decide to interpret the words as a warning. If, on the other hand, these same words are uttered by a parent in an episode of "joking around," you'll interpret the meaning as a move in a game of teasing.

To respond to the speech act, you have to consider regulative rules. Remember that these rules tell us what speech acts are appropriate given your goals and understanding of the context. In the case of the professor, your regulative rules for this academic episode might be, "Given that I want to pass this course, the proper speech act for me to perform is a polite request for further information."

LANGUAGE AND CULTURE

Does the language we speak influence how we perceive the world? In 1921 Edward Sapir suggested that it did. He, along with his student, Benjamin Whorf, suggested that language did affect a culture's behavior and habits of thinking. As Sapir indicates (quoted in Whorf, 1956):

> Human beings do not live in the objective world alone, nor alone in the world of social activity as ordinarily understood, but are very much at the mercy of the particular language which has become the medium of expression for their society. . . . The fact is that the "real world" is to a large extent unconsciously built up on the language habits of the group. . . . We see and hear and otherwise experience the world very much as we do because the language habits of our community predispose certain choices of interpretation. (p. 134)

The Sapir-Whorf hypothesis has two versions: linguistic determinism and linguistic relativity. *Linguistic determinism* suggests that our language determines the way we interpret the world. *Linguistic relativity* suggests that since language affects thought, speakers of different languages will perceive the world differently. Most students of language today adhere to the linguistic relativity version.

Lewis (1996) tells the story of how linguistic relativity "works." He was interested in why the Zulu language has 39 words for "green," whereas English has only one. So he asked a Zulu chief. The Zulu chief explained that prior to national highways the Zulu had to make long treks across the savannah grasslands. Because there were no signposts or maps, the lengthy journeys had to be described by those who had traveled the road before. The language changed to accommodate the need for "finely wrought, beautiful logical descriptions of nature, causation, repetition, duration and results" (p. 16). Lewis describes the conversation:

> "But give me some examples of different green-words," I persisted.
>> My friend picked up a leaf. "What color is this?" he asked.
> "Green," I replied.
>> The sun was shining. He waited until a cloud intervened. "What color is the leaf now?" he asked.
> "Green," I answered, already sensing my inadequacy.
> "It isn't the same green, is it?"
> "No, it isn't."
> "We have a different word in Zulu." He dipped the leaf in water and held it out again. "Has the color changed?"
> "Yes."
> "In Zulu we have a word for 'green shining wet.'"
>> The sun came out again and I needed another word (leaf-green-wet-but-with-sunshine-on-it!).
>> My friend retreated 20 meters and showed me the leaf. "Has the color changed again?"

"Yes," I screamed.

"We have another word," he said with a smile.

He went on to indicate how different Zulu greens would deal with tree leaves, bush leaves, leaves vibrating in the wind, river greens, pool greens, tree trunk greens, crocodile greens . . . he got to 39 without even raising a sweat. (p. 160)

Language also tells us about relationships; it can tell us how to talk with others based on intimacy and rank. As we indicated in Chapter 1, the German language has formal and informal pronouns. If you know someone quite well, you would use the *du* form of "you." If you did not know that person well or you wanted to show respect, you would use the *Sie* form of "you." Languages such as French and Spanish also have various forms of "you" depending on the relationship. In Mandarin Chinese there are terms for younger sister (*mei-mei*), older sister (*jiejie*), younger brother (*didi*), older brother (*gege*), paternal grandfather (*yeye*), paternal grandmother (*nainai*), maternal grandfather (*laoye*), maternal grandmother (*laolao*), your son's son (*sunzi*), your daughter's son (*waisun*), and so forth. In the Hindu language, there are no single words for the English words *aunt* and *uncle*. Hindi have different words for your mother's older brother and younger brother, and your mother's older brother-in-law, father's older brother, younger brother, and so on. The Thai language uses different pronouns, nouns, and verbs to represent rank and intimacy.

Not only does language tell us how to talk to one another but it also tells us what we talk about. The Navaho language contains five terms to designate color. Hoijer (1994) explains:

The Navaho color vocabulary includes, among others, five terms: ligai, dilxl, lizin, lici, and dokiz, to be taken as one way of categorizing certain color impressions. Ligai is roughly equivalent to English white, dilxl and lizin to English black, lici to English red, and dokiz to English blue or green. Clearly then, the Navaho five-point system is not the same as English white-black-red-blue-green, which also has five categories. English black is divided into two categories in Navaho (dilxl and lizin), while Navaho has but one category (do-kiz) for the English blue and green.

All this is not to say that English speakers cannot perceive the difference between the two "blacks" of the Navaho or that Navaho speakers cannot differentiate "blue" and "green." It is to say that it will be harder. If we don't have words for something, it takes longer to distinguish that thing from others.

In sum, the Sapir-Whorf hypothesis suggests that the way one culture sees the world may not be the same as the way another culture sees the world. What you believe to be true is based on the language you speak. Thus, when you come into contact with a speaker of a different language, you are entering a different view of the world. One final example makes this clear (Dickey, 1991):

Differences in language, rhetoric, religion, logic, notions of truth and freedom, honor, trust, family, friendship, hospitality—all account for misunderstandings that persist between Arabs and the West. But they are not the core of the incomprehension. The essence can be summed up in a single word: history. It is an always present force in Arab life, and this is what so many Westerners find impossible to grasp. Americans, especially, have very little sense of their own past, and virtually no sense of the Middle East's. Given a problem to confront, an American typically will ask what comes next. An Arab will talk about what came before. "We don't dare to talk about the future, or even the present. Our refuge is the past," says Amin Mahmoud, a Palestinian history professor from Kuwait University who lost his savings and his home in the Iraqi invasion. "We always go back to the roots."

VERBAL COMMUNICATION STYLES

In their analysis of verbal and nonverbal communication styles across cultures, Gudykunst and Ting-Toomey (1988) present four verbal communication styles. *Style* is "a meta message that contextualizes how individuals should accept and interpret a verbal message" (p. 100). As you read this section, think about the style of your culture, and how you might need to adapt this style as you venture to other cultures.

Direct versus Indirect Style

The direct versus indirect style refers to the extent that speakers reveal their intentions through explicit verbal communication. The primary function of language in a *direct style* is to express feelings, ideas, and thoughts as clearly and logically as possible. In other words, all the information is in the explicit coded message. Such a style occurs in low-context cultures, primarily Western nations. In these nations speakers value specificity, clarity, and precision. Members talk more, find verbal people more attractive, and are relatively insensitive to nonverbal cues (to the context surrounding the verbal message).

In contrast, an *indirect style* occurs in high-context cultures in which the message is highly dependent on the context or internalized with the people who are communicating and less on the actual words that are spoken. Thus, the meaning of the message lies in when and where it is said as well as who says it and to whom.

People in high-context cultures who use an indirect style of communication often find people in low-context cultures loud and insensitive. On the other hand, people in low-context cultures, who use a direct style, cannot understand why high-context speakers don't say what they mean. The following example from Okabe (1983) clarifies these ideas:

> Reflecting the cultural value of precision, [North] Americans' tendency to use explicit words is the most noteworthy characteristic of their communicative style. They prefer to employ such categorical words as "absolutely," "certainly," and "positively." . . . The English syntax dictates that the absolute "I" be placed at the beginning of a sentence in most cases, and that the subject-predicate relation be constructed in an ordinary sentence. . . . By contrast, the cultural assumptions of interdependence and harmony require that Japanese speakers limit themselves to implicit and even ambiguous use of words. In order to avoid leaving an assertive impression, they like to depend more frequently on qualifiers such as "maybe," "perhaps," "probably," and "somewhat." Since Japanese syntax does not require the use of a subject in a sentence, the qualifier-predicate is a predominant form of sentence construction. (p. 36)

Elaborate versus Succinct Style

The elaborate versus succinct style concerns the quantity of talk that is valued in different cultures. An *elaborate style* is the use of rich, expressive language in everyday conversation. On the other end of the continuum is the *succinct style,* which includes the use of understatement, silences, and pauses in everyday conversation. In the middle of the continuum is the exacting style—one should give neither more nor less information than is required.

Arab speakers use an elaborate style of communication. Their conversations are filled with exaggerations, assertions, proverbs, cultural idioms, and metaphors. Similarly, Mexican speakers delight in verbal play. They use double entendres, turn of phrases, and old quotations expressed at just the right moment in everyday conversation.

In contrast, the Japanese have a succinct style. Silence, or *ma,* is prevalent in Japanese communication. The Japanese believe that it is the silence between words that is significant to conveying meaning. In addition, they use circumlocution and indirectness. This is true in many Asian countries. For example, rather than telling you directly, "I don't agree with you" (as someone using an exacting style would do), a Korean speaker will be less direct, saying something like, "I agree with you in principle." Exacting style is characteristic of many Northern European cultures and the U.S. culture. People from these cultures tend to "say what they mean."

Personal versus Contextual Style

Verbal *personal style* is individual-centered language, whereas verbal *contextual style* is role-centered language. In a verbal personal style, linguistic devices are used to emphasize the "I" identity. Meanings are expressed for the purpose of emphasizing "personhood." In a verbal contextual style, linguistic devices are used to emphasize the "role" identity. Meanings are expressed for the purpose of emphasizing prescribed role relationships.

English speakers tend to stress informality and power relationships, whereas Chinese speakers, using a contextual style language, stress formality and asymmetrical power relationships. U.S. Americans shun formal codes of conduct, titles, and honorifics in interaction with others. They prefer a first-name basis and direct address. Chinese, on the other hand, believe formality is essential to their human relationships. Similarly, Koreans use Confucian ethical rules of hierarchical human relationships. They have separate vocabularies for different sexes, different degrees of intimacy, different formal occasions, and different degrees of social status.

Instrumental versus Affective Style

The *instrumental verbal style* is sender oriented, goal oriented, and relies heavily on the digital code to accomplish goals. The *affective verbal style* is receiver oriented, process oriented, and relies heavily on the analogic code to negotiate relational definition and approval. Western cultures, such as that of the United States, use an instrumental style. Most Arab, Asian, and Latin American cultures use an affective style. Note that the former are low-context cultures; the latter are high-context cultures.

Comparing North Americans to South Koreans, Park (1979) suggests:

> In an instrumental communication pattern, like that of the [North] Americans, people assert themselves or make themselves understood by talking . . . whereas in a situation communication style like that of Koreans or Japanese, people try to defend themselves either by vague expressions or by not talking. [North] Americans try to persuade their listeners in the step-by-step process [regardless of] whether their listeners accept them totally. But a Korean or a Japanese tends to refuse to talk any further in the course of a conversation with someone once he [or she] decides that he [or she] cannot accept the other's attitude, his [or her] way of thinking and feeling in totality. (pp. 92–93)

LINGUISTIC PREJUDICE

Prejudice, as we discussed earlier, involves making a prejudgment based on membership in a social category. In general, we tend to think of prejudice as negative—an unfair or biased attitude toward another person or group. One form of prejudice is linguistic prejudice. The language others use and that is used to describe them can affect our perception of them. According to Spender (1985), the English language is prejudiced against women. Men have controlled the language, provided themselves with more positive words to describe themselves, and given themselves more opportunities to use those words. For example, there is no feminine generic—that is, feminine words used to represent both the feminine and the masculine form of a word (Smith, 1985). According to Ayim (1993), the term *woman* is not even generic for all females, since it usually focuses on white women, excluding Black women, Native American women, and other women of color. In the first reading at the end of this chapter, Houston suggests the same idea.

A major way that we make boundaries between our ethnic group and the ethnic group of others is by the language we speak. Often we use the language styles of ethnic groups to support our stereotypes about them. For example, Kochman (1981) observes that African American speakers favor forceful outputs (e.g., volume of voice) during conflicts, whereas White speakers prefer subdued outputs. Whites perceive African Americans' responses in bad taste, whereas African Americans view Whites' responses as lifeless.

One final note before we leave the idea of linguistic prejudice. We need to be aware of the fact that we may engage in prejudiced talk ourselves. Often when we are going to say something negative about a group, we preface it by saying, "I'm not prejudiced, but . . ." and then we go on to engage in prejudiced talk. Van Dijk (1984, p. 70) clusters prejudiced talk into four categories: (1) "they are different" (in culture, mentality), (2) "they do not adapt themselves," (3) "they threaten our (social, economic) interests," and (4) "they are involved in negative acts" (nuisances, crime).

Being aware of our communication can help us eliminate prejudiced talk from our communication. In addition, when we hear others using prejudiced talk, we can indicate to them that this form of communication is not acceptable to us.

CONCLUSION

As the narratives with which we began this chapter suggest, we may often be confused when the language of our native culture comes into contact with the language of other cultures. When we communicate with people from cultures different from our own, our confusion as well as frustration mounts. Being attuned to the language differences we have discussed in this chapter may lessen that confusion and frustration. Knowing differences exist and knowing what form these differences may take can help prepare you for using language in another culture (Kranhold et al., 2004). The readings in this chapter help us understand how language affects culture. Marsha Houston describes the talk between Blacks and Whites as perceived by Black women. Ting-Toomey and Oetzel examine conflict interaction styles of various cultures.

FOR DISCUSSION

1. Describe a situation in which language differences caused an intercultural communication misunderstanding. How did you handle the situation? Was your way effective? Why or why not?
2. Think about the Sapir-Whorf hypothesis in terms of your own native language. Can you think of examples in your language that support this hypothesis? Refute it?
3. Define linguistic prejudice. In your journal, keep track of examples of linguistic prejudice you hear during the next week.
4. When traveling to another country do you consider it important to learn the language of the people of that country? If so, how much? If not, why not? How do you feel about foreigners who come to your country and don't know your language?
5. Analyze your communication style. Given your communication style, what problems might you encounter as you travel?

REFERENCES

Ayim, M. (1993). Issues in language and gender: An annotated bibliography. *Resources for Feminist Research, 22* (1/2), 1–35.

Banks, J. (1984). *Teaching strategies for ethnic studies,* 3rd ed. Boston: Allyn and Bacon.

Bernstein, B. (1971). *Class, codes and control: Theoretical studies toward a sociology of language.* London: Routledge & Kegan Paul.

Chideya, F. (1995). *Don't believe the hype: Fighting cultural misinformation about African Americans.* New York: Penguin.

Cronen, V., Pearce, B., and Harris, L. (1982). The coordinated management of meaning: A theory of communication. In F. Dance (Ed.), *Communication theory: Comparative essays* (pp. 61–89). New York: Harper & Row.

Dodd, C. (1998). *Dynamics of intercultural communication,* 5th ed. Boston: McGraw-Hill.

Gudykunst, W. (1994). *Bridging differences,* 2nd ed. Thousand Oaks, CA: Sage.

Gudykunst, W., and Kim, Y. Y. (1997). *Communicating with strangers: An approach to intercultural communication,* 3rd ed. New York: McGraw-Hill.

Gudykunst, W., and Ting-Toomey, S. (1988). *Culture and interpersonal communication.* Newbury Park, CA: Sage.

Harre, R. (1979). *Social being: A theory for social psychology.* Totowa, NJ: Rowan and Littlefield.

Hoijer, J. (1994). The Sapir-Whorf hypothesis. In L. Samovar and R. Porter (Eds.), *Intercultural communication: A reader* (pp. 194–200). Belmont, CA: Wadsworth.

Honig, B. (1992). *Handbook for teaching Korean-American students.* Sacramento: California Department of Education.

Infante, D. A., and Rancer, A. S. (1982). A conceptualization and measure of argumentativeness. *Journal of Personality Assessment, 46,* 19–170.

Katzner, K. (1995). *The languages of the world.* New York: Routledge.

Kochman, T. (1981). *Black and white: Styles in conflict.* Chicago: University of Chicago Press.

Kranhold, K., Bilefsky, D., Karnitschnig, M., and Parker, G. (2004, May 28). Lost in translation. *The Wall Street Journal,* pp. B1, B6.

Lewis, R. (1996). *When cultures collide: Managing successfully across cultures.* London: Nicholas Brealey.

Littlejohn, S. (1996). *Theories of human communication,* 5th ed. Belmont, CA: Wadsworth.

Lustig, M., and Koester, J. (1996). *Intercultural competence: Interpersonal communication across cultures,* 2nd ed. New York: HarperCollins.

Martin, J., and Nakayama, T. (1997). *Intercultural communication in context.* Mountain View, CA: Mayfield.

Ogden, C. K., and Richards, I. A. (1927). *The meaning of meaning.* New York: Harcourt Brace.

Okabe, R. (1983). Cultural assumptions of east and west: Japan and the United States. In W. M. Gudykunst (Ed.), *Intercultural communication theory.* Beverly Hills, CA: Sage.

Park, M. (1979). *Communication styles in two different cultures: Korean and American.* Seoul, Korea: Han Shin Publishing Company.

Philipsen, G. (1992). *Speaking culturally.* Albany: State University of New York Press.

Samovar, L., Porter, R., and Stefani, L. (1998). *Communicating between cultures,* 3rd ed. Belmont, CA: Wadsworth.

Schutz, A. (1970). *On phenomenology and social relations.* Chicago: University of Chicago Press.

Shotter, J. (1984). *Social accountability and selfhood.* Oxford, England: Blackwell.

Smith, P. (1985). *Language, the sexes and society.* Oxford, England: Blackwell.

Spender, D. (1985). *Man made language,* 2nd ed. London: Routledge and Kegan Paul.

Trenholm, S., and Jensen, A. (1992). *Interpersonal communication.* Belmont, CA: Wadsworth.

Van Dijk, T. (1984). *Prejudice in discourse.* Amsterdam: Benjamins.

Wallach, J., and Metcalf, G. (1995). *Working with Americans: A practical guide for Asians on how to succeed with U.S. managers.* New York: McGraw-Hill.

Whorf, B. (1956). *Language, thought and reality.* New York: John Wiley & Sons.

Zajonic, R. B. (1980). Feeling and thinking: Preferences need no inferences. *American Psychologist, 35,* 152–155.

Multiple Perspectives: African American Women Conceive Their Talk

Marsha Houston

"Double jeopardy" (Beale, 1970) is often considered the fundamental insight into the lived experiences of African American women. African American feminist thinkers, from nineteenth-century orator Maria Stewart to contemporary cultural critic bell hooks, have pointed out that African American womanhood is experienced holistically. Black[1] women experience womanhood *in the context* of blackness; they do not experience their gender and ethnic identities as separate "parts" of who they are (Collins, 2000; Davis, 1981; hooks, 1981; 1984). The outcome of being African American *and* woman in a social order rife with both racism *and* sexism is that black women's experiences of womanhood may overlap with those of both white women and other women of color, but will also differ from them in important ways; and their experience of blackness may overlap with those of African American men, but will significantly differ from them as well. When the fundamental insight of "double jeopardy" is extended to other aspects of African American women's identities (e.g., socio-economic class, sexual orientation) the "multiple jeopardy" and "multiple consciousness"[2] that characterize African American womanhood become apparent (King, 1988).

For individual African American women, these twin concepts suggest both the risks of many sorts of disadvantage and marginalization and the possibilities of simultaneous, multiple, self- and group-affirming ways of seeing every aspect of human social life. For African American women as a social group, "multiple jeopardy" and "multiple consciousness" suggest a heterogeneity of social relationships, experiences, and outlooks that preclude essentializing black womanhood.

Any explanation of African American women's communication must, in some way, account for the heterogeneity of black women's lived experiences suggested by multiple jeopardy and multiple consciousness. In this essay, I endeavor to account for that heterogeneity by exploring three contrasting perspectives taken by African American women in response to my request that they write free descriptions of "black women's talk." One hundred thirty-four middle-class professional women and aspiring middle-class women (college students) responded to this request. This is not a report of the responses they gave, but an interpretation of the ways they approached the question, that is, the ways they conceived "black women's talk," as a distinct communication style or repertoire of styles. Some women evaded the idea of "black women's talk," others saw style-switching as its central feature, but most celebrated one or more of three dimensions of black women's interpersonal style: wisdom, fortitude, and caring.

Hecht, Ribeau and Alberts (1989) suggest that cultural *speaking perspectives* are ways of thinking about and talking about talk that reveal the discursive forms a cultural group regards as ideal and perceives as typical of particular speakers and situations. Perspectives also reveal the personal qualities and types of interpersonal relationships that are valued by the group. My goal is to connect the three contrasting, gendered cultural perspectives African American women expressed about their talk to one aspect of "multiple jeopardy," the disparaging stereotypes that have formed the dominant consensus about black womanhood and black women's speech throughout most of U.S. history. These stereotypes are central elements of the discourse environment (van Dijk, 1987) in which African American women speak and develop their attitudes toward their own language and speaking styles. I suggest that each of the perspectives represents African American women's effort to positively conceive their talk in the face of the disparaging conceptions they routinely encounter in both the dominant and ethnic cultures that are the predominate settings for their communicative lives. In other words, I offer an inquiry into some of the socio-political bases for black women's conceptions of their communication styles. As Henley and Kramarae (1994) point out, feminist scholars recognize that descriptions of women's talk are of limited value unless they advance understanding of women's relationship to the social order.

THE PARTICIPANTS AND THE STUDY

I set out to gather and interpret qualitative data about how middle-class and aspiring middle-class African American women view their communication styles in relation to those of African American men and white women and men. I used a seven-item free-response questionnaire in which I asked, "How would you describe the following ways of speaking: 'women's talk,' 'black talk,' 'black women's talk,' 'black men's talk,' 'white talk,' 'white women's talk,' or 'white men's talk?'" The questionnaire was not intended as a quantifiable, "scientific" measure, but as a source of narrative descriptions.

The 134 African American women who responded to the questionnaire varied in age, socio-economic class, regional provenance, and the racial configuration of the neighborhoods in which they grew up. Most (104) were undergraduate students enrolled in introductory communication, English, sociology, and psychology classes at a black women's college located in the Southeast with a student body recruited from throughout the nation. The remainder (30) were professional women (aged 22 to above 50) who grew up in various regions of the U.S. and were currently working in the Southeast; their responses were solicited by students enrolled in an upper-level communication and gender seminar. Because all of the participants had or were acquiring college degrees and professional jobs, it is not surprising that most (110) self-identified as "middle class." Although 58 described themselves as growing up in "mostly black" neighborhoods, 72 described their neighborhoods as "mostly white" or "multi-racial" (the remaining 4 had lived in several different types of neighborhoods while growing up).

I encouraged participants to make their responses as lengthy or brief as they wished; the majority (109) were in the form of word lists, phrases or single sentences; 11 were narratives of two sentences or more. As I began a content analysis of the responses,[3] the most glaring, and troubling, results that emerged were that 14 of the women who completed the questionnaire chose not to describe "black women's talk," and another 13 wrote statements that suggested they resisted (or resented) the request to describe it. These resistant responses and non-responses came from women in all the demographic groups described above. Why would 20% of the participants in this study (27 African American women) evade the task of describing their own talk?

As a feminist scholar, I wanted to account for all responses in some manner, even the non-responses; to use a metaphor familiar to feminist researchers, I wanted to listen to all the voices in the text and to attend to the silences as well. It was reflection on the non-responses as well as the full range of written responses that led me to consider the perspectives participants took on the idea that "black women's talk" can or should be described as a distinct, identifiable style or repertoire of styles. In the remainder of this discussion, I describe what I have labeled the evasive, accommodating, and celebratory perspectives on black women's talk and their relationships women routinely construct definitions of their talk and conduct their communicative lives.

PERSPECTIVES ON BLACK WOMEN'S TALK

Evasion

In this perspective I include the 27 women who either did not respond or who wrote responses that resisted the question, such as the following:

- [Black women's talk] suggests nothing in particular.
- [Black women's talk] is no different from women's talk in general.
- I can't describe talking like a black woman because all black women don't talk alike; you can't generalize.

All written evasive responses were brief, that is, one sentence or phrase, such as those above; their tone was self-assured and sometimes vehement:

- There is no description for talking like a black woman.
- How would I describe black women's talk? I wouldn't!

Of the many possible reasons for evasive responses, I suggest the following two. First, Susan Ervin-Tripp has pointed out that it is often difficult for speakers to sufficiently objectify their own speech in order to discern its features (Ervin-Tripp, 1968). Both a non-response and a resistant response may be the result of a woman's inability to distance herself enough from her own talk to perceive its gendered cultural markings.

The second, more compelling reason for evasive responses, I believe, has to do with how black women speakers and black women's speech is constructed in the U.S. American social order. Because the U.S. is a hierarchically structured, multi-cultural society in which marginalized groups have little control over the dominant consensus about any of their culture-based behaviors, some members of marginalized groups inevitably internalize dominant cultural evaluations of their ethnic language and communication style, even if those evaluations are overtly prejudiced (van Dijk, 1987). One black feminist scholar has described the dominant consensus about black women within U.S. American society in the following rather striking manner:

> Black women embody by their sheer physical presence two of the most hated identities in this . . . country. Whiteness and maleness . . . have not only been seen as physical identities but codified into states of being and worldviews. The codification of Blackness and femaleness by whites and males is contained in the terms "thinking like a woman" and "acting like a nigger." White/male worldview would be that of thinking and acting like a "nigger woman" (Bethel, 1982).

There is abundant evidence of the "negative coding" of black womanhood in the U.S. Qualities the dominant culture defines as undesirable in women in general are frequently projected onto individual African American women (Manning-Marable & Houston, 1995) as well as onto African American women as a social group (Anderson, 1997). Historically, almost all the undesirable feminine qualities, from promiscuity to intellectual inferiority to outspokenness, have been used to disparage black women (Collins, 2000; Essed, 1991; Guy-Sheftall, 1990, 1995).

In popular entertainment, for example, black women who were loud, smart-alecky, and/or ungrammatical speakers were stock characters in early nineteenth- and early twentieth-century minstrel shows and continued to be reproduced in such mass media characters as "Sapphire" of the *Amos and Andy* radio and television programs, "Mammy" of the film *Gone With the Wind,* and "Florence" of television's *The Jeffersons* (Anderson, 1997; Merritt, 1997). When producers of pseudo-realistic daytime television talk shows encourage teenage and young adult black women guests to be particularly obstreperous, the long-standing stereotype that uncivil, ungrammatical, and traditionally unfeminine communication are central features of black women's talk is reinforced.

The mass media are not the only dominant cultural contexts in which black women's speech and black women speakers are coded negatively. In her study of black women's interpersonal interracial encounters, Philomena Essed (1991) demonstrates that any speaker or any discourse marked as black and female is likely to be pejoratively evaluated. Essed argues that racism and sexism are inseparable interpretations of African American women's discourse, and that the dominant culture exerts tremendous pressure on African American women to assimilate by communicating in ways that are as non-black as possible. (See also Etter-Lewis, 1993; St. Jean & Feagin, 1998.)

But African American women not only encounter negative coding and an urge to assimilate in dominant cultural contexts. Members of marginalized groups do not develop speaking norms and values in isolation from those of the dominant group; thus some African Americans who recognize pragmatic reasons for not conforming to dominant cultural norms nevertheless valorize those norms as ideal behaviors (Hannerz, 1970). This tension between ethnic and dominant cultural norms and behaviors is implied in the concept of multiple consciousness. For example, a black woman may recognize that black women's tradition of work outside the home has resulted in cultural expectations of egalitarian male-female relational communication (Ladner, 1971; Houston Stanback, 1985); nevertheless, she may idealize the more passive, submissive communication style considered traditional for white women. The valorization of dominant cultural norms for women's talk seems to underlie black men's portrayal of black women as domineering speakers, for example as "verbal castrators" (Abrahams, 1975; Bond & Peery, 1970; Rogers-Rose, 1980; Spillers, 1979), or as contentious "hard mouths" (Folb, 1980).

Nowhere was the tension between African American and dominant cultural linguistic norms more apparent than in the controversy over teaching "Ebonics" in the Oakland public schools which erupted in the national media in December 1996 (Locke, 1996). In her contribution to a special issue of *The Black Scholar* on "Ebonics," Rosina Lippi-Green (1997) summarizes the dialectical language attitudes of the masses of African Americans:

> The greater African American community seems to accept the inevitability of linguistic assimilation to mainstream U.S. English in certain settings, but there is also deep unhappiness about the necessity in many quarters. . . . To make two statements: *I acknowledge that my home language is viable and adequate, and I acknowledge that my home language will never be accepted*, is to set up an unresolvable conflict. (p. 9)

I suggest that evasive responses are one way respondents to my study endeavored to resolve this conflict. Because African American womanhood and Af-

rican American women's talk so often are maligned in both the dominant and ethnic cultures, the women who responded evasively, with silence or verbal resistance to the idea of *black* women's talk, may have conceived the question as a request for pejorative stereotypes of their language and speaking style (e.g., talking like a "nigger woman"). Those who had internalized the dominant consensus about "black women's talk" as linguistically unacceptable and stylistically unfeminine may have been unable to conceive a self-affirming way of describing their talk as black women except as singular (not generalizable to other *black* women) or as "no different" from the talk of women who are not black. When we consider the socio-political context in which respondents endeavored to describe their talk, evasive responses that appear to deny the existence of distinct black women's speaking styles can be more usefully understood as strategies for resisting racist and sexist stereotypes of those styles.

Accommodation

A small number (4) of the women who participated in the study took what I call the accommodationist perspective on black women's talk. This perspective is illustrated by the following response:

- If [a black woman] is around her friends, she will use slang . . . and if she is speaking with a group of business associates she will talk intellectually.

Rather than evading the idea of black women's talk, the woman who wrote this response valorized speakers who can use both an informal African American speaking style and a formal, mainstream American style.

By recognizing the need to switch styles, the women who took this perspective, like those who took the evasive perspective, indicated awareness of the dominant consensus that speech marked as "black" and "female" is inferior, lacking in prestige and social power. But they were more explicit about the components of their style, specifying an African American English lexicon, context sensitivity, and communicative flexibility as characterizing black women's talk:

- Talking like a black woman would depend on [the] social conditions and what education the woman had, but there could be talk about black men and how blacks, especially women, are treated.
- [Black women's talk is] anything [from what is] said between individuals living in a rural setting to communication that takes place in the world of "high society" Blacks. It takes on many different forms given the scope of the topics and situation.

Respondents' descriptions of style-switching parallel those of language and communication scholars who also argue that style-switching is most often situation dependent, and that in order for African American speakers to alternate styles they must acquire a command of African American styles through socialization in African American speech communities, and of a mainstream style through formal education, or through a combination of education and modeling (e.g., by bi-stylistic parents) (Baugh, 1983; Nelson, 1990).

Like evasion, accommodation can be traced to the tension created by a social order that engenders multiple consciousness in African American women. Bi-cultural behaviors, such as communication style-switching, are one way of resolving that tension, especially for educated professional women whose lives require them to meet the communicative demands of both the ethnic and dominant cultural milieus (Bell, 1983; Bucholtz, 1966; Dill, 1979; Rubin & Garner, 1984; St. Jean & Feagin, 1998).

Celebration

Most of the respondents (107) resisted and transcended stereotypic perceptions of black women's talk to offer alternative descriptions that spoke to the self-affirming interpersonal qualities that they considered central to their communication styles. This is the perspective that I call "celebratory." Celebratory responses were characterized by positive evolutions of black women's communication behaviors, including those that are often pejoratively stereotyped by others. The largest number of celebratory responses (49) focused on underlying social and interpersonal functions of talk, that is, on communication strategies and attributes of the speaker. Here are a few examples:

- [Black women's talk is] talking with intimacy [and] deep caring; [it is] highly intuitive, and charged with an other-worldly quality. It connotes that the conversation is humanistic, principled, and based on inner convictions.
- A black woman's talk may be out of protest so she's going to be heard. Talking like a black woman also suggests that the conversation may be really down to earth.
- [Black women's talk is] candidness, use of emphasis and intensity, "joaning,"[4] loudness; often entertaining and comical in her use of expressions ("honey," "child," "sugar"), especially characteristic of Southern black women.

Three dimensions of black women's interpersonal communication style are suggested by the celebra-tory descriptions, each indicating the goals, strategies, and outcomes of talk that are valued by black women speakers: wisdom, fortitude, and caring.

Wisdom Geneva Smitherman (1997) agues that communication scholars often place so much emphasis on the dynamic expressive style of black speakers, they ignore the high value blacks place on the substance of talk. Citing the criticism of dynamic but vacuous discourse in a once-popular soul song entitled, "Talkin' Loud, but Sayin' Nothin'," Smitherman reminds us that through the "rich verbal interplay among everyday people, lessons and precepts about [black] life and survival are handed down from generation to generation" (p. 73).

The ethnic cultural priority placed on the substance of talk is reflected in responses that describe what I term the wisdom dimension of black women's talk. The emphasis on wisdom and knowledge is one of two important distinctions between the stereotypes of black women's talk (as smart-alecky, domineering, obstreperous) and black women's own experience and understanding of their talk.

The women who took the celebratory perspective not only constructed black women's talk as substantive but constructed themselves as authorities. They described a variety of bases for their authority, including intellect, formal education, life experiences, common sense, moral principles, and intuition. While many responses described black women as generally knowledgeable, those that focused on the topics of black women's talk (30) gave some sense of respondents' perceptions of the domains of black women's knowledge. Topical responses can be grouped into two major categories: talk about black men and talk about black women's personal and professional lives. The women referred to talk that criticized certain black male behaviors (e.g., infidelity) as well as talk that supported individual black men or empathized with the situation of black men as a social group. The majority of topical descriptors referred to talk about women's personal and professional lives, including "how black women are treated in the white patriarchal society," "sisterhood," "single motherhood," "being a working woman," "female strength and independence," and "bettering yourself."

Fortitude In their study of black perspectives on interracial communication, Hecht, Ribeau and Alberts (1989) make several references to black women's talk as "tough"; their two black women informants told them that black women "have had to be so tough as the head of the household throughout history that they 'tend to talk tough and make fun of white women who are soft'" and that "'Talking tough' is a way of carrying oneself. . . . Black females historically have had to take charge, and this has led to strength" (pp. 385–410). The word "tough" was never used by the women who responded to my questionnaire; however, they used a total of 27 other, more positively connoted words and phrases to describe what I term the dimension of fortitude in black women's talk. This was, by far, the largest number of descriptors used for any category; they included: "strong," "stern," "firm," "challenging," "with authority," "direct," "candid," "with assertion," and "says exactly what's on her mind."

In expressing fortitude, respondents frequently combined descriptions of strength and assertiveness. Unlike the African American women quoted by Hecht and his co-authors (1989), those in this study did not consider themselves to have been forced by circumstances to adopt a façade of strength. Instead, they constructed fortitude as a desirable quality in women communicators and women's communication. Their descriptions related fortitude to forthrightness ("getting down to the heart of the matter"), seriousness ("in-depth conversation"), sincerity ("meaning everything they say"), and the absence of pretension ("down to earth"). In addition, they often coupled descriptors related to fortitude (e.g., "powerful," "firm," "determined") with descriptors related to self-esteem (e.g., "self-assured," "confident," "speaks with pride and dignity"). The following are typical responses:

- [Black women's talk is the talk of] a strong woman with a lot of pride in who she is and what she believes in.
- [Black women's talk is] talking like you believe in yourself. You are speaking with strength.
- [Black women's talk is] assertive and proud talk.

This dimension of black women's talk is best understood when we keep in mind that it is realized and valued in the context of wisdom. Taken together, the two dimensions indicate that black women value speaking out and speaking strongly, but not without a basis in knowledge and experience. They do *not* value talking loud but saying nothing. In addition, we should not confuse fortitude or strength with dominance, an error that leads to stereotyping black women as domineering and obstreperous. An assertive speaker who conveys strongly held opinions and ideas is not necessarily one who wishes to exert undue control over the conversation, to silence others. My analysis of conversations among black women, between black and white women, and between black women and men demonstrates that black women do not engage in

such dominance behaviors as monopolizing talk time, controlling topics, or interrupting more than they are interrupted by their conversational partners (Houston Stanback, 1983; Houston, forthcoming).

Caring Collins (2000) emphasizes an "ethic of care" as a central element of black feminist epistemology and describes it as most often manifest in the high value placed on personal expressiveness and the interrelationship between cognitive and affective involvement in interaction. Earlier, I noted that the wisdom dimension was one important distinction between the stereotypes of black women's talk and black women's own experience of their talk. Their emphasis on caring is another important distinction. The relationship between expressions of caring and fortitude is illustrated in the following descriptions:

- [Black women's talk] reflects a warmth and sensitivity that is characteristic of their personalities; since they have to face so much in this society they are more nurturing to their families and husbands; caring.
- [Black women] will tell the truth if asked, even if it hurts (provided it's for the better).

The second response emphasizes the context-sensitive nature of black women's forthright speech. In contrast to whites who eschew confrontational talk (Foeman & Pressley, 1987), black women perceive forthrightness as caring, supportive discourse in some contexts, "if asked . . . [and] provided it's for the better." Most descriptors of the caring dimension of black women's talk were embedded in lists or narratives describing the other two dimensions as well; descriptors respondents frequently used were "concerned," "compassionate," "sensitive," "warm," and "humanistic."

SUMMARY

Despite a discourse environment rife with racist and sexist stereotypes of their communication, both within and outside their own social group, most of the African American women in my study constructed an alternative, self-affirming, celebratory vision of their talk that emphasizes speaking knowledgably, assertively, and sensitively. This majority perspective stresses the social and interpersonal goals and strategies of talk. While the linguistic style-switching entailed in the accommodation perspective is dependent on socio-economic class and/or education (Seymour & Seymour, 1979; Nelson, 1990), the features of talk emphasized in the celebratory perspective are not necessarily linked to class or educational status. Further research is needed to determine whether the speaking perspectives of African American working-class women are similar to those of the middle-class (and aspiring middle-class) women in this study, as well as whether there are class-related differences in African American women's ways of *expressing* wisdom, fortitude, and caring interpersonal interactions.

CONCLUSION

Throughout their history in the United States, African American women have actively constructed an alternative definition of themselves and their behavior that defied the derogatory judgments of their intellectual abilities and disproved the pejorative stereotypes of their moral character promulgated by the dominant culture (Collins, 2000; Guy-Sheftall, 1995). In this discussion, evasion, accommodation, and celebration were designated as three perspectives taken by African American women in describing their talk. Admittedly, speaking perspectives tell us how individuals think about talk, but not how they use language in actual communication interactions. Yet they provide vital information about the communication behaviors speakers value and expect. In addition, perspectives suggest key elements of the frames speakers use to interpret talk.

The heterogeneity of African American women's lived experiences, suggested by the concepts "multiple jeopardy" and "multiple consciousness" (King, 1988), is reflected in the contrasting perspectives on their talk described in this discussion. Although a majority expressed the celebratory perspective, focusing on wisdom, fortitude, and caring as desirable features of their interpersonal style, a few chose to describe their talk as accommodating the language and communication demands of both the ethnic and dominant cultures, and others evaded the task of offering a specific description. Each of these ways of conceiving their talk demonstrated the respondent's struggle to positively construct her voice in the midst of a discourse environment that continues to disparage speech and speakers marked as black *and* woman.

NOTES

1. Throughout this discussion the terms "black" and "African American" will be used interchangeably.
2. "Multiple consciousness" is an extension of the concept "double consciousness" developed by the African American sociologist W. E. B. DuBois (1937) to

describe the social outlooks of blacks in the United States.

3. Content analysis was done by the author using a combination of repeated manual searches of the responses and the list-processing computer program PC-File III (Button, 1984). Details can be found in Houston (1992, April), obtainable from the author.
4. "Joaning" is one contemporary term for those African American speech events that involve using teasing or kidding to criticize or "talk about" another (e.g., "signifying" [Smitherman, 1977; Garner, 1983], "loud-talking" and "marking" [Mitchell-Kernan, 1972]).

REFERENCES

Abrahams, R. D. (1975). Negotiating respect: Patterns of presentation among black women. *Journal of American Folklore, 88,* 58–80.

Anderson, L. M. (1997). *Mammies no more: The changing image of black women on stage and screen.* Lanham, MD: Rowman & Littlefield.

Baugh, J. (1983). *Black street speech.* Austin, TX: University of Texas Press.

Beale, F. (1970). Double jeopardy: To be black and female. In T. Cade (Ed.), *The black woman* (pp. 90–100). New York: Signet.

Bell, M. J. (1983). *The world from Brown's Lounge: An ethnography of black middle class play.* Urbana, IL: University of Illinois Press.

Bethel, L. (1982). This infinity of conscious pain: Zora Neal Hurston and the black female literary tradition. In G. T. Hull, P. Bell Scott, & B. Smith (Eds.), *All the women are white, all the blacks are men: But some of us are brave.* Old Westbury, NY: The Feminist Press.

Bond, J. C. & Peery, P. (1970). Is the black male castrated? In T. Cade (Ed.), *The black woman* (pp. 101–110). New York: Signet.

Bucholtz, M. (1996). Black feminist theory and African American women's linguistic practice. In V. L. Bergvall, J. M. Bing & A. F. Freed (Eds.), *Rethinking language and gender research: Theory and practice* (pp. 267–290). London: Longman.

Button, J. (1984). PC-File III [Computer program]. Bellevue, WA: Buttonware.

Collins, P. H. (2000). *Black feminist thought: Knowledge, consciousness, and the politics of empowerment,* rev. ed. New York: Routledge.

Davis, A. Y. (1981). *Women, race, and class.* New York: Random House.

Dill, B. T. (1979). The dialectics of black womanhood. *Signs, 4,* 543–57.

Dubois, W. E. B. (1937). *The souls of black folk* (21st ed.). Chicago: McClug.

Ervin-Tripp, S. (1968). An analysis of the interaction of language, topic, and listener. In Joshua Fishman (Ed.),

Readings in the sociology of language (pp. 192–211). The Hague, Netherlands: Mouton.

Essed, P. (1991). *Understanding everyday racism: An interdisciplinary theory.* Newbury Park, CA: Sage.

Etter-Lewis, G. (1993). *My soul is my own: Oral narratives of African American women in the professions.* New York: Routledge.

Foeman, A. K. & Pressley, G. (1987). Ethnic culture and corporate culture: using black styles in organizations. *Communication Quarterly, 33,* 293–307.

Folb, E. (1980). Gender. In her *Runnin' down some lines: The language and culture of black teenagers* (pp. 193–98). Cambridge, MA: Harvard University Press.

Garner, T. (1983). Playing the dozens: Folklore as strategies for living. *Quarterly Journal of Speech, 69,* 47–57.

Guy-Sheftall, B. (1990). *Daughters of sorrow: Attitudes toward black women, 1880–1920.* New York: Carlson Publishing.

Guy-Sheftall, B. (1995). Introduction: The evolution of feminist consciousness among African American women. In her *Words of fire: An anthology of African American feminist thought* (pp. 1–24). New York: New Press.

Hannerz, U. (1970). The notion of ghetto culture. In J. F. Szwed (Ed.), *Black America* (pp. 99–109). New York: Basic Books.

Hecht, M., Ribeau, S., & Alberts, J. K. (1989). An Afro-American perspective on interethnic communication. *Communication Monographs,* 56, 385–410.

Henley, N. & Kramarae, C. (1994). Gender, power, and miscommunication. In C. Roman, S. Juhasz, & C. Miller (Eds.), *The women and language debate: A sourcebook* (pp. 383–406). New Brunswick, NJ: Rutgers University Press.

hooks, b. (1981). *Ain't I a woman?: Black women and feminism.* Boston: South End Press.

hooks, b. (1984). *Feminist theory: From margin to center.* Boston: South End Press.

Houston, M. (1992, April). *Listening to ourselves: African-American women's perspectives on their communication style.* Paper presented to Gender Studies Division, Southern States Communication Association, San Antonio, TX.

Houston, M. (Forthcoming). Triumph stories: Caring and accountability in African American women's conversation narratives. In M. Houston & O. I. Davis (Eds.), *Centering ourselves: African American feminist and womanist studies of discourse.* Cresskill, NJ: Hampton Press.

Houston Stanback, M. (1983). Code-switching in black women's speech (Doctoral dissertation, University of Massachusetts). *Dissertation Abstracts International, 84* (01), 105 (University Microfilms No. TX1–384–886).

Houston Stanback, M. (1985). Language and black woman's place: Evidence from the black middle class. In P. A. Treichler, C. Kramarae, & B. Stafford (Eds.), *For alma mater: Theory and practice in feminist scholarship* (pp. 177–93). Urbana, IL: University of Illinois Press.

King, D. K. (1988). Multiple jeopardy, multiple consciousness: The context of a black feminist ideology. *Signs, 14* (Autumn), 42–72.

Ladner, J. (1971). *Tomorrow's tomorrow: The black women.* Garden City, NY: Doubleday-Anchor.

Lippi-Green, R. (1997). What we talk about when we talk about Ebonics: Why definitions matter. *The Black Scholar, 27* (2), 7–11.

Locke, M. (22 December 1996). Debate over Black English heats up: Critics call it an insult to students. *The New Orleans Times-Picayune,* p. A24.

Manning-Marable, C. & Houston, M. (1995). Toward an understanding of agenda-building discourse by African American women: The case of Lani Guinier. *Women and Language, 18* (1), 34–36.

Merritt, B. (1997). Illusive reflections: African American women in primetime television. In A. Gonzalez, M. Houston, & V. Chen (Eds.), *Our voices: Essays in culture, ethnicity and communication* (2nd ed.) (pp. 52–60). Los Angeles, CA: Roxbury.

Mitchell-Kernan, C. (1972). Signifying, loud-talking, and marking. In T. Kochman (Ed.), *Rappin' and stylin' out* (pp. 315–335). Urbana, IL: University of Illinois Press.

Nelson, L. W. (1990). Code-switching in the oral life narratives of African American women: Challenges to linguistic hegemony. *Journal of Education, 172* (3), 142–55.

Rogers-Rose, L. (1980). Dialectics of black male-female relationships. In her *The black woman* (pp. 251–264). Newbury Park, CA: Sage.

Rubin, D. & Garner, T. (1984, November). *Middle class blacks' perceptions of dialect and style switching.* Paper presented to Speech Communication Association, Chicago, IL.

Seymour, H. & Seymour, C. (1979). The symbolism of Ebonics: I'd rather switch than fight. *Journal of Black Studies, 9,* 367–82.

Smitherman, G. (1977). *Talkin' and testifyin': The language of Black America.* Boston: Houghton Mifflin.

Spillers, H. (1979). The politics of intimacy: A discussion. In R. Bell, B. Parker, & B. Guy-Sheftall (Eds.), *Sturdy black bridges: Visions of black women in literature* (pp. 87–106). New York: Anchor.

St. Jean, Y. & Feagin, J. R. (1998). *Double burden: Black women and everyday racism.* Armonk, NY: M. E. Sharpe.

van Dijk, T. A. (1987). *Communicating racism: Ethnic prejudice in thought and talk.* Newbury Park, CA: Sage.

CHECK YOUR UNDERSTANDING

1. In what ways did African American women conceive of their talk?
2. Describe the talk of women in your cultural group. How does this talk compare with Houston's account of African American women's talk?
3. What is "multiple jeopardy"?
4. Can you think of examples of negative coding in the media of Latino women's talk? Asian women's talk? White women's talk?
5. Do you agree that it is often difficult for people to metacommunicate? Suppose Houston asked you to describe you talk. What would you say?

Intercultural Conflict: A Culture-Based Situational Model

Stella Ting-Toomey and John Oetzel

Competent conflict management requires us to communicate adaptively and flexibly in diverse conflict situations. It requires us to be sensitive to the differences and similarities across a wide range of cultural and situational factors that affect the intercultural conflict episode. Effective conflict negotiation demands that we be mindful of our own ethnocentric biases when making hasty judgments of other people's conflict styles. It also demands that we be attuned to the multiple layers of the antecedent, process, and outcome of an intercultural encounter episode.

Although the study of intercultural conflict is a complex phenomenon, understanding conflict along a cultural variability perspective serves as the beginning step in understanding conflict variations among different clusters of cultures. A *cultural variability perspective* emphasizes the value variation dimensions of individualism-collectivism and power distance and how these dimensions influence conflict management processes. These value dimensions, in conjunction with individual personality attributes and situational factors, influence the expectations and attitudes we hold in approaching or side-stepping various conflicts in our everyday lives. Cultural value dimensions, as mediated through situational features, affect the way we experience the conflict, define the conflict, and attribute meanings to the micro-events that take place in the conflict.

Many factors affect our competent management of an intercultural conflict episode. To explain these factors, we need a model to organize, relate, and explain concepts in a coherent fashion. This chapter introduces a culture-based situational model and examines some of the cultural, personal, and situational factors that shape face-to-face intercultural conflict. We identify four clusters of factors in this model: (1) primary orientation factors: cultural value patterns, personal attributes, conflict norms, and face concerns; (2) situational and relationship boundary features: intergroup boundaries, relationship parameters, conflict goal assessments, and conflict intensity; (3) conflict communication process factors: conflict styles, facework strategies, emotional expressions, and conflict rhythms; and (4) conflict competence features (see Figure 1).

A CULTURE-BASED SITUATIONAL CONFLICT MODEL: PRIMARY ORIENTATION FACTORS

In conflict episodes that include two polarized intercultural parties, the participants often carry with them different cultural lenses and values, face concerns, and distinctive conflict styles in dealing with the escalatory conflict spirals. These different conflict lenses and patterns often affect the core expectations and attitudes indicating how an intercultural conflict should be approached, managed, and resolved. In an intercultural conflict situation, different conflict lenses often sustain the conflict and serve as major obstacles to

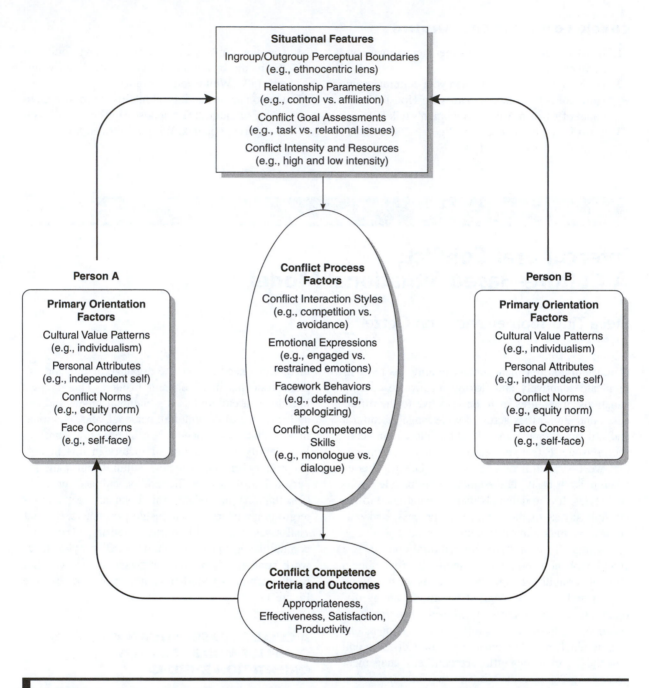

FIGURE 1 An Intercultural Conflict Episode: A Culture-Based Situational Conflict Model

genuine intercultural and interpersonal understanding. By understanding the larger cultural grounding and situational features that influence the use of various conflict styles and facework behaviors, we can understand the logic that motivates actions by intercultural others. We begin with a discussion of primary cultural value patterns.

Cultural Value Patterns

The hidden dimensions of intercultural conflict often stem, in part, from differences in cultural values that give rise to different ideals that determine how conflicts should be managed. Although national cultures differ in many value orientations, two value frameworks that have received consistent attention from intercultural researchers are individualism-collectivism and power distance (Gudykunst & Ting-Toomey, 1988; Hofstede, 1991; Ting-Toomey, 1999; Triandis, 1995).

Personal Attributes

An alternative way to understand individualism and collectivism and power distance focuses on how individuals conceptualize the sense of self. We must remember that within-culture variations exist in each culture. In individualistic cultures, there are those who act just like collectivists. Likewise, in collectivistic cultures, there are people who behave just like individualists. We must also keep in mind that behavior is only a partial indicator of a person's identity. To understand a "full-fledged" independent or interdependent person, we must also examine the thinking and affective pattern of this individual. Markus and Kitayama (1991) argue that our self-conception within our culture profoundly influences our communication with others: Individuals with a strong independent sense of self tend to see themselves as autonomous, self-reliant, unencumbered, and rational choice makers; individuals with a strong interdependent sense of self tend to see themselves as ingroup-bound, obligatory agents, and relational peacemakers. Both types of self-construal exist within a culture. Overall, however, independent concepts of self are more common in individualistic cultures, and interdependent concepts of self are more common in collectivistic cultures.

Independent-self individuals tend to make sense of their environment through autonomous-self lenses. In comparison, interdependent-self individuals tend to make sense of their surrounding through ingroup-self lenses. Independent-self types tend to worry about whether they present their unique self credibly and competently in front of others. Interdependent-self types tend to be more attuned to what others think of their face image in the context of ingroup-outgroup relations. When communicating with others, high independents believe in voicing their personal opinions, striving for personal goals, and assertively expressing their conflict needs. On the other hand, high interdependents tend to be more circumspect in an interpersonal conflict situation. They prefer self-restraint and self-monitoring strategies to approach a conflict in order not to bring relational chaos or disharmony. They practice other-centered communication in anticipating the thoughts and feelings of the other person in the conflict situation (Gudykunst et al., 1996).

Juxtaposed to the above self-construal idea, we can examine power distance from a personal level. In-

dividuals and their behaviors can be conceptualized as either moving toward the "horizontal-self" spectrum or the "vertical-self" spectrum. Individuals who endorse horizontal self-construals prefer informal-symmetrical interactions (i.e., equal treatment) regardless of one's position, status, rank, or age. In comparison, individuals who emphasize vertical self-construals prefer formal-asymmetrical interactions (i.e., deferential treatment) with due respect to one's position, title, and age. As Triandis (1995) observes,

> This [conceptualization] means that people will seek different kinds of relationships and when possible "convert" a relationship to the kind that they are most comfortable with. Thus, a professor from a horizontal-based self may convert a professor-student relationship to a friend-friend relationship, which may well confuse a student from a vertical-based self. (p. 164)

Although horizontal selves tend to predominate in small power distance cultures, vertical selves tend to predominate in large power distance cultures.

Conflict Norms

Cultural values and personal attributes influence the norms that we use in a conflict interaction episode. Norms are prescriptive standards that we apply to assess culturally "reasonable" or "unreasonable" behaviors in a conflict situation. Norms are implicit or explicit guidelines for evaluating competent or incompetent conflict behavior, such as listening to a high-status person's perspective during a conflict. They are reflected through our expectations of what constitutes appropriate or effective actions in a given setting. Norms are driven by the underlying beliefs and value patterns in a cultural system. . . .

Face Concerns

Hu (1944) provided one of the earliest definitions of face when he argued that there are two types of face in Chinese culture: *lien* and *mianzi*. *Lien* refers to the moral character of an individual, whereas *mianzi* refers to the social status achieved through success in life. The two concepts can be viewed as interdependent constructs; they can also be understood separately. To understand the concept of face on the deep level, we have to understand the moral conditioning or moral drives (e.g., shame, guilt) of the self. However, in the context of explaining intercultural conflict, the concept of face is cast at a midrange level—that is, the concept of a negotiated social self-image.

Face is an important social self-concept in China (Gao & Ting-Toomey, 1998), Japan (Morisaki &

Gudykunst, 1994), Korea (Lim & Choi, 1996), Colombia (Fitch, 1998), Mexico (Garcia, 1996), and many Arab countries (Katriel, 1986). Morisaki and Gudykunst (1994), for example, pointed out that there are two types of social face in Japanese culture; one is *mentsu* and the other is *taimen*. *Mentsu* is similar to the social status concept of *mianzi* in Chinese culture, whereas *taimen* refers to the appearance of impression one presents to others.

Although the concept of face originated in Eastern cultures, people in all cultures share aspects of face. Face can be lost, saved, and protected. All members of a society want to present and protect their own public images (Brown & Levinson, 1978; Goffman, 1959). Previous studies indicate that the concept of face is used across cultures; however, the meanings and usages are different depending on the culture (Condon, 1984; Ting-Toomey, 1988).

We define *face* as the claimed sense of favorable social self-worth and the simultaneous assessment of other-worth in an interpersonal situation (Ting-Toomey & Kurogi, 1998). It is a vulnerable resource in social interaction because this resource can be threatened, enhanced, bargained over, and maintained. Face is a cluster of identity- and relations-based issues that simmer and surface before, during, and after the conflict process. Face is associated with respect, honor, status, reputation, credibility, competence, network connection, and relational obligation issues. Face has simultaneous affective (e.g., feelings of shame and pride), cognitive (e.g., calculating how much to give and to receive), and behavioral levels.

Face consists of three dimensions: (1) locus of face—concern for self, other, or both; (2) face valence—whether face is being defended, maintained, or honored; and (3) temporality—whether face is being restored or proactively protected (Rogan & Hammer, 1994; Ting-Toomey & Cole, 1990). We focus our discussion on the locus of face because it is the primary dimension of face and determines the direction of the subsequent conflict messages. *Self-face* is the protective concern for one's own image when one's own face is threatened in the conflict situation. *Other-face,* on the other hand, is the concern for accommodating the other conflict party's image in the conflict crisis situation. *Mutual-face* is the concern for both parties' images, the image of the relationship, or all three (Ting-Toomey, 1988; Ting-Toomey & Kurogi, 1998).

Whereas individualists or independents tend to be more concerned with protecting or preserving self-face images during an ongoing conflict episode, collectivists or interdependents tend to more concerned with either accommodating the other-face images or saving mutual-face images during a conflict. . . .

Situational and Relationship Boundary Features

Situational and relationship boundary features refer to two aspects: (1) the physical setting and work activity in a particular interaction and (2) the nature of the relationship that you have with the other party. To manage intercultural conflict mindfully, we have to understand the features that mediate between the primary orientation factors on the one hand, and the conflict communication process factors on the other. How individuals draw ingroup–outgroup boundaries, how they perceive the nature of their relationship, and how they evaluate the different goal types will have a profound influence on the conflict styles and facework behaviors exhibited in an intercultural conflict episode. We discuss each of these features in this section.

Ingroup–Outgroup Perceptual Boundaries The drawing of an ingroup–outgroup boundary involves intergroup perceptions and attributions. Intergroup perception is the process of selecting cues from the social environment, organizing the cues into some coherent pattern, and interpreting and dissecting the pattern into a dichotomy of "Us versus Them." According to Triandis (1995), *ingroups* are groups of individuals "about whose welfare a person is concerned, with whom that person is willing to cooperate without demanding equitable returns, and separation from whom leads to anxiety" (p. 9). Ingroups are usually characterized by members who perceive a common fate or shared attributes among them. *Outgroups* are groups of individuals that are perceived as disconnected, unequal, or threatening in some way. Outgroups are groups that carry very different characteristics or attributes, and often these attributes are in conflict with one's ingroup standards.

It is important to note that members of collectivistic cultures make a greater distinction between ingroups and outgroups than do members of individualistic cultures (Triandis, 1995). It usually takes time, patience, and a long-term commitment to move from the outgroup to the ingroup boundary in a collectivistic-based culture. Collectivists tend to practice greater other-face concerns with ingroup members and greater self-face concerns with outgroup members. In contrast, individualists have greater self-face concerns in dealing with *both* ingroup and outgroup members. For highly important conflicts, both collectivists and individualists prefer the use of the equity norm when competing with outgroup members for needed resources. For example, both individualistic and collectivistic managers from different companies would compete with each other for a contract by showing that they deserve it more than other bidders. For less important conflicts, however, collectivists prefer the use of the communal norm with either ingroup or outgroup members, opting for maintaining surface relational harmony over getting too "worked up" dealing with irritants (Leung & Iwawaki, 1988). . . .

Relationship Parameters Another feature of situational and relationship boundary features is relationship parameters. *Relationship parameters* can be understood in terms of three dimensions: competition–cooperation, affiliation–control, and trust–distrust (Lewicki & Bunker, 1995; Rubin & Levinger, 1995). In an intercultural conflict episode, conflict combatants may emphasize different features of the perceived relationship parameters. Relationship parameters affect how we frame a conflict. Framing is critical to how two conflict parties view one another and how they view their relationship and the conflict task. Framing directs our attention and steers our focus to what is at stake in a conflict.

The first set of relationship parameters concerns the competitive cooperative dimension. If members frame the relationship as purely competitive, they are likely to use conflict and facework strategies that enhance individual (or ingroup) gains and minimize individual (or ingroup) loss. If members frame the relationship as somewhat cooperative in nature, they are more likely to maximize mutual gains and less likely to push away the other conflict party in their negotiation behavior.

At some point, conflict disputants may realize that the conflict is a mixed-motive arrangement that requires both cooperative and competitive moves—especially if the relationship is highly interdependent. If two disputants each have something that the other wants or needs, then some degree of cooperation will be essential, whether it is dividing the resources equally, trading off different resources, or expanding the resource pie collaboratively.

The second set of relationship parameters concerns the affiliation–control dimension. *Affiliation* involves social ties and intimacy issues, as well as relational rapport and support. On the other hand, *control* involves social dominance and submission issues, as well as respect and deference orientations.

For example, an intercultural couple may argue over time spent together—the collectivistic wife wants to spend more time with her family, whereas the individualistic husband wants the couple to have more private time together. The wife perceives the conflict relationship as a high controlling one, whereas the husband views the conflict relationship as a low affiliative problem. . . .

A third set of relationship parameters is the trust–distrust dimension. Trust is often viewed as the single most important element of good working relationship (Fisher & Brown, 1988). Whereas *trust* is about reliability and sustained faith issues, *distrust* is about reliability violations and sustained skepticism issues. When trust is nonexistent, disputants will often second-guess each other's intentions and actions. In a tension-filled intercultural conflict scenario, adversaries will often view the relationship with distrust because interpersonal faith is broken and the other party is perceived from an outgroup—one of the distant "them."

Interpersonal trust begins with one side's perception that the other's verbal or nonverbal gesture is reliable or trustworthy. This perception is often followed by direct experience that the other's action is highly dependable. Repeated reliability and dependability across time further cultivate attachment accompanied by faith in the other person's responsiveness to one's needs (Rubin & Levinger, 1995). Thus, trust building depends heavily on reliable words and dependable actions. Being trusted by someone means promises that are kept and commitments that are honored. It also means we have the sustained faith that the other conflict party will perform as promised. For individualists, trust may be tested in a short to medium time frame, a monochronic basis. For collectivists, however, trust may entail a long-term, polychronic focus that entails mutual patience and longitudinal network reciprocity. . . .

Conflict Goal Assessments . . . People experience conflict in intimate and nonintimate relationships across a diverse range of cultures. How we perceive the conflict, whether we choose to engage in or disengage from it, and how we attribute different weights to the different goals in a conflict episode can vary greatly across cultural lines. The perceived or actual conflict differences often rotate around the following goal issues: content, relational, and identity (Wilmot & Hocker, 1998).

By *content conflict goals* we mean the substantive issues external to the individual involved. For example, an intercultural couple might argue about whether they should entertain their visiting in-laws at home or in a restaurant. They might disagree whether they should raise their children as monolinguals or bilinguals. . . .

By *relational conflict goals* we refer to how individuals define, or would like to define, the particular relationship (e.g., nonintimate vs. intimate, formal vs. informal) in that conflict episode. Nonintimate–intimate and formal–informal are two ways individuals might relate to one another. In the business setting, for example, one business partner from the United States might opt to scribble a note and fax it to another international partner from Japan. The latter might well view this hastily prepared communication as a cavalier and unfriendly gesture. The Japanese partner may have perceived and experienced face threat and relationship threat. However, the U.S. American business partner may not even realize that he or she has committed a faux pas by sending this offhand message. The U.S. American perceived the informal note as signaling affiliation or friendliness to minimize the formal relationship distance.

Identity-based goals revolve around issues of validation–rejection, approval–disapproval, respect–disrespect, and valuing disconfirming of the individuals in the conflict episode. In a given interaction, identity goals are directly linked to face-saving and face-honoring issues. Over the course of many interactions, identity goals are broadly linked to the underlying beliefs and value patterns of the culture and the individuals. Thus, to reject someone's proposal or idea in a conflict can mean rejecting that person's deeply held beliefs and convictions. . . .

Identity-based conflict goals often underlie content-based and relational-based conflict issues. On the overt level, people may be arguing or disagreeing over content or relational issues; however, beneath the surface rest identity conflict problems. From the collectivistic cultural perspective, relational conflict goals usually supersede content goals. The reasoning from the collectivistic point of view is that if the relationship is in jeopardy and mutual-face images have been threatened, there is no advantage to spending time talking about content issues. In contrast, from the individualistic perspective, content issues usually supersede relational issues. The reasoning from the individualistic perspective is that we can use actions and concrete steps to resolve the content goal problem decisively and have closure to the problem. An action orientation and a content problem-solving mode reflect the individualistic conflict worldview. By tackling the content problem first, individualists then can relax and deal with an interpersonal relationship problem. At the heart of all recurring conflict problems often rest unresolved identity conflict issues.

Conflict Intensity and Resources   . . . *High intensity conflict* means that high stakes are involved in the conflict and gains and losses can severely affect the individual, the organization, or both. The calculation of gains and losses can be content based, relationship based, or both. In contrast, *low intensity conflict* means that low stakes are involved and low incentives and costs are tied to the process and outcome. Conflict intensity holds both cultural-overlap and cultural-distinctive meanings.

The cultural-overlap meanings can be that both group membership teams realize that if they do not find a way to work collaboratively together they will lose their jobs. The cultural-distinctive meanings can involve collectivists wanting to emphasize the relationship trust issue and individualists wanting to consider substantive solution. As a result, individualists and collectivists may develop different "punctuation points" of what constitute the salient aspects of the conflict, as well as the scarce resources that are involved in the conflict episode.

Conflict resources refer to tangible or intangible rewards that people strive for in the dispute. The rewards or commodities may be scarce, or perceived as scarce, by individuals in the conflict. Perceived scarce resources may spark the initial impetus for conflict. Tangible resources may include a salary increase, a promotion, a new office, or a bonus vacation trip. Some tangible commodities are indeed scarce or limited (e.g., only one promotion for three analysts). Other tangible resources are only perceived to be limited (e.g., not enough computers for everyone when abundant supplies are hidden in a storage room) rather than involving actual scarcity. Intangible resources, on the other hand, may include deeply felt desires or needs such as psychological/emotional security, including connection, respect, control, and meaning issues. Many recurring conflicts between disputants involve unmet (or frustrated) intangible needs rather than conflicting tangible wants. Scarce tangible resources can be real or perceived as real (e.g., two children fighting for the perceived scarcity of attention of their parent) by individuals in the conflict episode. . . .

Intercultural Conflict Communication: Process Factors

Drawing from the conceptual explanations of Ting-Toomey's (1988; see also Ting-Toomey & Kurogi, 1998) face negotiation theory, we examine the process-based factors of conflict interaction styles and conflict facework behaviors. We conclude the section by examining two additional factors—conflict emotional expressions and conflict rhythms—in the intercultural conflict process. The four factors are the communication behaviors that individuals employ during intercultural conflict.

Conflict Interaction Styles   Conflict interaction style refers to patterned responses to conflict in a variety of dissenting conflict situations (Ting-Toomey, 1994a, 1994b). Findings in many past studies indicate that people display consistent styles across a variety of conflict situations in different cultures. Conflict style is learned within the primary socialization process of one's cultural or ethnic group.

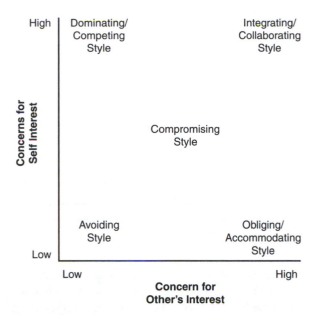

FIGURE 2 A Five-Style Conflict Grid: A Western Approach

Many researchers conceptualize conflict styles along two dimensions (Blake & Mouton, 1964; Putnam & Wilson, 1982; Thomas & Kilmann, 1974). Rahim (1983, 1992) bases his classification of conflict styles on the two conceptual dimensions of concern for self and concern for others. The first dimension illustrates the degree (high or low) to which a person seeks to satisfy his or her own interest or own face need. The second dimension represents the degree (high or low) to which a person desires to incorporate the other's conflict interest. The two dimensions are combined, resulting in five styles of handling interpersonal conflict: dominating, avoiding, obliging, compromising, and integrating (see Figure 2).

Briefly, the *dominating* (or *competitive/controlling*) style emphasizes conflict tactics that push for one's own position or goal above and beyond the other person's conflict interest. The *avoiding* style involves eluding the conflict topic, the conflict party, or the conflict situation altogether. The *obliging* (or *accommodating*) style is characterized by a high concern for the other person's conflict interest above and beyond one's own conflict interest. The *compromising* style involves a give-and-take concession approach to reach a midpoint agreement concerning the conflict issue. Finally, the *integrating* (or *collaborative*) style reflects a need for solution closure in conflict and involves high concern for self and high concern for others in conflict substantive negotiation. It should be noted that, in the U.S. conflict management literature,

obliging and avoiding conflict styles often take on a Western slant of being negatively disengaged (i.e., placating or flight from the conflict scene). However, collectivists do not perceive obliging and avoiding conflict styles as negative. Typically, these two styles are employed to maintain mutual-face interests and relational network interests (Ting-Toomey, 1988).

Furthermore, the five-style model misses subtle nuances of conflict behavior. Therefore, we have added three other conflict styles to account for the potentially rich areas of cultural and ethnic differences in conflict: emotional expression, third-party help, and neglect (Ting-Toomey et al., 2000). *Emotional expression* refers to using one's emotions to guide communication behaviors during conflict. *Third-party help* involves using an outsider to mediate the conflict. *Neglect* is characterized by using passive-aggressive responses to sidestep the conflict but at the same time getting an indirect reaction from the other conflict party. Further conceptual discussions and measurements of these eight conflict styles can be found in Ting-Toomey et al.'s article (2000). Based on our research in recent years, we have refined and updated the model to an eight-style conflict model (see Figure 3).

Face-negotiation theory helps to explain how individualism-collectivism, power distance, and self-construals influence conflict style (Ting-Toomey, 1988, 1997; Ting-Toomey & Kurogi, 1998). The premise of the theory is that members who subscribe to individualistic values tend to be more self-face oriented

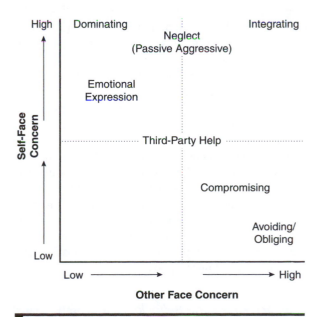

FIGURE 3 An Eight-Style Conflict Grid: An Intercultural Approach

and members who subscribe to group-oriented values tend to be more other- or mutual-face oriented in conflict negotiation. In addition, cultural members who subscribe to small power distance values tend to be more sensitive to horizontal face treatment, and cultural members who subscribe to large power distance values tend to be more attuned to vertical face treatment (Ting-Toomey & Kurogi, 1998). Parallel to the cultural-level predictions, personal attributes such as independent/interdependent self and horizontal/vertical self also assert a strong influence on conflict styles. Finally, different situational contexts and goals call for different rituals of conflict styles and facework appropriateness and effectiveness.

The face orientations, influenced by the various cultural and individual factors, affect conflict styles. Research across cultures (e.g., in China, Hong Kong, Japan, Korea, Taiwan, Mexico, and the United States) clearly indicates that individualists tend to use more self-defensive, controlling, dominating, and competitive styles in managing conflict than do collectivists. By comparison, collectivists tend to use more integrative and compromising styles in dealing with conflict than do individualists. Furthermore, collectivists tend to use more obliging and avoiding styles in task-related conflicts than do individualists (Chua & Gudykunst, 1987; Ting-Toomey et al., 1991; Ting-Toomey et al., 2000; Trubisky, Ting-Toomey, & Lin, 1991).

On the personal attributes level, independent-self individuals tend to use more dominating conflict styles than interdependent-self individuals, whereas interdependent-self individuals tend to use more avoiding, obliging, integrating, and compromising styles than independent-self individuals (Oetzel, 1998). Further research helps to illustrate how self-construals affect conflict styles by considering four types that result from a combination of the two components of self: biconstrual, independent, interdependent, and ambivalent (Ting-Toomey, Oetzel, & Yee-Jung, in press) (see Figure 4). Overall, it seems that the biconstruals have a wide range of conflict repertoires to deal with different conflict situations. They appear to be more flexible and adaptable in handling different conflict issues than the other three self-construal types. In addition, biconstruals, independents, and interdependents prefer to use integrating and compromising conflict styles more than do ambivalents. Finally, ambivalents prefer to use neglecting conflict style more than do biconstruals, independents, and interdependents.

Conflict Facework Behaviors   A closely related concept to conflict style is facework behavior. *Facework* is the combination of communication strategies

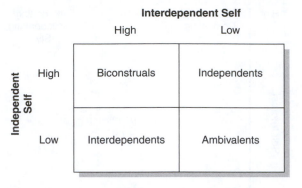

FIGURE 4   A Self-Construal Typological Model

used to uphold, support, and challenge self-face and the other's face. Facework can be specific behaviors of a broad conflict style. For example, the integrating conflict style reflects a need for finding a solution during conflict and involves both parties working together to substantively resolve the issue (Rahim, 1983). Facework behaviors consistent with the integrating style include (but are not limited to) listening to the other person, respecting the feelings of the other, and sharing personal viewpoints. During conflict, facework has a variety of functions. Facework is employed to resolve a conflict, exacerbate a conflict, avoid a conflict, threaten or challenge another person, protect a person's image, and so on. These functions are part of the process of maintaining and upholding face. Facework is linked closely with identity and relationship conflict goal issues.

In examining facework strategies in saving self-face or giving consideration to the other's face, research indicates that whereas individualists tend to use self-oriented face-saving strategies in conflicts, collectivists tend to use other- or mutual-oriented face-saving strategies in such situations. In addition, individualists (e.g., U.S. European American respondents) tend to use more direct face-threatening conflict behaviors than collectivists, whereas collectivists (e.g., Taiwanese and Chinese respondents) tend to use more indirect other-oriented face-saving conflict behaviors than individualists (Cocroft & Ting-Toomey, 1994; Ting-Toomey et al., 1991). Self-face is reflected through behaviors such as defending a position and confrontation of the other party's position. Other-face is reflected through behaviors such as avoiding the conflict, seeking a third party to help resolve the conflict, and giving in to the other party. Mutual-face is reflected through behaviors such as attempting to solve the problem with the other person, compromising, signaling relational solidarity, having private discussions with the other party, and apologizing for behavior (Oetzel, Ting-Toomey, Masumoto, Yokochi, & Takai, in press). . . .

Conflict Emotional Expressions Regarding norms of emotional expression, conflict is an emotionally distressing experience. In two extensive, detailed reviews of culture and emotions (Mesquita & Frijida, 1992; Russell, 1991), clear cross-cultural emotional expression and interpretation differences are uncovered. Based on these reviews, we can conclude that cultural norms, or *cultural display rules,* exist in conflict, which regulate displays of aggressive or negative emotional reactions such as anger, fear, shame, frustration, resentment, and hostility. For example, in many Western, individualistic cultures, open expressions of emotions in conflict are viewed as honest, engaging signals. However, in many Asian, collectivistic cultures, maintaining restrained emotional composure is viewed as the self-disciplined, mature way to handle conflict. This norm does not mean, however, that collectivists deal with each other harmoniously all the time. As Triandis (1994) observes,

> In collectivist cultures . . . norms are very powerful regulators of behavior. . . . [Japanese returnees] after spending some time abroad are frequently criticized, teased, and bullied by their peers . . . for non-Japanese behaviors such as having a sun tan or a permanent-wave hairstyle. . . . The threat of ostracism is an especially powerful source of fear in collectivist cultures. (p. 302)

Individuals vary in terms of their tempos, pacing, and rhythms in managing various conflict schedules and issues. In *monochromic time* (M-time) cultures, time is experienced and used in a linear way. "Comparable to a road . . . M-time is divided quite naturally into segments; it is scheduled and compartmentalized, making it possible for a person to concentrate on one thing at a time" (Hall & Hall, 1987, p. 16). Intercultural researchers have identified Germany, the Scandinavian countries, Switzerland, and the United States as prime M-time examples. In comparison, *polychronic time* (P-time) cultures are characterized by the "simultaneous occurrence of many things and by a great involvement with people. There is also more emphasis on completing human transactions than on holding schedules. . . . P-time is experienced as much less tangible than M-time, and can better be compared to a single point than to a road" (Hall & Hall, 1987, pp. 17–18). Many African, Asian, Latin American, Eastern European, Caribbean, and Mediterranean cultures are prime examples of P-time cultures. It also appears that cultural members who subscribe to individualistic value patterns also favor a monochronic-time approach to conflict.

Conversely, cultural members who subscribe to collectivistic value patterns also tend to favor a polychronic-time approach to conflict.

Monochronic-time people prefer to deal with conflict from a linear-sequential approach (either through inductive or deductive means); polychronic-time people prefer to handle conflict from a spiral-holistic viewpoint. For M-time individuals, conflict management time should be filled with problem-solving or decision-making activities. For P-time individuals, time is an idea governed by the smooth implicit rhythms in the interaction between people. When conflict occurs between two P-time individuals, they will be more concerned with restoring the disjunctive rhythms in the interaction than in dealing directly with issues of substance.

REFERENCES

Blake, R. R., & Mouton, J. S. (1964). *The managerial grid.* Houston, TX: Gulf Publishing.

Brown, P., & Levinson, S. (1978). Universals in language usage: Politeness phenomenon. In E. Goody (Ed.), *Questions and politeness: Strategies in social interaction* (pp. 56–289). Cambridge, UK: Cambridge University Press.

Chen, G. M. (Ed.). (1997). Conflict resolution in Chinese [Special Issue]. *Intercultural Communication Studies, 8.*

Chua, E., & Gudykunst, W. B. (1987). Conflict resolution style in low- and high-context cultures. *Communication Research Reports, 4,* 32–37.

Cocroft, B., & Ting-Toomey, S. (1994). Facework in Japan and the United States. *International Journal of Intercultural Relations, 18,* 469–506.

Condon, J. C. (1984). *With respect to the Japanese: A guide for Americans.* Yarmouth, ME: Intercultural Press.

Fisher, R., & Brown, S. (1988). *Getting together: Building relationships as we negotiate.* New York: Penguin.

Fitch, K. (1998). *Speaking relationally: Culture, communication, and interpersonal communication.* New York: Guilford.

Gao, G., & Ting-Toomey, S. (1998). *Communicating effectively with the Chinese.* Thousand Oaks, CA: Sage.

Garcia, W. R. (1996). *Respeto:* A Mexican base for interpersonal relationships. In W. Gudykunst, S. Ting-Toomey, & T. Nishida (Eds.), *Communication in personal relationships across cultures* (pp. 137–155). Thousand Oaks, CA: Sage.

Goffman, E. (1959). *The presentation of self in everyday life.* Garden City, NY: Anchor/Doubleday.

Gudykunst, W., & Ting-Toomey, S. (1988). *Culture and interpersonal communication.* Newbury Park, CA: Sage.

Gudykunst, W. B., Matsumoto, Y., Ting-Toomey, S., Nishida, T., Kim, K. S., & Heyman, S. (1996). The influence of cultural individualism-collectivism, self construals, and individual values on communication styles across cultures. *Human Communication Research, 22,* 510–543.

Hall, E. T., & Hall, M. (1987). *Hidden differences: Doing business with the Japanese.* Garden City, NY: Anchor/Doubleday.

Hofstede, G. (1991). *Culture and organizations: Software of the mind.* London: McGraw-Hill.

Hu, H. C. (1944). The Chinese concept of "face." *American Anthropologist, 46,* 45–64.

Katriel, T. (1986). *Talking straight: Dugri speech in Israeli Sabra culture.* Cambridge, UK: Cambridge University Press.

Leung, K., & Bond, M. (1984). The impact of cultural collectivism on reward allocation. *Journal of Personality and Social Psychology, 47,* 793–804.

Leung, K., & Iwawaki, S. (1988). Cultural collectivism and distributive behavior. *Journal of Cross-Cultural Psychology, 19,* 35–49.

Lewicki, R. J., & Bunker, B. B. (1995). Trust in relationships: A model of development and decline. In B. Bunker, J. Rubin, & associates (Eds.), *Conflict, cooperation and justice* (pp. 39–57). San Francisco: Jossey-Bass.

Lim, T.-S., & Choi, S. (1996). Interpersonal relationships in Korea. In W. B. Gudykunst, S. Ting-Toomey, & T. Nishida (Eds.), *Communication in personal relationships across cultures* (pp. 122–136). Thousand Oaks, CA: Sage.

Markus, H. R., & Kitayama, S. (1991). Culture and self: Implication for cognition, emotion, and motivation. *Psychological Review, 98,* 224–253.

Mesquita, B., & Frijida, N. (1992). Cultural variations in emotions: A review. *Psychological Bulletin, 112,* 179–204.

Morisaki, S., & Gudykunst, W. B. (1994). Face in Japan and the United States. In S. Ting-Toomey (Ed.), *The challenge of facework* (pp. 47–94). Albany: State University of New York Press.

Oetzel, J. G. (1998). The effects of self-construals and ethnicity on self-reported conflict styles. *Communication Reports, 11,* 133–144.

Oetzel, J. G., Ting-Toomey, S., Masumoto, T., Yokochi, Y., & Takai, J. (in press). Developing a cross-cultural typology of facework behaviors in interpersonal conflicts. *Communication Quarterly.*

Putnam, L., & Wilson, C. E. (1982). Communicative strategies in organizational conflicts: Reliability and validity of a measurement scale. In M. Burgoon (Ed.), *Communication Yearbook 6* (pp. 629–652). Beverly Hills, CA: Sage.

Rahim, M. A. (1983). A measure of styles of handling interpersonal conflict. *Academy of Management Journal, 26,* 368–376.

Rahim, M. A. (1992). *Managing conflict in organizations* (2nd ed.). Westport, CT: Praeger.

Rogan, R. G., & Hammer, M. R. (1994). Crisis negotiations: A preliminary investigation of facework in naturalistic conflict discourse. *Journal of Applied Communication Research, 22,* 216–231.

Rubin, J. Z., & Levinger, G. (1995). Levels of analysis: In search of generalizable knowledge. In B. Bunker, J. Rubin, & associates (Eds.), *Conflict, cooperation and justice* (pp. 13–38). San Francisco: Jossey-Bass.

Russell, J. (1991). Culture and the categorization of emotions. *Psychological Bulletin, 110,* 426–450.

Thomas, K. W., & Kilmann, R. H. (1974). *Thomas-Kilmann conflict MODE instrument.* New York: XICOM, Tuxedo.

Thomas, R. R. (1990, March–April). From affirmative action to affirming diversity. *Harvard Business Review, 68,* 107–117.

Ting-Toomey, S. (1988). Intercultural conflict styles: A face-negotiation theory. In Y. Kim & W. Gudykunst (Eds.), *Theories in intercultural communication* (pp. 213–235). Newbury Park, CA: Sage.

Ting-Toomey, S. (1994a). Managing conflict in intimate intercultural relationships. In D. Cahn (Ed.), *Intimate conflict in personal relationships* (pp. 120–147). Hillsdale, NJ: Lawrence Erlbaum.

Ting-Toomey, S. (1994b). Managing intercultural conflicts effectively. In I. Samovar & R. Porter (Eds.), *Intercultural communication: A reader* (7th ed., pp. 360–372). Belmont, CA: Wadsworth.

Ting-Toomey, S. (1997). Intercultural conflict competence. In W. R. Cupach & D. J. Canary (Eds.), *Competence in interpersonal conflict* (pp. 120–147). New York: McGraw-Hill.

Ting-Toomey, S. (1999). *Communicating across cultures.* New York: Guilford.

Ting-Toomey, S., & Cole, M. (1990). Intergroup diplomatic communication: A face-negotiation perspective. In P. Korzenny & S. Ting-Toomey (Eds), *Communicating for peace: Diplomacy and negotiation* (pp. 77–95). Newbury Park, CA: Sage.

Ting-Toomey, S., Gao, G., Trubisky, P., Yang, Z., Kim, H. S., Lin, S.-L., & Nishida, T. (1991). Culture, face maintenance, and styles of handling interpersonal conflict: A study in five cultures. *International Journal of Conflict Management, 2,* 275–296.

Ting-Toomey, S., & Kurogi, A. (1998). Facework competence in intercultural conflict: An updated face-negotiation theory. *International Journal of Intercultural Relations, 22,* 187–225.

Ting-Toomey, S., Oetzel, J. G., & Yee-Jung. K. (in press). Self-construal types and conflict management styles. *Communication Reports.*

Ting-Toomey, S., Yee-Jung, K., Shapiro, R., Garcia, W., Wright, T., & Oetzel, J. G. (2000). Cultural/ethnic identity salience and conflict styles in four U.S. ethnic groups. *International Journal of Intercultural Relations, 24,* 47–81.

Triandis, H. C. (1994). *Culture and social behavior.* New York: McGraw-Hill.

Triandis, H. C. (1995). *Individualism and collectivism.* Boulder, CO: Westview.

Trubisky P., Ting-Toomey, S., & Lin, S.-L. (1991). The influence of individualism-collectivism and self-monitoring on conflict styles. *International Journal of Intercultural Relations, 15,* 65–84.

Wilmot, W., & Hocker, J. (1998). *Interpersonal conflict* (5th ed.). Boston: McGraw-Hill.

CHECK YOUR UNDERSTANDING

1. According to the authors, one's conflict style is learned within "the primary socialization process of one's cultural or ethnic group." Describe the conflict style you have learned. How did your family, friends, educational, religious, and political institutions influence this style?

2. Discuss how the following factors affect your intercultural conflict style: sense of self, face concerns, conflict norms, situational and relationship boundary features, and emotional expression.

3. Plot your conflict style on Figures 2, 3, and 4. How does examining your style on all three figures aid in your understanding of your conflict style?

4. Consider a conflict you have had with a person from another culture. Explain the conflict using the concept of conflict styles.

CHAPTER ACTIVITIES

1. Write a personal narrative in which you describe a time when language differences caused communication difficulties for you.

2. In your journal write proverbs of various cultures as you come across them in your reading or conversations. There are numerous books containing proverbs of other countries. You might browse through some of those and choose proverbs you particularly like. After you have gathered proverbs from different cultures, analyze the common values or lessons expressed. Analyze the differences as well and suggest ways these differences might affect intercultural communication.

3. Interview several people. Ask them to complete this sentence: Culture is _____. What metaphors are used to complete the sentence?

4. In a small group create your own language. For example, you may be familiar with Pig Latin in which the first letter of a word is placed at the end of the word and a long "a" sound is added to the end of the word. The term *Pig Latin* becomes "igpay atinlay." Another language creation is "Burley Furble (thanks to Beth Cooper for this one). In Burley Furble you add an "l" at the end of a syllable and an "f" at the beginning of the next syllable. If the word is only one syllable, the "l" and "f" combine in the middle of the word. For example, "cat" becomes "calft." The sentence, "I'll tell you something" becomes "Ilf telf youlf somelfthing."

5. Try to communicate with people from the other groups who have created a language. Ask questions such as

   What is your name?
   How far is it to Kalamazoo?
   Where is the bathroom?
   Which direction do I go to get to the Hotel Maria?
   When does the next plane for Beijing leave?

6. How did you communicate? Did you communicate your meaning? When others could not understand your language, did you just talk louder or did you try to use nonverbal communication?

7. Choose an abstract term such as *family, marriage, education,* or *beauty.* Ask a person from another culture to define this word for you. Compare her or his definition to your own. How might differences in your meanings create intercultural communication problems? How might similarities enhance your communication?

8. Bring to class examples from newspapers of intercultural communication problems that result from language differences. In small groups discuss the causes of misunderstanding and possible ways of alleviating the misunderstanding.

CHAPTER 6

NONVERBAL INTERCULTURAL COMMUNICATION

SHOPPING WITH THE BEDOUINS

It was near the end of our trip. My mother and I had been in Israel for two weeks. She had finally seen "where Jesus walked," and was content and exhausted. We were in our church tour bus, late at night, driving through the mountainous desert. The night was black—no moon and only a few stars. The only light was the headlights of the bus. The road was winding and rugged, leaving little room for our bus, and the gasps of the passengers were audible as each curve seemed to go off into space. We were all sitting on the edge of our seats. I wondered if our trip was to end in disaster. I imagined us falling to the desert floor below.

With a jerk, our bus stopped. On the side of the road was a family of Bedouins—desert dwellers. We had often seen them as we traveled the countryside. Most Bedouin camps we had seen consisted of five to ten tents. Each tent houses a nuclear family and perhaps an unmarried uncle or sister. The tents have two sections—one for the men and one for the women. The tents can be moved within two hours. Bedouins move often—every couple of weeks. Their need for pasture and water for their livestock (camels, sheep, and goats) necessitates the moves. Living in the highlands during the hottest part of the year, and the lowlands during the winter, theirs is a life of constant movement. During our trip we had all talked about what a difficult life it must be. Yet, these people had lived in this manner for centuries.

Our guide and driver exited the bus and talked to the Bedouins and soon returned, urging us to leave the bus and come with the Bedouins, who had brought various merchandise for us—camel blankets, goat's milk, and an assortment of Bedouin clothing. What struck me was the jewelry. It is one of the few art forms of the Bedouins. I was amazed at how beautiful the jewelry was—a stark contrast to the bleakness of the desert. By Western standards, the jewelry was gaudy—multiple chains, bells, pendants, and coins decorated with strands of filigree and inlaid with colored stones. A particular salesman had a *kaff*—a connected piece of jewelry with rings for each finger, a piece for the back of the hand, and a bracelet. Earrings, rings, bracelets, necklaces, nose rings—the variety of pieces was astounding. Some were truly works of art, while others were crude. The designs were thousands of years old. Bedouins discourage individuality and creativity, so a new design is rare.

Here, in the dark of night, on a deserted road, was a jewelry store—in fact, a general store! I was most interested in the jewelry: first, because I love jewelry and second, because I knew that in this culture, the women owned the jewelry. In Bedouin culture, most people cannot read or write, so the men entertain as well as tell stories and recite poems that impart their history as well as entertain. But the women own the jewelry. The bride receives her first pieces as a part of her dowry. Ownership shows she is a woman of property. As her family gains wealth, that wealth is reflected in livestock and her jewelry.

This jewelry reflected the culture of the Bedouins. Surviving in the desert alone is not possible, so family becomes extremely important. Dependence and loyalty are fostered. Theirs is a collectivist culture. And in the night, the family comes together to meet the bus.

In terms of Kluckhohn and Strodbeck's dimensions, Bedouins are a "being" rather than a "doing" culture—an orientation defined as people, events, and ideas flowing spontaneously within the moment. It was not surprising then that the moment of the bus, the merchandise, and the people all came together spontaneously and the Bedouins made the most of it. The present is important. And in this case, the present was an opportunity to sell tourists merchandise!

OBJECTIVES

After reading this chapter and completing the readings and activities, you should be able to

- Define the importance of nonverbal communication in the overall communication process.
- List five universal characteristics of nonverbal communication.
- Discuss three cultural variations in nonverbal communication.
- Explain the functions of nonverbal communication.
- Provide an intercultural difference for each of the codes of nonverbal communication presented in this chapter.

IMPORTANCE OF NONVERBAL COMMUNICATION

Nonverbal communication (all communication except that which is coded through words) is an extremely important variable in the intercultural communication process. Yet it is difficult to understand because it is usually performed spontaneously and often subconsciously. That is, until people begin to communicate interculturally, they are unaware of their own nonverbal behaviors. According to Andersen (1999), "Most aspects of one's culture are learned through observation and imitation rather than through explicit verbal instruction or expression" (p. 75).

Mehrabian (1982) estimates that only 7 percent of the meaning of any message is carried through the verbal message—through words. He calculates that 93 percent of the meaning is carried through the nonverbal communication channels: 38 percent through the voice, and 55 percent through the face. Birdwhistell (1970) presents a more conservative estimate, suggesting 65 percent of the message's meaning is conveyed through nonverbal channels.

UNIVERSALITY OF NONVERBAL COMMUNICATION

Nonverbal communication reveals our attitudes, personalities, emotions, and relationships with others. By understanding how nonverbal communication influences us and others, we can understand other cultures better, as well as understand our own ethnocentrism. Hindus greet one another by placing their palms together in front of them while bowing their heads slightly. This greeting behavior reflects the Hindu belief that the deity exists in everyone. Patting the top of a child's head in Thailand or Malaysia is forbidden. The spiritual center of a person is in the head. Patting the head would cause damage to the spirit.

Although we humans are a species with universal facial expressions for most of our basic emotions (sadness, happiness, anger, distrust, surprise, and fear), when, where, and to whom we display these emotions are culturally bound. They are learned within the culture to which we were born and in which we were raised (Ekman and Friesen, 1971). In addition, the rules regarding these are not taught verbally. Rather, we learn them through observation and personal experience in our culture. Thus, an examination of nonverbal communication in various cultures can help us understand another culture better. For example, U.S. Americans tend to see nonverbal communication as ancillary to verbal communication, but elsewhere in the world (e.g., Japan) the nonverbal code may be used to convey the major message. In either case, nonverbal behavior is representative of deep cultural values. Stewart and Bennett (1991) provide the following example, which makes this point clear. An American visitor to Mexico was describing his family to a Mexican. To describe his young children, the American tried to convey their ages by indicating their height. He held up his right hand, the palm open and facing down horizontally at the height of his child from the ground. At first the American did not notice the look of dismay on the face of the Mexican in response to the hand gesture. It was only later that the visitor found out what had gone wrong with the conversation. The gesture he had used is similar to the movement of the hand in petting a dog or some other animal on the head. Mexicans accept that hand gesture as the height of a dog, pig, or some other animal, but human beings are measured with the palm open and held vertical to the ground at the appropriate height (p. 59).

Some researchers suggest that there are universal nonverbal behaviors across cultures. For example, Ekman and Friesen (1971) and Fridlund and associates (1987) report research indicating that the ability to produce emotional displays such as anger and happiness is consistent across cultures. Thus, there is probably a genetic or biological basis that allows these emotions to be produced by all humans. Whether these emotions are recognized universally is still under debate. For example, Shioiri and colleagues state (1999) that the expressions of surprise and happiness were well understood by both Japanese and Americans; however, anger, contempt, disgust, fear, and sadness were not always recognized by people in Japan. According to Jandt (2004), "It was Darwin's idea that these expressions evolved because they allow us to know immediately the difference between strangers who are friendly and those who might attack" (p. 121).

Argyle (1975) outlines five characteristics of nonverbal communication that are universal across cultures: (1) the same body parts are used for nonverbal expressions; (2) nonverbal channels are used to convey similar information, emotions, norms, values, and self-disclosures; (3) nonverbal messages accompany verbal communication and are used in ritual and art; (4) the motives for using the nonverbal channels (such as when speech is impossible) are similar across cultures; and (5) nonverbal messages are used to coordinate and control a range of contexts and relationships that are similar across cultures (p. 95).

Although research suggests that there are nonverbal universals, how these are manifested across cultures differ. In other words, these may "look" different as we experience other cultures. Lustig and Koester (2002) outline three cultural variations in nonverbal communication. First, cultures differ in their specific repertoire of behaviors. Movements, gestures, and spatial requirements are specific to a particular culture. Second, all cultures have display rules. These "indicate such things as how far apart people should stand while talking, whom to touch and where, the speed and timing of movements and gestures, when to look directly at others in a conversation and when to look away, whether loud talking and expansive gestures or quietness and controlled movements should be used, when to smile and when to frown, and the overall pacing of communication" (p. 191). Thus, display rules govern when and in what situations various nonverbal expressions are required, permitted, preferred, or prohibited, and they differ across cultures. Third, as the examples in this chapter indicate, the meanings that are attributed to particular nonverbal behaviors differ across cultures.

FUNCTIONS OF NONVERBAL COMMUNICATION

Nonverbal communication can be used independently or in conjunction with verbal communication. While Andersen (1999) suggests that one of the most basic and obvious functions of nonverbal communication is to communicate one's culture, Knapp and Hall (1997) provide six primary functions of nonverbal communication. The nonverbal cue may simply repeat the verbal—for instance, waving good-bye while saying "Good-bye." Nonverbal cues may contradict the verbal, such as when a friend has a sad expression but says, "No, I don't feel sad." If the verbal and nonverbal are contradictory, we adults most often believe the nonverbal because we consider nonverbal communication as more spontaneous and less likely to be contrived than verbal communication. Nonverbal cues can substitute for the verbal—for example, waving good-bye with no accompanying verbal communication. Nonverbal cues can complement verbal cues, like saying "I love you" while hugging the person. Nonverbal cues can accent the verbal message, such as a child yelling, "I hate you!" while stomping his or her feet. Although complementing and accenting are similar, as the previous examples indicate, they differ in intensity. Finally, nonverbal cues can regulate the verbal communication—for example, nodding your head in agreement, thereby signaling your communication partner to continue talking.

Regardless of how nonverbal communication is used, it, like verbal communication, uses a culturally agreed upon set of symbols. As Ramsey (1979) suggests:

> According to culturally prescribed codes, we use eye movement and contact to manage conversations and to regulate interactions; we follow rigid rules governing intra- and interpersonal touch, our bodies synchronously join in the rhythm of others in a group, and gestures modulate our speech. We must internalize all of this in order to become and remain fully functioning and socially appropriate members of our culture. (p. 111)

NONVERBAL COMMUNICATION CODES

As indicated previously, nonverbal communication is multichanneled. In other words, several codes of nonverbal behavior can be generated by a single person at any given time. For example, we observe the person's dress, gestures, and voice tone and make some assumptions about the person using these nonverbal cues.

There are numerous categories of nonverbal behavior. In this section we will examine seven that are particularly important in intercultural communication: kinesics, chronemics, proxemics, haptics, artifacts, physical characteristics, and paralanguage.

Kinesics

Kinesics, the study of body language, includes such cues as gestures, head movements, facial expressions, and eye contact. Each culture has its own interpretation of various kinesic behaviors.

In general, U.S. Americans tend to be moderately expressive in their kinesic behavior. In contrast to many Asian cultures, people in the United States use gestures freely. But compared to those in Mediterranean, Latin, or Arab cultures, U.S. Americans seem quite restrained.

A smile in Western culture generally means happiness. In Chinese society a smile can disguise embarrassment, mask bereavement, or conceal rage. In general, the Chinese don't show their emotions because displaying emotions violates face-saving norms by disrupting harmony and causing conflict (Wenzhong and Grove, 1991).

Gestures signify different meanings in different cultures. The simple gesture of nodding "yes" differs across cultures. A Westerner's head nod for "yes" signifies "no" in Thailand. In Turkey, this same movement means "I don't understand." The Korean gesture for "come" is similar to the Western "good-bye." When a Westerner waves to a Korean from a distance, the Korean may think he is being asked to "come here." Koreans wave good-bye by waving their arm from side to side. Winston Churchill's famous victory sign is considered an obscene gesture in South America. Showing the bottoms of your feet is considered an insult in Egyptian culture. Harper and colleagues (1991) indicate that "making a circle with one's thumb and index finger while extending the others is emblematic of the word 'OK'; in Japan (and Korea) it signifies 'money' (okane); and among Arabs this gesture is usually accompanied by a baring of teeth, and together they signify extreme hostility" (p. 164). Standing with your hands on your hips is interpreted as an aggressive posture in the Philippines as well as in Mexico and Malaysia. Any gesture that displays an extended thumb, including the "thumbs-up" gesture or a hitchhiker's gesture, is offensive throughout the Middle East. Yet, the hitchhiker's gesture in Indonesia means "You go first." The left hand is considered unclean in the Arab world, so one should always eat with the right hand.

Whereas North Americans expect others to "look them in the eye" while communicating, and in fact may distrust someone who does not, Chinese and Indonesians lower their eyes as a sign of respect. Prolonged eye contact is considered rude in Japan and the Philippines, but expected in Arab cultures as a sign of interest in what the other person is saying. In France, eye contact among people is frequent and intense and sometimes intimidating to U.S. Americans.

Chronemics

In a lighthearted article titled, "What If There Weren't Any Clocks to Watch?" Zarembo (1997) describes the beginning of time—that is, chronemics: "Three centuries ago, a Dutch mathematician named Christiaan Huygens invented a new religion. He didn't mean to. All he did was build a pendulum clock that allowed people, for the first time in history, to keep track of hours and minutes accurately. But over the decades, this power attracted millions of followers" (p. 14).

Hall (1983) distinguishes two types of time that govern different cultures: monochronic time (M-time) and polychronic time (P-time). People who use *M-time* usually engage in one activity at a time, compartmentalize time, and separate task-oriented time from socioemotional time. In general, monochronic cultures value punctuality, completing tasks, and keeping on a schedule. Time is linear and is viewed as something that can be saved or wasted. People who use *P-time* usually engage in several tasks at once, hold a more fluid attitude toward time, and integrate task time and socioemotional time. Appointments can be broken easily, schedules ignored, and deadlines broken. If a family member or friend requires attention, this relationship is more important than any schedule.

Members of individualistic cultures such as Northern European, German, and North American are representative of M-time. Collectivist cultures such as Latin American, Middle Eastern, Asian, and French cultures are representative of P-time. Table 6.1 summarizes the basic differences between these two time perspectives in terms of behavior.

Time can also be viewed from a past, present, and future perspective. Individualistic cultures view time from a linear perspective—past, present, future. Those cultures that are past oriented emphasize tradition and the wisdom passed down from generation to generation. Present-oriented cultures emphasize experiencing each moment fully and spontaneity and immediacy. Future-oriented cultures emphasize the importance of present activity to future outcomes. As indicated by Gonzalez and Zimbardo (1985), differences in time orientations can cause difficulties in intercultural communication. A person from a future-oriented perspective might perceive a person from a present orientation as hedonistic, self-centered, foolish, and inefficient. On the other hand, a present-oriented person might perceive a past-oriented person as too tied to tradition and a future-oriented person as materialistic.

Proxemics

Proxemics is the use of space. It includes territoriality and personal space. Territoriality is space that is claimed by individuals either permanently or temporarily. Personal space has been compared to a bubble surrounding us that we carry with us wherever we go and expand or contract depending on the situation.

TABLE 6.1 Comparison of Monochronic and Polychronic People	
Monochronic People	**Polychronic People**
Do one thing at a time.	Do many things at once.
Concentrate on the job.	Are easily distracted and subject to interruptions.
Take time commitments (deadlines, schedules) seriously.	Consider time commitments an objective to be achieved, if possible.
Are low context and need information.	Are high context and already have information.
Are committed to the job.	Are committed to people and human relationships.
Adhere to plans.	Change plans often and easily.
Are concerned about not disturbing others; follow rules of privacy.	Are more concerned with those close to them (family, friends, close business associates) than with privacy.
Emphasize promptness.	Base promptness on the relationship.
Are accustomed to short-term relationships.	Have strong tendency to build lifetime relationships.

Source: Adapted from Edward T. Hall and Mildred Reed Hall, *Understanding Cultural Differences: German, French and American* (Yarmouth, ME: Intercultural Press, 1990), p. 15.

How culture uses space is linked to its value system. For example, people from individualistic cultures require more space because they value privacy. Collectivist cultures are interdependent and require less space. Thus, people work, play, and live in close proximity to one another. For example, in collectivist cultures the middle-class home environment is integrated with a central plaza, a community center, or a neighborhood dwelling. In individualistic cultures the middle-class home environment is often separated from the community at large by a fence or through the use of frontyards or backyards (Gudykunst et al., 1996).

Every culture has its rules for the use of space. In the Netherlands you might find yourself giving a sales pitch from a chair that seems uncomfortably far away. To move your chair closer would be an insult. Privacy is very important to Germans, both at work and home. Doors are kept closed and one must knock before entering. In Japan the person with the most authority sits at the head of the table, the lowest person in the hierarchy is nearest the door at the opposite end of the table from the person with the most authority (McDaniel, 2003). Chinese prefer side-by-side seating rather than arrangements that facilitate direct eye contact.

In terms of personal space, Hall (1959) analyzed U.S. Americans' use of personal space. In general, Hall found that people in the United States use personal space at varying distances for varying purposes. For example, the closer the space between people, the more intimate the communication. Very close (0 to 1½ feet) is for intimate communication, such as comforting, protecting, and lovemaking. Most dyadic encounters occur from 1 to 4½ feet. Social gatherings and business transactions take place between 4 to 12 feet, and the largest distance between persons (over 12 feet) occurs in public speaking situations.

Because of our ethnocentrism, many U.S. Americans might think that all cultures use personal space in the same way we do. However, as Stewart and Bennett (1991) indicate:

> Standing close in conversation may signal fight or flight from Americans while representing the appropriate distance for conversational interaction prescribed by another person's culture. Both spacing and touching are rather precisely coded with social and sexual meaning for Americans.

Thus, the norms of Arabs, and to a lesser degree, of Latinos, may suggest to Americans that these people are socially aggressive and sexually promiscuous. (p. 58)

What happens when one's personal space is violated? Bond and Iwata (1976) indicate that members of individualistic cultures take an active, aggressive stance when their space is violated. Members of collectivist cultures assume a passive, withdrawal stance when their space is "invaded" by another person. While living in an Asian culture, one of the authors had great difficulty with this issue of space. The pushing and shoving while in public places seemed "rude" from her Western perspective. She wanted to push back! However, the Chinese people simply kept walking. They did not see this closeness as invasive, but as normal.

Haptics

Different cultures view touching behavior in different ways. In Southeast Asia people engage in very little touching behavior. As Kim (1992) observes, "Southeastern Asians do not ordinarily touch during a conversation, especially one between opposite sexes, because many Asian cultures adhere to norms that forbid public displays of affection and intimacy" (p. 322).

In general, cultures that believe in emotional restraint and rigid status distinctions (such as the German, Scandinavian, and English) touch less than cultures that stress collectivism and outward signs of affection (such as Middle Eastern, Latin American, and Eastern Europe). What happens to intercultural communication as a result of these differences? As Lustig and Koester (1996) suggest, "Germans, Scandinavians, and Japanese, for example, may be perceived as cold and aloof by Brazilians and Italians, who in turn may be regarded as aggressive, pushy and overly familiar by northern Europeans" (p. 204).

Gudykunst and Ting-Toomey (1988) review research that suggests that Japanese tend to engage in same-sex touch behavior more than North Americans, and North Americans tend to engage in opposite-sex touch behavior more often than do the Japanese. Japanese females tend to touch more than do Japanese males. In Mediterranean cultures male-male touch behavior is more common than is female-female touch behavior. People in the Near East are less touch avoidant to opposite-sex touching than people from the Mediterranean area and the Far East. The Far Eastern group is the most touch-avoidant cultural group in opposite-sex touch behavior among the four groups. These findings suggest that Far Eastern cultures are low-contact cultures, the North American culture is a moderate-contact culture, and the Arab and Mediterranean cultures are high nonverbal contact cultures.

Cultures vary in terms of their rules as to who touches whom, as well as the settings or occasions in which touch is acceptable. For example, in Thailand, the rules of touch that are important to know are:

1. Don't touch anyone's head for any reason. The head is the most important part of the body. It is the seat of the soul.
2. Do not touch a female on any part of her body.
3. The feet are considered the "dirtiest" part of the body. They are used only for walking. Thus, it is an insult to rest your feet on someone else's backrest, such as in the cinema or on a train.
4. Women must never touch a monk or his robe. Even in a bus or train, women cannot sit next to a monk.
5. Always accept things with your right hand. The left hand is used to wash the posterior and is therefore regarded as unclean.

As is the case with all nonverbal variables, it is extremely important to understand that the culture of our roots teaches us the appropriate form of touch for our culture. However, as we move along other routes, touching behaviors will differ, and we need to adapt to them.

Artifacts

A popular intercultural activity asks participants to choose 10 items to put in a time capsule (size and cost notwithstanding). Once these items or artifacts are selected, participants are asked to consider what these material possessions say about their culture. Would someone from Asia or Africa select items similar to someone from the United States? Understanding how artifacts (the material side of culture) relate to intercultural interactions can aid in the understanding of problems in development aid, technology transfer, marketing, and personal intercultural interactions (Roth, 2001). Artifacts may include technology (cellular telephone, pocket computers, etc.), homes, cars, symbols (flags, insignias, etc.), jewelry, clothing, or any other object that is used to communicate meaning. Some examples of artifacts communicating interculturally follow.

In Shanghai, China, persons of status like nothing more than to slip into their pajamas after work and head out on the town. According to Fackler (2002), pajamas are considered a sign of comfort and status and wearing them in public is a symbol of luxury and a way to flaunt wealth. However, another item of clothing in Afghanistan, the *burka,* worn by women in public, is considered a sign of oppression. Each culture determines what is appropriate attire and what is attractive. In Arab cultures women might wear the *hijab,* a long raincoat-like garment with a scarf placed on the head to cover the hair completely. This form of dress evolved because women in Islam are supposed to be covered completely except for their faces, hands, and feet. In Kuwait, women dress very modestly. To respect that culture, female visitors should do the same—the neckline should be high and the sleeves come to at least the elbows. Hemlines should be well below the knee. The entire effect should be one of concealment—a full-length outfit that is tight and revealing is not acceptable (Morrison et al., 1994).

Many other artifacts are symbolic in nature. Durham (2001) conducted a study of the nose ring as a South Asian symbol made popular by Western culture. She employed a critical analysis of media images of White women adorned in the symbols of Indian femininity to explore the circulating economy. Finally, rhetorical scholars have examined the U.S. Senate's decision whether to grant a 14-year extension of the design patent for the United Daughters of the Confederacy insignia because it contained a representation of the Confederate flag—a historical symbol of racism (Crenshaw, 1997).

Physical Characteristics

Perceptions of physical characteristics such as attractiveness and body preference vary across gender and ethnicity. According to Patel and Gray (2001), women are more dissatisfied with their bodies than are men and Caucasian women are more dissatisfied than are African American women. A cursory glance at glamour magazines for each group might explain these differences in perceptions. The ideal woman in a U.S. American magazine is extremely tall and thin, whereas African American women are portrayed more realistically in magazines that are targeted to that audience.

In Malaysia both sexes receive many tattoos, both for protection and decoration. Many tribes place long weights or simple wooden plugs in the ears of children in order to stretch the earlobe. However, only women wear the heaviest weights so that their ear lobes eventually stretch down to their chests. Long lobes are considered a sign of great beauty in Malaysia.

In Bali it is essential for every Balinese to have his or her teeth filed, so much so that in the event of the death of a youth, the teeth are filed before cremation. The purpose of teeth filing is to reduce the power of greed, jealousy, anger, lust, drunkenness, and "confusion"—emotions more suitable to animals than to humans. Thus, the two upper canine teeth and the four incisors between them are filed down. A similar ritual, but for different reasons, is performed in Sudanese tribes in Africa. To welcome preteens into adulthood, six bottom teeth are removed (without benefit of anesthesia). The resulting collapsed lip and toothless grins may be a sign of pride in Africa, but these refugees have difficulty in the United States getting jobs where English is required and eating American food (Zaslow, 2002).

Paralanguage

Paralanguage consists of *how* something is said, not *what* is said. It includes vocal qualifiers (volume, pitch, rhythm, tone), vocal segregates ("uh," "um," "shh"), and vocal characteristics (sobbing, laughing, whispering). Cultural differences exist in each of these. For example, in terms of volume, Arabs tend to speak loudly because this suggests strength and sincerity. Thai and Japanese people speak softly because it is a sign of good manners and education. As Hoskin (1992) suggests:

> In Thailand, the voice should always be soft and calm. Those who had witnessed a car accident would have noted that even in such a grave situation, there was none of the shouting, accusing, finger-pointing, wild gestures, name-calling and everything else that is so common in the supposedly more advanced West. Don't raise your voice anywhere or anytime even when you feel cheated and you need to demand an explanation. To do so is to "lower yourself" and be seen as uncultured; perhaps a barbarian as one would say? (p. 118)

The high-pitched voice of the French should not be mistaken for anger. It generally means a great interest in the subject. The rate of speech also differs across cultures. Arabs, Jews, and Italians tend to speak faster than U.S. Americans.

In China, people use "hai" ("yes") as a vocal segregate. In fact, they often use it continually, even while the other person is speaking. U.S. Americans view this as rude because they view it as a violation of turn-taking cues. Vocal characteristics and their meaning also differ across cultures. The Japanese use laughter not only for joy but also to mask anger, sorrow, or displeasure.

CONCLUSION

Interpreting the meaning of nonverbal communication across cultures is tricky. The rules of nonverbal communication are rarely verbally discussed. One must observe closely in order to understand the appropriate roles and behaviors.

We'll close this chapter with an example of the problems a lack of understanding of nonverbal communication can cause (Storti, 1990, p. 24–25). It is an apocryphal story of the American couple invited to a Moroccan family's home for dinner:

> Having pressed their host to fix a time, they arrive half an hour late and are shown into the "guest" room. After a decent interval, they ask after the host wife, who has yet to appear, and are told that she is busy in the kitchen. At one point their host's little son wanders in, and the couple remark on his good looks. Just before the meal is served, the guests ask to be shown to the toilet so they may wash their hands. The main course is served in and eaten from a large, common platter, and the couple choose morsels of food from wherever they can reach, trying to keep up polite conversation throughout the meal. Soon after tea and cookies they take their leave.

What did they do wrong? Almost everything. They confused their host by asking him to fix the hour, for in the Muslim world an invitation to a meal is really an invitation to come and spend time with your friends, during the course of which time, God willing, a meal may very well appear. To ask what time you should come is tantamount to asking your host how long he wants you around and implies, as well, that you are more interested in the meal than in his company.

> One should be careful about asking after a Moslem man's wife; she frequently does not eat with foreign guests, even if female spouses are present, nor would she necessarily even be introduced. In any case, she belongs in the kitchen, guaranteeing the meal is as good as she can produce, thereby showing respect for her guests and bringing honor on her and her husband's house. Nor should one praise the intelligence or good looks of small children, for this will alert evil spirits

to the presence of a prized object in the home, and they may come and cause harm. It was not appropriate to ask to be shown the toilet either, for a decorative basin would have been offered for the washing of hands (and the nicer it is, the more honor it conveys upon the family). Nor should one talk during the meal; it interferes with the enjoyment of the food to have to keep up a conversation and may even be interpreted as a slight against the cooking. And one should only take food from the part of the platter directly in front, not from anywhere within reach. Not only is it rude to reach, but doing so deprives the host of one of his chief duties and pleasures: finding the best pieces of chicken or lamb and ostentatiously placing them before the guest.

In the readings that follow, two authors suggest the importance of nonverbal communication in the Chinese cultures. Forney discusses "online" grave sweeping and Cooper discusses the concept of beauty.

FOR DISCUSSION

1. Choose one nonverbal communication code such as kinesics, chronemics, or proxemics. How will the concept you choose influence communication with a person from a culture different from your own?
2. Review the percentages presented at the beginning of this chapter. Does your own personal experience support or refute the percentages? Give an example.
3. Describe an intercultural communication episode you have encountered in which nonverbal communication differences caused a misunderstanding.

REFERENCES

Andersen, P. A. (1999). Cultural cues: Nonverbal communication in a diverse world. In *Nonverbal communication: Forms and functions.* Mountain View, CA: Mayfield.

Argyle, M. (1975). *Bodily communication.* New York: International Universities Press.

Birdwhistell, R. (1970). *Kinesics and context.* Philadelphia: University of Pennsylvania Press.

Bond, M., and Iwata, Y. (1976). Proxemics and observation anxiety in Japan: Nonverbal and cognitive responses. *Psychologia, 19,* 110–126.

Crenshaw, C. (1997). Resisting whiteness' rhetorical silence. *Western Journal of Communication, 61* (3), 253–278.

Durham, M. G. (2001). Displaced persons: Symbols of south Asian femininity and the returned gaze in U.S. media culture. *International Communication Association, 11* (2), 201–217.

Ekman, P., and Friesen, W. (1971). Constants across cultures in the face and emotion. *Journal of Personality and Social Psychology, 17,* 124–129.

Fackler, M. (2002, September 15). On the streets of Shanghai, life is one big pajama party. *Milwaukee Journal Sentinel,* p. 32A.

Fridlund, A., Ekman, P., and Oster, H. (1987). Facial expression of emotion: Review of literature, 1970–1983. In A. Siegman and S. Feldstein (Eds.), *Nonverbal behavior and communication,* 2nd ed. (pp. 143–224). Hillsdale, NJ: Erlbaum.

Gonzalez, A., and Zimbardo, P. (1985). Time in perspective. *Psychology Today, 19,* 20–26.

Gudykunst, W., and Ting-Toomey, S. (1988). *Culture and interpersonal communication.* Newbury Park, CA: Sage

Gudykunst, W., Ting-Toomey, S., Sudweeks, S., and Steward, L. P. (1996). *Building bridges: Interpersonal skills for a changing world.* Boston: Houghton Mifflin.

Hall, E. T. (1959). *The silent language.* New York: Fawcett.

Hall, E. T. (1983). *The dance of life.* New York: Doubleday.

Hall, E. T., and Hall, M. R. (1990). *Understanding cultural differences: German, French and American.* Yarmouth, ME: Intercultural Press.

Harper, R., Wiens, A., and Matarazzo, J. (1991). *Nonverbal communication: The state of the art.* New York: Wiley.

Hoskin, J. (1992). *Introduction to Thailand.* Hong Kong: Odyssey Guide.

Jandt, F. E. (2004). Nonverbal communication. In *An introduction to intercultural communication: Identities in a global community,* 4th ed. Thousand Oaks, CA: Sage.

Kim, M. S. (1992). A comparative analysis of nonverbal expression as portrayed by Korean and American print-media advertising. *Howard Journal of Communication, 3,* 320–324.

Knapp, M., and Hall, J. (1997). *Nonverbal communication in human interaction,* 4th ed. Philadelphia: Harcourt, Brace, Jovanovich.

Lustig, M., and Koester, J. (1996). *Intercultural competence: Interpersonal communication across cultures.* New York: HarperCollins.

Lustig, M., and Koester, J. (2002). *Intercultural competence: Interpersonal communication across cultures,* 4th ed. New York: HarperCollins.

McDaniel, E. (2003). Nonverbal communication: A reflection of cultural themes. In L. Samovar and R. Porter (Eds.), *Intercultural communication: A reader,* 10th ed. (pp. 253–261). Belmont, CA: Wadsworth.

Mehrabian, A. (1982). *Silent messages: Implicit communication of emotion and attitudes,* 2nd ed. Belmont, CA: Wadsworth.

Morrison, T., Conway, W., and Borden, G. (1994). *Kiss now or shake hands: How to do business in sixty countries.* Holbrook, MA: Adams Media Corporation.

Patel, K. A., and Gray, J. J. (2001). Judgement accuracy in body preferences among African Americans. *Sex Roles, 44,* (3–4), 227–235.

Ramsey, S. (1979). Nonverbal behavior: An intercultural perspective. In M. Asante, E. Newmark, and C. Blake (Eds.), *Handbook of intercultural communication.* Beverly Hills, CA: Sage.

Roth, K. (2001, October). Material culture and intercultural communication. *International Journal of Intercultural Relations, 25* (5), 563–577.

Shioiri, T., Someya, T., Helmeste, D., and Tang, S. (1999). Misinterpretation of facial expression: A cross-cultural study. *Psychiatry and Clinical Neurosciences, 53,* 45–50.

Stewart, E., and Bennett, M. (1991). *American cultural patterns: A cross-cultural perspective.* Yarmouth, ME: Intercultural Press.

Storti, C. (1990). *The art of crossing cultures.* Yarmouth, ME: Intercultural Press.

Wenzhong, H., and Grove, C. (1991). *Encountering the Chinese.* Yarmouth, ME: Intercultural Press.

Zarembo, A. (1997, June 30). What if there weren't any clocks to watch? *Newsweek,* p. 14.

Zaslow, J. (2002, October 15). A Nebraska dentist offers African refugees rare gift: Their smile. *Wall Street Journal,* p. A12.

Virtual Grave Sites Play Host to Filial But Busy Chinese

Matt Forney

Life for filial but busy Chinese just got easier. Now, they can venerate their ancestors online at China's first virtual graveyard.

Just in time, too. Today is the annual grave-sweeping holiday, one of the biggest festivals of the year when Chinese tramp out to the countryside to pluck weeds from the burial mounds of their forebears, burn incense and pile food by tombstones. An unkempt grave shows disrespect and could lead to trouble from angry ghosts.

But the old ways of expressing piety don't fit modern lifestyles. "People work hard, and traffic on the roads to cemeteries can be terrible," says Li Xinghua, a manager of the Yuanbao Cemetery, which sponsors the site for free.

Shanghai officials predict that four million people will travel to a neighboring province for this year's holiday. "The Web is a better way to bring people together to memorialize the dead," says Mr. Li.

The Chinese-language site, Qingming.net, allows relatives of the deceased to design a virtual tomb for their late beloved. For ambience, Qingming—named after the Chinese festival—offers five types of background music, including the songs from *The Godfather* and *Titanic*. At the center of the computer screen monument is a choice of five tombstone designs, upon which one may type an inscription.

So far the site, which was launched two weeks ago, hasn't caught on. It receives fewer than 50 hits a day, and roughly 25 people have chosen to create "prayer rooms" for their dead relatives. No venture capitalist has visited the owners, who have no plans for an initial public offering. Yet Qu Gong, the man who administers the site on behalf of the cemetery, which is based in the port city of Tianjin, is certain it will make a killing.

"If you leave some fruit on the grave of a loved one, it will be gone when you visit the next year," Mr. Qu explains. "With the Web site, the virtual food or poems you leave will stay for 10 years, or forever," he says.

CHECK YOUR UNDERSTANDING

1. What are the burial practices in your culture? How do these differ from the one described in this news clipping? How are they similar?
2. What values and beliefs about life, the afterlife, and good and evil are communicated by these practices?

3. What artifacts are important symbols in your culture? What do these artifacts communicate about your culture?

Bound for Beauty: Narratives of Chinese Footbinding

Pamela Cooper

I remember the day the footbinding began. My mother told me that I could not be beautiful if I did not have bound feet. Ugly girls couldn't marry. The binding of my feet began when I was five years old. I hated it. I cried. It was so very, very painful. No matter how much I cried or begged, my mother never relented. If I loosened the bandages at night, my mother would beat me in the morning and bind the feet even tighter. So, what could I do? Nothing. So, my feet were bound. I remember the first time my mother unwrapped them. They were rotting. They smelled very bad and were full of pus. (Mrs. Kuo, Taiwan, 1995)

While teaching at the Chinese University of Hong Kong during 1992–1994, I began to study Chinese folktales as one way of understanding Chinese culture. Through a series of events, this study led me to an interest in footbinding. As I tried to gather information, it became apparent that little on the topic existed. What did exist, except for a book by Levy, was sketchy (1994). Interestingly, this definitive work on footbinding was written by a man. Even more recent works written by women lack the actual stories women told (Ping, 2000; Cooper, 2000; Lee, 1998; Jackson, 1997). Because I think it important to (1) gather the stories of women with bound feet before firsthand knowledge of this practice is unattainable due to the death of these women and (2) because I believe it important to tell these stories from a woman's perspective, I became engaged in this research study.

HISTORICAL PERSPECTIVE

Throughout history, in nearly every culture, women have "changed" their bodies to try to meet the standard of attractiveness designated by men. Several writers suggest the importance of beauty to women and the extremes women will go to both financially and emotionally to achieve the beauty standard set by men (see, for example, Wolf, 1991; Friday, 1993; Harris, 1994; Halprin, 1995; Brumberg, 1997). Rarely have women been asked to describe their experiences in relationship to these practices. In terms of footbinding, Ko suggests (1994, 169):

> Our present understanding of footbinding is based on four sources, all written by men: missionary accounts, literati studies of the custom's origins, erotica, and abolition literature, which sometimes include interviews with women. These sources naturally perpetuate our current reading of footbinding as a man-to-woman story. The other half of the picture, footbinding as a woman-to-woman story, has to be sought in the voices of the women themselves, both the binder and the bound.

Harris (1994, 4) creates a fitting metaphor—both for this struggle to meet society's image of beauty in general, and for this research specifically:

> I am reminded of the story of Cinderella's stepsisters who, in an effort to attain the prince, squeezed their feet into a slipper that was too tight and constricting. One of the sisters was compelled to cut off her toes, the other to amputate her heel, all in an attempt to fit into a shoe that belonged to someone else. Generally, when we read the story of Cinderella we see these sisters as unsympathetic characters. It is Cinderella waiting for her prince who is the heroine of the story. Yet these sisters present us with a story which resonates with the experiences of many modern women. Unable to fit into the images that have been presented to us, we often do damage to our essential selves, amputating important parts of who we are so that we can squeeze ourselves into the images that have been constructed by others. Not insignificantly, the slipper that the sisters tried to fit was made of glass. It was never intended for a real woman who would obviously be unable to walk in a glass slipper; only a woman who existed as a figment of our imagination could wear a glass slipper; only a woman who ceased to be real and had ascended the pedestal of an idealized image of femininity could possibly own a slipper made of glass.

HISTORY OF FOOTBINDING

The practice of footbinding began in the tenth century (around 950). Legend has it that the practice began with emperor Li Yu who had a favorite concubine named Lovely Maiden who was not only beautiful, but also a gifted dancer. Li Yu had a six-foot–high lotus constructed for her out of gold; it was decorated with pearls and had a carmine lotus carpel in the center. He ordered Lovely Maiden to bind her feet with white silk cloth to make the tips look like the points of a moon sickle. She then danced in the center of the lotus, whirling about like a rising cloud. Other concubines in the palace also bound their feet in order to gain favor with the emperor. Thus, the practice of footbinding began. It spread to the upper classes and eventually even to the peasants. The practice was quite widespread. It is estimated that 4.5 million Chinese women had their feet bound during the thousand years it was practiced in China.

Bound feet became known as "golden lotuses" because they resembled a lotus pod with the petals removed. The smaller the feet, the more beautiful they were considered to be. In fact, the ideal length was three inches. In addition to length, one writer set forth nine traditions of excellence in terms of shape (Hsun in Levy, 1994, 108–120). There were seventy-six different styles of footbinding in China (Becker, 1995). In the south, for example, men admired longer and slimmer feet. In western China, the preference was for curved feet.

As early as 1664 a ban on footbinding was issued but was rescinded in 1668. Footbinding was formally outlawed after the fall of the Manchu Dynasty in 1911, partly in response to a campaign by Western missionaries. This law too was later rescinded. However, once the Communists took over in 1949, footbinding was outlawed for the final time. The Kuomintang government employed "foot inspectors" whose duty it was to travel through the countryside and enforce the ban on footbinding. However, as late as 1947, young girls' feet were still being bound in remote villages in China (Zhang, 1989).

Footbinding was an exclusively female affair. Usually a young girl's feet were bound by her mother. The binding was started between the ages of five and seven. The mother gathered the materials: a bandage two inches wide and ten feet long (lightly starched and free of wrinkles), five pairs of cloth shoes with flat bottoms, three pairs of cloth slippers for bed (women made the shoes; in fact women took great pride in the shoes—the intricate embroidery used to decorate them), several pairs of tight socks, alum, an astringent, scissors, nail clippers, needle and thread. The success or failure of footbinding was dependent on the skillful application of a bandage, about two inches wide and ten feet long. One end of the bandage was placed on the inside of the instep and from there it was carried over the small so as to force the toes in and towards the sole. The large toe was left unbound. The bandage was then wrapped around the heel forcefully, so that the toe and heel were drawn closer together. The process was then repeated from beginning to end until the bandage was completely wrapped. The object was to make the toes bend under and into the sole and bring the sole and heel as close together as was physically possible.

Two interesting facts emerged from this and other studies of this practice. First, the myth has been that only wealthy women had their feet bound. However, if a woman was a member of the ethnic group of Han Chinese, her feet were bound—even if she came from a peasant family. Second, although this practice was one of the Han, evidence suggests that other ethnic groups were affected by this practice. For example, in her review of Cantonese love songs, Cooper (1994) found that several of the songs refer to the desire for bound feet and references to desiring a mate with bound feet rather than a "big-footed" woman.

The process of footbinding was sometimes launched with a prayer to the gods. Ko (1994, 149–150) indicates some of the rituals associated with footbinding:

A Ming household almanac printed in Fujian stipulated rules for picking an auspicious day to inaugurate this rite of passage. In Suzhou, binding customarily started on the twenty-fourth day of the eighth month, when the Tiny-Foot Maiden (Ziaojiao Guniang), the deity in charge of footbinding, enjoyed offerings from her devotees. On that day, girls shaped rice balls from glutinous rice and red beans, praying that their bones would be just as soft. Offerings to the stove god were also made. The date was chosen in part for practical reasons; it was more pleasant for a girl to start binding in the cool of autumn. Both the starting date and rituals varied from area to area. In some areas of China Guanyin, the omnipotent protector of women. Before binding was to start, a mother would sew and embroider a tiny pair of shoes and place it on top of an incense burner in front of a Guanyin statue.

REASONS FOR FOOTBINDING

One purpose for the footbinding was to restrain women. As Seagrave writes, "Confucians barely tolerated females, and by crippling their feet it was certain that they could not stray far from their well-guarded quarters, or run from beatings" (1985, 159).

However, most historians agree that the main purpose was one of sexual attractiveness. Men found bound feet erotic (Levy, 1994, 62):

A woman's sexual attraction came to center in the mystery of her bound feet, which were almost never bared to view. The caressing of the diminutive foot in innumerable ways became part of the prelude to the sex act. The rationale came about that binding the foot resulted in a heavier thigh and that the genital region tightened and became much more developed. These scientifically invalid ideas were, nonetheless, widely believed.

Thus, in order to be seen as sexually attractive, women needed to have bound feet. The women in this study indicated that having bound feet was a prerequisite to marriage. In Chinese culture, it was imperative that a woman be married. She had no value in Chinese society unless she was married and bore sons. In fact, women were not even considered adults until they were married (Clayre, 1984). In a society in which women were seen as inferior to men and whose only real value lay in the ability to bear sons, it was imperative for survival that women be found attractive enough to be married (Ko, 1997).

Ko indicates that footbinding was seen as a sign of civility (1997, 12):

Correct attire—headdress, dress, and shoes—was the quintessential expression of civility, culture, and humanity, all being ramifications of "wen." Attire played a central role in both the external and internal definitions of Chinese identities: clothing differentiated the Chinese from their (inferior) neighbors while marking social and gender distinctions within society. . . . If properly clothed bodies marked the civility and orderliness of the Chinese, unadorned bodies and feet recurred as visible signs of the savagery of peoples on the peripheries.

Thus, footbinding was seen as an expression of civility and as a marker separating Han from other ethnic groups. In addition, footbinding was seen as ornament or embellishment (Ko, 1997, 18, 19):

That is to say, in the classical Chinese formulation, what signifies a body is its cosmological location, not physicality in itself . . . This perception of the body as primarily a social body that is neither self-contained nor isolated illuminates the significance of Chinese clothing as social, moral, and ethnic markers. It also resonates with the imperial Chinese notion of dressing as embodiment, a corollary to the conception of the body as attire. . . . This expansive conception of the body also helps explain why the predominant view of footbinding before the eighteenth century was one of attire and adornment, not bodily mutilation.

THE INTERVIEWS

As suggested earlier, the extant literature contains little of women's personal narratives of footbinding. As Ko (1997, 9) suggests, "And most important, how did women feel about it?"

Before examining what women said about footbinding, it is important to understand three cultural factors that greatly influenced this study. The first is the sexual nature of footbinding. The Chinese are traditionally reluctant to talk about sexual matters.

The second factor is that the Chinese are reluctant to talk about this practice because it is now seen as "barbaric." I was told time and time again, "Oh, those women are all dead. We don't do that anymore. You should just forget it." It is rare to see bound feet shoes in museums in China. It is rarely referred to in recent books of Chinese history.

The third factor is the concept of "guanxi" or connections. Little can be accomplished in the Chinese culture "on your own." Thus, I spent over a year and a half locating the seven women I interviewed. I contacted colleagues, friends, and acquaintances in China, Taiwan, Hong Kong, and in my professional organizations both here and abroad. These "connections," or the "connections" these people had or could make, resulted in finding the seven women.

Seven women (ranging in age from 77 to 96) were interviewed over the course of two summers in the mid-1990s. Three women lived in Taiwan, one in Hong Kong, and three in Beijing. Four other women who either still had or who previously had bound feet were located, but could not be interviewed. One woman who was ninety had agreed to be interviewed, but when I arrived with the interpreter at the nursing home, she was sleeping and did not awaken during the hour and half I was at the nursing home interviewing another woman. The son of one woman (who had bound her own feet when she was an adolescent) refused to allow me to interview his mother. This was also the case with two other women. One woman's son told me that footbinding was a very private affair and his family did not want me to talk about it.

No audio or videotaping of the conversations was allowed. During all but one interview, I was allowed to take notes. One woman's feet were bared when I entered her cubicle at the nursing home, so she allowed me to take pictures of her feet. Three of the seven women allowed me to take their picture. I had a female interpreter since my command of Mandarin is quite limited. After each interview was completed, the interpreter and I returned to our hotel room and wrote our field notes. We then compared the field notes for discrepancies.

All interviews took place in the residences of the women. I have included two narratives from two transcripts.

Mrs. Wang

(I interviewed Mrs. Wang and Mrs. Huo at an apartment complex in Beijing. Mrs. Wang began talking as soon as she entered the room. She asked me, "Did you come to have your feet bound?" and she chuckled. She began telling her story. Both she and Mrs. Huo talked nearly nonstop about their experience. I had the feeling that they had a story to tell and someone to finally listen, and they were going to tell it! Mrs. Wang's daughter and granddaughter sat in the room during the interview. They had never heard the story before.)

My feet were bound by my mother when I was five and unbound when I was fourteen. I am now seventy-seven. On the day my feet were first bound, my mother told me she was sorry, but if she didn't bind them, no man would marry me—not even a bad man! She said, "Only little feet are beautiful." I was very unhappy when the President of China ordered feet to be unbound!

My feet were bound with a long, white cloth, nearly one and two-thirds meters long. At first the binding was not tight, but every day my mother bound it tighter and tighter. It was hard to walk. When I walked my hips swayed a lot (she got up from her chair and demonstrated for us). Men thought the swaying was very beautiful.

My feet were bound twice a day—once in the morning and once at night. They were bound very tight at night, but not so tight during the day so I could walk. After a while, I learned to bind my own feet so my mother no longer had to. The pain was very bad. I cried. There was nothing for the pain—no medicine.

Men had no part in footbinding. Women bound each other's feet. My father told my mother to bind my feet because it was her job.

I made my own shoes—very beautiful. Everyone made their own shoes. You couldn't buy them. I was very proud of my beautiful embroidered shoes.

I bound my younger sister's feet. Hers weren't bound long, because the government ordered feet unbound.

I am so glad someone has finally asked me about my bound feet. I never talked to anyone about it before. No one talked to each other about it. It was private. I was afraid I would die before anyone asked me about my bound feet.

You ask how my life would be different if I didn't ever have bound feet. I don't know. I lived this life. That's all I know.

(When I left, Mrs. Wang took her cane and walked down three flights of stairs with me, out to the main street, and stood, tears running down her cheeks, as I drove away in the taxi.)

Mrs. Huo

I am 85 years old. My feet were bound by my mother when I was five, but unbound when I was eight. My mother told me, "If you don't bind your feet, you won't get a husband. The smaller your feet, the more beautiful, the more men will like you." I always obeyed my parents, so I did not argue. Whatever parents say, you must do.

At first it wasn't painful. The feet were bound loosely. When I went to bed, they were bound tighter. They hurt so much I couldn't have them covered. I washed them every three days. That helped the pain some. But, if you bound the feet too tight, the finger (little toe) would stick out and then the feet were ugly. You had to be careful about that.

The government told women to let out their feet or they had to pay lots of money. I didn't have lots of money, so I let them out. Besides, I was ashamed to have bound feet. First we were supposed to have them, then we weren't. The pain when they were unbound was much. I had to learn to walk again on unbound feet.

I never talked to anyone about this—not my husband, mother, sister, no one. It was something you had, but didn't talk about. It just was. Now I will talk to you about it because I am not ashamed now; I am "liberated." Also, you are my *pengyou* (friend).

(When I left, Mrs. Huo asked me to come back. She said, "You are my friend. Come to see me. Please, come to see me again.")

CONCLUSION

It is interesting that although I did not ask women to explain how their feet were bound, all but one did so. It seemed to be extremely important to them that I understood the physical pain and suffering they had been through. Even if the feet had been bound for only a few years, the damage was done. All these women showed physical effects of the binding.

Only one of the women had talked about footbinding previous to our conversation. Unlike American culture, where nearly everything is talked about, in Chinese culture there was no need to talk. This practice was one that had been passed down for a thousand years. When a parent tells a child to do something, the child does it—no questions asked. Only one woman's mother had explained the process. The women had no say in whether it was to be done or not. They never talked about it until I arrived to ask them about it.

Two forces can explain the lack of communication about footbinding. The first is the role of women in China. During the time this practice occurred, women had no rights and their only hope of any societal position was marriage. In her book, *Changing Identities of Chinese Women,* Croll (1995) indicates that during the time of footbinding, this practice was just one more way to keep women confined. The sexes were separated. Women were not allowed to venture from their homes or to take part in various rituals such as ancestor worship. In a culture in which women had no status, no real value except to give birth to sons, it is little wonder that no discussion of footbinding was seen as necessary. It was the means to the appropriate end of any woman—marriage.

The second force is the cultural one. In collectivist societies such as China, the good of the whole is most important, not the desires of a single individual. If females had refused to have their feet bound, they, their mother, and their entire family would have lost face. To refuse would have been unthinkable in the culture, and thus, there was no need to discuss it, explain it, or complain about it. In addition, as these interviews as well as historical writings and art suggest, the bound foot was extremely erotic. Such sexual matters are not discussed in Chinese culture.

These women, by sharing their stories, have, as Vickers and Thomas (1989) suggest, validated their life experience—not only for themselves but for all women who have had their bodies "altered" for the sake of societal and cultural concepts of beauty.

REFERENCES

Becker, Jasper. (September 1995). Agony in the name of beauty. *South China Morning Post,* 16, p. 26.

Brumberg, Joan Jacobs. (1997). *The body project: An intimate history of American girls.* New York: Random House.

Christ, Carol. (1986). *Diving deep and surfacing.* Boston: Beacon Press.

Clayre, Alasdair. (1984). *The heart of the dragon.* Boston: Houghton Mifflin.

Cooper, Pamela. (1994). *The role of women in Cantonese love songs.* Paper presented at the annual meetings of the Central States Communication Association, Lexington, KY.

Cooper, Pamela. (2000). Twists and turns: An autobiography. *Human Communication,* 3, 85–96.

Croll, Elaine. (1995). *Changing identities of Chinese women.* Hong Kong: Hong Kong University Press.

Fisher, Walter. (1989). *Human communication as narration: Toward a philosophy of reason, value and action.* Columbia, SC: University of South Carolina Press.

Friday, Nancy. (1993). *The power of beauty.* New York: HarperCollins.

Halprin, Sara. (1995). *Look at my ugly face.* New York: Penguin.

Harris, Maxine. (1994). *Down from the pedestal.* New York: Doubleday.

Heilbrun, Carolyn. (1988). *Writing a woman's life.* New York: Ballantine Books.

Jackson, Beverly. (1997). *Splendid slippers: A thousand years of an erotic tradition.* Berkeley, CA: Speed Press.

Hong, Fan. (1997). *Footbinding, feminism and freedom: The liberation of women's bodies in modern China.* London: Frank Cass.

Ko, Dorothy. (1994). *Teachers of the inner chambers: women and culture in seventeenth-century China.* Stanford, CA: Stanford University Press.

Ko, Dorothy. (1997). The body as attire: The shifting meanings of footbinding in seventeenth-century China. *The Journal of Women's History,* 8, 8–27.

Lee, Wenshu. (1998). Patriotic breeders or colonized converts: A postcolonial feminist approach to antifootbinding discourse in China. In Delores Tanno and Alberto Gonzalez (Eds.), *Communication and identity across cultures.* Thousand Oaks, CA: Sage, pp. 11–33.

Levy, Howard. (1968, 1994). *The lotus lovers: The complete history of the curious erotic custom of footbinding in China.* Buffalo, NY: Prometheus Books.

Ping, Wang. (2000). *Aching for beauty.* Minneapolis, MN: University of Minnesota Press.

Roberts, Glenn and Steele, Valerie. (March/April 1997). The three inch golden lotus: A collection of Chinese bound feet shoes. *Arts of Asia,* 27, 69–85.

Seagrave, Sterling. (1985). *The Soong Dynasty.* New York: Harper and Row.

Vickers, Joanne and Thomas, Barbara. (1989). *No more frogs, no more princes.* Freedom, CA: The Crossing Press.

Wolf, Naomi. (1991). *The beauty myth: How images of beauty are used against women.* New York: Doubleday.

Zhang, Jiafen. (September 1989). Free bound feet. *Women in China,* 43–45.

CHECK YOUR UNDERSTANDING

1. What is considered beautiful in your culture?
2. Is there any practice women use in your culture to obtain beauty that is similar to that of footbinding?

CHAPTER ACTIVITIES

1. With a classmate, view a foreign film. After viewing the film, discuss the differences you observed between the culture in the film and your own culture.
2. Visit an ethnic area in your city. Observe nonverbal variables such as greeting behavior, speech volume, spatial relationships, artifacts, haptics, chronemics, and kinesics. How do these differ from your own culture? What do these differences tell you about being an effective communicator in that culture versus your own culture?
3. Interview a person from a culture different from your own about nonverbal rules in her or his culture. Share with him or her how these rules are different from or similar to your culture.

CHAPTER 7

LISTENING

LISTENING IN A JAPANESE GARDEN

The sounds of Tokyo had become too much. The hustle and bustle, the noise, the pollution. I needed to escape, if only for a moment of solitude, and peace, and quiet.

I walked and found myself in a park with a beautiful Japanese garden. I entered. Here was just what I needed. The street noises subsided and I found myself listening to the sounds of the garden. Other people were there also, but each seemed to know the sacredness of this place and were reverent. I thought of one of my favorite hymns, *In the Garden*.

This was a landscape garden. It had water and a pond. Unlike the dry Buddhist gardens which have no water, but rather raked pebbles to simulate water. Both types of gardens create an atmosphere for meditation. The sound of the water over the rocks, the beautifully landscaped gardens, ponds and water falls, the groupings of stones, shrubs, and trees all combined into a symphony of silence. I sat quietly and began to think of how this garden reflected the nature of the Japanese people.

Japanese are a collectivist culture and value harmony (*wa*) between individuals and between nature and individuals. The garden certainly reflected such harmony. Each element of the garden created a natural refuge. In addition, no Japanese would dream of upsetting the garden by littering. Just as they strive to protect "face" and thus maintain harmony, the Japanese garden with its emphasis on the beauties of nature and the placement of one element in the garden to another reflects this value on harmony. Part of the harmony also results from the silence of the garden. Silence truly is "golden" in Japan, and much can be communicated by it. In fact, Japanese suggest that real communication—the understanding of emotions and feelings—can only take place in silence. A Japanese proverb states: Those who know do not speak; those who speak do not know.

The garden also reflected the Japanese concept of *seishin* (spirit). Seishin stresses devotion to duty and the importance of self-discipline. Without *seishin*, harmony is destroyed. Thus, the gardener does not "force" the garden. Rather, he allows it to express itself through the seasons. Unlike his American counterpart, the Japanese gardener does not try to impose form and order on the garden. Rather, he seeks to capture its intrinsic being: I knew this garden would be as beautiful in winter as it was on this hot day in July. I longed to see this garden in winter. No doubt the trees had been planted in such a way that the bare branches in winter would have their own appeal. I thought of a picture I had seen of a Japanese garden in winter with snow on the tree branches.

Two Japanese words came to mind as I sat and walked in the garden. *Wabi*—the aesthetic feeling of discovering serenity and richness in simplicity, and *sabi*—the feeling of quiet grandeur enjoyed in solitude. I began to think of the sounds I had heard in the garden. The water falling over rocks, the singing of birds and the sound as they flew, the chirping of insects. When I talked about my experience with a Japanese friend, she said, "Ah yes. We Japanese can hear the cherry blossoms falling!"

Time passed and I left the garden. I returned often during my visit. In stillness, in simplicity, and in serenity I began to really listen—to focus on the sounds and sights around me, and to listen not only with my ears and eyes, but with my heart. And, the lesson of the Japanese garden is that solitude prepares us again for the hustle and bustle of life—perhaps as better listeners.

OBJECTIVES

After reading this chapter and completing the readings and activities, you should be able to

- Define listening.
- Understand the importance of active listening.
- Describe the levels of listening.
- Understand the barriers to effective listening.
- Describe principles for listening interculturally.
- Describe steps to listening effectively across cultures.

DEFINITION OF LISTENING

Take a moment, close your eyes, and attend to the sounds around you. What did you hear? The hum of the heating system, birds outside your window, footsteps of someone walking down the hall? These sounds are around us all the time, but because we are not listening, we are not aware of their presence. It is one thing to hear a sound, but quite another to listen to it. Hearing is the first step in the listening process. It is necessary, but not sufficient for listening to occur. While hearing involves the physiological reception of sounds, listening is a much more complicated process.

HURIER MODEL

Brownell (2002) describes listening according to the HURIER model, which represents six interrelated activities associated with listening; hearing, understanding, remembering, interpreting, evaluating, and responding. Let's analyze the experiences of the author in the narrative of "Listening in a Japanese Garden" according to this model.

Hearing

Since hearing involves the accurate receiving of sounds, you must focus your attention and concentrate to begin the process of listening. For example, the author in the narrative was attempting to escape the street noises and found herself listening to the sounds of the garden. She describes the water falling over the rocks, the singing of the birds and the sound of their flight, and chirping insects. These are the things she hears and attends to.

Understanding

You may hear sounds but not always comprehend them. Listening for comprehension improves with practice. It involves an intrapersonal thought process and requires reflection. The author in the garden began to think of the sounds in the garden and what they meant. She describes the aesthetic feeling of discovering serenity and the quiet grandeur of solitude.

Remembering

According to Brownell (2002), "Remembering is essential if you intend to apply what you have heard in future situations" (p. 15). How often have you been introduced to someone and forgotten his or her name only moments later? Perhaps this is because you are not attending to the name; rather, you are forming in your mind first impressions of the person. Remembering requires a conscious effort on the part of the listener. The author of "Listening in a Japanese Garden" takes time to reflect on the nature of the garden. She is rehearsing every aspect of the beauty of the garden so she may never forget and she recalls a favorite song that will allow her to associate the garden with her own experiences. She even reflects on how the garden might look at different times of the year and is applying these memories to future situations.

Interpreting

Interpreting messages involves the ability to empathize—to see a situation from another person's perspective. In addition, interpreting "requires that you pay attention to emotional meaning and to the communication context" (Brownell, 2002, p. 15). This is exemplified perfectly in the Japanese Garden as the author considers how the garden reflects the nature of the Japanese people. She reflects on how someone from a culture other than her own will respond to the garden. She indicates to others in the garden that she understands the serenity and sanctity of the garden by remaining silent.

Evaluating

You evaluate messages through your past experiences, attitudes, and values. Based on these predispositions, you evaluate the messages you receive. Are they consistent with your beliefs? If not, how are they different, and will you accept or reject the messages? The author evaluates the garden by concluding that the solitude it provides will better prepare her for life and listening.

Responding

Once you have listened to a message, you must decide how you will respond. What will you do with the information? Will you use it to form new information? Or will you reject it because it is not consistent with what you already know? The author of the narrative makes a conscious decision to remember the garden and to return to it often, and she reflects on how the garden allows her to appreciate the process of listening. She decides to focus on the sounds and sights around her, and to listen not only with her ears but also with her heart.

IMPORTANCE OF ACTIVE LISTENING

The HURIER model describes the process of active listening. In other words, listening requires a lot of time and effort. But why is it important to listen? First, we spend most of our time listening. According to Cooper and Simonds (2003), 70 percent of our waking time is spent in some form of communication. Of that time, 9 percent is spent writing, 16 percent reading, 30 percent talking, and 57 percent listening. Interestingly, although listening is the activity we engage in the most, it is a skill we are seldom taught. Communication textbooks offer few sections on listening, and even fewer departments offer courses, but this is the skill with which we are expected to perform at very competent levels.

Finally, listening is an important survival skill. For example, Wolvin and Coakley (1991) cite listening as the top skill necessary for success in the business community. We acquire knowledge, develop language, learn professions, enhance relationships, and communicate respect through listening. Brownell (2002) describes two very important functions of listening. First, listening helps you accomplish tasks through understanding, recall, feedback, decision making, and problem solving. Second, as mentioned earlier, listening promotes relationships by attending to emotions, understanding needs, self-disclosure, enhancing authentic trust, and valuing diversity and respect for others. These functions will ultimately allow us to communicate better interpersonally as well as interculturally.

LEVELS OF LISTENING

In a chapter on listening between co-cultures, Chen and Starosta (1998) describe three levels of listening: (1) intrapersonal, (2) interpersonal, and (3) intercultural listening.

Intrapersonal

Intrapersonal listening involves self-monitoring and reflection. You might ask, How can I listen if no one is talking? Have you ever had a conversation with yourself? Did you make decisions about future behaviors in light of that conversation? According to Brownell (2002), self-monitoring involves self-awareness. It involves the awareness about how your behavior affects the ability to do your job or build relationships. The author of "Listening in a Japanese Garden" was engaging in intrapersonal listening. Although there was no conversation with another person, she was reflecting on the meaning and nature of the garden in her own mind. In doing so, she was listening to herself. People who tend to engage in self-listening behaviors develop the ability to listen better to others.

Interpersonal

Interpersonal listening occurs when we communicate with people who are similar to us. That is, they speak the same language and hold similar cultural values as us. A perfect example of this type of listening is that shared between family members. The more time you spend with another person, the more history you share, the better able you are to listen to one another. This happens because shared experiences allow you to predict more accurately what the other person is thinking. This common symbol base lends itself to effective listening and communication, but what happens when people are dissimilar?

Intercultural

Because our past experiences, language, values, and predispositions affect the way we listen and communicate, intercultural communication can become problematic if we are not sensitive to these differences. Even someone who speaks the same language may have difficulty listening effectively to a person from another region. Differences in vocal rhythm or pronunciation may cause problems in listening. Chen and Starosta (1998) list three issues that affect our ability to listen interculturally: (1) listening across emotions, (2) fusing horizons, and (3) selective listening.

Lack of shared history, context, and meaning can block openness of exchange. Speicher (1994) suggests that the person who speaks emotionally across cultures usually speaks rationally. Because certain emotions are more universal, effective intercultural communicators should be attuned to emotions. People can be both passionate and logical. Although someone from another culture may not understand the logic, they may be better suited to understand the emotion behind the logic.

We all have our own worldview that is comprised of our language, patterns of thought, values, and beliefs. When we become locked into that worldview, effective interactions with people from another culture are blocked (Chen & Starosta, 1998). We engage in ethnocentrism as we defend our own interpretations of events. It is not until we can learn to fuse horizons by putting aside our own historical and cultural references that we can appreciate how others see us.

Sometimes, we listen and accept what we expect to hear and dismiss messages that are inconsistent with our own thinking, These prejudices and history limit us from authentic listening. For example, Lewis (1999) suggests that in negotiations, U.S. Americans expect to hear humor, catch phrases, jokes, and a "hard sell"; Japanese expect a formal presentation; Germans expect to hear technical information and no jokes; French expect a logical presentation; and Arabs expect eloquence. This form of selective listening does not allow us to communicate interculturally and can lead to barriers to effective listening.

BARRIERS TO EFFECTIVE LISTENING

It's no wonder we have difficulty listening. There are so many interferences that can get in the way, especially when people communicating do not share the same culture. In order to communicate effectively, we must learn to deal with physical, mental, factual, and semantic distractions.

Physical distractions include external interferences from the environment that keep you from focusing on the speaker and the message. Examples may include loud music, people talking, strong smells, temperature in the room, or time of day. These distractions may inhibit your ability to hear the message which would certainly inhibit your ability to complete the listening process. The next three types of interference are internal distractions.

A *mental distraction* causes you not to concentrate on the message. You may hear it, but you don't attend to it, so understanding is not achieved. Your mind may wander because you are hungry or upset. You may be thinking about what you are going to say next rather than listening to what is being said to you. You may be nervous or confused. All of these distractions inhibit your ability to process the message. For example, in a job interview, you are so concerned with how you are portraying yourself and the first impressions that are being received, you forget to listen to the next interview question.

The third type of internal interference is a *factual distraction*. This can occur when there are too many details to attend to. You may become overwhelmed with information overload and miss the main point of the message. Perhaps you are paying attention to the facts, or particular details, but miss the overall message. For example, in a history class, you may be so concerned with remembering dates and places that you lose sight of the implications of the events.

The last type of internal interference is most likely to occur while communicating interculturally. *Semantic distractions* occur when someone uses unfamiliar words or terminology or when you react emotionally to a word or phrase. In other words, language barriers create semantic distractions as well as emotional barriers. As these barriers may affect our ability to listen and develop relationships with people from other cultures, it is important to discuss strategies for listening interculturally

EFFECTIVE LISTENING ACROSS CULTURES

It is not until we understand the process of listening as well as the implications for communicating across cultures that we can become more effective listeners. It is important to note that improving listening skills will require time and effort as well as motivation. We will first discuss general strategies for improving listening and then focus on particular strategies for improving intercultural listening. First, Cooper and Simonds (2003) outline several behaviors that can improve listening.

1. *Remove, if possible, the physical barriers to listening.* You might simply move to another room or move the furniture in the room, turn the thermostat up or down, or close the door. Manipulate your environment to fit your needs.
2. *Focus on the speaker's main idea.* You can always request specific facts and figures later. Your initial purpose as a listener should be to answer the question. What is the person's main idea?
3. *Listen for the intent, as well as the content, of the messages.* Ask yourself, why is this person saying this?
4. *Give the other person a full hearing.* Do not begin your evaluation until you have listened to the entire message. Too often, as listeners we spend our listening time creating our messages rather than concentrating on the content and intent of the other's message.

5. *Remember the saying that meanings are in people, not in words.* Try to overcome your emotional reactions to words. Focus on what you can agree with in the message and use this as common ground as you move into more controversial issues.

6. *Concentrate on the other person as a communicator and as a human being.* All of us have ideas, and we have feelings about those ideas. Listen with all your senses, not just with your ears. The well-known admonition to "stop, look, and listen" is an excellent one to follow when listening. Focus on questions such as: What does she mean verbally? Nonverbally? What's the feeling behind the message? Is this message consistent with those she has expressed in previous conversations? (pp. 70–71).

In an article titled, "Listening in the Global Marketplace," Jean Harris (2002) provides several strategies for listening interculturally. They include (1) Listen for your own cultural/individual values; (2) When you are being introduced to someone from another culture, listen for his or her cultural/individual values; (3) Expand your knowledge of the cultural norms of other peoples; and (4) Listen with your eyes open and an open mind. These strategies allow one to become a global listener. Harris describes the global listener as one who has:

I. *Knowledge*—You will have the capacity to:
   - Identify your own cultural values and their effects on your listening ability style.
   - Learn about the cultural values and listening behaviors of others by reading and by seeking out opportunities to meet people from different cultures.
   - Know your strengths and weaknesses as they relate to listening across cultures. Include knowing your emotional responses and biases when you listen to someone from another culture.

II. *Attitude*—You will have the will to:
   - Adopt an open, respectful approach towards cultural differences.
   - Acknowledge and suspend your assumptions about the speaker who is culturally different.
   - Check any judgmental tendencies you may have.
   - Be prepared for the unexpected.
   - Develop patience.

III. *Skill*—You will have the ability to:
   - Practice listening to people who have a distinct accent.
   - Practice interpreting nonverbals of people from other countries.
   - Modify your listening style to accommodate the speaker who is culturally different.
   - Remember that questions are not always appropriate. One might be offended by a question about a basic assumption.
   - Listen for the use of "I" and "we" to indicate individualistic or group outlook.
   - Listen for silence that differs from its use in the United States.
   - Listen for introductions that may reveal values.
   - Listen for a different use of "yes" and "no."
   - Listen for emphasis on transparency.
   - Approach each intercultural encounter as a unique experience. Remind yourself that you may be listening to someone who has modified the cultural norm of his/her group. (p. 26)

CONCLUSION

Harris's advice brings together the concepts discussed in this chapter in a very practical way. Once we understand how listening works and that it takes time, effort, and motivation to master, we can begin to understand the implications of how listening may be different across cultures. It is important to engage in active listening behaviors regardless of the level at which it is taking place. Barriers to effective listening can create misunderstanding and tension even among those who are similar and can certainly become the impetus for even larger conflicts when people are dissimilar. This chapter provides many guidelines for listening interculturally as well as suggestions for improving your listening skills at home and abroad. This information is furthered in the reading by Beall in this chapter. The advice of the author of "Listening in a Japanese Garden" is well taken. When we learn to listen with our hearts as well as our eyes and ears, we can begin to break down the barriers to effective cross-cultural relationships.

FOR DISCUSSION

1. How does the HURIER model of listening make it an active rather than a passive activity?
2. Describe an event where listening has helped you accomplish a task. Maintain a relationship with another person? Communicate respect to another person?
3. What are the implications that levels of listening have on the way you communicate with yourself and others?
4. Consider the barriers to effective listening. Which one of these is most likely to affect your ability to communicate with someone from another culture? Explain.
5. Describe some strategies you will use to begin listening more effectively.

REFERENCES

Brownell, J. (2002). *Listening: Attitudes, principles, and skills.* Boston: Allyn and Bacon.

Chen, G. M., and Starosta, W. J. (1998). *Foundations of intercultural communication.* Boston: Allyn and Bacon.

Cooper, P. J., and Simonds, C. J. (2003). *Communication for the classroom teacher.* Boston: Allyn and Bacon.

Harris, J. A. (2002). Listening in the global marketplace. *EarPiece: Magazine of the International Listening Association, 1* (1), 24–27.

Lewis, R. (1999). *When cultures collide.* London: Nicholas Brealey.

Speicher, B. L. (1994). Interethnic conflict: Attribution and cultural ignorance. *Howard Journal of Communication, 5* (3), 195–213.

Wolvin, A., and Coakley, C. (1991). A survey of the status of listening training in some Fortune 500 corporations. *Communication Education, 40,* 152–164.

Perspectives on Intercultural Listening

Melissa Beall

In the past two decades, the world has become much more aware of cultural practices. Intercultural awareness is usually viewed as a positive characteristic in today's global society. In many elementary and secondary classrooms around the world, "multiculturalism" is a required part of the curriculum and many colleges require a course in multiculturalism or, more specifically, in intercultural communication. And, college and university general education requirements usually include or at least strongly encourage study of various cultures. Many require at least one course in non-Western culture as a part of core requirements.

While many courses focus on differences, there are, in fact, many similarities between and among various cultures that we choose not to think about or even recognize. What is apparent, however, is that unless the interactants in diverse communication events are aware of both similarities and differences, problems may occur. Culture is the basis for the ways people think, talk, and act. Culture, however, is not contained within just different ethnic or national boundaries. There are many layers of cultures within any given country or society. Thus, while it may be easy to refer to cultural perspectives, it is not always easy to define what we mean by the term. Culture pervades everything people do, and varies from country to country, workplace to workplace, and group to group. Despite the awareness of the need to know more about other cultures, unless there's an employer mandate, or another significant reason to learn more about others and their culture, little or no emphasis is placed on intercultural listening. And, despite the prevalence of the need for effective listening, listening is often not included in the training provided by employers for personnel sent on global assignments. Furthermore, the concept of intercultural listening also almost defies categorization. Thomlison (1997, p. 91) asserts that "Western cultures as a whole place much greater emphasis on speaking than on listening. . . . Western cultures take listening for granted. . . . In contrast, many non-Western cultures emphasize listening rather than speaking." Thus, it would seem that trainers and educators should expend greater effort to raise people's awareness of the importance of listening, in general, and intercultural listening, specifically.

While we do not yet have all the answers to the question, "What is intercultural listening?" there are some characteristics that we can use as a guideline to understand listening in our own culture and in other cultures. In this essay, we will explore what we already "know" about intercultural listening, identify some of the characteristics of intercultural listening within different cultures (based on a review of the literature and interviews with international students), and posit some concerns for needed research in the area.

A BRIEF REVIEW OF THE LITERATURE

Clinard (1985, p. 39) suggests that listening may be the best tool for understanding the people with whom we work. Wolvin and Coakley (1996, p. 124) offer "ten factors influencing the listening process." Significantly, the first factor is culture and the authors suggest that "Communication scholars have come to recognize that culture is a primary determinant of all communication behaviors—including listening—because one's culture essentially serves to define who one is and how one will communicate through one's perceptual filter." Wolvin and Coakley (1996, p. 125) further suggest that [cultures and] subcultures within the United States

illustrate differences that require adaptation for the listener to understand and to respond appropriately. They further state that "communication between blacks and whites is shaped by cultural influences." Intercultural communication scholars, Samovar and Porter (1994, p. 19), describe the profound impact of culture on listening behavior as follows: "The ways in which we communicate, the circumstances of our communication, the language and language style we use, and our nonverbal behaviors are all a response to and a function of our culture. And, as cultures differ from one another, the communication practices and behaviors of individuals reared in those cultures will also be different." Thomlison (1991) indicates that just as communication and culture are inseparable, so too are listening and culture. He also suggests, "The ultimate goal of the cross cultural listener is to reduce uncertainty in the communication process" and that what may be "effective listening in one culture is totally inappropriate or misunderstood in another culture." In a series of research reports with a focus on nonverbal effects on intercultural listening, Ostermeier (1987, 1989, 1992, 1993, 1995, 1996, 1997a, 1997b, 1999) suggests that "intercultural listening is a challenging arena for participants to enter. Factors other than language such as cultural values and nonverbal cues take on significant importance."

Wolvin (1987), in a study of perceptions of listening behavior found that international students perceived Americans to be less willing and less patient as listeners than they perceived listeners in African, South American, or European cultures to be. The respondents in Wolvin's study indicated that "good listeners in any culture are those who care about their relationships with others." Wolvin and Coakley (1996, p. 126) cite K. C. Chan-Herur, who recommends that when Americans conduct business internationally, they should: "1. Observe. 2. Listen. 3. Speak." These recommendations are the direct opposite of the usual pattern for people in the United States. Chan-Herur's suggestions should also be considered whenever U.S. citizens interact with anyone, but especially when interacting with people from other cultures or co-cultures.

Anthropologist Edward T. Hall identified cultures as either high context or low context. The United States and Canada are both low-context cultures; this means that communicators expect to gain most of the information in communication events in the words of the messages. The high-context perspective, however, found in many parts of Asia and the Middle East, occurs where more information is contained in the communication setting and in the communicators themselves than is contained in the words uttered. In the high-context culture, then, according to Hall, messages tend to be shorter, more general, and faster. Speakers and listeners in high-context cultures rely on a common understanding of values and rules. So, in the (low-context) United States, speakers believe that it is their responsibility to help their listeners understand their messages, whereas people in high-context cultures believe it is the responsibility of the listener to understand. For this reason, when some Asian students, for example, interact with others, whether it is in a class or in an interpersonal communication event, they expect to understand what is being said, and if they do not, they usually will not express their lack of understanding because in their own cultures, it is their duty to understand without asking questions or making their lack of knowledge or understanding known to others. Americans who believe that it is their responsibility to "make people understand" may be seen as overbearing, patronizing, and even pompous when they explain and repeat things in an effort to help the listener, especially if the listener is from a high-context culture. Thus, we can see that effective communication may be difficult to attain, unless all concerned parties are aware of both the similarities and differences and able to work around them.

THE EFFECT OF SPECIFIC BEHAVIORS ON INTERCULTURAL LISTENING

Ostermeier (1995) provides an excellent overview of the effects of nonverbal behavior on intercultural listening. He reports that American students who interviewed international students from Africa, Asia, Europe, Latin America, and the Middle East, indicated that five nonverbal behaviors affected the Americans' perception of listening: Use of Voice, Conversational Space, Eye Behavior, Facial Expressions, and Hand Gestures. Ostermeier concludes:

> It would appear that the type of nonverbal cue may make it easier or more difficult to listen. Listeners reported that differences in meanings for voice and conversational space made it more likely to be difficult to listen to the international persons. On the other hand, they felt differences in the meanings for facial expressions and hand gestures made it more likely to be easier to listen. Differences in meanings for eye behavior were no more likely to be a help or a hindrance to listening. The adverse impact on listening due to differences in nonverbal cue meanings may be in the perception of the listener that something negative is being directed at them personally or it may be the perception that some-

thing negative is being directed at what they are saying. Either outcome, of course, could result in misunderstandings between the participants. The differences in meanings for nonverbal cues appear more likely to make it easier or more difficult to listen depending on the cultural area of the world of the international person. From these interviews, differences in meanings would seem more likely to make it more difficult to listen to persons from the Middle East and Latin America. On the other hand, differences in these cues seem to make it easier to listen to Africans. Nonverbal differences appear to be as likely a help as a hindrance in listening to Asians and Europeans. These generalizations, of course, must be viewed in the context of the sample of 103 subjects being analyzed in the categories of cultural areas of the world. It is apparent that persons from one country within a particular cultural group may very well exhibit behaviors differently than persons from another country within the same cultural group. Thus, one always must be cautioned to be prepared to adapt to a particular country within a particular cultural area, and, in fact, to that particular individual. (1995, p. 33)

A number of essays and research reports suggest that collectivist cultures (e.g., Japan, Korea, and China) place a higher value on listening than do individualistic cultures (the U.S. and Canada). Native Americans tend to be more collectivist and are similar to people from Asia in their views of storytelling as means of preserving and maintaining the traditions of the culture. Presenters at past International Listening Association Conventions have suggested that a great deal of research remains to be completed in the arena of intercultural listening. We have much to learn about culture and listening if we are to successfully interact in this global community, the world. Visitors to other countries need to learn about the people, their culture, their language, and their views on listening. Only through an awareness of and sensitivity to the cultural practices and traditions of others, will we be able to effectively communicate with the people around us.

A STUDY ON THE ROLE OF INTERCULTURAL LISTENING

Given Ostermeier's findings, it would seem that we should all be aware of the role of intercultural listening in our exchanges with others. And given the relative currency of intercultural listening research, and the relative paucity of information on intercultural listening, this author decided to interview people from different world areas to determine the role of listening in various countries and cultures. While this is a work in progress, and is not yet complete, there are some interesting generalizations that would seem to corroborate what previous researchers have found.

International graduate students from Denmark, Sweden and Norway seemed surprised that listening is an area of study. These students commented that "listening is just something you do." "Why would you be concerned about listening?" The students from Scandinavia indicate that little time is spent on communication in their educational systems, and listening is something that is taken for granted—you listen because you have to in order to understand messages. Scandinavian business persons stated similar ideas: "What can you study about listening? You just do it!" A woman with whom we struck up a conversation in a Swedish shopping mall was amazed that people would study and conduct research on listening. We exchanged email addresses and have continued to correspond for the past three months about the nature of listening. She has decided "there is something to this idea of listening," even though she really had never thought about listening as a skill one could separate from the communication process. Native-speaking German professors in the Modern Language department at this writer's home institution, the University of Northern Iowa, responded to questions about the role of listening in their own country and culture with these statements: "Well, of course, we are interested in listening! We teach language." "One cannot teach or learn language without listening. But, in our home country, it is just expected that people will listen and understand."

Asian Perspectives on Listening

Asians, however, indicate different perspectives on listening. Three Chinese graduate student women were interviewed in several lengthy sessions. There were three major questions given to them prior to the interview to facilitate the process: (1) Tell me about listening in your province and culture. What is the role of listening in your culture? (2) What is a "good listener"? (3) Are there differences in listening between your province [in China] as compared to the United States?

One of the women, "Christine," is from the Haka race of Taipei, Taiwan, but she explained that she is really "Chinese" because her ancestors were mainlanders who fled China to a safer place. She says her family "still practices customs similar to those in their native homeland." Her family speaks Fukan and she indicates the Haka race and culture is isolated from the rest of the Taiwanese people because they are "not really Taiwanese." This young woman has been in the United States for four years and speaks English, Fukan, and Manda-

rin Chinese. Christine pointed out that she comes from a hierarchical society where one listens to one's elders and where listening is an expectation. Young people are expected to distance themselves from their elders and be humble in their behaviors. In her culture, young people make eye contact with each other when they speak, but "with our elders, we look away, down, or at their chins, but not right at the person's eyes." Listeners don't have many gestures, she said, unless with their peers, and then they are like young people in the West. Christine indicates that young people in her culture are "trained not to show emotions nor opinions." Furthermore, Christine says that words and content are not the message: "You have to read between the lines, so to speak. When you listen, you use your ears, eyes, and heart to determine *the* meaning. The eyes are actually more important than the ears. You have to learn to listen to the content, but you have to *know* what people *mean*." (Christine also indicated to this writer that the ILA shirt with the Chinese character for listening on it, actually says, listen with your eyes, your ears, and your heart.)

Christine explained that teachers and professors in Taiwan lecture and students take notes and memorize everything. "We take notes. We don't ask questions or even look at the teacher, or anything. The teacher may think the student does not like the teacher if students ask questions. Teachers have rules. Students have rules. We learn to survive but not really communicate in school." Christine added that, in her experience, it is easier to communicate with Chinese people than with Taiwanese because "5,000 years of culture influences Taiwan as well as China because without Chinese tradition, Taiwan has not much! But, China's culture is of such long standing that it is impossible to think in any way except what you are expected to think and act."

When asked what advice she would give Americans, Christine said:

> Don't use your culture's style when you're in another culture. Learn about the culture. If you want to know and learn, listen and follow. You cannot just do what you want. There's a line between us. If you want to be a good listener in my culture, watch, learn the language, learn a little about my culture. Listen to nature. Know about Chinese religion and the emphasis on spirits. Our ancestors' spirits protect us, and nature is where the spirits are found, so we must listen to everything around us in order not to miss anything. Nature is more important than people, so keep that in mind when you communicate with anyone from my culture.

A second woman, "Jan," is from the Hebei Province in north China, in the Beijing area. She has been in the United States for two years and has traveled extensively in that time period. Jan says she sees herself as a "low-context person who is very direct" and she probably is not really very much like other Chinese. In fact, Jan wanted to make sure the interviewer knew that she "may not answer the same way other Chinese people do." Jan often serves as an interpreter for Chinese business persons who come to the U.S. to learn more about products or practices.

Jan indicates that there really are not that many distinct differences in cultural communication nor in listening. While she was never overtly told to "listen," you first learn to be a good listener from your family and society, friends, and school reinforces that. She says that a "good listening is a good personality trait." In her culture, listening is the way to show respect, concern, and caring, and that a good listener makes many friends. She knows that good listening is very important to how well work can be done. In the Hebei Province, Jan says lower-status people are better listeners than those of a higher status and this is reflected in the fact that leaders (whether in government or business) do not listen very well to the suggestions from those of a lower status. She indicates that parents in the Hebei province expect their children to listen very well and they expect their children to follow what the parents say. But, she says that she often listens to what her parents say, and considers it carefully, but she does not always do what they want. "I compromise to not disappoint my family, but I don't always do what they want me to do!" In the classroom, Jan says that it is not a practice for students to interrupt their professors, nor to ask questions of them. "It is not polite to interrupt a speaker during the speech, but it is *now* okay to ask a question privately, after class."

When Jan was asked what it means to "listen well," she said, "You listen and at the same time you think about what the speaker means by saying that. And, you accompany your thoughts with head nods and looking into the speaker's eyes. Sometimes you can ask questions and respond." A good listener in the Hebei province is one who "follows through at least in terms of carefully thinking about what was said, if not the same exact way as the person suggested." And, Jan says a good listener will "remember and acknowledge ideas from others even a long time later." One of the themes in Jan's view of listening in her culture as well as in the United States was this: "One must listen not only to what is said, but what is meant." Jan identified the following as indicators of good listening behavior: responding to messages with facial expressions, demonstrating that you are thinking about what

is said, being "calm and not scattered," having some eye contact unless you're too shy to do so. When asked about the differences between her culture and the U.S., Jan said that professors are equally good listeners in both cultures, but that the hierarchy of China is not evident here in the U.S., and so it is sometimes hard to know what to do or what is expected. Jan felt that her Chinese peers are better listeners than are her college classmates in the U.S. She characterized the U.S. culture as "an impatient, fast culture where interests don't linger for longer than five to eight minutes." Jan says that people in her country value traditions much more than Americans do, and so there are more long-term friendships than she sees here in the U.S. Furthermore, she says, "what was planted in people's minds is the comfort or spiritual bonds with long-term friendships, and this influences behaviors." Jan stated that listening is more important than speaking in her culture, especially in social and general contexts. (This is similar to what was previously reported in the research on intercultural listening.) "Listening is very important in China." When asked what advice she would give to Americans about listening to Chinese people, Jan made these suggestions:

> Do not only listen to me, but try to understand me. Try to understand the cultural differences. Ask questions, especially if things don't quite make sense—get more information so you can analyze the situation. Keep your own opinions out of it for a time, at least until you understand for sure. Ask questions before giving advice! Think about what was said before jumping in. International people do not expect immediate, quick responses. When people really listen, they may be slower, and they will try to understand others. International students appreciate it when someone expends an effort to understand.

The third woman, "Allison," is from Guilin in the Guangxi Province of South China and she indicated that Guilin's dialect is very close to the Mandarin dialect so she can understand and be easily understood by people in the Mandarin Province in Northern China. Also, she said her native dialect helps when she is expected to speak and understand the official language of the People's Republic of China. Allison says that listening has a far greater role than speaking in her culture. Allison, too, talked about the hierarchical society, and the need for the young to respect their elders and not even to be thought to question their authority. The Chinese in the Guangxi province are taught to listen because it is a "virtue to be a good listener, and to do what adults tell you to do."

Allison talked about the difference between people from a high-context culture and those from a low-context culture such as in the United States. She says in her culture, it is the listener's "duty to get the meanings." Allison, like the other two Chinese women, indicates that a good listener is taught to "learn more between the lines" rather than just to listen to the words of the message. She said, "I was pretty impressed my first time in the U.S. when people expressed their emotions so directly. I was surprised and astonished! In China, you're not supposed to admit to strong feelings. So, I was so shocked when an American woman argued with a Chinese professor that I could not say anything. Direct is easier to understand and deal with, but it's just not a part of my culture." The student's role is to listen. Children are taught not to question, and not to challenge, and that's the expectation both at home and in school. They are allowed to ask questions, but, "We are told to ask questions when we need to do so, but we are reminded that we need to consider the group and the place. And, we are encouraged to ask questions only about certain areas. Do not ask a question that is not on track. Listening is a core rule in the home and in the classroom."

Allison says there are differences between Chinese in the North (Jan's province) and South. Allison says people in the North are more open and direct. They bring up questions more readily, and fit better into a low-context culture than those in the South, where people "speak more like the soft, gentle rain." Allison says they learn that "Silence is gold," and that one must maintain dignity at all times, both for oneself, and for others. Thus, silence, not asking questions, and not challenging others is what is expected.

Allison said in her culture one is taught to "never argue with your parents, teachers, and adults. We often never utter a word, we just listen. In school we listen and take notes. We are always required to raise our hands to get permission to even ask a question. Allison used the Great Cultural Revolution as being typical of the way the Chinese have traditionally been expected to behave: It doesn't matter if you understand, just do as you're told."

After four years in the United States, Allison says that her impression is that Chinese listeners will consider and think about comments and suggestions more deeply; they will look at more than what is said, and will interpret things exactly as a person said or promised. In China, she says, people take more time to listen and think about what others say. It's hard to understand when your expectations are not met in this culture. "U.S. culture is so busy. Everyone has so much to do. It's totally different in China. Chinese people take more time for other people." Allison provided an example: In the U.S. people meet and greet each other with something like "How are you?" but they don't want or expect a real answer. In China, Allison suggests, there are many different phrases and ways of saying "ni hao?" or "ni hao ma?" (literally translated "How are you" and, "How are you, really?") but the inflection and the addition of words indicates the person really wants to listen to you tell about how you are. "In the U.S., people ask the question and keep walking, so a Chinese person learns early that it's just a question, but not very meaningful."

DISCUSSION

The three Chinese women's responses to the questions in the interview affirm previous research findings suggesting that people in Asian cultures view listening as a much stronger and much more valuable skill or trait than speaking or reading. While these students say they are not *directly* taught to be good listeners, Chinese cultural traditions create expectations that listening is much more valuable than any other attribute. And, everything in the culture provides implications for appropriate behaviors. The four themes pervading the interviews with the three Chinese students were: (1) Listening Is Important, (2) Listening Is Expected, (3) Listening Is Learned by Example and by Expectation, and (4) One Must Listen for What is *not* Said. All three interviewees indicated that listening is very important in their own cultures, and they were surprised that it was less so here in the United States. In their own cultures, they indicate that there are punishments for failure to listen, especially to one's parents or teachers. While they were hesitant to state that they were taught to listen, they were quite descriptive about the ways that good, careful listening is expected, and that parents, elders, and teachers expect to only say something once, and that the listener will receive, comprehend and comply with the message. All three students provided numerous examples of how one must listen to not just the words, but to the meaning intended. This listening with the mind also includes listening with the heart, the eyes, and the ears. "We must listen to what is not said," was a common phrase they offered about listening. Many of their examples of good listening also included instances of listening to more than the words, and with more than the ears. It was clear in these interviews that in their culture, listening can indeed be defined as it has been delimited by the International Listening Association (1996): *Listening* is the process of receiving, constructing meaning from, and responding to spoken and/or nonverbal messages.

The informal interviews with the western European students and faculty, and the lengthy interviews with the three Chinese women suggest that we can learn a great deal about another's culture, and the world's view of intercultural listening if we will take the time to learn about the culture and, especially, to learn to listen with the ears, eyes, mind and heart.

For more information about listening, visit the International Listening Association website at www.listen.org.

REFERENCES

Brownell, Judi. (2002). *Listening: Attitudes, principles and skills,* 2nd ed. Boston: Allyn and Bacon. (See, esp., Chapter 10, Listening Challenges.)

Chen, Guo-Ming, and Starosta, William J. (1998). *Foundations of intercultural communication,* 1st ed. Boston: Allyn and Bacon.

Chen, Guo-Ming, and Starosta, William J. (Eds.) (2000). *Communication and global society.* New York: Peter Lang Publishers. See Chapter 15, pp. 279–293, "Listening Across Diversity in Global Society," William J. Starosta and Guo-Ming Chen.

Clinard, H. (1985). Listen for the difference. *Training and Development Journal, 39* (10), 39.

International Listening Association Definition of Listening (1994). Cited by Andrew Wolvin, "On Competent Listening," *The Listening Post, 54* (July 1995).

Franks, Parthenia. (2001). *Native Americans and the value of silence/listening.* Unpublished paper presented at the 2001 International Listening Association Convention, Chicago, IL.

Hall, Edward T. (1959). *The silent language.* Greenwich, CT: Fawcett.

Harris, Jean. (2000). *Listening across culture: From theory to practice.* Unpublished paper presented at the 2000 International Listening Association Convention, Virginia Beach, VA.

Ostermeier, Terry. (1987, July). *Learning intercultural listening concepts through participating in intercultural communication exercises/simulations.* Paper presented at the International Listening Association Summer Conference, Toronto, Canada.

Ostermeier, Terry. (1989). Perceptions of cultural values and communicating interculturally: A simulation experience. *World Communication Journal,* 18.1, 33–47.

Ostermeier, Terry. (1992, March). *The intercultural interview: An experience in intercultural listening.* Paper presented at the meeting of the International Listening Association, Seattle, WA.

Ostermeier, Terry. (1993). Perception of nonverbal cues in dialogic listening in an intercultural interview. *Journal of the International Listening Association,* Special Issue.

Ostermeier, Terry. (1995, Summer). Meaning differences for nonverbal cues: Easier or more difficult for the intercultural listener?" *Intercultural Communication Studies, V* (1), 19–40.

Ostermeier, Terry. (1996). *Intercultural listening and facial/vocal cues: The gender factor.* Unpublished paper presented at the 1996 International Listening Association Convention, Sacramento, CA.

Ostermeier, Terry. (1997a). *Gender, nonverbal cues, and intercultural listening: Part II Conversational space and hand gestures.* Paper presented at the International Listening Association Convention, Mobile, AL.

Ostermeier, Terry. (1997b). *An intercultural student to student interview project: A descriptive study.* Paper presented at the 14th Biennial Conference of the World Communication Association, San Jose, Costa Rica.

Ostermeier, Terry. (1999). *Confronting the challenges of intercultural listening.* Paper presented at the 7th Annual International Conference on Cross Cultural Communication, Louisville, KY.

Purdy, Michael W. (2000). Listening, culture, and structures of consciousness. *International Journal of Listening, 14,* 47–68.

Samovar, L., and Porter, R. (1994). *Communication between cultures,* 2nd ed. Belmont, CA: Wadsworth Publishing.

Thomlison, T. Dean. (1997). Intercultural listening. In Michael Purdy and Deborah Borisoff (Eds.), *Listening in everyday life: A personal and professional approach,* 2nd ed. Lanham, MD: University Press of America, pp. 79–120.

Waxwood, Vincenne A. (2000). *The multicultural factor in decision-making.* Unpublished paper presented at the International Listening Association Convention, Virginia Beach, VA.

Wolvin, Andrew D. (1987). *Culture as a listening variable.* Unpublished paper presented at the International Listening Association Summer Conference, Toronto, Canada.

Wolvin, Andrew D. (1999). *Listening in the quality organization.* Ithaca, NY: Finger Lakes Press.

Wolvin, Andrew D. and Coakley, Carolyn. (1996). *Listening,* 5th ed. Madison, WI: Brown & Benchmark Publishers.

CHECK YOUR UNDERSTANDING

1. How do you define effective listening? What behaviors (for example, direct eye contact) define good listening in your culture?
2. According to Beall, how is listening viewed in Scandinavian countries? In the Chinese culture? What impact would these different views have on intercultural communication?
3. Discuss with a classmate a time when your view of listening caused difficulty in intercultural communication.
4. What does it mean to listen for what is not said? Do people from the United States consider this idea important? Why or why not? Give personal examples to support your answer.

CHAPTER ACTIVITIES

1. As the opening of the chapter suggests, close your eyes for 60 seconds. Record all the sounds you hear. Choose one sound and follow the steps of the listening process according to the HURIER model.

2. For one day, keep a journal of your communication activities. How much time did you spend reading, writing, speaking, and listening? Of the time you spent listening, how much time did you spend listening intrapersonally, interpersonally, and interculturally?

3. Find someone from another culture and spend the day with her or him. Before your visit, make an inventory of your own cultural/individual values. Plan, in advance, your strategies for listening interculturally using the suggestions provided in this chapter. What were the other person's cultural/individual values? How did you adapt your communication to listen more effectively during your interaction? What did you learn about this person that you wouldn't have known otherwise? Now, use this experience to help you communicate/listen more effectively with another person from another culture.

CHAPTER 8

FAMILY AND FRIENDS

THE SPACES IN BETWEEN

Laura Elizabeth Pearson Cooper

This House of mine has a Person,
You can't see It but It's there—
It fills this house to bursting and Its heartbeat is everywhere.
You shrug a bit and laugh and say, "My sense is not so keen.
I only see the walls and doors and spaces in between."
And there you have the answer,
It's not the things you see
That make my pulses leap with joy and mean so much to me.
Rather, it is the laughter that rings out within these walls,
And the love that is here, and happiness,
And the sadness that befalls at time to every house.
And so it is that all these unseen things combine to mean
That the Being of this house lives in the spaces in between.
Yes, this house has a Soul.
Don't glance with such chagrin,
For the Soul of this house is composed of all those who dwell within.

OBJECTIVES

After reading this chapter and completing the readings and the activities, you should be able to

- Understand the stages of relationship development.
- Define the universal dimensions of relationships.
- Compare the relationship model of Knapp and Vangelisti to that of Chen.
- Understand how family relationships differ across cultures.
- Understand how friendship relationships differ across cultures.

DEFINING RELATIONSHIPS

Regardless of the culture, all cultures have relationships that connect the people in that culture. The most important relationships are those of family and friends. In this chapter we will first discuss the development of relationships and then examine relationships in the contexts of family and friends.

We live in the context of relationships. Simply defined, relationships are how we deal with others in our everyday lives. Like communication, relationships are dynamic—ever changing. In addition relationships are reciprocal when the parties in the relationship can meet each other's needs. According to Schultz (1966) these needs are inclusion (sense of belonging), control (the ability to be in charge of our own life and to influence others around us), and affection (our desire to love and be loved). How we fulfill these needs varies depending on the culture in which we live. For example, the degree of self-disclosure in relationships differs from culture to culture. In the United States, we use self-disclosure as a means of developing relationships—to feel included, to control, and to give and gain affection. In Chinese culture, self-disclosure is more conservative. As Changsheng Xi (1994) explains:

> For a Chinese, self-centered speech would be considered boastful and pretentious. Chinese tend to scorn those who often talk about themselves and doubt their motives when they do so. Chinese seem to prefer talking about external matters, such as world events. For Americans, self-disclosure is a strategy to make various types of relationships work; for Chinese, it is a gift shared only with the most intimate relatives and friends. (p. 155)

UNIVERSAL DIMENSIONS OF RELATIONSHIPS

Although relationships have different characteristics in various cultures, Triandis (1977) suggests four universal dimensions of social relationships: association–disassociation, superordination–subordination, intimacy–formality, overt–covert. Triandis provides an example behavior of each dimension. Association behaviors include being helpful, cooperative, and supportive. Disassociation behaviors include fighting or avoiding the other person. Superordinate behaviors include giving orders or criticizing. Subordinate behaviors involve obeying or asking for help. Intimate behaviors consist of self-disclosure, touching, and expressing emotions. Formality behaviors involve behaviors such as sending written invitations. Overt behaviors are visible to others, whereas covert behaviors are not.

Triandis (1984) argues that although these four dimensions are universal, the degree to which they are manifested varies across cultures. For example, Asian families tend to be more associative, subordinate, formal, and covert than U.S. families. Triandis explains this difference in degree by relating the four dimensions to the dimensions of culture discussed by other theorists. Triandis suggests that the association–dissociation is related to the human nature value orientation of Kluckhohn and Strodtbeck. In cultures where people believe that humans are inherently good, associative behaviors are most important; in cultures that view human nature as inherently evil, disassociative behaviors are most important. The superordination–subordination behaviors can be linked to Hofstede's power dimension. In high-power distance cultures, subordination and superordination are viewed as natural characteristics with which people are born. In low-power cultures, superordination and subordination behaviors are not viewed as natural. Rather, these are viewed as a function of the roles individuals play in the culture. The intimacy–formality dimension relates to the degree of contact people in a given culture have. In high-contact cultures, people stand closer, face one another, look one another in the eye, and use more emotional expression than those in noncontact cultures. Finally, Triandis suggests that the overt–covert dimension relates to the cultural variations in tightness and looseness. Tightness is defined in terms of the number of roles and role relationships, and the nature of the bonds among the roles (Boldt, 1978). The more roles and the more tightly they are bonded together, the tighter the culture. As you might guess, Triandis argues that there is greater overt behavior in loose cultures and more covert behaviors in tight cultures.

RELATIONSHIP DEVELOPMENT

We all begin relationships as strangers. We have to build our relationships, developing it in stages. In other words, I must learn to be in the relationship of daughter, mother, wife, acquaintance, friend, co-worker, and so on. Several communication researchers have discussed relationship development (Berger and Calabrese, 1975; Devito, 2003; Knapp and Vangelisti, 1992; Chen, 1995). In this section we will outline and compare the models presented by Knapp and Vangelisti as well as Chen.

Knapp and Vangelisti's Model of Relationship Development

Knapp and Vangelisti suggest that relationship development occurs in two parts: coming together (the development of relationships) and coming apart (the dissolving of relationships). Both parts involve five stages.

Coming Together   The first stage of coming together is *initiating*. In this stage, we initiate a relationship. We try to "put our best foot forward." We talk in "small talk"—the "What's your name? What do you do? Nice party, huh?" kind of communication. In this stage we are reducing our uncertainty about the other person in order to determine whether we want to move to the second stage.

In the second stage is *experimenting*. Here, we want to find out more than the superficial information we gained in the initiating stage. We want to learn about our similarities. We are not yet ready to make a commitment. Our relationship is a casual one.

In the third stage, *intensifying,* we increase the amount of personal and psychological information. Using Altman and Taylor's social penetration concept (1973), we penetrate deeper into the other's "self." We cover a wide range of topics (breadth), and we disclose more to one another (depth).

Integrating is the fourth stage of coming together. This stage is characterized by frequency of interaction, exclusiveness of the interaction between ourselves and the other person, and increased depth and breadth of topics. We are committed to this relationship.

Finally, *bonding* is a public declaration of our commitment. This final stage signals to the world that we are in a secure, stable, committed relationship. A good example of this stage is the ritual wedding ceremony.

Coming Apart   Relationships change; some do not last. This brings us to the five stages of coming apart. The first stage is *differentiating*. We begin to feel we are different from one another. Our similarities don't appear as similar as they once did. We begin to think in terms of "I" rather than the "we" of the bonding stage.

The next stage is *circumscribing*. We seek to limit our communication with one another. We avoid sensitive or intimate topics; our communication shifts to a superficial level.

Stagnating follows circumscribing. In this stage, we no longer see a need to communicate with one another. Often the parties think they know the outcome of the communication, so why communicate? The communication is awkward, much like in the initial stages of coming together.

As a result of this awkwardness and desire to avoid communication, we begin the *avoiding* stage. We find excuses to avoid the other person. We may interpret the other's communication as unfriendly or antagonistic.

Thus, the scene is set for the final stage of coming apart—*termination*. In short, we no longer contact one another. In the case of marriage, divorce is the termination stage. It is important to note that we may move in and out of stages. In other words, the development of a relationship and the termination of a relationship are not strictly linear. For example, we may be at the intensifying stage of a relationship, enter the integrating stage, and then step back to the intensifying stage.

Chen's Model of Relationship Development

Knapp and Vangelisti's model of relationships is a Western view of relationships. Researchers are examining relationship development from non-Western perspectives. One well-developed non-Western model is that of Chen (1995). Chen bases his model of relationship development on the eight trigrams of the classical Chinese text, *The Book of Changes (I Ching)*. Three assumptions underlie Chen's approach:

1. The universe is a whole in which everything is a transitional process (including human relationships).
2. This transforming process of the universe is an endless cycle (human relationships change according to this cycle).
3. There is no ending of the transforming process of the universe (human relationships are never complete or finished).

Based on these three assumptions, Chen uses the movement of the eight trigrams to explain the development of a relationship. Figure 8.1 shows Chen's mode of relationship development. Each trigram represents an attribute of human nature and each attribute is associated with a part of a 24-hour day. Each stage of the model is both a cause and effect—the cause of the next stage and an effect of the previous stage. Let's examine each of these eight stages.

The first stage, *Chen* (thunder—the arousing), is the birth stage (4:30–7:30 A.M.). This stage is the internal process of our need to develop an emotional attachment to someone else. The process is an intrapersonal one dominated by our personality factors.

The second stage, *Sun* (breeze—the penetrating; 7:30–10:30 A.M.), represents the externalization of stage 1. We begin to contact the person with whom we wish to have a relationship. We reduce our uncertainty about the other by gathering information. We increase our understanding of one another and as we do so, we feel confident to disclose our enthusiasm and passion.

Li (fire—the clinging; 10:30 A.M.–1:30 P.M.) is the third stage. Our passion and enthusiasm "burst into flame" like the sun at noon. We express our desire to emotionally and psychologically cling to one another. Successful clinging depends on the response from our partner—the element of fire needs the element of wood to survive. If we receive a positive response from the other, we continue to stage 4.

Kun (earth—the receptive; 1:30–4:30 P.M.) is the stage of acceptance of the relationship by both parties. The time of rest (night) is approaching. Similarly, this stage is the preparation time for reaping the consequences of our behavior and action. Our minds are open. This stage is the bud, a flower ready to bloom.

Stage 5, *Tu* (lake—the joyous; 4:30–7:30 P.M.), is the enjoyment of the harvest, symbolized by the lake in which the two parties mirror one another in the transparent water of the lake. The feeling of joy binds the two parties together.

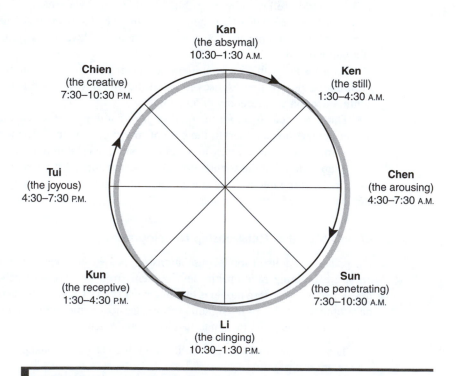

FIGURE 8.1   Chen's Model of Relationship Development

Source: From Guo-Ming Chen and William J. Soraston, *Foundations of Intercultural Communication,* published by Allyn and Bacon, Boston, MA. Copyright ©1998 by Pearson Education. Reprinted by permission of the publisher.

Chien (heaven—the creative; 7:30–10:30 P.M.) symbolizes the intimate relationship. This stage is the apex of the relationship. Yet, as soon as the relationship reaches this apex it begins to reverse its course. The strong, creative, pure state of the relationship cannot be sustained, leading to the seventh stage.

The seventh stage is *Kan* (water—the abysmal; 10:30 P.M.–1:30 A.M.). The relationship is no longer harmonious. Only patience, perseverance, sincerity, and lasting virtue can rescue the relationship at this stage.

The last stage is *Ken* (mountain—keeping still; 1:30–4:40 A.M.). Unlike the rushing water of stage 6, this stage is the mountain standing still. The relationship "stands" or rests. Yet, time moves on and the cyclical process continues. Thus, Chen begins—either in the form of the redevelopment of the relationship or the beginning of a new relationship—with someone else.

As these two models show, relationship development is based on cultural values. Yum (1988) suggests that the values of Confucianism influence East Asian relationships. Confucian philosophy delineates four principles that affect how relationships are developed: *jen* (humanism), *I* (faithfulness, loyalty, or justice), *li* (propriety, rite, or respect for social forms), and *chih* (wisdom or a liberal education). These values lead to major differences between East Asians and North Americans in terms of interpersonal relationship patterns. East Asians are oriented to particularistic relationships (those in which communication is ruled by the hierarchical structure of human relationships), long-term and asymmetrical reciprocity (relationships are permanent and obligatory), sharp distinctions between in-group and out-group members, informal intermediaries, and overlapping personal and public relationships. In contrast, North Americans are oriented toward universalistic relationships, short-term and symmetrical reciprocity or contractual reciprocity (relationships are neither long term nor obligatory), less sharp distinctions between in-group and out-group members, contractual intermediaries, and separate personal and public relationships.

FAMILIES

Families come in a variety of forms. In the United States, the family structure has changed significantly over the past several years. The family no longer consists of the so-called norm: mother, father, and one or two children. Instead, families come in a variety of forms: single-parent families, step-families, homosexual partner families, extended families, and so on. Thus, even in the U.S. culture, family structures are not the same. Within each family structure, the rules, themes, decision making, ways of dealing with conflict, degree of support for one another, boundaries, roles, and cohesion (the closeness of the family) all may differ, and each affects communication within that family (Galvin et al., 2003).

Similarly, families differ across cultures (Gudykunst and Lee, 2001). In the United States, extended families usually do not live together. In Latin America, members of the extended family often live together. Roles in the United States are not as strictly defined in other cultures. For example, the family roles in Argentina are strictly defined. The mother raises the children, takes care of the household, and shows deference to her husband. In China, parents play a major role in making decisions for the children. Where to go to college, what profession to enter, and even who to marry are all decisions greatly influenced by parents. As you no doubt have begun to realize, many of these differences can be explained by Hofstede's individualist versus collectivist dimension.

In collectivist families, such as those in China, Japan, Korea, and Latin America, the family consists of numerous members living closely together—grandparents, uncles, aunts, cousins. Thus, children grow up defining themselves as members of this large group. In fact, they define themselves in relation to this "we" of family rather than as an "I." Lifelong loyalty is owed to this group. Since harmony is a major value, "speaking one's mind" is not encouraged. The word *no* is seldom used. Rather, "We will think about it" or "You may be right" are used. Also, the word *yes* does not necessarily mean agreement. "Yes" often means that the speaker was heard, as in "Yes, I understand you."

In three surveys of Chinese family structure (China Internet Information Center, 2001), Chinese families were classified into seven types: the single family (consisting of a single man or woman), the "dink" family (well-off young working couple with no children), the empty nest family (the children have grown up and left the home), the core family (a mother, a father, and a child), the "trunk" family (a couple living with their parents and their children), the joint family (a couple living with their parents and in-laws), and "other" (all other types).

The obligation to the family in collectivist cultures is financial. Resources are shared. If a member of a collectivist family does not have a job, the others in the family support the unemployed member. Yet, the obligation is not just financial. Ritual obligation is also owed to the family. All occasions—births, deaths, marriages—are very important and the celebrations must be attended by all family members.

One final important concept in collectivist cultures is face. Face describes the proper relationship between a person and her or his social environment. "Losing face" is synonymous with humiliation. Because of the "we" of the family, if one individual in the family loses face, all members lose face. One loses face if she or he (or someone close to her or him) fails to meet the essential requirements placed on her or him by society. In addition to losing face, one can "give face"—prestige and honor—by the way one acts toward another.

The Western family, which is individualistic, differs considerably from its Eastern counterpart. Western families emphasize the "I" rather than the "we" and it is this difference that makes all the difference. A Western family member is much more likely to speak her or his mind and disagree with her or his parents. The individual decides, for the most part, which college to attend, which profession to enter, and who to marry. Obligations to the family are looser, both financially and in terms of rituals. Parents focus on helping their children to become independent. Eastern parents focus on maintaining their children's dependence on the family.

One particularly interesting variable across and within cultures is courting and marriage. For example, although the majority of China's ethnic groups follow a patrilineal tradition, the ethnic group known as the Mosuo emphasizes matrilineal ties (Lu and Mitchell, 2000). Women of this ethnic group prefer a visiting relationship among lovers rather than the marriage of other cultures. This relation is referred to as *sisi* (walking back and forth). When a girl is age 12, she is given a coming-of-age ceremony, and after puberty, she receives male visitors. The male may stay the night, but he returns to his own mother's house the next morning. Any children born from such a relationship live with their mother, and her brothers are responsible for helping to look after the children. Although a child may know who his or her father is, and may even have a close relationship with him, the father has no social or economic obligation. Lovers can end their relationship at anytime. A woman signals her change of heart simply by no longer opening the door, signaling a man not to visit.

The Bari of Venezuela believe that a fetus is built up over time with repeated washes of sperm. The first act of sex, which plants the seed, should occur between husband and wife. Then the fetus must be nourished by repeated anointing of semen. In order not to wear the husband out, the wife takes a lover to help in this nourishment process. This "secondary father" has an obligation to the mother and the child. He is expected to give gifts of fish and game while continuing to support his own wife and children (Small, 2003).

Omiai (honorable seeing-meetings), matchmaking, still determines roughly half of all Japanese marriages today, although the outcome is generally left up to the couple concerned. Relatives or trusted parental friends (generally female) act as *nakodo* (go-betweens). The *nakado* initiate contact between the families by presenting prints or snapshots to the prospective family. If interest is expressed, the two families meet, usually in a restaurant. The male's father extols his son's academic achievements and prospects; the woman's father extols her virtuous nature, schooling, hobbies, housekeeping abilities, and fondness for children.

During the next week, if the man does not like the woman, he withdraws with a range of polite excuses. If he likes her, he asks her out on a date. If the woman likes him, she will accept. If they continue to "hit it off," they may end up at the Shinto alter. It is important to note that not all marriages in Japan are *omiai* (arranged-marriage introductions). *Renai kekkon* (love marriages) also occur.

Most unions in Iraq are arranged by families. In Iraq's deeply religious society, where most men and women cannot date without a father or brother present, marriage offers an independent life. It is not about love. As Akil Abbas indicates, "I don't have time for such tales (about love). My mother said if you marry you will be on the right path, and Allah will bless you" (al-Anbaki and Potter, 2004).

The societal changes in a culture can affect marriage and family life. In Iraq the number of marriages each month is believed to have increased 20 percent since the fall of Saddam Hussein's regime. Experts suggest that an increase in government salaries and an end to compulsory military service (freeing more young men for marriage) are behind the marriage rise (al-Anbaki and Potter, 2004).

Families differ across cultures. We have provided you with just a few examples to demonstrate these differences. This sampling suggests that regardless of the form, families are key to the survival of a culture.

FRIENDS

Intercultural friendships vary in a number of ways: selection (who can be a friend), duration (how long the friendship lasts), the number of friends, the responsibilities and prerogatives of a friend, and how long a relationship exists before it can be considered a friendship. Western Europeans feel that close friends can be developed within a few months. Asian Americans, African Americans, and Latinos take about a year to develop a friendship they would consider close (Collier, 1991). African American friends can criticize one another, often quite loudly, whereas Western European friends do not consider this behavior appropriate (Hecht et al., 1993). Hispanic, Asian American, African American, and Anglo American students report that trust and acceptance are important characteristics of friendship. Yet, each group emphasizes a slightly different aspect of these characteristics: Latinos emphasize relational support in friendship; African Americans emphasize respect and acceptance; Asian Americans emphasize a positive, caring exchange of ideas; and Anglo Americans emphasize recognizing the needs of the individual (Collier, 1991).

In addition, Anglo American friendships are often compartmentalized. For example, an Anglo American might have friends with whom he or she plays tennis, friends with whom she or he studies, friends with whom she or he goes to the movies, and so on. In other words, friends are for specific purposes. European Americans tend to classify others into what they can do rather than who they are. Not so with Thais. In Thailand, a friend is chosen for the person as a whole. A Thai would not choose a friend whose values, beliefs, or lifestyle did not correspond to her or his own.

People in the United States tend to be quite mobile, moving from job to job, location to location. As they move, they make new friends. However, friendships do not usually last after one has moved to a different area. In other words, friendships are often transient. In

Asian cultures, a friend is for a lifetime. Once you are friends, you remain so, no matter the distance between you or the time that has passed since you last met. It is not uncommon in the United States for people to lose track of the people who were in their wedding party. Such an event would never occur in Asian countries.

Rawlins (1992) and Baxter and Montgomery (1996) suggest that all relationships experience dialectical tensions that reflect conflicting and contradictory needs. These dialectical tensions are:

• Instrumentality and affection: the tension between requesting help and expressing affection
• Openness and closedness: the tension between expectations for honesty and caution about information sharing
• Autonomy and connection: the tension between the benefits of contacts of friends and the possibility that ongoing contact may provide little autonomy for each friend
• Judgment and acceptance: the tension between expectations of mutual affirmation and acceptance among friends and relational requirements of honest critique
• Impartiality and favoritism: the tension between organizational norms of impartial and objective treatment of employees and friendship expectations of unconditional support

Using these tensions as the basis for their study, Chen and her associates (2001) examined the dialectical tensions between international Taiwanese students in the United States. In addition to the dialectics just outlined, Taiwanese in the United States exhibited another dialectical tension—affinity and resentment. Taiwanese international students in the study indicated that no matter how much one disliked another Taiwanese, "Taiwanese still needs Taiwanese" (p. 63). This need resulted primarily from feelings of familiarity and comfort with those from the same culture who spoke the same language, but prohibited the formation of intercultural friendships with U.S. students.

CONCLUSION

In this chapter we have discussed human relationships in general and, in particular, within the contexts of family and friends. We have seen that although there are certain universals in relationships across cultures, each culture puts its own special mark on how these universals are "played out" in day-to-day communication. In the readings that follow, the family relationships in two cultures are described. Bhatt describes the marriage and mate selection rituals of Asian Indian communities in the United States—specifically the use of matrimonial advertisements. Galvin examines the communication in Irish families.

FOR DISCUSSION

1. Define relationship. Survey 10 people and ask them to define *relationship*. What are the similarities and differences in definition? What do these indicate about how relationships are viewed in your culture?
2. Choose a family ritual—birth, death, baptism, marriage—and describe your family's rituals surrounding this ritual. Compare your ritual with the same ritual from a friend's family. Consider what the similarities and differences tell you about family rituals in your culture.
3. All families have rituals and traditions. Bring a photo taken at one of your family's holiday celebrations. Write a short story about the event. Identify the family members, describe the activities and traditions that took place, and analyze what this information tells you about the culture of your family.

4. Ask 10 people to list the three major characteristics they consider most important to friendship. What do the similarities and differences in the answers indicate about friendship in your culture?

REFERENCES

al-Anbaki, S., and Potter, S. (2004, November 12). Iraqis looking to marry find the time is right. *USA Today,* p. 11A.

Altman, I., and Taylor, D. (1973). *Social penetration: The development of interpersonal relationships.* New York: Rinehart and Winston.

Baxter, L. A., and Montgomery, B. (1996). *Relating: Dialogues and dialectics.* New York: Guilford.

Berger, C., and Calabrese, R. (1975). Some explorations in initial interactions and beyond: Toward a developmental theory of interpersonal communication. *Human Communication Research, 1,* 99–112.

Boldt, E. (1978). Structural tightness and cross-cultural research. *Journal of Cross-Cultural Psychology, 9,* 151–165.

Chen, G. M. (1995). A model of intercultural communication competence. *Mass Communication Journal, 50,* 81–96.

Chen, L. (2002). Communication in intercultural relationships. In W. Gudykunst and B. Mody (Eds.), *Handbook of international and intercultural communication* (pp. 241–260). Thousand Oaks, CA: Sage.

Chen, T., Drzewiecke, J., and Sias, P. (2001). Dialectical tensions in Taiwanese International student friendships. *Qualitative Research Reports in Communication, 2,* 57–65.

China Internet Information Center. (2001, February 5). What's a typical Chinese family like? *China Daily.* www.china.org.cn.

Collier, M. J. (1991). Conflict competence within African, Mexican and Anglo American friendships. In S. Ting-Toomey and F. Korzenny (Eds.), *Cross-cultural interpersonal communication* (pp. 132–154). Newbury Park, CA: Sage.

Devito, J. (2003). *The interpersonal communication book.* Boston: Allyn and Bacon.

Galvin, K., Bylund, C., and Brommel, B. (2003). *Family communication: Cohesion and change.* Boston: Allyn and Bacon.

Gudykunst, W., and Kim, Y. Y. (2003). *Communication with strangers: An approach to intercultural communication.* Boston: McGraw-Hill.

Gudykunst, W., and Lee, C. (2001). An agenda for studying ethnicity and family communication. *Journal of Family Communication, 1* (1), 75–85.

Hecht, M., Collier, M. J., and Ribeau, A. (1993). *African American communication: Ethnic identity and cultural interpretation.* Newbury Park, CA: Sage.

Knapp, M., and Vangelisti, A. (2000). *Interpersonal communication and human relationships.* Boston: Allyn and Bacon.

Lu, Yuan, and Mitchell, S. (2000) *Land of the walking marriage: Natural history.* New York: The American Museum of Natural History.

Rawlins, W. K. (1992). *Friendship matters: Communication, dialectics, and the life course.* New York: Aldine De Gruyter.

Schutz, W. (1958). *Firo: A three-dimensional theory of interpersonal behavior.* New York: Holt, Rinehart and Winston

Small, M. (2003, April). *Discover,* pp. 54–61.

Triandis, H. C. (1977). *Interpersonal behavior.* Monterey, CA: Brooks/Cole.

Triandis, H. C. (1984). A theoretical framework for the more efficient construction of culture assimilators. *International Journal of Intercultural Relations, 8,* 301–330.

Xi, Changsheng. (1994). Individualism and collectivism in American and Chinese societies. In A. Gonzalez, M. Houston, and V. Chen (Eds.), *Our voices: Essays in culture, ethnicity, and communication* (pp. 125–167). Los Angeles: Roxbury.

Yum, J. O. (1988). The impact of Confucianism on interpersonal relationships and communication patterns in East Asia. *Communication Monographs, 55,* 374–388.

Mate Selection among Asian Indians Living in America: A Quest for Traditional Ritual

Archana J. Bhatt

Charotar Patel, handsome, affectionate, and intelligent, 29, 5'10", U.S. citizen, well-settled, electrical engineer with NASA invites correspondence from Patel girl with Indian values. Prefers pharmacist, medical doctor, or lawyer. Call (xxx) xxx-xxxx.

When we think of personal ads, many of us conjure an image of a desperately lonely individual who is seeking companionship at all costs. However, this is not the only depiction of personal ads. In the South Asian communities, specifically amongst Indian Americans, marital ads serve as a viable resource for finding a mate. Ads such as the one above are a wealth of information and often used by family members who participate in the process of selecting a mate for young adults in the family.

Diversity brings with it many unique elements to our everyday lives. One such element is the increasing exposure to different traditions and rituals from all over the world. As the United States' population continues to change and grow, the traditions of various immigrant groups warrant attention. The latest large influx of immigrants has come to the United States from Asia (Fernandez & Liu, 1986) and they have brought with them distinctly unique cultures. In fact, *Newsweek* (September 18, 2000) in a recent special report on race, noted that California's Silicon Valley has had a statistical majority of Asians since 1998. Most of these Asians are Chinese and Indian. The American Medical Association identifies Asian Indians as their largest majority group. And, UC Berkeley cites 45% of its incoming freshmen are Asian American. Despite these rapidly growing numbers, scholarship about the Asian Americans and the Asian Indian community specifically is relatively basic and focuses primarily on immigration statistics and patterns. This focus is due, in part, to the immigration options available to this group and to the lack of visibility of the Asian Indian community prior to 1965. Only since 1965 has United States immigration policy allowed a large influx of Asians into the United States.

Like all immigrant groups, the Asian Indian community strives to hold onto its traditional cultural norms while in the United States. However, unlike some other immigrant groups, the Asian Indian community has been able to obtain this goal while obtaining a certain upper middle class America status as well. In virtually all major cities within the United States, there are "little Indias" where the Indian community has access to its traditional foods, traditional wares, and other members of the Indian community.[1] One interesting aspect of the Asian Indian community is how the community has tailored its rituals to work for them within the United States. A primary example of this is the utilization of marriage and mate selection rituals.

The Indian American community has many community newspapers of which several are major English written newspapers based out of Los Angeles, Chicago and New York. These newspapers dedicate, on average, two to three pages to matrimonial advertisements. Unlike the American image of personal ads as a last resort for those who cannot find partners, Indian matrimonials are considered a normal and expected aspect of the arranged marriage process. These advertisements offer an interesting display of the Asian Indian community and its efforts to create a world of "Indianness" in the United States.

As Asian Indians move physically further and further away from the physical source of their culture, they try to re-create a psychic/social connection to support their sense of cultural identity. The matrimonial advertisements found in virtually all of the Asian Indian community newspapers in the United States serve a function that extends far beyond finding mates. These advertisements are clear, physical proclamations of cultural affiliation and identity. These advertisements serve to proclaim that the families who advertise are Indian in the purest sense of the word and they have actively raised Indian children. This notion of "Indian" children refers to children who are proud

The author wishes to thank Dr. D. Lawrence Wieder for his invaluable guidance during the writing of this paper, the members of the Indian community for their participation in the previous research that informed this paper, and the Drs. Ambarish and Divya Pathak for providing access into the Indian American community.

of their heritage and actively participate in community events; uphold specific Indian cultural values, customs and beliefs. This notion of Indianness will be discussed later in the [reading].

Paradoxically, these advertisements also then reflect a family's success in North America. As people live in a host culture, a sense of cultural fusion occurs, whether that fusion is recognized or not. Thus, these advertisements show how families have succeeded in this country while upholding their native culture. This success is evidenced through the emphasis on indicators of financial success throughout the advertisements. Even as these advertisements call for a "blend of East/West cultures" from the respondents, the actual advertisements are a unique blend of the two cultures in and of themselves. This blend presents an interesting point in the history of Asian Indians in America. There are a multitude of issues embedded in these ads, their use and how they are perceived in the Indian-American community. In examining these advertisements, the following questions present an approach toward understanding the Asian Indian mate selection process.

1. How do Asian Indians fulfill the ritual of mate selection in the United States?
2. What does this ritual say about the "Indianness" of the people involved to other Indians?
3. What are some of the implied embedded elements in the matrimonial advertisements?

Before examining each of these questions, a brief background of the Asian Indian community and the existing literature about the mate selection ritual is warranted.

REVIEW OF LITERATURE AND BACKGROUND

Saran and Eames (1980) posited that the greatest issues to face the Asian Indian community within the next 15 to 20 years would be issues of marriage and parent/child conflict. [Their] prediction was accurate given the topic areas that are currently researched within the Asian Indian community. The literature focuses on issues of identity maintenance, matrimonial advertisements, and cultural integrity within the United States. Matrimonial advertisements represent a concerted effort by the Indian community to maintain their cultural norms within the United States.[2] To understand these advertisements, it is first necessary to have a brief understanding of arranged marriages. Ancient traditional arranged marriages were often set up throughout Indian communities by social networking. Families of potential mates were often approached by

mutual friends who instigated the communication between the families. Since a majority of the marriages, approximately 95%, were arranged within sub-castes, this allowed for potential mates to know each other or each other's families at a social level. Additionally, since arrangements were suggested by mutual friends, potential spouses were described in detail. This transmitted vital information about physical attributes, education, personality traits and family background. As the Indian community continued to grow, newspaper advertisements became a mode of expressing availability of potential mates. Furthermore, as Indians began to migrate to other countries, these advertisements became a necessity in efforts to continue the arranged marriage ritual. These advertisements have proven to be highly effective here in the United States in terms of popularity and utilization.[3]

In a content analysis of 1,000 matrimonials throughout the 1980's, Ryali (1989) found that personal attributes (age, education, profession, height, appearance) were more often mentioned than social attributes (caste, religion, language, state). Ryali's article is representative of the current research on matrimonial advertisements. Other research on the Asian Indian community focuses on the analysis of demographic data, such as the 1980 United States census (e.g., Fernandez & Liu, 1986), which was the first United States census that listed Asian Indians as a separate ethnic group. More recent research examines the migration experience and issues of ethnic identity for Asian Indian immigrants (Jensen, 1988; Saran & Eames, 1980; Segal, 1991). Finally, the most recent crop of articles on Asian Indians in America comes from a critical, cultural perspective. Much of this comes from the critical ethnographic tradition. There has also been an emergence of popular literature dealing with the issues of adaptation and assimilation into mainstream America. While this research opens the door to the more complex issues within the community, the research on the Asian Indian community is limited and does not extensively explore the community's deeper issues. As mentioned earlier, much of the matrimonial advertisement research is content analysis that does not provide interpretation of the advertisements. For this reason, this [reading] provides an ethnographic examination of the themes in United States matrimonial advertisements.[4]

METHOD

This study primarily utilizes an ethnographic approach. While ethnography stands as a valid methodological approach to research, several key points about method warrant attention. As social sciences are influenced by the post-modern movement, several issues regarding research begin to overlap and intersect. Specific to this research, the question of researcher and researched is vital and warrants attention. In traditional ethnography, the prime goal has been to describe and present a clear view of a culture, its peoples and its rituals. As we begin to examine the intersection of cultures, this goal becomes somewhat more difficult to achieve. When examining a "culture" as it is transplanted into another culture, the research questions inherently presume questions of the boundaries as well as the center. The questions "which culture? where? and when? to what degree?" focus the research on the boundaries of a culture rather than focusing solely on descriptions of cultural acts, as has been common in past traditional ethnographies. Additionally, movements within research such as feminism and post-colonialism bring to the forefront questions about the researchers' motives and politics. These movements focus on and critique the politics and power of social science itself and strive to illuminate those power structures so that the reader is aware of the researcher's biases within the research. It is important to note, however, that the intent here is not to call ethnography itself into question. Rather, we call into question ethnographic authority and the inherent power structures of fieldwork which are most often ignored (Marcus, 1994, p. 565).

As researchers, it is imperative that we are aware of and make clear our positionality and subjectivity in our research. Specifically in ethnographic observation, there is a need to acknowledge the role the researcher plays in "creating" the results. For example, as an Indian American, my position as researcher co-constitutes the field in a very specific way. I engage interaction with a group of "participants" through the advertisements I observe and describe. As a researcher, I am not an invisible filter through which the advertisements are read. I, with the unnamed participants, through the reading of these advertisements co-constitute the field, the interaction and the rhetoric, which I then "report." Geertz (1973, p. 9) explains this as "that what we call our data are really our own constructions of other people's constructions of what they and their compatriots are up to . . ." He continues to explain that "there is nothing really wrong with this, and is in any case inevitable."

This does not imply in any way that it is not possible to engage in meaningful research. Rather, it is an indication of what is necessary for one to engage in meaningful research. The positionality and subjectivity of the researcher is as much a part of the field as observations.

Ethnography has long been a popular method with which to study culture and offers a broad scope through which to examine cultural practices. Geertz (1973) presents his method of thick description of ethnography. Geertz borrows this term from Gilbert Ryle. In explaining thick versus thin description, Geertz relies on Ryle's example of two young boys and the movements of their eyelids. Though at a phenomenalistic level, a wink and a twitch are the same movement, thick description incorporates motive and meaning of the actual action. Thin description would take the position of being a camera, reporting mere movement without examining beyond that movement. Thick description is the examination of the communication that is occurring with and by the specific movement. The move from movement to gesture is the focus of thick description. Geertz explains that at a point between thin description and thick description lies the object of ethnography: "a stratified hierarchy of meaningful structures in terms of which twitches, winks, fake-winks, parodies, rehearsals of parodies are produced, perceived, and interpreted, and without which they would not in fact exist, no matter what anyone did or didn't do with his eyelids" (1973, p. 7). Thus, ethnography is an interpretive method, one which takes thin description to thick description; one that examines meaning and motive, not mere behavior.

Thus, utilizing interpretive critical ethnography, I observe these advertisements and address the themes as they emerge from the text. A major weekly English language, Indian community newspaper (specifically the marital advertisements pages) was utilized for this study. Ads were collected over a period of 4 months, with a representative sample of advertisements utilized for analysis. As some ads were run over a period of time, ads were collected once for the data pool and checked for consistency throughout.[5]

THEMES

Introduction

In examining the matrimonial advertisements, two key topic areas warrant attention. First is an examination of the actual make-up of the advertisements. Through detailed ethnographic observation, certain topics are found as central in these advertisements. Additionally, the physical design of these advertisements also led to an examination of the embedded elements within these advertisements.

In the *India Journal* of Los Angeles, the last few pages are marked with matrimonial advertisements. These advertisements, divided by the folk categories, "Matrimonial Female," "Matrimonial Male," and

"Matrimonial Services," are a primary source for mate selection in the Indian community in the United States. The advertisements focus on the qualities of the advertised individual and preferred qualities of the potential mate. Under these umbrella categories are sub-categories that reveal the issues, themes and values that are of the greatest concern to the members of the immigrant Asian Indian population within the United States. References are made in these advertisements to education, personality type, height, and source of advertisement. The element of caste is predominant, either as a direct reference or as an indication that caste has no bar in the selection process. Also, a more recent element within the advertisements has been a reference to the value system of the females advertised. Statements such as "east/west values" indicate that the female has blended both the American and Indian worlds, a matter to be discussed later in the [reading].

Fulfilling the Ritual of Mate Selection

Regardless of gender of the advertised party, all of these advertisements begin with similar phrases.[6] The phrases include statements such as, "Parents invite correspondence . . . Match invited for . . . [caste, relationship] seek . . ." Though these phrases tend to come within the first two lines of the ad, some advertisements do provide a description of the advertiser first and then incorporate these phrases. For example:

> Charotar Patel, handsome, affectionate, and intelligent, 29, 5'1", U.S. citizen, well-settled, electrical engineer with NASA invites correspondence from Patel girl with Indian values. Prefers pharmacist, medical doctor, or lawyer. Call (xxx) xxx-xxxx.

Regardless of their placement, these phrases are considered appropriate language within the advertisements. The advertisement above also points out a few of the distinct elements within Indian matrimonials. One such element being the focus on physical characteristics. Height is frequently mentioned as is age. Age is sometimes referred to in acceptable ranges, rather than as a specific age. For example:

> Parents invite correspondence with a returnable photo from 28–31 yrs. Gujrati professionals with University degree, vegetarian and min. height of 5'7", for a 25 year daughter, B.A. psychology, B.S.W., raised in Canada with East/West culture. Reply. . . .

Other physical attributes that are also mentioned refer to female's skin tone, usually indicating that the female is fair skinned. Males are often referred to as attractive or handsome. Females are referred to as pretty, beautiful, or attractive. Advertisements also indicate females' weight with terms such as slim.

Expressing a Family's Indianness through Advertisements

The next major topic of these matrimonial advertisements is a direct reference to the advertiser's region, language and caste. The first two elements, region and language, are stated for the advertiser and for the potential respondents. Though the advertisements may not directly state that the advertisers are looking for someone from a specific region, the reference to the advertiser's region often implies that only those from that region need reply. As is common with the transliteration of Indian languages to English, region also refers to the native language of the advertising family.

The element of caste is a much more complex and deeper issue. Though caste is not an overt, visible element of American society, for the Asian Indian community in the United States, caste still plays a partly submerged role in matrimonial decisions. Granted, for certain individuals, caste plays a role in that they make a point of indicating that caste does not matter for them. While acknowledging the existence of these individuals, it is important to examine the communities that do express caste in their advertisements.[7] One such community is the Patel community, especially known in the United States for its presence in hotel and motel ownership and management. Patel is a surname within the Indian Gujrati community and refers to a specific sub-caste.[8] Central to caste for the Patel community is geographical region. As with the advertisement shown earlier in the text, many advertisements from the Patel community include reference to the village or area of their origin. Within the Patel community, there is a formal, yet tacit understanding of acceptable unions between members of specific villages or areas. Examples of terms that refer to region are Charotar and schagam (6gam).[9] By clearly stating these regions, the advertisers send an implied message about whose replies will be considered. Patel community members who are not as concerned about sub-caste will often simply refer to themselves as "Patel family" or "Patel male" to indicate their main caste.

Another example of a community that often refers to caste in their advertisements is the Sikh community. Sikhs are a religious sect of the Indian population most recognized in popular culture by their turbans. Advertisements placed by members of this community tend to refer to sub-castes within their community.

Brahmins also tend to clearly state their caste in advertisements, sometimes including reference to one's *gotra.* Though no longer a common sight, some advertisements do mention specific references to *gotra,* exogamous marital units within the caste system. A final point about caste is the integrated elements of caste and surname. Though many of these advertisements claim no caste bar, the reference to surnames within the advertisements indicates basic caste affiliation. Indian surnames reflect regional background and major caste affiliation. Here, advertisers presume that someone in the respondent's family has the historical oral knowledge of caste to derive necessary interpretation about the respondent's familial affiliation based on surname. Furthermore, though these advertisements claim "caste no bar," indicating no problem with respondents from any caste, further meetings in the arranged marriage process most likely do deal with the issue in much greater detail. Finally, it is important to note that while caste has become an inappropriate issue for many Asian Indians, even the denial of its importance reflects its power within the community. True indifference to caste is not so easily achieved within the Asian Indian American community.

Expressing a Candidate's Indianness through Ads

Once the elements of caste, language and region are referred to in the advertisements, the advertisers describe the personality attributes of the person they represent and the preferred personality attributes of the potential respondents. For men, the words commonly used include: intelligent, ambitious, qualified, established, clean-shaven, well settled. As these words indicate, the focus is often on the male's ability to provide financial and social security in the marriage. Females are described as: attractive, educated, down to earth, homely, sincere, cultured, traditional, slim, professional, good looking, creative, open minded.[10] These terms show the great value placed on a female's appearance as well as her ability to adapt to her married home. These terms seem to be words that would describe the perfect hostess. The terms traditional, homely and down to earth are coded descriptors alluding to the issue of which Eastern/Western values are ideally held by Indian American women.

The longer Asian Indians live in the United States, the more pressing the issue of value orientation becomes. Many families are unwilling to arrange marriages for their sons with Indian-American women who are perceived as having completely adopted American/Western values. However, these same families and their sons do recognize that some commitment to Western values is necessary for success in the United States and ideally prefer a very specific

blend of Indian and American/Western values. For Indian parents and sons, ideal females are Western in their beliefs about working outside the home and in their social skills. For many sons, these women should also be Western enough to be comfortable with their husband's somewhat "Western" behavior. For example, wives should be comfortable with his social drinking and be able to perform appropriately at corporate dinners. However, that is the limit to the acceptable meaning of "Western values." The families would like Eastern values in regard to the female's interactions within her marital home; and in regard to the female's interactions with her in-laws and her extended family. The wife should be willing to stay with her in-laws and other members of the extended family. She should not be overly outspoken and should overtly honor her husband. It is important to note that, in regard to family interactions, the expectations on women are higher than the expectations on men. Additionally, what is defined as an "ideal woman" for the Indian-American community is somewhat more conservative than the definition of "ideal woman" in India.[11]

Though the term "values" is utilized to express these ideal attributes, it is important to recognize that the term is meant somewhat differently than the academic, social scientific definition and that families are often more interested in behavior than values and other internal states. Many young couples coordinate their own ways of presenting what is considered an acceptable image in the eyes of in-laws while otherwise maintaining a Western relationship. This is an issue of generation as well as culture. This issue will be further discussed later in the [reading].

Having discussed the major topics within these advertisements, it is now important to examine other external topics that appear within the advertisements. One such topic is that of food preferences. Many advertisements distinguish specific needs such as vegetarianism, non-drinker, and non-smoker. One ad went so far as to indicate minimal drinking. As Asian Indians westernize, the issue of non-vegetarianism and social drinking are areas where there is much more leeway within the society.

Another feature of the advertiser and potential respondents that is explicitly mentioned is immigration status. Though the social networking system within Indian castes is not as well developed as in the ancient past, it is still a vital part of the caste. Many of these advertisements use green card status or citizenship as an enticement for potential mates from India. Many people in India have family members representing them in the United States who are active participants in the family's search for a mate. Also it is common practice for Asian Indians to obtain visitor's visas and visit the United States in hopes of finding a mate. The reverse is also common, with Indian-Americans traveling to India to find potential mates. Green card status and citizenship implies a well-settled individual with familial support in the United States. These well-settled families are seen as good families to marry into as, most likely, there are several extended family members in the U.S. and an already existent, strong social network, assuring that the newly married couple would not be totally alone and without family support in the United States.[12]

Hand in hand with immigrant status is the issue of employment. In a quest for indicating security, many advertisements focus on the level of education and employment of the person represented in the ad. In fact, one ad indicated that the person was an electrical engineer for NASA, showing that the person has an appropriate education and a prime, stable job.

Advertisers and respondents share a set of conventional understandings about employment that they use in constructing and interpreting advertisements. Within these conventions, reference to a female's education serves a two-fold purpose. It is understood that in this modern world, it is vital to have a mate who can work and has the education to obtain a financially rewarding job. The overt reason for stating a female's education is to indicate her earning capacity. In the conventional view, it is also important to show a female's compatibility with potential partners, which provides a deeper reason for mentioning her education. It is understood that a woman's education reflects her ability to converse on various topics and understand the issues facing her husband in everyday life. As some advertisements indicate, certain education is more preferred, as shown in the earlier ad. The reference to a female's education shows her potential to work as well as what areas interest her. The premise of match making in the Indian community relies on the concept of similarity. Those who have a similar background have a better chance of getting along. This also indicates why the previous ad indicated that a pharmacist was preferred, since pharmacists and engineers may not seem adequately similar. More suitable matches may be a pharmacist and a doctor or an engineer and an urban planner.

The final issue in regard to security is the references to type of family. In the Indian tradition, marriage is a union between two families. To uphold this tradition, some families refer to the fact that they are "good families." This refers to the family background. Good families are families that have high status in their caste, no divorce within the extended family and a tendency to uphold tradition. The reference to "good

family" implies a more traditional family and solicits responses from a traditional family.

Knowing what topics are appropriate is only the first part of matrimonial advertisements. The next obvious part is the process of making connections between potential mates. As is common in the Indian community, elder family members instigate the meetings between potential spouses. Making the choice of who to contact for further information is usually based on the biodata and sometimes a picture. A biodata is a type of matrimonial resume. It includes physical information such as height, weight, age, and possible unique physical features. It also includes information about the individual's education, hobbies, and personal interests. Some biodatas also incorporate information about extended family members and future plans of the potential spouse. Though all advertisements do not require pictures, most request a returnable photo to gauge the attractiveness of the respondent. Most newspapers, such as *The India Journal, India Tribune, India West,* and *The Gujarat Times* provide a blind box service. This provides the advertiser a post office box under the name of the newspaper where replies can be sent. Some advertisements provide phone numbers, though this is not as common. Many advertisements also provide addresses, or refer to the location of their home. This reference provides the respondent an understanding of where the family has settled in the United States. Certain addresses are familiar as exclusive neighborhoods, or as large Indian communities. These addresses provide the respondents with information about the advertiser's financial status, a general understanding of the security of the extended family in the United States and the advertiser's connection to the Indian community. It also gives the respondents a place to start their research about the advertiser's family. For example, many advertisements come from Mississauga, Ontario, Canada. Ontario has a large Asian Indian population. Such an address tells the potential respondents that the advertiser is a member of a well-established Indian-Canadian enclave and opens the door for the potential respondents to inquire among their friends in Ontario about the advertiser. Once biodatas and pictures are examined, further contact is made with potential mates and the rest of the arranged marriage ritual is initiated.

Embedded/Implied Elements of Advertisements

Having examined the components of matrimonial advertisements in the Asian Indian community, it is only natural to ask what the impact of such information is on the community which supports and perpetuates such a system as well the impact on the individuals who participate in the advertisements. This essay provides a forum from which to posit a hypothesis regarding the function and impact of such a system on the Asian Indian-American community and individual community members. The hypothesis presented is based on the data generated from this study and from previous works about arranged marriage.

First, I posit that the use of newspapers as a forum for matrimonial advertisements is a pragmatic function of adaptation to a technological world. As modernity becomes a mode of function in all parts of the world, ancient traditions of oral culture are diminished and ultimately replaced. The ancient culture of knowing caste, recalling lineage and verbally reinforcing complex structures of exogamy and endogamy is lost in this era of mobility. Thus, advertisements offer a replacement for finding members of various groups, tribes and collectives within larger castes. This is evident in India as well as in Indian communities abroad. Given the rapid rate of urbanization and the easy access to international travel, newspapers provide an ideal forum to connect with members of one's social group despite physical distance.

Furthermore, as Indians move physically further and further away from their cultural source, they try to recreate a psychological and physical connection between themselves to support their sense of cultural identity. These advertisements serve a function that extends much beyond finding mates. These advertisements are clear, physical proclamations of cultural affiliation and identity. These advertisements serve to proclaim that the families who advertise are "Indian" in the purest sense of the word and that they have actively raised "Indian" children.

Paradoxically, the very fact of these advertisements also reflects a family's success in North America and indicates at least as much incorporation of American/Western values as required to achieve that success. Thus, by their emphasis on indicators of financial success, these advertisements show how families have succeeded in the United States and/or Canada while simultaneously upholding their native culture and incorporating some American culture. Just as these advertisements call for a "blend of East/West cultures," the actual advertisements themselves are a unique blend of cultures.

However, this blend of East and West is a key concern for the individuals who participate in the advertisements. The impact of the advertisements on individual members of the community is very controversial. For every bit of cultural reinforcement these advertisements provide at a mass community scale,

they bring into question the cultural identity of individuals and make the issue of cultural identity a public topic of discussion. In many ways, for Indian-American youth, cultural identity is a battle between a Western world and Eastern world.[13]

The most obvious issue facing the community is the "inappropriateness" of American born/raised Indian females.[14] Many women speak of the emphasis on their domesticity and traditionalism as oppressive and problematic. Furthermore, there are even further embedded issues of mate selection systems for Indian youth, both male and female. Whether parents agree or not, most Indian youth participate in the American dating system until family intervention occurs to reinforce the traditional arrangement system. Many Indian youth feel anger and confusion about this experience because they perceive a sudden shift by and within their parents. Up until dating and mate selection become an issue, most Indian parents encourage and aid their children in the utilization, internalization, and manifestation of American modes of behavior to assure the child's success. This support is then directly contradicted when the children make the natural extension of their behavior to choosing a mate. At this point, the parents make it clear the children are expected to uphold and engage in traditional Indian behavior.

Beyond this issue is the tenuous balance between behavior and values. As mentioned earlier in the [reading], there is often a gap between what the extended family wants and what occurs between the actual spouses. Here, the key issue is the blend of Indian and American/Western values. The implied element of most Indian communities in the United States is the emphasis on cultural preservation. The matrimonial advertisements are utilized for the purpose of bringing two people together who will engage in behaviors that ultimately uphold the Indian culture. However, for many younger Indians, the issue is not one of cultural preservation, it is simply a matter of presenting an acceptable image within the older Indian community.[15] Oftentimes, the assumed extension of behavior to value orientation is lost in the mate selection process. The inherent values that are the essential focus for the older Indian-American community are seen as irrelevant or obsolete by the younger Indian-American community. Thus, younger Indian-Americans engage in appropriate behaviors in the presence of elders, yet ultimately, they adhere to an essentially different value system. This struggle somewhat defeats the community's efforts to maintain a static cultural identity and uphold cultural preservation. Much of this dynamic is present in the United States because most

Indian parents living in the United States envision an India of the 1950s or 1960s when creating standards of behavior for their children. What these parents fail to recognize is that India has Westernized beyond that point.[16]

Another aspect of this dynamic is the powerful return to fundamental cultural identity for many Indians living in the United States. These fundamental Indians are often the children of Indians who settled in the United States over 20 years ago and still see India the way it was in the late 1950s. The parents have instilled in their children an older historic tradition of Indian cultural identity that comes across as strident fundamentalism in today's era. Note that there are two very distinct reactions by the children of parents from the same cohort. Though there is minimal data to support the claim, there is still room to make the inference that Indian males in the U.S. tend to gravitate toward the fundamental identity while Indian females engage in culturally acceptable behaviors while being committed to a vastly different belief system. This may be due to a simple cost/benefit analysis. The males benefit from a traditional value orientation, whereas the women benefit from a more modern ideology. Regardless, these issues clearly point to concerns in the marriages between two individuals who may seem similar on the outside, but are ideologically so different.

Keep in mind that this argument solely addresses Indians in America, not Indian youth in India. An interesting extension of this study could be a comparison between Indian cohorts in India and the United States. Again, preliminary probes indicate that the female cohorts are somewhat similar in both countries; yet, the male cohorts are vastly different.

CONCLUSION

Though these advertisements are small boxes paid for by the line, to the informed reader, they are a wealth of information about potential spouses. Matrimonials are a vital part of the Indian community both in India and abroad. For Asian Indians in the United States, these advertisements represent a sense of ritual and a sense of identity. Unlike the mate selection process of the Western world, the matrimonials open up communication between individuals who could not and would not meet under the circumstances of migration. Many of these marriages take place between individuals from cities that are a continent apart or even from countries an ocean apart.

Engaging in the process of finding a spouse for their offspring provides a sense of community for Asian Indians outside of India. Asian Indians abroad are a group that exists through its conventionalized practices, through the way it does things. By providing themselves with specific services catered to the Indian population, Indians in the United States have found a way to establish community and ethnic identity while existing in another world. Further research on matrimonial advertisements and other rituals within the Indian community provide a rich domain for understanding the concepts of identity and community.

NOTES

1. Examples of this would be Artesia, CA, near Los Angeles; Devon Street in Chicago, IL; Jackson Heights in New York City, NY; and Edison, NJ.
2. This is so in a complex manner. It does not require deliberations or agreement in the community. Depending as it does on the organization of a market, it does not require agreement in the community to pursue the maintenance of cultural norms.
3. This study cannot and does not measure effectiveness of these advertisements. Popularity is reflected in the large preponderance of these adverstisements and utilization is reflected in the response rate for ads as well as the daily reference to these ads throughout the process of arrangement.
4. Ethnographic work allows for observational data as well as an insider perspective. As I use a clear insider perspective, this methodology offers the best approach to the data.
5. None of the ads were changed, with the exception of address corrections. Because this [reading] focused on advertisement utility and function, no data was collected regarding length of time for ads.
6. In examining the topics within the advertisements, it is convenient to organize the sequence of the discussion so that it mirrors the order of topics in the advertisements. Despite this chronology in the paper, clear overarching themes emerge.
7. Here, community is not used in its technical social scientific sense, but is employed to designate what Asian Indians mean when they speak words like *nathe* and *samaj*.
8. Many members of the Asian Indian community in the United States come from the western part of India known as Gujarat. The members of this region, Gujaratis, are often categorized as Patels or non-Patels.
9. 6gam is the abbreviation used in ads. *Schagam* literally means six villages and refers to a network of Patel villages in Gujarat State, India.
10. In this context, the term homely refers to an Indian woman's domestic nature, her simplicity, and her marked lack of pretentiousness. A homely woman is one who does not put on airs, is not vain, and not

boastful of her talent as a homemaker. It does not mean unattractive or socially unskilled.

11. While this [reading] focuses solely on Indian-Americans, an examination of youth in India also warrants attention as a source of comparative analysis.

12. Well settled families are families that have secure financial status in the U.S., a fair number of family members in North America, and a history within the Indian abroad community.

13. I have explored this notion of residing in many worlds at once in my other works. This discussion offers a preliminary examination of a series of complex issues.

14. The following hypotheses regarding Indian American women are based on previous research.

15. Here, the term community refers to direct members of an individual's family and the Indian community at large.

16. This notion of recalling an older India is referred to as frozen-in-time memory.

REFERENCES

Agarwal, P. (1991). *Post-1965 immigrants into the U.S.* Palo Alto, CA: Yuvati Press.

Bacon, J. (1996). *Life lines: Community, family, and assimilation among Asian Indian immigrants.* New York: Oxford University Press.

Barringer H. & Kassebaum, G. (1989). Asian Indians as a minority in the United States: The effect of education, occupations, and gender on income. *Sociological Perspectives, 32,* 501–520.

Chandrasekhar, S. (Ed.). (1983). *From India to America: A brief history of immigration, problems of discrimination admission and assimilation.* La Jolla, CA: Population Review.

Dasgupta, S. S. (1989). *On the trail of an uncertain dream: Indian immigrant experience in America.* New York: AMS Press.

Fernandez, M. & Liu, W. T. (1986). Asian Indians in the United States: Economic, educational, and family profiles from the 1980 census. *Studies in Third World Societies, 38,* 149–177.

Fisher, M. P. (1978). Creating ethnic identity: Asian Indians in the New York City area. *Urban Anthropology, 7,* 271–285.

Fisher, M. P. (1980). *The Indians of New York City: A study of immigrants from India.* Columbia, MO: South Asia Books.

Geertz, C. (1973). *The interpretation of cultures.* New York: Basic Books.

Gibson, M. A. (1988). *Accommodation without assimilation: Sikh immigrants in an American high school.* Ithaca, NY: Cornell University Press.

Goffman, E. (1959). *The presentation of self in everyday life.* Garden City, NY: Doubleday Anchor.

Gudykunst, W. B. & Kim, Y. Y. (1992). *Communicating with strangers: An approach to intercultural communication.* New York: McGraw-Hill.

Helweg, A. W. (1987) Why leave India for America? A case study approach to understanding migrant behaviour. *International Migration, 25,* 165–178.

Helweg, A. W. & Helweg, U. M. (1990). *An immigrant success story: East Indians in America.* Philadelphia: University of Pennsylvania Press.

Jensen, J. M. (1988). *Passage from India: Asian Indian immigrants in North America.* New Haven, CT: Yale University Press.

Kurian, G. & Srivastava, R. P. (1983). *Overseas Indians: A study in adaptation.* Delhi, India: Vikas Publishing House.

Lee, J. F. J. (1991). *Asian American experiences in the United States: Oral histories of first to fourth generations Americans from China, the Philippines, Japan, India, the Pacific Islands, Vietnam and Cambodia.* Jefferson, NC: McFarland & Company.

Lofland, J. & Lofland, L. H. (1984). *Analyzing social settings: A guide to qualitative observation and analysis.* Belmont, CA: Wadsworth

Marcus, G. E. (1994). What comes (just) after the "post"? The case of ethnography. In N. K. Denzin & Y. S. Lincoln (Eds.), *Handbook of qualitative research.* Thousand Oaks, CA: Sage.

Mehta, R. & Belk, R. W. (1988). Artifacts, identity, and transition: Favorite possessions of Indians and Indian immigrants to the United States. *Journal of Consumer Research, 1,* 398–411.

Melendy, H. B. (1977) *Asians in America: Filipinos, Koreans, and East Indians.* Boston, MA: Twayne Publishers.

Radhakrishnan, R. (1996). *Diasporic mediations.* Carbondale, IL: Southern Illinois University Press.

Ryali, R. (1989). Ethnic identity: Spouse selection among Asian-American Indians. *Free Inquiry in Creative Sociology, 17,* 131–139.

Saran, P. (1985). *The Asian Indian experience in the United States.* Cambridge, MA: Shenckman Publishing Company.

Saran, P. & Eames, E. (1980). *The new ethnics: Asian Indians in the United States.* New York: Praeger.

Segal, U. A. (1991). Cultural variables in Asian Indian families. *The Journal of Contemporary Human Services,* 233–242.

Sheth, M. (1995). Asian Indian Americans, in P. G. Min (Ed.), *Asian Americans: Contemporary trends and issues.* Thousand Oaks, CA: Sage.

Sridhar, K. L. (1988). Language maintenance and language shift among Asian-Indians: Kannadigas in the New York area. *International Journal of the Sociology of Language, 69,* 73–87.

Takaki, R. (1989). *India in the West: South Asians in America.* New York: Chelsea House.

Van Maanen, J. (1988). *Tales of the field: On writing ethnography.* Chicago: University of Chicago Press.

CHECK YOUR UNDERSTANDING

1. What are the marriage and mate selection rituals in your culture?
2. How do these differ from the ones described by Bhatt? How are they similar?
3. What do these differences and similarities suggest about intercultural communication?

4. Look in the personal ads of your local newspaper. How do these compare with those described by Bhatt.

It's Not All Blarney: Intergenerational Transmission of Communication Patterns in Irish-American Families

Kathleen Galvin

Families come from families. The communication in each family system reflects the patterns of the adults' families-of-origin as well as their cultural heritage's norms for interaction (Galvin & Brommel, 1999). Frequently overlooked, ethnic communication patterns that serve as a proving ground for values, expectations and patterns of behavior contribute to family communication patterns (Collins, 1978; Socha & Diggs, 1999). According to McGoldrick and Giordano (1996), ethnicity, "a common ancestry through which individuals have evolved shared values and customs . . . is deeply tied to the family, through which it is transmitted" (p. 1). In addition to the basic characteristics of race, religion, national or geographic origin, ethnicity also involves "conscious and unconscious processes that fulfill a deep psychological need for identity and a sense of historical continuity." Family members view the world through their own ethnic filters although they may not be aware of the existence or power of such filters.

Multiple ethnicities and family life have been intertwined within the United States reflecting the waves of immigrants who settled, and continue to settle here. Contrary to the image that ethnic groups, particularly English-speaking ones, quickly become assimilated and "Americanized" or homogenized, current thinking suggests a cross generational continuity of ethnicity. If the first generation lives within an ethnic context and the second generation is likely to reject some of the parental attitudes, behaviors, and strive to appear "American," while the third and fourth generations are more likely to reclaim aspects of their identity (Sluzki, 1979).

There is increasing evidence that certain ethnic values are retained throughout multiple generations and affect aspects of family life including communication patterns (Donohue, 2000; McGoldrick, Giordano & Pearce, 1996). Based on her clinical work with ethnic families, McGoldrick (1993) suggests the following factors influence the extent to which traditional ethnic patterns will be salient for a particular family (pp. 341–342).

1. The reasons for immigration—what the family was seeking and what it was leaving behind (religious or political persecution, poverty, wish for adventure, etc.).
2. The length of time since immigration and the impact of generational acculturation conflicts on the family.
3. The family's place of residence—whether or not the family lives or has lived in an ethnic neighborhood.
4. The order of migration—whether one member migrated alone or whether a large portion of the family, community or nation came together.
5. The socioeconomic status, education, and upward nobility of family members.
6. The political and religious ties to the ethnic group.
7. The languages spoken by family members.
8. The extent of family intermarriage with or connection to other ethnic groups.
9. The family members' attitudes toward the ethnic group and its values.

The complexity of the ethnic experience cannot be overstated. The previous list presents numerous issues of concern to any researcher concerned with the effect of ethnicity on a specific individual or family system. It also implies that physical and linguistic differences need not be the sole determinants of a strong ethnic heritage.

Intercultural scholars pay limited attention to the subtleties of the ethnicity of European-American groups long established in the United States. Few family-oriented scholars have focused on communication within the generations of descendants of American immigrants representing a Northern European, English-speaking background. In fact, many individuals from such a background describe themselves as a "plain vanilla or un-hyphenated American."

Thus the effect of ethnicity on the communication patterns within three- or four-generation Northern-European ethnic families, specifically those of Irish American heritage, is thought to be lost through assimilation. This position overlooks the previously noted conscious and unconscious processes that fulfill a need for identity and a sense of historical continuity. Ethnic patterns continue to affect the family communication patterns of multigenerational Irish American families, especially those that retain strong religious and community roots.

The Irish and American heritage has been intertwined since the United States was founded. The first U.S. census (1790) reported 44,000 Irish immigrants and 150,000 of Irish ancestry among the population and by the Famine, which started in 1845, more than another million had arrived; then "between 1845 and 1860 nearly two million Irish immigrants—a quarter of the Irish nation—were flung onto the shores of America" (Golway, 1997, p. 4). After the turn of the century the numbers decline, and since the 1960s when immigrant quotas restricted numbers of Northern Europeans only a few hundred Irish entered the U.S legally (Horgan, 1998). Almost all Irish immigrants settled permanently in the United States to partake in the economic opportunities until the late 1990s when the first reverse immigration wave occurred due to improved economic opportunities in Ireland.

In order to examine the effect of Irish ethnicity on the family members' communication patterns it is necessary to explore major characteristics of an Irish American background relying on relevant literature, selected interviews from an earlier study and further observations of three generations of Irish American, Catholic women in one extended immigrant family (Galvin, 1982). This study included a grandparent generation born in Ireland, a parent generation born in Ireland, the U.S. or England and a third generation born in the United States. This examination will demonstrate that an English-speaking, Northern-European heritage, such as an Irish heritage, impacts the communication patterns of multiple generations due to underlying ingrained values and practices no longer understood to be cultural in nature.

THE IRISH AMERICAN EXPERIENCE

Most Americans, whether or not of Irish heritage, recognize the commercial symbols of Ireland—the shamrock, the St. Patrick's Day parade, the step dancing of *River Dance* and phrases such as "Top o' the mornin'"—the paddywhackery or exaggerated self-caricature of the Irish. Some scholars maintain paddywhackery is all that is left of the Irish heritage in America, a remnant of the Paddy caricature that became popular in the late 1800s in magazines such as *Puck* and *Harper's Weekly*. Others contend ethnic influence continues to be strong even within the apparently assimilated Irish American, Catholic families. The former argue that many of the young middle class Irish Americans who sing ballads and support the I.R.A. are ignorant of Irish history, untouched by Irish culture, and are only romantically reacting to the enthusiasm of youth, the Irishness of their names, the beat of the music, and the need for a cause (McCaffrey, 1997). They believe upward mobility has resulted in their entrance into all levels of educational and career successes but at the same time the American-Irish have lost their ethnic identity due to lack of knowledge of Irish culture, history and literature.

Opponents argue for the continuation of an Irish culture in the descendants of Irish immigrants, reasoning that even Irish Americans who do not have cognitive knowledge of their heritage retain cultural characteristics. This reflects a belief that ethnic groups, even those such as the Irish who might appear assimilated, maintain cultural patterns whose origins can be traced to their past and which do not seem to be eroding with education, time in America, movement to the suburbs and, in some cases, intermarriage (Greeley, 1981). Such proponents suggest Irish cultural attributes may be found in their patterns of family structure, religious behavior, political activities, reaction to death, perceptions of women, and drinking. McGoldrick (1996) presents an analysis that includes: the Irish historical context, the Church, linguistic characteristics, respectability, emotional problems, alcohol use, death and family patterns. Most authors draw distinctions about the Irish based on religious affiliation because of the power of the Catholic experience in shaping the Irish

American heritage. Even that has changed in the past decades as the Second Vatican Council affected how Irish American families function because of the Catholic diminished sense of guilt and increased sense of religious options, suggesting this change appears to have altered rather than ended the Irish American experience (McGoldrick & Pearce, 1981). The current Irish American experience will be explored in terms of historical patterns related to selected issues including: (1) boundary management, (2) language, (3) tough topics (sex and death) and (4) values, each of which are relevant to family communication patterns. Some of these reflect the Irish heritage and others are influenced by the early American experiences that included extensive discrimination due in part to the immigrants' lack of education, poverty and Catholic religious traditions.

BOUNDARIES

The Irish culture exhibits a powerful respect for family and individual boundaries. Traditionally, one does not share highly personal information and deep feelings with the surrounding community, such as the neighbors, and often one does not share pain or praise with other family members. Psychological walls constructed around the individual, the family and the extended family remain firm. These boundaries may be best understood through an examination of the issues of respectability, suffering and distancing.

RESPECTABILITY

Propriety has been the curse of the Irish since their arrival in the United States. Irish immigrants desired to appear respectable in the eyes of others, particularly the non-Irish. Even contemporary Irish American families are likely to be more concerned than other groups about exhibiting any different behavior and concerned with achieving good appearances and acceptance (McGoldrick, 1995).

Two questions traditionally raised in every Irish family reflect this focus on respectability, (1) "Who do you think you are?" and (2) "What will people say?" (Greeley, 1979). Boasting or showing off would call attention to oneself, an undesirable behavior, because any kind of unusual behavior could lead to critical comments from others. Respectability is achieved by following the straight and narrow path. Such pressures forced young people into the professions, thus proving the stability and respectability of the family, but providing limited options for alternative career growth. Success depended on making conventional choices and not calling undue attention to oneself. Family life

reflected the norms of politeness, obedience, and discipline. Typical parental messages included, "What will the neighbors think?" "Don't make a scene," or "That's a sin," and "Know your place." Phrases such as "Who do you think you are?" and "What will people say?" are repeated across generations often to warn a child that based on a historically formed culture that may have long been forgotten, conformity is more valuable than individuality, and, out of the historical context, this merely undercut the child's self-confidence and creativity" (Donohue 2000, p. 8). Among the three generations of Irish American women, respondents of each generation identified immediately with the phrases "What will people say?" and "What will other people think?" One Irish grandmother stated, "I would never want my neighbors to know we had an argument" while her daughter said, "Even if we are just sitting on the porch on Saturday night my father will get hysterical if the voices are too high and he'll say, 'Keep your voices down. You don't want the neighbors to hear.'"

Much of the respectability was maintained through strict injunctions against sharing the family business outside the family. Such a call for privacy serves to keep attention from the Irish American individual and family and perpetuates respectability. Every respondent had a variation of the theme of privacy. These included the following family injunctions:

- "What you see and hear in this house goes no further."
- "This is just within our own family."
- "This doesn't leave the house" or "This doesn't leave this table."
- "Don't advertise your business. Handle it on the q.t."

Such admonitions reflected the strong Irish bid for respectability and the belief that respectability was gained by a show of propriety.

SUFFERING

Suffering and privacy stand as twin supports to the Irish American orientation to sin and religion. The Irish tend to assume that anything that goes wrong is tied to their sins and that their problems are private matters between individuals and God (McGoldrick, 1993). Relief and release is found in "offering up" the pain to Christ through prayer. Suffering in silence is respected and valued, as well as the ability to be outwardly hospitable and cheerful while suffering.

The Irish are less likely than other ethnic groups to seek medical or psychotherapeutic relief, instead finding religion with its promise of a better world, to be the outlet for their pain. The "stiff upper lip" refers to individual privacy rather than to emotional responses to the woes of their country or their superficial sensitivity. There is a pride tied to the ability to suffer without complaint. Frequently the happy-go-lucky image remains just that; personal boundaries are too powerful to allow open reflection of an inner life.

Suffering as part of a religious orientation had been taught to most of the Irish women respondents although some of the younger ones no longer accepted the expectation that one should suffer silently for sins. Most still retained some variation of the belief as indicated by one grandmother, "I wouldn't tell my troubles to nobody. If I had a problem I kept it inside." One mother said, "If you had bad news within the family, you just suffered within yourself. You didn't ask others to share your problems. You held it within yourself. You held your head high and you just prayed to God that it would pass." And a granddaughter revealed, "All emotions were denied. It was 'keep the exterior calm, cool and collected.' Whenever I got angry I left the room."

DISTANCING

Tied to their sense of strong personal boundaries the Irish tend to distance from outsiders and from family in an exhibition of emotional isolation. In comparison to Southern European families, Northern European families have far less intense interactions and are more likely to deal with problems by distancing. The Irish pragmatic orientation to marriage and the de-emphasis of romance contributes to distancing patterns.

> Partners tend to resign themselves to an emotionally distant relationship. Physical or emotional separation has been the primary way of dealing with problems. . . . Whereas for the Irish, distancing is merely the best temporary solution to interpersonal problems, it may be interpreted by others as abandonment (McGoldrick & Pearce, 1981, p. 231)

Donohue (2000) provides one explanation for this saying,

> First colonized by Roman Catholicism, then the British, then forced into exile where they were treated poorly, the Irish may have been forced to adopt a victim's distrust of others a way of distancing themselves with humor and stories that deflect any real intimacy. (p. 1)

The cutoff as a conflict strategy applies to more aggressive familial situations. Because of the Irish avoidance of direct anger, when the humorous expression such as sarcasm or ridicule does not work, relational cutoffs occur. These may range from traumatic events such as running away, to refusing to communicate with a family member who remains nearby, to resorting to ritualized, impersonal communication at family events (Kramer, 1985). In any case the "other" is disconfirmed or treated as if invisible.

Anger may be dealt with by a silent building up of resentments, culminating in cutting off the relationship, often without a word or by invoking the silent treatment for a period of time as a type of punishment. The Irish may never talk about the cutoff: they just live with it, suffering in silence and maintaining their boundaries. Even with their sense of humor and fun, extended family relationships among the Irish may be activated only in "duty visits" on holidays but emotional support may not be drawn from this extended membership. Frank McCourt's personal memoir, *Angela's Ashes,* contains a powerful example:

> Grandma won't talk to Mam anymore because of what I did with god in her backyard. Mam doesn't talk to her sister, Aunt Aggie, or her brother Uncle Tom. Dad doesn't talk to any one in Mam's family and they don't talk to him. (1996, p. 132)

Most female interviewees reported growing up with a sense of distrust of others and a history of keeping things to themselves although few had experienced an intense cutoff. Their extended family interactions occurred predictably at weddings, graduations and funerals. There appears to be little emotional sharing between the family strands although within each family unit emotional support exists. The overall family appears to function according "duty visits" remaining politely distant or reserved most of the time.

LANGUAGE

In examining the language of the Irish it is important to consider the effect of the patterns of speech which appear to be politic and romantic, but which may cloak whatever is really intended. The "gift of talk," the extreme of paddywhackery and the reality of plain or straightforward talk provide ways to explore the use of language.

The English have long referred to "the talking Irish" to describe the Irish capacity to both communicate and not communicate at the same time. The gift of talk has been an undisputed Irish talent. The poet has always been revered in Ireland and, although in America "respectability" has discouraged such creative/artistic careers, the appreciation still remains. McGoldrick (1995) suggests the Irish use words to buffer experience, "They call upon poetry or the humor of language to make reality somehow more tolerable" (p. 265). Famine and hardship have given rise to fantasy and dreams. Additionally, in keeping with the traditions of other oppressed peoples, the Irish developed a pattern of speech designed to exclude others, such as the British.

> The original purpose of blarney was to preserve the fiction of compliance while maintaining one's own ideas of justice. To speak out directly against the system imposed by the British was a dangerous activity. The alternatives, then, were either discreet silence or skilled speech. . . . Thus, "soft deception" cloaked in elaborate evasiveness became one of the main features of that unique phenomenon called Irish blarney. (Spaulding, 1978, pp. 11–12)

The more modern Irish and Irish Americans' sense of blarney tends toward a lighter purpose although it still may serve to cover difficult topics. The writer Mary Gordon grew up with the admonition, "Don't tell anyone our secrets. Laugh, and smile and lie" (Donohue, 2000, p. 1). Blarney may also be used to flatter, to ingratiate, to tease, to play with words. The oldest members of the Chicago family retained the predicted Irish gift of talk. One daughter explained her mother's expressions, saying, "She invents them. They're sure original. It relates to her Irish wit." Her grandchildren remember many of their grandmother's witticisms or sayings such as her predictable accompaniment to any gift, "Well to wear and many better." One woman remembered how her mother countered her son's argument that since he was born on English soil he must be English. She replied: "If a cat has kittens in the oven, you wouldn't call them muffins." During the interviews one grandmother stated, "If I was to knit my years together there's really a lot of loose stitches there." In a recent *New York Times* article Irish poet Brendan Kennelly addresses the Irish talent for composing narratives saying, "We live on stories. I always think of that phrase, 'I am the way, the truth and the light.' You see, the truth comes second; it's the way that matters. Its how you tell things. And that is the oldest Irish tradition" (Hoge, 2000, p. 2).

Plain/Straightforward Talk

Language has given the Irish their fantasy release but while they have the most highly developed skill with words of any culture, they may be at a loss to describe their own inner feelings and emotions (McGoldrick, 1996). Such limitations influence family interactions and cohesion. Although historically there have been extensive marital and parent-child conversations in Irish families, the conversations tend to avoid quarreling. Thus, both conflict and affection are carefully controlled in the Irish Catholic family.

There was great variability in response to open, leveling conversations among the women interviewed. In most cases such conversations were carefully self-monitored and people were careful not to disclose too much, particularly to extended family or those outside the family.

Humor

More than other cultures, the Irish are noted for their wit which is a source of personal pride and a delight to outsiders. Yet humor serves as a great Irish defense against life's problems; sarcasm, ridicule, and joking serve as ways of covering feelings and protecting self and avoiding personal attacks.

> The Irish form of banter says one thing and means another. It is often used to avoid responsibility or closeness with others. Teasing and ridicule are especially common in Irish family relationships. Unfortunately, their facile ability to joke can leave family members frozen in emotional isolation and unable to get close to anyone. (McGoldrick & Pearce, 1981, p. 227)

Obvious hostility is likely to be directed outward but feelings of anger within the family may be buried in indirect humor until the pain becomes too great and a person may be cut off. Three typical speech patterns of Irish American Catholic families are understatement, put downs and ridicule (Biddle, 1976).

Most female respondents related to the witticism level of humor, recalling funny stories of older members or their ability to make others laugh. One set of granddaughters recounted what their father taught them about humor.

> When you were angry—turn it to humor. So no one really knew how to deal with it (anger) to the point where no one could identify it when it was there. . . . He would never allow you to say anything against her (Mother) except in humor—only where it wouldn't hurt. If someone teased me he'd say, "Don't be angry—laugh it off." No one said it's not real. You're not a pig or ape or whatever they called you. No one taught you how to deal with it. It was "deny it" and "laugh at it."

Paddywhackery involves "exaggerating Irish characteristics to the point of self-caricature, though generally the distortion gently ridicules the beholder rather than the subject" (O'Connor, 1971, p. 365). Some consider it "blarney with a bite." The Irish and Irish Americans who specialize in "begorra" and effusive blarney may provide an extensive put-on for the listener. There are countless sayings, spontaneous jigs, songs or poems that may be interjected at key moments to distract or add lightness to a moment.

COMMUNICATION OF FEELINGS

There is a story of the old Irishman whose wife kept asking him, "Colin, do you love me? You haven't said you loved me in the 40 years since our wedding." The old man was most reluctant to express his feelings but finally he said "Peggy, I told you I loved you when I married you. If I change my mind I'll let you know." It appears that "although the Irish have a marvelous ability to tell stories, when it comes to their emotions they have no words" (McGoldrick & Pearce, 1981, p. 226). The poetic nature of the Irish both permits expressions of feeling at superficial levels yet prevents such expression at deeper levels. The Irish American patterns of communicating feelings may be explored by looking at communication of affection and communication of anger, particularly related to discipline

Even when the Irish care deeply it is hard for them to put their feelings into words. In terms of ethnic comparisons, Greeley argues that the Irish do not love their family members so differently but rather "we find that the words of affection get stuck in their throats" (1981). Affection varied across the strands of the families interviewed. One grandfather was perceived as very outgoing and demonstrative, thereby breaking traditional Irish norms. His daughter remembers:

> There was always the hugging . . . just the family closeness. It was more instinct probably than outward show or whatever. . . . It was more demonstrative than actually saying.

One of her daughters remembers her grandfather as very affectionate and warm.

> Poppa always says, "I love you. I love you kids for everything." I just remember when I wore my brace, he just hugged me to death and he'd say, "I went to church two times . . . and I prayed for you." When he'd say how much he prayed for you—that let you know.

This man's other granddaughters also related to the physical expression of emotion. "The physical is pretty standard. It's Irish to be hugging and kissing but that's (verbal expression) showing emotion—showing weakness."

Yet this second set of granddaughters also experienced the exchange favors as the relational currency for sharing affection ("Although we have to pay for them") and giving of gifts ("If my mother feels she hurt one of us she'd buy something for us") instead of direct statements of affection or feeling. One young woman reported that after writing a very special letter in a Father's Day card thanking her father for all he had done over the years she received the following response, "It was a nice card." Yet she interpreted this

as expressing deep gratitude. The respondents in a different family strand reported limited physical or verbal expression of affection particularly between the first two generations but indicated they "knew" they were loved. This grandmother said as a child she "took it for granted" that her parents loved her, concluding "they had you, so they must love you."

Yet this woman's daughters knew they were loved. One daughter remembered that when she was a child in England her mother expressed love in special ways.

> When I was sick my Mom would put me into her bed, in the lightest room. She would make hot tea and toast and cut it in buttered fingers and always bring it up to me. And when she would go to the store she would bring home an orange. . . . And we really didn't have the money for something like that.

She and her sister both said they knew their mother loved them "because she was always there" and still remembered the one or two times their mother was not home during their childhood. She knew her father loved her because

> on Sundays he would take us and walk for miles and miles. We would stop at farms . . . that was my Dad's contribution. . . . Also when he worked until ten a child would go across the street and bring home a beer for him and all the kids would come downstairs saying, "Could I have a mouthful of beer, Dad?" and he would always give it to us.

She never experienced kissing and hugging in Ireland and "I never saw my Mom and Dad kiss until they were here and I was delighted." Yet this woman has consciously chosen to be more affectionate with her husband and children, proudly stating, "I'll say to my boys in the morning, 'I love you.'"

Distancing behaviors affect the discipline in the household by creating a reliance on ridicule, blaming, shaming and, in some cases the cutoff, whereby a child is given the silent treatment or disconfirmed for a given period of time (McGoldrick, 1996). Usually a spanking or a scolding is a relief if a child has been treated as invisible. No respondent could identify with the cutoff and most had not experienced the silent treatment. Each older member indicated "you talked things out" and their children concurred. One daughter stated, "If something happened we got hollered at right then and there, we got spanked right then and there. That was it. It was the end of it. And you knew you better never to do it again."

One grandmother did remember experiencing silence as discipline when she was a child. In addition to hitting, her mother might be "silent for a day" to an offending child. Although this respondent thought she might have disciplined through silence, her daughters did not remember it. One mother remembered, "I learned growing up to 'talk and speak your piece and then forget it.'" In general most respondents reported that they talked things out. One set of granddaughters reported guilt was a major discipline technique and cited the following quote: "Jewish mothers invented guilt; Irish mothers perfected it." In addition, spankings, screaming and hitting with brooms or shoes occurred regularly in some of these families.

TOUGH TOPICS: SEX AND DEATH

Although these may appear as a unique and arbitrary combination of topics the Irish appear to manage communication about these critical issues in ways quite different from other cultures due, in part, to their religious affiliations. Such Irish variations have a direct bearing on communication related to such sensitive topics as sex and death.

Historically sex has been considered the "lack of the Irish" (Messinger, 1971). The experience of growing up in an environment of sexual repression applies to previous generations of mainland Irish. McGoldrick and Pearce (1981) cite the jig, Ireland's traditional dance, as a caricature of the historical repression of bodily experiences—"the skilled dancer agilely moves only his or her feet, while keeping the rest of the body as motionless as possible" (p. 225). Historically marriage was viewed as "permission to sin" and discussion about sexuality was almost non-existent. Many older Irish American Catholics were taught to view sex solely as a means of procreation. Greeley maintains there is little evidence of sexual repression experienced by modern Irish Americans, saying "There are virtually no differences between Irish-Catholics and other Americans in attitudes toward premarital or extramarital sex and Irish-Americans are more tolerant of homosexuality than other Americans" (1981, p. 126).

Almost all respondents learned about sex outside the home and if it was talked about at home it was done so in a clinical manner. The older members spoke about their learning about sex in terms of it "coming naturally," therefore it was unnecessary to talk about the subject. One grandmother remembered:

Oh, there was none of that (talk about sex). It was never discussed. The priest he never discussed it. Over there (Ireland) they'd matchmaker for a girl and a fellow. And they'd never meet before they were almost to the altar. . . . But sex, they never even mentioned it in the schools. Even when our kids went to school that was a closed subject. It was a closed subject. We never discussed it

with our kids. You know what? They never asked a word about it and we never discussed it with them because they didn't have it in the schools in their day. They're teaching sex now to them little kids in grade school.

When asked about how she learned about sex another older respondent stated, "It never be mentioned." She views sex as a "very sacred word" that belongs "between a man and wife and not discussed again." She said she "never heard it in school" and worried that today when sex is "every place" it might be "worse."

The middle generation reported an experience of familial silence. Responses to the question "Where did you learn about sex?" included:

- "It wasn't from our parents. Mostly from school—biology class."
- "From my girlfriends. Then I told the younger ones."
- "Certainly not in the home . . . I learned from friends, a little bit here and a little bit there, some right and a lot of it wrong."

Although talking of sex was uncomfortable, these mothers have broached the subject with at least some of their family members. One mother related that during a recent trip to the internist the doctor asked her and her husband if they had had sex since trying some new medicine and "My husband said 'No,' I said 'Yes' and then we both looked down embarrassed." Yet she said that since her own mother started working in a hospital the two of them could discuss sexually related issues such as venereal disease. She believed her daughter was still very uncomfortable with the topic and did not want to discuss it.

One young respondent provided the following description of the struggle ensuing when a mother tried to break the pattern:

My mother explained the act of sex in the most metallic, cold, mechanical, scientific, factual way she could. And she told me everything and I was embarrassed. And I couldn't look at her face. And she finished it and all I knew was that it was very difficult for her, but the fact that her mother had not told her at all, and she had let her get married and go on a honeymoon without any knowledge of what was going to happen made her, and she told me this made her tell me, and her last words to me were, "Do you understand what I've told you?" She made a point of saying, "After marriage . . ."

In attributing a reason to the clinical attitude this young woman suggested that her mother

could not have transmitted any affection because she never felt any pleasure or if she did feel it she denied that. It was her duty or something that she could get through.

Her younger sister responded that her mother

> asked me at 16, "Do you know about sex?" and I said, "Sure." And she said, "Well why didn't you ever ask me anything?" And I said, "Cause I didn't want you to explain it." I was always angry with her. I never wanted her to be close to me.

Thus, at least within this extended Irish family sex remains a restricted and often scary topic although each younger respondent indicated a strong desire to break the pattern with her future children.

In contrast to other cultures, the Irish attitude toward death differs from that of many other cultures in its attitude of welcome and/or acceptance. The traditional Catholic position that recognizes death as a release from life's struggles and entrance into heavenly reward, combined with the frustrations of living under British subjugation, undergird the Irish view that death is a time for celebration rather than deep mourning. Current Irish Americans are likely to identify with the religious rather than the political orientation toward death. Within the Irish American tradition the wake and funeral still remain a family gathering time while reflecting the "duty visit." In traditional Irish American wakes, "Much of the talk was of happy or humorous events concerning the dead person and the reminiscing helped families to mourn publicly and without embarrassment" (Horgan, 1998, p. 57).

In discussing the Irish wake as a celebration of release from suffering and entrance into a new life, McGoldrick and Pearce (1981) say, "The Irish loved to get together for any social occasion, but the most prominent social gathering was always the wake. The extended family would gather, tell jokes, drink, and reminisce about the deceased" (p. 230).

Respondents of all three generations held similar views on death. It was viewed as "sad rather than scary," as a time for mourning and religious celebration, and as a reason to come together as an extended family.

The older Maloney members reflected the beliefs that death signaled an entrance into a new life

- "They used to tell us at home not to be afraid of someone dying. They'd go to heaven and everything else."
- "We learned the Lord called them to heaven. He wanted them there, and they're up there praying for everybody and they got reconciled to the fact."

All older members believed that children should be included in wakes or funerals depending on their ages; one stated, "It's good for the kids really."

Most respondents attended wakes or funerals from childhood and experienced a comfort with the idea of death because, after paying their respects, the mourners reflect on the lighter side of the deceased's life. Two young sisters described their experiences as follows. One girl stated:

> They (the Irish) look at the brighter side. The fact that its more a celebration, like they've gone to new life. They look at it that way rather than they've gone. . . . I remember when we all sat and watched the Notre Dame football game at Grandma's wake. Grandma would have been the first one to be mad at that if they weren't sitting there watching the ballgame.

Her sister added:

> They always make sure they go to the wakes and things like that, but again, they make light of it once the person is laid to rest in that they'll just think, "Well, Joe would have liked it this way." I've gone to some wakes and you just don't talk and, well, people are crying. And you walk into a (Irish) funeral and the first thing is, "Oh, he looks good." Here's a person dead in the casket and you're saying he looks good and I don't hear that at any other kind of wake. (At Irish wakes) they talk all the time and its always open conversations.

The traditional Irish reluctance to discuss sex and ease of talking about death distinguishes them from other cultures.

VALUES

The Catholic tradition undergirds any consideration of Irish American values, making it critical to examine the role of religion, respect and self-esteem, and nationalism (Horgan, 1998). In addressing questions of value the respondents consistently indicated the importance of religion. This was followed by a variable order of topics related to respect and self-esteem, often called "Irish pride" and a sense of "Irishness."

Religion is the centerpiece of the Irish American Catholic identity. In 1971, O'Connor described the Irish as "more Catholic than the Pope" (p. 115) an apt picture of how many Irish Catholics were raised; in 1998 Horgan suggests religion is sill highly important. In contrast to other cultures:

> The authority of the Roman Catholic Church was the major unifier for the Irish, to such an extent that the Church came before the family . . . Irish Catholics have traditionally viewed most things moralistically, following the rules of the Church without question. This, of course, has changed in recent years but the underlying rigidity often remains. (McGoldrick, 1993, p. 344)

A mainstay of this identity is found in the parish, the geographically defined church community led by priests and supportive parishioners, "an enclave of

American Irish families of the second, third and sometimes fourth generation living dispersed among native-born people and a few families from other ethnic groups" (Horgan, 1998, p. 49). As the Irish immigrated to America they sent their children to parochial school and became the mainstay of the parish Catholic school system, a tradition that continues in certain suburban areas today.

Catholicism represents the source of guilt for many Irish families who respond more strongly to the concept than other cultures. McGoldrick and Pearce (1981) maintain

> More than other ethnic groups, the Irish struggled with their sense of sin and guilt. Italians, for instance, though also Catholic, tended to place responsibility for their problems outside themselves; their experience of guilt was limited primarily to violations of family loyalty. (p. 225)

For many Irish immigrants to be Catholic meant to go to church and sacraments, assist the parish, raise one's children in parochial schools or provide access to religious instruction, to follow the ritual—fasts, vows, rosaries—and to feel guilty about sins. This created a worldview and established rituals which set them apart from other groups.

The grandmother generation of respondents experienced the parish as "the place to belong" and helped to establish the local church. They and their children worked actively in the parish and their joy knew no bounds when one son and nephew became a priest—and, in his sister's words, became "the Irish Prince," or the spoiled and cared-for Irish male. One older woman stated, "Without the Faith we wouldn't have had anything. The Faith was it . . . in storms, in sickness, everything." Just as the elder women would only consider marrying an Irish-Catholic so too they expected that of their daughters. As one of their daughters said, "If you met somebody and you found they weren't Catholic you'd just disassociate yourself with them. You just talk small talk and bop off. You wouldn't do it knowing it would upset your parents." One granddaughter suggested, "I'm sure my (future) family would eat dinner together and for sure say prayers before."

All family members interviewed grew up with a Catholic education and a strong religious tradition. There was a clear identification of being Irish-Catholic with the belief expressed by many that the Catholic part was more precious than the Irish part. At the current time the youngest family members have broken the traditions of marrying Irish and Catholic as some have brought non-Catholics or person of various ethnic backgrounds into the family, thus altering the cultural mix.

In addition to religion, part of the Irish American self-image includes a potent mixture of inferiority and pride (Mulcrone, 1999). The long-term hunger for respect creates heightened awareness of any real or imagined insult. The history of Anglophobia may appear in bravado and deep sensitivity to slights. Praise in the Irish family is seen as the road to a conceited or spoiled individual. Irish American families are reluctant to praise their children for fear of giving them a "swelled head." To call attention to yourself through self-praise was to invite a response of "Who do you think you are?" One learned never to claim that they had more talent or skills than siblings or age-peers. Very often Irish praise, if it existed at all, became intertwined with the paradoxical language strategy such that a mother may say, "my favorite daughter," when Maureen is also her only daughter.

The pressure for constant respectability resulted in praise being seen as a potential mistake, because the person might behave inappropriately in the future. Phrases such as, "You never know how long this (good behavior) will last," or "Who knows how he'll be acting two years from now," tempered any tendency to rush in and praise some current success. It was better to keep the person in his or her place, and treat the good behavior as expected, rather than to lose some respectability later if the person acted inappropriately due to a "swelled head."

One of the respondents almost mirrored the exact language of the cultural writers in her comments:

- "I never praise my children because *you never know from one month to the next* what will happen."
- "I never brag on my kids. Someone has to ask how they are doing, since *you never know when they could embarrass or hurt you.*"
- "Yes, I have good kids—now."

Her mother described her lack of praise for her children or grandchildren saying, "I mustn't be blowing their trumpets," and explained at length that parents should not brag about their children.

One grandmother espoused the often-repeated theme "Self praise is no praise at all," and her daughter agreed that one was expected to control the use of praise but her husband was famous for breaking the stereotypical image. As his daughter described him

> It's hard to contain him. He is so proud of not only, way back, his parents, his brothers and his sisters, but his nieces and nephews, his wife, his children, his grandchildren, his son-in-laws—you name it. My father is proud. He excels in that. He wouldn't care if you put it on the first page of the newspaper—He's the other extreme.

Almost all respondents mentioned the pride of the Irish—for being Irish. One younger respondent named the "real" pride of the Irish—for being Irish. She asserted, "Irish people seem to have a lot more pride than any other nationality. I think it's just pride to be Irish." Yet self pride was to be kept contained. As the Maloney girls' grandmother said, "The average Irish family doesn't blow about themselves. They let someone else blow about them if there's any blowin' to be done."

Finally, a fierce sense of nationalism provided a sense of pride and connection. The immigrant Irish were particularly skilled at building parallel institutions to create venues for mutual support. These included social, charitable and political organizations, which served to isolate members and reinforce their Irish ties (Horgan, 1998). Many parishes served this purpose but social clubs and political causes reinforced an ethnic identity. Because of the large size of Irish communities in urban areas there was always news of Ireland, new arrivals with current stories and customs, as well as a network of physical and psychological support for those in need.

The three strands of family respondents value their Irish heritage at varying levels. One grandmother suggests her Irish heritage is not critically important because "I didn't get that much out of over there. The second generation here gets more out of Ireland than we do." The family who lived in England for years experienced greater Irishness since moving to the United States because, in the words of their matriarch they "mixed more with Irish" and "your company can do a lot for you."

The third family expressed the strongest Irish ties. Much of the extended family's obvious Irishness is attributed to this strand's collection of Irish music and to their Sunday dinners after which family members would listen to the music and then begin their own songfest. One mother said:

> Irish songs—O Lord yes—when we were little kids Dad would be teaching us the Irish songs. One thing he always wanted to do was win the sweepstakes and take us all to Ireland. . . . When my sister and I would go on a Notre Dame trip she and I knew all the Irish songs, but the others didn't.

Many children remembered "Grandma's music" and believe their sense of Irish tradition ties directly to the Irish family parties.

In addition to the parties and music some of their Irish identification can be seen through the following comments:

- "We are loyal . . . simply on the grounds of someone being Irish. We learned from Nana, "You're 100% Irish and maybe a little French."

- "We are expected to carry on at Irish Fest, go to Irish bars."

Part of the transmission of Irish culture includes the pishogues or the superstitions passed through the generations. In the early nineteenth century when superstitions were common in Ireland people would consult the pishogue or the "wise old woman of the village, a purveyor of charms, old saws and other rural incantations" (Delaney, 1973, p. 112). Many of the old attitudes did not survive the famine, or were countered by the Church influence but part of the mystique of Ireland includes concern with the supernatural, involving good or bad luck.

The current attitude toward superstitions is best captured in the phrase "There's no sense taking chances." This allows the quaint recitation and following of pishogues in Irish American families who are unlikely to believe the superstitions but follow the rituals because "it can't hurt."

The transmission and valuing of pishogues occurs primarily in one of the families. Another strand appears to have lost most of this folk wisdom during their time in England although they could remember hearing about some superstitions and could name some specific statements. The third grandmother recognized them but "paid them no mind."

Some pishogues collected from the respondents include:

- "Don't count cars in a funeral procession—that's bad luck or someone might die."
- "Company should always leave by the door they entered or more company will arrive very shortly."
- "Never put new shoes on the table—that's bad luck." (Really any elevated spot—in or out of the box.)
- "If a bird flies into your house it is a sign of death."
- "In a thunderstorm you bless all the rooms of the house with holy water and light a candle."
- "If you spill salt you throw some over your left shoulder with your right hand to keep bad luck from happening."
- "If a fork falls on the floor a family is coming to visit, if a knife falls there will be a man visitor and if a spoon falls a woman is coming" (or some slight variation).
- "You never carry a broom from one home to another. If you move you leave the old broom and get a new one—that's bad luck."

Even the granddaughters could reel off a list of them, saying they "learned them from Grandma." As an indication of their continuing power a second generation mother reported that she does bless her house, "I do it . . . I bless the house with holy water . . . just in storms." She also does not count funeral cars because she experienced bad luck after doing so. She also relayed a story of a death following the appearance of a bird in a relative's home. Their pishogues seemed to bind some family members to their Irish heritage and provide a relatively easy way to maintain an ethnic identification.

FAMILY

Every member of the extended family expressed directly or indirectly a strong belief in, and concern for, the family. Almost all were taught to value their brothers and sisters and all the older members came to this country because other family members "brought us over."

In explaining her attempts to emphasize the importance of family to her boys one mother indicated that as a child she always heard the reprimand "You always take the strangers before your own" if she tried to leave the house without a sibling. Now she actively informs her boys, "Years from now when you're in trouble you'll call your brother," and "Years from now they'll (friends) be gone and you'll still have him to live with."

A granddaughter recalls that as a child she learned:

> If anyone touches or makes fun of anyone in your family, you are allowed to beat them up. You stick up for your family no matter what. . . . You could trust, you could depend on your brothers and sisters.

Her sister articulated the theme, "Family always first . . . above and beyond anything."

Each three generation family strand maintained a strong internal phone network. The other family members maintain contact with each other regularly. The older parents talk to each daughter once a day and the daughters attempt to follow suit with their children although some of the younger generation sees this as intrusive. Today there is limited contact across the strands except for special news or information about special events. These cross-strand conversations usually occur among the older members.

Thus the family stands as a critical and valued part of each member's life with the focus remaining on the immediate family rather than the broadly extended family. One granddaughter's comments reaffirm the sense of continuity and identification. When asked to think about what she wished to pass on to her future children she replied:

> I'd like to pass on that my grandmother came over when she was 13 and she worked all her life for her children lived her life in such a way that she bettered her offspring who in turn did the same. The whole continuity . . . the whole idea of being 13, taking the boat by yourself . . . that to me is like a pride. If I had children I'd like to pass on the history, the music, the customs, the funny stories, the folklore, not as truth, not as fact as they were passed on to me . . . but in quaintness.

Thus many values remain in altered form—losing some strength but retaining the flavor. Many of the patterns and worldviews of older generations have been unconsciously passed down without explicit ethnic identification.

This examination of Irish American families examines an immigrant tradition reflecting a Northern European, English-speaking background, one often overlooked on the assumption that ethnicity is no longer relevant. Although today there are many variations in form and style among the younger generations descended from Irish immigrants, certain unconscious patterns are likely to remain viable. Current Irish Americans may not associate ethnicity with the way they communicate with others. For example, the emphasis on boundaries to protect privacy and the emphasis on pride in the Irish tradition might restrict self-disclosure outside the immediate family system. Discussions of topics, such as sex or death, may be significantly different from the patterns of other cultures. Strategies for conflict management may continue without clarity of origin. In short the culturally created boundaries, language strategies, management of particular topics and importance of selected values are likely to affect members' development of interpersonal relationships inside and outside the family. There's more to such an ethnic tradition than blarney, pishogues and paddywhackery.

REFERENCES

Biddle, E. H. (1976). The American Catholic Irish family. In C. H. Mindel & R. W. Hebenstein (Eds.), *Ethnic families in America* (pp. 89–123). New York: Elsevier.

Collins, C. (1978). *The family unit: Conduit for communication patterns of a culture.* Paper presented at the Central States Speech Association, Chicago, IL.

Delaney, M. M. (1973). *Of Irish ways.* New York: Barnes and Noble.

Donohue, S. L. (2000, June 2) Confessing culture: Mary Gordon's Irish Catholics and Jews in Protestant America. www.cocc.edu/sdonohue/confessingculture.htm

Galvin, K. M. (1982). *Pishogues and paddywhackery: Transmission of communication Patterns and values through three generations of an Irish-American family.* Paper presented at Speech Communication Association Conference, Louisville, KY.

Galvin, K. & Brommel, B. (1999). *Family communication: Cohesion and change* (5th ed.). Boston, MA: Allyn and Bacon.

Greeley, A. (1979). Creativity in the Irish family: The cost of immigration. *International Journal of Family Therapy,* 1, 295–303.

Greeley. A. (1981). *The Irish-Americans.* New York: Harper and Row.

Golway, T. (1997). The great famine: between hunger and the White House. In M. Coffey (Ed.), *The Irish in America* (pp. 3–39). New York: Hyperion.

Hoge, W. (2000, July 17). Money, jobs, big cars: How's an Irishman to cope? *New York Times,* p. 2.

Horgan, E. S. (1998). The Irish American family. In C. H. Mindel, R. W. Habenstein & R. Wright (Eds.), *Ethnic families in America* (4th ed., pp. 39–67). Englewood Cliffs, NJ: Prentice Hall.

Kramer, J. R. (1985). *Family interface: Transgenerational patterns.* New York: Brunner/Mazel.

McCaffrey, L. J. (1997). *The Irish Catholic diaspora in America.* Bloomington, IN: Indiana University Press.

McCourt, F. (1996). *Angela's ashes.* New York: Scribner.

McGoldrick, M. (1993). Normal families: An ethnic perspective. In F. Walsh (Ed.), *Normal family processes* (2nd ed., pp. 331–360). New York: Guilford Press.

McGoldrick, M. (1995). *You can go home again.* New York: W. W. Norton.

McGoldrick. M. (1996). Irish families. In M. McGoldrick., J. Giordano & J. Pearce (Eds.), *Ethnicity and family*

therapy (2nd ed., pp. 544–566). New York: Guilford Press

McGoldrick, M. & Giordano, J. (1996). Overview: Ethnicity and family therapy. In M. McGoldrick, J. Giordano & J. K. Pearce (Eds.), *Ethnicity and family therapy* (2nd ed., pp. 1–30). New York: Guilford Press.

McGoldrick, M., Giordano, J., & Pearce, J. (Eds.). (1983). *Ethnicity and family therapy.* New York: Guilford Press.

McGoldrick, M. & Pearce, J. (1981). Family therapy with Irish Americans. *Family Process,* 20, 223–244.

Messinger, J. C. (1971). Sexuality: The lack of the Irish. *Psychology Today,* 4, 41–42, 68.

Mulcrone, M. (1999). The family and collective memory. In A. Gribbin (Ed.), *The great famine and the Irish diaspora in America* (pp. 219–238). Amherst: University of Massachusetts Press.

O'Connor, R. (1971). *The Irish: Portrait of a people.* New York: G. P. Putnam's Sons.

Sluzki, C. (1979). Migration and family conflict. *Family Process,* 18, 4, 370–390.

Socha, T. J. & Diggs, R. C. (Eds.). (1999). *Communication, race and family.* Mahwah, NJ.: Lawrence Erlbaum

Spaulding, H. (1978). *The lilt of the Irish: An encyclopedia of Irish folklore and humor.* Middle Village, NY: Johnathan David Publishers.

CHECK YOUR UNDERSTANDING

1. Define paddywhackery.
2. Compare how members of your family communicate their love to one another. How is this similar to and different from those described by Galvin?
3. All families have boundaries. Describe the boundaries in your family. How would these boundaries influence your intercultural communication?
4. How do the values of your culture affect the communication patterns in your family?
5. How does your family talk about sex and death? Compare this to Galvin's description of these topics in Irish American families.

CHAPTER ACTIVITIES

1. Choose a video that highlights intercultural relationships. For example, *The Joy Luck Club, Mississippi Masala,* or *Fools Rush In.* After viewing the video, write a journal entry describing how the relationships in the video differ from relationships in your own culture.
2. Choose a culture and investigate family and friendship relationships in that culture. Answer questions such as:
   • How do people in the culture define friendship?
   • What family structures exist in the culture?
   • What are the roles of family members?
   • What are courtship customs?
   • What are the wedding customs?
3. Go to the Intercultural E-Mail Classroom Connections website (www.iecc.org). Here you can subscribe and begin to write to a student pen pal in a different country.
4. Look at the website http://novaonline.nvcc.edu and connect to the Family Structures and Communication link. Here you will find interesting information about all types of families. Choose a family type and present a report to the class.

CHAPTER 9

EDUCATION

WHY CAN'T WE DISCUSS IT?

It began in September 1992. I had just walked into a classroom at the Chinese University of Hong Kong to begin my first international teaching experience. Perhaps more than any other time since I'd moved to Hong Kong, I knew I was no longer in Illinois! A sea of Chinese faces watched me walk into the classroom. I was unsure about their English proficiency, and I spoke enough Mandarin to fill a thimble, and even less Cantonese. Here I was, the teacher of the basic oral communication course. There they were, staring at me. My heart sank. I asked myself, "What am I doing here?" Everything I'd learned about teaching in the past 25 years suddenly appeared useless. I was indeed a stranger in a strange land. My environment, my academic discipline, my sense of self were all strangers to me.

After a disastrous first class period, I returned to my office, closed the door, sat down, and asked myself, "How can I teach communication when they don't communicate?" After some contemplation I began to devise a plan.

The plan began with the Chinese culture. The Chinese culture is one in which talk is not paramount. The traditional teaching method of lecture is the model. Students are not to disagree or discuss with the teacher. Rather, they are to sit silently, respectfully, and take notes. This is, no doubt, a hangover from the Imperial Exams when receptive skills rather than production skills were emphasized. Explanation, not performance, rote learning, not comprehension, written work, not oral work, uniformity, not individuality are the keystones of the Chinese classroom. All of these characteristics are inherent in the collectivist culture of the Chinese where group membership, face issues, and hierarchical relationships are the norm.

So, the first part of my plan focused on understanding that what I could expect from these students, in terms of class discussion, was not the same as what I could expect from my students in the United States. So, I began to lecture more than I had ever done, interspersing it with stories, and asking students if they had ever had a similar experience.

Unsure of their English, they were naturally reluctant to communicate in front of a large group, so I had devised the second step of my plan—students would discuss the assignments and text materials in pairs or small groups rather than individually in front of the class. This would make them more comfortable talking when we "report back" to the class as a whole.

Step 3: I decided that story was universal. All cultures tell stories, and I believe all communication is story. So, my teaching plan focused on story. The informative speech assignment turned into a storytelling assignment, the small group assignment turned into solving a murder mystery, the speech to entertain turned into a speech of tribute based on a story of the person to whom they paid tribute, and the persuasion speech turned into an advertisement for a product to be sold to Chinese and then to Americans.

Armed with my new approach, I entered the classroom. The story has a happy ending! This approach worked! My own story of teaching basic oral communication in a culture other than my own is one of frustration and fascination. It was never, however, a boring story!

OBJECTIVES

After reading this chapter and completing the readings and activities, you should be able to

- Explain the functions of schools.
- Identify the cultural dimensions that affect the classroom.
- Recognize differences in culture that affect learning.
- Understand cultural differences in an educational context.
- Outline ways to communicate effectively in an intercultural classroom.

FUNCTIONS OF SCHOOLS

The educational environment is fraught with intercultural stumbling blocks as the following quote indicates:

> The familiar nursery school activity of having children mix flour and water to make paste fails completely when Native American children refuse to make the paste because flour is food and one does not play with food. (Rivlin, 1977, p. 109)

Yet most teachers are not trained to work in multicultural settings. In fact, as Condon (1986) argues, the classroom culture is, to a great extent, an extension of mainstream U.S. American culture. For example, the values of the U.S. American classroom are those of independence, individualism, and concern for relevance and application. As a result, students whose backgrounds are different from this dominant culture may have a difficult time adjusting to the classroom culture.

This is true because, as Bowman (1989) tells us, culture influences both behavior and psychological processes. It affects the way we perceive the world. Culture "forms a prism through which members of a group see the world and create shared meanings" (p. 118).

Education, both formal and informal, seeks to help form the prism of each culture. Thus, in every culture, schools serve a variety of functions. Samovar and colleagues (2001, pp. 198–199) suggest three. According to these authors, schools

1. Help fashion the individual since they offer children a set of guidelines and values and make them aware of what they need to know in order to become productive and successful members of their culture.
2. Are a primary means by which a culture's history and tradition are passed from one generation to the next.
3. Teach the informal knowledge of a culture such as the rules of correct conduct, hierarchy of cultural values, gender-role expectations, and how to treat others.

Cultural background affects attitudes, beliefs, and values about education—ideas about how classes ought to be conducted, how students and teachers ought to interact, and what types of relationships are appropriate for students and teachers (Collier and Powell, 1990). As classrooms in the United States become more diverse culturally, it is important for both teachers and students to understand some of the cultural factors that affect learning. In an article in *Education Week* (April 10, 1986), Debra Viadero demonstrates this in the following example:

> Ms. White, a teacher in an isolated rural community, is teaching her first graders how to tell time. She points to a clock, telling her students that it's ten o'clock because the big hand is on the twelve and the little hand is on the ten.
>
> "What time is it?" she asks the students. Many of the white children raise their hands, eager to answer. The black students sit silently. A few give her a puzzled look. Ms. White concludes that many of her black students do not know the answer, and she silently makes a note to herself to revisit the concept with them later. But researchers who study the role that culture plays in learning say that Ms. White may have the wrong take on what is going on with her students. What is really happening, they say, is that two distinct cultures are bumping up against one

another, forming an invisible wall that stands in the way of learning and communication. Like their teacher, the white children in this community grew up in families where adults routinely quizzed children the way their teacher does. "What color is this?" a parent might say, pointing to a red ball. In the African American children's families, such questions were posed only when someone genuinely needed to know the answer. "What is she asking us for?" some of the black children might have wondered. "She just told us it was ten o'clock." (pp. 39–40)

No doubt roadblocks such as this one will become more and more common since our classrooms are becoming increasingly multicultural. In fact, Hodgkinson (2004) projects that about 65 percent of the U.S. population growth in the next two decades will be from minorities, mostly Hispanic and Asian immigrants. However, the majority of teachers are White and research suggests this will continue to be the case (Viadero, 1986). African American, Asian American, Hispanic American, and Native American teachers now make up just 10 percent of the teaching force (Viadero, 1986). In addition, 6.3 million children in the United States report speaking a non-English language at home (National Association of Bilingual Education, 1993).

The cultural differences in classrooms are important to understand for three major reasons: (1) cultural differences may result in differences in learning style, (2) cultural differences affect relationships in the educational environment, and (3) understanding cultural differences can help us communicate more effectively with our classmates. Before we explore each of these three areas it is useful to examine the cultural dimensions that affect classroom communication.

CULTURAL DIMENSIONS

In Chapter 2 we discussed the work of Hofstede (1991). Hofstede suggests four cultural dimensions that affect what occurs in a classroom. The first of these is *individualism/collectivism*. Individualist cultures assume that any person looks primarily after his or her own interest and the interest of his or her immediate family (husband, wife, and children). The collectivist society (whether extended family, clan, or organization) protects the interest of its members, but in turn expects their permanent loyalty.

In terms of classroom behavior, the dimensions suggest that in collectivist cultures students expect to speak up in class only when called on personally to by the teacher. Formal harmony is important and neither a teacher nor any student should ever be made to lose face (Hwang et al., 2003). For example, Vietnamese students are always taught to be respectful of their teacher and never to criticize (Ha, 2001). On the other hand, in individualistic cultures, students expect to speak up in class in response to a general invitation by the teacher. In addition, confrontation is not necessarily avoided; conflicts can be brought into the open; and face-consciousness is weak.

In a collectivist culture, harmony with nature, circularity, and the group is emphasized rather than the individual. That is why Native American children learn better in an environment that is noncompetitive, holistic, and cooperative (Lustig and Koester, 1996). Mexican children, because their culture emphasizes cooperation, allow others to share their homework or answers. This shows group solidarity, helpfulness, and generosity—important characteristics of their collectivist culture (Grossman, 1984). Contrast this with the U.S. educational system, which emphasizes competition and the individual. If a U.S. American student shares his or her homework, he or she is seen as dishonest, perhaps even a cheater!

A second dimension is *power distance*. Power distance as a characteristic of a culture defines the extent to which the less powerful persons in a society accept inequality in power and consider it normal. Inequality exists within any culture, but the degree of it that is tolerated varies between one culture and another.

If the power distance of a culture is small, appropriate behaviors are different from those of a culture that has a large power distance. In terms of classroom behavior, the power dimension suggests that in small power distance societies, the educational process is student centered. The students initiate communication, outline their own paths to learning, and can contradict the teacher.

In large power distance societies, the educational process is teacher centered. The teacher initiates all communication, outlines the paths of learning that students should follow, and is never publicly criticized or contradicted. In large power distance societies, the emphasis is on the personal "wisdom" of the teacher; in small power distance societies, the emphasis is on impersonal "truth" that can be obtained by any competent person.

In Asian societies, the teacher is given much respect. There is a large power distance between teacher and student (Ha, 2001). A Chinese or Vietnamese student would never consider arguing with a teacher. The role of the Asian student is to accept and respect the wisdom of the teacher. The teacher presents information and the student accepts it without question. Asking questions is seen as a challenge to the teacher's authority or as an admission of the student's ignorance. Neither is desirable (Wallach and Metcalf, 1995).

In the United States, where the power difference is small, students are encouraged to challenge the teacher and one another. The teacher encourages students to discuss and debate issues, learn how to solve problems, and create their own answers to the questions posed. In general, U.S. Americans prefer to learn through personal discovery and problem solving rather than through memorizing facts presented to them by an authority figure.

Uncertainty avoidance is the third of Hofstede's dimensions. As a characteristic of a culture, it defines the extent to which people within a culture are made nervous by situations that they perceive as unstructured, unclear, or unpredictable—situations that they therefore try to avoid by maintaining strict codes of behavior and a belief in absolute truths. Cultures with a strong uncertainty avoidance are active, aggressive, emotional, compulsive, security seeking, and intolerant; cultures with a weak uncertainty avoidance are contemplative, less aggressive, unemotional, relaxed, personal risk takers, and relatively tolerant.

In a weak uncertainty avoidance society, students feel comfortable in unstructured learning situations (vague objectives, no timetables, broad assignments) and are rewarded for innovative approaches to problem solving. Teachers are allowed to say, "I don't know," interpret intellectual disagreement as stimulating, and seek parents' ideas.

In strong uncertainty avoidance societies, students feel comfortable in structured learning situations (precise objectives, strict timetables, detailed assignments) and are rewarded for accuracy in problem solving. Teachers are expected to have all the answers, interpret intellectual disagreement as personal disloyalty, and consider themselves experts who do not need parents' ideas (and parents agree).

In a strong uncertainty avoidance culture, students prefer clear instructions, avoid conflict, and dislike competition. Examples of cultures with strong uncertainty avoidance are France, Chile, Spain, Portugal, Japan, Peru, and Argentina. By comparison, the United States, Great Britain, Denmark, Ireland, and India are characterized by weak uncertainty avoidance. Students in these countries are competitive, need fewer instructions, and see conflict as stimulating.

The final dimension is *masculinity/femininity*. Masculinity as a characteristic of a culture opposes femininity. The two differ in the social roles attributed to men. The cultures labeled as masculine strive for maximal distinction between what men are expected to do and what women are expected to do. They expect men to be assertive, ambitious, and competitive; to strive for material success; and to respect whatever is big, strong, and fast. They expect women to serve and to care for the nonmaterial quality of life, for children, and for the weak. Feminine cultures, on the other hand, define relatively overlapping social roles for the sexes, in which, in particular, men need not be ambitious or competitive but may go for a different quality of life than material success; men may respect whatever is small, weak, and slow. In both masculine and feminine cultures, the dominant values within political and work organizations are those of men. So, in masculine cultures, these politicalizational values stress material success and assertiveness; in feminine cultures, they stress other types of quality of life, interpersonal relationships, and concern for the weak (Hofstede, 1991).

In terms of the classroom, we can again make some assumptions about behavior, depending on whether a culture is feminine or masculine. In feminine societies, teachers avoid openly praising students because academic achievement is less important than successful interpersonal relationships, and cooperation among students is fostered. Teachers use average students as the "norm." In feminine societies, a student's failure in school is a relatively minor event. The system rewards students' social adaptations.

In masculine societies, teachers openly praise good students because academic achievement is highly regarded and competition is fostered. Teachers use the best students as the "norm." Academic failure is a severe blow to the self-image. The system rewards academic performance.

A masculine culture values assertiveness and competitiveness. High masculinity countries include Japan, Mexico, Ireland, Austria, Venezuela, Switzerland, Great Britain, and Germany. High feminine countries include Chile, Portugal, Thailand, Sweden, Norway, the Netherlands, Denmark, and Finland. These countries place a high value on interpersonal relationships, compassion, and nurturing.

RECOGNIZING DIFFERENCES IN LEARNING

These cultural dimensions lead to differences in terms of how students learn. Researchers and teachers have, in recent years, been giving increased attention to the way people learn in intercultural settings (e.g., Cole and Means, 1981; Cooper and Simonds, 2003; Cushner, 1990; Cushner et al., 1992). The underlying assumption of this increased attention is the idea that the way students in one culture learn may not be the way students of a different culture learn (Brislin and Yoshida, 1996; Taylor, 1994). For example, after lecturing to a class of Chinese students at the Chinese University of Hong Kong, one of the authors of this book asked students if they understood and all responded that they did. However, their subsequent actions made it clear that they did not. It became clear that students often said they understood, whether they did or not, out of respect for the professor, or their desire not to lose face.

Learning style refers to a student's preference for learning. For example, one student may be an auditory learner, whereas another is visual or kinesthetic. *Cognitive style* refers to the way in which a student processes information and is a part of a person's overall learning style (Vermunt and Verloop, 2000). Specifically, a cognitive style is a person's typical or habitual mode of problem solving, thinking, perceiving, and remembering (Riding and Cheema, 1991) and will determine the way people go about performing a task. One distinction should be made about learning or cognitive styles and ability. Simply because people possess a particular type of style does not necessarily indicate increased ability to perform a particular task such as learning (Rickards et al., 1997). It merely indicates a preference for how to learn or process information.

As Dunn and colleagues (1989) indicate, no style is better or worse than another. In fact, all learning styles are found within all ethnic groups to a varying degree but with a dominant style for each ethnicity (Hollins et al., 1994). What is important, however, is the fact that the closer the match between a student's style and the teacher's style, the higher the student's grade-point average. When students are permitted to learn difficult academic information or skills through their identified learning style preferences, they tend to achieve statistically higher test and aptitude scores than when instruction is dissonant with their preferences.

Another example of learning style is a preference for groups versus individual learning. In Euro-American cultures, education typically emphasizes individual learning. Each student strives for his or her individual grade or praise. In many collectivist cultures, group learning is expected. For example, children of Hawaiian ancestry come under the guidance of their older siblings very early in life. Parents interact with their children as a group, not so much as individuals. As a result of this kind of upbringing, children learn best from siblings and peers in group situations, not from one adult, as is typical in Euro-American cultures as well as in the school setting (Cushner and Brislin, 1996).

In other words, some cultures emphasize cooperation while others emphasize competition. African Americans, Asian Americans, and Hispanic Americans raise their children cooperatively, and the educational system perpetuates this cooperativeness. Peers offer help to one another. In contrast, U.S. students are encouraged to work alone. Even when they work in groups, each student is expected to "carry his or her own weight."

An example of cognitive style is field dependent versus field independent. Figure 9.1 summarizes the differences in characteristics between field-dependent and -independent learners. Field-dependent learners tend to "take elements or background variables from the environment into account . . . [and] perceive the event holistically, including the emotionality and the feelings associated with the entire event" (Lieberman, 1994, p. 179). By contrast, field-independent learners are analytical and use strategies to isolate elements of the field (Brown, 1987). Field-dependent learners prefer to work with others, seek guidance from the teacher, and receive rewards based on their relationship with the group. In contrast, field-independent learners prefer to work alone, are task oriented, and would rather receive rewards based on individual competition (Lieberman, 1997). To put it simply, some people see the forest; some see the trees. Field-dependent style is prevalent in group-oriented, high-context, collectivist societies. Field-independent styles predominate in low-context, highly competitive, highly industrialized societies (Lieberman, 1994).

Kleinfield (1994) indicates that "the concept of learning styles is useful when it reminds teachers to create rich and interesting classrooms where children can learn in many different ways" (p. 156). She provides an example of how this might be done. In a remote Eskimo village a teacher tried to introduce the concepts of "calories" and "energy formation" through a lecture. But the expressions on the children's faces indicated that they were bored. So, the teacher later asked the children to attend a steambath, an important event in the village's culture. As they observed what happened to the water when it was gas, solid, and liquid, they asked questions such as, "What happens to the steam when

FIGURE 9.1   Examples of Characteristics Exhibited by People Who Possess the Field-Dependent or Field-Independent Cognitive Style

Field Dependent	Field Independent
Low tolerance for ambiguity	High tolerance for ambiguity or uncertainty
Less developed sense of identity	Less developed sense of identity and do not mind being alone
Tend to have more social or interpersonal orientation	
Have greater need for externally provided structure and benefit from teacher providing examples, charts, graphs, etc.	Perform better on short-term memory tests thought to involve extensive interference, underscoring ability to focus attention on relevant aspects of the field
Respond well to teacher feedback	Score better on reading and math tests
Desire to understand the social and personal meaning of the learning experience	Able to encode more words than field-dependent learners
Perform poorly on memory tests	More likely to enroll in and flourish in distance education courses
Recall more information when provided with cues such as structural maps	More likely to work independently and less likely to ask teacher for assistance
Aspire to careers that require involvement with people such as teaching or counseling	Aspire to careers dealing with the subject areas of natural sciences, mathematics, and engineering

Source: Data compiled by Steve Hunt (1998). Reprinted with permission.

it goes out the steambath when someone opens the door?" Kleinfeld points out that the teacher adapted the science lesson to the cultural setting and to the learning styles of the children.

UNDERSTANDING CULTURAL DIFFERENCES

It is important to note that not only will learning or cognitive styles affect the way students respond to information in the classroom, but cultural characteristics will as well. There are many elements of culture that are universal. That is, all cultures have elements of these characteristics but may ascribe different meanings to them. Such cultural universals important to consider for the classroom include language (verbal and nonverbal symbols), patterns of thought (learning or cognitive styles), and values or beliefs (individualism/collectivism). Once we understand the things that cultures have in common, we can begin to understand the different meanings various cultures ascribe to these universals. For example, time is considered a nonverbal symbol. All cultures have a sense of time. Some cultures are monochronic (can do only one thing at a time); other cultures are polychronic (can do multiple things at a time). Consider the implications of a classroom where the teacher is monochronic and a student is polychronic. What misperceptions might the teacher have about the student's attentiveness if the student is working on math while the teacher is reading a story?

Anderson and Powell (2000), in their article on cultural influences on education processes, review research that highlights intercultural differences. For example, there is virtually no classroom interaction in Vietnamese, Mexican, or Chinese classrooms. In contrast, in an Israeli kibbutz students talk among themselves, address teachers by their first names, and criticize teachers when they feel teachers are wrong.

Cooper and Simonds (2003) outline research suggesting that in Italian classrooms, children greet their teacher with a kiss on both cheeks, and students and teachers touch one another frequently. Black children may use back channeling—a vocal response that is meant to encourage or reinforce the speaker ("yeah," "go on," "right on," etc.). Often Anglo-American teachers view this interaction as an interruption rather than a reinforcer. Looking at the teacher is a sign of disrespect in Jamaican and Black African cultures, but in the United States it is a sign of respect.

The Anglo-American culture values punctuality and a monochronic view of time; other cultures may not. This can cause problems in the educational process. For example, Hispanic students are not conditioned to use every moment in a productive, task-oriented way. American Indians have a polychronic view of time—things are done when the time is right, not by the time on a clock or a date on the calendar.

COMMUNICATING EFFECTIVELY IN AN INTERCULTURAL CLASSROOM

Past research has indicated that White teachers interact differently with students of color. In fact, Cooper and Allen (1998) believe that teachers interact less, provide more negative feedback, and offer less praise with African American and Latino students. These inequities in the classroom can cause defensive climates as well as an increase in disruptions. We, as educators, need to become more aware of these inequities in addition to taking steps to become more culturally sensitive.

Teaching in a multicultural classroom can be both challenging and rewarding. Using the work of Condon (1986), Cooper and Simonds (2005) suggest that in order to communicate effectively in a multicultural classroom, it is necessary to consider the following:

1. *Our expectation for appropriate student behavior.* We may, for example, expect students to use Standard English in both speaking and writing.
2. *The student's actual behavior.* The student may or may not use Standard English.

3. *Our feeling about the student's behavior as well as the basis for this feeling.* ("I'm angry because the student refuses to learn Standard English.")
4. *Our explanations for the behavior.* ("The student isn't motivated to learn"), remembering that these explanations reflect our cultural values.
5. *Our response to the student's behavior.* We may reprimand the student—either publicly or privately. Again, our response reflects our cultural values and norms.

When teachers are aware of the cultural differences in their classrooms, understand their attitudes concerning them, and understand the five steps outlined here, they can begin to structure their classroom so that they communicate effectively with all students. They can, for example, respect the ethnic background of their students and demonstrate that respect by reading stories with varied ethnic and racial content in literature class, or have students study world events from different cultural perspectives in social studies class. However, multicultural education is not content alone: A teacher's attitude toward culturally diverse students and how she or he communicates that attitude is extremely important.

Gail Sorensen (1989) suggests that although there is much research in multicultural issues, little of it is helpful in guiding teachers. She shares an example of what she learned from public school teachers in Fresno, California:

> First, never touch Hmong children on the top of the head. This is where the spirits reside and they become angry when touched. Second, allow children to wear strings around their wrists and ankles. Blue string keeps the good spirits in, while red string keeps the evil spirits out. Third, watch for signs of a sore throat and subsequent distress. Many of the Asians treat sore throats by having their children eat sand. Fourth, contact the family if students are absent for prolonged periods. When a member of the family is believed to be dying, children may be kept home to protect the ailing person from evil spirits. Fifth, if homework is rarely completed, check on the living conditions at home. Many refugees come here in extended families. No matter what housing arrangements are made, they may be living with more than 10 people in a two-bedroom apartment. Additionally, it has been discovered that some refugees have brought in dirt and "grow lights" to raise their own food in one room of the apartment. The school children may have no place to do their work. (p. 52)

One of the authors of this book taught Chinese students at the Chinese University of Hong Kong. Teaching strategies common in the United States can be problematic for the Chinese. For example, never ask Chinese students, "Are there any questions?" To ask a question would show one's ignorance, and a loss of face would result. However, if a teacher asks, "Have I explained this clearly?" students are free to ask questions because it is the teacher's "fault" that they don't understand. If the teacher had explained clearly, there would be no need for questions!

These examples tell us that teaching in a culturally diverse classroom is not an easy task. Teachers need special training. In preparing to work with a diverse group, Chism and colleagues (1989) suggest the following:

1. Understand nontraditional learning styles.
2. Learn about the history and culture of nontraditional groups.
3. Research the contributions of women and ethnic minorities.
4. Uncover your own biases.
5. Learn about bias in instructional materials.
6. Learn about your school's resources for nontraditional students.

Finally, teachers should use a variety of teaching methods—discussion, simulations, role plays, lectures, hands-on experiences, and more. In addition, teachers should provide opportunities for students to work cooperatively as well as individually, to stress cooperation as well as competition. Students should also be given choices in how to complete an assignment—a paper, an art project, an oral report, or another choice.

CONCLUSION

Culture affects the way we perceive the world and the way we communicate. In this chapter we have discussed how cultural differences affect educational environments. How simple it sometimes can be to avoid problems in the classroom if we simply understand that culture affects how students learn. Imagine if the teacher in the opening quote of this chapter had considered the culture of the students!

If we hope to be effective communicators in the educational environment we need to understand that cultural differences may result in differences in learning and/or cognitive style and affect the student–teacher relationship as well as the relationships among students in the educational environment. In addition, we need to remember that understanding cultural differences can help us avoid problems such as that presented at the beginning of this chapter. In the reading that follows, the problems and the joys of teaching interculturally are presented. MacLennan describes her journey of learning to communicate effectively in a Puerto Rican classroom.

FOR DISCUSSION

1. Describe your learning and/or cognitive style. How might your style cause you difficulties in another culture?
2. Consider a classroom in which you are a member. Describe how the teacher does or does not take into account Hofstede's four cultural dimensions.
3. Using the list of cultural universals (language, patterns of thought, values, and beliefs) analyze your own culture. What communication problems might occur in educational environments as a result of the differences between the two cultures?
4. Examine the textbooks used in the courses you are taking. What biases do you see? What effect might these have in the educational environment?

REFERENCES

Anderson, J., and Powell, R. (2000). Cultural influences on educational processes. In L. Samovar and L. Porter (Eds.), *Intercultural communication: A reader* (pp. 207–214). Belmont, CA: Wadsworth.

Berger, E., and Goldberger, L. (1979). Field dependence and short-term memory. *Perceptual and Motor Skills, 49,* 87–96.

Bochner, S. (1994). Cross-cultural differences in the self-concept. A test of Hofstede's individualism-collectivism distinction. *Journal of Cross-Cultural Psychology, 25,* 273–283.

Bosacki, S., Innerd, W., and Towson, S. (1997). Field independence-dependence and self-esteem in preadolescents: Does gender make a difference? *Journal of Youth and Adolescence, 26,* 691–703.

Bowman, B. (1989). Educating language minority children: Challenges and opportunities. *Phi Delta Kappan, 1,* 18–120.

Brislin, R. W., and Yoshida, T. (Eds.). (1996). *Improving intercultural interactions: Modules for cross-cultural training programs,* 2nd ed. Thousand Oaks, CA: Sage.

Brown, H. D. (1987). *Principles of language learning and teaching,* 2nd ed. Englewood Cliffs, NJ: Prentice-Hall.

Chism, N., Cano, J., and Pruitt, A. (1989). Teaching in a diverse environment: Knowledge and skills needed by TAs. In J. Nyquist, R. Abbott, and D. Wulff (Eds.), *Teaching assistant training in the 1990s: New directions for teaching and learning* (pp. 23–35). San Francisco: Jossey-Bass.

Chmielewski, T. L., Dansereau, D. F., and Moreland, J. L. (1998). Using common region in node-link displays: The roles of field dependence/independence. *Journal of Experimental Education, 66,* 197–207.

Cole, M., and Means, B. (1981). *Comparative studies of how people think.* Cambridge, MA: Harvard University Press.

Collier, M. J., and Powell, R. (1990). Ethnicity, instructional communication and classroom systems. *Communication Quarterly, 38,* 334–349.

Condon, J. (1986). The ethnocentric classroom. In J. Civikly (Ed.), *Communicating in college classrooms* (pp. 11–20). San Francisco: Jossey-Bass.

Cooper, E., and Allen, M. (1998). A meta-analytic examination of the impact of student race on classroom interaction. *Communication Research Reports, 15,* 151–161.

Cooper, P., and Simonds, C. (2005). *Communication for the classroom teacher,* 7th ed. Boston: Allyn and Bacon.

Cornett, C. (1983). *What you should know about teaching and learning styles.* Bloomington, IN: Phi Delta Kappa Education Foundation.

Cushner, K. (1990). Cross-cultural psychology and the formal classroom. In R. W. Brislin (Ed.), *Applied cross-cultural psychology* (pp. 98–120). Newbury Park, CA: Sage.

Cushner, K., and Brislin, R. (1996). *Intercultural interactions: A practical guide,* 2nd ed. Thousand Oaks, CA: Sage.

Cushner, K., McClelland, A., and Safford, P. (1992). *Human diversity in education: An* integrative approach. New York: McGraw-Hill.

Dunn, R., Beaudry, J., and Klavas, A. (1989). A survey of research on learning styles. *Educational Leadership,* 50–58.

Dunn, R., Dunn, K., and Price, G. (1979). Identifying individual learning styles. In E. Kieman (Ed.), *Student learning styles: Diagnosing and prescribing programs* (pp. 51–60). Reston, VA: National Association of Secondary School Principals.

Frankel, C. (1965). *The neglected aspect of foreign affairs.* Washington, DC: Brookings Institute.

Gibb, J. (1961). Defensive communication. *Journal of Communication, 2,* 141–148.

Grossman, H. (1984). *Educating Hispanic students: Cultural implications for instruction, classroom management, and assessment.* Springfield, IL: Charles C. Thomas.

Ha, P. (2001). How do culturally situated notions of 'polite' forms influence the way Vietnamese postgraduate students write academic English in Australia? *Australian Journal of Education, 45,* 296–308.

Hodgkinson, H. (2004). Educational demographics: What teachers should know. In F. Shultz (Ed.), *Multicultural Education* (pp. 24–27). Guilford, CT: McGraw-Hill/Dushkin.

Hofstede, G. (1991). *Cultures and organizations: Software of the mind.* London: McGraw-Hill.

Hollins, E. R., King, J. E., and Hayman, W. C. (1994). *Teaching diverse populations: Formulating a knowledge base.* New York: State University of New York Press.

Hunt, S. K. (1998). *Cognition and communication: Students' cognitive styles and the argumentation and debate course.* Unpublished doctoral dissertation, Southern Illinois University, Carbondale.

Hwang, A., Francesco, A. M., and Kessler, E. (2003). The relationship between individualism-collectivism, face, and feedback and learning processes in Hong Kong, Singapore, and the United States. *Journal of Cross-Cultural Psychology, 34,* 72–88.

Jonassen, D., and Grabowski, B. (1993). *Handbook of individual differences, learning and instruction.* Hillsdale, NJ: Lawrence Erlbaum Associates.

Keefe, J. (1982). *Student learning styles and brain behavior.* Reston, VA: National Association of Secondary School Principals.

Kiewra, K. A., and Frank, B. M. (1988). Encoding and external-storage effects of personal lecture notes, skeletal notes, and detailed notes for field-independent and field-dependent learners. *Journal of Educational Research, 81,* 143–148.

Kleinfeld, J. (1994). Learning styles and culture. In W. J. Lonner and R. S. Malpass (Eds.), *Psychology and culture* (pp. 151–156). Boston: Allyn and Bacon.

Lieberman, D. (1994). Ethnocognitivism, problem solving and hemisphericity. In L. Samovar and R. Porter (Eds.), *Intercultural communication: A reader,* 7th ed. (pp. 178–193). Belmont, CA: Wadsworth.

Lieberman, D. (1997). Culture, problem solving, and pedagogical style. In L. Samovar and R. Porter (Eds.), *Intercultural communication: A reader,* 8th ed. (pp. 191–207). Belmont, CA: Wadsworth.

Lustig, M., and Koester, J. (1996). *Interpersonal competence: Interpersonal communication across cultures,* 2nd ed. New York: HarperCollins.

Mahlios, M. C. (1981). Effects of teacher-student cognitive style on patterns of dyadic classroom interaction. *Journal of Experimental Education, 49,* 147–157.

Myers, L. (1981). The nature of pluralism and the African American case. *Theory Into Practice, 20,* 3–4.

National Association of Bilingual Education. (1993). Census reports sharp increase in number of non-English speaking Americans. *NABE News, 16,* (6), 1, 25.

Pusch, M. (1979). *Multicultural education: A cross cultural training approach.* Yarmouth, ME: Intercultural Press.

Reiff, J. (1996). Multiple intelligences: Different ways of learning. Retrieved December 20, 2003, from www.udel.edu/bateman/acei/multint9.htm.

Richardson, J., and Turner, A. (2000). A large-scale "local" evaluation of students' learning experiences using virtual learning environments. *Educational Technology and Society, 3,* 108–125.

Rickards, J. P., Fajen, B., Sullivan, J., and Gillespie, G. (1997). Signaling, notetaking and field independence/dependence in text comprehension and recall. *Journal of Educational Psychology, 89,* 508–517.

Riding, R., and Cheema, I. (1991). Cognitive styles—an overview and integration. *Educational Psychology, 11,* 193–215.

Rivlin, H. (1977). Research and development in multicultural education. In F. Klassen and D. Golnick (Eds.), *Pluralism and the American teacher: Issues and case studies.* Washington, DC: American Association of Colleges for Teacher Education.

Samovar, L., Porter, R., and Stefani, L. (2001). *Communication between cultures,* 4th ed. Belmont, CA: Wadsworth.

Sinatra, R. (1986). *Visual literacy connections to thinking, reading and writing.* Springfield, IL: Charles C. Thomas.

Sorensen, G. (1989). Teaching teachers from east to west: A look at common myths. *Communication Education, 38,* 330–335.

Taylor, E. (1994). A learning model for becoming interculturally competent. *International Journal of Intercultural Relations, 18,* 389–408.

Vermunt, J. D., and Verloop, N. (2000, August). *Dissonance in students' regulation of learning processes.* Paper presented at the International Conference on Innovations in Higher Education 2000, Helsinki, Finland.

Viadero, D. (1986, April 10). Culture class. *Education Week,* 39–42.

Wallach, J., and Metcalf, G. (1995). *Working with Americans: A practical guide for Asians on how to succeed with U.S. managers.* New York: McGraw-Hill.

Witkin, H. A. (1976). Cognitive style in academic performance and in teacher-student relations. In S. Messick (Ed.) *Individuality in learning* (pp. 38–72). San Francisco: Jossey-Bass.

Witkin, H. A., Dyk, R. B., Faterson, H. F., and Karp, S. A. (1962). *Psychological differentiation studies of development.* New York: John Wiley and Sons, Inc.

Witkin, H. A., Moore, C. A., Goodenough, D. R., and Cox, P. W. (1977). Field-dependent and field-independent cognitive styles and their educational implications. *Review of Education Research, 47,* 1–64.

Witkin, H. A., Moore, C. A., Oltman, P. K., Goodenough, D. R., Friedman, F., Owen, D. R., and Raskin E. (1977). Role of field dependent and field independent cognitive styles in academic evolution: A longitudinal study. *Journal of Educational Psychology, 69,* 197–211.

There's a Lizard in My Living Room and a Pigeon in My Classroom: A Personal Reflection on What It Takes to Teach in a Different Culture

Janet MacLennan

My first year of being a professor instead of a teaching associate, of being a faculty member instead of a lowly graduate student, was also my first year of teaching in a new and different-to-me culture. Learning how to teach in a different culture was an opportunity I embraced, yet that did not necessarily make it easy. . . .

Taking this opportunity to reflect, I have devised a picture of what I think it takes to teach in a different culture. I will go through and describe each facet of this picture until the whole picture is complete. This is my snapshot; yours could be different because you are different or because of the influence of an immersion into a different culture. . . .

BE COMFORTABLE WITH THE UNCOMFORTABLE

Certainly I am the kind of person who likes to be prepared, even overly prepared. But I simply could not be prepared for what was unknown about my new students—what would be the same from my previous teaching experience, what would be different, what would be unexpected—in terms of this new culture. So one ingredient for success in cross-cultural teaching has to be a measure of comfort with that icky feeling of being unsure of yourself, not just in the beginning but over and over and over again. It is a feeling that is uncomfortable, strange and strange-making. And it does not go away entirely, even with time.

I experienced several overlapping layers of discomfort with uncertainty. As informed by the intercultural communication contribution of Hofstede's body of research, we can realize that one of the dimensions for evaluating culture is uncertainty avoidance (1980). . . .

One of the most significant areas of uncertainty for me early on was that, as my first semester progressed, it became increasingly difficult for me to have confidence that I was going to be able to achieve my course goals in any of my classes due to the constant and unexpected interruptions of class time. In my previous teaching experience, it was generally a given that there would be class as the schedule indicated. What I would do or how it might go or which students would be in attendance, that remained to be seen, but the class would certainly take place. In my new culture, even *having* class was not a given, not a given at all: There was the day of the bomb threat, one of an power outage, several water outages, student assemblies. Or how about the day I arrived on campus only to be told to go home for a week. And then there were the strikes when you could not tell if you would be back to class the next day or the next semester. My students took it all in stride. They seemed to know to expect the unexpected and it was only once I realized to expect this as well that some of the icky feeling, the uncomfortable uncertainty, finally subsided. From then on, when it came to doing any kind of course planning, I just planned to expect the unexpected. (Notice I did not give up entirely on the idea of planning.) . . .

I learned over and over those first months: that avoiding that icky feeling of uncomfortable uncertainty would only be achieved when I had drastically altered my expectations, pretty much in every way, and even in some ways I had never anticipated. Around here, some days, getting to work is the main challenge; after that, you can enjoy just being there.

THIS MAY BE A COMMUNICATION CLASS BUT NO, I DON'T KNOW WHAT YOU'RE SAYING

In my communication classes, likely similar to your classes, I try to foster a learning environment in which students feel confident and comfortable in sharing thoughts, discussing ideas, and even making mistakes. This makes learning about communication and applying new learning easier, even possible. I quickly discovered that although I still had the same goal of developing this type of environment, I had one major barrier and that was that I did not speak the students' native language of Spanish. I did not speak it, did not understand it, not one word. And even though my students have very highly developed skills in English, it is still their second language for the most part and this led to problems, such as when a student could not remember the words in English and instead would simply say them in Spanish, or else when they resorted to discussing amongst themselves in Spanish at length what the words would be in English. Sometimes a student speaks English but with an accent heavily influenced by Spanish, making it difficult for me to interpret *my* native language. Before class when students engage in before-class chatter, you never know what is being said, what is so interesting or so funny. In view of this, I had to give up the sense of control that comes from knowing everything that is being discussed in my classroom. It is not exactly the paranoia that everyone is talking behind your back; on the other hand, they *could* be, and you would not know it. . . . Just as one small but significant example, there was the time when I quizzed the students about the single most important contributor to happiness in our lives, according to DeVito's (1998) interpersonal communication textbook. The answer: close relationships. The answer one student gave: God. Whatever my own beliefs, could I mark that answer wrong? If I did, what was I getting into?

My new best response to all of this was to admit my lack of knowledge of their language, to joke about the problems that arose because of that lack of knowledge, and to share with them stories of my struggle as I was beginning to learn what had always been second nature for most of them: communicating from within their own culture. . . .

DON'T HIDE YOUR CULTURE SHOCK

In a very self-effacing manner, I have to laugh at this title. I realize now that when I was in the peak of my culture shock I could not have hidden it even if I had wanted to. Just as my blue eyes, light hair, and fair skin (my students refer to it as "pink," just the color I have always wanted to be) immediately call attention to the likelihood of my outsider status, so too did my culture shock come across loud and clear.

Even at the time, I realized that the larger culture shock I was experiencing was not at all something that I could hide. Indeed, in terms of developing my relationship with my students, it was not something that I would *want* to hide. Instead, it was something that helped us to understand each other and connect. I told them my stories as they happened to me: my worries about hurricanes, the tarantula I killed in my kitchen, learning about the political events of the Island and strikes, adapting to the feeling of constantly being watched (Do I have something hanging from my nose?), different ways of greeting and getting to know people, adapting to the new climate and the to-me freaky weather patterns, adapting to new rules for the use of time, and many more. I would share stories and sometimes I would ask them questions. Did they think this talk of a strike had merit? Did they think this hurricane hurtling toward us was going to hit or miss? As to the ways of the culture they were experts, I was not. . . .

REMEMBER THAT YOU ARE PRACTICING WHAT YOU TEACH

I teach communication, but of course that does not mean I am especially or automatically good at communicating. The expectation is often that you must be a good communicator and have perfect relationships because, after all, you have a doctorate in that subject. Along with the expectation comes the scrutiny. Although I do not agree with the expression "Those who can, do; those who can't, teach," I sometimes secretly worry there might be a glimmer of truth in it somewhere.

No matter, this situation of teaching communication always sets up an interesting dynamic: as you teach your students about what constitutes good communication, they look to you to see if you are doing it, if you are being a good model. A great deal of the substance behind successful interpersonal communica-

tion especially involves anticipating the other, having an open and inquisitive way of engaging with others, being critical of our own perception processes, and reflecting constantly. By sharing my experiences in their new culture—positive and negative, successful and otherwise—I hope that in some ways I was practicing what I was teaching. . . .

IT DOESN'T MATTER WHAT YOU WEAR, YOU'RE STILL GOING TO STAND OUT

It is a little daunting to be always identified as an outsider. A saleslady in J. C. Penney once dropped her jaw in surprised confusion because I was buying household goods and she so obviously had concluded I must be a tourist. Shop owners where I lived in Old San Juan would notice my interest in an item for sale and quickly assure me that they ship anywhere in the world, obviously having concluded I was fresh off a cruise ship, when in reality I lived one street up and two blocks over. Do you ship there? When I landed in parts of the city not frequented by tourists is when I received the most open stares, and still do. Until people learn that I live here, they will talk to me just a bit differently, and share information differently too. . . . Once I asked someone in the tourist trade how late the A5 bus ran. She told me that after dark they recommend taxis. When I told her I lived here she laughed, shook off the tourist trade talk, and shared easily the answer.

I remain visibly an outsider. Due to this, I am anticipating that I will be perpetually paused at stage three culture shock entitled "gradual adjustment" (Furnham & Bochner, 1986) where I enjoy the culture, am more comfortable in it, and can function at a high level without feeling so isolated, but can never feel fully embraced and adjusted, a process which can take many years. Still, you have to take your advantages where you can. The advantage of the situation created by this outsider-ness is discussed next.

RETHINK EVERYTHING

Being more on the outside opens up the opportunity to rethink everything. Whatever standard practices you have come to rely on in your teaching, you quickly discover you cannot fall back on so easily any more. Things that have worked in the past no longer work. Things that never worked in the past suddenly work like you never thought possible. Things you struggled with before are no longer an issue, yet you have to figure out the nature of new, unpredictable struggles. You begin to look at the material you are teaching with a different eye, more critical than before. You see flaws in the material and begin to question it more. But simultaneously you envision new applications, new openings, new connections. If you are overly comfortable in the ways of being a teacher that you have established over time, I guess you might not enjoy this process of rethinking practically everything. But if you are open to it, it can be thrilling and energizing. . . .

COMING UNDER CRITIQUE

I do not want to paint an overly rosy picture. As much as rethinking and thinking anew about teaching and about communication can be energizing, it can also be energy-consuming and energy-draining. Some days I just felt so inadequate as a teacher that I was sure someone would meet me at the door at the end of the day and fire me. Sure, it was a feeling I had felt before in my teaching, but I felt it a lot more often after switching cultures.

Moreover, there is a larger context for your presence in this new culture that cannot be ignored. In other words, I came here to teach, to live, to do what I have been trained to do. But the context and the structure of the dynamic of my outsider-ness enters in always, whether I am willing to examine implications of this or not. I just suggest it is important to be aware of the broader political and social implications that are implicitly and explicitly affecting how you do your job and even whether or not you can do the job you have set out to do.

CANADA? BUT IT'S COLD THERE!

You come under critique, but you are also critiquing your new culture. It goes both ways. As much as I was learning about a new culture I was also sharing my own cultural identity, that most firmly associated with the country of Canada. It is not just a matter of fitting in to a new culture, it is also about understanding and appreciating both the qualities and constraints of the culture in which I was raised. And even after you start to fit in, you have to answer this question for yourself: do *I like* this new culture? . . .

Being ever careful not to overestimate differences between cultures—a communication habit identified as a barrier to competent intercultural communication (Jandt, 2001)—I can look for connections between my island experience of my home called Cape Breton Island and the island experience of Puerto Rico, between the bilingualism language issues of French and English in Canada and the bilingualism language is-

sues of Spanish and English here, between the political struggle to preserve cultural identity of minority groups in Canada and the political struggle to preserve cultural identity of what is a minority group to the United States.

While I am sharing my own cultural identity, I am also in the process of learning what I want to uphold from each culture, what I value, and what I would like to transform within me. The best example of this has to do with time orientation. Most people who have experienced Puerto Rico would probably readily agree with me that one difference here as compared to North America is that Puerto Ricans have a present-focused time orientation compared to a more future-focused time orientation in the United States and Canada. This one difference, so easy to describe on paper, is so immensely difficult to adjust to in practice. In the beginning, while I struggled through the second stage of culture shock entitled "irritation and hostility"—need I explain more?—I ranted, roared, and railed about and against the "inefficiency" of just about everything here. Let me put it this way: the golden arches may shine here but what is served in the establishment could never be called *fast* food. Gradually, moving into the adjustment of stage three culture shock, I came to see it differently. All that rushing around, always thinking of the next things that must get done, always living just ahead of yourself and rarely actually in the moment, was that so great? The loaded label of inefficiency faded to a possibly better pace of life. . . .

HOW RUDE! ASSIMILATING ASSIMILATION

2001 in Atlanta. . . . I was the one standing still on the elevator . . . at the Marriott with my jaw on the floor and a look of disgust on my face. What could cause such offense? Only that everyone on the elevator—in particular the men—had pushed themselves through the doors ahead of me without a thought.

Actually, that would be only part of the reason my jaw was on the floor; the other reason would be the sudden realization as to the extent of my assimilation into a Latin macho culture. How did it happen? How did I actually come to expect men to give way and give me priority for exiting even the most packed elevator? And I am a feminist!

How? I already used the word: *assimilation*. Truthfully, I was not really prepared for this. I had anticipated adjusting to a new culture but I had never anticipated that I would actually change and become like *them*. It has been the different gender roles that I find especially difficult to understand, and yet it was in this area that I seemed to assimilate the soonest in small, subtle ways. More evidence of this came to me one day while I was waiting for the bus and I accidentally dropped my bus fare. A "normal" course of action would dictate that I bend and pick it up; however, having experienced the knocking of heads brought about when my head got in the way of any male in a 300 foot radius who would inevitably rush in to get the dropped item for me, I instead had a revelation and said to myself, "He'll get it for me." Indeed, the "he" in question walked ten feet to graciously recapture and return my dropped change.

Were these changes so bad? When I started teaching the course in intercultural communication, I could identify some of my experiences as connected to the tensions between moving from a more feminine culture, where social roles overlap, to a masculine culture where social roles are distinct and discrete (Hofstede, 1980). Part of my assimilation was to recognize the more masculine nature of this culture with less overlapping of social roles, a culture where women get off elevators first and men pick things up whenever a woman drops them. . . .

INTERPRETING THE TITLE: NEW WALLS, NEW WINDOWS

I chose the first part of the title of my [reading], "There's a Lizard in My Living Room and a Pigeon in My Classroom," not just because it was true, but also for a more significant reason. The fact of these two experiences was definitely new and startling for me. The thing that made it possible for various creatures to freely roam my home and work is simply because, by definition, walls and windows are different here in Puerto Rico. In my first apartment, I had no windows in the way that I had come to understand that concept. Instead, I had wooden shutters. They did not stop anything from coming in—especially outside noise and prying eyes—and even made it difficult to see out. As for walls, I was missing one in the entire back half of the building which opened into a courtyard open to the world. In my classrooms, many were situated along a corridor that, again, had no windows in the sense I am used to, and was a few walls short of a building by *my* traditional notions of building construction. My students, being used to this kind of construction, did not think it odd that a pigeon flew right in one day while I was mid-sentence. But me? I thought that a little different.

These new walls and windows—or lack thereof—can also be understood in a more symbolic manner. In my new culture, I could not shut-out outside influences just because it might be convenient or because I was feeling overloaded or overwhelmed. Everything came in any way; there was nothing to stop it. So you either go with it or . . .

THE THRILL OF TEACHING IS UNIVERSAL

One thing I have learned with confidence is that if you enjoy teaching, that passion will stay with you no matter what adjustments you have to make or challenges you have to face. Indeed, with all these new experiences, I enjoy teaching much more now in my adopted (adopting?) culture than I ever did before, or ever could have imagined. It is satisfying to realize that the experience of learning how to teach in a new culture is making me a better educator in many ways. . . .

The thrill of teaching is universal, but in many ways, so is that thrill of being a student, a lifelong learner.

REFERENCES

Furnham, A. & Bochner, S. (1986). *Culture shock: Psychological reactions to unfamiliar environments.* New York: Methuen.

DeVito, J. A. (1998). *The interpersonal communication book* (8th ed.). New York: Longman.

Hofstede, G. (1980). *Culture's consequences.* Beverly Hills, CA: Sage.

Jandt, F. E. (2001). *Intercultural communication: An introduction,* 3rd ed. Sage: Thousand Oak.

CHECK YOUR UNDERSTANDING

1. Explain the title of this reading.
2. What is culture shock?
3. What is assimilation?

4. Why is it important to "rethink everything" when you are in a culture different from your own?

CHAPTER ACTIVITIES

Using the principles discussed in this chapter, read the following critical incident from Cushner and Brislin (1996) and decide what is the best course of action.

The New ESL Teacher

After two years of travel throughout Asia and Europe and a year of study and preparation in a master's program in English as a Second Language (ESL), George felt quite confident. Although he had not had any real classroom experience, he had taught English informally to a Malaysian student he met while traveling, had studied all the latest approaches to teaching English, was keen to employ intercultural dimensions in his teaching, and was quite eager to get to know as many international students coming to the United States as he could. He was, not surprisingly, excited to be offered his first position at a nearby university to teach in a special ESL summer program for a group of visiting Japanese students. He eagerly prepared for his upcoming teaching assignment. The first day of class arrived. George had found out earlier that the majority of his students would be business majors, because the importance of English for business purposes had become quite evident. From the very first day, even though he had learned a bit of Japanese during his earlier travels, George made sure to only use English in class to communicate and to teach his students. He tried to be as friendly as he could and to maintain interaction with his students. It puzzled him that when he approached a student with a question, the student inevitably looked down at his or her textbook and would not give an answer to the question he asked. This behavior continued down the line, with each student maintaining an embarrassed silence. The students were not the only ones embarrassed by the silence—George was also in a quandary. He did not know how to manage the situation. He decided to sit next to one of his students in order to communicate better. To his dismay, he noticed after he tried this that more and more students started sitting at the back of the classroom rather than filling the chairs up front.

Things finally flared up when George asked a particular student to summarize the points made in the previous class. What he had neglected to notice was that the student he chose had been absent the previous day. As a result, the student maintained a long and uncomfortable silence. George had had enough. He told the student to look at him directly and tell him if she knew the material. After this confrontation, most of the students stopped coming to class.

What insights might you offer George that would help him better understand what was going on?

1. Japanese students revere and respect elderly teachers. There was not enough of an age gap between George and his students.
2. In Japanese custom, in order to gain full respect, it is necessary to greet people in the Japanese language. Because George made a point of using only English, he never really gained the respect of his students.
3. George's style of teaching was in direct conflict with the manner in which Japanese students learn.
4. George was struggling because he was a new teacher. The situation would certainly improve as he gained experience and confidence. (Cushner and Brislin, 1996, pp. 200–201)

Answers

1. It is true that Japanese students revere and respect elderly teachers, but Japanese students tend to revere and respect any and all teachers. The title *sansei,* given to teachers, is a sign of honor and respect. George would most probably have been afforded all the respect coming to any teacher by Japanese students—certainly far more respect than would be given by most American students. Please select an alternative explanation.
2. It is true that there may be certain customs for greeting that are important to the maintenance of interpersonal relationships. However, these students came to the United States with the express intention of learning English in an American context. There is no indication in the story that George's use of English only was the problem. Please select an alternative explanation.
3. This explanation provides the most insight into this situation. In George's classroom there were many instances where instructional style and learning style seemed to be in conflict. George's attempts at friendliness and informality would have been rather uncomfortable for students accustomed to a more formal, structured interaction between teacher and student. In addition, in Japan, where group conformity is strongly encouraged, a teacher would rarely single individual students out from the group. Students thus singled out would become quite uncomfortable, which would explain George's students' reluctance to return to class. On another level, this incident demonstrates how many people who are well-traveled believe they know how to be effective when working intimately with those from other cultures; George's problems clearly suggest that this is not always the case.
4. It is true that George was a new teacher and was probably learning to adapt all that he had in school to the real world of teaching. However, in this case, without attending to the cultural differences in learning and teaching style, it was unlikely things would change. There is a better explanation for the problems George experienced. Please choose again. (Cushner and Brislin, 1996, pp. 222)

CHAPTER 10

ECONOMICS, BUSINESS, AND INTERCULTURAL COMMUNICATION

HOW DO I CRITICIZE? LET ME COUNT THE WAYS

Rick Hoel

When we lived in Hong Kong, I taught a class to some of our mid-level managers. It was a course designed to help our Chinese employees improve their skills in making Western-style presentations to groups both inside and outside the company. The class consisted of about 20 employees and we met twice a month. I assigned five people to prepare and to give individual presentations at each class session. The presenter's classmates and I would then critique the presentations in class. I was aware of the fact that direct criticism of individuals in the Chinese culture, particularly in front of others, needed to be handled delicately. I had already seen instances where what I thought was constructive criticism caused an embarrassing situation for the recipient. I even went so far as to candidly address this issue with the class, explaining that I wanted everyone, including me, to feel free to offer critiques with the goal not of offending anyone but of encouraging improvement. No one spoke up and objected to this approach and I felt confident that I was on the right track.

Despite my precautions, I found that my critiques were not well received and despite the fact that many of the employees had worked with Western companies for some time, few were willing to criticize anyone's presentation. Whenever anyone did offer some form of criticism it was striking that everyone's head in the class went down. Everyone seemed genuinely embarrassed to allow themselves to witness another's shame. No matter how hard I tried to couch my criticism in the form of encouragement ("That was a tremendous presentation and could have been even more effective if . . ."), anything that hinted that the presentation could use improvement generated some degree of this type of reaction.

Finally, I asked for help. I met privately with several of the better students in the class and asked what I could do to get over this hurdle. I suggested that perhaps I needed to meet alone with each student to offer my critiques or simply put it in writing. My students offered a better suggestion. They suggested that I form presentation teams that would work together to develop and make group presentations to the class. This was in fact the way the Chinese culture best approached problem solving. Historically the great events in Chinese history often involved famine and poverty and have cried out for collective solutions. Confucianism stresses the collective over the individual. In contrast, in America, both the frontier experience and the Industrial Revolution and an abundance of natural resources encouraged the development of self-reliance and stress on the individual.

We approached the course in this way. Each team developed and presented the material together and when I opened the floor for discussion of the presentations, candid criticism flowed easily about the ways in which each group could improve. Eventually we were able to evolve to individual presentations with much better appreciation for constructive criticism.

OBJECTIVES

After reading this chapter and completing the readings and activities, you should be able to

- Explain the relationship between economics and culture.
- Explain how changes in the global economic community influence intercultural dynamics.
- Define uncertainty reduction.
- Explain how language and relationships influence the business context.
- Explain how evidence, reasoning, and persuasive style differ across cultures.
- Explain how negotiation differs across cultures.

Worldwide, we are being forced to rethink our economic role in human culture. Our understanding of the relationship between economics and culture and the fact that cultural tensions are created by economic transformations, is key to our understanding of intercultural communication in the business context. In this chapter we focus on the relationship between economics, culture, and communication, and we discuss the intercultural communication business context.

ECONOMIC GLOBAL TRANSFORMATIONS

Global transformations refer to the worldwide economic and technological changes that influence how people relate to one another. For example, the global economy links people in desert and rural isolation in Mongolia via the Internet with those in urban areas of Minnesota (Ohmae, 1995, p. l). People in nearly every part of the world can buy blue jeans! East Indian movies are viewed throughout Southeast Asia and Africa. In 1991, while visiting a remote, pristine area of the Gambia, one of the authors was struck by sweet, musical sounds coming from a transistor radio, as a village elder vigorously pounded yams using a centuries-old pestle!

In each instance, these changes are occurring because of information and communications technologies and global market forces. Without knowledge of these changes, it is unlikely that we will understand the attitudes and behaviors that accompany such dramatic economic and cultural shifts. Consequently, we will not know how to respond to new and different cultural situations.

Alvin Toffler (1980) identifies several characteristics of global transformations that influence our ability to communicate competently with people from other cultures: (1) The ground rules of social life are changing; (2) the restructuring of time is intensifying loneliness and social isolation; (3) we are becoming an information society; (4) human tensions are being spawned by technological changes; (5) old values are clashing with technology; and (6) our role models of reality are changing from the teacher, the priest, and the family to multiple outside channels, such as mass media, including television, newspapers, radio, and magazines.

Paul Kennedy's (1993) research on increased immigration and what happens when money and jobs cross borders also demonstrates the challenges and opportunities facing individuals of different backgrounds who live and work together. Kennedy believes that our social attitudes, religious beliefs, and culture are probably the most important influences on how quickly we respond to change. For example, it is believed that people who worship their ancestors, or have deeply rooted beliefs in extended families, will have a more difficult time adjusting to global and technological changes.

Another concern is what happens interpersonally when cultural products are transported across boundaries. A controversy in France over the Walt Disney Company's dress code illustrates these effects. The Walt Disney Company insisted that its French workers shave their beards in keeping with Disney's image. The French saw this requirement as insensitive to their cultural norms. As we can see, even though global transformations have made it possible for companies to relocate in outside countries with greater ease, such arrangements threaten existing habits and ways of life. In the case of the Disney example, a basic dress requirement became an assault on French social and cultural standards ("A Disney Dress Code," 1991). Although the dress code was changed, the damage to intercultural relationships remained.

Economic and technological jolts and jars are bound to affect how we communicate interculturally. The following is a list of some basic characteristics that are tied to the workplace:

1. *Rising levels of stress.* Research indicates that people are more prone to strike out against others in times of stress. As Young Yun Kim (1994) observes, "Stress . . . is part and parcel of strangers' adaptation and growth experiences over time" (p. 393). Feelings of stress are readily translated into outward behavior. Psychologist Craig Brod cites the example of an office worker who "becomes impatient with phone callers who take too long to get to the point" (Rifkin, 1995, p. 187). When people have a lot to do, and too little time to do it, they often become impatient, curt, and sometimes rude.

Stress frames our interaction with others. An individual who was once calm, cool, and collected could turn into a proverbial monster if suddenly his or her livelihood is jeopardized. It is easier to understand the transgressions of a co-worker if we know that she not only holds down a 20-hour job and attends university classes but is also forced to compete for a smaller slice of the economic pie.

2. *Loss of hope.* Although cultures differ concerning their attitudes toward the future, hope is tied to anticipation about the future—that is, whether we can see positive benefits instead of negative ones, a mode of perception that we refer to as *congenial expectation.* In the United States, this general feeling is tied to the belief that the future will be better and brighter. Edward C. Stewart observes that "most Americans feel that through their efforts a better future can be brought about which will not compromise the welfare and progress of others" (Stewart, 1972, p. 64). As you learned in Chapter 2, this is still an American belief. An absence of hope can create a bitterness that presents challenges to communication across cultures.

3. *Feelings of redundancy.* All of the things that we have mentioned thus far can indeed be a bitter curse for those enduring them; however, when we add to these problems a feeling that our skills might become useless in the workplace, our way of life is doubly threatened. For example, in China, traditional labor-intensive sectors are declining. A typical example is the mineral exploration in which income topped other sectors in 1990, but fell to third from the bottom of the income list in 1999. In addition, as a natural result of urbanization, more and more farmers will leave their farms and flood into the cities. These farmers will have none of the skills necessary to an urban environment (www.china.org. cn/english/2001/May/13426.htm).

4. *Expressions of virtue.* Finally, tensions occur because of the way groups express their virtues. Although most people work hard, some groups assign more importance to certain virtues than do other groups. For example, Thomas Sowell (1983) notes that in the United States, as in Southeast Asia, the Chinese became objects of hatred because of their virtues of endurance and frugality. In the United States, anti-Chinese feelings were so strong that labor unions and political groups organized against Chinese companies, and in some instances ran these companies out of business.

NEW PEOPLE IN THE WORKPLACE

The complexion of the workplace is changing. People who are employed in corporations, universities, fast-food restaurants, and the government are coming from increasingly different cultural backgrounds. African Americans, Latinos, Japanese Americans, gays and lesbians, people with disabilities, as well as newly arriving immigrants, are occupying positions as managers, corporate executives, computer analysts, scientists, writers, gardeners, factory stewards, and farm workers.

This growing diversity is exacerbating ethnic tensions, as between Mexican immigrants and other Americans because of the immigrants' willingness to accept lower wages and fewer benefits ("A Manifesto for Immigration," 1996). Ponterotto and Pedersen (1993) provide some examples of the conditions that produce or exacerbate tensions between groups. These conditions include (1) a heterogeneous society, (2) rapid social change, (3) large or increasing minority groups, (4) upward mobility, and (5) increasing competition and threat from minority groups. These characteristics define economic changes that are currently happening in the United States.

As we interact with an increasingly multicultural workforce, we can improve our interpersonal competence if we follow a few general rules:

1. *Learn acceptable verbal patterns of address.* People from different cultures have different ways to greet and address other people. Some relationships between people, such as student–teacher, father–son, customer–waiter, and boss–clerk, are heavily power coded, whereas others are not. In Korea, before addressing someone, relative rank must be assessed. In Belgium, you don't address somebody you don't know in a jovial way (Pinxten, 1993). In Bantu, names are frequently avoided in an address in order to express deference and/or intimacy (Mufwene, 1993). However, because of North Americans' insistence on the "perception of equality," we value first names and even use nicknames, forms of address that members of other cultures may find rude, or even offensive.

2. *Learn about other groups in the workplace.* A good place to start is to learn other cultures' histories, because they provide important clues about how to behave and what to say or not say. For example, a man hired a student to help him with some chores around his house. One day, before Father's Day, the man asked the worker what he had gotten for his father. "I am a Jehovah's Witness and we don't celebrate Father's Day," replied the worker. The employer was embarrassed. Of course, it will not be possible to learn every aspect of a specific culture, but we should try to learn as much as possible.

3. *Know how friendship rules apply.* Styles of friendships differ and are culturally generated. People in the United States have friendships that develop around work, children, or political opinion—around charities, games, various occasions for sharing food and alcohol, and so on. Because these divisions of friendship are kept separate, it is possible for a person to have different work-related and social-related friendships. Other cultural groups, such as Russians, tend to embrace the whole person in their friendships, rather than relegating them to separate divisions.

4. *Recognize that information-based cultures differ from agricultural, industrial, or postindustrial cultures.* Economic structures help to explain many of the beliefs, values, and norms of a culture (Carr-Ruffino, 1996). For example, people migrating from agriculturally based economies will normally have the values, myths, concepts, and morals of an agricultural society, such as dependency on an extended family. Such a family structure also carries much clearer decision-making processes and lines of authority, whereas more decisions may be made outside of the family in information-based cultures.

5. *Place communication and meanings in context.* In our discussion of Hall's conception of high- and low-context cultures, we noted that some groups are more "We" oriented while others are more "I" oriented. Because the setting in which communication occurs organizes meanings, and because more unspoken meaning is taken for granted in some cultures than in others, it is important to remember that ignoring this rule can create cultural mischief. For example, an administrative assistant of a faculty council at a Big Ten university, observing that the president pro tem was absent, took it upon herself to tell the African American secretary of the faculty council the smallest details about how to conduct business, including calling the roll. She was accustomed to following her culture's rules of spelling things out and taking very little for granted. As an associate professor, the secretary could easily have taken offense at what looked like racially based condescension. Instead of responding negatively, however, the secretary replied by simply saying, "Thank you."

When messages are made very explicit, if users of such language are not careful, they can be construed as talking in a condescending manner. Knowledge and understanding of the role of such contextual dynamics in the workplace can facilitate interpersonal effectiveness.

6. *Observe "because of" and "in spite of" behavioral differences.* We may distinguish between things that happen to us because of our race, ethnicity, age, sex, size, or occupation, and things that happen to us "in spite of" these and other factors. For example, if a Native American is next in line at the office copy machine and a White American approaches the machine, becomes momentarily distracted, and then cuts in front of the Native American, did this behavior occur "because of" ethnicity or "in spite of" ethnicity?

Remember that change is inevitable, and yet it often brings anguish, disruption, and a rearranging of our lives. All around us are instances of change in everything from how we talk to others, to the music that we listen to, to how we manage our time. Clashes between traditional and new ways of doing things can influence interpersonal relationships. For example, before the advent of television, most families in the United States shared meals together and sat around the kitchen table discussing the events and activities of the day. It was even possible for us to visit rural India and not hear CNN there!

CHANGING CONCEPT OF GLOBAL ECONOMIC COMMUNITY

To understand the changing dynamics of the current economic global community and its influence on intercultural behavior, it is essential to begin with the breakup of the former Soviet Union. Prior to 1991, the world was clearly ideologically divided and full of "isms." The West, which included the United States, Western Europe, and their allies, were on one side, and the Soviet bloc countries of Eastern Europe, which included Poland, Yugoslavia, and Czechoslovakia, were on the other. These bipolar groups were held together by a unifying concept of the "enemy." The Soviet Union and its allies supported communism while the United States and its allies supported democracy and a capitalist economy.

What is important in terms of communication is the fact that the two differing forms of thought served as a powerful means of unifying those who supported the respective doctrines. In a sense, the world was much simpler then; individuals could readily distinguish "friend" from "enemy" based on the geographical area in which a person lived. Then the proverbial "enemy from without" was clearly noticeable and North Americans could and did rally around things that were anti-Communist. In fact, it used to be acceptable to use terms such as "better dead than red," or to speak of the Soviet empire and its people disdainfully. And, of course, the opposite also was true: The Soviet Union and its supporters were equally disdainful of the United States and its citizens.

As we increasingly interact with others, we must assume a burden of complexity, because it is no longer acceptable to place people in tight ideological boxes. The rejection of easy categorization encourages thinking about the many-sidedness of others. For example, when a Russian and North American student communicate today, it is likely that they will have more in common with one another than with their parents. Mass media, including television, have played a tremendous role in making this communication possible.

UNCERTAINTY REDUCTION

Geert Hofstede (1992) suggests that individuals carry with them images of their past that are rooted in childhood. These unconscious orientations strongly affect behavior in work situations. As you recall from Chapter 2, in determining the role of culture in work situations, Hofstede studied a large multinational corporation and the employees of its subsidiaries in 67 countries. He was careful to compare employees working in similar jobs so that any difference would not be due to occupation but to nationality.

Uncertainty avoidance, one of the dimensions Hofstede found, is "the extent to which the members of a society feel comfortable with uncertainty and ambiguity" (1992, p. 91). Unpredictability about the future creates anxiety. For example, how will individuals react to the fact that there is a new global economic game with new rules? And to the foreboding fact that in the United States jobs that used to require only a high school degree are increasingly being held by people with college degrees? It is important to remember that the powerful economic forces that are occurring as a result of globalization are testing our deeply rooted beliefs about the future.

When tensions about the future are paramount, the "how" of our economic lives is questioned. For example, the congressional sponsors of a bill for restricting immigration used the argument that immigration destroys the quality of life in the United States. ("A Manifesto for Immigration," 1996). People are likely to feel more threatened by other cultures during periods of economic uncertainty. Another way to think about the impact of global economic changes on our future is to consider the very notion of change itself. Lester C. Thurow (1996), a professor of economics at Massachusetts Institute of Technology, argues that despite the conception that people like to change, in reality "all humans hate to change." The Chinese curse, "May you live in interesting times" (which is comparable in damning intent to the North American saying, "May you burn in hell"), is a more realistic representation of reaction to change, says Thurow (p. 232). The following basic elements should help us to understand why we resist change and how this resistance influences our interpersonal interactions with others:

1. *Old modes of behavior do not work; new ones are required.* Think of all the things that are affected by economic change: habits of dress, what we eat, rules of courtesy, how to talk to newcomers, competition for jobs, worker stress, how to interact with computers, and a shift from face-to-face communication to communication with machines. These are only a few of the things that require new rules in the face of economic change.

2. *Cherished values are threatened.* Links between economic values and the economic uncertainty of not knowing what lies ahead threaten cherished beliefs (Thurow, 1996). For example, in the United States, abortion doctors have been shot because they are viewed as tampering with virtues that are firmly rooted in Christian morality. Other examples of defense of cherished values include the war against obscene music lyrics led by Vice President Albert Gore's wife, Tipper, and the National Baptist Convention's 1996 promise to boycott Disney films because the company recognizes the civil rights of gays and lesbians.

3. *There is a tendency to retreat into religious fundamentalism.* Because people do not react well to threats to their economic way of life, some individuals retreat into religious fundamentalism as a source of stability. For example, during the Middle Ages, when the world seemed to hold fewer certainties, people sought solace in religious fundamentalism, where the rules were clearer (Bredero, 1986). Today, economic instability has also triggered a rise of religious fundamentalism among many groups, including Hindu, Muslim, Jewish, Christian, and Buddhist (Thurow, 1996).

The major lesson in this section is that economic forces are powerful factors in intercultural communication. What can you do to lessen the tension and the uncertainty that comes from changes in our economic condition?

• *Convince yourself that the world is changing and that you must change with it.* The world is complex and various but you can learn enough about change to adjust. Just think of when the Model T Ford was invented. Some people could not envision themselves without the horse and buggy; obviously, however, they soon adjusted. In his book, *Who Moved My Cheese?,* Johnson (2004) suggests that if we can't make changes as we need to, we will be left behind.

• *Adjust your attitude.* Develop a perspective that invites an intellectual knowledge of other participants in the new world economics and objectify the concept of change. Think of how, for instance, changes in technology, economics, trading, and other aspects of the global economy are affecting the lives of everyone. An objectification of your attitude should give you a fresh perspective on dealing with change.

• *Avoid blaming others.* Because the rules for interacting in the new world order are still being made, it is counterproductive to look for scapegoats. Use your energy to focus on yourself instead, and find new ways of coping.

• *Look for comfort zones.* In times of stress, it is essential to find outlets to help you release the stress. For example, you might join an exercise club, a book club, or do a few hours of volunteer work. One of the authors joined a spinning guild while in graduate school. For one night every two weeks, she took her spinning wheel and went to the home of another guild member and spun wool.

• *Demonstrate civil verbal and nonverbal behavior.* Chances are very good that competition over jobs, and the tension caused by a new economic game with new rules, will test our linguistic habits. Be especially tactful and appropriate in your language and behavior around people of different cultures. For example, one of the authors and her friend were en route to a wilderness area in Indiana when they came to a four-way stop. The author signaled that she was legally supposed to go first, but the other driver signaled his own desire to go first. Instead of turning this incident into an uncivil nonverbal competition, however, the author simply smiled, and motioned for the other driver to proceed, a gesture that was met with appreciation by the other driver.

• *Observe and record.* Moments of intense anxiety especially require that the facts fit the situation. If you can establish who, why, when, where, how, and with what effect something happened to you, chances are that your attitude will accord with the facts of the situation. For example, misunderstandings sometimes occur over matters such as affirmative action and equal opportunity.

USING ECONOMIC ARRANGEMENTS TO EXPLAIN INTERCULTURAL COMMUNICATION

Values and Lifestyle Patterns

"It feels great here. This is a friendly home," says the feng shui (pronounced fung shway) consultant William Spear, walking through the entrance of an apartment. "It's not a formal family when there are books in the hall. You're very open, and spreading." This conversation took place between Joanne Kaufman, a writer in New York, and her feng shui consultant. Feng shui, the 3000-year-old Asian art of the study of electromagnetic energy lines, is a popular lifestyle choice among wealthy Westerners ("Feng Shui Puts Your Furniture," 1996).

Lifestyle patterns help to explain what people value. These patterns are concerned with the role of economics and culture in influencing how we live. These days multicultural lifestyle choices related to how we spend our leisure time and the uses we make of our material existence can act as class markers. For example, because of changing lifestyle patterns, upscale, pricy, fashionable, fast-food establishments are thriving in cities such as New York and Dallas, promoting foods such as salmon with mango salsa, Thai noodles, and sushi.

To improve interpersonal relationships, then, it is necessary to accept diverse lifestyle preferences and manage differences in perception and expectations. For example, people who read *Gourmet* and *Yachting* magazines differ at some level from those who read *MAD* and *Glamour.*

Information and Decision Making

Today's global economic revolution also is influencing the way people manage information and make decisions. For example, until recently the flow of information in most Western European and North American companies was from the top down. This meant that chief executives, professional managers, field staff, and production workers were arranged in a pyramid-like form, and that each person was assigned tasks and held accountable for specific jobs. There was a clear separation of physical from mental work. Since the 1980s, however, there has been a trend toward teamwork with more workers participating in decision making, from production workers to distribution workers to problem solvers.

This new approach, called a *team-based model of work,* is rooted in the Japanese cultural conception that all workers should contribute to decision making. It is one of the many examples of changes in work styles that have been brought about by intercultural communication.

INTERCULTURAL COMMUNICATION IN THE BUSINESS CONTEXT

With this understanding of the relationship among economics, culture, and communication, we are now ready to move on to the intercultural business context. We will examine language, relationships, the use of evidence, and persuasive style as well as negotiation strategies.

Language

As you recall from Chapter 5, language plays an important role in intercultural communication. In the business context, our language differences can cause significant problems both economically and personally. U.S. Americans sometimes view persons who use an indirect style of communication as deceptive or untrustworthy; conversely, U.S. Americans are often perceived as rude or insensitive because of their direct style of communication. Engholm (1991) provides an interesting example. The Westerner asks the question, "Has my proposal been accepted?" If the proposal has not been accepted, the Asian business person, rather than saying a direct, "No," could reply in any of the following ways:

- *The conditional "Yes":* "If everything proceeds as planned, the proposal will be approved."
- *The counterquestion:* "Have you submitted a copy of your proposal to the Ministry of Electronics?"
- *The question is criticized:* "Your question is difficult to answer."
- *The question is refused:* "We cannot answer this question at this time."
- *The tangential reply:* "Will you be staying longer than you originally planned?"
- *The "yes, but . . ." reply:* "Yes, approval looks likely, but . . ." (The word "but" may mean "It might not be approved.")
- *The answer is delayed:* "You will know soon." (pp. 115–116)

But it is not just the language itself that can cause problems. A communicator's style can also be problematic. Engholm and Rowland (1996) suggest that the timing of speech utterances can cause difficulty:

Brazilians frequently have two people talking at once in a conversation, with almost no pauses. Americans sometimes have brief pauses between speakers and sometimes have a little overlay of speakers. If you are speaking with people from a culture that has many verbal overlays, such as the Brazilians, you may have to be more assertive if you want to participate in the conversation. . . . If you are speaking with people from a culture with more verbal pauses, you may have to learn to pause more often to make sure others get a chance to speak. When talking with a Japanese, it is typical for Americans to wait just long enough to become uncomfortable and then begin speaking again. The Japanese person, however, has remained silent to show respect for the speaker or the comment, and by the time he feels it is appropriate to say something, the American is already speaking again. The result is that we end up monopolizing conversations. (pp. 81–82)

Relationships

The pacing of the business transaction differs across cultures. This is due in part to the ways in which people from various cultures develop and maintain relationships. For example, in the initial stages of a negotiation, German business managers may ask numerous questions concerning technical details; Scandinavians tend to want to get right down to business; French emphasize laying out all the aspects of the potential deal; and Italian managers emphasize getting to know the individuals of the "opposing party" by socializing before getting down to business. In fact, several days may be required in this initial phase of negotiation if you are in Spain or Mexico, where relational concerns are extremely important.

In fact, interpersonal relationships may be a key factor in intercultural negotiations. In some countries, such as Columbia and other Latin American countries, as well as India, using interpersonal contacts to obtain jobs, supplies, contracts, and so on, are commonplace and considered appropriate. In addition, in countries such as China, the social hierarchy of relationships is extremely important.

Notice that we have referred to the "man with the key." In many cultures, women do not have the same status or position as men. When I attended the UGO Forum in China in the mid-1990s, I was amazed to discover just how many struggles women worldwide have. Equal rights for women is a Western idea and has a long way to go before the concept can be universal. It is not surprising, given the status of women in many cultures, that women are not in positions of power in the organization. In male-dominated societies, it may be difficult for a female to be the primary negotiator. Many cultures feel that you should not send a woman to do a man's job. Thus, in intercultural communication, gender becomes another important relational issue.

Evidence, Reasoning, and Persuasive Style

Reasoning plays an important part in business contexts. Yet, not every culture reasons in the same way (Toulmin, 1972). Cultures differ in what is considered acceptable evidence, reasonable, and persuasive styles (the preferred way to convince others).

European Americans prefer facts as evidence. The myriad detective stories on television suggest this emphasis on facts: the physical aspects of the crime scene, the accounts of people who saw the events, the scientific data from DNA. These facts lead investigators to not only the behavior of individuals involved in the crime, but also their motivation.

For some cultures, facts are not as acceptable. For Muslims, stories or parables, particularly from the Koran, are acceptable as well as powerful forms of evidence. The story is told and the lesson from the story is assumed conclusive. In cultures influenced by Confucianism, metaphors and analogies are used for evidence. In African cultures, testimony is not a powerful form of evidence as it is in the U.S. legal system. Some African cultures believe that the word of a witness should be disregarded because if the person speaks up about seeing something, she or he must have an agenda and is therefore not objective.

Another factor closely related to the idea of what evidence and claims are considered "good" is the idea of persuasive style—the way people prefer to arrange evidence, claims, and assumptions. Cultures differ in terms of what style they prefer: quasilogical, presentational, or analogical (Johnstone, 1989).

The *quasilogical* style is preferred by Westerners. Statistics, testimony from experts, and objective witnesses are used as evidence. This evidence is then connected to a conclusion. Usually words such as *therefore, as a result,* and *thus* are used to signal that the evidence is being connected to the conclusion. Westerners believe that if the idea is "true," it only needs to be presented in a logical way so that others can also see that it is "true." In short, the quasilogical style is based on the premise that the truth or falsity of a particular experience or idea can be discovered.

The *presentational* style takes quite a different approach. The speaker using this style appeals to and emphasizes the emotional aspect of persuasion. It is the people, not the idea, that makes an idea persuasive. In other words, how the idea is presented is what makes it persuasive. The speaker makes the idea real through the use of words related to our senses: words that force the listener to see, feel, and hear the idea, and, finally, to believe it.

The *analogic* style takes yet another approach. The speaker establishes the conclusion she or he want her or his audience to accept by using an analogy, a story, or a parable in which a lesson (explicit or implicit) is to be learned. Underlying this persuasive style is the idea that the collective experience of groups of people (culture) is what is persuasive. Again, as with the presentational style, it is not the idea that is persuasive in and of itself. Neither is the presentation of the speaker the persuasive factor. Rather, it is the discovery and narration of an appropriate story—one that captures the essence of what the speaker wants the audience to believe.

As you might guess, such differences in persuasive style can cause communication difficulties. For example, to Westerners, who prefer the quasilogical style, the presentational style will seem emotional and the analogical style will seem irrelevant. On the other hand, speakers using the presentational style will find those using the quasilogical dull and insignificant. To the analogical-style speaker, the quasilogical style seems unappealing and too direct.

QUESTIONS TO CONSIDER WHEN DOING BUSINESS INTERNATIONALLY

There are several concerns that must be addressed in an intercultural business environment. Some of these revolve around the cultural patterns we discussed earlier in this text. For example, Hofstede's dimensions of masculinity/femininity, individualism/collectivism, power distance, and uncertainty avoidance will affect how business is conducted in any culture. In a collectivist culture, relationships are extremely important. For example, a Chinese business person would want to get to know an American, build a relationship, and then conduct business. Remember that a collectivist culture such as the Chinese emphasizes the collective, not the individual. So to do business, you must become a part of the collective—at least to a degree. Americans doing business in China separate business and social activities. "Get the job done *and then* socialize." For the Chinese it is "Socialize *and* get the job done." In other words, for the Chinese the relationship must be built in order to do business.

Another concern is the way decisions are made. Whereas in the United States it might be a top management team, in Japan a middle-line team would decide through consensus. In other words, it is important to make sure that the person you are dealing with has the authority to make the decision.

How is time viewed? Are you negotiating with a culture that takes a relatively short time to make a decision, such as in the United States ("Time is of the essence") or a culture that views time as circular, such as in China ("If the decision is not made today, it can be made tomorrow")?

Language is important as well. Not only is the degree of formality important, but the methods of verbal persuasion are also important. Does the culture value open and direct communication? Does it value indirect, cooperative language? Or is it a culture that uses flattery and emotional language?

What is the world view? This is a term taken from the German word *Weltanschauung,* meaning a "look onto the world." Your world view is your comprehensive conception of the world, humanity, and life. It answers such questions as: What is the world like? How can we explain it? Where are we heading? What should we do? How should we attain our goals? What is true? What is false? Related to this world view is the cultural dimension of universalism/particularism (Trompenaars, 1994). In a universalistic culture, business decisions are based on a consistent application of rules (universals). In a particularistic culture, individuals adapt the rules based on the particular circumstances of the business transaction. Similarly, we might look at this same idea another way. Individualistic cultures tend to be universalistic while collectivist cultures tend to be particularistic (Gudykunst and Matsumoto, 1996). Thus, individualistic countries apply the same standards to all situations. Collectivist cultures apply different standards as the situation requires. Suppose you are an American business person negotiating a contract in China. You sign the contract. So does your Chinese counterpart. The problem is that the contract is not viewed the same in both cultures. You are from a universalistic/individualistic culture where a contract is binding for the time stated in the contract. The Chinese person is from a particularistic/collectivist culture. The contract is binding as long as the circumstances under which it was signed remain the same. Thus, if the Chinese person who signed the contract left the company, the Chinese would no longer consider the contract binding.

Elashmawi and Harris (2000) suggest that there are numerous concerns in business negotiations between Americans, Japanese, and Arabs. These concerns are not only time, relationships, world view, and language, but also how offers change from the first to the final offer, space orientation, number of negotiators involved, the group composition of the negotiators, risk-taking, and the information exchanged. In terms of the latter, whereas Americans prefer documented, step-by-step multimedia information exchange, Japanese prefer extensive concentration on the receiving side, and Arab business people prefer less emphasis on technology and more on relationship.

So, how might one approach the intercultural business context? In a sense, the approach is no different from other contexts. Kohls (2001) lists the following characteristics as most important to intercultural success:

Tolerance for ambiguity	Warmth in relationships
Low goal/task orientation	Motivation
Open-mindedness	Self-reliance
Nonjudgmental approach	Strong sense of self
Empathy	Tolerance for differences
Communicativeness	Perceptiveness
Flexibility; adaptability	Ability to fail
Curiosity	

On a scale of 1 (low) to 5 (high) rate yourself on each of these characteristics. Write the number next to each characteristic and add the numbers. If you scored less than 55, you need to work on these characteristics. Now, circle the traits you think are most important to successful intercultural encounters. According to Kohls, the three most important characteristics are a sense of humor, low goal/task orientation, and ability to fail. Have a sense of humor. Working in the international arena is challenging and frustrating. Being able to laugh at ourselves will help us deal with anger, anxiety, embarrassment, and discouragement.

Have an ability to fail. Ours is a success driven culture. Thus, an ability to fail is critical, because everyone fails at something when living and working in other cultures. We have perhaps been successful all our lives, but intercultural exchanges are failure ridden. What we did to be successful in our culture may be the very thing that keeps us from succeeding in another culture. Failure, when used as a learning experience, can make us effective intercultural communicators.

Finally, have a low goal/task orientation. We come from a culture of doing. Most of us have a long "to do" list each day. However, when living in another culture, the "to do" list has to be shortened. We simply can't accomplish as many goals or tasks when we are dealing with people from another culture. Language barriers, differing values, norms, and beliefs can slow down our progress. The solution is to set goals and tasks that can be accomplished in a time that is possible in that particular culture.

In addition to the above, we would list a few other suggestions:

- Be cognizant of the communication issues that arise such as those discussed above.
- Don't jump to conclusions but rather try to assume similarities. In those instances where common ground is not readily apparent, accept the other person's fundamental humaneness as a starting point for genuine communication.
- Be flexible. Few people find it easy to accept those they view as different, whether the differences are of creed, ways of thinking, or color. When old, musty views of the "other" are challenged, be willing to act on the basis of new, factual information.

CONCLUSION

In this chapter we have provided background information on the connection among communication, culture, and communication. Learning to interpret our perceptions of others correctly increasingly depends on our ability to understand those whose lives are being radically affected by economic changes. Based on that background, intercultural communication in the business context was discussed. We suggested some ways that we might adjust to our current economic situation as we confront a more diverse and changing workplace.

In the readings that follow, the authors further our understanding of this context. Hoel provides an overall introduction to doing business in another culture. Trujillo discusses the role of proverbs in negotiation.

FOR DISCUSSION

1. In what ways do economic factors influence your relationship with others?
2. What is the relationship between communication, culture, and economics?
3. What is your reaction to the team-based approach to doing business?
4. What language characteristic do you have that might be problematic in intercultural communication encounters? Why? What should you do to minimize the problems these characteristics might cause you?
5. What is your persuasive style? Have you ever communicated with someone whose style differed from yours? What happened? How did you adjust to the other person's style?

REFERENCES

A Disney dress code chafes in the land of haute couture. (1991, December 25). *New York Times,* p. 1.

Affirmative action, on the merit system. (1995, August 7). *New York Times,* p. A11.

A manifesto for immigration. (1996, February 29). *Wall Street Journal,* p. A14.

Brake, T., and Walker, D. (1995). *Doing business internationally.* Princeton, NJ: Princeton Training Press.

Bredero, A. (1986). *Christendom and Christianity in the middle ages.* Grand Rapids, MI: William B. Eerdmans.

Burke, J., and Ornstein, R. (1995). *The axemaker's gift: A double-edged history of human culture.* New York: G. P. Putnam's Sons.

Carr-Ruffino, N. (1996). *Managing diversity: People skills for a multicultural workplace.* Salt Lake City, UT: International Thomson Publishing.

Cheney, L., and Martin, J. (2000). *Intercultural business communication.* Upper Saddle River, NJ: Prentice-Hall.

Elashmawi, F., and Harris, P. (1998*). Multicultural management 2000: Essential cultural insights for global business success* (pp. 196, 198). Houston, TX: Gulf.

Engholm, C. (1991). *When business East meets business West: The guide to practice and protocol in the Pacific Rim.* New York: Wiley.

Engholm, C., and Rowland, D. (1996). *International excellence: Seven breakthrough strategies for personal and professional success.* New York: Kodansha International.

Feng shui puts your furniture and your life in order. (1996, January 18). *Wall Street Journal,* p. A12.

Ferraro, G. (2002). *The cultural dimension of international business.* Upper Saddle River, NJ: Prentice-Hall.

Furnham, A. (1992). Strangers adaptation. In W. Gudykunst and Y. Y. Kim (Eds.), *Readings on communicating with strangers: An approach to intercultural communication* (pp. 336–345). New York: McGraw-Hill.

Glenn, E. S. (1966). *Mind, culture, politics.* Mimeographed.

Gudykunst, W., and Matsumoto, Y. (1996). Cross-cultural variability of communication in personal relationships. In W. Gudykunst, S. Ting-Toomey, and T. Nishida (Eds.), *Communication in personal relationships across cultures.* Thousand Oaks, CA: Sage.

Hofstede, G. (1992). Cultural dimensions in management and planning. In W. Gudykunst and Y. Kim (Eds.), *Readings on communicating with strangers: An approach to intercultural communication* (pp. 89–109). New York: McGraw-Hill.

Johnson, S. (2004). *Who moved my cheese?* New York: G. P. Putnam.

Johnstone, B. (1989). Linguistic strategies for persuasive discourse. In S. Ting-Toomey and Felipe Korzenny (Eds.), *Language, communication, and culture: Current directions* (pp. 139–156). Newbury Park, CA: Sage.

Kennedy, P. (1993). *Preparing for the twenty-first century.* New York: Vintage Books.

Kim, Y. Y. (1994). Adapting to a new culture. In L. A. Samovar and R. Porter (Eds.), *Intercultural communication: A reader* (pp. 393–404). Belmont, CA: Wadsworth.

Kim, Y. Y., and Paulk, S. (1994). Interpersonal challenges and personal adjustments: A qualitative analysis of the experiences of American and Japanese coworkers. In R. Wiseman and R. Shuter (Eds.), *Communicating in multinational organizations* (pp. 117–140). Thousand Oaks, CA: Sage.

Mufwene, S. (1993). Forms of address: How their social functions may vary. In P. Devita and J. Armstrong (Eds.), *America as a foreign culture* (pp. 60–65). Belmont, CA: Wadsworth.

Ohmae, K. (1995). *The end of the nation state: The rise of regional economics.* New York: Free Press.

Pinxten, R. (1993). America for Americans. In P. Devita and J. Armstrong (Eds.), *America as a foreign culture* (pp. 93–102). Belmont, CA: Wadsworth.

Ponterotto, J., and Pedersen, P. (1993). *Preventing prejudice.* Thousand Oaks, CA: Sage.

Rifkin, J. (1995). *The end of work: The decline of the global labor force and the dawn of the post-market era.* New York: G. P. Putnam's Sons.

Sowell, T. (1983). *The economics and politics of race: An international perspective.* New York: William Morrow.

Sowell, T. (1994). *Race and culture: A world view.* New York: BasicBooks.

Stephan, W., and Stephan, C. (1992). Intergroup anxiety. In W. Gudykunst and Y. Kim (Eds.), *Readings on communicating with strangers: An approach to intercultural communication* (pp. 16–29). New York: McGraw-Hill.

Stewart, E. (1972). *American cultural patterns: A cross-cultural perspective.* Pittsburgh, PA: Intercultural Communications Network.

Taijfel, H., and Turner, J. (1992). The social identity theory of intergroup behavior. In W. Gudykunst and Y. Kim (Eds.), *Readings on communicating with strangers: An approach to communicating with strangers* (pp. 112–119). New York: McGraw-Hill.

Thurow, L. (1996). *The future of capitalism: How today's economic forces shape tomorrow's world.* New York: William Morrow.

Tilly, C. (1990). *Short hours, short shrift: Causes and consequences of part-time work.* Washington, DC: Economic Policy Institute.

Toffler, A. (1980). *The third wave.* New York: Bantam Books.

Toulmin, S. (1972). *Human understanding, volume I: The collective use and evolution of concepts.* Princeton, NJ: Princeton University Press.

Trompenaars, F. (1994). *Riding the waves of culture: Understanding diversity in global business.* Burr Ridge, IL: Irwin.

Xiao Mao and Nan-tzu. (1990). *The man with the key is not here.* Dallas, TX: Pacific Venture Text.

The Cultural Practice of Law or How to Successfully Do a Deal in a Foreign Jurisdiction

J. Richard Hoel, Jr.

Although I did not know it at the time, I was fortunate to have my first cultural misstep happen so soon after my arrival in Hong Kong. Two weeks into my assignment as regional counsel for a U.S. multinational company with Asian headquarters in Hong Kong, our personnel director thought it would be a good idea to have a Feng Shui practitioner survey our offices. Feng Shui is the ancient Chinese art of analyzing and, where possible, altering the interaction between people and their environment to maximize positive energy or "chi" and thereby improve their quality of life.

I was out of town when the practitioner surveyed all of the offices on our floor. I am told that all was going very well—with the practitioner making modest suggestions for the rearrangement of some furniture and the addition here or there of a mirror or possibly a fish tank—until he entered my office. The practitioner recoiled as he stared in shock at the layout of my furniture. The arrangement of my desk and credenza formed a triangular prison in which imaginary lines extending from two piers in the Hong Kong Harbor, visible through a window, converged to seal my fate.

"Is he well?" the practitioner had asked. "Has Mr. Hoel been ill, or is his business doing poorly?" He had rarely seen things so grave.

I returned that evening to the bad news: rearrange my furniture or pay the consequences. When I laughingly said I would take the risk, our personnel director warned me that I was not the only one affected. In deadly earnest, the practitioner had predicted that any office in our building with such bad chi could cause company profits in China, perhaps in all of Asia, to plummet. The health of those around me could suffer. Still, I stalled.

It was not long before I noticed that our Chinese employees were not spending much time in my office. Finally, my secretary, who now was dropping things quickly on my desk and darting out, stepped out of character and confronted me, albeit indirectly, by volunteering the assistance of people who would be more than happy to help move my furniture. A week later, I was stunned to hear that representatives of one of our largest customers in China refused to conduct contract discussions in my office. How did they know?

I relented, and the Feng Shui practitioner swiftly returned to chalk the locations where my furniture should be moved. With the help of several complex charts, he noted the optimum dates and times in the upcoming weeks for the move. When the time arrived, my secretary interrupted a meeting I was having with several visitors from the United States, whom I enlisted to help rearrange the office. As we dismantled my triangular cell, I tried to alleviate suspicions by explaining to my guests that this was a new approach to growing the bottom line.

This experience became more valuable to me over time as I gained a deeper appreciation for the Chinese culture. I realize now that, although my co-workers were polite, never expressing anger at my attitude, my indifference was a serious display of disrespect. Fortunately, the incident ended happily, and I learned a valuable lesson. If we lawyers are to bridge cultural divides meaningfully, we must do more than take a brief predeparture course in etiquette. If we are to deal effectively in a different country, we must regard our cultural education as a continuous process that often requires real attitudinal change. The payoff, however, can be immense.

COMMON TRUTHS

Those who have practiced law for any length of time in the international arena have encountered, and benefited from, a wealth of literature about the various cultures in which we conduct business. Without a doubt, when we prepare to do a deal in a foreign jurisdiction, we should learn as much as we can about the new culture. The world is not yet so small that significant differences do not exist between cultures; a socially graceful act in one country can still be an egregious faux pas in another. Sadly, the ugly American has not retired, as my Feng Shui story illustrates. Too often, Americans act as if the world were moving steadily in the direction of a global western culture and underestimate the value of striving to learn about and understand other cultures.

I once commented to a Japanese friend that I was astounded at how many American trappings I found among the Tokyo populace, such as Lee Jeans, Michael Jordan apparel, and western business suits. I asked him, "Is the rest of the world becoming more western? Is it only a matter of time until cultural barriers disappear and western norms predominate?" After all, I rarely saw Americans in traditional Japanese attire. My friend gently warned me not to fall into this trap. Becoming modern is not the same as becoming western, he said, stressing that external trappings belie the important and unique transformation that occurs when a culture modernizes.

I believe we can glean from our significant collective international experiences as lawyers certain common truths about dealing generally with cultural differences, certain principles and approaches that will serve us well when doing business in any culture. I have traveled to South America, Europe, and Africa, lived for three years in Asia, and made as many mistakes as I am entitled to in each, but as a result, I have learned what I believe are universal axioms that will help attorneys recognize the powerful tools at their disposal to help bridge cultural gaps and build lasting relationships that translate to successful deals. I offer the principles in this article to help lawyers in effectively addressing and taking advantage of factors that draw cultures together. A few may sound basic, even commonsensical, yet it is startling how many of us pay them no heed. In all of the successful international deals that I have seen, more often than not, the attorneys drew upon many of these principles.

PEOPLE CULTIVATING RELATIONSHIPS IS AN ART THAT PAYS DIVIDENDS

There are few international players who will not trumpet the importance of building and sustaining relationships. Not all, however, understand the significant complexity and work involved in this process. There is more to establishing and fostering successful and meaningful relationships with our foreign counterparts than getting to know one another. Below, I highlight the areas in which we all can benefit from more diligent effort and preparation. It is important to understand and study the various concepts that combine to make one culture different from another, as well as the qualities that appear to be universal, drawing people from different cultures naturally together: our own attitude toward others, differing perceptions of similar factors, unique cultural approaches toward authority and the use of time, listening behaviors, and gender. Each culture is a unique mosaic of myriad qualities. Those who strive to understand this notion will not only consummate successful transactions but also learn a great deal more about themselves in the process.

EMBRACING HUMILITY

Before I embark upon a trip or tackle a project in a foreign country, I find it useful to spend some time thinking about how much I do not know. That idea may sound strange, but I believe that humility is the most successful attitude to effect in another culture. I could easily jump to conclusions based upon my initial observations abroad, or at home for that matter, only to discover later that I simply had not understood the underlying cultural dynamics at play. In a new culture, my initial observations are almost certainly going to be wrong. And yet, successful international players do not embark upon a foreign challenge with a sense of fear or dread, but with a sense of wonder and adventure, born of humility.

When I first started practicing international law, an insightful attorney from Singapore, who is now a good friend, explained this attitude to me by drawing an analogy to "The Story of the Cave" told by Plato in *The Republic*. Plato used this myth to explain his theory of knowledge as the search for the pure forms of all people and things in our lives. The story describes a group of people who have lived chained within the recesses of a cave, bound together in a way that prevents them from seeing one another or the world outside. With their backs to the entryway, the cave dwellers see only a cave wall that displays shadows cast by figures passing before a fire as they move about outside.

Breaking free, one of the dwellers escapes into the daylight and sees the real world for the first time. He returns to the cave to tell the others that all they have experienced thus far are shadows, which they have mistakenly, although understandably, believed to be real. The real world awaits them if they are willing to struggle free of their bonds.

My Singaporean friend used this story as one of his tools to reach a deeper understanding with attorneys from different parts of the world. He was constantly enthused with the pure joy of learning about others, and his enthusiasm was infectious. Yet, he was humble, constantly asking questions about the way we lived, what we believed, and how we perceived the world. I watched in awe as my friend was able to gain the trust of everyone involved in our deal, not because of his grasp of the substantive aspects of the transac-

tion, but because of his sincere interest in the lives of those around him and his desire to learn. People naturally wanted to communicate with my friend.

In my view, the international lawyer's success flows from this humble approach. This perspective may generate decisions that seem counterintuitive to many lawyers, but they usually lead to a more successful intercultural experience. The time-honored position of always negotiating on home turf, for example, does not hold up when we recognize how much there is to learn about the other party's culture and the benefits of doing so. Today, writes a distinguished U.S. international law professor, "the effective global deal maker sees the negotiation as an opportunity to learn, and the best way to learn is to visit the other side's territory to conduct the negotiations."[1] The visit demonstrates commitment and often transforms the visitor into the driving force in structuring a deal. Within each culture, we meet people like my Singaporean friend who seem to embody a multicultural temperament. It is important that we seek these people out even as we strive to develop the characteristics of such a temperament in ourselves.

ANTICIPATING CULTURAL DIFFERENCES

All attorneys understand the need for thorough preparation. But preparation becomes more complex when we deal in a different culture. If we just read a book about the country we are about to enter on the flight over, we only scratch the surface.

When negotiating a transaction in a foreign country, we must learn as much as we can about the customs and negotiating styles of our counterparts. We also must learn as much as we can about the individuals with whom we will be dealing. What are their roles within their enterprise and their relationships to one another? Who has the authority to make decisions? If authority does not exist within the group with which we are dealing, where and with whom does it reside?

Frequently, a cultural interpreter, someone in the country whom we know and trust, is our best source of preparation. Much like a language interpreter, a person who knows both us and his or her own culture can prove invaluable in providing general cultural insights and in framing a clearer picture of the people with whom we deal. Such a person can be especially helpful during negotiations by deciphering what is really happening on the other side, thus giving us an opportunity to step outside of our cultural caves.

I met such a person in Vietnam while negotiating a contract with a local customer. A college student in Hanoi, whom we originally hired as a translator, this young man spoke excellent English and was exceptionally skilled at discerning intentions from the words and actions of our Vietnamese hosts. Interestingly, because of his excellent translation skills, he also helped our hosts and soon became an integral part of the negotiation process, playing a mediating role as we struggled with some of the more difficult issues. His insights into the internal debates occurring among our Vietnamese counterparts were particularly useful. During these tough negotiations, he often encouraged our team not to lose patience and not to display our growing frustration openly. I frankly did not have as much confidence in the process as he did, but his advice proved accurate. Our interpreter had correctly assessed a growing willingness on the part of our hosts to compromise.

UNDERSTANDING PERCEPTIONS OF THE UNITED STATES

And what about our culture? Rarely do we focus on our unique culture, but we should try to imagine how others will be looking at us. I find it tremendously useful to consult a book or other literature written for non-Americans that describes us and counsels readers on how to deal with us.[2]

Americans have been described as a collection of immigrants who are individualistic, hedonistic, and materialistic. We have been characterized as some of the world's toughest negotiators, yet easier to deal with than many because of our open, straightforward philosophy that we want to earn as much as we can as quickly as possible through hard work, opportunism, and, if necessary, raw power.[3] But each culture brings its own perspective to bear upon this American assessment, and as a result, different cultures highlight, and often exaggerate, different qualities. The Japanese, for example, tend to regard Americans as nationalistic, decisive, frequently rude, and self-indulgent, while the Germans view us as energetic, inventive, sophisticated, and intelligent.

How prepared are we to help others to understand us? Inasmuch as our effectiveness will increase as our understanding of our counterpart's culture does, it is only logical to conclude that our deal-effectiveness quotient will double if we facilitate the other side's understanding of our culture. We have a tremendous, largely untapped opportunity to educate our counterparts about the best we Americans have to offer.

I often identify for my foreign counterparts the qualities that I believe Americans possess, such as forthrightness, persistence, tolerance, and compassion, and think of ways to help them truly understand these attributes and their genesis in our country. I have found that simply describing these qualities is of little value in an intercultural setting. But as my Singaporean friend understood, storytelling is an excellent tool. The myths, folklore, legends, and proverbs of a culture, and the personal experiences that its people share with one another constitute the knowledge about that culture. Storytelling transmits culture.[4] To appreciate an American value, someone from a different culture needs first to visualize the notion and then to understand it in the context of an anecdote or story. I therefore am more likely to read Lincoln's Gettysburg Address on my flight over than a book on cultural manners.

We attorneys have the training and a particularly useful platform to help others understand the American character and thus facilitate a degree of mutual understanding that can encourage successful deals. People remember points better if they are conveyed in the form of stories, not charts. This notion seems to be a universal truth. Before we begin negotiating in a foreign country, we need to find stories, anecdotes, and other creative means by which to describe our culture, our companies, ourselves, and the legal system in which we operate.

APPRECIATING DIFFERENT VIEWS ON AUTHORITY

Members of different cultures have very different ways of perceiving and dealing with authority. At one end of the authority spectrum, Americans embody the single leader view of authority, exemplified in fact and lore by the rugged individualist who leads loyal troops into battle or stands alone bravely against overwhelming odds. From George Washington to Gary Cooper, the image endures. As a result, the personality of the leader is a very important factor with American business teams and often the focus of attention during negotiations. At the other end are the Japanese, who play down the importance of a leader and stress teamwork and building consensus. The real leader of a Japanese negotiating team is often not obvious. The Chinese, although governed autocratically, deal with authority in a manner similar to the Japanese; we should never be surprised to have our team of three met by a Chinese or Japanese delegation of twelve.[5]

The way in which a culture handles authority can significantly influence intercultural business interactions. For example, one consequence of the American style is that the leader often becomes the team in the eyes of Asian negotiators. I have seen numerous situations in which progress made over the course of several meetings evaporated when the American team showed up with a new leader, a commonplace occurrence in our fast-paced environment. To be successful, American attorneys must carefully prepare the other side for this eventuality.

One cultural study on attitudes regarding authority looked at how members of different societies regard inequality and deal with it on a regular basis.[6] Local IBM employees in more than 50 countries answered three questions designed to elicit (1) subordinates' fear of superiors; (2) subordinates' perception of the type of authority, autocratic or paternalistic, wielded by their superiors; and (3) subordinates' preference for an autocratic or paternalistic style of authority.

Interestingly, perception correlated very closely with preference. For example, in Malaysia, the country ranking highest (most autocratic) on the resulting Power Distance Index (PDI), citizens/employees perceived their leadership as very autocratic and preferred it that way. Members of such a highly autocratic culture would be likely to view someone in authority as distant and difficult to approach, expecting and preferring that the leader make important decisions alone. Austria ranked in the study as the least autocratic society. Accordingly, we would expect most Austrians to view authority figures with less deference and fear and prefer consultative decision-making processes. I find it very useful to know where a country ranks on the PDI scale before I embark on a project.[7]

DISCERNING TIME AND LISTENING APTITUDES

As a young attorney, I had the opportunity to participate in a complex litigation battle between two aggressive, privately owned companies. An initial dispute in one jurisdiction quickly escalated with a series of seizure and attachment actions commenced by each party against the assets of the other in various locations, including Europe, Canada, the Cayman Islands, the United States, and Singapore. After several months, I attended a meeting of our client's attorneys from Great Britain, Canada, Portugal, and Singapore. I often reflect upon the significant role that cultural differences played in our deliberations.

The British attorney chaired the meeting. He adhered to a very strict agenda, scheduling time for everything, including bathroom breaks. While exchanging pleasantries, most of us became aware that our Singaporean associate was not very comfortable with small talk. He was so reserved that we had difficulty knowing whether or not he understood the conversations. During the meeting, he often asked questions, rather than make statements, which only heightened our impression that he was not understanding. Conversely, the attorney from Lisbon was more talkative than any of us and not very impressed with the rigid meeting format. He often interrupted with ideas and proposals that were not on the agenda and did not appear to listen to others' comments. He also requested frequent breaks to call his office on unrelated matters. We had a terrible time making progress, and we were all on the same side!

I know now, but did not appreciate then, that I was witnessing classic examples of three different cultural approaches to the concept of time.[8] Linear-active people, exemplified by the British, Germans, Swiss, Swedes, and, to a lesser extent, Americans, think and work in a linear manner, attaching great importance to agendas, timetables, and deadlines. They see a logical progression to life. If they do A, they next do B, and C follows.

At the opposite end, multi-active people, such as the Portuguese, Italians, and other southern European and many Latin American cultures, are less concerned with timetables and punctuality than with flexibility and the ability to manage a number of things at once. If circumstances change, an Italian is apt not to see the sense in sticking to an agenda or keeping an appointment that may no longer have any real significance. Our meeting agenda made little sense to our Portuguese associate once he felt that it failed to address some of the real issues we faced. From his point of view, he would expect others to dispense willingly with such an agenda also.

The third group consists of the listeners, who come from reactive cultures in which members typically wait until the other side presents the facts or a position, then often pause before responding. In reactive cultures, such as Japan, China, Taiwan, Singapore, Korea, and Finland, we find the world's best listeners. They frequently respond with more questions to elicit additional facts and even then are reluctant to state a firm position, relying often upon the unspoken and on evolving consensus. People in these cultures are much more comfortable with silence than westerners, who frequently leap to fill a gap in conversation, often before a position has been thoroughly considered.

Is one culture right and another wrong? Was the Portuguese attorney rude to have interrupted or was the British attorney missing the boat by not being more flexible with his agenda? Did the Singaporean attorney have a particular strength to offer that others could not see because they concluded too abruptly that his silence and unwillingness to engage in small talk were signs of indifference, ignorance, or disrespect?

I was reminded of this meeting years later during a conversation with a Chinese friend about the different ways we view each other's culture. He confessed that Chinese often see Americans and Europeans as impatient, selfish, and opportunistic, with a singular focus upon individual needs and goals. I noted that Americans often view the Chinese as much too dependent on what others think (the face concept) and lacking in self-confidence. Some portion of each characterization is accurate because of our respective nation's history. The American frontier experience and the Industrial Revolution bred a country of self-reliant individuals. In China, famine and poverty naturally fostered a community need to rely on others, and Confucianism taught patience.

Our meeting of intelligent attorneys from all corners of the world could have led to some of the most creative solutions the world has to offer. Unfortunately, the things we did not understand about one another stood in the way; in the final analysis, little was accomplished. Had we been more aware of our cultural differences, I suspect that our initial judgmental reactions would have been different. We might not have seen the Portuguese attorney as necessarily rude for interrupting. The lawyer from Singapore was almost certainly not confused or disrespectful in choosing not to participate more vigorously. And our British leader was probably not protecting his lead role by insisting on sticking to an agenda. Had we focused upon our respective cultural strengths of discipline, flexibility, and patience, rather than on superficial conflicts, we could have achieved our potential. The recognition of cultural differences is the first step toward effective communication; in the international arena, compromise opens doors to creative opportunities to structure successful deals.

EVALUATING GENDER DIFFERENCES

There are several ways of looking at gender as a cultural issue. Each culture has at least some unique characteristics that reflect the roles of men and women in that society. It is common, for example, to find that most dentists in Belgium and most doctors in Russia are women. In Japan you need to look hard to find a female manager, while many managers in the Philippines and Thailand are women. In Pakistan, most typists are male.[9] Certainly, the role of women in Arab countries is far different from that in the West. In Japan and many other "masculine" cultures, parents reinforce stereotypical gender roles from birth.[10]

Despite these differences, some well-known gender-role characteristics are common to all cultures. Based in large measure upon biological development and reinforced to some extent in all societies by sex-role stereotypes, most cultures see men as more interested in roles outside of the home and associate such traits as assertiveness, toughness, and ambitiousness, with an emphasis upon material success, as masculine. Most cultures typically view women as home-oriented and more modest, tender, and concerned with the quality of life.

Although individual exceptions often shatter these role definitions, one prominent study has classified cultures based upon a predominance of masculine or feminine attributes.[11] In the most masculine countries, Japan, Austria, and Italy, both men and women express a strong preference for distinct masculine and feminine roles with each sex preferring its traditional behavioral model. But in the most feminine countries, Denmark, Sweden, Norway, and the Netherlands, no difference exists between the responses of men and women, both indicating a preference for a tender and nurturing value system, as well as a personal desire for a tender, nurturing role.

I find it very helpful to know where a country ranks on the masculine–feminine scale.[12] Countries seem to reflect predictable characteristics in business practices based upon their position on this scale. Masculine societies do tend toward heavy manufacturing industries, while feminine cultures lean toward service industries. Members of masculine cultures conduct business in a more aggressive style, viewing meetings as opportunities to express themselves and to sell ideas. In feminine cultures, meetings are opportunities for cooperative consensus building.

ESTABLISHING PERSONAL CONNECTIONS

Shortly before leaving Hong Kong, I asked a Chinese friend what she thought was the single biggest mistake that Americans make in conducting business in China. She said she was constantly surprised that Americans do not take an interest in Chinese culture or in the stories of Chinese people. She could not understand how anyone could do business with someone else before knowing that person, before establishing a relationship. Western SWAT teams, as she called them, paid little heed to personal connections. She thought, as a result, that deals that could have been completed with a little more patience were not and that some deals that had been consummated quickly did not survive.

Whenever we deal with people from different countries, we should bear in mind that two types of culture are at play: the vertical and the horizontal. As Americans, we are all members of the same vertical culture. But as lawyers, we have cultural kin in every country in the world, members of the horizontal culture of lawyers. Often, there is more common ground between two lawyers from different vertical cultures, than between a lawyer and a member of another profession in the same vertical culture.

We need to realize that, often with a purely domestic transaction, both sides know and understand equally the various ways to structure the deal. But when two different cultures are involved, synergistic forms of structuring a deal may occur by combining traditional approaches from each culture. If lawyers do not establish relationships and understandings that maximize the potential for creative alternatives, these new approaches often go undiscovered. All of the principles that I have described so far come to bear upon this process. I am convinced that many creative options never emerge because the lawyers have not established relationships that leverage the wealth of horizontal synergies. And yet, lawyers may be the only people in the deal-making group with the training and skills necessary to bridge difficult differences and find a creative solution.

Before moving to Hong Kong, I worked in Brazil to structure a joint venture with several Brazilian entities in order to bid on a government project. It was only after I had spent a great deal of time with my Brazilian counterparts negotiating the terms of the joint-venture agreement that we were able to see beyond the government's very rigid requirements for the venture structure. Repeated delays in the bid process actually gave me an opportunity to know my counterpart very well. After he had explained the history of his country's struggles with privatization in the context of an entrenched bureaucracy and I had described similar stories about deregulation in the United States, we discovered that we had had certain common experiences with the legislative process in our respective countries. Our talks led to a mutual decision to bring a government lawyer into the process to help us better understand our challenges. Ultimately, this step encouraged a fresh approach that resulted in liberalizing the bid requirements, a solution that may not have been possible if all of the attorneys involved had not been willing to think outside of the box.

THE DEAL: EVERY AGREEMENT HAS A CULTURE OF ITS OWN

Observing the principles discussed above will put lawyers in a position to do what they do best: structure, negotiate, and close a successful transaction that will last. Although much of our deal preparation must focus on the deal's specifics, we also need to learn as much as we can about similar deals in the foreign culture. What are the precedents for what we are doing, and how have others overcome some of the difficulties that we are encountering?

Creating Rules of the Deal

I once worked with a team negotiating an extremely complex deal with the commercial arm of a government ministry in China. We spent a week getting to know each other, wining and dining in the traditional way, but skirting the key issues. Despite our best efforts, we were stiff in negotiations, in part because of the size of each team: six members on our side and eight on the other. Rigid hierarchical reporting relationships among our counterparts also restricted the free flow of horizontal discussion.

Although these formidable barriers threatened to undermine the deal, we all had a strong desire to succeed, and we made slow progress. One day as we struggled with a particular structure that involved several interlocking relationships with various subsidiaries in and out of the country, several of us started to move coffee cups and glasses around the conference table. Eventually, everyone joined in, using cups, glasses, and cans to illustrate the complex arrangement. Suddenly, we realized that, with pencils, coffee cups, and Coca-Cola cans, we had diagrammed a deal that we all thought would work.

Before we knew it, a waitress started to pick up the cans and cups. As one, we rose in protest. We all stared at one another in a terror that quickly ripened into the first real group laughter of the week. Much work remained to be done, but our breakthrough was significant. We photographed the table from various angles and used the photos as a reminder of the week. When we finally signed the deal, we each got a coffee cup inscribed with the name of the transaction and a framed picture of the table.

This story may seem trivial, but it is an example of a phenomenon that typically will occur with any lengthy negotiation. If recognized, such breakthrough collaboration can be built upon and lead to much greater understanding. I do not, by the way, arm myself with pop bottles before all international negotiations. That was one deal, and the accidental approach fit well. But I do now start all new sessions by candidly discussing with my counterpart the agendas and items that we can agree upon, such as the daily starting time or the seating arrangements. I suggest we put together a working statement of deal rules, which are separate from more formal documents, such as letters of intent or other memoranda of understanding. The other attorney is often excited to explore this exercise because it sets the stage for deeper understanding. It also presents an excellent opportunity for developing significant cultural compromises based upon honest discussions about the cultural differences that tend to prevent successful negotiation. As noted earlier, agendas may not suit all cultures, and any discussion of process should not shy away from stylistic differences.

I know that the sooner I can establish links with the foreign parties, the sooner we will be able to view ourselves as one team rather than two or more, and the better the chances are that the deal will be based on a full and candid discussion of all issues. We lawyers can play a key role in defining the new team and its unique culture.

Forging Genuine Understanding

Often, true negotiation stops in international negotiations when the deal is struck. At this stage, I become concerned if the other side does not dedicate as much effort to drafting the agreement documents as it did to negotiating the business terms. Its indifference raises the likelihood for me that the party does not intend to adhere to the contract terms. If I did not respond to this indifference, I would squander a critical opportunity to strengthen the relationship between the parties and to expose issues that may derail the relationship in the future.

My company was one of the first to set up a representative office in Vietnam after the United States had lifted its trade embargo. Much to our welcome surprise, Vietnamese businesspeople had a tremendous pent-up desire to do business with the West, particularly the United States. Resentments from the war appeared to be gone. The Vietnamese seemed to be genuinely fascinated with Americans and their products and services. We were deluged with opportunities.

We negotiated deals quickly. In one case, my Vietnamese counterpart asked that I prepare the contract, which was not a surprising request in a developing country. Much of the Vietnamese corporate law had recently been enacted and was largely a cut-and-paste job, using a great deal of U.S. statutory language even though many of the provisions were clearly inapplicable to the new markets of Vietnam. In much the same vein, the Vietnamese lawyer with whom I was dealing suggested that we use my form contract and did not propose many changes. I certainly thought that the contract protected our side and would have been proud to walk away with a deal in this form. But what would its true value have been? I remembered an adage that a law school professor had repeated ad nauseam: "Never let 'I didn't understand' be the legitimate basis for a contractual dispute."

When this type of situation arises, contrary to my first instinct, I force everyone to sit down and truly negotiate the terms of the contract, so that we all understand to what we are agreeing. I find that when I do this, my contracts tend to pattern the deal more particularly and often take form in a completely different way from that originally planned. I am not always as pleased with the substantive aspects of the document as I was when my form was pristine, but I am satisfied that the contract reflects the deal and the understanding of the parties. Most important, the deal takes on a life that cannot easily be denied at a later date.

More and more, I believe that successful negotiation is not getting my way, but getting a complete meeting of the minds. This point was driven home one day after I had spent the better part of a year negotiating a breakthrough sales agreement with a state-owned enterprise in the People's Republic of China. We signed the agreement with much fanfare, and all seemed well until the buyer suddenly demanded a steep reduction in the price of our product. My product manager's counterpart told him that if the reduction were not forthcoming, the customer would simply deal with a more competitive supplier. He asked me the obvious question, "Can they do this?"

I had felt pretty good when I had explained to my management team the year before that the contract had no provision requiring a reduction in price under these or any other circumstances. Unfortunately, the customer just told my team that it didn't care what the contract said. "Why," the buyer had asked in sincere surprise, "would we look to a contract that was signed a year ago, when circumstances have now changed so significantly?" In many Asian cultures, the concept of contract does have a different meaning from that which we apply in the West; Asians view a contract as a statement of present intent rather than as a roadmap to govern future dealings between the parties.

We managed to deal with these problems and keep the relationship intact, but this experience forced me to think about what could have been done earlier in the process to avoid this situation. Obviously, sitting down and truly negotiating all phases of the contract would likely have flushed out the possibility that one of the parties might not honor the contract if the price went up, an uncomfortable eventuality to face perhaps, but much easier to address at the outset. Certainly, I could have learned more about the different attitude that my counterparts had toward contracts generally. My role as the lawyer is to probe such issues and, if need be, to let my people know that they should take little comfort in a deal that reads well for them, but that is not fully understood and less likely to be observed by the other side.

Defining Language and Terms

I have found that, when efforts are made to truly negotiate the terms of an agreement and parties undertake the process honestly with the intent to inform, we can draft unique contracts. In many instances, the definition section becomes the most critical component of the entire agreement. The lawyer's role in this process is much more than that of a scribe or a negotiator; lawyers on both sides become educators, as well.

During this process, I am always surprised by how much we take for granted and typically find that many terms familiar to us are understood by our counterparts in a completely different way. Whenever I start to assume that all of us must have the same understanding of a basic term, I recall my wife's experience when she was first teaching at the Chinese University in Hong Kong. As she does in the United States, she had hung a sign on her door that read: "Please make an appointment to see me." The first day, she was inundated with people knocking on her door to make an appointment. People who were not taking her class and had no reason to see her took this message as a directive, not as a scheduling mechanism for those who otherwise wanted to see Pam.

But Americans also stumble over language. One of the most common mistakes committed by westerners in Asia is their failure to appreciate the tendency by Asian people to avoid directly saying "no" to anything. In part, they do not wish to offend, but they also have a cultural preference for avoiding direct confrontation. More likely than not, when an Asian negotiator says "maybe," "I will think about it," and "possibly," he is strongly hinting that a deal is headed in the wrong direction.

We must use all of the tools at our disposal to elicit a clear understanding of the real meaning of language and terms. We can never spend too much time on definitions. But defining our western terms is only half the story. I know the process is in full bloom when my counterparts are also adding to the definitional mix, helping me to understand the importance of their legal terms and definitions. Particularly in emerging markets, this process can mean the difference between a contract that lasts and one that is quickly ignored when crisis occurs. Some of my most successful contracts contain definition sections that are longer than the rest of the agreement.

Fashioning a Creative, Flexible Contract

Negotiating and drafting a contract is a much more exciting process when we view it as an opportunity to learn, teach, and build understanding. We must be creative. We should not be wedded to the forms that have come to be accepted in our country or any other for that matter. We should incorporate into our contracts the cultural bridges that we have built during our negotiations. Legal language is often unduly complex in our country; our legal jargon has to confuse lawyers

from different cultures. To express the true bond that we have established with our foreign counterparts, we should create our own language. The contract should be a living embodiment of our business achievement, not some neutral, detached recitation of one lawyer's view of the deal.

I have a particularly effective approach for doing this in Asian countries, where relationships are so important. I learned that I could avoid or at least lessen the chances of a later circumstances-have-changed argument by addressing the relationship issue head-on in the contract. We hear repeatedly from many of our Asian partners that the contract itself is only words and that the true success of the deal will depend upon the strength of the bonds that the parties have formed and will cultivate this notion. This notion is undoubtedly true and a point that we in the West should focus upon more frequently. But there is validity to our point of view, as well; a written contract can and should be the basis of our dealings now and into the future. Not only do we expect the contract to be honored, but also we expect both parties to value it and to work within its guidelines.

The solution, I find, is to reflect in the agreement the parties' desire to cultivate the relationship continually and to rely upon that relationship to address problems before turning to mediation, arbitration, litigation, or another mechanism for dispute resolution. I use a relationship management clause in those cultures that stress the overriding importance of relationship. (A sample relationship management clause is provided at the end of this reading.) It is a useful vehicle to head off disputes before they reach a serious level. We can always customize a contract so that it is truly meaningful to both parties. It is much more difficult to deny the applicability of an agreement when it is, in part, a creation and reflection of our own values and efforts.

CONCLUSION

In order to glean similarities between cultures and establish platforms that will lead to creative, cooperative deal-making, we first have to recognize and understand core differences that have not disappeared as the world has become smaller. There are no shortcuts to this process. Although it is important to learn the proper way to shake hands or to exchange business cards in another country, we initially need to activate our intellectual curiosity and be willing to engage in the hard work of understanding the key cultural characteristics of our counterparts and ourselves.

When I consider the effort involved and the payoff, I can't help but think of my friend from Singapore and others like him. The one characteristic more than any other that makes these people so successful in this intercultural endeavor is their genuineness. Those who take a real interest in another's culture are those who take an equally genuine interest in their own and cultivate creative ways of teaching others about themselves. Lawyers who seriously engage in this dialogue establish an environment in which the very best qualities of each culture can be identified and blended to maximize the chances of long-term success.

We all have experienced deal failures. I see too many transactions in the international arena break down because of a fundamental misunderstanding that never surfaced during the negotiation either because the lawyers had failed to recognize it or because they had thought at the time that it would be easier to accept certain ambiguities in order to get a deal signed. Thankfully, we have also been involved in deals that survive crisis, often repeatedly. In these deals, the lawyers build a strong and lasting relationship and play an important role in structuring a culturally meaningful agreement. They also have more fun. Once I have successfully completed a deal, my relationships with the people with whom I have worked abroad are just beginning. My effectiveness grows as I cultivate those relationships from the United States and reinforce what I have learned by passing my experiences on to others at home. In turn, people provide me their rich experiences, enabling me to reload my arsenal with stories and strategies for the next deal.

SAMPLE RELATIONSHIP MANAGEMENT CLAUSE

1. Relationship Management

The parties agree that the maintenance of a trusting and candid relationship is vital to the success of the Agreement. Accordingly, both parties will exercise their best efforts to identify and resolve any disputes before it becomes necessary to resort to arbitration, litigation, or any other form of alternative dispute resolution described later in this agreement.

With this goal in mind, the parties agree as follows:

Each Party shall appoint a relationship manager ("Manager") who shall be an individual who has been involved in and understands the history of the negotiations leading to this Agreement. Additionally, both Managers shall be familiar with all of the terms of this Agreement and Exhibit and shall be responsible for reviewing the same on a regular basis. To the extent that either Manager at any time feels that a portion of the Agreement is not clear and requires clarifica-

tion, he will seek advice from that Party's appropriate representative.

Party A appoints _____ as its Manager, and Party B appoints _____ as its Manager.

The Managers will meet on a regular and frequent basis but no less than once every two weeks. The purpose of these meetings will be to discuss and identify any potential sources of misunderstanding that may have arisen with respect to the Agreement and the relationship between the Parties. Following such meetings, each Manager will report back to the Parties' respective Management on the status of the Agreement.

In the event that any problems are identified, the Managers will discuss those problems with their respective management and attempt to resolve any issues together. At such time as both Managers agree that a problem has not been resolved and may lead to a dispute, the Managers will advise their respective managements and arrange a meeting between appropriate representatives of each Party for the purpose of resolving the issue.

Once the problem has been resolved, the Managers will prepare a joint written report and submit the report to their Management with a clear explanation of the problem, as well as the resolution.

2. Alternative Dispute Resolution

The Parties shall attempt to resolve all disputes relating to the Agreement as described in Section 1 and through good faith negotiations. If the Parties are unable to resolve such disputes through negotiations within thirty (30) days, they shall submit the dispute to a mutually acceptable professional mediator who shall assist the Parties to reach an acceptable solution to their dispute. Should the Parties be unable to resolve their dispute through mediation, then the Parties shall submit their dispute to arbitration as set out below.

3. Arbitration

All disputes that cannot be resolved as stated above shall be submitted to arbitration before _____ _____ (example: the International Chamber of Commerce in Paris, France) for resolution according to its rules then in effect. The arbitration shall be in _____ _____ (English). The award shall be final and binding upon the Parties, and any judgment consistent therewith may be entered in any court having jurisdiction over the Parties.

NOTES

1. Jeswald W. Salacuse, *Making global deals,* p. 17 (1991).
2. See, e.g., Richard D. Lewis, *When cultures collide,* pp. 165–71 (1996).
3. Id. at p. 167.
4. For basic reference, see, e.g., Rives Collins & Pamela J. Cooper, *The power of story* (2000); Audrey Fisher, *Human communication as narration: Toward a philosophy of reason, value and action* (1989).
5. See Salacuse, supra note 1, at pp. 68–69.
6. See Geert H. Hofstede, *Cultures and organizations,* pp. 23–48 (1997).
7. See id. at p. 26. The five highest-ranking countries were Malaysia, Guatemala, Panama, the Philippines, and Mexico. The five least autocratic cultures were Austria, Israel, Denmark, New Zealand, and Ireland. Other country rankings, with the lower number indicating a more autocratic culture, include India (10), South Korea (27), Spain (31), Japan (33), Italy (34), United States (38), Germany (42), Britain (43), and Sweden (48). Note that some of these rankings do not readily correlate with the country's traditional views of leadership. The United States has a relatively low PDI, for example, in light of our focus upon the individual and a single-leader structure. But this situation makes sense when we consider that, despite the American desire for strong leaders and hierarchy, our culture does not evidence a great distance between leader and follower nor are we afraid to confront our bosses.
8. See Lewis, supra note 2, at pp. 52–64.
9. See Hofstede, supra note 5, at pp. 80–81.
10. See Norine Dresser, *Multicultural manners,* pp. 125–26 (1996). In Japan, it is not uncommon for parents to pack sweets in their little boys' school lunches while girls receive none. Parents have higher expectations for boys and treat them accordingly. Id. at p. 125.
11. See Hofstede, supra note 5, at pp. 79–108.
12. See id. at p. 84. Some sample country rankings, with lower numbers indicating masculinity, include Japan (1), Italy (4), Mexico (6), Germany (9), United States (15), India (20), Brazil (27), Israel (29), France (35), Spain (36), Thailand (44), and Finland (47).

CHECK YOUR UNDERSTANDING

1. Although Hoel works in the international law arena, what lessons does his experience have for all of us?

2. According to Hoel, why must we be aware of gender differences as these relate to cultural differences?

"Even the White Ants Confer Before They Scatter": The Use of the Proverb in West African Peacemaking Traditions

Mary Adams Trujillo

Although conflict is as old as time, recent identity-based disputes around the globe seem to require new strategies for resolving these disputes. Yet, most conflict theory suggests that conflicts that involve identity, values, and high-stakes distribution are intractable. Perhaps the truth is not that the issues are irresolvable, but rather that the problem solving method is inadequate. . . .

Western approaches generally promote and esteem independence, individual rights and power, and linear resolution processes. Despite their presumed universal appeal, these values are, in fact, representative of a particular tradition, history, and worldview. It stands to reason that since conflict is an ancient and diverse phenomenon, there should exist a wealth of conflict resolution and peacemaking traditions from which to develop theory and practice. If, as Ross (1993) suggests, causes and modes of expression are culturally informed, then there should also be specific cultural contexts available for the resolution of identity-based or intercultural conflicts. Blake (1998) suggests that examining cultural warrants—religious beliefs, practices and documents; historical kinship structures and inter-ethnic relations; and customs, laws and traditions—will show measurable processes for peacemaking. This [reading] will examine the proverb as a cultural warrant of West Africa, a region with rich and deeply embedded traditions (Khapoya, 1994), with an eye toward generating an alternative paradigm for conflict resolution and theory. . . .

Conflict occupies a central role in the community's experience by virtue of its sociopolitical, economic, and racial minority status, as well as differences in worldview and communication styles. . . .

In looking at West Africa, we may test DuBois' hypothesis that "He (the African American) knows that Negro blood has a message for the world." An African conceptual framework posits "peace" as a process of building interconnected relationships that transform individual identity into community. In contrast, the predominant U.S. negotiation model constructs conflict resolution as a competitive transaction, with both parties being told that they can "win." In the language of dispute resolution, individuals are referred to as "positions," "interests," or "parties." Negotiators are taught to "separate the parties from the positions" (Fisher, Ury, & Patton, 1991) and encouraged, as third party interveners, to maintain "neutrality."

Donohue (1988) constructs peace as a reflection of relational conditions along dimensions of affiliation and interdependence. Relational order theory asserts that individuals (negotiators) are engaged in a continuous and tacit process in which relational limits are negotiated in order to develop constraining parameters. His emphasis on relationship in negotiating contexts bears some resemblance to the traditional African way of peacemaking. A traditional or pre-colonial African worldview is characterized by collectivism of such intensity that it is more accurately termed an extended kinship or communocentric system (Mbiti, cited in Opoku, 1997). Ross contends that a given society will resolve its disputes within its particular cultural traditions—its collection of norms, practices, and institutions. As an example, Ross (1993) recalls scholarly work with the Mbuti people of Zaire's rain forest. The Mbuti are hunters and gatherers who have no formal leaders. Cooperation is critical and all members of the community share the meat from a successful hunt. When individuals get into disputes, even though tempers may flare, the dispute is resolved through community discussion and ends with a solution acceptable to all members of the community. These issues are generally resolved with little reference to the alleged rights or wrongs of the case but mainly with the goal of restoring peace to the entire community. The Mbuti ritualize acceptance of collective physical and spiritual responsibility for babies born into the community, affirmation of the connection between the natural world and the ancestors, and the bonds between each other. On Donahue's axes, the Mbuti would be characterized as having and promoting high interdependence and high affiliation. All of the group's rituals and interactions serve to underscore relations between individuals for the purpose of preserving community.

Western approaches to conflict resolution presume that conflict occurs, in part, due to competition for resources. Socioeconomic complexity, in particular, increases competition and therefore conflict. It should be noted, however, that values around competitiveness are culturally informed. In the context of the Mbuti, for example, competition and aggression are not acceptable motives for intragroup behavior. In the Mbuti's dealings with nearby Bantu villagers, for example, Ross (1993) reports that the Mbuti seek to maintain autonomy, even though both groups are mutually dependent on each other for goods and services. In this relational condition, both groups still share values of cooperation, respect for life, and nonviolence. In this respect, the Mbuti are not atypical of African ethnic groups. Paradoxically, Africa has also been the site of extreme intranational and identity-based conflicts, such as those recently witnessed in Rwanda. Blake (1998) observes that the effectiveness of the process that he terms "peace communication" in Africa is marred by nonessential factors. Without question, the impact of the colonial experience profoundly and irretrievably altered social, political, and economic relationships between the peoples of Africa. These effects are well documented throughout the literatures of various disciplines and do not require reiteration here. The scholar who wishes to construct a model of peacemaking from cultural traditions, however, must recognize that the colonial past essentially makes impossible the teasing out of "pure" tradition. The nature of culture is such that while some "traditions" were erased by colonialism, other "traditions" were formed by the interaction of the dominant and subdominant groups. Similarly, African ontology asserts that time is continuous and flowing, as opposed to linear (Myers, 1993). Past, present, and future can never be fully demarcated; pre- and post-colonial "traditions" influence, reinforce, and reproduce each other.

Relative to conflict resolution practices, a review of the cultural warrants suggests that a traditional African dispute resolution model does exist and can be summarized as follows:

1. *The entire community is involved in the process of dispute resolution.* There is often some form of council or consensus, where members of the community can express their concerns and offer their opinions.

2. *All individuals, including the disputants, are situated within the context of a larger community.* This larger community consists of the natural world, the spirit world, and the familial unit, past, present, and future. Ancestors are living beings who have passed beyond the physical dimension of earthly life but who maintain contact and influence with those living in the earthly realm.

3. *Interpersonal relationships are primary because the individual exists in relation to others.* Human beings are seen as part of a spiritual web that connects them to the natural world, to God and other spiritual forces, and to other human beings living, passed on, and yet to come. Further, since "community" encompasses such a large network, a conflict between individuals is said to "stain the soil," affecting crops and incurring the disapproval of the ancestors.

4. *Mutual cooperation is the norm.* Conflict represents a break in the relationship of the community. The focus remains on interdependence and synergistic collectivism—a value that allows community members to achieve objectives greater than through any one individual.

This model can be further delineated into seven principles specific to West Africa. However, before examining these specific principles, we must first understand the context for the cultural warrants which explicate the principles. We turn now to the nature and use of the proverb in West Africa.

THE PROVERB IN WEST AFRICA

In the West, we construct emotion, thought, and spirit as separate and distinct processes. Throughout traditional Africa, however, cognition is integrated with all other aspects of being. "Cognition" includes thinking, feeling, faith, imagination, consciousness, wisdom, and experience and aims at a holistic form of impression and expression. The proverb is used to convey areas of cognition in a manner that requires listening, analyzing, interpreting, and applying the information. Proverbs are indirect and figurative speech acts, which instruct, correct, inform, inquire, give advice, encourage, warn, and at the same time entertain. One is not considered intelligent without these competencies. A Yoruba proverb asserts, "Half a word will do for an intelligent boy" (Pachocinski, 1996). Proverbs adorn and beautify language (Mbiti, 1991). Nigerian novelist Chinua Achebe describes proverbs as "the palm oil with which the yam is eaten." These examples illustrate how structure and purpose inform each other.

Proverbs operate on multiple levels and may have multiple applications of meaning. An Akan proverb explains, "The proverb does not stay in one place, it flies." Rhetorically, the proverb encapsulates beliefs, practices, and norms (Yankah, 1985). Conceptually, the proverb is a statement of cultural "truth," expressing the collective wisdom of previous generations and providing a common reference point. Contextually, the proverb is the expression of opinion of the speaker; the speaker of the proverb is not neutral. The proverb operates simultaneously as performance and as the means by which to enjoin previous generations to contemporary hearers.

As the physical embodiment of this enjoining, elders are presumed to have acquired wisdom through their lifetimes. Elders typically serve as repositories of history, stories, folklore and the wisdom stored in proverbs. They have the responsibility for passing on all that is important: the need for mutual cooperation; life and death; how to maintain relationships with spouses, children, neighbors, and extended kin; discerning the nature and will of God; and individual character. Their interpretation is considered the correct one. An Oye elder said, "The words of elders not followed in the morning will surely come to pass before the evening tide" (Pachocinski, 1996). Some proverbs have been passed down through the ages, others represent a spontaneous creation. Generally proverbs are introduced by phrases like "the elders say," or "as the old people have said." The cultural belief is that by virtue of their longevity, elders must be treated with absolute respect. In contrast, as a society, Westerners tend to believe that wisdom is democratic and respect is to be earned.

When elders mediate disputes, which is their role, they may speak in proverbs in order to give the disputing parties "the water of patience to drink." Their words are "words of wisdom, and the intelligent [one] bears it and becomes wise" (Pachocinski, 1996). Proverbs are considered better than ordinary speech because they are instrumental in helping speakers to emphasize their communication prowess. In her study of quoting behavior among the Igbo of Nigeria, Joyce Penfield (1983) identifies five functional properties of quoting behavior in conflict resolution.

The first functional property is *depersonalization.* In this instance the message is indirect, and the speaker is not the originator of the message. This strategy permits the speaker/mediator to address a sensitive topic indirectly or obliquely without threatening the recipient's face. This lessens the possibility of overt conflict between the disputants. A second function of quoting behavior is *foregrounding*. Here the proverb is simultaneously part of the interactional discourse but because of the oblique, formal and metaphorical qualities of language, the proverb is also set apart from the rest of the discourse. This separation catches the attention of the listener and forces the listener to think differently about what has been said.

The third function of the use of proverbs in conflict situations is to bestow *authoritativeness*. Credibility is given to the statement, and by extension to the speaker, because the proverb is identified with some recognized authority or with community acceptance of the ideas. The example is given of a young married female student (A) who often studies with her male colleagues. A female friend (B) says to her, "Remove the hand of the monkey from your stew or it might be taken as a human hand." The interactional meaning is that people might assume that (A) is having an extramarital affair. In a communocentric environment, one would care what people might think. By inference the human hand and the monkey's hand might be similar enough in appearance to be mistaken for each other. In this case, it is assumed that the friend's role involves protection for potential censure by identifying the offending behavior.

A fourth functional property of quoting behavior is to reference societal norms and values. In this way, the speaker persuades by referring to *values* which are highly esteemed in the community. For example, one proverb asks "He who eats others' things, when will others eat his own?" In a communocentric society where sharing and reciprocity are expected, if one is a partaker of the hospitality and generosity of others, one is expected to return the favor. A Western example of this principle might be, "One good turn deserves another."

A fifth property of quoting behavior is to increase the *prestige* of the speaker. Proficiency in quoting behavior brings a certain amount of respect and admiration to the speaker. Skillful talkers can use their tongues to avoid conflict, smooth over conflict, or redirect conflict. Africa's oral tradition is both reflected in, and a reflection of, the collective appreciation of rhetorical skills that are highly valued for entertainment as well as utility. Although his purpose was not to increase his personal prestige, the example of Dr. Martin Luther King illustrates this property. King's espousal of the cause of peace and justice was greatly enhanced by his eloquence as an orator. Similarly, the speaker who knows and can use proverbs well is highly regarded.

THE PROVERB DOES NOT STAY IN ONE PLACE

Consistent with the traditional African model of peacemaking presented previously, there are seven general principles for resolving conflict that can be distilled from the proverbs. The primary principle is that God, articulated either as God or as some other ultimate creative force, is the source of all relationships and has established justice and order for those relationships. For example, "It is God who settles the case of the man who shares a piece of meat between two people with His teeth" (Idoma). More colorfully, the Akan people of Ghana declare, "If you cheat the crab, God sees your buttocks." The meaning of this proverb is literally, when bending over to interact with the crab, or metaphorically, to act in an immoral or unethical manner, one exposes his or her vulnerability, and is subject to Divine justice (Yankah, 1985). . . .

A second principle governing conflict resolution is that human beings have intrinsic worth. By extension, if one respects the Creator, one must respect (His) creations. Among the Ewe, one might hear, "Even if the mosquito has not got much to boast of, it has a voice for humming songs." However, it is only through being in community that the individual can be fully realized. For example, the Yoruba assert, "I am, because we are," or similarly, "A single hand cannot cover the sky." . . .

Third, mutual cooperation is essential. Members of a community, like the parts of the body, are spiritually and physically interdependent. This relationship is expressed rhetorically through proverbial metaphors that connect the part to a larger whole. From the Akan, "If one tree alone faces a windstorm, it breaks." Several additional proverbs also reflect the principle of mutual cooperation including: "It takes one person to kill the elephant, but the whole community consumes its meat," "The left hand washes the right and right hand washes the left," and "You can't snap your fingers without your thumb." Not only is interdependence and connection the expectation, but failure to abide by these norms brings disharmony to the individual and the community as well. For example, as the Akan assert, "If one person alone eats all the honey, it bloats the stomach."

A fourth principle concerns the inevitability of conflict, especially when interests are divergent. The Hausa say, "Two pieces of meat confuse the mind of the fly." The avoidable emergence of conflict is seen as akin to the natural order of things. This can be seen in proverb: "We are mice of the same hole, if we don't meet going in, we meet coming out." Thus, parties in conflict are obligated to resolve what causes disunity. Among the Igbo people, one might hear, "Two calabashes on the same water are bound to touch each other."

A fifth principle establishes reconciliation as the desired outcome of conflict. Forgiveness is necessary, even though abusive words do damage and are not easily forgotten. For example, when the Akan say, "Some of the blood on the tongue is spewed out, the rest is swallowed," they acknowledge literally and metaphorically that conflict may be painful, because one may have to "bite one's tongue." Reconciliation requires a willingness to place one's immediate concerns beneath the greater good of the community. The Igbo say, "Hawk and Eagle perched on a tree. If the hawk does not allow the eagle to perch, his wing should break off." What one says is as important as what one does, as words have the power to build, as well as to destroy. Therefore, the effect of words spoken in anger, even though they may be ultimately forgiven, are never really erased. In other words, "Water may cover the footprint on the ground, but it does not cover the words of the mouth" (Ewe). In addition to recognizing the inherent power of words, these proverbs speak to the necessity of "thinking before speaking."

A sixth principle delineates the process of situational analysis which should be done before arriving at a conclusion. In other words, consider the issue and the possible outcomes from the perspectives of all concerned. "Wisdom is not in the head of only one person" (Akan). It also indicates the value of focusing on solving specific (smaller) parts of the conflict instead of trying to solve the entire conflict at once. This is represented in an Akan proverb which reminds us, "A whole animal is not smoked on the fire." Further, the Mbuti assert, "A calabash breaks by the pulling of two people." If the desired goal is reconciliation and cooperation, then parties must work together. In contrast, if two parties in conflict do not cooperate, then their "pulling" breaks apart the calabash, causing it to be unusable for anyone.

A seventh principle affirms that resolution is in the best interest of everyone. "You don't know where you are going, you only know where you have been" (Makongo). Life is such that one does not know what the future will require. A Western equivalent might be, "Don't burn your bridges behind you." The Yoruba say, "Ashes always fly back in the face of him that throws them." Finally, as encouragement, the Igbo say, "Even the white ants confer before they scatter," meaning that humans can learn lessons from

the natural world about the importance of seeking consensus and being of one mind. In closing, we turn to a specific peacemaking context to examine how the proverb can be incorporated into intergroup conflict resolution.

PEACEMAKING IN THE IGBO TRADITION

In the Igbo language, the words *idozi okwu* describe both peacemaking and mediation. The folk definition of this process is "putting things in order" or "settling a dispute." *Idozi okwu* is likely to involve the use of an advisor to help the conflicting parties work through several stages of conflict development. Penfield (1983) has identified four stages of conflict and notes that there are proverbs appropriate for each stage. In the initial phase, for example, the advisor's goal is to contain the conflict. She or he is likely to use language that warns the individual of the consequences of his/her behavior. If the conflict escalates, the advisor/mediator's language is geared toward reducing insult, intimidation, or provocative language. If *idozi okwu* fails, the parties might ultimately end up going to court or using some other formal means of dispute resolution.

In contrast to Western negotiating, the mediator/advisor does not claim to be neutral, but is chosen because he or she (usually he) has a reputation for fairness and wisdom. Potential mediators might include the male heads—fathers of the husband or wife, husbands, government heads, teachers, chiefs. Women might be mediators when they are elderly or when the disputants are women or children. The mediator/advisor's role is to encourage a compromise solution and get the parties back to a place of mutual respect and harmony. The mediator may also observe as an arbitrator, determining guilt and establishing restitution. In each of the escalating stages, the mediator becomes more of an arbitrator, with success ultimately depending on the parties' willingness to accept the mediator's judgment. There is, however, a great social pressure to seek peace. Individuals who make public their nursing of grudges, or who attempt to slander the reputation of another, face social ostracism. The process of having one's reputation destroyed in a communocentric culture is devastating.

The inherent danger in looking at the proverb as a cultural warrant and as a peacemaking tool is that of oversimplifying of the process of conflict and its resolution. The unfortunate reality in the twenty-first century is that there are no simple solutions. However, just as there are African traditions in peacemaking, one can assume that other indigenous or local cultures have similar principles that govern the practice of making peace. In intercultural conflicts, examining traditional peacemaking structures may provide relatively easy access to peaceful solutions. For mediators and human rights workers, reconceptualizing conflict cross culturally (Ting-Toomey, 1997), as well as over time, offers a tremendous opportunity to work with parties in conflict in ways that are contextually respectful and relevant. Future research directions are many. Relative to African Americans, a direction for future research is to examine how these traditions survived the Atlantic crossing and the institution of slavery. What evidence is there of these beliefs and practices in contemporary African American communication (Ribeau, Baldwin, & Hecht, 1997)? How might these traditions impact the practice of resolving interracial *and* intraracial conflict? For other ethnic groups, in the United States and elsewhere, how does assimilation affect the maintenance of peacemaking traditions? In short, human rights workers and intergroup relations practitioners could benefit from understanding cultural traditions in peacemaking. As asserted in this [reading], they might specifically explore the extent to which the conflict resolution strategies of traditional West Africa can serve to bring a "message to the world."

REFERENCES

Blake, C. (1998). The role of peace communication in conflict resolution in Africa. *Journal of Black Studies, 28,* 309–319.

Donohue, W. (1988). Managing equivocally and relational paradox in the Oslo peace negotiations. *Journal of Language and Social Psychology, 17,* 72–96.

Du Bois, W. E. B. (1982). *The souls of Black folks.* New York: Signet. (Original work published in 1903).

Fisher, R., Ury, W., and Patton, B. (1991). *Getting to yes: Negotiating Agreement without giving in.* New York: Penguin.

Khapoya, V. (1994). *The Africa experience: An introduction.* Englewood Cliffs, NJ: Prentice-Hall.

Mbiti, J. S. (1991). *Introduction to African religion.* Portsmouth, NH: Heineman Educational Books.

Myers, L. (1993). *Understanding an Afrocentric worldview: Introduction to optimal psychology.* Dubuque, IA: Kendall-Hunt Publishing.

Opoku, K. (1997). *Hearing and keeping.* Pretoria, South Africa: Unisa Press.

Pachocinski, R. (1996). *Proverbs of Africa.* St. Paul, MN: Professors World Peace Academy.

Penfield, J. (1983). *Communicating with quotes.* Westport, CT: Greenwood Press.

Ribeau, S., Baldwin, J., and Hecht, M. (1997). An African American communication perspective. In L. Samovar and R. Porter (Eds.), *Intercultural communication: A reader* (pp. 147–153). Belmont, CA: Wadsworth.

Ross, M. (1993). *The culture of conflict: Interpretations and interests in comparative perspective.* New Haven, CT: Yale University Press.

Ting-Toomey, S. (1997). Managing intercultural conflict effectively. In L. Samovar and R. Porter (Eds.), *Intercultural communication: A reader* (pp. 392–403). Belmont, CA: Wadsworth.

Yankah, K. (1985). *The proverb in the context of Akan rhetoric.* Unpublished doctoral dissertation, Indiana University, Bloomington.

CHECK YOUR UNDERSTANDING

1. Think of the proverbs of your culture. List two of them. What do they tell you about the values of your culture?
2. What are proverbs used for in your culture? Is this use similar to the use of proverbs in West Africa?
3. Talk to a person from a culture different from yours about the proverbs in her or his culture. What similarities and differences do you find in the values expressed in the proverbs? What do these similarities and differences tell you about communication styles in the two cultures?

CHAPTER ACTIVITIES

1. Select a book such as J. C. Beaglehole's *The Journals of Captain Cook on His Voyages of Discovery,* Augustus Earle's *Narrative of a Nine Month's Residence in New Zealand,* or a book from your university library that tells a story of one group's first encounter with another group. Chart the journey that the writer took when he or she first came into contact with cultural diversity. Note in particular the author's encounters with artifacts and tools, such as jewelry, cowrie beads, and other symbols of economic power or wealth. Describe some of the strategies that both sides in the interpersonal exchange used to communicate with one another. To what extent do struggles over economic goods alter the course of intercultural events?

2. Hugh Duncan notes that there is a relationship between the goods and services that we surround ourselves with and our sense of who we are—our identity. How do consumer goods, such as Nike shoes, Calvin Klein jeans, or Gucci bags reveal a sense of identity? Do such goods create divisions between classes and cultures, or do they serve as unifying symbols?

3. Make a list of the various economic and social contributions that ethnic groups have made to human culture. Then explain how the ecology of the area and geographic features—mountains, rivers, climate, soil, and so on—helped to shape the culture's contributions. For instance, the first examples of writings occurred in the Near East and grew out of a need for the people to mark quantity and ownership.

CHAPTER 11

HEALTH

THE MALAYSIAN DOCTOR

Anyone who has been ill while in another country knows the difficulties that event causes. It is bad enough to become ill while away from home, even in one's own country, but it is extremely bad when in another country. My visit to the Malaysian doctor makes this point painfully (no pun intended) clear.

My husband and I were on a long overdue vacation. As a surprise, I had called his secretary and had her clear his calendar for a week. I packed his bags and whisked him away from his office. I had planned a wonderful vacation of lying in the sun, snorkeling, watching sunsets, and just relaxing at a beautiful resort in Malaysia. All went well for the first three days.

On the fourth day I woke up with a tremendous pain on my backside. I had a huge swelling, great pain, and could not sit down. My husband insisted I go to the doctor, so we checked with the hotel, and the management gave us the name and address of a clinic. We found the clinic—a run-down building in great need of paint and repair. I hesitated. My husband took my hand and we entered.

People of all ages and in all types of conditions were seated in the waiting room. Most were in Muslim attire. No seats were available, and since I had to stand anyway, this was not a problem. We explained my condition to the receptionist as best we could, given that she spoke no English and we did not speak her language. We finally understood that we should wait and the doctor would see me.

I looked around the waiting room as the patients stared at us. The chairs were folding chairs—no comfortable couches as in my doctor's office at home. The walls were dingy gray and completely bare. The light was a single bulb hanging from the ceiling. The floor appeared to have been swept sometime during the last century. I began to be concerned about the lack of cleanliness. Would I leave with something worse than I had come in with? It seemed likely. My husband kept telling me to relax, that we were not going to leave, and that the doctor's actual office was probably quite different. I assured him that if it wasn't, I would leave.

My name was called, or a facsimile of it, and my husband and I entered the doctor's office. She greeted us in perfect English. I had never been so happy to hear my native tongue! The room was clean—not the brightly polished, well-lit, decorated doctor's office of the United States, but certainly sanitary. The equipment was not the latest, but my problem didn't require any, so I was comfortable. She washed her hands, examined me, and explained that I had been bitten by either a spider or something in the ocean. She couldn't say for sure, but did assure me that the bite was not life threatening. I kept wondering how she knew that if she didn't know what had bitten me! She gave me some ointment and sent me on my way.

By the next day the swelling was much less and the pain had, for the most part, subsided. By the end of the week, I was fine. She was right—the bite wasn't life-threatening. I began to think about the sterile appearances of our hospitals and doctors' offices in the United States. Cleanliness in health-care facilities is so important to us. Yet, personnel are currently fighting infections that are spread in their hospitals despite the emphasis on sterile conditions. Don't get me wrong. The more sterile, the better. But the Malaysian experience taught me that good care can be given despite the facilities in which it is given.

OBJECTIVES

After reading this chapter and completing the activities and readings, you should be able to

- Explain how different perceptions of health and healing shape intercultural interactions.
- Explain the relationship among the following intercultural concepts: family, power, religion, spirituality, and ethical issues.
- Discuss ways of reducing potential breakdowns and misunderstandings in intercultural health communication contexts.

"His deeds remind me of Gao Yaojie, a doctor in the Henan province. In the face of AIDS transmission, Gao did not keep silent but participated in dissemination of knowledge and cooperated with both domestic and international media and through them revealed the truth" (Fudong, 2003, p. 1). Han Fudong is referring here to the heroic deeds of the "honest doctor," Jiang Yanhong, a 72-year-old Chinese man who disclosed to the media the truth about the scale of severe acute respiratory syndrome (SARS) in China. In doing so, Yanhong broke the silence about the nature and extent of the outbreak of the disease. In acting boldly, Yanhong's disclosure not only forced the Chinese government to develop a strategy for combating SARS but it also protected people worldwide from the potentially deadly disease. Dr. Yanhong's actions also revealed the tenuous nature of public health in a highly globalized world.

In today's interconnected world where people can literally have dinner in New York City and breakfast in Paris, the challenges to public health are enormous, because infectious diseases can travel rapidly from Bernice, Louisiana, to Budapest, Hungary. As Eugene Linden, author of *The Future in Plain Sight* (2002) notes, "With the ever-increasing integration of the world economy, problems that arise in one city can very quickly become global. . . . The health of the first-world cities depends in some measure on the success of developing nations in controlling the diseases incubating in slums. The West ignores these issues at its own peril" (p. 55). Linden's argument further underlines the seriousness of Dr. Yanghong's informing the public about SARS and the importance of health communication at all levels—an aspect of public health that has only recently begun to gain the attention that it deserves. We are, of course, referring to the critical role that culture plays in our attitudes toward health communication. Clearly, culture influenced China's initial response to the SARS outbreak, from an imposed code of silence to an inclination to undercount the number of people who had been infected by SARS.

In this chapter we examine the ways in which culture shapes our attitudes and behavior toward health, from familial support to religion and spirituality to matters such as linguistic interference in the health arena. We have already noted the importance of effective health communication from a global perspective. However, we must take into account other factors such as how communicating with others provides a way for individuals to interact or connect, as well as how not communicating effectively "directly influences our physical well-being" (Wood, 2000, p. 11). Research indicates, for example, that "intimacy promotes health while isolation fosters stress, disease and early death" (*Newsweek,* March 6, 1998). Research also reveals that "life threatening medical problems are affected by healthy interaction with others," and that "heart disease is more common among people who lack strong interpersonal relationships" (Wood, 2000, p. 11). Similarly, researchers report that "social isolation is statistically as dangerous as high blood pressure, smoking, obesity, or high cholesterol" (p. 11).

The significance of health communication in these studies is clear. If people are to interact with other people worldwide, it is important to understand how sociocultural forces shape the well-being of others.

HEALTH BELIEF SYSTEMS

When Lia, a young Hmong girl who lived in Merced, California, was diagnosed as an epileptic, her parents, Foua and Nao Kao Lee, said that the cause of her illness was *qaug dab peg*—the spirit catches you and you fall down—a kind of wandering of the soul. Lia's North American doctors, in contrast, attributed her seizures to the misfiring of her cerebral neurons, leading to a biological interpretation of illness (Fadiman, 1997). Lia's parents also believe that the body contains a finite or limited amount of blood and that one cannot replenish it; for this reason, "repeated blood sampling from small children may be fatal" (p. 33). When we interact with others we must also be mindful that cultures use different belief systems to explain the causes and treatment of illnesses.

According to Angelucci (1995) and Samovar and Porter (2001), three belief systems are used to account for such differences: biomedical, personalistic, and naturalistic.

Biomedical System

The biomedical belief system posits the notion that illness has an objective, scientific basis; in other words, illness is caused by germs, bacteria, viruses, or a physical condition such as an injury or aging. Although the biomedical belief system is the dominant belief system in the United States, we must remember that there are some cultural groups residing within North America who do not completely accept this view. German Americans, for example, believe in the "germ theory of infection" (Spector, 2004, p. 288), but they also believe that illness can be caused by drafts, environmental changes, and the evil eye (p. 288).

Treatment in the biomedical system "involves avoiding pathogens, agents, or activities known to cause abnormalities" (Angelucci, 1995, p. 8).

Personalistic System

Lia's story is a good example of the personalistic system, which, according to Angelucci (1995) is "the result of active intervention by a supernatural being (deity or god), a non-human being (ghost or evil spirit) or a human (witch or sorcerer)" (p. 8). Recall that Lia's parents attributed her illness to spiritual matters and to a human event that happened when Lia was three months old. Lia's older sister, Yer, slammed the front door of the Lees' apartment, "and this caused her illness. For this reason, the Lees preferred animal sacrifice as a way of curing her illness instead of anticonvulsants that the doctors prescribed."

Treatment in the personalistic system "involves assuring positive association with spirits, deities, etc." (Angelucci, 1995, p. 8).

Naturalistic System

The third and final belief system is naturalistic, which is caused by an imbalance between the hot and cold elements of the body. This practice will be discussed in more detail later. In this system, illness is prevented by maintaining the proper hot–cold balance in the body (Spector, 2004). In Puerto Rican culture, for example, such foods as avocado, banana, coconut, sugar cane, and white beans are classified as cold foods. Treatment in the naturalistic system involves prescribing hot remedies for cold illnesses and cold remedies for hot illnesses, as we reveal later (Spector, 2004; Angelucci, 1995).

INTERCULTURAL BARRIERS OF EFFECTIVE HEALTH CARE

In this section we highlight the fact that what is rooted in the stories we tell can act as barriers of effective health care primarily because of the diversity of beliefs, assumptions, and attitudes that we bring to the intercultural encounter.

According to Hodgkinson (Fact sheet, 2000, Indiana University), one of four premier demographers in the United States, there are about 200-plus nations containing our species, and the United States has a representative from each of these countries living within its borders. This means that on any given day in the United States, doctors are confronted with patients from Bangladesh, Nigeria, or India who manifest different conceptions of health and the healing process than North American doctors. Patients also bring with them *cultural rationales,* or conceptions about the nature, causes, and consequences of illness.

"Conceptualizations about illness that a patient brings to the health communication exchange are referred to as an explanatory model" (Carillo, 1999). The explanatory model "is inextricably linked to the social factors that make up" a person's "social environment," and the model includes such factors as patient beliefs, attitudes toward illness, the meaning of sickness, expectations, and various other assumptions that help to determine one's response to sickness (see Figure 11.1).

Think of an explanatory model as the meaning that a person attaches to illness (Carrillo, 1999, p. 829) as well as the social factors that influence meaning, such as socioeconomic status, level of education, and religious beliefs. For example, Navajo believe that illness occurs when one is "out of congruence" with the beauty of one's surroundings and creation. For this reason, Navajo engage in ceremonies called "sings," which are designed to "restore beauty" (Hall, 1994, p. 112).

George (2001, p. 393) argues that our ability to explain and understand illness involves two major strands, which are often at odds with one another. First, she notes that clinicians diagnose and treat *diseases* with an eye toward "pathophysiologic abnormalities of the body." Note the strategic emphasis on disease; few sick patients define their plight in this manner!

Second, a layperson's view of illness is highly "confined" to science-like biophysical explanations provided by the health professional and measured by subjective and objective data. This suggests that patients see illness as "an interpretation given to the *experience of being ill.*" Significantly, this is a knowledge-based approach to intercultural interactions, and both patient and caregiver can learn from one another. Care must be taken not to overstate the importance of a knowledge-based approach to generating cross-cultural understanding about matters of health care, however. Studies (George, 2001; Galanti, 1997; Spector, 2004) reveal that knowing about a culture and using the knowledge in a refined and helpful way are two different things.

Nevertheless, George's explanation of the two divergent views of illness serves as a way of understanding cross-cultural aspects of healing. This means that clinicians and others who fail to take into consideration the fact that people from different cultures bring differing explanations of health and disease to the table can jeopardize the well-being of human beings.

▌FIGURE 11.1 An Explanatory Model

1. *Social environment* (our relationship to people in terms of social class, history, social network, education)

2. *People's beliefs and attitudes* (influence of worldview on the perception of what will or will not influence health and well-being such as older Catholic Italian and Mexican women wearing rosaries or a Native American displaying a "soul catcher" [a circular frame with feathers hanging from it] as a way of helping to cure illness)

3. *Meaning of illness* (how to interpret the place of illness in one's life—for example, is illness stress related or episodic?)

4. Expectations toward illness (the total sum of items 1, 2, and 3; the sum equals what is required or demanded in understanding health cross culturally)

Because communicating health matters interculturally invites a confrontation with diversity of ideas, concepts, beliefs, attitudes, and practices, it can involve a radical jolt to both patient and health-care provider. For example, when a Hmong mother who has just delivered a baby tells the doctor she wants to take the placenta home with her, a physician who is ignorant of the ways of the Hmong can be taken aback by such a request, because the activity is not customarily done in North America (Fadiman, 1997). Anthropologist Susan McCombie, who worked as an infection control epidemiologist in a county health department in Arizona, observed that some patients "had a concept of flu" (which she called "folk flu") and that this conception caused some patients not to seek treatment (quoted in Hahn, 1995, p. 276).

In general, because people are taught so well in childhood what to value or devalue, appreciate or denigrate, love or hate with regard to the healing process, such orientations carry with them profound sentiments that can and do determine the pursuit of medical information and diagnosis. The point is that cultural barriers such as family history, power, and religion can greatly influence a person's health.

Family

In her book, *Caring for Patients from Different Cultures,* Geri-Ann Galanti (1997) recounts the following incident:

> A sixty-five-year old Filipino woman named Carlita Ricos lay dying for six months. Although she was in a coma, her fourteen children were with her constantly, bathing her, grooming her, rubbing her favorite lotion on her skin. Her failure to respond did nothing to diminish their devotion. (p. 61)

This story illustrates the strong influence that familial attachments can have on intercultural interactions. Although not all families behave similarly, kinship groups exert a powerful influence culturally and determine to a large extent what families value and, by extension, how they care for their loved ones. Hahn (1995) notes, for example, that "humans are born into societies that inform them how the world is and how to behave in it" (p. 76). As we learned in Chapter 8, the family is the basic governing unit of society that establishes basic norms of conduct. Kinship ties range all the way from those of the nuclear family, which contains mother, father, and children, to those of a Nigerian extended family, which includes mother, father, children, uncles, and aunts.

Today, anthropologists use two terms to define the complexity of the family unit: family of orientation versus family of procreation. The *family of orientation* is the one that "a person is born into, the one to which one first orients oneself" (Galanti, 1997, p. 11). It includes mother, father, brothers, and sisters, and any other household members. The *family of procreation* is the "one formed through marrying and procreating," or not procreating, as the case may be. Regardless of the pattern of orientation, families provide a sense of continuity and sustainability and give the individual an anchor in times of stress and sickness.

In trying to give you a sense of the complexity of familial habits that can shape intercultural behavior among human beings, the discussion will center on two main areas: the nature of personal care and the respect and obligation that are required in different cultures. As we will see, these orientations can and do interfere with the delivery of health care and, by extension, health communication. In one study, when nurses were asked to "name their most common problem in dealing with non-Anglo ethnic groups," most nurses responded, "Their families" (Galanti, 1997). This striking statement is an example of how cultures frame "what people pay attention to and what they ignore" (Hall, 1976, p. 74). In discussing the resilient hold that people's stories have on how they behave, it is nevertheless important to remember that although we are discussing cultural trends and tendencies, experiences vary from family to family.

Respect and Obligation When people enter a hospital, they take their experiential background with them and because attitudes and values are not unidirectional, sometimes both patient and health-care giver can bump up against each other with serious consequences. This is especially the case when the beliefs, values, and habits of mind between patient and health care provider are notably different. Such cultural divergences increase the likelihood that conflicts will result. If we are to understand such influences, we must grasp some of the cultural dynamics in the process.

The case of the Chinese is one such example. Chinese culture emphasizes loyalty to family and devotion to group. Chinese also place great importance on filial duty (i.e., the proper behavior of child to parent), and they maintain strong and cohesive social bonds. For Confucian-oriented societies, the social glue is very strong and encourages duty, loyalty, and responsibility. According to Confucianism, relationships are expressed through the responsibilities of each participant in the five Confucian relationships: "king-justice, subject-loyalty," "father-love, son-filiality," "husband-initiative, wife-obedience," "elder brother-brotherly love, younger brother-reverence," and "friends-mutual faith" (Robinson, 2003, p. 59). Within these dyads are patterns for behavior that naturally extend to discourses on health care and how issues of responsibility are ultimately addressed.

In Chinese culture this suggests that people are expected to take care of their family—both immediate and extended. In this way, the family is both honored and respected. Edwin Hui (1999) writes, "It is not shameful for a Chinese elderly sick person to be dependent on her children, but rather it is something to which she is entitled" (p. 131). According to the Chinese *Book of Rites,* the rules are "When a ruler is ill, and has to drink medicine, the minister first tastes it. The same is true for a son and an ailing parent" (Hui, 1999, p. 131). Furthermore, as a result of the deep responsibility that resides within Confucian ethics, and as a result of mutual interdependence, Chinese children are expected to assume several roles, including caregiver, protector, and surrogate decision maker.

The traditional Chinese approach contrasts greatly with North American traditions, where family input is not determinative. Hui (1999) notes further that according to the "rule of filial piety" in Chinese culture, it is "inexcusable to disclose a terminal illness which may add further harm to the patient" (p. 132). This cultural value is greatly at odds with North American values, which govern relationships between patient and physician. In the United States, physicians are expected to provide relevant and full information to the patient. Clearly this can be a significant barrier in health care. In a later section of this chapter we will return to the crucial point of ethics and how they govern what can and cannot be done or said based on cultural norms and patterns of behavior.

Other cultures also have strong family ties that have implications for providing health care and interpersonal interactions, including Russians, the Hmong, Mexican Americans, and Navajo. Navajo culture relies very heavily on the extended family and a network of people, including parents, children, and a host of other relatives, for care and well-being. Because of the centrality of the family in Navajo culture, to be without family is tantamount to being very poor. So, when a Navajo person is ill in the hospital, it is not uncommon for a family member to stay there until the relative has been discharged. Knowing this piece of information, one would expect conflict to occur between patient and physician unless there is mutual respect and some form of accommodation to specific Navajo cultural needs within medical settings (Giger and Davidhizar, 1999, p. 242).

Stories that become embedded within Navajo culture are circulated fairly early to children such that they learn the proper relationship that should exist between parent and child and between adult and child. Navajo children, for example, receive important and lively traditions that are passed down from the elderly; these focus on such values as respect, honor, and wisdom (Geiger and Davidhizar, 1999, p. 243). The significant point for our purposes is that family members' attitudes toward their loved ones not only symbolize the culture but also guide the members' way of thinking and behaving that can interfere with the delivery of health care, and, by extension, can influence everyday interaction with others.

For this reason, we should take such matters very seriously. Consider the following story about 27-year-old Alfredo Gomez, who was in the hospital in traction with multiple fractures following a traffic accident. For some time, he whined continuously and incessantly buzzed Helga, his German nurse, with the call light. After a while, Helga became irritated and angry with Alfredo and ultimately adopted a stern and direct attitude. However, when Alfredo's wife and sister arrived at hospital, his entire demeanor changed. Why? Because they not only gave him their full attention but they also anticipated his every need, fluffing his pillow and moistening his lips (Galanti, 1997, p. 25).

Gomez's wife and sister reacted according to the dictates of Mexican American culture, which highly values *familismo*. *Familismo* is a term used to describe the collective loyalty that Mexican Americans have to their family members. In his study of culture and the patient–physician relationship, Flores (2000) identifies three basic aspects of *familism:* (1) familial obligations (giving both material and emotional support to family members); (2) support from the family (a keen perception that one can count on family members to be reliable and supportive providers); and (3) family as referents (one should be pleasant and consult with family members [http://gatewah1.olvidweb.cgi, p. 4]).

Familismo can serve as a powerful way of communicating to health-care providers and as a compelling signal of how we should behave toward others. In the story about Alfredo and his German nurse, Helga, Helga noticed how Alfredo's family interacted with him and began to use a softer, less harsh tone with him. In fact, she learned how to become a more effective intercultural communicator because she was attentive and willing to learn. Specifically, nurse Helga learned that Mexican Americans are emotionally expressive toward family members; this was in sharp contrast to her own culture, which required unemotionality, according to German customs.

Nurse Helga also learned that Alfredo behaved as he did because he was not receiving the care and concern that his own culture dictated that he should receive. As a result of nurse Helga's lesson in intercultural comportment, she identified the optimal communicative conditions for healing to take place and, as a consequence, added to her repertoire of theoretical and practical information regarding cross-cultural demeanor and communication styles (Galanti, 1997, p. 25).

There is another valuable lesson nestled inside of Alfredo's and nurse Helga's moving story, and it is this: People must try as best they can to honor the expectations that others have of situations and conditions, whether they be illness or otherwise. Later, we will talk more about the role of expectations in governing one's behavior toward others. In this chapter, however, we keep our attention focused on how familial culture can serve as a barrier in health communication. So far, we have discussed aspects of Chinese and Mexican American familial culture. Let us now turn to another dimension of intercultural barriers of effective health care: the role of gender.

Gender

In Chapter 4 we discussed how gender can greatly disadvantage and exclude women from participating meaningfully in communication exchanges. Gender also plays a role in how patients, their families, and staff interact when a person's health is at risk in hospitals. To understand fully the implications of gender, we need to consider for a moment the importance of gender in culture. Women, as we know, traditionally have had a historical and cultural experience significantly different from that of men. Based on these differences, men assumed roles of ruler and protector and developed a family organizational structure known as *patriarchy* (Lerner, 1986).

Although we are concerned about the role of gender and its impact on human interaction, it is not necessary for us to detail all aspects of patriarchy. We should stress, however, that patriarchy refers to a system of rule by men in which many of the groups they dominate exchange responsibilities and obligations for their protection. For example, men have historically dominated women in exchange for the responsibility of their economic support and protection. In some cultures, patriarchal structures have led men to make most decisions for women. Although changes are occurring worldwide in terms of how women are treated, certain patterns still persist.

The instance of an upper-class 25-year-old Iranian male is a case in point. When Hamid Sadeghi entered an unnamed hospital, not only was he uncooperative but he also refused to care for his own personal needs. Instead, he gave vigorous orders to the nurses; for example, he routinely rang for the nurses and demanded, "You get here right now and do this" (Galanti, 1997, p. 25). He even posted a note on his door saying, "Do not enter without knocking, including the nurses." Needless to say, his behavior caused the nurses and others much grief. Finally, when Hamid was confronted with the question, "Why are you behaving in this fashion?" the nurses received the following reply: "This is the way it is done" (Galanti, 1997, p. 25). Clearly, male-oriented demands had entered the hospital!

Hamid's culture dictated that he should give orders to women regardless of their situation or status, and he had acted on such dictates. In accepting the traditional roles of his culture, Hamid's thinking and ways of behaving had become *natural* or *commonsensical* to him, including the expectation that he should give orders and that women should accept them, despite his horizontal status. Thus, when people are socialized with a tendency toward masculine or feminine behavior, it can disturb intercultural relationships.

In the case of Hamid, one should also note the role of the Koran in offering guidelines to him for the proper course of conduct. As Galanti (1997) points out, "Nursing is a low-level position in the Middle East because the job requires a woman to violate the laws of the Koran—she must both look at and touch the bodies of naked male strangers" (p. 25). Of course, the Koran is not the only canonical work that restricts what women do, when, how, and under what conditions. Despite this caveat, evidence is piling up that differences in approaches to what constitutes appropriate behavior in hospitals and other health settings are primary causes of tension and friction between the sexes.

Power

Recall Hofstede's (2001) four dimensions of culture that we discussed in Chapter 2, including power distance. Recall further that the power dimension of culture refers to the extent to which the less powerful persons in a society accept inequality as natural. If the power distance of a culture is small, appropriate behaviors are different from those of a culture that has a large power distance. In terms of intercultural barriers, areas of health care also include power dynamics that can and do interfere with human relationships between and among patients, their families, and staff.

Let us begin with what doctors wear daily—a special kind of white cloth that at once instantly symbolizes connections between power and status. Burke and Ornstein (1995), in commenting on the "medicalizing" role of doctors in the twentieth century and what it symbolized, note "the seductive attraction of the physician's world, with its white coats, gleaming instruments, and life-saving gifts" (p. 248). The authors further observe that the doctor, "the new shaman," brought along with him a science-like orientation. Thus, when one considers how physicians dress and the response that patients are likely to have toward this "aura-like, authority-giving" uniform, it is clear that symbolic clothing can act as a real deterrent to decision making among different groups, especially for people whose stories grow out of soil that is rooted in a high-power distance orientation to the world.

In a real sense, the presence of "white coats" and "gleaming instruments" combined with the "scientific-imbuing behavior" of the physician can, in effect, separate the patient from the physician as well as the family from the physician. When one adds the vocabulary that the average doctor uses, another complex layer is added to the power dimension of culture. For example, some patients are not likely to ask questions that they should for the good of their health because of the technical language that some physicians use when talking to patients. Furthermore, when one adds still another dimension to the process—the reverence and respect that some cultures have for authority figures—it is highly unlikely that specific and necessary questions about one's health will be asked.

To dramatize the nature of power arrangements between doctor and patient, consider the following story of Dr. Mehraban, a Middle Eastern male physician, and a White American female, Roberta Hansen, who was Dr. Mehraban's patient. When Dr. Mehraban was called in to consult with Roberta's personal physician about her health, he gave no reasons for his medical decision, nor did he include Roberta in the decision-making process. When Roberta tried to question the doctor regarding his decisions, she was met with vague and imprecise answers. Finally, in anger, Dr. Mehraban removed himself from Roberta's case (Galanti, 1997, p. 86).

This story illustrates the important effect that both power and gender relations can have on health-seeking behavior. The reason for Dr. Mehraban's actions can be explained by his culture. In the Middle East, doctors are viewed as strong authoritative figures, and patients fully expect such individuals to make medical decisions on their behalf.

A major point that we should bear in mind is that definitions of what constitutes a "good doctor" also reside within cultures. In the case of people who come from some Middle Eastern cultures, and in the case of many people from Native American and Asian cultures, a "good doctor" is one who "knows" what is in the best interest of the patient, and for this reason, members of such cultures do not readily pepper their doctors with questions. Such behavior would violate the rules of social agreement between doctor and patient. In China and Japan, for example, because high-power distance rules govern the hierarchy, it is not unusual for patients to learn little, if anything, about their condition. By contrast, in the United States, doctors are socialized to ask their patients questions. In intercultural settings, if one is unmindful of such differences, real conflicts can result in real damage to intercultural relationships.

Finally, an even more critical reason why we should care about doctor–patient power dynamics is because the consequences can be very serious, indeed. As Dr. Sherrie H. Kaplan observes, patient passivity, or failure to talk to the doctor, "should be treated as a risk factor in chronic disease" (quoted in Levine, 2004, p. D6). Sometimes "a more dominant tone of voice," can prevent patients from speaking out; in fact, evidence shows that doctors who use a more dominant tone of voice are sued more often than those who have warmer voices (p. D6). One reason for this is that patients "who sue often feel abandoned" (p. D6). This means that both doctor and patient can suffer from a communication breakdown.

Imagine other things that can go horribly wrong when patients feel overpowered by a doctor's tone of voice. The patient might neglect to tell the doctor about feelings of dizziness, which could signal the onset of diabetes, because he or she is afraid to interrupt the doctor or to ask the doctor questions. The patient might also omit other major indicators that signal the presence of such diseases as heart disease, stroke, arthritis, gallbladder disease, and multiple other diseases that require honest and forthright communication between doctor and patient. Brody (2003, p. D7) reports that more cancers are now being linked to excess weight; such relationships can be missed if the patient is fearful of asking the doctor questions that seriously bear on his or her health. When one adds such matters as ethnicity and gender to the health equation, the dynamics of power can also be daunting, as noted previously.

Religion and Spirituality

To this point we have discussed the importance of effective health communication and noted how family and power dimensions can serve as barriers to health care. Here, we outline how religion—a nearly universal feature of human life—can have a profound impact on health and intercultural encounters. As Spector (2004) points out, "Religion strongly affects the way people interpret and respond to the signs and signals of illness" (p. 105). And as we noted in Chapter 4, although religion can be defined in many ways, it can mean different things to different people, depending on whether they are from the New Guinea highlands or from the highlands of Scotland. At the center of religion, however, is a "belief in supernatural beings and in their ability to influence the world of man [and woman]" (Benderly et al., 1977, p. 206). Religion is closely related to but also different from the concept of spirituality. By spirituality, we mean "a person's or group's relationship with the transcendent, however that may be construed. Spirituality is about the search for transcendent meaning" (Astrow et al., 2001, p. 4). Spirituality is a spacious concept and for this reason it may be expressed through music, the arts, philosophical beliefs, or one's relationship to nature or with friends and family (http://gateway1.ovid.com/ovidweb. cgi?Full+Text, p. 4).

At the beginning of recorded history, "healing could only come about through appeasement of the gods and the quelling of their wrath, and the conduct of healing rituals were entrusted to shamans and witch doctors" (Astrow et al., 2001, pp. 1–2). In the early Renaissance period, however, at least in the West, there arose a division between science and religion. This can be seen in the church's confrontation with the scientist Galileo, who was "condemned to be silent" because his views clashed with the views of the Church (Van Doren, 1991, p. 202).

Despite such responses from the West, and despite the separation of science and religion, people in many parts of the world, including the United States, take their religion seriously and, for this reason, it, along with spirituality, enters the domain of culture and health. "Science," according to Astrow and colleagues (2001) "provides no answers to the questions that are inevitably raised by illness: Why am I ill? Is there any meaning to my suffering?" As a result of an absence of answers to such existential questions, people inevitably turn to religion and spirituality in search of answers. Thus, religious and spiritual beliefs provide people with *explanatory* reasons for their illness and cultural guides for their reaction to it.

A crucial point for our purposes is that religion and spirituality go to the heart of humans trying to give their world and its attendant illnesses meaning. In her study of the religious beliefs and practices of Taiwanese parents of pediatric patients with cancer, for example, Yeh (2001) found that "an average of 81% of adult patients with cancer were found to use religious practices" (p. 2).

Despite the fact that Taiwanese are polytheistic, they still have "a strong cultural value and belief in religion," according to Yeh (2001). These beliefs are expressed in such rituals as praying alone or with family members. "'I went to the temple to query why my child was sick,' said one mother. 'I brought some offerings, such as fruits and foods to the temple. After I burned incense and paper currency (which was used as cash in the supernatural world), I prayed for the answer to why my child was sick and supplicated so to give us a sign'" (p. 5). Then, following the mother's prayers, she "shook the bamboo sticks from a tube and picked the single one which stood out from others. The divining blocks (Jiaobei, which were carved out from wood or bamboo root) were used to communicate with God asking if the bamboo stick picked was the right one" (p. 5). These religious practices take on added weight when one considers the flow of immigrants across cultural borders who take their orientation to the spirit world with them to other intercultural spaces and places.

Let us examine another story. A 75-year-old very religious Black woman, Agnes Jones, is in a hospital, recovering from a heart attack. She spent most of her day engaged in prayer along with her "brothers and sisters" from the church. While in the hospital, Mrs. Jones would accept only the procedures and medicines that she believed were divinely inspired. During her daily bathing rituals, she constantly "preached" to the nurses and other workers about her religion. Pretty soon, the workers began to avoid her.

We can discern several elements in the communication encounter between Mrs. Jones and the health-care providers that are particularly relevant to understanding why religious beliefs and values can create conflict across cultures. First, many African Americans believe in religion and spirituality, and these components are a central aspect of their life. Furthermore, some Blacks believe that God is the giver and the sustainer of their life and that it is necessary to "call" on the Lord and to seek his guidance and help, especially in matters relating to health and wellness. Prayer is a large part of such beliefs.

Second, in the case of the hospital staff, they might have been more mindful of the relationship between health, religion, and healing. Instead of avoiding Mrs. Jones, "they should have had a team conference to discuss her beliefs and perhaps invited a minister from her church to attend" (Galanti, 1977, p. 45).

The transformative power of religion can also be seen in a research study conducted by Newlin and others (2002). To understand the role of African American spirituality in the delivery of competent health care, Newlin and his colleagues conducted a literature review of 20 studies to get a sense of "the antecedents, attributes, consequences, related terms, and surrogate terms used to describe the concept of African American spirituality." Their study revealed that African American spirituality serves as a "salient source" of guidance, coping, and peace, especially in the face of adversity (p. 10).

To become more interculturally competent in understanding the central role of religion in human affairs, we must be prepared to understand culturally appropriate care for each individual, regardless of that person's cultural or religious background. Admittedly, it might not be possible to accommodate every conceivable request; however, in the world of sickness, it is important to understand why patients behave as they do and under what health circumstances. For example, in the following narrative of a 20-year-old Buddhist monk from Cambodia, had the treating nurse known that a monk is not supposed to be touched by a woman, all might have ended well. However, it did not.

When Lisa, the monk's nurse, touched him on his head, he "suddenly jumped from her in horror" (Gilanti, 1997). The monk's "mother and aunt lunged at Lisa, shouting at her in Cambodian. Lisa fled the room and called a 'code gray,' which summoned all male hospital personnel to the area" (p. 45). Of all the things that have the potential to alter what we do interculturally, few are as important as knowing the rules of conduct that help us to determine how we should act in specific intercultural situations.

To understand the role of religion and spirituality is to understand as well how diet can constrain human behavior in health settings. In some instances, specific illnesses limit the range of options available to patients in terms of calories and food choices. George (2001) points out, for example, that Muslim communities such as those in Pakistan, Indonesia, North Africa, and India observe the ninth month of the calendar, *Hijra,* which requires Muslims to fast during the month of Ramadan. During the month of Ramadan "post pubescent persons are required to eat 2 times a day, a light meal before sunrise and a large meal after sunset" (p. 394). George surmises that if an asthma patient is required to abstain from oral medications during Ramadam, this can portend illness for a patient.

Hot and Cold/Yin and Yang   Other difficulties can also arise from cultural practices—for example, beliefs that are tied to how to keep the body healthy as well as how to prevent illness. Table 11.1 lists some cultures and practices that are used to ward off illness.

In Islamic, East Indian, Asian, and Latin American cultures hot–cold theories of health and disease are pretty common. Hot–cold theories posit the idea that certain illnesses are categorized into "hot" or "cold" states and may be treated by consuming food and drinks that possess the opposite effects. "Hot and cold terms are used to refer to the cooling or heating effects of the foodstuff, rather than to its actual temperatures" (Chan, 1995, p. 30).

The concept of Yin and Yang (see Figure 11.2) is also closely tied to concepts of hot and cold. According to Chan (1995), the concept of Ying and Yang "is probably the single

TABLE 11.1 Cultural Practices to Ward Off Ill Health

Ethnic Group	Practice
Vietnamese, Cambodian, Korean, Chinese	Coin rubbing
Armenian	Cupping—heating glass and placing it on the body
Japanese	Cooling the body—removing regular blankets and placing "ice blankets" under the patient
Chinese	*Qi gong*—regulation of breathing to improve circulation and enhance the immune system
Indian	*Ayurvedic*—diet and natural herbs to increase longevity and improve quality of life
African American	*Pica*—eating laundry starch during pregnancy to "build up the blood"
German	*Hydrotherapy*—using water internally and externally to keep the body healthy
East Indian, Asian, Latin America	*Hot/cold treatment*—using hot remedies to treat cold illnesses and cold remedies to treat hot diseases; for example, a hot person must not drink cold water because it causes colic
Taiwanese	Using hairs of certain rare turtles to cure cancer
Chinese	Using tiny sea animals (seahorses) to cure heart and kidney nuisances

Source: Adapted from Spector (2004, p. 95), Galanti (1997, pp. 122–125), and Mulyana (2004).

most distinctive theory in Chinese medicine." She further argues that "all Chinese medical knowledge is eventually reduced to this concept" (p. 31). Although we are not prepared to reduce the totality of Chinese medical knowledge to this one concept, it is noteworthy that the Chinese concept of Yin and Yang has a long history, extending as far back as 700 B.C., where the idea is recorded in the *Book of Changes*. Yin and Yang is naturalistic in origin and promotes the belief that all things in the universe consist of "two opposing forces or elements" (p. 31). This includes the human body and the relationship of the body to health and disease. Using this philosophy, some Chinese believe that illnesses are caused by an imbalance between Yin and Yang.

Although the nature of Yin and Yang is very complex, the sources of such cultural values are very much rooted in Chinese's belief in harmony in life. Harmony is facilitated by regulating Yin and Yang. As Chan (1995) notes, "Although the Yin and Yang forces work by opposing each other, they are in fact complementary, forming a united whole. Furthermore, the concepts are facilitated by regulating such dichotomies as cold (*leung*) and hot (*yeh*); female and male; negative and positive; darkness and light; emptiness and fullness" (p. 32).

The extension of such beliefs carries with them specific healing remedies. For example, the Southeast Asian practices of "coin-rubbing" and "cupping" dictate particular health rituals. Cupping "is the placement, by use of a vacuum, of a small glass or bamboo cup over the posterior lung fields to promote drainage of excess cold," and "coin-rubbing involves rubbing quarter-sized coins in ointment over ailing body parts until they produce welts" (George, 2001, p. 6). The latter is supposed to be particularly effective in curing asthma, which is perceived to be a "cold" disease.

According to George (2001, p. 6), Latinos also perceive asthma as a cold disease and for this reason members of this culture will not only seek herbal and prescribed medicines to cure asthma but they also use "warm" therapies. George notes further that stories

FIGURE 11.2   Yin and Yang

circulate about Puerto Rican mothers dressing their children warmly and keeping their homes nicely heated as a way of warding off illness. One of the authors of this textbook recalls an African-derived version of the hot–cold concept when she was growing up in Louisiana. Her parents and other relatives generally believed that going out into cold, wintry weather insufficiently "bundled" would cause one to "catch a cold," and that going out into the damp air following a bath would also cause one to "catch a cold."

Thus, we see that beliefs circulate widely and deeply and translate into the notion that our attention to appropriate folk beliefs is related to illness and well-being. Indeed, these accumulated stories are passed on from generation to generation, which is why they stay alive and flourish. The lesson that one can draw from these theories is that health-care providers should be cognizant of such practices when treating certain cultural groups to ensure that there are no known cultural barriers to the medical plan of action, however defined. Knowing these two pieces of information in combination, and knowing that different cultures have different explanations for why one is ill and what to do about it goes a long way in helping to cure sick patients and in understanding why people think and act as they do in specific situations.

Ethical Issues

When doctors and patients interact on matters of health, questions of morality are likely to occur. Our moral sense helps us to explain a great deal about why we behave as we do. Because we are rarely indifferent to our environment, we are called on to make judgments about what we "ought" to do as opposed to "what we want to do" in specific situations. To understand why we behave as we do, and under what health circumstances, it is necessary for us to learn about how moral sentiments, the wellsprings of human emotions, shape interactions in health settings. Scholars argue that although all people remote in time and space share basic emotions in common, the rules for resolving moral dilemmas are rooted in families and in cultures. In this section we examine how people respond to health information, especially in terms of cultural diversity and ethical issues.

Consider the case of a 76-year-old Mexican man who had been receiving radiation and chemotherapy for the treatment of cancer on an outpatient basis. As his illness progressed, he found it necessary to be hospitalized and under the care of a physician for the first time.

In the process of talking with the physician about the Mexican's illness, family members, using Mexican cultural values as a guide, told the doctor that the patient did not know the extent of his illness. How come? Why wasn't the patient informed about the nature of his illness? (Orr et al., 1995). What should the physician do? In the United States, the cultural orientation is that the patient has "a right to know" about his or her illness. Physicians, nurses, and other health-care providers face such difficult questions daily and must be ready to grapple with their magnitude.

McDonald (1999, p. 15) argues that two basic questions are central to issues that undergird the ethics of health. The first question is, "What are health, disease, life and death from the viewpoints of various cultural, religious, and secular perspectives?" and the second question is, "What is it to be a health care provider?" (p. 92). For our purposes, we need not be concerned with answering the second question, because it is specific to a particular profession. Rather, our focus is on the first question, which raises the issue of whether culturally different people can construct an "ethic of health" that is "sensitive to cultural, religious, and other differences, and yet be mindful of the things that humans share in common."

What are some factors that figure prominently in ethical considerations of health? As individuals from diverse backgrounds interact, knotty and thorny ethical issues are inevitable. One such issue is this: Given the various ethnic and cultural groups and their specific values, beliefs, and habits of mind, how should conflict between minority and mainstream cultures be handled? (Hoffmaster, 1999, p. 117). Think about the range of issues that can develop over matters of health, ranging from who has the power of informed consent to issues of health and dying. For example, the Chinese culture holds that dying patients must be protected from bad news, which is at odds with the Western view. In such matters, how much sway should Chinese values have in hospital settings? To what extent might such views be injurious to the patient? Prevent the physician from functioning in the best interest of the patient? Risk a lawsuit?

In China, the physician is likely to follow the dictates of the family in order to meet the cognitive, behavioral, hierarchal, and filial demands of the culture. In the United States, however, the doctor might find it ethically and professionally troubling to withhold information from the patient. What, then, should one do? Clearly, the matter has significant ethical implications for how physicians in a multicultural world do medical business.

Another ethical issue that is fraught with anguish is the extent of "this tolerance or cultural sensitivity" (Hoffmaster, 1999). At what point can a medical doctor say to a Southeast Asian family, or anyone else for that matter, "For the good of the patient, this is the way it must be" and still maintain a semblance of humanity? This is a weighty question and it deserves a seriously open and engaging answer (p. 118). How might we answer Hoffmaster's overarching question: "Can defense to the views of the majority . . . legitimately be demanded, and what justifies this cultural imperialism? . . . What are the ramifications?" Although these are undoubtedly two most troubling issues to be addressed in the area of health-care ethics, admittedly, we do not have hard and fast answers for such complex and intricate questions.

Still another complicating concern, as Howard and Ratanakul (1999) argue, is that "modern medicine is itself a culture alongside the other cultures—Muslim, Buddhist, Hindu, Chinese, etc." (p. 3). Think about such cultural complexities. Not only does one have to be concerned with ethics pertaining to various cultures but also with a culture—medicine—nestled inside others—African American, Hispanic, Asian American, and the like.

The key point is that we must be mindful of such issues and try to find a way out of such limiting views. One answer is that each society or community needs to discuss what Daniels, quoted in McDonald (1999), refers to as "the normal opportunity range for that specific society . . . [that is] the array of life-plans reasonable people in it are likely to construct for themselves" (p. 108). This means that one should think about the various dimensions of health from a cultural and religious perspective and the relationship that exists between meaning and such dimensions. In other words, one needs a constructive dialogue to deal with health issues. How else will a person find himself or herself out of the wilderness of confusion that can result from ethical considerations?

Daniels's (1999) suggestion is paramount to intercultural understanding because it reveals much about the human capacity to address ethical issues that sustain harmonious and cooperative social behavior within a community. In fact, as McDonald (1999) observes, "The essential ethical question . . . is about the kind of community that reflects a society's moral sensibilities" (p. 108). This point of view is indeed attractive, and it is the foundation of much confidence we have in interacting well with others, especially with regard to difficult questions centered on health issues.

By focusing ethical issues "around various communities' collective provision for meeting significant health care needs" (McDonald, 1999, p. 108), one goes a long way toward understanding the impact of ethics on interpersonal interactions.

CONCLUSION

In concluding this chapter, it is noteworthy to observe that people in all cultures go about their daily lives enacting health practices and values that are deeply rooted in their cultural experiences. To sum up our discussion on health and communication, we must recognize that such factors as diversity, familial health traditions, folk medicine, power, and gender provide the essential signals and rules of conduct necessary for us to understand what makes people tick. These materials are building blocks for our understanding of how health factors help to shape what we think, feel, and do as we interact with others. Anne Fadiman's reading, "Do Doctors Eat Brains?" and Sunwolf's "Telling Multicultural Tales in Applied Contexts" provide striking ways of looking at what happens when people use different stories to explain their encounters with others. It should enhance your understanding of the lived experiences of humans as well as your understanding of what happens to cultural lore when it crosses intercultural borders.

FOR DISCUSSION

1. Compare and contrast your own views of health and culture with those of representative groups discussed in this chapter.
2. To what extent will traditional views of health and healing in the twenty-first century be shaped by modern, technological, and scientific changes? And how will such changes impact our understanding of globalization?
3. If you were required to defend or destroy the following thesis, which position would you take and why? *Thesis:* Our deepest health sentiments are the products of the culture in which we have been raised and are therefore relative.

REFERENCES

Angelucci, P. (1995, 26 August). Notes from the field: Cultural diversity health belief systems. *Nursing Management.*

Astrow, A. B., Puchalski, C. M., and Sulmasy, D. P. (2001). Religion, spirituality, and health care: Social, ethical, and practical considerations. *American Journal of Medicine, 110* (4), 283–287.

Benderly, B., Gallagher, M., and Young, J. (1977). *Discovering culture: An introduction to anthropology.* New York: D. Van Nostrand Company.

Brody, J. (2003, May 6). Another study finds a link between excess weight and cancer. *New York Times,* p. D7.

Burke, J., and Ornstein, R. (1995). *The axemaker's gift: A double-edged history of human culture.* New York: G. P. Putnam's Sons.

Carillo, J. E. (1999). Cross-cultural primary care: A patient-based approach. *Annals of Internal Medicine, 30,* 829–834.

Chan, J. (1995). Dietary beliefs of Chinese patients. *Nursing Standard, 9* (27), 30–34.

Ching, I. (1977). *Book of changes* (C. F. Baynes, trans.). Princeton, NJ: Princeton University Press.

Coward, H., and Ratanakul P. (Eds.). (1999). *A cross-cultural dialogue on health care ethics.* Waterloo, Ontario, Canada: Wilfrid Laurier University Press.

Fadiman, A. (1997). *The spirit catches you and you fall down: A Hmong child, her American doctors, and the collision of two cultures.* New York: Farrar, Straus and Giroux.

Flores, G. (2000). Culture and the patient-physician relationship: Achieving cultural competency in health care. *The Journal of Pediatrics, 1* (36), 14–23.

Fudong, H. (2003). http://ww.sinofile.net/Saiweng/swsite.nsf/FullStory?readform&AD41F9DE79A 3545D48.

Galanti, G-T. (1997). *Caring for patients from different cultures: Case studies from American hospitals.* Philadelphia: University of Pennsylvania Press.

George, M. (2001). The challenge of culturally competent health care: Applications for asthma. *Heart & Lung, 30,* 392–400.

Giger, J. N., and Davidhizar, R. E. (1999). *Transcultural nursing: Assessment and intervention.* St. Louis, MO: Mosby.

Hahn, R. A. (1995). *Sickness and healing: An anthropological perspective.* New Haven, CT: Yale University Press.

Hall, E. (1976). *Beyond culture.* New York: Anchor Press/Doubleday.

Hall, E. T. (1994). *West of the thirties: Discoveries among the Navaho and Hopi.* New York: Anchor Books Doubleday.

Hoffmaster, B. (1999). Conclusion. In H. Coward and P. Ratanakul (Eds.) *A cross-cultural dialogue on health care ethics* (pp. 146–156). Waterloo, Ontario, Canada: Wilfrid Laurier University Press.

Hofstede, G. (2001). *Culture's consequences: Comparing values, behaviors, institutions, and organizations across nations,* 2nd ed. Thousand Oaks, CA: Sage.

Hui, E. (1999). Concepts of health and disease in traditional Chinese medicine. In H. Coward and P. Ratanakul (Eds.), *A cross-cultural dialogue on health care ethics* (pp. 34–46). Waterloo, Ontario, Canada: Wilfrid Laurier University Press.

Lerner, G. (1986). *The creation of patriarchy.* New York: Oxford University Press.

Levine, M. (2004, June 6). Tell the doctor all your problems, but keep it to less than a minute. *New York Times,* p. D6.

Linden, E. (2002). *The future in plain sight: The rise of the "true believers" and other clues to the coming instability.* New York: A Plume Book.

McDonald, M. (1999). Health, health care, and culture: Diverse meanings, shared agendas. In H. Coward and P. Ratanakul (Eds.), *A cross-cultural dialogue on health care ethics* (pp. 92–112). Waterloo, Ontario, Canada: Wilfrid Laurier University Press.

Mulyana, D. (2004). *Cross cultural health communication.* Lecture.

Newlin, K., Knall, K., and Melkus, G. D'E. (2002). African-American spirituality: A concept analysis. *ANS Adv. Nurs. Sci., 25* (2), 57–70.

Orr, R. D., Marshall, P. A., and Osborn, J. (1995). Cross-cultural considerations in clinical ethics consultations. *Archives of Family Medicine, 4* (2), 159–164.

Robinson, J. H. (2003). Communication in Korea: Playing things by eye. In L. Samovar and R. Porter (Eds.), *Intercultural communication: A reader* (pp. 57–64). Belmont, CA: Wadsworth.

Samovar, L., and Porter, R. (2001). *Communication between cultures.* Belmont, CA: Wadsworth.

Spector, R. E. (2004). *Cultural diversity in health and illness.* Upper Saddle River, NJ: Pearson/Prentice Hall.

Van Doren, C. (1991). A *history of knowledge past, present, and future.* New York: Ballantine Books.

Wood, J. T. (2000). *Communication in our lives.* Australia: Wadsworth.

Yeh, C-H (2001). Religious beliefs and practices of Taiwanese parents of pediatric patients with cancer. *Cancer Nursing, 24* (6), 476–482.

Do Doctors Eat Brains?

Anne Fadiman

In 1982, Mao Thao, a Hmong woman from Laos who had resettled in St. Paul, Minnesota, visited Ban Vinai, the refugee camp in Thailand where she had lived for a year after her escape from Laos in 1975. She was the first Hmong-American ever to return there, and when an officer of the United Nations High Commissioner for Refugees, which administered the camp, asked her to speak about life in the United States, 15,000 Hmong, more than a third of the population of Ban Vini, assembled in a soccer field and questioned her for nearly four hours. Some of the questions they asked her were: Is it forbidden to use a *tixv neeb* to heal an illness in the United States? Why do American doctors take so much blood from their patients? After you die, why do American doctors try to open up your head and take out your brains? Do American doctors eat the livers, kidneys, and brains of Hmong patients? When Hmong people die in the United States, is it true that they are cut into pieces and put in tin cans and sold as food?

The general drift of these questions suggests that the accounts of the American health care system that had filtered back to Asia were not exactly enthusiastic. The limited contact the Hmong had already had with Western medicine in the camp hospitals and clinics had done little to instill confidence, especially when compared to the experiences with shamanistic healing to which they were accustomed. A *txiv neeb* might spend as much as eight hours in a sick person's home; doctors forced their patients, no matter how weak they were, to come to the hospital, and then might spend only twenty minutes at their bedsides.

Txiv neebs were polite and never needed to ask questions; doctors asked many rude and intimate questions about patients' lives, right down to their sexual and excretory habits. *Txiv neebs* could render an immediate diagnosis; doctors often demanded samples of blood (or even urine or feces, which they liked to keep in little bottles), took X-rays, and waited for days for the results to come back from the laboratory—and then, after all that, sometimes they were unable to identify the cause of the problem. *Txiv neebs* never undressed their patients; doctors asked patients to take off all their clothes, and sometimes dared to put their fingers inside women's vaginas. *Txiv neebs* know that to treat the body without treating the soul was an act

of patent folly; doctors never even mentioned the soul. *Txiv neebs* could preserve unblemished reputations even if their patients didn't get well, since the blame was laid on the intransigence of the spirits rather than the competence of the negotiators, whose stock might even rise if they had had to do battle with particularly dangerous opponents; when doctors failed to heal, it was their own fault.

To add injury to insult, some of the doctors' procedures actually seemed more likely to threaten their patients' health than to restore it. Most Hmong believe that the body contains a finite amount of blood that it is unable to replenish, so repeated blood sampling, especially from small children, may be fatal. When people are unconscious, their souls are at large, so anesthesia may lead to illness or death. If the body is cut or disfigured, or if it loses any of its parts, it will remain in a condition of perpetual imbalance, and the damaged person not only will become frequently ill but may be physically incomplete during the next incarnation; so surgery is taboo. If people lose their vital organs after death, their souls cannot be reborn into new bodies and may take revenge on living relatives; so autopsies and embalming are also taboo. (Some of the questions on the Ban Vinai soccer field were obviously inspired by reports of the widespread practice of autopsy and embalming in the United States. To make the leap from hearing that doctors removed organs to believing that they ate them was probably no crazier than to assume, as did American doctors, that the Hmong ate human placentas—but it was certainly scarier.)

The only form of medical treatment that was gratefully accepted by at least some of the Hmong in the Thai camps was antibiotic therapy, either oral or by injection. Most Hmong have little fear of needles, perhaps because some of their own healers (not *txiv neebs,* who never touch their patients) attempt to release fevers and toxicity through acupuncture and other forms of dermal treatment, such as massage; pinching; scraping the skin with coins, spoons, silver jewelry, or pieces of bamboo; applying a heated cup to the skin; or burning the skin with a sheaf of grass or a wad of cotton wool. An antibiotic shot that could heal an infection almost overnight was welcomed. A shot to immunize someone against a disease he did not yet have was something else again. In his book, *Les Naufrages de la Liberte,* the French physician Jean-Pierre Willem, who worked as a volunteer in the hospital at the Nam Yao camp, related how during a typhoid epidemic, the Hmong refugees refused to be vaccinated until they were told that only those who got shots would receive their usual allotments of rice—whereupon 14,000 people showed up at the hospital, including at least a thousand who came twice in order to get seconds.

When Foua Yang and Nao Kao Lee brought their three sick children to the hospital at Mae Jarim, they were engaging in behavior that many of the other camp inhabitants would have considered positively aberrant. Hospitals were regarded not as places of healing but as charnel houses. They were populated by the spirits of people who had died there, a lonesome and rapacious crew who were eager to swell their own ranks. Catherine Pake, a public health nurse who spent six months working at Phanat Nikhom (a camp where refugees from Laos, Vietnam, and Cambodia came for their final "processing" before they were sent to a country of permanent asylum), concluded from a study of the hospital log that "in comparison to refugees of other ethnic groups, the Hmong have the lowest per capita rate of visits." (Pake also discovered, not coincidentally, that the Hmong had an extremely "high utilization rate" of indigenous healing arts: shamanism, dermal treatments, herbalism. She published an article in the *Journal of Ethnobiology* identifying 20 medicinal plants she had collected under the tutelage of Hmong herbalists, which, in various forms—chopped, crushed, dried, shredded, powdered, decocted, infused with hot water, infused with cold water, mixed with ashes, mixed with sulphur, mixed with egg, mixed with chicken—were indicated for burns, fever, weakness, poor vision, broken bones, stomachaches, painful urination, prolapsed uterus, insufficient breast milk, arthritis, anemia, tuberculosis, rabies, scabies, gonorrhea, dysentery, constipation, impotence, and attacks by a *dab ntxaug,* a spirit who lives in the jungle and causes epidemics when he is disturbed. In this last case, the plant, *Fatropha curcas,* is crushed and its oil left in a cup, to be consumed not by the patient but by the *dab.)*

Wendy Walker-Moffat, an educational consultant who spent three years teaching and working on nutritional and agricultural projects in Phanat Nikhom and Ban Vinai, suggests that one reason the Hmong avoided the camp hospitals is that so many of the medical staff members were excessively zealous volunteers from Christian charitable organizations. "They were there to provide medical aid, but they were also there—though not overtly—to convert people," Walker-Moffat told me. "And part of becoming converted was believing in Western medicine. I'll never forget one conversation I

overheard when I was working in the hospital area at Ban Vinai. A group of doctors and nurses were talking to a Hmong man whom they had converted and ordained as a Protestant minister. They had decided that in order to get the Hmong to come into the hospital, they were going to allow a traditional healer, a shaman, to practice there. I knew they all thought shamanism was witch-doctoring. So I heard them tell this Hmong minister that if they let a shaman work in the medical center, he could only give out herbs, and not perform any actual work with the spirits. At this point they asked the poor Hmong minister, 'Now *you* never go to a shaman, do you?' He was a Christian convert, he knew you cannot tell a lie, so he said, 'Well, yes, I do.' But then their reaction was so shocked that he said, 'No, no, no, I've never been. I've just heard that *other* people go.' What they didn't realize was that—to my knowledge, at least—no Hmong is ever fully converted."

In 1985, the International Rescue Committee assigned Dwight Conquergood, a young ethnographer with a special interest in shamanism and performance art, to design an environmental health program for Ban Vinai. He later wrote:

> I heard horror story after horror story from the refugees about people who went to the hospital for treatment, but before being admitted had their spirit-strings cut from their wrists by a nurse because "the strings were unsanitary and carried germs." Doctors confidently cut off neckrings that held the life-souls of babies intact.
>
> Instead of working to cooperate with the shamans, they did everything to disconfirm them and undermine their authority. . . . Is it any wonder that the Hmong community regarded the camp hospital as the last choice of available health care options? In the local hierarchy of values, consulting a shaman or herbalist, or purchasing medicine available in the Thai market just outside the entrance to the camp, was much preferred and more prestigious than going to the camp hospital.
>
> The refugees told me that only the very poorest people who had no relatives or resources whatsoever would subject themselves to the camp hospital treatment. To say that the camp hospital was underutilized would be an understatement.

Unlike the other camp volunteers, who commuted from an expatriate enclave an hour away, Conquergood insisted on living in Ban Vinai, sharing the corner of a thatched hut with seven chickens and a pig. His first day in the camp, Conquergood noticed a Hmong woman sitting on a bench, singing folksongs. Her face was decorated with little blue moons and golden suns, which he recognized as stickers the camp clinic placed on medication bottles to inform illiterate patients whether the pills should be taken morning or night. The fact that Conquergood considered this a delightful example of creative costume design rather than an act of medical noncompliance suggests some of the reasons why the program he designed turned out to be the most (indeed, possibly the only) completely successful attempt at health care delivery Ban Vinai had ever seen.

Conquergood's first challenge came after an outbreak of rabies among the camp dogs prompted a mass dog-vaccination campaign by the medical staff, during which the Ban Vinai inhabitants failed to bring in a single dog to be inoculated. Conquergood was asked to come up with a new campaign. He decided on a Rabies Parade, a procession led by three important characters from Hmong folktales—a tiger, a chicken, and a *dab*—dressed in homemade costumes. The cast, like its audience, was one hundred percent Hmong. As the parade snaked through the camp, the tiger danced and played the *qeej,* the *dab* sang and banged a drum, and the chicken (chosen for this crucial role because of its traditional powers of augury) explained the etiology of rabies through a bullhorn. The next morning, the vaccination stations were so besieged by dogs—dogs carried in their owner's arms, dogs dragged on rope leashes, dogs rolled in on two-wheeled pushcarts—that the health workers could hardly inoculate them fast enough. Conquergood's next production, a sanitation campaign in which a parade of children led by Mother Clean (a huge, insanely grinning figure on a bamboo frame) and the Garbage Troll (dressed in ragged clothes plastered with trash) sang songs about latrine use and refuse disposal, was equally well received.

During Conquergood's five months in Ban Vinai, he himself was successfully treated with Hmong herbs for diarrhea and a gashed toe. When he contracted dengue fever (for which he also sought conventional medical treatment), a *txiv neeb* informed him that his homesick soul had wandered back to Chicago, and two chickens were sacrificed to expedite its return. Conquergood considered his relationship with the Hmong to be a form of barter, "a productive and mutually invigorating dialog, with neither side dominating or winning out." In his opinion, the physicians and nurses at Ban Vinai failed to win the cooperation of the camp inhabitants because they considered the relationship one-sided, with the Westerners holding all the knowledge. As long as they persisted in this view, Conquergood believed that what the medical establishment was offering would continue to be rejected, since the Hmong would view it not as a gift but as a form of coercion.

CHECK YOUR UNDERSTANDING

1. What is your reaction to Fadiman's description of the culture clash between the Hmong and American doctors?
2. What role did differences in perceptions play in misunderstanding?
3. Describe a situation in which you experienced "culture clash." What variables caused the clash?

How could your understanding of the concepts presented in this text have helped you understand and cope with the situation in an effective way?

4. How might Fisher's concept of mindset help both the Hmong and the American medical personnel to avoid or a least minimize misunderstanding?

Telling Multicultural Tales in Applied Contexts: Unexpected Journeys into Healing and Interconnectedness in Hospitals and Courtrooms

Sunwolf

story (stor•e), *n.* **1.** a narrative, either true or fictitious. **2.** a way of knowing and remembering information; a shape or pattern into which information can be arranged and experiences preserved. **3.** an ancient, natural order of the mind. **4.** isolated and disconnected scraps of human experience, bound into a meaningful whole.

Technologies replace tales, news supersedes narrative, and videos increasingly seduce viewers. We have created vast data sets from sophisticated communication technologies, yet individuals in the western world have never had fewer stories to pass on to one another in interpersonal dialogues. Feeling the lack of stories to tell, people gravitate toward media-generated tales; rather than *doing story* with one another, they invite one another to *watch* it. Strange times.

Human beings think, perceive, imagine, and make moral choices according to narrative structures (Sarbin, 1986). Storytelling is one of the oldest forms of communication and has been used by every culture (Collins & Cooper, 1997). Nonetheless, the accessibility, appeal, and variety of home videos and multiple cable movie channels have contributed to the separation of individuals from the powerful stories of people around them, and has further isolated many from a full awareness of their own rich stories. Livo and Rietz (1986) argue that in story we are shown a truth about who we are and even why we are, since a tale takes the ordinary and binds it into all of human existence, revealing the significance of the trivial. When I ask college students to tell me stories that were told in their families, they stare at me blankly; they were not, they explain, *told* stories—though some of them confess to being read to (the latter practice, however, stopping abruptly at the time the child demonstrated independent reading ability). Curious times.

Stories are among our most basic units of communication. We are socialized by narrativity, although we may be educated by rationality (Fisher, 1984). The role of stories in social explanation has been analyzed in fields as diverse as psychology, sociolinguistics, political science, history, anthropology, law, and communication (summarized by Bennett, 1992). Fisher (1985, 1987) suggests that humans are essentially storytellers, and proposes that all forms of communication are most usefully interpreted from a narrational perspective, since people inherently pursue a *narrative* logic. A recently proposed decision-making theory of communication is based upon the narrative-imagining people experience during ordinary circumstances (Sunwolf, 2001b). Decisional Regret Theory argues that people facing important decisions create imaginary stories with alternate choices and outcomes, in an attempt to anticipate and avoid feeling regret later. Story*thinking* is pervasive and unavoidable.

The Storied Audience Bridge

A Zuni kachina emerged from the underworld and attached to his back was a being from an alien world. There they were, back-to-back, facing in opposite directions. The alien couldn't see the world of the Zuni

and so, of course, he didn't understand it. Yet, they were attached. But still he had hope; for there was always the possibility that the Zuni would learn to turn around, and then each could learn who the other was and what the other might become. (Stotter, 1994a)

Media-delivered storytelling shares the theater's traditional "fourth wall" relationship with audiences: the audience is not immediate. Instead of allowing themselves to see their audience, theater actors create a fourth wall where the audience passively sits—encouraged to watch, but not interact with, the performance. Interpersonal storytelling, however, is lost without the audience connection (Cordi, 1997). The story is projected through the teller's unique personality and performance style, rather than an assumed temporary role. The storyteller's goal is not, as with the actor, to make the audience believe they are seeing someone other than the teller—in fact, a personal audience-connection is actually much sought after. Oral storytelling creates a relationship (Collins & Cooper, 1997). The teller-quest for a communication connection with audience is illustrated by the experience of one storytelling troupe of middle-school students, sponsored by the California Arts Council, who began giving weekly performances at a day care center for senior citizens. Unfortunately, students found that listeners often interrupted with questions or comments. To draw deeper connections, students started stimulating their senior audience members before the tellings using memory-prompts (i.e., Who was your first love? Your favorite pet? Your best friend?), which connected young tellers to their older audience in advance of the tellings (Loya, 1997). Poignant *audience* tales emerged:

> Frank told amazing stories. With each passing year, however, his personality deteriorated, ravaged by Alzheimer's disease. By the third year he barely talked and never told stories. One day a young teller, Yarra, told about dancing. When she finished, Frank spoke for the first time in months. He had been a champion dancer, had won lots of competitions. Would Yarra like to dance? She accepted. They moved gracefully about the room in a wonderful dance, then he brought her back to her chair. As he sat down, the light left his eyes for the last time. He never spoke again after that. (Loya, 1997, p. 10)

COMMUNICATION EFFECTS OF STORYLISTENING

"What do stories do? Affect us, nothing else" (St. John, 1990).

"Tale" comes from the Anglo-Saxon *talu*, which means "speech"—and so, tales are meant to be told, both in the etymological sense and in a historical sense

(Yolen, 1986). Traditionally, laws, news, customs, values and beliefs were passed on through the years through oral tales. Paleontologists argue that it is the very capacity to make pictures in our brain that compensated for our comparatively weak senses of smell, sight, touch, hearing, and taste (Birch & Heckler, 1996). Storytelling has been proposed as the engine, the expressive heart of human communication systems in all cultures (Birch & Heckler, 1996). Oral storytelling has been vanishing, however, in a technologically video-driven Internet world.

Stories are themselves commentaries on the narratives a community finds valid or compelling, and constitute a form of persuasive argument (Kirkwood, 1985). Four theoretical explanations for the powerful effects of storytelling from research on social influence processes have been suggested in Table 1.

Contemporary tellers are attempting to restore the effects of story wisdom (see, for example, Mellon, 1992). Story is widely viewed as a method both for learning about the world and a way to share knowledge (Berger, 1997). Fisher (1987) argues that people evaluate persuasive reasons for moral action based upon narrative assessments of the stories they experience, while Kirkwood (1992) suggests that stories function to open the mind to creative possibilities when the tales exceed people's values, beliefs, and experiences. Bruner (1986) has helped popularize within educational research a conception of the mind that gives renewed prominence to the role of story in our ways of making sense of the world and of experience. Stories perform both an epistemological function (passing on specific knowledge to the listener) and transformative function (suggesting new ways of thinking or behaving). Using storytelling in classrooms and workshops fulfills multiple curricula and administrative directives for teachers and team leaders because it is interdisciplinary, embodies whole language pedagogy, addresses the needs of group members with different learning styles,

and teaches high level thinking skills. Storytelling can be used to construct a cooperative learning experience (Stotter, 1994b). Kirkwood and Gold (1983) use teaching stories to explore philosophical themes in the classroom. Cargile and Sunwolf (1998) offer folktales from Nigeria and India to teach constructs in an intercultural communication course, and African Dilemma tales, Native American lesson stories, and Sufi wisdom tales are suggested for provoking discussion in a variety of teaching and persuasive tasks (Sunwolf, 1999a; see also, Appendix A). Egan (1995) demonstrates how the narrative nature of mind might affect our ideas about learning principles in college classrooms.

The search for community is enhanced by storytelling, as listeners and tellers become for a moment "all one blood, but many minds" (McGee & Nelson, 1985). Oral storytelling may be a more effective teaching tool than traditional lecture format, allowing powerful indirect instruction, prompting dialogue, providing an easily retrievable format, enhancing listening skills, as well as providing opportunities for the appreciation of the beauty and rhythm of language (Sunwolf, 1997). Witherell, Tran, and Othus (1995) argue that oral storytelling allows the audience to engage in a leap of empathy, binding them into wider relationships that provide bridges across cultures. Stories have a legitimate and valuable function in public debate, offering an essential moral element to public discussion (McGee & Nelson, 1985), and expanding the human capacity to "become what we are not" (Kirkwood, 1992). Listeners benefit from exposure to real and inevitable paradoxes in the human condition offered in African dilemma tales, involving the clash of love and duty, the need for both belongingness and independence, the relative benefits of science or art, the duty to the group or the individual, and the acts of freedom and their restrictive consequences (Sunwolf, 1999a). Further, oral stories aid students in crossing the barrier from collecting the known, to approaching the unknown. The

TABLE 1 Theoretical Explanation for Effects of Storytelling

Theoretical Dynamic	Process
Persuasion through self-generated thoughts	It is not simply the external story that triggers the attitude change, but the inner listener-thinking that may be provoked by a story.
Persuasion through active participation	People automatically role-play as they listen to tales, supplying their own reasoning to dilemmas presented in the tales.
Persuasion through modeling	Attitudes and beliefs are influenced as listeners consider the behaviors and choices made by various story characters.
Persuasion through conscious deliberation	Listeners calculate costs and rewards of future behaviors by observing the consequences and results described in story plots.

Source: Sunwolf, (1999a).

emphasis upon gaining information from lectures and texts (passivity of knowledge-getting) may be supplemented by both telling and listening to stories (activity of imagining knowledge), as wisdom tales *engage* students in ways that connect with their own experiences (Fried, 1995; Sunwolf, 1999a).

In the United States today, there has been a revival of oral storytelling. By the mid-twentieth century, there were only a few pockets of back-porch tellers. In contrast, in many other cultures storytelling was an apprenticed occupation: Irish ollahms and shanachies, African griots, Norse skalds, German minnesingers, French troubadors, Anglo-Saxon gleemen, Norman minstrels (Yolen, 1986). Now, more than one hundred local festivals take place each year across the United States (Martin, 1996). Embracing the technology that has seemed in opposition to such an ancient interpersonal art, storytelling has spread to the Internet, with mailing lists, net newsgroups, and dozens of World Wide Web cites (Weaver, 1996). Colleges offer graduate degrees or educational certificates in storytelling (e.g., University of San Diego, Dominican College, Southern Connecticut State University, Wesleyan University, University of North Florida, Northwestern University, Northern Illinois University, Lesley College–Cambridge, Wayne State University, Kent State University, University of Oregon, Mansfield University, Temple University, East Tennessee State University, Texas Women's University, Hardin-Simmons University, University of Wisconsin–Milwaukee, and the University of Alberta–Edmonton). Clubs of high school student storytellers (e.g., Voices Across America) have been formed in the last two years. The art of storytelling has spread to schools, libraries, museums, camps, colleges, ministries, corporate offices, and therapists' offices. Tales are thriving and increasing, preserving the stories of many cultures: ghost stories, urban legends, oral histories, nature fables, fairy tales, personal remembrances, and regional folklore are increasingly abundant. Today there are thousands more (teachers, librarians, ministers, lawyers, salespeople, psychotherapists, motivational speakers) who have made storytelling an integral part of their lives and work. This chapter describes two such applied story settings, the health care and legal domains, in which telling folktales from many cultures is emerging as an innovative training tool for professionals charged with the healing of patients or the representation of clients.

Can Stories Heal?

Stories have power. The impact of stories that *hurt* has been experienced by all of us in our personal and professional lives: gossip, slander, or distorted rumors have devastating effects on the emotional and physical health of the victims of this dark side of storytelling. In the Jewish tradition the ancient rabbis coined a term to describe the power of negative stories, *lashon hara,* which means "speaking with an evil tongue." Limits were placed on what stories could be repeated, as it was understood that the very act of speaking a story gives weight to its words (Stone, 1998). The *hurting* power is counterbalanced by the *healing* power of story.

Indigenous people around the world still tell ancestral stories to evoke healing spirits and inspire change. Aristotle believed that written stories aroused emotions that had a healing effect (Bristow, 1997). Meade (1995), a therapist who trains other therapists on the use of "healing stories," believes that new meanings hatch each time a story is told, both for the listeners and the teller. Lipman (1998) argues that stories help the emotional healing process by (1) undoing the effects of past painful experiences, (2) reminding us of things that happened in the past, and (3) reminding us that past events are now over. Sunwolf and Frey (2001) review the healing effects of storied therapy by doctors and psychotherapists.

On a basic level, stories are effective during lengthy illnesses or healing journeys by providing a bit of distance from the stress and anxiety inherent in hospital settings and medical procedures (Klingler, 1997). Benson (1975) described the Relaxation Response, synthesizing western medical data with eastern religious practices. When listeners are relaxed, they are open to more active retention of what is being said, less defensive, and the internal processes of their own wonderful bodies begin "healing" (blood pressure lowers, pains fade, breathing becomes softly rhythmic, the heart beat slows, and stress hormones cease production). Some researchers explain the healing power of story by arguing that story listening allows the mind to enter a deeper, more imaginative state of consciousness. Stallings (1988) describes storytelling's power to hypnotize ("wrinkles melt, lips part, and even elderly faces glow like the youngest" [p. 6]). Folklore and fairy tales come with familiar "inductions" for trance states built in: It was a dark and stormy night; Once upon a time in a far away land. The spoken tale itself continues the trance, and does not duplicate the literary tale: repetitions, rhythms of voice, silences, whispers, all enhance deeper relaxation (Sunwolf, 2001a). When unfamiliar multicultural tales are told, audiences may be in a receptive storytrance that opens them to receive new values and world views with a less critical mind.

Bristow (1997), a 30-year veteran psychotherapist, argues that while therapy for emotional problems can be threatening, storytelling can be a powerful alternative. "Holding an audience spellbound" is often used to describe an audience's altered state of listening to a great tale told well, and psychologists have claimed that storytelling performances contain many of the conditions necessary for inducing trances (Martin, 1993). A former nurse turned teller explains that for both the storyteller and health care provider, the use of story can help to establish a safe, slower paced, receptive human environment in which patients can feel more relaxed and empowered to express questions, concerns, and needs (Klingler, 1997).

Early research was supportive of the use of stories to help heal emotional wounds of children in therapeutic settings (see annotated bibliography compiled by Langenbrunner & Disque, 1998). The "mutual storytelling technique" was outlined in the early 1970s by Gardner as an effective method for revealing conflicts troubled children experience (Gardner, 1972). Gardner advocated the role of the therapist in "retelling" the child's life story in a way that became both more acceptable and empowering. The metaphoric power of stories for children in therapy became popular among many therapists (Mills & Crowley, 1986; Rosen, 1991), as children's own stories became a tool for the therapist to use in symbolically gaining access to a child's experiences. Milton Erickson combined both the hypnotic trance and storytelling methods to help people address suppressed and painful information in their lives (Rosen, 1991). More recently Barker (1996) demonstrated the use of existing stories in the public domain which he reworked to fit the needs and lives of his clients in order to help them develop alternative perspectives of their own lives. Thematic Fantasy Play was developed as a strategy allowing children to role play stories from children's literature to increase social competence (Williamson, 1993).

While narrative has been generally recommended as a therapeutic tool in psychiatry and psychotherapy (e.g., Eron & Lund, 1996; Monk, Winslade, Crocket, & Epston, 1997; Parry & Doan, 1994; Roberts & Holmes, 1999, Sunwolf & Frey, 2001), the specific use of folklore and fairy tales has received limited attention. Bettelheim (1977) and von Franz (1980) are generally cited as reinstituting a psychoanalytic approach to the buried meanings in fairy tales. More recently, however, active therapists have described the powerful effects on both adults and children of hearing oral folklore as they cope with personal challenges. Narrative Therapy was brought to the attention of many academics outside the world of child therapy by White and Epston (1990), who borrowed from the field of cultural anthropology and the work of Foucault to argue that therapists should help their clients view their lives as stories during the clinical process. A psychiatric nurse,

who is also trained in hypnosis, reports that she regularly uses the combination of storytelling and hypnosis in her work with clients (Martin, 1993). A Boulder, Colorado, psychotherapist–storyteller describes the story trance as an inner-directed state of consciousness, such that eyes may be on the storyteller, but consciousness is turned inward (Martin, 1993).

Not only story*telling,* but story *listening* may have specific health benefits. Three studies were undertaken exploring the coping benefits and limitations of stories people *hear* about others undergoing similar stressful events (Taylor, Aspinwall, Giuliano, Dakof, & Reardon, 1993). Interestingly, cancer patients reported that positive stories about other patients were more helpful than negative stories, yet negative stories were the most commonly told. Relatively few patients were interested in *seeking* stories about other cancer patients, though participants repeatedly reported that they had been told one or more stories about other cancer patients, usually by friends or relatives who were not cancer patients (two-thirds of these stories were about others who had died or done poorly with cancer). The source of a story may influence how it is perceived, even when the story parallels a patient's own situation; Taylor and colleagues postulated that the most effective stories may come from similar others or experts. When the valence and source of stories told to college students facing midterm exams were manipulated, stories with positive endings and those relayed by expert sources were regarded more positively than negative stories and those told by nonexperts (Taylor et al., 1993). In a third study, three groups of students listened either to stories of another student's poor college adjustment, average level of adjustment, or excellent success; there were further two story conditions (*informative story* condition, containing information relevant to improving college adjustment, or *uninformative story* condition). Findings supported that the reason a story may be perceived as helpful depended on valence (negative stories made students feel lucky by comparison, positive stories were perceived as offering a better role model and sense of hope).

Who do stories heal? Stories may have the inherent power to heal both the listener and the teller (Cotter, 1998). Michael Cotter, a Minnesota farmer, led a workshop on storytelling for 22 terminally ill people at Cape May, New Jersey. The location selected was powerful: a wildlife laboratory, where the enormous glass windows of the large room overlooked a marsh that fed into the Atlantic Ocean. Most of the patients were suffering from AIDS or cancer; all had been waiting expectantly for this unique unknown experience. Because of the fragile condition of the participants and the novelty of the approach, therapists, doctors, and nurses were present, too. Cotter's job was to tell his most vulnerable stories, to create a safe place, and to help these patients see the powerful stories embedded in their years of painful experiences (Cotter, 1998). A circle of anxious patients and caregivers was created in the room, led by a farmer who had never lived more than 60 feet from the spot where he had been born more than 60 years before.

Which stories should be told? Cotter finally settled on telling them two stories about his life on the farm, both of which revealed in diverse ways his own uncertainties and vulnerabilities. It is challenging, however, to lead listeners even further into the role of tellers. He provided a transition distant from their current fears, yet reaching to the genesis of who they were: he asked each person to share the story of their name. This was a "story" each participant knew and could tell without planning: "When their stories began to come—hesitant at first, fragile and vulnerable, then with more power and humor and force—they came like a tidal wave. Sad, tender, at times humorous, they were the stories of people looking at life's end" (p. 4). In enacting storytelling with one another, and making the transition from listeners to Cotter's tales to tellers of their own stories, the participants seemed to gain a sense of mission as they moved from names to individual life-dream-identity stories:

> Of the 22 participants, 21 told their stories. An 11-year old boy with brain cancer just wanted his classmates to treat him normally. There was a young father of three whose six-year-old daughter had only known him as ill. That was the only kind of father she knew, though he longed to be a normal one to her ... There was a woman who lived in a setting surrounded by birds and trees and natural sounds. She told of having to go from the well world of nature with its sounds and colors, into the sterile shut-in sounds of the hospital where she had only herself and her fear and her pain. (p. 4)

When the workshop was over, the woman who had remained silent found the farmer and poured out her story—such a powerful one that the farmer–teller experienced some inner healing of his own.

Other storytellers who are taking their tales into health care settings report similar examples of dying patients with a story to tell. One teller was directed by a doctor to a man who had been in hospice for more than six months, receiving no visitors, no mail, not even a single phone call (Oceanna, 1998). By all medical standards he should have been dead. She sat down and explained who she was but he said nothing, and they sat together quietly for awhile. They she began telling a tale. The patient suddenly reached out his hand and touched her arm gently: "If you don't mind, I'd like to tell you *my* story, my life's story. I'm dying, you know,

AIDS. There isn't anyone to tell it all to, and I can't die until I've told the whole thing. Will you listen?" (p. 20). They sat there for hours as his stories poured out. When the hospice nurse called the storyteller the next day to report the man had died peacefully in his sleep that night, storytelling took on a new dimension for the teller, as she confronted the phenomenon she called "Transitional Story Listening." Oceanna's hospice work began to actively include story listening. She had often used stories to ease the transition between life and death, but now she realized that sometimes the dying have a need to tell their own stories, to be heard and accepted by other human beings before they can let go of life. She began asking the people she visited if they wanted to tell her their stories—many patients specifically gave her permission to tell their stories: "One elderly English gentleman called me his personal bard. In his mind's eye, he said, he saw me singing songs and passing down stories about his life like the troubadours of old. He claimed it made him feel immortal" (p. 20).

Richard Stone (1994) has developed a guide to help health care practitioners elicit story memories from patients, and actively conducts workshops across the country on such topics as the healing power of humor in storytelling, enhancing communication skills through the power of storytelling, improving physician communication through positive listening attitudes, transforming a hospital's culture through the power of storytelling, and building a community of caring and support in health care institutions. His storytelling workshops are intensive and experiential—designed not only for nurses and doctors, but including therapists, social workers, volunteers, patient advocates, interns, and clergy who constitute additional accessible avenues for eliciting stories from anxious patients. Bristow (1997) has developed a "storyboard" to aid in the process of putting together some orderly sequence to a patient's told story.

Health care workers routinely rely upon the self-reports of their patients in measuring the healing effects of listening to and telling stories. One unique effort to quantify such effects is the use of a "Death Anxiety Scale," which gauges the degree to which an individual experiences anxiety at the prospect of dying. This scale is being applied in storytelling applications to help create emotional and spiritual healing at life's end (Stone, 1998). The Missoula Quality at Life's End Demonstration Project is currently finalizing results from a study in which two groups of 30 residents living in a congregate living facility participated in research over a period of six to eight weeks. The Death Anxiety Scale, as well as other scales, were administered before, at the conclusion of the story treatment, and then six to eight weeks later. A matched control group was led by a facilitator in general discussions about events of the day at the same time each week, while the experimental group participants worked with story exercises designed to facilitate reminiscence sharing (Stone, 1998). Another research project is examining the biochemical effects of storytelling, testing story listeners for the presence of an immune substance known as immunoglobulin A and the hormone cortisol, which have been connected with the trance state (Martin, 1993).

Many national health care organizations now regularly offer training programs designed to help patients heal through storytelling, including the National Hospice Organization and the Spiritual Caregivers Association. The growing use of oral storytelling by health care practitioners is predicated on the belief that storytelling is a natural outcome of speech, and that all people, therefore, are storytellers, whether they know it or not. One radical prediction foresees a change in America's health care system (Klingler, 1997):

> Hospital settings and other health care environments should make room for institutional models of healing that incorporate storytelling and other art form . . . even traditionalists are opening themselves to the possibility that the quickest route to healing the body is through the psyche and the soul. Like shamans in tribal societies, storytellers may soon be walking the halls of hallowed medical institutions dispensing their remedies one tale at a time. (pp. 21–22)

The National Storytelling Network (www.storynet.org), has recently organized the Healing Arts Special Interest Group, offering references, resources, and networking for health care workers wishing to read and train in narrative healing.

Can Stories Obtain Justice?

> I don't know, I'd kind of like to make a story. Then have everybody believe the same story that happened. (Foreperson, robbery trial; Sunwolf, 1999b)

Most lawyers prefer to win; they have this preference in common with their clients. Stories and narratives constitute a form of argument with inherent powers of persuasion (Bennett & Edelman, 1985; Kirkwood, 1985; Lucaites & Condit, 1985; Sunwolf, 1999a). Fisher (1987) argues that people evaluate persuasive reasons for moral action based upon narrative assessments of the stories they experience, while Kirkwood (1992) suggests that stories function to open the mind to creative possibilities when the tales exceed people's values, beliefs, and experiences. The narrative paradigm postulates that people are acutely aware

of narrative probability in making sense of the world: they are inherently aware of what constitutes a good story, and whether a story rings true with stories they know to be true from their own lives (Fisher, 1985). Juries are always multicultural groups; each juror consciously or unconscious carries powerful inner stories from their own cultural traditions that will influence their views of justice.

In the legal arena, it has been argued that trial advocates must become effective storytellers in order to persuade juries. Some researchers have theorized that jurors organize and interpret trial evidence by using story structures (Bennett, 1978, 1979; Pennington & Hastie, 1981, 1986, 1992). One early study analyzing the content of recorded deliberations found that jurors shared personal stories, though the researchers concluded these shared personal experiences may have been triggered by the court's instructions to share with other jurors "relevant personal experiences" (James, 1959). It has been argued that ordinary people who become jurors judge disputed versions in criminal trials by reducing them to their most common everyday communicational form, the story (Bennett, 1979). Stories provide useful structures: plot, characters, time frames, motives, settings. Bennett and Feldman (1981) suggest that jurors use story structures to manage complex evidence, thus solving the problem of information overload in trials by making it possible to continuously organize and reorganize large amounts of constantly changing evidence.

Trials are essentially *story*-battles. In the courtroom, each attorney will tell the jury a different story, call witnesses to support that story, and make contrasting arguments for what a just verdict might be according to the plot of the story told. After hearing the tales, the judge or jury is faced with choosing between these competing stories. The stories may disagree on plot (*what* actually happened), they may disagree on the motive of central characters (*why* it happened), or they may disagree on what the consequences of the events should be (what would constitute *justice*). Bennett and Feldman (1981) attempted to study why and how jurors make the decisions they do and concluded that jurors place the scattered bits of information presented at trial into narratives, then compare these reconstructed narratives with the stories they construct privately (from experience, logic, bias, myth, social convention) about how the situation described in the trial should have taken place. A recent study of real jurors in criminal cases (Sunwolf, 1999b) revealed that deliberative communication was story-laden, as jurors imported their own life stories, engaged in symbolic story-battles with other jurors about fantasized story-possibilities, as well as *fictionalized* trial evidence by engaging in imaginative storytelling. Seven story types were revealed (what-if stories, if-only stories, common knowledge stories, personal knowledge stories, reasonable-person stories, what-probably-happened stories, and story invitations). Jurors are hungry for fairness, and seek it in constructed stories.

Professional storytellers are now offering workshops for trial attorneys to help them develop and intensify their skills as storytellers, and increase their awareness of the power of a well-told story. Creeden (1994), a prosecutor-turned-storyteller (*"I wanted to tell stories more than I wanted to try cases"*), collected stories of justice from around the world that shed light on issues people struggle with today. Two professional storytellers have recently received a good deal of publicity in California for their "story consultation" service to attorneys. Their company, Anecdotal Evidence, offers to provide the stories, anecdotes, and metaphors that juries will be most persuaded by ("great legal tales from legend and history," "making jurors want to listen," "David v. Goliath—When Goliath Is Your Client"), as well as coach the lawyer in developing storytelling skills. In their workshops, attorneys learn how to present cases the way storytellers spin tales.

Building on the work with storytelling in health care settings, this author (a storyteller as well as former criminal defense attorney and Training Director for Colorado's Public Defender Office) has joined with storyteller Michael Cotter to offer trial advocacy seminars for trial attorneys focusing on the powerful effects of both storytelling and storylistening. "Radical Advocacy: A Journey and a Joining" is a workshop in which a thorough theoretical foundation in communication theory is laid for explanatory power, followed by a participatory series of tales and exercises. A triangulated approach to story and trial advocacy is taken in which three sets of stories are harvested and connected: (1) stories from clients, (2) the attorney's personal stories, and (3) stories from jurors. Going beyond the power of personal or historical narratives, this author and Jim May, an Illinois Emmy Award–winning national teller and workshop leader, use multicultural stories in their work with trial lawyers (see Appendix B). Attorneys are trained in the use of multicultural tales of justice to touch the value systems of diverse jurors and give a sampling of justice tales to use in legal arguments. The power of story is extended further in these workshops with intensive hands-on sharings, in which attorney–participants are led to see how storylistening can expand the relationships they have with their clients, and assist them in finding more powerful stories to tell jurors about the people and value systems

their clients represent. Recognition is given to the fact that trial attorneys may be so submerged in the tales of their clients that they become disconnected from their own powerful narratives (Jim May's powerful workshops on inner experiences of men influenced exercises on "Healing the Wounded Warrior: Finding Your Own Personal Tales"). As attorneys become skilled at encouraging clients to tell their tales and in sharing their own personal stories, they move on to techniques that allow them to harvest and connect with the tales every juror carries with them into the courtroom that will influence how each juror perceives the evidence and what story will best touch their hearts. Stories that come from the jurors are at once more compelling and more credible than those imported by the attorney paid to advocate for one side or the other.

The spoken narrative tradition in criminal defense discourse has been recognized for some time (Webster, 1991). Webster is a law professor who encourages her students to explore the narrative tradition in the cases they study in order to see the stories behind written decisions. Webster points out that most of the stories of successful trials never get told in the case books, because not-guilty verdicts are not appealed and thus do not get examined by appellate courts or result in written opinions; only criminal defense *losses* get appealed. It is a peculiar deficiency of the justice system. Instead, tales of criminal defense *victories* are passed along, from one generation of attorneys to the next, through the spoken tradition of telling "war stories," in which is embedded vital knowledge of successful advocacy techniques.

NEW DIRECTIONS: HAPPILY-EVER-AFTERING

Storytelling as an empathy-building and healing tool for health care workers or lawyers is in its infancy. Methodological designs to study its effects and measure its success or limitations are sorely lacking. In this gap, one thing appears clear, however. Storytelling offers lawyers a unique tool to create connected persuasion, both with clients and with the jurors who will ultimately decide what's fair. Health care settings are uniquely suited to the importation of multicultural tales, which require no expensive equipment and offer a tool that supplements without compromising more traditional medical interventions. The challenge for both groups of professionals is to actively step into the world of oral storytellers, and initially experience the power of being a story *listener* (Sunwolf, 2001a). Experiencing their own brand of listening, they can import the gift of story for clients—at the same time having a tool that may enrich the life of the helper as well as the helped.

> All stories are true on the *inside,* but not always true on the *outside.* —A kindergarten child (Meade, 1995)

REFERENCES

Barker, P. (1996). *Psychotherapeutic metaphors: A guide to theory and practice.* New York: Brunner/Mazel.

Bennett, W. L. (1978). Storytelling in criminal trials: A model of social judgment. *Quarterly Journal of Speech, 64,* 1–22.

Bennett, W. L. (1979). Rhetorical transformation of evidence in criminal trials: Creating grounds for legal judgment. *Quarterly Journal of Speech, 65,* 311–323.

Bennett, W. L. (1985). Toward a new political narrative. *Journal of Communication, 35,* 156–171.

Bennett, W. L. (1992). Legal fictions: Telling stories and doing justice. In M. L. McLaughlin, M. J. Cody, & S. J. Read (Eds.), *Explaining one's self to others: Reason-giving in a social context* (pp. 149–165). Hillsdale, NJ: Lawrence Erlbaum.

Bennett, W. L., & Feldman, M. S. (1981). *Reconstructing reality in the courtroom: Justice and judgment in American culture.* New Brunswick, NJ: Rutgers University Press.

Benson, H. (1975). *The relaxation response.* New York: Avon.

Berger, A. A. (1997). *Narratives in popular culture, media, and everyday life.* Thousand Oaks, CA: Sage.

Bettelheim, B. (1977). *The uses of enchantment: The meaning and importance of fairy tales.* New York: Vintage.

Birch, C. L., & Heckler, M. A. (1996). *Who says? Essays on pivotal issues in contemporary storytelling.* Little Rock, AR: August House.

Bristow, T. (1997). Finding the healing story. *Storytelling Magazine, 9(4),* 18–20.

Bruner, J. (1986). *Actual minds, possible worlds.* Cambridge, MA: Harvard University Press.

Burnstein, E., Vinokur, A., & Trope, V. (1973). Interpersonal comparison versus persuasive argumentation: A more direct test of alternative explanations for group induced shifts in individual choice. *Journal of Experimental Social Psychology, 9,* 236–245.

Cargile, A. C., & Sunwolf. (1998). Does the squeaky wheel get the grease? Understanding direct and indirect communication. In T. Singelis (Ed.), *Teaching about race, culture and diversity* (pp. 221–229). Thousand Oaks, CA: Sage.

Collins, R., & Cooper, P. J. (1997). *The power of storytelling: Teaching through storytelling* (2nd ed.). Scottsdale, AZ: Gorsuch Scarisbrick.

Cordi, K. (1997). Storytelling and theater. *Storytelling World, 12,* 15.

Cotter, M. (1998). Can stories heal? *Storytelling World, 14,* 4.

Creeden, S. (1994). *Fair is fair: World folktales of justice.* Little Rock, AR: August House.

Egan, K. (1995). Narrative and learning: A voyage of implications. In H. McEwan & K. Egan (Eds.), *Narrative in teaching, learning, and research* (pp. 116–124). New York: Teachers College Press.

Eron, J. B., & Lund, T. W. (1996). *Narrative solutions in brief therapy.* New York: Guilford.

Fishbein, M., & Ajzen, I. (1981). Attitudes and voting behavior: An application of the theory of reasoned action. In G. M. Stephenson & J. M. Davis (Eds.), *Progress in applied social psychology* (Vol. 1, pp. 253–313). New York: Wiley.

Fisher, B. A. (1984). Narration as a human communication paradigm: The case of public moral argument. *Communication Monographs, 51,* 1–22.

Fisher, W. R. (1985). The narrative paradigm: In the beginning. *Journal of Communication, 35,* 74–89.

Fisher, W. R. (1987). *Human communication as narration: Toward a philosophy of reason, value, and action.* Columbia, SC: University of South Carolina.

Fried, R. L. (1995). *The passionate teacher: A practical guide.* Boston, MA: Beacon Press.

Gardner, R. A. (1972). *Therapeutic communication with children: The mutual storytelling technique.* New York: Science House.

Garner, T. (1983). Playing the dozens: Folklore as strategies for living. *Quarterly Journal of Speech, 69,* 47–57.

James, R. (1959). Status and competence of jurors. *The American Journal of Sociology, 64,* 563–570.

Kirkwood, W. G. (1983). Storytelling and self-confrontation: Parables as communication strategies. *Quarterly Journal of Speech, 69,* 58–74.

Kirkwood, W. G. (1985). Parables as metaphors and examples. *Quarterly Journal of Speech, 71,* 422–440.

Kirkwood, W. G. (1992). Narrative and the rhetoric of possibility. *Communication* Monographs, *59,* 30–47.

Kirkwood, W. G., & Gold, J. B. (1983). Using teaching stories to explore philosophical themes in the classroom. *Metaphilosophy, 14,* 341–352.

Klingler, A. (1997). The storyteller in healthcare settings. *Storytelling Magazine, 9(4),* 21–23.

Langenbrunner, M. R., & Disque, J. G. (1998). The healing power of stories for children: An annotated bibliography. *Storytelling World, 14,* 23–25.

Lipman, D. (1998). Tips from the storytelling coach. *Storytelling World, 14,* 22.

Livo, N., & Rietz, S. (1986). *Storytelling: Process and practice.* Littleton, CO: Libraries Unlimited.

Loya, O. (1997). Special audiences. *Storytelling World, 12,* 10.

Lozano, E. (1992). The force of myth on popular narratives: The case of melodramatic serials. *Communication Theory, 2,* 207–220.

Lucaites, J. L., & Condit, C. M. (1985). Re-constructing narrative theory: A functional perspective. *Journal of Communication, 35,* 90–108.

Martin, S. (1993). Altered states. *Storytelling Magazine, 5(3),* 20–23.

Martin, S. (1996). A storytelling guidebook: Introduction. In *1996 National Storytelling Directory* (pp. 99–101). Jonesborough, TN: National Storytelling Association.

McGee, M. C., & Nelson, J. S. (1985). Narrative reason in the public argument. *Journal of Communication, 35,* 139–155.

Meade, E. H. (1995). *Tell it by heart: Women and the healing power of a story.* Chicago: Open Court.

Mellon, N. (1992). *Storytelling and the art of imagination.* Rockport, MA: Element.

Monk, G., Winslade, J., Crocket, K., & Epston, D. (Eds.). (1997). *Narrative therapy in practice: The archaeology of hope.* San Francisco: Jossey-Bass.

Oceanna. (1998). The healing power of story listening. *Storytelling World, 14,* 20.

Parry, A., & Doan, R. E. (1994). *Story re-visions: Narrative therapy in the postmodern world.* New York: Guilford.

Pennington, N., & Hastie, R. (1981). Juror decision-making models: The generalization gap. *Psychological Bulletin, 89,* 246–287.

Pennington, N., & Hastie, R. (1986). Evidence evaluation in complex decision making. *Journal of Personality and Social Psychology, 51,* 242–256.

Pennington, N., & Hastie, R. (1992). Explaining the evidence: Tests of the story model for juror decision making. *Journal of Personality and Social Psychology, 62,* 189–206.

Perloff, R. M. (1993). *The dynamics of persuasion.* Hillsdale, NJ: Erlbaum.

Perloff, R. M., & Brock, T. C. (1980). "And thinking makes it so": Cognitive responses to persuasion. In M. E. Roloff & G. R. Miller (Eds.), *Persuasion: New directions in theory and research* (pp. 67–99). Beverly Hills, CA: Sage.

Petty, R. E., & Cacioppo, J. T. (1981). *Attitudes and persuasion: Classic and contemporary approaches.* Dubuque, IA: William C. Brown.

Roberts, G., & Holmes, J. (Eds.). (1999). *Healing stories: Narrative in psychiatry and psychotherapy.* New York: Oxford University Press.

Rosen, S. (Ed.). (1991). *My voice will go with you.* New York: W. W. Norton.

Sarbin, T. R. (1986). *Narrative psychology: The storied nature of human conduct.* New York: Praeger.

Silko, L. (1977). *Ceremony.* New York: Viking.

Stallings, F. (1988). The web of silence: The story listening trance. *National Storytelling Journal, 5,* 6–19.

St. John, P. (1990). *Dreamer.* Pittsburgh, PA: Carnegie Mellon University Press.

Stone, R. (1994). *Stories: The family legacy, a guide for recollection and sharing.* Maitland, FL: Storywork Institute Press.

Stone, R. (1998). Storytelling research with Missoula demonstration project. *Storywork Institute Newsletter,* Winter & Spring, 2.

Stotter, R. (1994a). The storyteller: Bridge between cultures. In R. Stotter (Ed.), *About story: Writings on stories and storytelling 1980–1984.* Stinson Beach, CA: Stotter Press.

Stotter, R. (1994b). Storytelling as a cooperative learning experience. In R. Stotter (Ed.), *About story: Writings on stories and storytelling 1980–1994.* Stinson Beach, CA: Stotter Press.

Sunwolf. (1997). *Story spells: Powerful techniques for teaching the small group, intergroup, intercultural or interpersonal communication course.* Paper presented at the Central States Communication Association Convention, St. Louis, MO.

Sunwolf. (1999a). The pedagogical and persuasive effects of Native American lesson stories, African dilemma tales, and Sufi wisdom tales. *Howard Journal of Communications, 10,* 47–71.

Sunwolf. (1999b). *Telling tales in jury deliberations: Jurors' uses of fictionalized and factually-based storytelling in argument.* Paper presented at the Group Communication Division of the National Communication Association Convention, Chicago.

Sunwolf. (2000). *Restorying reality in the juryroom: Real jurors' uses of what-if and if-only stories in both deadlocked and verdict-producing deliberations.* Paper presented to the Commission on Communication and Law of the National Communication Association Convention, Seattle.

Sunwolf. (2001a). *Grief tales: The therapeutic power of folklore and storytelling to heal grief and loss.* Paper presented to the Counseling for Grief and Loss Symposium, Department of Counseling Psychology, Santa Clara, California.

Sunwolf. (2001b). *Decisional regret theory: Reducing the anxiety of group decision making through shared counterfactual storytelling.* Paper presented to the Group Communication Division of the National Communication Association Convention, Atlanta.

Sunwolf, & Frey, L. R. (2001). Storytelling: The power of narrative communication and interpretation. In W. P. Robinson & H. Giles (Eds.), *The new handbook of language and social psychology* (pp. 119–135). Sussex: Wiley.

Taylor, S. E., Aspinwall, L. G., Giuliano, T. A., Dakof, G. A., & Reardon, K. K. (1993). Storytelling and coping with stressful events. *Journal of Applied Social Psychology, 23,* 703–733.

Von Franz, M.-L. (1980). *The psychological meaning of redemption motifs in fairytales.* Toronto: Inner City Books.

Weaver, Mary C. (1996). Storytelling in cyberspace. In *1996 National Storytelling Directory* (pp. 99–101). Jonesborough, TN: National Storytelling Association.

Webster, L. G. (1991). Telling stories: The spoken narrative tradition in criminal defense discourse. *Mercer Law Review, 42,* 553–568.

White, M., & Epston, D. (1990). *Narrative means to therapeutic ends.* New York: W. W. Norton.

Williamson, P. A. (1993). Encouraging social competence and story comprehension through thematic fantasy play. *Dimensions of Early Childhood, 21,* 17–20.

Witherell, C. S., Tran, H. T., & Othus, J. (1995). Narrative landscapes and the moral imagination: Taking the story to heart. In H. McEwan & K. Egan (Eds.), *Narrative in teaching, learning, and research* (pp. 39–49). New York: Teachers College Press.

Yolen, J. (1986). *Favorite folktales from around the world.* New York: Pantheon Books.

Zipes, J. (1995). *Creative storytelling: Building community, changing lives.* New York: Routledge.

APPENDIX A: AFRICAN DILEMMA TALES

> **dilemma** (di•lem•ma), *n., pl.,* **1.** a situation requiring equally undesirable alternatives. **2.** any perplexing situation or problem. Syn. See PREDICAMENT.

• [Nkundo] The drum asked the canoe what use it was. The canoe replied, "I carry our master wherever he goes, carry others who pay him for the ride, and because of me our master catches fish. Of what use are you?" The drum replied, "I am the mouth of our master and of the entire clan. I warn people when war comes, and I send messages when our master wants to speak with someone at a distance. During the dances my voice speaks with joy and gives enthusiasm to the dancers. Am I not the most important of our master's servants?" They went to their master to settle the argument. He bent over to think but has not yet spoken. Which has the noblest work?

• [Kono] A man was traveling with his wife, his mother, and his mother-in-law. While they were crossing a river, a large crocodile stopped their canoe and climbed in with them. It said that it would let the man go, but he must give it one of the three women. What would you do?

• [Nkundo] A man and his wife had no children and they were very old. The man wept constantly for children—before eating, before sleeping, and in conversation—because he had a great desire for them. A ghost promised him twenty children, but all of the same sex. It asked the man whether he wanted girls or boys. The man asked his friends for advice. They went into council but still have not returned. Should he choose only boys or only girls? Which is better?

• [Pygmy] A young man wanted to get married and went to visit three girls suggested by his father. The first was an expert at fishing, the second was an excellent cook, and the third knew well how to make love. Which one should he choose?

APPENDIX B: THE STOLEN SMELLS*

What is Fair? It all depends:

Once there was a baker who was a stingy man. He was stingy with his smiles. He was stingy with his greetings. And he never gave free cookies to children. But he was a skilled baker and his breads were finely made. People flocked to buy them. Everyone was drawn into his shop by the sweet smells wafting into the street.

One day while the baker was kneading and twisting the dough, complaining to himself about the price of flour, he noticed someone peering in the window. It was a man in a shabby coat. The man gazed at the rows of bread in the window and hungrily breathed in great chunks of the fragrant smells. The very sight of him angered the baker. "There's a thief, stealing my smells, filling his belly, and not a penny for me!"

The baker stormed from his shop, flung open the door and grabbed the poor man, demanding payment. The startled man said, "Pay you for what?"

"For the smells you have stolen," raged the baker.

"Please, sir. I have stolen nothing. I breathed the air, which is free."

"It's not free when it's full of the smells from my shop! Pay me now—or I will have you arrested."

When the man did not pay, the baker had him arrested. The judge asked the baker to explain the charges and listened patiently. Then he listened to the plea of the poor man about free air. Finally he turned to the poor man and asked him if he had any money. The man reached into his pocket and brought out three coins of the smallest denomination, explaining that it was all the money he had in the world. But the judge ordered him to surrender it while the baker smiled.

"I find that the baker owned the smells coming from his shop, and that this man breathed in these smells without permission or payment. Therefore the baker is entitled to just compensation." The baker held out his hand to receive the coins. The judge raised the coins into the air and rattled and jingled them together. The baker smiled still more, greedily anticipating even these few coins as his own just reward. "The punishment should fit the crime," declared the judge. "I have decided that the price for the *smell* of bread shall be— the *sound* of money," and he returned the coins to the poor man.

*From an adapted folktale by Sunwolf.

CHECK YOUR UNDERSTANDING

1. Why do you think oral storytelling is experiencing a revival in the United States?
2. Watch a television program such as *Law and Order* or *Boston Legal* or rent a video such as *To Kill a Mockingbird*. How do the courtroom scenes epitomize Sunwolf's idea of trials as story-battles?
3. How can listening to someone else's story heal us?
4. Begin to collect the stories of your family members. How can these stories help you understand your culture?

CHAPTER ACTIVITIES

1. Collect at least three stories from a culture different from your own. Break them down into categories based on themes such as folk medicine, health-care philosophies, familial health traditions, and definitions of health and illness. Next, examine how the authors of the stories that you selected developed their arguments. Were examples used? Forms of imagery? What do the forms of argument reveal about the culture that you chose?
2. Interview a doctor, a nurse, or a religious leader. Ask the person the following questions:
   a. How do questions of value and philosophy about health and healing influence the decisions that you make daily?
   b. Can you think of an instance in which your own view of healing differed from the healing principles of a person from another culture? If yes, how did you manage the moral difficulty? What was the nature of the difficulty?
   c. What are some new views of health and healing that you have gleaned from other cultures?

MEDIA AND TECHNOLOGY

A CELL PHONE ON THE GREAT WALL?

Jamie, my daughter, and I decided to go to a remote area of the Great Wall. We had visited the Great Wall numerous times, but always at a tourist site. We decided to go to a remote area that had yet to have enough tourist facilities that people would want to visit.

The day was a beautiful summer day—sunny, bright blue skies. We climbed the wall—quite a task given that the Wall was in ruins and no renovation had been done. It was also an extremely high section of the Wall. We climbed for over an hour. Sometimes on our hands and knees because the ascent was so steep. As we turned and looked, the Wall ran as far as the eye could see—up hill and down. After resting and congratulating ourselves on our non-tourist adventure, we began our descent.

About half-way down we hear a cell phone ring behind us. At first we could not believe it! We looked at one another with questioning looks. How could this be? We turned around and a man in a business suit was descending the Wall, cell phone in hand, talking in Chinese. He passed us and continued to talk on the cell phone.

So, we discovered, there is no way to escape modern-day telecommunication—even on a remote stretch of China's Great Wall.

OBJECTIVES

After reading this chapter and completing the readings and activities, you should be able to

- Define the role of the media in propagating cultural norms.
- Explain and describe the dimensions of popular culture.
- Explain how the media handle race, gender, and class issues.
- Discuss international dimensions of media and culture.

In the July 27, 2003, issue of the *New York Times,* under the heading "Learning to Be Very Rich, and a Little Famous," Anita Gates describes *The Family,* a then popular reality show. The purpose of the show is to create "a heightened sense of what rich people do, and it joins a host of other so-called reality television programs that are instructive about the nature of popular culture in modern-day life" (p. 12). In this section we examine the nature, boundaries, content, and characteristics of popular culture. We are particularly interested in the prominence and workings of popular culture and technology and their relationship to the production of meaning in a globalized world.

POPULAR CULTURE

What is popular culture? In trying to define a question often discussed in the literature, we are reminded of the query that a former director of the Smithsonian Institution raised. In great despair over the rising interest in popular and mass culture displays at the National Museum of American History, the director waved his hands in the air and sharply asked,

"How the hell do you define pop culture any way?" (Kammen, 1999, p. 7). Although there are almost as many definitions of popular culture as there are books and authors, it is possible to offer a reasonably clear definition.

The term *cultura popular* is the Latin term for "the culture of the people." As Lull (2000) notes, popular culture "comes from the people . . . it is not just given to them." This is an important distinction to make because sometimes people interpret *popular* simply to mean "widespread," "mainstream," "dominant," or "commercially successful." Although it may encompass some of these features, popular culture means that "artifacts and styles of human expression develop from the creativity of ordinary people, and circulate among people according to their interests, preferences, and tastes" (p. 165).

Popular culture stands in great contrast to what is commonly referred to as "highbrow" or elite culture. Kammen (1999) notes that the terms *highbrow* and *lowbrow* gained currency during the Victorian period when people were fascinated with "cranial capacity," or the size of one's intelligence. This "curiously racist" orientation, to use Kammen's words, equated one (*highbrow*) with high intelligence and the other (*lowbrow*) with very limited mental ability (p. 74). By mid-twentieth century, the way in which people viewed these two terms had changed considerably. In defining popular culture, it is important to note this cultural and historical change, because it has noticeable bearing on the way in which popular culture is viewed today. Although a number of individuals today still view popular culture in negative ways, for our purposes, we need not be detained by a recitation of such views. Just bear in mind that popular culture has its critics (Ravitch, 2003; McWhorter, 2003). Instead, let us focus on the nature of what is generally called popular culture (see Figure 12.1).

Popular culture embraces such cultural products as advertisements, music videos, video games, variety shows, children's cartoons, talk shows, situation comedies, soap operas, made-for-television movies, and sport (Dyson, 1996, p. 140). This means that at any given moment you are bombarded by the television program, *Survivor,* the *Harry Potter* book and film series, and hip-hop artist 50 Cent. Scholars suggest that these forms of popular culture specialize in or are rooted in entertainment (Cusic, 2001, p. 1; Dyson, 1996, p. 140). Although some popular culture may be viewed as "art," entertainment is the primary engine that drives the medium, providing viewers with a mixture of relaxation, escape, and excitement. In other words, people use popular culture as a way of cooling down after a hard day's work, or, in the case of university students, as a way of escaping stress after a particularly difficult final examination. Popular culture, however, extends far beyond merely an escapist route for individuals. Because media are carriers of popular culture, the latter can and does provide individuals with a dynamic way of looking at their world.

Consider, for example, an incident that happened in Puerto Rico in 1997 that stirred much controversy after a Barbie doll was introduced to the island by Mattel as part of the company's "Dolls of the World" line. Although the doll was received enthusiastically

---

■ FIGURE 12.1   Components of Popular Culture Forms

Advertisements	Talk shows
Soap operas	Situation comedies
Music videos	Video games
Variety shows	Movies
Sport	Cartoons
Primary engine =	Entertainment
End products =	Mixture of enjoyment, relation, escape, and excitement
Overall impact =	Major vehicle for circulating messages and images that shape human perception

in Puerto Rico, it created a heated debate among mainland Puerto Ricans. Mainlanders objected to the doll's light skin, her colonial-style tiered dress, and other features. "I was insulted," said Gina Rosario, a 46-year-old school art director of Puerto Rican descent who lives in Virginia. Rosario objected to the doll on the grounds that it looked "very, very Anglo" (Navarro, 1997, p. 1).

In this example, Mattel failed to consider cultural definitions of beauty in trying to diversify Barbie and neglected the facial features of Puerto Rican children. Furthermore, the example reveals the tantalizing power of symbols and how they can reconstruct images of people. Consider still another example that makes a strong argument for the ability of popular images to circulate globally and influence what and how people view the world. Neal Gabler, author of *Art Empire of Their Own* and *How the Jews Invented Hollywood,* writes that popular movies have the ability to appeal to people of all ages, classes, ethnicities, and religions. This universal feature of popular culture means that some images are circulated more than other images. For example, although television programs such as *Sex and the City, CSI,* and *The West Wing* are somewhat more difficult to adapt to universal audiences because of their local nature, movies have a striking ability to engage people globally (Gabler, 2003).

In fact, Gabler and others argue that U.S. movies rule global culture. What are some implications of this fact for the student of intercultural communication? Are movies basically forms of entertainment or do they provide not only excitement but also a worldview? These are questions that you should consider as you think about the role of popular culture in society. In any case, popular culture can shape humans' attitudes and beliefs despite its purpose, which is to entertain, delight, amuse, and, in some instances, educate.

Popular culture is also a marketing medium. The values that prevail are indeed the values of the marketplace, as Hunter (2000, p. 224) points out. Hunter is not alone in his assessment of popular culture. Dr. David Marx, executive director of the Coastal Rainforest Coalition based in San Francisco, California, places popular culture on a par with large corporations and missionaries—past and present—in terms of function and interest. Provocatively, he argues that just as missionaries sold and still sell their culture and values, so, too, does popular culture. Furthermore, Marx maintains that "pop culture's idolized icons are the new global missionaries. They not only sell their own products (CDs, TV shows, computer games, T-shirts, and so on) they also (intentionally or not) sell Western economies' values of materialism over consumption, and waste" (cited in Lull, 2000, p. 227). Although Marx's comments are emotionally charged, he provides another view of the compelling strength of popular culture's global reach.

In explaining how popular culture works, Marx delves into popular culture's ability to circulate messages and images widely and easily, because of its ability to provide a striking contrast between what is present in one culture and what is absent in another. For example, MTV videos with their images of sumptuous houses, fancy cars, and stylish clothes send messages to youths in Malaysia, Pakistan, Africa, and other places. The message is that they, too, can have such fabulous wealth if they emulate American culture (Lull, 2000, p. 227). Marx believes that the impact of popular culture on the fabric of world culture is striking and meaningful. In this regard, Marx's comments are similar to Burke's (1962) definition of identification: "You can persuade a man only insofar as you can talk his language by speech, gesture, tonality, order, image, attitude, idea, *identifying* your way with his" (p. 579).

In effect, both Marx and Burke tell the dramatic and important story of why Western modes of popular culture have spread to other cultures, carrying with them U.S. American values. Through their explanations, we get a sense of how images shape the world in which we live. Of course, we do not wish to suggest that the flow of images, data, and points of view necessarily result in changing the deep structure of cultures. By deep structure, we mean intangibles such as values and beliefs, which are not readily changed. Surface structure, in contrast, refers to tangibles such as cars, boats, videos, and broccoli.

Marx's and Burke's comments do, however, illustrate another feature of popular culture. Popular culture is, as Fowles (1996) points out, "reception oriented." In this way, individuals receive specific messages in anticipation of the sensations of pleasure, as we noted previously. Here, we call attention to one of the reasons why popular culture is "popular." There is an element of choice involved in the reception process. In other words, people voluntarily choose to participate in the product that brings them satisfaction and gratification. In this regard, popular culture may be viewed as an imaginative space for play and restitution that all are free to enter. The release of psychic energy, in turn, reinforces or augments feelings, creating a dynamic allure.

One of the reasons why this allure occurs is because of the shape that messages take when they are delivered to popular audiences. That shape is in the form of a narrative. As we have stated previously, narratives and stories are one of humankind's most basic and appealing vehicles for delivering messages, whether local, national, or international. Narratives and popular culture—television and film, in particular—serve as ways of "encasing" media content, pushed along by the very compelling nature of storytelling, which has a beginning, a middle, and an end. Fowles (1996, p. 107) believes that the encasing process works well and can be generalized to all of popular culture, including television, film, and videos, because of narratives' directional qualities (see Figure 12.2).

First, the beginning of the narrative, much like an elixir, invokes the emotions, which, by implication, will be satisfactorily resolved in the end. Second, much like a vessel that needs to be filled, so does the narrative fill our souls with tantalizing promises of things to come and feelings to be resolved. The narrative, then, acts as a "bonding" agent or a solvent, cementing our ways and feelings with the ways and feelings of others wherever they are in time and space.

Finally, the narrative power of popular culture offers a special kind of content that "affirms the operant social codes" (Fowles, 1996, p. 107). This is particularly noticeable in rap music, which encourages people to rebel against authority or to define and redefine the way that their lives might be lived. The movement of the popular culture narrative is directional; that is, it moves from the "plane of emotions to the plane of norms" (p. 107). Fowles collapses this narrative form into two parts: an interior part and an exterior part. The interior (feelings) aspect of the narrative corresponds to the pleasure dimensions, whereas the exterior (design) aspect provides "patterns for making sense out of the world" (p. 7). The exterior dimension of the narrative has significant implications for changing social mores and creating new and different cultural norms. For example, popular culture has been instrumental in "reconstituting" images of U.S. Blacks and other minorities. At the beginning of the twentieth century, for instance, Blacks were often depicted in demeaning and degrading images. Today, however, Blacks are not portrayed as "Aunt Jemima" or as "happy-go-lucky" souls.

Popular culture—television and film—has changed how audiences view Blacks because of narrative's power to shift audience emotions from a negative orientation to a more positive one. In this regard, popular culture serves a didactic or teaching function as well as a rehabilitative function. By rehabilitative, we mean the capacity of popular culture to restore images or bring about a condition of health to demeaned images.

▌FIGURE 12.2   Role of Storytelling in Popular Culture

Stories "encase" media content *(messages)*,
using a beginning *(evokes emotions)*,
a middle *(fills our minds with promises)*, and an ending *(affirms social codes)*
(directional qualities in terms of emotions and norms)

NORMS AND THE MEDIA

Norms and the media are intricately linked. "*Norms* are social agreements that the members of a community are expected to abide by and that can be enforced by sanctions, both positive and negative" (Mueller, 1973, p. 109; Adler and Rodman, 1982, p. 238; Wood, 1999, p. 99). Other terms for norms are *rules* and *laws*. Norms define the limits of permissible behavior in various situations, such as what is required in church as opposed to what is required at a football game.

Although norms may be explicitly or overtly stated, many are implicitly stated or inferred from previous behavior that we pick up from people in our social environment. For example, you probably won't find a written description of how to behave on an elevator in a large department store, yet if called on to do so you could certainly describe the implicit rules that govern behavior on an elevator. One implicit or unstated rule of elevator behavior is that you should look straight ahead and read the numbers on the panel near the door instead of making eye contact with fellow elevator riders. In Belgium, when greeting a person, you are expected to kiss the other person on the cheek three times, whereas in the United States, you are normally expected to shake hands, using a vigorous pumping motion. Of course, other cultures observe other rich modes of greeting behavior.

Norms are reflections of the culture in which we live and are rooted in tradition. Among the Yoruba of Nigeria, for instance, norms apply to respect for the elderly, how to address outsiders, when food is served, and who eats first. If we understand media as instruction in the normative order, then the relationship between norms and media becomes very clear. Media, including television, films, newspapers, books, and magazines, are often sanctions or reflections of the norms of a specific culture; this does not mean that everyone in a particular culture subscribes to such norms, however. Media norms sanction or reflect what is "out there." They may also be mirrors of reality, as some scholars believe, or, according to others, help create the norms of a culture. For example, during the colonial period (Takaki, 1990) in the United Stares, and well into the twentieth century, Native Americans were referred to as the "red race on our borders," as "savage bloodhounds," and as "bloodthirsty barbarians" (pp. 80, 95). These descriptions were sanctioned by such notable magazines as the *North American Review* and even by the seventh president of the United States, Andrew Jackson. Today, the focus is more on positive images of Native Americans and other ethnic groups.

Media are cultural couriers and contain a cluster of images of Blacks, Native Americans, women, and others, as we will reveal in the following section.

GENDER, CLASS, RACE, AND THE MEDIA

Gender

Writing in a December 2001 issue of the *New York Times,* Natalie Angier asserts in an engaging banner headline that "In the Movies, Women Age Faster." In the article, Angier quotes actress Goldie Hawn as saying that, in Hollywood, there are three ages of woman: "babe, district attorney and *Driving Miss Daisy*" (p. 3). Although Hawn uses hyperbole and humor to make her point, in many respects, she goes to the heart of the image-making machine matter in terms of the characterization of women in the media. Clearly, when juxtaposed against men, the image of women in the media is far less complex and various. For example, men play a range of characters, including dentists, architects, husbands of much younger wives, lawyers, and there is not, as Angier notes, "a pathetic pantaloon among them" (p. 5).

Media are especially effective in conveying messages and stereotypes about gender, particularly in the case of women, and invariably these stereotypes are at odds with the reality of women. Several scholars have commented on the cultural feminine ideal, which focuses on youth and thinness perpetuated by beautiful women who are models, actresses, news reporters, and anchors. In the film *Slim Hopes,* Kilbourne (1995) observes that media, especially advertising, promote the idea that women should be "young and beautiful" if they want to be loved. From such images, we learn a great deal about how media work and how they represent and influence cultural values. In any given television show or movie, viewers are able to scrutinize the characters against their own value systems and categorize the character as, for example, lovely, mean, desirable, a villain, or a heroine. As Stuart Hall (1996) notes, "There is a natural connection between how people look, be, and do."

In Kenya, for example, because of media's influence, Black women are beginning to bleach their skin so that they will be more attractive to some Kenyan men, who prefer lighter-skinned African women. In Korea, some women who have thick calves have begun to undergo surgery to pare down their so-called radish legs to manageable, Western-appearing sizes. And in China, as Johansson (1999) argues, television is now saturated with images of anything Western, including the most prevalent Western image, the "blond, blue-eyed woman" (p. 377). Johansson's research findings demonstrate the reach of a globalized commodity culture, where symbols regarding gender are promoted and exchanged.

Class

Media and ideology not only provide us with images of feminine or masculine ideals, they also serve as a prism through which to view elements of class. For starters, no one has come up with a clear definition of what the word *class* means, as we noted in Chapter 4. Here, we extend aspects of class with an eye toward media. Some people use the word *class* to mean status; others use the word to mean a stratum within a stratified society, in which membership is determined by economic standing and style of life. Regardless of where one begins with this complex term, it is fair to say that the term *class* suggests that people are classified as either upward or downward, rich or poor, employer or employee, landlord or tenant, bourgeois or proletariat. Furthermore, it is reasonable to observe that class demarcates a way of noting who gets what and why (Kerbo, 1996). Since Roman times some characteristics of what we call class have existed. After the advent of industrial societies, the term gained more currency and spread around the world. By spread around the world, we do not mean to suggest that the markings of class stratifications are identical worldwide. Rather, we mean to suggest that cultures tend to delineate class in two basic ways, on the basis of achievement and on the basis of ascription.

Class achievement posits the idea that those who work hard and have the greatest ability will be rewarded most highly. For example, a person who works hard for Company A will likely be rewarded with the position of president of the company. *Ascription,* by contrast, means that placement in the hierarchy is beyond the control of the individual. In Great Britain, until fairly recently, for example, it was expected that one born of "noble" birth would also ascend to that status without regard for merit or achievement. Another way of looking at class that has a particular bearing on our story about media's role in marking class is that people are generally classified as members of an elite versus members of the working class, and this tends to hold true whether one lives in Japan or in India.

Today, despite the fact that people are better off materially than they were in the feudal period, certain individuals are still advantaged by social prestige and money, and media play a commanding role in promoting images of class, however subtle. A television commercial for a luxury car is likely to paint a picture of someone living in an upscale house with an impressive façade and a circular driveway surrounded by lush gardens. In other words, television programs, film, and other media forms not only hint at *how* the legitimation process operates but they also tell an informative and informed story of who *ought* to occupy what class, drive what car, or belong to a particular social organization.

Domhoff (1983), Kerbo (1996), and Dye (1995) argue that media play a large role in the process of legitimation. That is, because the owners and producers of news shows are members of the middle and upper class, they have the ability to "create some national issues and ignore others, elevate obscure people to national prominence" (Kerbo, 1996, p. 384). Thus, the media are overly "influenced" by the wealthy and corporate class. This means that CNN, NBC, CBS, FOX, ABC, ESPN, Discovery, and other media companies to a large extent determine what people will see and hear about the world in which they live.

The way that media elites use language is also a special way of signaling distinctions between people and class. Cable News Network (CNN) talk show host, Larry King, for example, elevates movie stars, journalists, and other authors above the level of the so-called ordinary person. This is signaled through the words that he uses. When introducing a highly visible person such as actress Elizabeth Taylor, for example, King typically uses such language as, "If you have not heard of this individual, you must have been hiding under a rock." His words are used to register or to advertise that the CNN viewers are in the presence of a mighty important person. The effect of this habitual, linguistic-making class distinction implicitly signals that some people are more important than others.

Such registers are used more often than one would think in a society where, as Fussell (1983) notes, "class is fraught with unpleasant associations" (p. 15). In a July 13, 2003, issue of the *New York Times,* Nil, a Northwestern University coed, was featured because of the reactions that she receives when she goes shopping at the upscale store, Abercrombie & Fitch. According to the story, most of the time when Nil shops in such stores, she is approached by a clerk who invites her to become a salesperson, because of Nil's "striking" good looks (p. 10). Closer scrutiny of the article reveals not only a bias in favor of good-looking people but also a striking class distinction. It turns out that Abercrombie & Fitch is keen to attract a certain class of people to its products, as its advertisements, website, and catalogs indicate. For example, Abercrombie & Fitch is interested in a particular class of college students, especially people who are members of sororities and fraternities. Thus, the story in the *New York Times* about Abercrombie & Fitch is not only about the commanding role of beauty; the story is also about the importance of class in North American culture and how media frame it—using both nuances and subtleties.

In contrast, Benetton touts class in a more global fashion, and men and women of all hues are featured in their advertisement. Under the banner, "United Colors of Benetton," Benetton uses such language as "A global brand, and one of the most well known in the world, United Colors that combine color, energy and practicality" to sell its brand of clothing (Greenhouse, 2003, p. 10). The Black, White, and Asian models who appear in the advertisement are clearly marked by their middle-class looks.

Consider as well the former "reality" television program *Manor House,* which was broadcast on Public Broadcasting System (PBS) in spring 2003, and which used class "markers" of not only the upper class but also of the lower class. All of the trappings were present, including cutlery, clothing, and speech. As John Brooks notes, "One's speech is still most clearly visible when you say things" (quoted in Fussell, 1992, p. 151).

Race

As we have seen, media have an impact on their treatment of gender and class. In order to see "the other" in clearest light, we need to be mindful of media's ability to distribute information, paint pictures, and regulate the dominant ideas of a culture. The presentation of race is also one way that media have helped to create an imbalance in the social construction of images about African Americans. According to Dates and Barlow (1990), "Racial images in the mass media are infused with color-coded positive and negative moralistic features" (p. 4). They further observe that once such images become familiar and accepted, "they fuel misperceptions and perpetuate misunderstandings among the races" (p. 4). During the twentieth century, and less so in the twenty-first century, the combined effect of the media has been to depict Black Americans as comical, hence their overrepresentation in situation comedies and entertainment variety (Gray, 2000, pp. 118–119).

Television programs such as *Living Single, Martin, Girlfriends, Bernie Mac, The Parkers, Fresh Prince of Bel Air, Eve,* and *Everybody Hates Chris* are examples of the dominant genre where Black Americans have been relegated during prime-time television. Merritt (2004) notes that Blacks appear in other network shows in "ensemble roles." According to Merritt, "Ensemble shows have multiple characters, that is, a set number of characters that one sees every week and through whom plots unfold."

Some of the roles that Blacks play in ensembles are prominent and some are tangential, meaning that the roles of characters appear during the last 5 or 10 minutes of a show. Examples of ensemble shows that feature Blacks are *CSI* and *ER*. In the beginning, *ER* had one Black female surgeon, two Black female nurses, one Black male nurse, and a Black male resident doctor. In contrast, in two of the most popular television programs during the 2002–2003 season, *Friends* and *Sex & the City*, no Blacks appeared, not even in the background, elevating the view that no Blacks live in the city of New York.

In *CSI Miami*, the pathologist is Black and in *Law & Order*, the supervisor of the homicide squad played by S. Epatha Merkerson, is Black. An interesting thing about Merkerson's character is that in the series, in keeping with audience expectations of what a Black policeperson should "look" like, Merkerson wears a wig, although in everyday life she has dreadlocks. In this example, note the intersection between media presentations and race. Such images, however, extend beyond the nonverbal domain into the area of discourse.

Discourse about Blacks and other minorities is often constructed such that discussions about these groups are often restricted to certain topics and events (van Dijik, 2000, p. 38). In an analysis of media treatment of ethnic groups in western Europe and North America, for example, van Dijik discovered that talk about these groups centered on the arrival of new immigrants (illegal), reception problems of housing, social problems (employment, welfare), negative characterization about how they are different from the powerfully dominant group, integration conflicts, and threats such as violence, crime, drugs, and prostitution (p. 38). Van Dijik's point is that fairly neutral topics such as immigration, housing, and employment may be "topicalized as a threat" when they are associated with ethnic groups.

In a more elaborate and detailed analysis of the way discourses about ethnic groups operate via the media, van Dijik (2000) studied newspaper texts of the British tabloid the *Sun*. He critically examined articles in the *Sun* which related to illegal immigrants, starting with the banner headline, "Britain Invaded by an Army of Illegals" (p. 42). Van Dijik's analysis revealed that the *Sun* used topicalized headlines, hyperbolic metaphors, rhetorical repetition, and in-group versus out-group designators to portray ethnic groups. Van Dijik concluded that the *Sun*'s overall strategy was to use positive self-presentation and negative other-presentations. By self-presentation, van Dijik means references to members of the *Sun*'s dominant *ethnic* group. Following is a list of some of his findings: (1) Immigrants are stereotypically represented as breaking the norms and the law—that is, as being different, deviant, and a threat to British culture; (2) Britain as a group or nation was represented as victims; and (3) the credibility and factual nature of reports about immigrants was enhanced by the frequent use of numbers and statistics (p. 48).

Van Dijik's (2000) research further reveals the role of the media in bifurcating perceptions of race. In constructing a sense of who one cultural group *is,* sometimes media are keen to construct a sense of who one cultural group *is not.* Such constructions, as Cottle (2000) points out, result in such designators as "us and them," "insider and outsider," "colonizer and colonized," "citizen and foreigner," "normal and deviant," "friend and foe," and "the west and the rest" (p. 2). In this way, media delineate one group from another and at the same time create boundaries based on cultural beliefs, ideologies, and values.

In an earlier section we discussed the ways that media serve as powerful agents of cultural transmission. Differences in ethnic and racial values are also borne out by a 1999 Nielsen Media Research ratings analysis of television programs from March 29 to June 27. Nielsen found that Black viewers and White viewers watch entirely different television programs. For example, the top programs that Black viewers watched were *The Steve Harvey Show, For Your Love, The Jamie Foxx Show,* and *The Wayan Brothers.* Among Whites, these shows ranked 150th, 145th, 145th, and 142nd, respectively. A striking feature of the highly watched Black shows is that they featured programs with Black characters and actors.

The statistics regarding the shows that Whites watched during the same Nielsen ratings period reveal an entirely different story. The first- through fourth-ranked shows for Whites during the 1999 viewing period were *Frazier,* followed by *ER, Friends,* and *Veronica's Closet.* Among Blacks, the same shows finished 105th, 22nd, 102nd, and 92nd (Goldberg, 2002, pp. 148–149). These statistics reveal, among other things, that television is a major vehicle through which culture and values are articulated.

MEDIA AND POWER

Lull (2000) writes that "mass and micro communications media easily reach across national and cultural borders" (p. 224). In this manner, media play an extraordinary role in such a reach, using hegemonic power. Hegemony "is a process of convergence, consent, and subordination" (p. 54). The process of hegemony works this way. Ways of living, social institutions, owners of the means of production, and industries are compressed into a mosaic or form that preserves the folkways and "cultural advantage of the already powerful" (p. 55). One of the most effective ways that this is done is through fewer and fewer people who own media outlets such as radio and television stations, film companies, magazines, and newspapers. For example, Disney owns ABC, and Westinghouse Broadcasting and Viacom owns the CBS network. Time Warner merged with Turner Broadcasting Service and then with America Online, and Disney merged with Capital Cities Broadcasting/ABC (p. 34).

These facts demonstrate the capacity of empowered individuals to control most images of how we see ourselves and others. Media elites create images in the sense that they select what will be presented and how it will be presented. In this manner, our views of different cultural groups are shaped by media elites. And such views greatly shape the experiences and realities of others. For example, most of the images of Ethiopians on television are of starving, fly-smitten, emaciated people, leading many people to believe that *all* Ethiopians are woe-smitten people. The example of Ethiopia also illustrates the fact that if images selected by media elites are repeated often enough, they ultimately function holistically; that is, they function such that a part stands for the whole. Such images, through powerful repetition over time, also function as if they are facts. When one of the authors of this textbook visited South Africa for the first time in 1999 she realized the inherent ability of the media to sculpt images. She noted, for instance, that not all of Southwest Township contained tarpaulin-covered "shacks," an image that had been propagated by the media.

The hegemonic commercial advantage of media elites extends even further into related industries. As Figure 12.3 illustrates, when it comes to media, a small elite group of men and corporations influence what we read and especially what we watch on television. For example, media mogul Rupert Murdoch's News Corporation owns the Fox Group in the United States, several British and Australian media outlets, along with television stations and newspapers in China—Phoenix InfoNews. In Australia, Murdoch owns at least five newspapers, including the *Daily Telegraph,* the *Herald Sun,* and the *Sunday Telegraph.* In Britain, Murdoch owns four newspapers, among them, the *Times of London* and *News of the World* (Kirkpatric, 2003, p. C7). Given this hegemonic power, potentially, at any given moment, it is possible for Murdoch to reach at least five billon humans worldwide, circulating his story about how viewers ought to interpret their world. Add to this the fact that some people are unmindful of the hegemonic reach of global media, and one has an extraordinary elixir!

Despite the corporate influence over human images, some hegemonic media groups feature diverse characters. For example, the Disney Channel in 2003 produced such programs as *The Proud Family* and *Sister, Sister.* In *The Proud Family* the show's main character, Penny Proud, is not only a good girl in the traditional sitcom sense "but she also has a wide knowledge of black culture, from highbrow to lowbrow" (Warschauer, 2003, p. 23).

CHAPTER 12 MEDIA AND TECHNOLOGY

FIGURE 12.3   The Power of Ownership

Here are some of New Corporation's major news outlets.

Newspapers

Australia

- *The Daily Telegraph*
- *The Herald Sun*
- *The Advertiser*
- *The Australian*
- *The Sunday Telegraph*

Britain

- *News of the World*
- *The Sun*
- *The Sunday Times*
- *The Times of London*

United States

- *The New York Post*

Television

• Fox News Channel	United States
• Phoenix Info News	China
• Sky News	Britain
• Star News	India

Magazines

• *The Weekly Standard*	United States

Source: Adapted from the *New York Times,* April 7, 2003, p. C7.

ADVERTISING AND THE MEDIA

In her riveting film about the role of advertising in shaping attitudes and behavior about North American women's fixation on ideal female beauty, Kilbourne (1995) uses the term "impossible beauty" as a way of dramatizing the point that the ideal female beauty body size excludes about 90 percent of U.S. women! Despite this dazzling statistic, many women worldwide continue to buy into such images about slimness and beauty. Why? Part of the answer lies in the way advertising does its cultural work, which we discuss below.

First, the *raison d'être* for advertising involves "subtle psychic engineering, attaching subconscious needs and wants to often unnecessary products" (Linden, 2002, p. 207). Put another way, advertising involves rearranging motives, needs, and desires. Thus, the goal of an advertisement is to get consumers to transfer "the positive associations of the noncommodity material onto the commodity" so that beauty and glamour equal Maybelline, and friendship and excitement equal Bud Light. In fact, Bud Light commercials have been highly successful in painting a cultural picture of socially happy individuals such that people tune in before football games simply to watch the commercials. Judith Williamson's comment about the purpose of advertisements is telling: "Things 'mean' to us, and we give this meaning to the product, on the basis of an irrational mental leap invited by the form of the advertisement" (quoted in Fowles, p. 13). In one of his films on advertising, television scholar Sut Jhally makes a telling point about advertising: It "does not merely tell us about things, but of how things are connected to important domains of our lives" (Jhally, 1998). In a word, advertising is about the business of "wrapping up emotions and selling them back to people" (Jhally, 1998).

Second, advertising messages include both print and electronic forms and range from newspapers to television to film to the Internet. Regardless of the form, advertisements have a capacity to tap into the wellsprings of human emotions. This ability exists, regardless of the length of the advertisement; For example, magazine advertisements rarely exceed two pages in text and yet they are capable of speaking provocatively to consumers and giving them a window on their cultural world. Jory (1999) writes that advertising's "use of frequent, short, simple, repetitive messages gives it an advantage over other more traditional forms of cultural expressions" (p. 463).

Third, advertisements rely on two basic strategies for their effect: culture bound and global advertising (Leach and Liu, 1998, p. 523). The two approaches correspond to basic ways that individuals can react to diversity in humans: locally (particularism) or globally (universalism). By locally, we mean the tendency to emphasize specific differences in processing and interpreting data when interacting with others. In contrast, the global approach emphasizes likenesses in processing and interpreting data when interacting with others. In terms of advertisements, culture-bound advertisements include products related to holiday items and food that invite adaptation to cultural norms of a specific group. This is referred to as localized advertising and the target is national or regional markets.

Despite the localized nature of such advertising, corporate organizations must also be aware of within-cultural differences in terms of both content and style. The importance of within-cultural differences can be seen in new advertising by Procter & Gamble, which is responsible for dozens of big brand items such as Crest toothpaste, Tide detergent, Bounty, Pampers, Charmin, and Pringles (Elliott, 2003, p. C5). Procter & Gamble launched a campaign to reach Black consumers, taking into consideration linkages between Black culture and the larger society. For example, a Procter & Gamble spokesperson noted the influence of Black and Hispanic music tastes, food, fashion, and hip-hop on White consumers: "We're recognizing that the influence of African-American market into our general-market consumer" (p. C5).

Earlier, Procter & Gamble had already shown interest in Spanish-speaking consumers. Paying specific attention to how consumers are likely to be touched by nuances of culture, Luke Visconti, a partner at Diversity, Inc., in New Brunswick, New Jersey, commented on how Blacks and Whites would likely view the new Proctor & Gamble advertising campaign: "A white audience will say, 'That's a nice picture of a mother and child,' whereas an African-American audience will say, 'Ah, an African-American mother and African-American child; this product gets me'" (Elliott, 2003, p. C5).

Visconti's story is also striking for what it reveals about the nature of identity, a topic that we addressed in Chapter 4. Furthermore, the Procter & Gamble example illustrates how advertising has adapted to the new era of the twenty-first century, with a mosaic of cultures capable of being reached by a variety of message sources. Another way of looking at this new sensitivity of advertising is to say that a confrontation with diversity is highly visible by members of corporate cultures that rely on media for message production.

Thus far, we have underlined the importance of one strategy of advertising, the culture-bound strategy. The second strategy, global advertising, in contrast, uses basically the same messages across cultures, with one notable exception; in global advertising, surface details are changed so that they will be in line with local values, customs, and attitudes.

CULTURE AND THE INTERNET

In his lecture on "Some Demographics Based on the 2000 Census," Harold "Bud" Hodgkinson (2002) made a striking point about the world of the haves and the have-nots. Said he, "The computer the U.S. worker can buy with one month's wages would require 8 *years* of work for the Bangladeshi worker."

The statement is insightful because it underlines the important role that technology plays in our cultural lives, and because it raises crucial questions about who has access to the virtual world of the Internet with its chatrooms, bulletin boards, websites, emails, portals, and information, and who does not. In terms of access to the Internet, Hill (2001) divides the world into the haves, who are for the most part "the rich, white, Asian, and urban-dwelling populations and the have-nots, the poor, Hispanic, black American Indian, or rural-dwelling populations" (p. 14). In our discussion of the Internet, we are concerned to address issues of community access and language, ever mindful of the underlying themes of sameness and difference. We use the term *Internet* to refer to the vast network of inter-connected "nodes" (Purves, 1998, p. 138) around the world. A primary purpose of the Internet is to communicate.

Communities of Access and Interaction

Harold Rheingold (Purves, 1998) refers to this vast network of "nodes" as "the virtual community," which consists of the flow of ideas, meanings, and information that circulate globally. Once connected to the Internet, cultural possibilities are open to the user. The possibilities range from paying one's bills on the Internet to making an airline reservation to chatting with a famous author or friend. This access means that people are united around the world in what Marshall McLuhan terms the "global village." Of course we are not talking about "village" in the traditional sense of a charming little town square; rather, we use the term *global village* to mean that although people are separated geographically, they are connected to an electronic world. This means that you can communicate with someone in Bangladesh in southern Africa as readily as you can with someone in Cheyenne, Wyoming.

The connections that one uses to build cultural community in cyberspace are through bulletin boards and chatrooms that allow for discussions over a long period of time, if need be. Although such visual cues as facial expressions, hand gestures, tone of voice, and head-nodding are usually absent in cyberspace, people still get to know one another, however superficially. Does this mean that one can interact in virtual space without regard to race, gender, or ethnicity? And does this mean that the Internet is totally devoid of what Kolko (2000) refers to as culturally "yucky stuff" such as race and gender? Can one suppress race and gender on the Internet?

Language and Cyberspace

Although the Internet is generally viewed as a democratic site because of its tendency to open up access to larger numbers of people worldwide, scholar Mark Warschauer (2000) believes that language in cyperspace can serve as an important indicator of identity. His point raises the question of the role of language in cyperspace and what it can and cannot reveal. As we discuss cultural identity and language, it is important to bear in mind that, according to Warschauer, "as of 1996, some 82 percent of the webpages in the world were in English" (p. 156). Despite the fact that matters relating to linguistic access have changed since 1996, and despite the fact that many sites are rapidly opening up in developing countries, think of the implications of an English-dominated Internet for global communications! The role of language? What are some issues?

First, the matter raises delicate questions about the role of language as a vehicle for revealing racial identity. For example, Gonzalez (2000) points out that when we think of race we generally think that it is limited to such concrete, visible signs as skin and hair color, size of lips, hair texture, eye color, and bone structure. However, representations of the human body in cyberspace can be manifest through language. In cyberspace, more choice is involved. Despite the element of choice, Warschauer's (2000) research about how language affects ethnic and racial identity reveals that language clearly influences cyberspace interactions, even the way that language is constructed.

In his ethnographic study, Warschauer (2000) examined the uses of online technologies in the Hawaiian language revitalization movement, a movement that is designed to help native Hawaiians reclaim their indigenous languages. After focusing on a computer-intensive Hawaiian language class at the University of Hawaii, Warschauer found that "interacting in cyberspace in the Hawaiian language provided students an opportunity to explore and strengthen their sense of individual and collective Hawaiian identity" (p. 61). According to Warschauer, this sense of keen identity gave students an opportunity to relate to their heritage and nationality and a chance to emphasize the importance of the Hawaiian language (p. 61). For example, one student in the "Hawaiian 201" class who had chosen Japanese as a foreign language because of its occupational value, said she "began to hate [studying Japanese] because it wasn't something I could relate to in terms of heritage or nationality" (p. 161). Even though this finding is important, we do not wish to overgeneralize about Warschauer's study. The point is, however, that people are using the Internet to assert their language rights. The study also underscores how the Internet can be used to magnify the role of language and identity in human affairs.

Second, according to Nelson and colleagues (2001), language about who uses the Internet typically casts people of color, especially Blacks and Latinos, as victims of economic and educational resources. As a result, according to these scholars, discussions about the digital divide (who has access to the Internet and who does not), place Blacks and Latinos at a comparative disadvantage, because, as the reasoning goes, if people of color are victims, then why entrust them with the tools of technology? Closer scrutiny of the technology as a problem for people of color argument reveals a more nuanced situation, however. For example, Nelson and colleagues (2001) note that people of color are also involved in many levels of technological work from production to content to design (p. 6). They further reveal that "Techno-savvy Asian whiz kids . . . have always had a place in the high-tech hierarchy" (p. 5). In sum, language, technology, and identity are intimately linked and one should look for complexities in human relations.

Finally, language is very much implicated in the "outsourcing" issue today that is stirring much controversy. *Outsourcing* refers to the process of relocating jobs from one country to another, especially call-center and software programming jobs that are being transferred to India, China, Mexico, and other places (Irwin, 2004; Friedman, 2004; Scheiber, 2004). Without the Internet and other forms of technology, business processing—including call-centers and offices that handle payroll, accounting, and human-resources functions—would not be possible on a global scale. This means that a person in Bangalore, India, or in Mexico City can process your airline reservations, credit card accounts, and other services without leaving home! With the movement of jobs from the United States to overseas, for example, some "companies have gotten themselves into a box because they're not telling people and that's alarming consumers," according to Chris Larsen (quoted in Drucker and Brown, 2004). In the previous quotation, note the role of the Internet in removing geographical borders and boundaries for conducting economic business.

An important thing to remember is that the power of the Internet also generates friction among ethnic groups because it is so easy to "press 1 for Delhi and 2 for Dallas," as Drucker and Brown (2004) note in their article of the same title. Because operators in call-centers are located in one part of the world and their customers are located in another, there is a need for callers to be trained interculturally. For example, in India callers are trained to use North American accents so that matters of ethnicity and race are minimized.

INTERNATIONAL DIMENSIONS AND FLOW OF INFORMATION

To this point we have examined aspects of popular culture; discussed the intersection between norms and the media; identified the relationship among gender, class, race, and media; defined the relationship between media and power; and looked at advertising and culture, especially the role of advertising in telling us how things are connected to important cultural domains of our lives. We have also examined the power of the Internet to change the dynamics of human relations. Here, we discuss international dimensions of media.

In our highly globalized world, a repertoire of images and information is produced and distributed by newspapers, magazines, television, and film. Omae (1999), Young-Bae Song, (2002), Huntington (1996), and other scholars argue that the collapse of the Soviet Union and the end of communism in the late 1980s have brought about a unified global market through the disappearance of economic boundaries.

The symbolic removal of national boundaries means that distinctions between the different nation-states are diminishing, making it easier for certain media groups to transport their images across geographic boundaries faster. Witness the development of CNN and Aljazeera networks, which are beamed across the world from the Middle East to Southeast Asia to South Central Los Angeles.

The flow of information and ideas suggests that increasingly people are exposed to similar images. In Thailand, for example, over 95 percent of urban households have television, according to Jory (1999, p. 463). Coca-Cola commercials, false fingernails, Tina Turner, Brittany Spears, images of Western-style homes, and household products such as toothpaste and shampoo are broadcast on Thai television and in print advertisements (Jory, 1999). We do not mean to suggest that the West has taken over the symbol-making image machine in Thailand. To the contrary, both local and national images circulate in Thailand and in other parts of the world. However, some scholars raise questions about the dominance of Western media and argue that the West has a clear advantage in the movement of images around the globe. For example, as we noted earlier, although U.S. television is losing its hold worldwide, it still is the case that movies from the United States dominate global culture, along with Indian movies, which are seen in many households throughout Southeast Asia, Africa, and India (Gabler, 2003, p. A27).

Hannerz (1992) points out, "The defining feature of the media is the use of technology to achieve an externalization of meaning in such a way that people can communicate with one another without being in one another's presence" (p. 26). However, some key questions that you should ponder as you consider international dimensions of culture and the flow of information across fluid boundaries are: Whose images are circulated the most externally and have the capacity to change the hearts and minds of people worldwide? Who is a player? Who is not? And Whose discourses will serve as a vehicle for distributing values, attitudes, and behavior internationally?

CONCLUSION

This chapter has focused mainly on the media and how they disseminate cultural norms and value orientations. Furthermore, we examined how the media depict race, gender, and class issues through television programming. We also discussed the position of advertising as an aspect of media that contributes to the dissemination of cultural norms and value orientations. Advertising is an important activity within the overall media structure of the United States and elsewhere because the media are privately owned and depend on advertising for revenues. With the spread of consumerism all over the world, advertising has taken center stage in sustaining the free-enterprise capitalist ideology.

Finally, we examined the intricacies involved with the Internet and the international dimensions of media and culture. We observed that national boundaries are collapsing because of media and that symbol-making machines change humans' perspective on the world, and, by extension, influence intercultural dynamics. As you read "Perceived Typicality: American Television as Seen by Mexicans, Turks, and Americans," pay particular attention to the role of perceptions in fostering images of the "other."

FOR DISCUSSION

1. To what extent, and in what way, are media "couriers of ideology"?
2. What are some implications of media and power for intercultural relations?
3. How have media changed the way people live, work, and think worldwide?

REFERENCES

Adler, R., and Rodman, G. (1982). *Understanding human communication.* New York: Holt, Rinehart and Winston.

Angier, N. (2001, December 9). Best years of their lives: In the movies, women age faster. *New York Times,* p. 3.

Burke, K. (1962). *A grammar of motives and a rhetoric of motives.* Cleveland, OH: World Publishing Company.

Cottle, S. (2000). Introduction: Media research and ethnic minorities: Mapping the field. In S. Cottle (Ed.), *Ethnic minorities and the media* (pp. 1–30). Philadelphia, PA: Open University Press.

Cusic, D. (2001). The popular economy. *Journal of Popular Culture,* 1–10.

Dates, J., and Barlow, W. (Eds.). (1990). *Split image: African Americans in the mass media.* Washington, DC: Howard University Press.

Domhoff, G. (1998). *Who rules America? Power and politics in the year 2000.* Mountain View, CA: Mayfield Publishing Company.

Drucker, J., and Brown, K. (2004, March 9). Press 1 for Delhi, 2 for Dallas. *Wall Street Journal,* p. B1.

Dye, T. (1995). *Who's running America?* Englewood Cliffs, NJ: Prentice Hall.

Dyson, K. (1996). On being passionate about standards: Promoting the voice of aesthetics in broadcasting and multimedia. In K. Dyston and W. Homolka (Eds.), *Culture first!: Promoting standards in the new media age* (pp. 129–170). New York: Cassell.

Elliott, S. (2003, June 13). Procter & Gamble is giving a higher priority to developing campaigns aimed at black consumers. *New York Times,* p. C5.

Fowles, J. (1996). *Advertising and popular culture.* Thousand Oaks, CA: Sage Publications.

Freidman, T. (2004, April 22). Losing our edge? *New York Times,* p. A27.

Fussell, P. (1983). *Class: A guide through the American status system.* New York: Simon & Schuster.

Gabler, N. (2003, January 9). The world still watches America. *New York Times,* p. A27.

Gates, A. (2003, July 27). Learning to be very rich, and a little famous. *New York Times,* p. 12.

Goldberg, B. (2002). *Bias: A CBS insider exposes how the media distort the news.* Washington, DC: Regnery Publishing.

Gonzalez, J. (2000). The appended subject: Race and identity as digital assemblage. In B. Kolko, L. Nakamura, and G. Rodman (Eds.), *Race in cyberspace.* New York: Routledge.

Gray, H. (2000). Black media representation in the post network, post civil rights world of global media. In S. Cottle (Ed.), *Ethnic minorities and the media: Changing cultural boundaries.* Philadelphia: Open University Press.

Greenhouse, S. (2003, July 13). Going for the look, but risking discrimination. *New York Times,* p. 10.

Hall, S. (1996). Film, *Race and the Floating Signifier.*

Hannerz, U. (1992). *Cultural complexity: Studies in the social organization of meaning.* New York. Columbia University Press.

Hill, L. (2001). Beyond access: Race, technology, community. In A. Nelson, T. Tu, and A. Hines (Eds.), *Technicolor: Race, technology and everyday life.* New York: New York University Press.

Hodgkinson, H. (2002, July). Some demographics based on the 2000 census. Lecture at Walden University.

Hunter, J. D. (2000). *The death of character: Moral education in an age without good or evil.* New York: Basic Books.

Huntington, S. (1996). *The clash of civilizations and the remaking of world order.* New York: Simon & Schuster.

Irwin, D. (2004, January 28) "Outsourcing" is good for America. *Wall Street Journal,* p. A16.

Jhally, S. (1998). Film, *Advertising and the End of the World.*

Johansson, P. (1999). Consuming the other: The fetish of the western woman in Chinese advertising and popular culture. *Postcolonial Studies: Culture, Politics, Economy, 2* (3), 377–388.

Jory, P. (1999). Thai identity, globalization and advertising culture. *Asian Studies Review, 23* (4), 461–487.

Kammen, M. (1999). *American culture American tastes: Social change and the 20th century.* New York: Alfred A. Knopf.

Kerbo, H. (1996). *Social stratification and inequality: Class conflict in historical and comparative perspective.* Boston: WCB McGraw-Hill.

Kilbourne, J. (1995). Film, *Slim Hopes.*

Kirkpatric, D. D. (2003, April 7). Mr. Murdock's war: Global news empire marches to chairman's political drum. *New York Times,* p. C1.

Kolko, B. (2000). Race in cyberspace: An introduction. In B. Kolko, L. Nakamura, and G. Rodman (Eds.), *Race in cyberspace.* New York: Routledge.

Leach, M. P., and Liu, A. H. (1998). The use of culturally relevant stimuli in international advertising. *Psychology & Marketing, 15* (6), 523–546.

Linden, E. (2002). *The future in plain sight: The rise of the "true believers" and other clues to the coming instability.* New York: A Plume Book.

Lull, J. (2000). *Media, communication, culture: A global perspective.* 2nd ed. New York: Columbia University Press.

McWhorter, J. (2003). *Doing our thing: The degradation of language and music and why we should like, care.* New York: Gotham.

Merritt, B. (2004, September 3). Telephone interview with Professor Bishetta Merritt.

Mueller, C. (1973). *The politics of communication: A study in the political sociology of language, socialization, and legitimation.* New York: Oxford University Press.

Navarro, M. (1997, December 27). A new Barbie in Puerto Rico divides island and Mainland. *New York Times,* p. 1.

Nelson, A., Tu, T., and Hines, A. (Eds.). (2001). *Introduction: Hidden circuits.* New York: New York University Press.

Omae, K. (1995). *The end of the nation state: The rise of regional economies.* New York: Simon & Schuster, Inc.

Purves, A. (1998). *The web of text and the web of God.* New York: Guilford Press.

Rai, S. (2003, December 15). In India, a high-tech outpost for U.S. patents. *New York Times,* p. C4.

Ravitch, D. (2003). *The language police: How pressure groups restrict what students learn.* New York: Alfred A. Knopf.

Scheiber, N. (2004, May 9). As a center for outsourcing, India could be losing its edge. *New York Times,* p. 3.

Song, Y-B. (2002). Crisis of cultural identity in East Asia: On the meaning of Confucian ethics in the age of globalization. *Asian Philosophy, 12* (2), 109–125.

Takaki, R. (1990). *Iron cages: Race and culture in 19th-century America.* New York: Oxford University Press.

van Dijk, T. A. (2000). New(s) racism: A discourse analytical approach. In S. Cottle (Ed.), *Ethnic minorities and the media* (pp. 33–50). Philadelphia, PA: Open University Press.

Waldman, A. (2004, May 6). Low tech or high, jobs are scarce in India's boom. *New York Times,* p. A4.

Warschauer, M. (2000). Language, identity, and the Internet. In B. Kolko, L. Nakamura, and G. Rodman (Eds.), *Race in cyberspace.* New York: Routledge.

Weingarten, M. (2003, May 25). At the Disney channel, it's a diverse world after all. *New York Times,* p. 23.

Wood, J. (2000). *Communication in our lives.* Belmont, CA: Wadsworth/Thomson Learning.

Perceived Typicality: American Television as Seen by Mexicans, Turks, and Americans

Alice Hall, Todd Anten, and Idil Cakim

A long tradition of work in audience reception has examined the way individuals' social identities and opinions affect the meanings they gather from media texts (e.g., Morley, 1980; Livingstone, 1990; Vidmar & Rokeach, 1974). However, relatively few works have investigated differences in audience interpretations across national or cultural boundaries. This would be a fruitful area of investigation because cultural and national identities can subsume many aspects of the differences in position and perspective that are believed to affect audience interpretations of texts. The differences between national and international audiences[1] of a text can include class and power positions, attitudes towards the society of the producer, membership in the society portrayed, and cultural norms and values. . . .

An aspect of interpretation that is likely to be affected by the differences that define the national and international audiences of a media portrayal is the extent to which a viewer sees a media representation as typical of the society it portrays. Differences in viewers' level of familiarity with the culture portrayed in a specific text often accompany differences in viewers' nationalities. The extent of viewers' real-world experience may shape their reliance on the content of the text in their formation of real-world beliefs and attitudes. This principle is perhaps expressed most clearly in Ball-Rokeach's dependency theory (Ball-Rokeach, 1985; Ball-Rokeach & DeFleur, 1976), which suggests that audiences that lack direct experience with a particular subject are forced to rely on the media to a greater extent than audiences that have this experience. The application of this principle to audiences' impressions of other social groups is supported by Greenberg's (1972) work on the impact of television on children's perceptions of African Americans. He found that children from areas with smaller African American populations were more likely to cite television as their principle source of information about African Americans. Hartmann and Husband (1974), in a study conducted in Great Britain, also found greater reported reliance on the media for information about people of color among those from areas with higher proportions of White residents. A more recent study by Armstrong, Neuendorf, and Brentar (1992) examined the relationship between audiences' real-world experience and dependence on media portrayals for information about other groups more directly. These researchers explored the effect of media content on White viewers' perceptions of African American affluence. They found the effect of viewership on real-world impressions to be stronger among those who came from areas that offered fewer opportunities for interpersonal interaction with African Americans. These findings suggest that as real-world experience with the subject of a text decreases, the text will be seen as more representative of or more informative about the community it portrays.

Comparisons of typicality perceptions of the national and international audiences of a specific text are scarce. However, the work done on the impact of imported television programming on audiences of a different nationality or background than the producers suggests that these texts have the power to shape viewers' perceptions of the country or society in which a text is created. For example, Weimann (1984) examined the effects of American television on Israeli viewers' perceptions of the affluence and lifestyle of

Americans. He found that heavy viewers tended to overestimate the income and amount of time Americans spent on recreation by a greater amount than light viewers did. Similar associations between viewership of American programming and understandings of the United States that are consistent with the programs' content have been found by researchers working in Australia (Pingree & Hawkins, 1981); Taiwan and Mexico (Tan, Li, & Simpson, 1986); Thailand (Tan & Suarchavarat, 1988), Hong Kong, China, and Singapore (Willnat, He, & Hao, 1996); and Japan (Saito, 1996). . . .

This work focuses on two aspects of media interpretation. The first is typicality, or the frequency with which the characteristics of a media portrayal are believed to be present among the portrayal's real-world counterparts. We suggest that the perceived typicality of a text varies according to an audience member's social distance from the society in which a text is produced and set. The second focus is on the criteria audience members use in making these typicality judgments. This is likely to vary as a result of the viewers' specific cultural backgrounds.

The inclusion of three distinct cultures in this study allows for the exploration of contrasts in both these aspects of textual interpretation. Viewers from a culture portrayed in the text, here the Americans, are expected to describe the program as less typical than those who have less experience with the culture, here the Mexican and Turkish participants. Since the texts examined in this study are all American-made programs portraying aspects of American life, viewers who have grown up in the United States will have more real-world experience with the subject of the portrayals than will the Turkish and Mexican viewers. The non-American viewers are more likely to be dependent on television for their understandings of American life. Members of both non-American groups are more likely to rate the U.S. programs as typical, especially when speaking retrospectively of their viewing in their home countries.

The specific cultural backgrounds of the viewers are also likely to affect the way they evaluate the text by influencing what is noticed or used as judgment criteria. As the three counties included in the study have distinct cultures, differences in the criteria used to make typicality judgments are expected to vary across the viewers from different countries. . . .

PERCEIVED TYPICALITY IN RETROSPECT

The Mexican and Turkish participants' retrospective accounts of their perceptions of the typicality of American television programs suggest that, for members of both groups, American television was felt to have served as a source of their understandings of the character of Americans and the nature of U.S. society. For example, a Turkish man, speaking of *The Cosby Show,* articulates his reliance on the program for understandings of what American family life is like as well as his lack of real-world experience that could have allowed him to criticize the portrayal or to have put the show into context. "I did not know what an American way of life is. That's what I saw on TV, so that's what I thought what American family is" (#T14, Turkish male, 21, 3½ years in the U.S.). A Mexican male respondent made similar points in reference to a more specific aspect of a show as he evaluated the typicality of the situation comedy, *Friends:*

> This is the first time I am living outside of Mexico . . . so it is the image that someone can get. I was used to . . . because of my job, to have a formal relationship with Americans, but not an informal image like the one you get in the program. So, yes, I would say that, to some extent, I thought it was typical. (#M1, Mexican male, 26, 3 months in the U.S.)

Each of these participants acknowledged that the program shaped his perception of the U.S. and attributed his faith in possibly inaccurate beliefs to his lack of real-world experience with subjects portrayed in the programs.

Most participants did not explicitly articulate a perceived cause of their reliance on television. However, many respondents recounted a similar pattern of the generalization of the characteristics of a television portrayal to Americans, or a particular group of Americans, in the real world. A Turkish woman discussing *The Cosby Show* spoke of the clothes she saw the characters wearing as being typical of Americans: "I thought they were American, that they were really American, because they were wearing all these cloths. They were always wearing clothes that were fashionable" (#T12, Turkish female, 27, 2½ years in the U.S.). This respondent focuses on specific characteristics of the text, clothes, and uses the example she saw on television to generalize to a larger American population.

This pattern of generalization occurred with both the perceptions of individuals' appearance and behaviors, and perceptions of attributes that pertained to larger groups such as families or peer groups. For example, the same respondent quoted above in her discussion of *The Cosby Show* not only compares the behavior of individual characters to American people in general, but the Huxtable family to American families in general. "I thought they were American. . . . Both of the Huxtables were working. They were professionals. Their children were going to school. . . . The way they

were treating each other was a very American way I thought, like how they talked with their children when the children had problems" (#T12, Turkish female, 27, 2½ years in the U.S.). The Mexican and Turkish participants seemed to find television informative not only about Americans as individuals but also about America as a society.

This interest in family interactions and structure was common, especially among Turkish participants. For example, another Turkish woman, again speaking of *The Cosby Show,* discussed the way in which the interactions among the family members on the program differed from those of her own family and her conception of the average Turkish family:

> I guess I compared their family and lifestyle to Turkish families. And, well, especially my family, you don't joke around like that. There's more of a respect relationship, like hierarchical relationship, with parents. And like they'd all go out and have dates. . . . My life wasn't like that, and I was an only child, so, like, it was very different for me. But I guess I thought, you know, the kind of house they had, and their kitchen, and the way they socialized together, and, like, their grandparents would come and even with their grandparents, they would . . . be so friendly, and, like, open and stuff. So I guess I thought [they were], like, Americans. (#T1, Turkish female, 21, 3 years in the U.S.)

In addition to this focus on family, there were several other themes and topics that were mentioned repeatedly in the typicality assessments of both the Turkish and Mexican participants' retrospective accounts. Comments about the relative wealth of many television characters were frequently present in the discussions of participants from both countries, as the following examples indicate:

"I thought, especially about life in California, it gave me the impression that everyone was so rich and lived in nice mansions" (#T15, Turkish male, 19, 1½ years in the U.S., discussing *Beverly Hills, 90210*).

> Oh, very typical. I don't know how you say it, the median class, the average class, the working class, but they live better than working class in Mexico. Very typical. The kids would have more education, the parents would both have jobs or mom would be a housewife. (#M16, Mexican female, 20, 1 year in the U.S., discussing *Family Matters*)

Another common topic among both Mexican and Turkish participants was the social lives of the characters.

> It is a show that has a lot of typical Americans, like a lot of American stereotypes of the blonde, the American girl that goes out with all the hot types, and these trivial incidents that happen to teenagers, or young people. I would say that . . . it shows a lot of fashion. What is in,

what is out. (#M13, Mexican female, 19, 2 months in the U.S., discussing *Beverly Hills, 90210*)

I guess I thought the kids were very typical . . . especially the oldest girl. The younger was more like the studious, kind of like, introverted, kind of person . . . but the one went out a lot . . . she looked like she would be a cheerleader and she was very social . . . she went out a lot on dates because she was always talking about guys, and she was blonde. She was very typical. (#T1, Turkish female, 21, 3 years in the U.S., discussing *Charles in Charge*)

I think they have some things about the typical Americans . . . because the typical American goes to a bar. I mean the typical working class American, not the majority. . . . They like to drink a lot. (#M12, Mexican male, 28, 1 year in the U.S., discussing *The Simpsons*)

This is not to say that all of the respondents perceived the shows they watched in their home countries as entirely representative of America or Americans, or that these viewers were unaware of the constraints and conventions that affect television programming. Several participants, including some of those quoted above, specified that they felt that particular characteristics of a program's content reflected only a particular subgroup of the American population. . . .

Several respondents described the ways in which their views of the typicality of American programming have changed since their arrival in the United States. For example, a Turkish man discussed *Beverly Hills, 90210* as follows:

I thought the college life would be a little bit like that, but it turned out to be not like that at all. . . . I thought people would be really beautiful or handsome . . . but, like, people are normal. Before I came here it gave me some fantastic idea about the life in the States, but it actually turned out to be pretty normal. (#T15, Turkish male, 19, 1½ years in the U.S.)

He suggests that television helped shape his expectations about what American life would be like, expectations that failed to be confirmed by his own experience. A Mexican respondent expressed a similar perception of a discrepancy between television-based expectations and real-world experience in his discussion of *ER*. He suggests that his impression of the relatively charmed lives Americans lead has been moderated after living in the United States.

Maybe [when I watched *ER* in Mexico], it was a little bit more, I think it was easier, the life. When I came here I see that it was the same as we have in Mexico, the problems. . . . When you come here, you say "OK, they have their problems. Maybe less, but they have their problems." (#M15, Mexican male, 33, 1½ years in the U.S.)

CURRENT PERCEPTIONS

As the examples above suggest, the notions of the typicality of American programs which Mexican and Turkish respondents held while they were viewing in their home countries seem to have been influenced not only by the content of the portrayals of Americans on television, but also by their lack of familiarity with daily American life. Once Mexican and Turkish students gathered direct experience with the United States, however, they were often able to amend their typicality judgments. . . . For example, in discussing situation comedies, the following Mexican, Turkish, and American respondents used working and middle-class life as a standard against which they judged the television portrayals. Respondents tended to criticize portrayals of shows that deviated from their vision of the American middle class and commended representations that were seen to adhere to this standard.

I have not been able to find Americans like that . . . because, well, usually the characters, they do not have to worry about their jobs. It is almost for sure or granted. Americans or real guys have to worry about how they are going to live. They have, like . . . they do not have to suffer too much . . . They live in an ideal world. (#M12, Mexican male, 28, 1 year in the U.S., discussing *Friends*)

It is . . . quite typical. They are a family in Chicago. They live in a house. A man, a woman, and two kids. The man is a shoe salesman. They are middle class, maybe lower middle. I think they are typical America. (#T10, Turkish male, 26, 1½ years in the U.S., discussing *Married . . . With Children*)

Not very [typical]. Because you've got three girls who live in this amazing loft in New York City and one of them doesn't have a job, and the other one's like. . . . They couldn't have the lifestyle they have, based on the jobs they have, at such a young age. (#A7, American female, 21, discussing *Friends*) . . .

Members of all the groups also made fairly complex evaluations about the way certain characteristics are exaggerated or essentialized in order to maintain the conventions of television programming.

Some of the traits are exaggerated, so it's not realistic, but . . . some of those exaggerations pertain to some truth, like certain situations. (#M2, Mexican female, 19, 2½ years in the U.S., discussing *The Simpsons*)

Well, I think it is being exposed in a very exaggerated way, but I think all of those sitcoms are very typical American. (#T6, Turkish female, 21, 3 years in the U.S., discussing *Beverly Hills, 90210*)

I don't [think] they're really are realistic portrayals of Americans because they are exaggerated. . . . And I think they are portrayed as being more so than

Americans really are because it's a caricature, but I think to a lesser extent that Americans really are that way. So I think people in America really have those qualities but not the extent that the characters do. (#A9, American male, 19, discussing *King of the Hill*) . . .

Use of Conditional Statements

In addition to overall typicality judgments, we also examined the ways in which the participants phrased and formatted these evaluations. An aspect of typicality evaluations that was common among viewers of all three countries was a tendency to specify the portion of American society that a specific portrayal represented—to argue that a text was typical of doctors, New Yorkers, young people, or some other subgroup of U.S. society. The three groups did this with similar frequency and using similar subgroups. However, contrast in the means of their expressions of these conditions suggest differences in the motivations and processes with which judgments of representativeness were made. The nature of these differences supports the argument that these viewers' evaluations of the typicality of American television were shaped by their need to make sense of their environment.

Turkish and Mexican students were often extremely explicit about their feelings that the characteristics of media portrayals are common to a subgroup of American society, but not to the population as a whole, as the examples below indicate.

> Well, I think it may be typical of New Yorkers, but I don't think New York represents America, the rest of America. I mean, New York is, I think, unique in the world. (#T8, Turkish female, 26, 1 year in the U.S., discussing *Friends*)

> I guess the characters are not the typical average Americans, but they are typical American who is doing that kind of job, you know what I am saying? . . . For example, in that profession, they are, like, typical, very involved with their work. They are scientific. So they are, like, the typical scientific or typical detective or the typical doctor who are, like, very interested in their job and workaholic. (#M9, Mexican male, 26, 1 year in the U.S., discussing *The X-Files*) . . .

Americans were rarely this cautious or explicit when making such qualifications. When discussing how typical a specific portrayal is of America, American respondents often assumed that it would be understood they were not generalizing to society as a whole. Their conditional statements did not seem to contain as many formal qualifiers such as "but only for" or "but not for." Rather, their elaborations felt much more general in nature:

These are people who deal with an incredible amount of pressure. Especially being police officers, they deal with so much pressure, you know? They're not fake. They're real. They get angry at people. They have emotions. I think that's how a lot of people deal with things that happen in their own lives. (#A6, American male, 20, discussing *NYPD Blues*) . . .

CRITERIA OF TYPICALITY JUDGMENTS

Participants often supported their judgments of typicality by focusing on specific aspects of the program they felt were particularly typical or atypical. These aspects of their discussions were examined to determine if different criteria were being used to come to an overall evaluation of the representativeness of a program's portrayals. While we found no distinct differences in the overall typicality assessments across groups, there did seem to be consistent differences in the use of family structure and general problems as criteria for evaluating the programs. . . .

Family

Family structures and interactions seemed to be more salient criteria in the evaluations of both Turkish and Mexican participants than in those of the American respondents. Some mentioned the composition of the American family, as in this discussion of *The Simpsons* by a Mexican man.

> The mother is like a mother to any other people in this country. They take care of the house. They do whatever they have to do around the house. The father supposedly goes out and works and does all these things, which is a low middle class trying to get up in life, you know? (#M4, Mexican male, 20, 1 year in the U.S.)

Similarly, a Turkish participant evaluating *The Cosby Show,* cited family behavior and interfamily relations in her discussion of what she considered when she judged the typicality of the program.

> I think about their way of living, like their friends would come over, the parents' friends would come over, the men would go outside and play, and the women would stay inside and gossip. And all the important episodes would take place in the kitchen. This kitchen thing stayed in my mind, because of the kitchen . . . culture. . . . They solve all their problems in the kitchen. (#T6, Turkish female, 21, 3 years in the U.S.)

American participants' use of family in these evaluations was markedly different. They cited family as a criterion less frequently, and when it was mentioned, these respondents' comments tended to differ from those of the Turkish and Mexican participants. When

Americans talked of family, they were more likely to characterize the portrayals as atypical of American families in general. For example, the following respondent, when discussing *The Simpsons,* argued that not only the specific program, but also TV in general was unrealistic in this regard.

> Actually, I think in some ways it's very typical in that they watch a lot of TV and they do mundane things. But it's not very typical in the fact that they have family that's actually together quite often, and I don't think that's typical of the American public. A lot of TV shows are like that, they show the family around together a lot, but I don't think that's the case with the American public. (#A13, American male, 21) . . .

Both Mexican and Turkish participants seemed to cite shows where the primary interactions were among families more frequently than did Americans. . . .

It is also possible that these differences reflect something other than contrasts in program selection or situational salience. This trend may indicate that family is more central to daily life in both Mexico and Turkey than in the United States, and is therefore routinely more salient to Mexican and Turkish participants. Alternatively, the family interactions portrayed on American programs may differ from the Mexican and Turkish participants' experiences, and therefore captured their attention. Furthermore, since these participants are college students, they are unlikely to have a great deal of personal knowledge about American family life. Their lack of experience may have led them to a greater dependence on television for a sense of what this aspect of U.S. culture is like, even after their time of residency in the United States.

Problems

A second difference in the aspects of the programs that were used to make evaluations of typicality is that Americans were considerably more likely than either Mexicans or Turks to use the kinds of problems that the TV characters face as a means of judging their representativeness. Several Americans' comments suggested that they consider programs that deal with on-going problems as generally more representative of America than programs that do not include these issues. This is readily apparent in an American respondent's explanation of what makes *ER* seem realistic to him.

> The fact that they deal with problems of, like, race relations, how . . . not everything is a happy ending. Obviously there is a conclusion to most of the problems they have, that is the problem with . . . television in general . . . but the fact is that . . . you have more of a

feeling of realism to it than I do with [*The*] *Cosby Show* or something—solving the problem of smoking in 30 minutes. I just don't buy it. . . . [*ER* has] things like people with AIDS getting scorned by their co-workers, that is why I think it is typical. (#A15, American male, 20) . . .

Although both Turkish and Mexican students often mentioned the income and occupations of TV characters as atypical, they rarely used "general problems" as a criterion of judgment. This characteristic could represent an idiosyncratic concern specific to Americans or could reflect an aspect of media portrayals that the American viewers found particularly discordant in relation to their own experiences.

CONCLUSION

The Mexican and Turkish participants' accounts of their impressions of American television programs they watched in their home countries suggest that these shows played an important role in shaping their beliefs about the United States. Their time spent in the United States, however, seems to have allowed them the opportunity to gather the information and experience they needed to become more critical in their interpretations of American TV. Their overall typicality evaluations became roughly comparable to those of American-born viewers. Differences emerged, however, in the ways that participants articulated the portion of American society that media portrayals represent suggesting that non-American participants were more actively trying to determine how television could inform them about U.S. society. Furthermore, some differences across national groups were found in the aspects of the shows that were cited as criteria of typicality. These contrasts may stem from the specific cultural backgrounds of the participants.

These interviews suggest that Mexican and Turkish viewers tended to evaluate the American society portrayed on TV in similar ways. However, it is important to remember that members of these two groups should not be collapsed into one. It is likely that many of the similarities in typicality ratings found here are not due to similarities between the cultures of the two countries. Rather, they are likely to have resulted from a shared, previous lack of familiarity with American culture and from the fact that these specific Mexican and Turkish participants are relatively recent exchange students who are trying to make sense of life and people in the United States. Members of both of these groups are likely to be in a process of sense making—of reconciling the images they see and have seen on television with what they are experiencing.

They are likely to be trying, on some level, to sort out what they can trust from television and what is misleading. . . .

NOTE

1. "National" and "international" are not intended to refer to a particular country. Rather, "national" represents the audience native of the country that created the text, and "international" refers to the audiences not native of the country that created the text.

REFERENCES

Armstrong, G. B., Neuendorf, K. A., & Brentar, J. E. (1992). TV entertainment, news, and racial perceptions of college students. *Journal of Communication, 42(3),* 153–176.

Ball-Rokeach, S. J. (1985). The origins of individual media-system dependency: A sociological framework. *Communication Research, 12,* 485–510.

Ball-Rokeach, S. J., & DeFleur, M. L. (1976). A dependency model of mass-media effects. *Communication Research, 3,* 3–21.

Greenberg, B. S. (1972). Children's reaction to TV blacks. *Journalism Quarterly, 49,* 5–14.

Hartmann, P., & Husband, G. (1974). *Racism and the mass media: A study of the role of the mass media in the formation of white beliefs and attitudes in Britain.* Totowa, NJ: Roman and Littlefield.

Livingstone, S. (1990). *Making sense of television: The psychology of audience interpretation.* Oxford: Pergamon Press.

Morley, D. (1980). *The "nationwide" audience.* London: British Film Institute.

Pingree, S., & Hawkins, R. (1981). U.S. programs on Australian television: The cultivation effect. *Journal of Communication, 31(1),* 97–105.

Saito, S. (1996). *The image of the partner: Television's contribution to Japanese perceptions of America.* Unpublished doctoral dissertation, The Annenberg School for Communication, University of Pennsylvania, Philadelphia.

Tan, A. S., Li, S., & Simpson, C. (1986). American television and social stereotypes of Americans in Taiwan and Mexico. *Journalism Quarterly, 63,* 649–654.

Tan, A. S., & Suarchavarat, K. (1988). American TV and social stereotypes of Americans in Thailand. *Journalism Quarterly, 65,* 649–654.

Vidmar, N., & Rokeach, M. (1974). Archie Bunker's bigotry: A study in elective perception and exposure. *Journalism of Communication, 24(1),* 36–47.

Weimann, G. (1984). Images of life in America: The impact of American TV in Israel. *International Journal of Intercultural Relations, 8,* 185–197.

Willnat, L., He, Z., & Hao, X. (1996). *The effects of foreign media exposure on cognitive and affective perceptions of Americans in Hong Kong, China, and Singapore.* Paper presented at the meeting of the International Communication Association, Chicago, IL.

CHECK YOUR UNDERSTANDING

1. Choose your favorite television program. Watch the program with a person from another culture. What does this program communicate to you about U.S. values and lifestyle? What does it communicate to your friend?

2. View a foreign film. What did you learn about the culture? Would you consider the portrayal of the culture in the film typical of that culture? Why or why not? How would viewing this film affect your communication with a person from the culture in the film?

3. Read a news magazine such as *Newsweek* or *Time* for a month. What images of other cultures are portrayed in these magazines? What effect might these images have on intercultural communication with persons from those countries?

CHAPTER ACTIVITIES

1. Select several articles from your local city and national newspapers, featuring different cultural groups such as French, Germans, or South Americans, and then note how these groups are portrayed. For example, what kinds of adjectives are used to describe these groups? Does the article reveal information about how specific groups use nonverbal behaviors, language, or values?

2. Review the film *Dirty Pretty Things.* Then determine to what extent the film mirrors the values and culture of England, Africa, and Turkey. Use the chapter headings from this textbook as a guide. For example, how does the film treat Africans' orientation toward gender? Toward others? To what extent does the film reflect the values of the director?

3. Select the film that you chose in #2 and then try to correct any erroneous (if any) assumptions that were presented by "setting the record straight." For example, you might say something like: "I noticed in the film, *Dirty Pretty Things,* that West Africans were portrayed as anti-spiritualist. Scholarly research, however, reveals that traditional Africans strongly embrace spiritualism." You might be inclined to cite specific references as well.

CHAPTER 13

ETHICS

CAN I KEEP THE DIAMOND BRACELET?

Gifts are tricky. In the business setting this is particularly true. We Americans view gift giving as bribery, but in many cultures, gift giving is standard business practice.

The ethical issues of receiving and giving gifts in a foreign country can lead to interesting situations. For example, one of my husband's Chinese business associates brought me a gift when visiting our home in Hong Kong. In general one would not open the gift in front of the giver, but the man insisted. Inside the small box was a diamond bracelet! I love jewelry and I was sorely tempted to keep it! However, my husband's company forbade such gifts, so we had to explain to our guest that although I would have loved to keep the gift, it was against the rules of my husband's company. As a result, he took the bracelet back, and indicated that this was a "stupid American policy." In a couple of days a package arrived from him. Inside was a pair of earrings—a pair that cost the appropriate amount for the company to allow me to keep them!

Gift giving has many rules and regulations. Whenever receiving or giving a gift, use both hands. When giving a gift, expect the Chinese receiver to decline two or three times when offered the gift. This is done in order to show modesty and avoid appearing greedy. It is customary in China to take a gift to the family when you are visiting. Fruit or flowers are appropriate. However, the number of flowers or fruits is important. For example, the number 4 is unlucky in China. The number 8 is lucky.

The following are inappropriate because they are associated with funerals:

- A clock (life is passing)
- Handkerchiefs (symbolize sadness)
- Scissors or knives (symbolize the severing of a relationship)

If the gift is wrapped, the color of the paper is important. White is the color of mourning in China. Red is a lucky color. During the Chinese New Year it is customary to give a gift of money in a red envelope to children and the service personnel with which you deal on a regular basis. This gift is called *hang bao*. Only new bills in even numbers and even amounts should be given.

OBJECTIVES

After reading this chapter and completing the reading and activities, you should be able to

- Define ethics.
- Demonstrate how the six stages of moral reasoning proposed by Kohlberg operate.
- Apply the principles and rules of intercultural communication to your own experiences.
- Explain how ethics influences intercultural communication.

ETHICS DEFINED

Our ethical sense helps to explain a great deal about why we behave as we do. We are often called to make judgments about what we *ought* to do as opposed to what we *want* to do in specific situations. To understand why we behave as we do, it is necessary for us to learn about ethics. According to Chen and Starosta (1998), "ethics considers how we should communicate. It asks what is right or wrong, good or bad, and what standards and rules should guide our conduct" (p. 284). Scholars argue that although all people share basic emotions in common, the rules for determining when and where to feel joy, pain, and other emotions are rooted in families and culture (Morris, 1994). In this chapter we consider the fact that there is diversity in conceptions of ethics, although much of what we do can be explained individually. We also examine how once we choose to act a certain way based on our moral codes, such codes can also lead to love or hate, indifference or antagonism (Wright, 1995).

MORAL REASONING

Kohlberg (1976, 1984) argues that our ability to make moral judgments consists of six stages, which are basic to all cultures. According to Kohlberg, we move through these stages in sequence, although the manner and rate of progression vary across cultures. We will consider each stage of moral reasoning in turn.

Stage 1: Obedience and punishment orientation. This stage involves avoiding breaking rules, obeying them for the sake of obeying them, and avoiding physical harm to persons and property. For example, a child realizes, "If I steal cookies from the cookie jar, I will be punished."

Stage 2: Instrumental purpose and exchange. During this stage we learn when it is in our interest and the interest of others to abide by specific rules. We follow these rules using an "only then and when" orientation: "If I refrain from stealing cookies from the cookie jar, then will I get a brand new bag for school."

Stage 3: Interpersonal accord and conformity. Here we learn that "being good is important," so we live up to the expectations of others: "When I refrain from stealing cookies from the cookie jar, I am being virtuous and I also make my mother and others very happy."

Stage 4: Social accord and system maintenance. During this stage, we move to fulfilling the actual duties obligated by laws and that our social contract with others obligate, except in extreme cases where these duties conflict with other important values. We learn as well that we are contributing to a social group, or social organization: "Refraining from stealing promotes the common welfare and establishes a system of trust among people."

Stage 5: Social contract, utility, and individual rights. According to Kohlberg, by the time we arrive at Stage 5 we are aware of the fact that people hold a variety of beliefs and opinions, and that although most values are relative to our group, they should usually be upheld because they are part of the social contract. We also learn that some values should be upheld in any society regardless of majority opinion. Refraining from stealing is normally such an overarching value.

Stage 6: Universal ethical principles. Following ethical principles, we reason that there are certain universal principles, such as justice, the equality of human rights, and respect for the dignity of human beings. We uphold these principles because of our personal sense of commitment to these values.

The important contribution of Kohlberg's research is that it is universally based. For example, Kohlberg and his colleagues studied children in the United States and other countries, including India, Turkey, and Israel. Using a research strategy that elicited responses to hypothetical situations that posed issues of moral choice, Kohlberg concluded that "major aspects of moral development are culturally universal because all cultures have common sources of social interaction, role-taking, and social conflict which require moral integration" (1984, p. 196). Kohlberg's findings are also significant to intercultural understanding because they reveal much about the human capacity to participate in rule-governed, organized social activities that sustain much harmonious and cooperative social behavior around the globe. As Kohlberg notes, the desire to be known as "good" and "nice" is universal because all socially adjusted people want others to see them as someone with the potential for a "profitable" and "decent" relationship. This point of view is indeed attractive; it is the foundation of much of the confidence we have in interacting well with others. As such, Kohlberg's stages of moral reasoning suggest the need for universal principles and rules for communicating interculturally.

PRINCIPLES AND RULES OF INTERCULTURAL COMMUNICATION

When we interact with others, we try to determine whether we are being treated fairly by them. In some sense, all people have methods for judging notions of fairness in these exchanges, which comes down to the idea that "I helped you, so you ought to help me" (Wilson, 1993, p. 60). The sociological term for this fair exchange is *reciprocity*. It is a "prominent 'universal' principle of ethical intercultural communication" (Chen and Starosta, 1998, p. 288). Its principal role is to teach cooperation, on which much of human behavior relies. Reciprocity is crucial to intercultural behavior, because once a favor is extended, return of the favor or the failure to return it can determine the nature and quality of subsequent interactions with others. The key to reciprocity is trying to strike a balance between expectation and behavior, which can be difficult to reconcile in intercultural communication. Chen and Starosta (1998) note that the general rule of reciprocity is balanced against four behavioral standards or principles: mutuality, nonjudgmentalism, honesty, and respect.

Principles

Mutuality   Mutuality suggests that we must try our best to find common understanding within an intercultural encounter. We should expect that the shared experience with the other person is guided neither by our cultural background nor theirs. In communicating with a person from another culture we should actively search for some mutual ground that allows for an authentic exchange of ideas. We must be willing to consider ideas that may not be consistent with our own notion of culture or ethics. According to Chen and Starosta (1998), "if either party demands that the interaction be conducted solely on his or her own cultural terms, without flexibility, that interactant has created barriers to successful intercultural communication" (p. 288).

Nonjudgmentalism   Nonjudgmentalism typifies the notion of open-mindedness. We should not only be willing to express ourselves openly, but to consider the expressions of others without judgment. This represents a willingness to recognize and appreciate different views where real learning of another culture can take place. When we understand that all cultures have values and beliefs, we can begin to recognize and understand how theirs are different without placing a value judgement on that difference.

Honesty   Honesty is a perception of the confidence we place in other people's promises. The general rule across cultures is there should be consistency between what an individual promises and what he or she delivers. To be honest, we must understand our own cultural biases and how they affect our communication with others. In other words, we should be honest with ourselves before we can begin to be honest with others. We should discuss things in terms of how they *are* rather than how we would *like* them to be. Honesty requires that the information is true and that the sender understands it in a way to communicate it effectively to another.

Respect   To respect another person means that we attempt to protect his or her basic human rights. This requires sensitivity and understanding to the other person's needs. A respectful communicator will consider how information will affect the other party as well as how to respond to information provided in a respectful manner. To be respectful, communication scholar Milton Bennett suggests replacing the Golden Rule of "Do unto others as you would have then do unto you" with the platinum rule "Do unto other as they themselves would have done unto them" (as cited in Martin, Nakayama, & Flores, 2001, p. 366).

Rules

These principles of intercultural communication create an environment where "authentic dialogue between people from different cultures can be fostered" (Chen & Starosta, 1998, p. 289). The principles serve to dictate several ethical guidelines or rules for intercultual interactions. They include promoting voluntary participation in the interaction; seeking individual focus prior to a cultural one; maintaining the right to freedom from harm; accepting the right to privacy of thought and action; and avoiding imposing personal biases.

Although these rules can vary interculturally, it is comforting to know that humans of all cultures can at least start out with the same sentiments necessary to building common ground, which is an essential ingredient for other-regarding behavior. To say through words and deeds, "I see you and I take you and your ethical codes seriously," is to provide a means for promoting ties of kinship and communication.

To help provide further guidance for communicating ethically, the National Communication Association developed a credo for the general public (Morreale & Andersen, 1999, p. 4). As you will notice, many of these guidelines adhere to and support the principles and rules discussed previously.

Credo for Ethical Communication

Questions of right and wrong arise whenever people communicate. Ethical communication is fundamental to responsible thinking, decision making, and the development of relationships and communities within and across contexts, cultures, channels, and media. Moreover, ethical communication enhances human worth and dignity by fostering truthfulness, fairness, responsibility, personal integrity and respect for self and others. We believe that unethical communication threatens the quality of all communication and consequently the well-being of individuals and the society in which we live. Therefore we, the members of the National Communication Association, endorse and are committed to practicing the following principles of ethical communication:

- We advocate truthfulness, accuracy, honesty, and reason as essential to the integrity of communication.
- We endorse freedom of expression, diversity of perspective, and tolerance of dissent to achieve the informed and responsible decision making fundamental to a civil society.
- We strive to understand and respect other communicators before evaluating and responding to their messages.
- We promote access to communication resources and opportunities as necessary to fulfill human potential and contribute to the well-being of families, communities, and society.
- We promote communication climates of caring and mutual understanding that respect the unique needs and characteristics of individual communicators.
- We condemn communication that degrades individuals and humanity through distortion, intimidation, coercion, and violence, and through the expression of intolerance and hatred.
- We are committed to the courageous expression of personal convictions in pursuit of fairness and justice.

- We advocate sharing information, opinions, and feelings when facing significant choices while also respecting privacy and confidentiality
- We accept responsibility for the short- and long-term consequences for our own communication and expect the same of others.

CONCLUSION

In this chapter we have discussed aspects of ethical communication that shape human realities and experiences. The stages of moral reasoning provided by Kohlberg help us understand the principles and rules of intercultural communication and how they inform our interactions with others. Mutuality, nonjudgmentalism, honesty, and respect provide the guidelines for conduct that help us to determine how we should act in specific intercultural situations. The ability to communicate competently will also be determined by our conception of the importance of moral reasoning. Although we have attempted to provide some general principles for ethical communication, it is important to note that ethics are deeply rooted in one's culture. Rober Shuter (2003) explains that "the intercultural ethical challenge, then, is to understand truly how deeply communication ethics are grounded in culture. With an intracultural perspective, people, society, and their communication can be approached and possibly undertood from each culture's terms" (p. 454).

FOR DISCUSSION

1. Why are the stages of moral reasoning important to our understanding of intercultural communication?
2. How might your own cultural biases keep you from communicating effectively interculturally?
3. How will the principles and guidelines provided in this chapter help you in future encounters?
4. If you were required to defend or destroy the following thesis, which position would you take and why? *Thesis:* Our deepest moral sentiments are the products of the culture in which we have been raised and are therefore relative.

REFERENCES

Bennett, M. J. (1979). Overcoming the Golden Rule: Sympathy and empathy. In D. S. Nimmo (Ed.), *Communication yearbook, 3* (pp. 407–422). New Brunswick, NJ: Transaction Books.

Chen, G. M., and Starosta, W. J. (1998). *Foundations of intercultural communication.* Boston: Allyn & Bacon.

Kohlberg, L. (1976). Moral stages and moralization. In T. Lickona (Ed.), *Moral development and behavior: Theory research and social issues* (pp. 31–53). New York: Holt, Rinehart and Winston.

Kohlberg, L. (1984). Essays on moral development (vol 2). *The psychology of moral development.* San Francisco: Harper & Row.

Martin, J. N., Nakayama, T. K., and Flores, L. A. (2001). Ethical issues in intercultural communication. In J. Martin, T. Nakayama, and L. Flores (Eds.) *Readings in intercultural communication: Experiences and contexts,* 2nd ed. Boston: McGraw-Hill.

Morreale, S., and Andersen, K. (1999). Intense discussion at summer conference yields draft of NCA credo for communication ethics. *Spectra.* National Communication Association.

Morris, D. (1994). *The human animal: A personal view of the human species.* New York: Crown.

Shuter, R. (2003). Ethics, culture, and communication: An intercultural perspective. In L. Samovar, and R. Porter (Eds.), *Intercultural communication: A reader,* 10th ed. Belmont, CA: Wadsworth.

Wilson, J. (1993). *The moral sense.* New York: The Free Press.

Wright, R. (1995). *The moral animal: The new science of evolutionary psychology.* New York: Vintage Books.

Building on Ethical Conflicts

J. Richard Hoel, Jr.

It is rare when doing business in different cultures not to encounter ethical conflicts, situations where one party may view certain conduct as ethical and the other does not. Often, however, shades of gray predominate and effective communication is the only way to fashion a solution where common ground can be found.

Perhaps one of the best and most common examples where ethical norms are not always clear between cultures is the practice of bribery. In the United States, we view bribery as one of the worst forms of corruption and our legal and regulatory infrastructure is designed to promote a "level playing field" where all participants have an equal opportunity to succeed based on talent and, in business, the quality of products or services provided to customers. In less developed countries, emphasis on this transparency may not be so well defined and many would argue that an informal system of "gift giving" is in fact necessary for the development of an environment conducive to economic growth, at least until the stability of government and laws has evolved to protect all concerned.

One of the most glaring examples of differing cultural attitudes toward bribery of public officials was witnessed recently with the investigation of the International Olympic Committee of Salt Lake City. I have also encountered this phenomenon while practicing law in Asia, particularly in China, where the art of Guanxi or "trading favors" to build relationships is an integral part of the culture. In Arabic a similar practice is referred to as "bakshish," in Russian it is "vzyatka." Practicing Guanxi does not necessarily generate bribery. In fact, the focus is directed toward the development of a network of long term relationships that can be relied upon over time to provide a resource of valuable connections. In its best form, it is a very valuable practice and helps people focus on long term benefits of treating people with respect even though in the short term a specific arrangement or business transaction cannot be fashioned. In its worst form, however, the practice can open the door to corruption from a Western perspective.

The U.S. Foreign Corrupt Practices Act (FCPA) establishes a firm prohibition against bribery of public officials of any country, with severe penalties. There is, however, an exception for "facilitating" payments, gifts of nominal value that might be viewed as a courtesy and friendly gesture to a new acquaintance. The problem arises where such a gift is requested but its value is anything but nominal.

At first blush, I am inclined of course to view our counterparts who may engage in or invite this type of activity through our own cultural prism, where bribery is simply illegal—end of discussion. But in China, centuries of building relationships has created a culture that often views such activity as part of the natural harmony of doing business and the question of legality doesn't enter the picture. From our world perspective in North America, we wonder why any clear thinking businessperson would support the practice. Characteristically, we ignore the history of graft and corruption in our country. What to do?

I have found that unique and creative solutions to this problem are often available within the confines of our laws if the principles described in this chapter—mutuality, nonjudgmentalism, honesty, and respect—are employed. I worked once with a Chinese Ministry interested in our services and it was agreed that officials from the Ministry would travel to our plant in the United States. It was an excellent way for both parties to learn more about our services, our company and each other and accommodation for facilitating such trips is made in our own laws. But we received a request for much more from our Chinese counterparts, including a proposal that more people travel than necessary and that the trip include several stops in points of interest in our country, such as Disneyland.

We certainly appreciated the desire to learn more about our country and in fact welcomed that interest, but our own ethical standards as well as the law prohibited us from paying for most of the trip. But we didn't give up. In fact we viewed this as a starting point and were able to use the resulting discussions to not only educate our counterparts about our own legal system and the reasons for our own restrictions but learn more about theirs. We hoped we could structure an agreement that would satisfy both sides but we were willing to focus on the process of communication, education, and relationship building with the goal that no matter what happened in the short term, we would develop a relationship based upon mutual respect that could very well benefit both parties in the long run. We were never critical. In this endeavor we learned quite a bit from our Chinese counterparts about patience and relationship building. In the end, we were able to work things out on both a short and long term basis.

CHAPTER ACTIVITIES

1. Observe a rite of passage that occurs in your culture. This may be a club initiation, a graduation, an academic honors ceremony, a wedding, or a promotion. Assume that this rite of passage reflects important moral values, then make a list of the values that that rite of passage reflects. You might also explain how the rite of passage helps to maintain the social order.

2. Collect at least three stories from a culture different from your own. Next, examine how the authors of the stories that you selected developed their arguments. Were examples used? Statistics? What do the forms of argument reveal about the culture that you chose? Did you see any ethical values demonstrated in the stories?

3. Interview a student, doctor, teacher, police officer, judge, or religious leader. Ask the person the following questions:

   a. How do questions of ethics influence the decisions that you make daily?

   b. Can you think of an instance in which your own sense of ethics differed from the moral principles of a person from another culture? If yes, how did you manage the difficulty? What was the nature of that difficulty?

   c. What is new or different about issues of morality now as opposed to the 1980s? 1950s?

CHAPTER 14

DEVELOPING INTERCULTURAL COMPETENCE

COMPETENCY PRACTICES

J. Richard Hoel, Jr.

In many ways my experiences living, traveling, and doing business outside of the United States have brought me full circle in my approach to intercultural communication and reinforced certain basic truisms that I have been taught since I was young. The first and most important perhaps is that the best way to bridge intercultural chasms is to treat everyone I meet as a unique individual. This is easier when I understand as many dynamics as I can about that person's culture but also recognize that it is the effort I make to relate to each individual that in the final analysis makes the difference.

With this in mind here are some practices I have developed that help me to participate better in the intercultural arena:

- *Document relationships.* I have found that organization and preparation do not extinguish spontaneity from personal relationships. I have made a practice of maintaining a detailed index card file of all of the people I have met in my international experiences. But unlike the typical Rolodex file, mine not only includes addresses and contact information but also as many interesting things that I can recall about the person. I recognize that I may not see my new friend again soon and also am not embarrassed to admit that as I get older my memory doesn't hold the little details it used to retain. A reminder of the interesting stories about my contact is very helpful.

- *Cultivate relationships.* The file I maintain is not static. I make a practice of continually going through my file from start to finish by committing to contact five people in the file every day. Email makes this much easier than it used to be but frequently my contact may be a phone call or a letter. Perhaps it's just a "hello" on a business card. But the contact is made and the relationship endures. I'll often get a return message and learn more about my friend.

- *Be a teacher.* I need to remind myself frequently that there are two sides to any intercultural relationship. And although I spend as much time as I can learning about the culture of my counterpart, it is important to remember that the relationship is enriched when the learning goes both ways. Frequently, I may be the primary way that my counterpart experiences U.S. American culture. I try to think of the best ways I can teach each new person I meet about my culture. Again, I always try to think of the best stories I can tell to help others understand the values and beliefs that U.S. Americans hold dear.

- *Bring experiences home.* Teaching others about what I learned helps reinforce my own experiences. When I am required to explain and defend my own beliefs and practices to others, I add a very rich layer to my own intercultural knowledge. I therefore try to take as many opportunities as I can to speak and write about my intercultural experiences.

- *Have fun.* Need I say more?

OBJECTIVES

After reading this chapter and completing the readings and activities, you should be able to

- Explain the factors that shape intercultural encounters.
- Describe in writing the components that influence intercultural competence.
- Explain the 10 basic rules of intercultural communication.

In Chapter 4 we began the section on region and identity with a fascinating story about an experience that Karmi's (2003) mother encountered on a trip to Cordova and Granada in Spain. Despite Karmi's mother's proclamation that she preferred interacting with Arab people to viewing "piles of stones" in England, the mother's story changed when she visited southern Spain and witnessed the "grand legacy of Spain's Arab past" (p. 263).

Karmi's mother's story tells us a great deal about the interplay among values, displacement, traditions, habits, customs, beliefs, loss, and nostalgia. The story also reveals the complexity of human behavior and encounters. Daily, it is possible for us to interact with people whose stories can be the source of much intercultural difficulty. How are we to know what special and sometimes vexed narratives are circulating in the heads of those whom we encounter? Trying to understand others' behaviors and values can be an opportunity or a limitation. And yet, despite sometimes daunting challenges, we must try to see the world through the lens of the other. Communication problems are compounded when the people communicating are different or strange to each other. This book has provided you with information about why and when diversity matters. All of the discussions have served one major purpose: to give you sufficient sense-making materials to help you better understand and respond to others' ideas, meanings, beliefs, experiences, and feelings. In this section we discuss more practical steps that you can take to become a more competent intercultural communicator.

FACTORS SHAPING INDIVIDUAL ABILITY

Many models (Spitzberg and Cupach, 1984a, 1984b; Spitzberg, 1989) exist to explain the rules and practices that individuals should observe in their efforts to improve or adapt interculturally. For example, Kim (1991) believes that the different approaches should be integrated and that individuals differ in their capacity to adapt. Rather than argue for one approach over another, here I simply list the factors that shape an individual's ability to manage intercultural encounters:

1. *The cognitive dimension.* The cognitive dimension refers to an individual's ability to change his or her knowledge base, or, as Kim (1991) observes, "the sense-making activities" for determining the meaning of nonverbal and verbal codes that one receives (p. 269)—for example, how to make sense of the sentence, "All Chinese are farmers."

2. *The affective dimension.* The affective component focuses on the emotional aspects of an individual. It is associated with feelings such as fear, love, anger, dread, panic, hatred, and so on—for example, "Ya Ping adores people who eat with their fingers."

3. *The behavioral dimension.* The behavioral dimension refers to an individual's ability to adapt or change his or her actions based on skills acquired in the cognitive and affective realms. For example, if you believe that communicating interculturally is important, one would expect you to interact with people from different cultures should the opportunity arise.

Before we discuss specific strategies for improving your intercultural skills, I need to mention two things that are essential to changing your cognitive, affective, and behavioral dimensions: *an appreciative orientation* and *empathy*.

An Appreciative Orientation

"I am not blind to what the Greeks valued—their values may not be mine, but I can grasp what it would be like to live by their light . . . ," philosopher Isaiah Berlin (1991, p. 11) wrote. His statement expresses a *willingness* to engage with people unlike ourselves. Without a will to understand other people whose myths, music, and tales may be different, there are grave doubts that you will participate in a personal journey of intercultural discovery. So, as the authors come to the end of our cultural journey with you, ask whether you are truly committed to a path marked by beliefs and behaviors different from your own.

Empathy

It is not enough, however, to be willing to communicate. You must also develop *empathy* or a *sufficient effort of imagination*. Sufficient effort of imagination refers to your ability to "grasp what the world" looks like to "creatures, remote in time or space" (Berlin, 1991, p. 60). It is the capacity to participate imaginatively in another person's cognitive, affective, and behavioral world. The key term is *imaginative participation* because it assumes movement from your perspective to the perspective of a person unlike yourself. The Indian saying "Walk a mile in my moccasins" expresses what is meant by *empathic communication*. The emphasis on empathic communication is guided by a belief that there is enough common to all of us to warrant human understanding.

For example, to appreciate Shakespeare's tragic story of Romeo and Juliet or Pocahontas's role in helping Captain Smith during the establishment of the Virginia colony, you must attempt to understand and interpret how these characters felt and behaved. Your human connection bestows on you the expectation that you can know what it is like for others to feel pity, to love, to pray, to fear, to dream, to fight, to care. A sufficient effort of imagination means that you can imagine what it would be like to roast your hotdog over a fire made from cow dung; win an Olympic gold medal as a Russian; live in Brazil; paint your body all over with ocher; lug firewood five miles daily; begin your arguments frequently with "Let me tell you a story . . ."; and touch your food with your left hand only at dinner.

Admittedly, trying to infer the feelings and thoughts of others is daunting. A number of observations should prove helpful.

FACTORS INFLUENCING INTERCULTURAL COMPETENCE: A SYNTHESIS

Knowledge of Self

In his classic book, *The Principles of Psychology,* William James (1890) wrote, "*A man has as many social selves as there are individuals who recognize him* and carry an image of him in their mind" (emphasis added) (p. 294). James's comment reminds us that we have multiple selves, such as student, parent, gardener, sorority sister, doctor, lawyer, plumber, teacher, and so on. Despite our multiple selves, we must not only know who we are but also how who we are affects our interaction with others, including the moral choices we make, our strengths and weaknesses, our sense of our own stories, our communication style, and our prejudices, as well as the emotions that guide our behavior.

For example, if you have a strong bias against people who wear fur coats, it might be difficult for you to communicate with them. Knowing that you are biased, however, should at least help you decide what you could say to such people and how to say it. In suggesting that you know yourself, then, I am exhorting you to do two basic things.

First, know what kind of person you are, or your own cultural content; that is, *know what makes you tick*. We are not suggesting that you undergo some deep psychological analysis by consulting a psychic phone hotline or your local psychologist. Rather, we are suggesting that you know your personal stories and have a pretty good idea of what constitutes your thinking, feeling, and acting lines. Thinking, feeling, and acting lines are those major characteristics, practices, and values that influence the way people see the world. For example, the basic notion of whether the proverbial glass is considered to be half-full or half-empty conveys much about how individuals perceive the world, and how that also, in turn, helps shape individuals' reactions to people who hold similar or dissimilar views. The following questions should guide your self-analysis: What are your likes and dislikes? What are your values? What moves you to action? What are your own qualities? What does it mean to be true to self? Which models should we live by? What is your place in society?

Once you have answered these questions, you should have a sense of how your self-regarding thoughts and behaviors potentially influence your other-regarding thoughts and behaviors. In other words, you should find a balance; as Selznick (1992) notes, "If we go too far in one direction we suffer loss of self; in the other direction we slight the claims of others" (p. 238). By claims of others, Selznick means other individuals' notions of what and how the world is or ought to be.

It should be noted that this discussion of self has a Western bent. If you asked the Gahuku-Gama of New Guinea, "Who are you?" they would probably find the question curious because their conception of man/woman "does not allow for any clearly recognized distinction between the individual and the status which he occupies" (Shweder, 1991, p. 123). In analyzing your own self if you are North American, you should acknowledge that the notion of human selves as understood in North American society is at odds with the notion of human selves in other cultures. Recognizing this bias, however, should not interfere with your efforts to become fully informed about your efforts to understanding your own self.

The second thing you should understand is your communication style. Communication style refers to "those communication characteristics that are part of your personality" (Samovar and Porter, 1991) and that "contextualize" how you "should accept and interpret a verbal message" (Gudykunst and Ting-Toomey, 1988, p. 100). In Chapter 5 this concept was introduced by noting that language is a powerful means of social communication and that it mirrors cultural beliefs and values. For example, a soft-spoken person can be valued highly by one individual and negatively by another.

Think of the last effective encounter that you had with an individual. Then consider the extent to which style affected the outcome. Here is a list of terms that should help you gain insight into your communication style: *direct, humorous, tough, superior, intuitive, affective, condescending, paternalistic, personal, indirect, aggressive, assertive,* and others. Once you identify your own communication style, you are ready for the next step, which is to recognize that your style can be used as a prototype for judging others. Hudson's (1980) explanation of how people use information in terms of prototypes is helpful: "If characteristics A and B are typically ('prototypically') associated with each other, we assume the presence of B whenever we observe the presence of A and vice versa" (p. 202).

For our purposes, prototypical communication style thinking works this way: If person A (who uses directness as a preferred style) interacts with person B (who uses indirectness as a preferred style), directness and indirectness serve as clues to personality, values, and beliefs. The next step is for person A or B, or both, to assign a value judgment, such as good or bad. Needless to say, communicating with individuals whose styles differ from your own requires not only knowledge of how your own subjective orientations influence your perceptions but also an open mind.

Sociocultural Roots

Rootedness is a primary determinant of our relationships with others. It can bind us firmly to a particular past, with little interest in people, places, and ideas beyond our own village or town, or it can give us freedom to participate in the folkways and practices of others, or it can render us neutral. But rarely are individuals neutral regarding others. Above all, though, as Tuan (1977), notes, "we are oriented, which is a fundamental source of confidence. We know where we are and we can find our way to the local drugstore. Striding down the path in complete confidence, we are shocked when we miss a step or when our body expects a step where none exists" (p. 99).

Communicating competently involves "finding our way" through the brambles and branches that make us who we are. A continuing theme of this book is that who we are influences, sustains, and shapes our world. In this section we focus on the most salient factors that we believe have the most potential to define or modify our basic (or commonsensical) approach to other cultures. It might be useful at this point to discuss some of the most important sociocultural factors that challenge our intercultural competence.

Family

As we learned in Chapters 8 and 11, the family is a basic element of all societies. Traditionally, in almost all human societies, this unit has consisted of a mother, a father, and children. Although today the conception of family, especially in Western societies, is in flux, one may say that however families are constituted, they bestow a kinship status. Kinship status, and the way we are oriented toward it, gives us a foundation with which to organize the content of our world. For example, among the Nayar in India, it is not unusual for a woman to go through a ritual marriage ceremony with a man who may well have no further role in her life (Murphy, 1986).

Families, as indicated previously, can be defined in a variety of ways. Among them are families of procreation and families of orientation. In addition to kinship networks, a family's interactional style is also bound up in the nature and types of relationships we have with others. Condon and Yousef (1975) note, for example, that in the Middle East, despite the fact that in most homes all rooms look alike, there are specific activities that take place in particular rooms. Because Middle Easterners are very concerned about *face, façade,* and *appearances,* they are careful to maintain guest–host, male–female interactional spaces. As an illustration, it is not unusual in the Middle East for two men to have known each other for a long period of time without either having met the female members of the household. Knowing this, you would not visit a Middle Eastern home and ask, "May I meet your wife?"

In Japanese-style homes, we can also see the potential for intercultural misunderstandings. For example, in traditional Japanese homes, the sense of privacy differs from the concept of privacy in the United States. In fact, some scholars note that there is no word for "privacy" in Japan. This suggests that Westerners' notions of a clear separation between a private room and a public room, and the ease with which they go into their own rooms and lock their own doors, differ significantly from the Japanese notions of separation. For example, in the United States, our bath and toilet areas generally are in the same room. In Japan, however, these two rooms are separate.

Inherent within this separation of the bath from the toilet area is also an idea of what constitutes cleanliness. Japanese see a distinction between a dirty place and a clean place. For example, Pollack (1995, p. A4) observes that at some laundromats in Japan, customers are permitted to wash out the machine quickly before inserting their dirty clothes, "to wash away any lingering effects from the last customer." It is crucial to note here how different cultural patterns can contribute to our knowledge and understanding. There are many other examples, but for now, let us turn to another sociocultural factor that provides additional insights into ways of managing intercultural relations.

Economics

Economic factors greatly influence our world and how we respond to others. Our means of earning a livelihood, the globalization of society, and the relationship of economic resources to social justice tend to heighten ethnic hostility. Chua (2003) describes the conflict that can and does occur among ethnic groups because of economics. She observes, for example, that one of the consequences of economic globalization is ethnic hatred. She notes further that much contested ground exists between market-dominant minorities and indigenous groups. By market-dominant minorities, she means "ethnic minorities who, for widely varying reasons, tend under market conditions to dominate economically, often to a startling extent, the 'indigenous' majorities around them" (p. 6).

To give you a sense of the economic disparities among groups that shape intercultural relations, consider the following startling statistics from Chua (2003):

1. Chinese Filipinos control as much as 60 percent of the private economy, including the country's four major airlines and almost all of the country's banks, hotels, and shopping malls.

2. In Brundi, where they comprise roughly 14 percent of the population, the Tutsi still control approximately 70 percent of the country's wealth.

3. In Sierra Leone by the early 1990s, the Lebanese—not even 1 percent of the population—dominated all the most productive sectors of the economy, including diamonds and gold, finance, retail, construction and real estate.

4. [In Indonesia], just 3 percent of the population, the Chinese controlled (by 1998) approximately 70 percent of the private economy. All of Indonesia's billionaires were ethnically Chinese and almost all of the country's largest conglomerates were owned by Sino-Indonesian families.

Chua's notion of how economics and global markets divide human beings into groups, and as a result, create ethnic conflict, also can be seen in Table 14.1.

Economist Joseph E. Stiglitz in *Globalization and Its Discontents* (2002) also describes the prickly effects that economics and globalization are having on developing countries, especially the poor within those countries. At any given moment, such imbalances serve as fuel for discontent and strained relationships among people. In France, for example, teenagers of Arab and African descent are finding themselves unemployed, isolated, and alienated not only from the indigenous French but also from their parents. However, French-born teenagers of Arab descent learned values and beliefs that stand in great contrast to the values and beliefs of their parents who grew up in and migrated from North Africa and Southwest Asia. As a result of such cultural and economic dynamics, Smith (2003) notes that Arab youths are "strangers in their own homeland and in the land of their fathers" (p. A3). Think of the implications of such matters for intercultural communication!

Although we cannot detail here all of the economic factors that contribute to intercultural difficulties, we should note that the following organizations and institutions play major roles in global economic dynamics: the International Monetary Fund, the World Bank, the National Economic Council, and the North American Free Trade Agreement

TABLE 14.1 Divisions That Foster Ethnic Conflict and Hostility

Market-Dominant Minorities	Indigenous People
Haves	Have-nots
Rich	Poor
Powerful	Less powerful
Customs/attitudes/beliefs	Customs/attitudes/beliefs
Skills and lifestyle	Skills and lifestyles

(NAFTA). The actions of such organizations help reshape economics, and by extension, human relations. For example, there is much controversy over such economic resources as jobs, water, fuel, and technology worldwide. Note the potential of the following statistics to shape the course of human events (Hodgkinson, 2003):

1. We can feed 11 billion people, with maybe clean air and drinking water, but there is no way 11 billion of us can have flush toilets.
2. When we think of the "developed" nations, we are talking about 11% of the species.
3. The computer the U.S. worker can buy with one month's wages would require 8 *years* for the Bangladeshi worker.
4. Two billion of the world's people *have never made a telephone call.*
5. Our species is either very rich or very poor. Bill Gates represents about 40% of the world's wealth.

In short, we respond as we do based on how economic resources impinge on our world and based on both our individual and collective socioeconomic cultural encounters. For example, the fact that middle management workers are being hit hard in the corporate hierarchy because some of their jobs are being eliminated or outsourced and the fact that some workers see affirmative action practices pertaining to women and minorities as a central reason for loss of jobs, should have an effect on intercultural contact. By the same token, knowing that "for starving children in the Brazilian city of Recife, to have a Barbie doll seems more important than having food" (Hannerz, 1992, p. 223) tells us much about the complexity of human perception. Keep in mind that economic differences can serve as stumbling blocks to competent communication.

Political

Here, *political* refers to the extent to which the *state* (e.g., the U.S. government) accommodates the "disparate urges, goals and motivations of people . . . to the need for public safety and order, and to the requirement that the work of life be done" (Murphy, 1986, p. 142). The way in which our political institutions serve our purposes for "primary goods," such as income, health care, education, the right to vote, and due process, help determine not only our orientations toward the state but also how we respond to others within it (Gutman, 1992, p. 4). For example, much of the discussion concerning affirmative action centers on African Americans', women's, Latinos', and Native Americans' sense of how they should be treated politically (Taylor, 1992). Think of the complex interpersonal interactions that characterize answers to the following key political questions: What is the relationship of particular ethnic and social groups to other citizens? Should people ignore cultural particularities and focus on universal themes that transcend race and class? Should the public recognize specific ethnic groups?

These important questions focus on the relationship between culture and political practice. In communicating with others, you can expect the interplay between politics and culture to have a distinct effect on your everyday talk, the image you form of people, and the meanings you attach to what people say. For example, consider the impact of President Bush's words, "axis of evil," on the national and international conversation. Recall that in his 2002 State of the Union Address, Bush used the words to describe the U.S. political relationship to the countries of Iraq, Iran, and North Korea, which "contain weapons of mass destruction." Then think about how President Bush's words rearranged political debate and discussion worldwide.

In communicating with others, you can expect the interplay between politics and culture to have a distinct effect on your everyday talk, the image you form of people, and the meanings you attach to what they say. Be prepared to reflect on or modify your own cultural heritage in order to improve your intercultural knowledge and skills. Rarely will this orientation toward flexibility involve a radical change from what you value.

Stereotypes and Prejudices

Barna (1994) identifies "preconceptions and stereotypes" as one of the six stumbling blocks in intercultural communication. Earlier, when discussing stereotypes and prejudices, we learned that these modes of thinking and behaving can blind us to the individuality of people. Barna indicates that stereotypes are stumbling blocks in intercultural communication for several reasons. First, they interfere with our ability to view the other objectively. Because prejudiced and stereotypical judgments are made in advance of our interaction with individuals, the person who is the object of hatred or aversion is not given a chance and is at a comparative disadvantage. The severity of this mode of thinking is evident in the innocent, yet disturbing question that a little girl put to her mother, "Mother, what is the name of the children I am supposed to hate?" Imagine a criminal court judge pronouncing sentence on a person before the lawyers and witnesses have presented all of the evidence!

Second, prejudiced and stereotypical attitudes "sabotage trust" (Carr-Ruffino, 1996). It is difficult to build trust-establishing relationships when a comment such as, "You can't trust Whites," "Beware of the Jews," or "Italians are excitable" is part of our linguistic repertoire. Trust-establishing relationships move us toward individuals; nontrust-establishing relationships move us away from individuals.

Third, prejudiced and stereotypical attitudes increase our tendency to view the other selectively—that is, to take portions of information that sustain our worldview. For example, the Indian visitor who is accustomed to a life of asceticism and denial cannot fail to experience North American culture as materialistic and wasteful.

Your efforts to become a competent intercultural communicator will be greatly facilitated if you learn to become more open and understanding of others. Openness involves listening to others' point of view, weighing evidence objectively, and developing mutual respect. Reflect for a moment on any prejudices that you might have. A good, solid reflection should yield a search for the facts and your willingness to change when you have been exposed to new information that contradicts your prejudgment.

Religion

For most people, religion serves as a major source of rootedness. As we saw in Chapter 4, because religion gives us a comprehensive "picture of the way things in sheer actuality are," and because our identity is partly shaped by religion, it is a source of much conflict and diversity in the world (Geertz, 1973, p. 89). Shweder (1991) gives us a fine feel for the diversity of religious practices. He notes that "if we look in the right places and with the right clearance," we can see human beings hunting for witches, propitiating dead ancestors, sacrificing animals to hungry gods, scapegoating their sins, waiting for messiahs, seeking salvation by meditating naked in a cave for several years, and wandering on a pilgrimage from one dilapidated shrine to the next (p. 30).

If these practices challenge your beliefs, you have confronted the many religious differences that exist worldwide. Regardless of your worldview, however, you must remember that most people feel strongly about their religion, and that *differences between religious beliefs and practices do matter.* For example, among the Oriya Brahman of Indian, it is considered "shameless for a husband and wife to eat together" (Shweder, 1973, p. 30). Among some Christian faiths, however, "people who pray together, stay together." The Igbo of Nigeria distinguish between the physical aspects of the sun and its spiritual aspects (Uchendu, 1965). In Italy, there has been great dispute over the wearing of crosses in classrooms (Bruni, 2003, p. A4). And in France, religious attire, including headscarves for Muslim girls, Christian crosses, and skullcaps for Jewish boys, have been banned from public high schools (Sciolino, 2003, p. 1).

Because various cultures differ radically, and because religions provide insights into actions and language, you should also expect such values to manifest themselves in the expressions that you use everyday, as well as how you behave everyday. For example, if you have been taught that "cleanliness is next to godliness," this tenet will not only guide your behavior but it will also incline you to judge others accordingly. Our religious norms are so internalized that they serve unconsciously as radar guiding, prompting, directing, moving, and urging on our thoughts and actions. As you communicate with others, be prepared to see manifestations of these throughout everyday talk. Expect norms to show up in discussions about notions of right and wrong, good and bad, in both form and content. Search for a way of framing your thoughts that will encourage you to "let go" of discussion over religious matters that lead to antagonism and hostility. Above all, try to develop sensitivity toward other religious practices and views.

Language and Context

In Chapters 3 and 4 we noted that factors in the social environment influence how people respond to interpersonal interactions. As you become increasingly more interested in sharing yourself with others, you will observe that the social situation in which talk unfolds is an important consideration.

The human need to make sense of who speaks what language, to whom, and on what occasion provides a framework for understanding what is meant by *context*. To behave appropriately and effectively in an intercultural exchange, you must make an accurate assessment about the social context in which communication occurs.

For example, as Hymes (1977) notes, this can be facilitated by a "knowledge of what kinds of codes, channels and expression to use, in what kinds of situations and to what kinds of people." For example, Mai-Li, a Chinese immigrant, arrived in the United States a decade ago and made a genuine effort to learn English, including metaphors, proverbs, humorous sayings, and slang. One of the slang expressions that she learned was "to kick the bucket," which is term that cowboys use to indicate that an individual has died or passed away. Soon after Li had learned the expression, her history professor's wife died. While standing in line to express her condolences to her professor, Li said, "Professor Akbar, I am sorry that your wife has kicked the bucket." Despite Li's great intentions (and despite multiple variations of this story), her comments were inappropriate because the informal expression "to kick the bucket" was unsuitable for the occasion.

As you might expect, there are some factors in the communication environment that limit and control what you say. One factor is a speaker's ability to make decisions from among a range of available language choices. For example, in the case of Mai-Li, she might have chosen an expression such as "passed away," "departed," or "final resting place." Obviously, this book cannot provide you with enough specifics to manage every intercultural encounter. To improve intercultural relationships, however, you must make a conscious effort to use the appropriate word in the appropriate interpersonal context (Lee, 1997).

Another factor that influences the context is "know[ing] when not to speak as well as when to speak and what to say" (Basso, 1972, p. 69). For example, Native Americans are more likely than White Americans to use silence. Basso (1972) studied how Western Apache use silence and found that they do not feel compelled to "introduce" persons who are unknown to each other; their rule is to wait for the stranger to speak first. Basso also notes that Western Apache remain silent after they have "been cussed out" because they believe that enraged persons are temporarily "crazy" (p. 76). In contrast, consider how often North Americans encourage others to speak because they are uncomfortable with silence.

Finally, communication and content are rule governed. This means that there are patterns or rules that guide interpersonal interactions and that these rules reflect cultural beliefs and knowledge. Once a group has established communication rules, there is an expectation that they will be observed. For example, there are communication rules governing when to pause and for how long. In one culture, a five-second pause is an invitation for an individual to speak, but in another culture, it simply means that the person is organizing his or her thoughts. To be a successful communicator, you must know which rules apply, to whom, when, and how.

LOCAL AND GLOBAL DIMENSIONS

Having looked at the notion of context, we shall now look at the interplay between local and global dimensions. A story relating to this follows in which Hannerz (1992) illustrates the power of these connections.

> Each year in the spring, the countries of Europe meet in a televised song contest, a media event watched by hundreds of millions of people. There is first a national contest in each country to choose its own entry for the international competition. A few years ago, a controversy erupted in Sweden after this national contest. It was quite acceptable that the tune which was first runner-up had been performed by a lady from Finland, and the second runner-up by an Afro-American lady who was by now a naturalized Swede. Both were highly thought of and somehow represented that new heterogeneity of Swedish society which had evolved over the last couple of decades. What was controversial was the winning tune, the refrain of which was "Four Buggs and a Coca Cola;" Bugg, like the name of the soft drink, was a brand name (for a chewing gum). Many thought it improper that the national entry in the European contest should revolve around two brand names. But of the two, Coca Cola was much the more controversial, as it was widely understood as a central symbol of "cultural imperialism." Indeed a synonym for the latter is the cococolonizattion of the world. (p. 217)

Hannerz's story is important for what it tells us about the interrelatedness of cultures. First, today it is more difficult to see the world as a cultural mosaic with separate and discrete parts. Coca-Cola, reggae music, Pepsi, and other cultural products are part and parcel of cultures worldwide. And they influence how people view the presentation of and use of such products. Note, for instance, that in Hannerz's story, the Swedes were concerned about whether a local song contest should use lyrics expressing a global orientation. The Swedes demanded lyrics closer to their own culture and folkways. What the Swedes paid less attention to, however, was the fact that the winning number was a calypso, which also represented global culture. Because local products and their accompanying messages are extending beyond specific borders, you can expect these changes to challenge deeply held values and beliefs worldwide.

Second, although there is cultural flow between borders, we should not conclude that old customs and traditions will easily fade away. Knowing this, we should adjust our communication practices and attitudes to reflect an ongoing, dynamic flow of ideas and meanings across borders. Again, the Swedish controversy over "Four Buggs and Coca Cola" struck at the heart of Swedish culture.

IMPROVING INTERCULTURAL COMMUNICATION COMPETENCE

As we have seen, the specter of factors haunts our ability to communicate competently. Knowledge of self, sociocultural roots, religion, stereotypes and prejudices, and local and global dimensions of culture encourage fidelity to communication practices, but they can also be "iron cages." This book has noted some ways that we might free ourselves of these "iron cages," but the text has as yet only hinted at the most important ways of doing so. Next, we discuss some concrete things that you can do in order to become an effective communicator. This is through a complex and challenging approach to intercultural competence.

Framing an Approach to Intercultural Competence

Our practical approach to intercultural competence is based on Shweder's (1991) notion of what happens when individuals "confront diversity in belief, desire and practice" (p. 30).

Before we outline our approaches to improving intercultural communication effectiveness, you should consider the following points.

Overcoming "Either-or-ism"   Either-or-ism is a form of human thought that uses binary opposition as a way of classifying people, ideas, and things into categories such as good or bad, virtue or vice, fat or thin, black or white. This mode of categorical, pair-forming thinking forces people to deny that there is a middle ground. For example, the categorization of certain groups in the United States as either Black or White means that children who are a mixture of Black and White are forced to belong to one group or the other, rather than to both.

The ability to overcome either-or-ism is a basic requirement of a competent communicator. The first step in overcoming either-or-ism is to accept that *human cultures are complex and various.* Because people and cultures differ in all sorts of ways, you should try to look beyond simplistic categories and search for significant or deeper ways of talking about your experiences and interacting with others. To take an example, suppose a White North American female is visiting the Zulu of South Africa because her company has sent her there. Then, suppose that the company president, who is a Black male, takes the female to dinner and insists that he enter the restaurant first (McNeil, 1996). Imagine the reaction this would bring! Some individuals would possibly classify this as either good or bad before learning that in South Africa, it is customary for Zulu men to go first to clear the way of danger.

The second step in overcoming either-or-ism is to test whether an idea or concept can be explained beyond "either-or." For example, in the preceding Zulus incident, there is a vast middle ground of options to which we might appeal by using qualifiers such as "unless," "assuming," "if," and "until." Thus, rather than denouncing the behavior of the Black, Zulu male as "bad," we could make a statement such as, assuming that this is a cultural rule of the Zulu, it is neither "good" nor "bad," but "just is." Or we could make a statement such as, "Until I learn more about the cultural practices of the Zulu, I shall simply withhold judgment." Our point is until we know more about the specifics of situations, events, and ideas, the general rule is to be especially cautious regarding cultural interpretations. I do not want to give you the impression that no categorical thinking should occur. People do think categorically; however, the thought pattern should flow directly from the available evidence.

Distinguish between "In Spite of" and "Because of" Thinking   As you consider your thoughts, actions, and feelings and how they relate to the thoughts, actions, and feelings of others, you can improve your overall intercultural competence by making distinctions between "in spite of" and "because of" thinking. Let us begin with definitions. *Because of* thinking is the assumption that A (one's race, sex, ethnicity, age, etc.) is responsible for B (whatever is happening as a result of human interaction). For example, you have probably heard people say things like, "Susie neglected to acknowledge Shinika's presence because Shinika is Black," or "Koreans don't like Roberto because of his Spanish accent," or "Don't hate me because I'm beautiful"—the line from a classic television commercial featuring a gorgeous female with silky hair. Statements of these kind clamor for additional information.

There is a mathematical and social equation inherent in "because of" thinking because it assumes there is a one-to-one, direct causal relationship between A and B. In our way of thinking, "because of" thinking is asymmetrical because it works against harmonious relationships with others.

In spite of thinking is accountability reasoning. It assumes that A (whatever is happening) might or might not cause B. It is symmetrical thinking because it promotes congenial relationships—for instance, "Although the store clerk, who is British and Protestant, serviced John Majors, a British Protestant, before servicing McIntosh, who is Irish Catholic, it is impossible to determine whether it is based on assumptions about religion."

Perhaps a concrete example can make the point clearer. A group of Puerto Rican students are having a wonderful time in the lobby of a Chicago hotel. There are three women and two men. As the conversation continues, Morales (male) sits down next to an elegantly scrubbed, middle-aged Jewish American female. As soon as he sits down, the Jewish woman leaves immediately, in about 10 seconds. The question is, Why did the Jewish woman leave suddenly? How many reasons can you think of? If you are adjusting your thoughts along the lines of "in spite of" symmetrical thinking, rather than "because of" thinking, some reasons might include:

- The Jewish woman suddenly remembered that she had to make a telephone call.
- She was scheduled to meet a friend at a restaurant and discovered she had left the street address in her car.
- She saw a person across the room whom she wished to avoid.
- Nature called.

This exercise illustrates that we must have enough pieces of the intercultural puzzle to arrive at appropriate decisions about human attitudes and behavior.

Developing a Both/and Orientation   In building your interpersonal competence, you might process similar incidents in the following way:

1. *Describe the situation.* We noticed that the Jewish woman left as soon as Morales sat down beside her. Include the other factors in the communication context, such as nonverbal behaviors. For example, did Mrs. Stein shrug her shoulders or utter a "nasty" word about Puerto Ricans before leaving?
2. *Identify your feelings.* Mrs. Stein was rude, but in the grand scheme of things, it doesn't matter.
3. *Try to infer others' feelings.* I believe Mrs. Stein felt awful about leaving suddenly, and I have no reason to believe that she is a bad person.

Seeking Common Ground   Our discussion of how to improve intercultural competence is nearly complete. We have defined "either-or-ism," examined the difference between "because of" and "in spite of" thinking, and considered how to develop a "both/and orientation." Our discussion of improving intercultural communication, however, is still incomplete, because we have not emphasized common ground.

Although there are fascinating variations in human culture—from region to region and from society to society—and although we have stressed diversity, if we are to succeed in communicating interculturally, we must also search for significant or deeper points of similarity within cultures. Some scholars assume that there are many things that unite us. Murdock (1945) reminds us that all people have a concept of beauty, follow rules of etiquette, tell jokes, dance, make music, feel anger, participate in sports, gather food, and use systems of economic exchange, ranging from cowrie beads to the European Union euro to the Nigerian nira.

In all sorts of ways, though, we tend to emphasize the things that divide us rather than the things that unite us. We are astonished to learn, for instance, that in some cultures people believe that a neighbor's envy can make you sick or that snakeskin can ward off evil. In your efforts at being adaptable, keep the similarities that bind you to others in the foreground. When you greet someone from another culture, what is the first thing that you focus on? If your powers of perception are similar to those of others, you will probably notice details such as hair color, facial features, skin color, height, weight, and clothing. Focusing on similarities means that you should also move to the next level of perception, which is to consider those human traits, attitudes, customs, and behaviors that you share with others.

Think of this emphasis on similarities as observing what commonalities remain in your interactions with others long after the immediate "strangeness" has disappeared. As Morris (1994) nicely puts it, "We may wear different hats but we all show the same smile; we may speak different languages but they are all rooted in the same basic grammar; we may have different marriage customs but we all fall in love" (p. 6).

Ten Basic Rules of Intercultural Effectives

To improve relations with others, observe the following rules:

1. Give people the benefit of the perceptual doubt. Assume goodwill. This rule assumes that most individuals seek psychological comfort and congeniality.
2. Minimize confrontations by asking questions such as, "How's that?" and "How so?" Or say, "Please help me to understand why you see A or B the way you do."
3. Ask for clarification, such as, "Would you give me an example of A or B?" or "I'm not sure I understand what you mean. Would you elaborate further?"
4. Use "I" instead of "you" to deflect blame. Say, "I'm having some difficulty understanding A or B" rather than "You are not explaining the origins of chopsticks very well."
5. Try to look at people as individuals rather than as members of ethnic groups. Some stereotyping will occur, of course, since we generally do not start each encounter with a clean slate of impressions.
6. Seek common ground. Learn about things that you share in common with others—for example, "My friend Yoshiko and I both love the singer Brittany Spears."
7. Be flexible in selecting words and actions. Learn how to respond positively to conditions, people, and situations as they arise.
8. Learn how to distinguish between things that happen to you *because* you are White, Latino, Chinese, male, or female, and things that happen to you *in spite* of your sex or ethnicity.
9. Recognize the fact that people communicate differently—for example, some people smile a lot, others do not.
10. Develop empathy. Try to infer the feelings and actions of others.

These are general rules and will, of course, vary from situation to situation and from person to person. Also, remember that sometimes it is most difficult to communicate with some individuals despite your good and noble intentions. This can lead to a special kind of anguish when communicating.

CONCLUSION

Certain principles and practices are basic to the achievement of competent intercultural communication. Competent intercultural communication (1) makes full use of cognitive, affective, and behavioral dimensions; (2) has an appreciative orientation and a movement in the direction of empathy; (3) relies on knowledge or self and sociocultural roots such as ties to one's family as well as connections to political, religious, and economic attitudinal structures; (4) does not permit stereotypes and prejudices to "sabotage trust" with others; (5) are positive and other directed; and (6) acknowledge both local and global dimensions of human relations.

Among the various ways of improving intercultural competence, learning to overcome "either-or-ism," and distinguishing between "because of" and "in spite of" events and situations are most necessary. A both/and orientation toward developing intercultural competence emphasizes the relatively rich complexity of human behavior. We have sought to offer you advice and counsel about human diversity. The 10 basic rules of intercultural communication should serve as guides for you to seek to minimize misunderstandings between yourself and others.

Revisit the advice that Barna gives for removing stumbling blocks in intercultural communication and note what Collier recommends for managing problematics in ethnic friendships.

FOR DISCUSSION

1. What are some crucial factors in developing intercultural competence?
2. How are cognitive, affective, and behavioral dimensions related to intercultural competence?
3. In what sense can one say that an individual is acting locally? Globally? What are some key differences between the two?

REFERENCES

Barna, L. (1994). Stumbling blocks in intercultural communication. In L. Samovar and R. Porter (Eds.), *Intercultural communication: A reader* (pp. 337–346). Belmont, CA: Wadsworth.

Basso, K. (1972). To give up on words: Silence in Western Apache culture. In P. P. Giglioli (Ed.), *Language and social context* (pp. 67–86). New York: Penguin.

Berlin, I. (1991). *The crooked timber of humanity: Chapters in the history of ideas.* New York: Knopf.

Bruni, F. (2003, October 30). On display in Italy: Classroom crosses, and a raw nerve. *New York Times,* p. A4.

Carr-Ruffino, N. (1996). *Managing diversity: People skills for a multicultural workplace.* New York: Thomason Executive Press.

Chua, A. (2003) *World on fire.* New York: Doubleday.

Condon, J., and Yousef, F. (1975). *An introduction to intercultural communication.* Indianapolis, IN: Bobbs-Merrill.

Geertz, C. (1973). *The interpretation of cultures.* New York: Basic Books.

Gudykunst, W., and Ting-Toomey, S. (1988). *Culture and interpersonal communication.* Newbury Park, CA: Sage.

Gutmann, A. (1992). Introduction. In C. Taylor (Ed.), *Multiculturalism and the politics of recognition.* Princeton, NJ: Princeton University Press.

Hannerz, U. (1992). *Cultural complexity: Studies in the social organization of meaning.* New York: Columbia University Press.

Hodgkinson, H. (2003, July). *Some demographics: Based on the 2000 census.* Walden University lecture.

Hudson, R. (1980). *Sociolinguistics.* New York: Cambridge University Press.

Hymes, D. (1973). Toward ethnographies of communication. In M. Prosser (Ed.), *Intercommunication among nations and peoples* (pp. 45–66). New York: Harper & Row.

James, W. (1890). *The principles of psychology* (p. 294). (Reprint) Dover, 1950.

Karmi, G. (2003). *In search of Fatima: A Palestinian story.* New York: VERSO.

Kim, Y. (1991). Intercultural communication competence. In S. Ting-Toomey and F. Korzenny (Eds.), *Cross-cultural and interpersonal communication* (pp. 259–275). Newbury Park, CA: Sage.

Lee, W-S. (1997). In L. Samovar and R. Porter (Eds.), *Intercultural communication: A reader* (pp. 213–220). Belmont, CA: Wadsworth.

McNeil, D. G., Jr. (1996, July 21). In Johannesburg? *New York Times,* p. B1.

Morris, D. (1994). *The human animal: A personal view of the human species.* New York: Crown Publishers.

Murdock, G. (1945). Common denominator of cultures. In R. Linton (Ed.), *Science of man in the world crises.* New York: Columbia.

Murphy, R. (1986). *Cultural and social anthropology: An overture.* Englewood Cliffs, NJ: Prentice-Hall.

Pollack, A. (1995, July 27). The pen is mightier than the germ? *New York Times,* p. A4.

Samovar, L., and Porter, R. (1991). *Communication between cultures.* Belmont, CA: Wadsworth.

Sciolino, E. (2003, December 12). Ban religious attire in school, French panel says. *New York Times,* p. l.

Selznick, P. (1992). *The moral commonwealth: Social theory and the promise of community.* Berkeley, CA: University of California Press.

Shweder, R. A. (1991). *Thinking through cultures: Expeditions in cultural psychology.* Cambridge, MA: Harvard University Press.

Smith, C. S. (2003, December 26). French-born Arabs, perpetually foreign, grow bitter. *New York Times,* p. A3.

Spitzberg, B. H. (1989). Issues in the development of a theory of interpersonal competence in the intercultural context. *International Journal of Intercultural Relations, 13,* 241–268.

Spitzberg, B. H., and Cupach, W. R. (1984b). *International communication competence.* Beverly Hills, CA: Sage.

Spitzberg, B. H., and Cupach, W. R. (1984a). *Handbook of interpersonal competence research.* New York: Springer-Verlag.

Stiglitz, J. E. (2002). *Globalization and its discontents.* New York: Norton.

Taylor, C. (1992). *Multiculturalism and the politics of recognition.* Princeton, NJ: Princeton University Press.

Tuan, Y-F. (1997). *Space and place: The perspective of experience.* Minneapolis: The University of Minnesota Press.

Uchendu, V. (1965). *The Igbo of southeast Nigeria.* New York: Holt, Rinehart and Winston.

Stumbling Blocks in Intercultural Communication

LaRay M. Barna

Why is it that contact with persons from other cultures so often is frustrating and fraught with misunderstanding? Good intentions, the use of what one considers to be a friendly approach, and even the possibility of mutual benefits don't seem to be sufficient—to many people's surprise. A worse scenario is when rejection occurs just because the group to which a person belongs is "different." It's appropriate at this time of major changes in the international scene to take a hard look at some of the reasons for this. New proximity and new types of relationships are presenting communication challenges that few people are ready to meet.

THE SIX STUMBLING BLOCKS

I. Assumption of Similarities

One answer to the question of why misunderstanding and/or rejection occurs is that many people naively assume there are sufficient similarities among peoples of the world to make communication easy. They expect that simply being human, having common requirements of food, shelter, security, and so on, makes everyone alike. Unfortunately they overlook the fact that the forms of adaptation to these common biological and social needs and the values, beliefs, and attitudes surrounding them are vastly different from culture to culture. The biological commonalities are not much

help when it comes to communication, where we need to exchange ideas and information, find ways to live and work together, or just make the kind of impression we want to make.

Another reason many people are lured into thinking that "people are people" is that it reduces the discomfort of dealing with difference. If someone acts or looks "strange" (different from them), it's then possible to evaluate this as "wrong" and treat everyone ethnocentrically.

The assumption of similarity does not often extend to the expectation of a common verbal language but it does interfere with caution in decoding nonverbal symbols, signs, and signals. No cross-cultural studies have proven the existence of a common nonverbal language except those in support of Darwin's theory that facial expressions are universal.[1] Ekman (1976) found that "the particular visible pattern on the face, the combination of muscles contracted for anger, fear, surprise, sadness, disgust, happiness (and probably also for interest) is the same for all members of our species" (pp. 19–20).

This seems helpful until it is realized that a person's cultural upbringing determines whether or not the emotion will be displayed or suppressed, as well as on which occasions and to what degree (Ekman & Friesen, 1969, p. 1). The situations that bring about the emotional feeling also differ from culture to culture; for example the death of a loved one may be a cause for joy, sorrow, or some other emotion, depending upon the accepted cultural belief.

Since there seem to be no universals of "human nature" that can be used as a basis for automatic understanding, we must treat each encounter as an individual case, searching for whatever perceptions and communication means are held in common and proceed from there. This is summarized by Vinh The Do: "If we realize that we are all culture bound and culturally modified, we will accept the fact that, being unlike, we do not really know what someone else 'is.' This is another way to view the 'people are people' idea. We now have to find a way to sort out the cultural modifiers in each separate encounter to find similarity."[2]

Persons from the United States seem to hold this assumption of similarity more strongly than some other cultures. The Japanese, for example, have the reverse belief that they are distinctively different from the rest of the world. This notion brings intercultural communication problems of its own. Expecting no similarities they work hard to figure out the foreign stranger but do not expect foreigners to be able to understand them. This results in exclusionary attitudes and only passive efforts toward mutual understanding (Tai, 1986, pp. 45–47).

As Western trappings permeate more and more of the world the illusion of similarity increases. A look-alike facade deceives representatives from contrasting cultures when each wears Western dress, speaks English, and uses similar greeting rituals. It is like assuming that New York, Tokyo, and Tehran are all alike because each has the appearance of a modern city. But without being alert to possible underlying differences and the need to learn new rules for functioning, persons going from one city to the other will be in immediate trouble, even when taking on such simple roles as pedestrian or driver. Also, unless a foreigner expects subtle differences it will take a long time of noninsulated living in a new culture (not in an enclave of his or her own kind) before he or she can be jarred into a new perceptual and nonevaluative thinking.

The confidence that comes with the myth of similarity is much stronger than with the assumption of differences, the latter requiring tentative assumptions and behaviors and a willingness to accept the anxiety of "not knowing." Only with the assumption of differences, however, can reactions and interpretations be adjusted to fit "what's happening." Without it someone is likely to misread signs and symbols and judge the scene ethnocentrically.

The stumbling block of assumed similarity is a *trouble,* as one English learner expressed it, not only for the foreigner but for the people in the host country (United States or any other) with whom the international visitor comes into contact. The native inhabitants are likely to be lulled into the expectation that, since the foreign person is dressed appropriately and speaks some of the language, he or she will also have similar nonverbal codes, thoughts, and feelings. In the United States nodding, smiling, and affirmative comments from a foreigner will probably be confidently interpreted by straightforward, friendly Americans as meaning that they have informed, helped, and pleased the newcomer. It is likely, however, that the foreigner actually understood very little of the verbal and nonverbal content and was merely indicating polite interest or trying not to embarrass himself or herself or the host with verbalized questions. The conversation may even have confirmed a stereotype that Americans are insensitive and ethnocentric.

In instances like this, parties seldom compare impressions and correct misinterpretations. One place where opportunities for achieving insights does occur is in an intercultural communication classroom. Here, for example, U.S. students often complain that international student members of a discussion or project group seem uncooperative or uninterested. One person who had been thus judged offered the following explanation.

> I was surrounded by Americans with whom I couldn't follow their tempo of discussion half of the time. I have difficulty to listen and speak, but also with the way they handle the group. I felt uncomfortable because sometimes they believe their opinion strongly. I had been very serious about the whole subject but I was afraid I would say something wrong. I had the idea but not the words.[3]

The classroom is also a good place to test whether one common nonverbal behavior, the smile, is actually the universal sign people assume it to be. The following enlightening comments came from international students newly arrived in the United States.[4]

> *Japanese student:* On my way to and from school I have received a smile by non-acquaintance American girls several times. I have finally learned they have no interest for me; it means only a kind of greeting to a foreigner. If someone smiles at a stranger in Japan, especially a girl, she can assume he is either a sexual maniac or an impolite person.

> *Korean student:* An American visited me in my country for one week. His inference was that people in Korea are not very friendly because they didn't smile or want to talk with foreign people. Most Korean people take time to get to be friendly with people. We never talk or smile at strangers.

Arabic student: When I walked around the campus my first day many people smiled at me. I was very embarrassed and rushed to the men's room to see if I had made a mistake with my clothes. But I could find nothing for them to smile at. Now I am used to all the smiles.

Vietnamese student: The reason why certain foreigners may think that Americans are superficial—and they are, some Americans even recognize this—is that they talk and smile too much. For people who come from placid cultures where nonverbal language is more used, and where a silence, a smile, a glance have their own meaning, it is true that Americans speak a lot. The superficiality of Americans can also be detected in their relations with others. Their friendships are, most of the time, so ephemeral compared to the friendships we have at home. Americans make friends very easily and leave their friends almost as quickly, while in my country it takes a long time to find out a possible friend and then she becomes your friend—with a very strong sense of the term.

Statements from two U.S. students follow.[5] The first comes from someone who has learned to look for differing perceptions, and the second, unfortunately, reflects the stumbling block of assumed similarity.

U.S. student: I was waiting for my husband on a downtown corner when a man with a baby and two young children approached. Judging by small quirks of fashion he had not been in the U.S. long. I have a baby about the same age and in appreciation of his family and obvious involvement as a father I smiled at him. Immediately I realized I did the wrong thing as he stopped, looked me over from head to toe and said, "Are you waiting for me? You meet me later?" Apparently I had acted as a prostitute would in his country.

U.S. student: In general it seems to me that foreign people are not necessarily snobs but are very unfriendly. Some class members have told me that you shouldn't smile at others while passing them by on the street in their country. To me I can't stop smiling. It's just natural to be smiling and friendly. I can see now why so many foreign people stick together. They are impossible to get to know. It's like Americans are big bad wolves. How do Americans break this barrier? I want friends from all over the world but how do you start to be friends without offending them or scaring them off—like sheep?"

The discussion thus far threatens the popular expectation that increased contact with representatives of diverse cultures through travel, student exchange programs, joint business ventures, and so on, will automatically result in better understanding and friendship. Indeed, tests of that assumption have been disappointing.[6] For example, research found that Vietnamese immigrants who speak English well and have the best jobs are suffering the most from psychosomatic complaints and mental problems and are less optimistic about the future than their counterparts who remain in ethnic enclaves without attempting to adjust to their new homeland. One explanation given is that these persons, unlike the less acculturated immigrants, "spend considerable time in the mainstream of society, regularly facing the challenges and stresses of dealing with American attitudes" (Horn, 1980, pp. 103–104).

After 24 years of listening to conversations between international and U.S. students and professors and seeing the frustrations of both groups as they try to understand each other, this author, for one, is inclined to agree with Charles Frankel (1965) who says, "Tensions exist within nations and between nations that never would have existed were these nations not in such intensive cultural communication with one another" (p. 1). Recent world events have proven this to be true.

From a communicative perspective it doesn't have to be that way. Just as more opportunities now exist for cross-cultural contact so does more information about how to meet this challenge. There are more orientation and training programs around the country, more courses in intercultural communication in educational institutions, and more published material.[7] Until persons can squarely face the likelihood of meeting up with difference and misunderstanding, however, they will not be motivated to take advantage of these resources.

Many potential travelers who do try to prepare for out-of-country travel (for business conferences, government negotiations, study tours, or whatever) might gather information about the customs of the other country and a smattering of the language. Behaviors and attitudes of its people are sometimes researched, but necessarily from a secondhand source, such as a friend who has "been there." Experts realize that information gained in this fashion is general, seldom sufficient, and may or may not be applicable to the specific situation and area that the traveler visits. Also, knowing "what to expect" often blinds the observer to all but what confirms his or her image. Any contradictory evidence that does filter through the screens of preconception is likely to be treated as an exception and thus discounted.

A better approach is to begin by studying the history, political structure, art, literature, and language of the country if time permits. This provides a framework for on-site observations. Even more important is to develop an investigation, nonjudgmental attitude, and a high tolerance for ambiguity—all of which require lowered defenses. Margaret Mead (1960) suggests sensitizing persons to the kinds of things that need to be taken into account instead of developing behavior and attitude stereotypes. She reasons that there are individual differences in each encounter and that changes occur regularly in cultural patterns, making research information obsolete.

Stewart and Bennett (1991) also warn against providing lists of "dos and don'ts" for travelers for several reasons, mainly that behavior is ambiguous; the same action can have different meanings in different situations and no one can be armed with prescriptions for every contingency. Instead they encourage persons to understand the assumptions and values on which their own behavior rests. This can then be compared with what is found in the other culture, and a "third culture" can be adopted based on expanded cross-cultural understanding (pp. 15–16).

II. Language Differences

The remainder of this [reading] will examine some of the variables of the intercultural communication process itself and point out danger zones therein. The first stumbling block has already been discussed at length, the hazard of *assuming similarity instead of difference*. A second danger will surprise no one: *language difference*. Vocabulary, syntax, idioms, slang, dialects, and so on, all cause difficulty, but the person struggling with a different language is at least aware of being in trouble.

A worse language problem is the tenacity with which someone will cling to just one meaning of a word or phrase in the new language, regardless of connotation or context. The infinite variations possible, especially if inflection and tonal qualities are present, are so difficult to cope with that they are often waved aside. This complacency will stop a search for understanding. The nationwide misinterpretation of Krushchev's statement "We'll bury you" is a classic example. Even "yes" and "no" cause trouble. When a non-native speaker first hears the English phrase, "Won't you have some tea?" he or she listens to the literal meaning of the sentence and answers, "No," meaning that he or she wants some. The U.S. hostess, on the other hand, ignores the double negative because of common usage, and the guest gets no tea. Also, in some cultures, it is polite to refuse the first or second offer of refreshment. Many foreign guests have gone hungry because they never got a third offer. This is another case of where "no" means "yes."

III. Nonverbal Misinterpretations

Learning the language, which most visitors to foreign countries consider their only barrier to understanding, is actually only the beginning. As Frankel (1965) says, "To enter into a culture is to be able to hear, in Lionel Trilling's phrase, its special hum and buzz of implication" (p. 103). This suggests the third stumbling block, *nonverbal misinterpretations*. People from different cultures inhabit different sensory realities. They see, hear, feel, and smell only that which has some meaning or importance for them. They abstract whatever fits into their personal world of recognition and then interpret it through the frame of reference of their own culture. An example follows.

An Oregon girl in an intercultural communication class asked a young man from Saudi Arabia how he would nonverbally signal that he liked her. His response was to smooth back his hair, which to her was just a common nervous gesture signifying nothing. She repeated her question three times. He smoothed his hair three times. Then, realizing that she was not recognizing this movement as his reply to her question, he automatically ducked his head and stuck out his tongue slightly in embarrassment. This behavior *was* noticed by the girl and she expressed astonishment that he would show liking for someone by sticking out his tongue.

The lack of comprehension of nonverbal signs and symbols that are easy to observe—such as gestures, postures, and other body movements—is a definite communication barrier. But it is possible to learn the meanings of these messages, usually in informal rather than formal ways. It is more difficult to note correctly the unspoken codes of the other culture that are less obvious such as the handling of time and spatial relationships and subtle signs of respect or formality.

IV. Preconceptions and Stereotypes

The fourth stumbling block is the presence of *preconceptions and stereotypes*. If the label "inscrutable" has preceded the Japanese guest, his behaviors (including the constant and seemingly inappropriate smile) will probably be seen as such. The stereotype that Arabs are "inflammable" may cause U.S. students to keep their distance or even alert authorities when an animated and noisy group from the Middle East gathers. A professor who expects everyone from Indonesia, Mexico, and many other countries to "bargain" may unfairly interrupt a hesitation or request from an international student as a move to manipulate preferential treatment.

Stereotypes help do what Ernest Becker (1962) asserts the anxiety-prone human race must do—reduce the threat of the unknown by making the world predictable (pp. 84–89). Indeed, this is one of the basic functions of culture: to lay out a predictable world in which the individual is firmly oriented. Stereotypes are overgeneralized, secondhand beliefs that provide conceptual bases from which we "make sense" out of what goes on around us, whether or not they are accurate or fit the circumstance. In a foreign land their use increases our feeling of security and is psychologically necessary to the degree that we cannot tolerate ambiguity or the sense of helplessness resulting from inability to understand and deal with people and situations beyond our comprehension.

Stereotypes are stumbling blocks for communicators because they interfere with objective viewing of stimuli—the sensitive search for cues to guide the imagination toward the other person's reality. They are not easy to overcome in ourselves or to correct in others, even with the presentation of evidence. Stereotypes persist because they are firmly established as myths or truisms by one's own national culture and because they sometimes rationalize prejudices. They are also sustained and fed by the tendency to perceive selectively only those pieces of new information that correspond to the image held. For example, the Asian or African visitor who is accustomed to privation and the values of self-denial and self-help cannot fail to experience American culture as materialistic and wasteful. The stereotype for the visitor becomes a reality.

V. Tendency to Evaluate

Another deterrent to understanding between persons of differing cultures or ethnic groups is the *tendency to evaluate,* to approve or disapprove, the statements and actions of the other person or group rather than to try to comprehend completely the thoughts and feelings expressed from the worldview of the other. Each person's culture or way of life always seems right, proper, and natural. This bias prevents the open-minded attention needed to look at the attitudes and behavior patterns from the other's point of view. A mid-day siesta changes from a "lazy habit" to a "pretty good idea" when someone listens long enough to realize the mid-day temperature in that country is over 115°F.

The author, fresh from a conference in Tokyo where Japanese professors had emphasized the preference of the people of Japan for simple natural settings of rocks, moss, and water and of muted greens and misty ethereal landscapes, visited the Katsura Imperial Gardens in Kyoto. At the appointed time of the tour a young Japanese guide approached the group of 20 waiting U.S. Americans and remarked how fortunate it was that the day was cloudy. This brought hesitant smiles to the group who were less than pleased at the prospect of a shower. The guide's next statement was that the timing of the summer visit was particularly appropriate in that the azalea and rhododendron blossoms were gone and the trees had not yet turned to their brilliant fall colors. The group laughed loudly, now convinced that the young man had a fine sense of humor. I winced at his bewildered expression, realizing that had I come before attending the conference I would have shared the group's inference that he could not be serious.

The communication cutoff caused by immediate evaluation is heightened when feelings and emotions are deeply involved; yet this is just the time when listening with understanding is most needed. As stated by Sherif, Sherif, and Nebergall (1965), "A person's commitment to his religion, politics, values of his family, and his stand on the virtue of his way of life are ingredients in his self-picture—intimately felt and cherished" (p. vi). It takes both the awareness of the tendency to close our minds and the courage to risk changing our own perceptions and values to dare to comprehend why someone thinks and acts differently from us. Religious wars and negotiation deadlocks everywhere are examples of this.

On an interpersonal level there are innumerable illustrations of the tendency to evaluate, resulting a breach in intercultural relationships. Two follow:[8]

> *U.S. Student:* A Persian friend got offended because when we got in an argument with a third party, I didn't take his side. He says back home you are supposed to take a friend's or family's side even when they are wrong. When you get home then you can attack the "wrongdoer" but you are never supposed to go against a relative or a friend to a stranger. This I found strange because even if it is my mother and I think she is wrong, I say so.

> *Korean student:* When I call on my American friend he said through window, "I am sorry. I have no time because of my study." Then he shut the window. I couldn't understand through my cultural background. House owner should have welcome visitor whether he likes or not and whether he is busy or not. Also the owner never speaks without opening his door.

The admonition to resist the tendency to immediately evaluate does not intend to suggest that one should not develop one's own sense of right and wrong. The goal is to look and listen emphatically rather than through a thick screen of value judgments that would cause one to fail to achieve a fair and total understanding. Once comprehension is complete it can be determined whether or not there is a clash in values or ideology. If so, some form of adjustment or conflict resolution can be put into place.

VI. High Anxiety

High anxiety or *tension,* also known as *stress,* is common in cross-cultural experiences due to the number of uncertainties present. The two words, *anxiety* and *tension,* are linked because one cannot be mentally anxious without also being physically tense. Moderate tension and positive attitudes prepare one to meet challenges with energy. Too much anxiety or tension requires some form of relief which too often comes in the form of defenses, such as the skewing of perceptions, withdrawal, or hostility. That's why it is considered a serious stumbling block. As stated by Kim (1991):

> Stress, indeed, is considered to be inherent in intercultural encounters, disturbing the internal equilibrium of the individual system. Accordingly, to be interculturally competent means to be able to manage such stress, regain internal balance, and carry out the communication process in such as way that contributes to successful interaction outcomes. (p. 267)

High anxiety or tension, unlike the other five stumbling blocks (assumption of similarity, language, nonverbal misinterpretations, preconception and stereotypes, and the practice of immediate evaluation), is not only distinct but often underlies and compounds the other stumbling blocks. The use of stereotypes and evaluations are defense mechanisms in themselves to alleviate the stress of the unknown or the intercultural encounter, as previously explained. If the person was tense or anxious to begin with, these would be used even more. Falling prey to the aura of similarity is also a protection from the stress of recognizing and accommodating to differences. Different language and nonverbal patterns are difficult to use or interpret under the best of conditions. The distraction of trying to reduce the feeling of anxiety (sometimes called "internal noise") makes mistakes even more likely. Jack Gibb (1961) remarks:

> Defense arousal prevents the listener from concentrating upon the message. Not only do defensive communicators send off multiple value, motive, and affect cues, but also defensive recipients distort what they receive. As a person becomes more and more defensive, he becomes less and less able to perceive accurately the motives, the values, and the emotions of the sender. (pp. 141–148)

Anxious feelings usually permeate both parties in an intercultural dialogue. The host national is uncomfortable when talking with a foreigner because he or she cannot maintain the normal flow of verbal and nonverbal interaction. There are language and perception barriers; silences are too long or too short; prox-emic and other norms may be violated. He or she is also threatened by the other's unknown knowledge, experience, and evaluation, the visitor's potential for scrutiny, and rejection of the person and/or the country. The inevitable question "How do you like it here?" which the foreigner abhors, is a quest for reassurance, or at least a "feeler" that reduces the unknown. The reply is usually more polite than honest but this is seldom realized.

The foreign members of dyads are even more threatened. They feel strange and vulnerable, helpless to cope with messages that swamp them. Their own "normal" reactions are inappropriate. Their self-esteem is often intolerably undermined unless they employ such defenses as withdrawal into their own reference group or into themselves, screen out or misperceive stimuli, use rationalization or overcompensation, or become aggressive or hostile. None of these defenses leads to effective communication.

CULTURE SHOCK

If a person remains in a foreign culture over time the stress of constantly being "on guard" to protect oneself against making "stupid mistakes" takes its toll and he or she will probably be affected by "culture fatigue," usually called *culture shock.* According to Barna (1983):

> The innate physiological makeup of the human animal is such that discomfort of varying degrees occurs in the presence of alien stimuli. Without the normal props of one's own culture there is unpredictably, helplessness, a threat to self-esteem, and a general feeling of "walking on ice"—all of which are stress producing. (pp. 42–43)

The result of several months of this sustained anxiety or tension (or excitation if the high activation is perceived positively) is that reserve energy supplies become depleted, the person's physical capacity is weakened, and a feeling of exhaustion, desperation, or depression may take over (Selye, 1969). He or she, consciously or unconsciously, would then use psychological defenses such as those described previously. If this temptation is resisted, the sojourner suffering from the strain of constant adjustment may find his or her body absorbing the stress in the form of stomach or back aches, insomnia, inability to concentrate, or other stress-related illnesses (Barna, 1983, pp. 29–30).

The following account by a sojourner to the United States illustrates the trauma of culture shock:

> Soon after arriving in the U.S. from Peru, I cried almost every day. I was so tense I heard without hearing, and

this made me feel foolish. I also escaped into sleeping more than twelve hours at a time and dreamed of my life, family, and friends in Lima. After three months of isolating myself in the house and speaking to no-one, I ventured out. I then began to have severe headaches. Finally I consulted a doctor, but she only gave me a lot of drugs to relieve the pain. Neither my doctor nor my teachers ever mentioned the two magic words that could have changed my life: culture shock! When I learned about this I began to see things from a new point of view and was better able to accept myself and my feelings.

I now realize most of the Americans I met in Lima before I came to the U.S. were also in one of the stages of culture shock. They demonstrated a somewhat hostile attitude toward Peru, which the Peruvians sensed and usually moved from an initially friendly attitude to a defensive, aggressive attitude or to avoidance. The Americans mostly stayed within the safe cultural familiarity of the embassy compound. Many seemed to feel that the difficulties they were experiencing in Peru were specially created by Peruvians to create discomfort for "gringos." In other words, they displaced their problem of adjustment and blamed everything on Peru.[9]

Culture shock is a state of dis-ease, and, like a disease, it has different effects, different degrees of severity, and different time spans for different people. It is the least troublesome to those who learn to accept cultural diversity with interest instead of anxiety and manage normal stress reactions by practicing positive coping mechanisms, such as conscious physical relaxation (Barna, 1983, pp. 33–39).

Physiological Reactions

Understanding the physiological component of the stumbling block of anxiety/tension helps in the search for ways to lessen its debilitating effects (Selye, 1974, 1976). It is hard to circumvent because, as human animals, our biological system is set so that anything that is perceived as being "not normal" automatically signals an alert (Toffler, 1970, pp. 334–342; Ursin, 1978). Depending on how serious the potential threat seems to be, extra adrenalin and noradrenalin pour into the system; muscles tighten; the heart rate, blood pressure, and breathing rate increase; the digestive process turns off; and other changes occur (Oken, 1974).

This "fight or flight" response was useful, actually a biological gift for survival or effective functioning, when the need was for vigorous action. However, if the "danger" is to one's social self, which is more often the case in today's world, too much anxi-

ety or tension just gets in the way. This is particularly true in an intercultural setting where the need is for understanding, calm deliberation, and empathy in order to untangle misperceptions and enter into smooth relationships.

All is not "doom and gloom," however. As stated by Ursin (1978), "The bodily response to changes in the environment and to threatening stimuli is simply activation" (p. 219). Researchers believe that individuals control their emotional response to that activation by their own cognitions (Brown, 1980; Keating, 1979; Schachter and Singer, 1962). If a person expects something to be exciting rather than frightening, he is more likely to interpret the somatic changes that he feels in his body as excitement. Selye (1978) would label that "the good stress" that does much less harm unless it continues for some time without relief. Feeling "challenged" facilitates functioning as opposed to a person who feels "threatened" (Lazarus, 1979).

People also differ in their stress tolerance. Whatever the reasons, everyone knows people who "fall apart at the least thing" and others who seem unflappable in any crisis. If you are one of the former there are positive ways to handle the stress of intercultural situations, whether these be one-time encounters; frequent dialogues in multicultural settings like a school or workplace; vacation trips; or whatever. For starters, you can find opportunities to become familiar with many types of people so that differences become normal and interesting instead of threatening. And you can practice body awareness so that changes that signify a stress reaction can be identified and counteracted.

CONCLUSION

Being aware of the six stumbling blocks is certainly the first stop in avoiding them, but it isn't easy. For most people it takes insight, training, and sometimes an alteration of long-standing habits or thinking patterns before progress can be made. The increasing need for global understanding, however, gives all of us the responsibility for giving it our best effort.

We can study other languages and learn to expect differences in nonverbal forms and other cultural aspects. We can train ourselves to meet intercultural encounters with more attention to situational details. We can use an investigative approach rather than stereotypes and preconceptions. We can gradually expose ourselves to differences so that they become less threatening. We can even learn to lower our tension level when needed to avoid triggering defensive reactions.

The overall goal should be to achieve *intercultural communication competence,* which is defined by Kim (1991) as "the overall internal capability of an individual to manage key challenging features of intercultural communication: namely, cultural differences and unfamiliarity, intergroup posture, and the accompanying experience of stress" (p. 259).

Roger Harrison (1966) adds a final thought:

The communicator cannot stop at knowing that the people he is working with have different customs, goals, and thought patterns from his own. He must be able to feel his way into intimate contact with these alien values, attitudes, and feelings. He must be able to work with them and within them, neither losing his own values in the confrontation nor protecting himself behind a wall of intellectual detachment. (p. 4)

NOTES

1. See Charles Darwin, *The Expression of Emotions in Man and Animals* (New York: Appleton, 1872); Irenaus Eibl-Eibesfeldt, *Ethology: The Biology of Behavior* (New York: Holt, Rinehart & Winston, 1970); Paul Ekman and Wallace V. Friesan, "Constants Across Cultures in the Face and Emotion," *Journal of Personality and Social Psychology, 17* (1971), pp. 124–129.
2. Personal correspondence. Mr. Do is a multicultural specialist, Portland Public Schools, Portland, Oregon.
3. Taken from student papers in a course on intercultural communication taught by the author.
4. Ibid.
5. Ibid.
6. See, for example, Bryant Wedge, *Visitors to the United States and How They See Us* (Princeton, NJ: D. Van Nostrand Company, 1965); and Milton Miller et al., "The Cross-Cultural Student: Lessons in Human Nature," *Bulletin of Menninger Clinic* (March 1971).
7. One good source is the Intercultural Press Inc., P. O. Box 768, Yarmouth, Maine 04096 U.S.A.
8. Taken from student papers in a course on intercultural communication taught by the author.
9. Personal correspondence.

REFERENCES

Barna, L. M. (1983). The stress factor in intercultural relations. In D. Landis and R. W. Brislin (Eds.), *Handbook of intercultural training,* Vol. II. New York: Pergamon Press.

Becker, E. (1962). *The birth and death of meaning.* New York: Free Press.

Brown, B. B. (1980). Perspectives on social stress. In H. Selye (Ed.), *Selye's guide to stress research,* Vol. 1. New York: Van Nostrand Reinhold.

Ekman, P. (1976). Movements with precise meanings. *Journal of Communication, 26,* Summer.

Ekman, P., and Friesen, W. (1969). The repertoire of nonverbal behavior—Categories, origins, usage and coding. *Semiotica 1.*

Frankel, C. (1965). *The neglected aspect of foreign affairs,* Washington, D.C.: Brookings Institution.

Gibb, J. R. (1961). Defensive communication. *Journal of Communication 2,* September.

Harrison, R. (1966). The design of cross-cultural training: An alternative to the university model. In *Explorations in human relations training and research.* Bethesda, MD: National Training Laboratories. NEA No. 2.

Horn, J. (1980). Vietnamese immigrants: Doing poorly by doing well. *Psychology Today,* June.

Keating, J. P. (1979). Environmental stressors: Misplaced emphasis crowding as stressor. In I. G. Sarason and C. D. Spielberger (Eds.), *Stress and anxiety,* Vol. 6. Washington, D.C.: Hemisphere.

Kim, Y. Y. (1991). Intercultural communication competence: A systems-theoretic view. In S. Ting-Toomey and F. Korzenny (Eds.), *Cross-cultural interpersonal communication* (International and Intercultural Communication Annual, Vol. XV). Newbury Park, CA: Sage.

Lazarus, R. S. (1979). Positive denial: The case for not facing reality. *Psychology Today,* November.

Mead, M. (1960). The cultural perspective. In Mary Capes (Ed.), *Communication or conflict.* Associated Press.

Oken, D. (1974). Stress—Our friend, our foe. In *Blue print for health.* Chicago: Blue Cross Association.

Schachter, S., and Singer, J. E. (1962). Cognitive, social and physiological determinants of emotional state. *Psychological Review, 69.*

Selye, H. (1969). Stress: It's a G. A. S. *Psychology Today,* September.

Selye, H. (1974). *Stress without distress.* New York: J. B. Lippincott.

Selye, H. (1976). *The stress of life.* New York: McGraw-Hill.

Selye, H. (1978). On the real benefits of eustress. *Psychology Today,* March.

Sherif, C. W., Sherif, W., and Nebergall, R. (1965). *Attitude and attitude change.* Philadelphia: W. B. Saunders.

Stewart, E. C., and Bennett, M. J. (1991). *American cultural patterns.* Yarmouth, ME: Intercultural Press.

Tai, E. (1986). *Modification of the Western approach to intercultural communication for the Japanese context.* Unpublished master's thesis, Portland State University, Portland, OR.

Toffler, A. (1970). *Future shock.* New York: Bantam.

Ursin, H. (1978). Activation, coping and psychosomatics. In E. Baade, S. Levine, and H. Ursin (Eds.), *Psychobiology of stress: A study of coping men.* New York: Academic Press.

CHECK YOUR UNDERSTANDING

1. Barna describes six stumbling blocks to effective intercultural communication? Define them.
2. Do you agree with Barna that persons from the United States seem to hold the assumption of similarity more strongly than persons from other cultures? Give specific examples from your own experience to support your answer.
3. Describe an incident in which your tendency to evaluate and/or your nonverbal misinterpretation caused ineffective intercultural communication.

4. How would you describe your "stress tolerance level"? What effect does your level have on your ability to be an effective intercultural communicator?
5. Why is a list of "dos and don'ts" for travelers so problematic from an intercultural perspective?

Communication Competence Problematic in Ethnic Friendships

Mary Jane Collier

Dialogue and debate about what constitutes friendship and how it should be studied have a long history. Aristotle defined friendship in *Rhetoric* as any relationship characterized by mutual liking, that is, by mutual well-wishing and well-doing out of concern for another (Cooper, 1980). Taylor and Altman (1987) describe friendship as characterized by affective exchange and increasing spontaneity.

Ideas about what friendship is, as well as norms for what friends should and should not do, are learned in national, ethnic, and socioeconomic class group contexts. Humans learn what a friend should be and should do from family, friends, and the media; patterns and norms emerge as behaviors are positively and negatively reinforced. In addition, individuals learn early in life to make ingroup and outgroup distinctions and compare themselves to members of other groups (Tajfel, 1978). Such social comparisons and perceived ingroup support affect judgments about friendship formation and development.

One of the goals of this study was to understand the communicative process used by ethnic friends and explain why they view some conduct as more competent than other conduct. . . . A further objective was to assess the role of ethnic background on the emergent identities in those friendships. Toward that end, the study focused on how and when cultural identities

become salient, norms become clear, and positive outcomes are experienced among friends. Multiple cultural identities, including ethnic and gender, as well as relational, identities, were examined, along with multiple outcomes. Such a focus on norms and outcomes for diverse cultural identities may be one window through which to view and begin to understand intra- and intergroup communication among friends.

REVIEW OF PREVIOUS SCHOLARSHIP

Cultural Background and Cultural Identity

One common approach to the conceptualization of culture is to define it as national or group affiliation and, hence, to presume that individuals from the same place share the same background and have undergone similar socialization. By definition, then, because groups of individuals come from a certain geographical area and share certain background characteristics, they are assumed to share values, worldviews, or patterns of verbal and nonverbal language. Arguably, if one spends more time with members of one group than with members of other groups and views himself or herself as similar to ingroup members, there is a likelihood that some similar communicative patterns or styles will emerge. As Martin (1986) notes, however, there are variables other than culture that influence behavior, and the contextual variations of group differences need to be acknowledged.

Ethnicity refers to a particular type of cultural background, a group affiliation based on shared heritage with which persons identify and in which they perceive acceptance (Banks, 1987; Collier & Thomas, 1988). Ethnolinguistic vitality and linguistic strategies of convergence and divergence occur as people negotiate the importance of their shared heritage, the changing degree of group solidarity, and the process of adaptation to other groups (Giles, Bourhis, & Taylor, 1977). Persons in and outside the ethnic group place varying degrees of emphasis on shared heritage and the importance of maintaining the ties with ethnic history. Ethnic background is important because of the influence of institutions, the media, family, and peer groups on ethnic identity formation, reinforcement, threat, and how persons define, as well as enact, friendships.

In addition to studying culture as group background/affiliation, it can also be studied as emergent identity. In the current research, emergent culture was defined as an historically transmitted system of symbols, meanings, and norms (Collier & Thomas, 1988; Geertz, 1973; Schneider, 1976). Cultural identity is an emergent, contextual phenomenon, identifiable through patterns of group conduct, meanings, and norms (Collier, 1989). Cultural groups may be defined by a wide array of features, including nationality, ethnicity, profession, corporation or institution, sex/gender, relationship, and physical ability/disability. Knowing the background or place of origin is insufficient to predict or explain group conduct because individuals have a range of potential group identities. In addition, group identities are affected by socioeconomic context, other persons, and the topic of conversation.

Hecht, Collier, and Ribeau (1993) developed a model of African American cultural identity that includes enduring but changing properties and characteristics. Philipsen (1989), as well as Hecht, Collier, and Ribeau (1993), point out that cultural identity, depending on whether the researcher takes the perspective of a communal, relational, or individual frame of reference, assumes a different character.

Cultural identity is negotiated along two dimensions of conduct: a constitutive dimension, including symbols and meanings, and a normative dimension, including rules and/or competencies for conduct (Geertz, 1973; Schneider, 1976). People enact and take on particular cultural identities and co-create norms and intersubjective interpretations in the same way that they negotiate self and other face (Goffman, 1959; Ting-Toomey, 1988). Thus, group members must know the code, as well as be able to use the code appropriately, to be considered competent, accepted members of the cultural group (Philipsen, 1989).

Friendship

Taylor and Altman (1987) characterize friendships as affective exchanges in which interactive engagements are "more free wheeling and casual . . . [with] heightened activity at intermediate layers of personality" (p. 259). Close friendships provide a mechanism for negotiation and validation of identity. Individuals, with others, initiate, develop, or terminate friendships. Jones (1991) found that positive affective characteristics associated with companionship and intimacy were the best predictors of friendship satisfaction for young adult men and women in the United States. Hays (1989) found further that close friends interacted more often across a greater range of settings and times and perceived more benefits from their encounters.

Much of the research on friendship and culture has dealt with explications of friendship within a particular national or cultural group. Adams and Blieszner (1994) note that most related social–psychological research tests the effect of individual characteristics on friendship patterns that vary by structural and cultural context. They also point out the frequency of use, as well as criticize, the problems inherent in the use of proxy measures. For instance, many researchers include sex and frequency of interaction in assessing the general effect of style on friendship processes. The same criticism can be made of some research on culture. As Duck (1990) aptly notes, if researchers do not give attention to the everyday negotiation processes, in effect, they are studying the relationships between ingredients and dinner without giving attention to the process of cooking.

The interest in this study was in the emergent cultural and gender identities of interactants. Emergent identities were investigated through attention to impressions of appropriate and effective conduct in interaction between friends. This focus may be a step toward building knowledge about everyday negotiation of identity.

Cross-cultural studies comparing national and ethnic group friendships are relatively uncommon. Japanese and U.S. American friendships have been compared and contrasted by several researchers; however, Gudykunst and Nishida (1986) found more similarities than differences in perceived intimacy of friends and close friends. Barnlund (1988) discovered similarities in preferences for companions from the same nationality and differences in frequency of interaction.

Collier and Shimizu (1993) concluded that Japanese maintain friendships for a longer period than their U.S. American counterparts. Argyle and Henderson (1984) proposed six rules common to friendship maintenance among British, Italian, Chinese, and Japanese groups: standing up for the other in his or her absence, sharing news of success, showing emotional support, trusting and confiding in each other, volunteering help in time of need, and striving to make him or her happy while in each other's company. Collier (1991) identified both similarities and differences in the rules that govern conflict management as perceived by African Americans, as well as Latinos and Anglo Americans. Whether friends from different ethnic groups utilize similar rules for friends or develop more specific rules reflecting their ethnic and gender identities is a question that remains open.

COMMUNICATION COMPETENCE

For this study, *communication competence* referred to conduct that is mutually appropriate and effective (Collier, 1988a, Spitzberg & Cupach, 1984). *Cultural competence* referred to mutually appropriate and effective conduct for the particular cultural identity shared by the group or relational partners in the particular situation. Communication competencies were identified by asking respondents to identify appropriate, rule-following conduct in a given friendship and then to describe outcomes experienced from following those rules.

Rules, as well as outcomes, can vary in scope (breadth) and salience (relative importance). The more specific the type of rules, the more precise the theoretical description and explanation. For example, discovering that Anglo male friends prefer to manage conflict with each other by means of direct and assertive messages is more useful than discovering that Anglos are typically assertive.

Rules concerning friendship vary for men and women. Friendships among women, in comparison to those among men, have been described as higher in personal disclosure (Taylor & Belgrave, 1986), showing concern for others, and expressiveness (Graham, 1983). Helgeson, Shaver, and Dyer (1987) report that men and women talk more to women about personal subjects. Similarly, rules pertaining to appropriate affirmation of ethnic identity may differ across ethnic groups. For example, Collier, Ribeau, and Hecht (1986) found that African American, Mexican American, and Anglo American acquaintances described different cues that would be viewed as appropriate for their ethnic identities. Mexican Americans appreci-

ated nonverbal greetings and support whereas African Americans preferred clear verbal articulation of position and assertiveness.

The rules pertaining to what constitutes appropriate conduct for friends may also be contextual. Gender identity may become salient in cross-sex friendships. Gender identity rules may be consistent within but different across ethnic groups as a result of cultural socialization. Hilliard (1994), for example, found both similarities and differences in the rules and outcomes experienced by multi-ethnic women in conversations with co-workers, friends, and family members. Sometimes, the women appreciated similar kinds of conduct from others that affirmed their identities as women; other times, they preferred conduct more relevant to one of their ethnic identities. Therefore, different types of rules, including those related to friendship, gender, and enacted ethnic identity, warrant greater attention.

Cultural and intercultural friendships are guided by sometimes explicit, more often implicit, rules of appropriate behavior. When friends enact different cultural identities, for instance, in a political discussion, one friend may be enacting the identity of a traditional Mexican friend and the other an African American activist, the two friends must create a process in which each appropriately affirms the identity of the other or create a process in which friendship norms of agreeing to disagree emerge. If there are patterns in the rules, or shared preferences among members of particular groups, such information could be valuable in developing research knowledge and training models for cultural and intercultural communication.

The outcomes from following or violating such rules for ethnic identity or gender identity require attention as well. Giving attention to the outcome or result of appropriate and inappropriate conduct provides evidence about the force or strength of the rule (Pearce & Cronen, 1980), as well as a partial explanation for why the behavior is perceived to be appropriate. Identifying the outcomes or functions of the conduct is also essential for creating a coherent picture of what it takes to be a competent and accepted member of the particular speech community being co-created by interlocutors (Hymes, 1962). Examples of types of outcomes that have been pinpointed in previous research on ethnic acquaintances and friends include the extent to which self-concept is affirmed, ethnic identity is affirmed, and the relationship is perceived to be maintained or further developed (Collier, 1988a; Collier, Ribeau, & Hecht, 1986). Also, Collier (1991) discovered that in conflict, perception of the future maintenance or development of ethnic friendships was related to the topic of the conflict.

Each individual may have different perceptions about others' conduct. Spitzberg and Cupach (1984) have shown that individuals differ in their impressions of one another's competence within a friendship. Acquaintances of unequal status and from different ethnic backgrounds often differ in their ideas concerning what is appropriate and effective in their relationships (Collier, 1988a; Collier, 1988b; Collier, Ribeau, & Hecht, 1986). Therefore, rules of appropriate behavior and outcomes experienced must be compared and contrasted across individuals if we are to understand how both individuals contribute to intercultural competence. . . .

RESEARCH QUESTIONS

The following research questions all deal with competencies: adherence to norms of appropriate conduct and positive outcomes from following the norms. The first set of questions focuses on different types of norms/rules: for conversation in the friendship, gender rules, and rules pertaining to enacted ethnic identity within the friendship. Since friends negotiate competencies and may or may not agree on their impressions of the rules and outcomes applicable to their friendship, individual and joint impressions were solicited from the friends.

Martin (1986), among others, has called for more research on conversations in order to see the congruence or incongruities in self and other judgments of cultural and intercultural competence. The questions of interest were:

RQ1: What are Latino, Asian American, African American, and Anglo close friends' individual and joint impressions of general conversational rules in their friendships?
RQ2: What are Latino, Asian American, African American, and Anglo close friends' individual and joint impressions of gender rules in their friendship?
RQ3: What are Latino, Asian American, African American, and Anglo close friends' individual and joint impressions of ethnic identity rules in their friendship?

Competence includes impressions of appropriate behavior and positive outcomes perceived to result from particular conversations (Collier, 1988b; Collier & Thomas, 1988; Spitzberg & Cupach, 1984). Attention to the consequences of rule-following conduct provides information about the force of the rule and the salience of particular types of rules as they relate to positive consequences. Several types of outcomes are salient for acquaintances and friends (Collier, 1988a; Collier, 1988b; Collier, Ribeau, & Hecht, 1986), such as perceptions of self, perceptions of the other person, and predictions about the relationship and its future.

Hecht (1984) studied individual impressions of outcomes and found that satisfaction with communication correlates with desire to maintain the friendship. Hecht and Ribeau (1984) found further that ethnic group members differed in the kinds of conduct that resulted in outcome perceptions of satisfaction with communication. Feelings about the relationship are an important indicator of the potential future of the relationship. Impressions of friends may differ with regard to perceived consequences from a particular recalled conversation. Thus, the following additional research questions were posed.

RQ4: What are individual Latino, Asian American, African American, and Anglo friends' impressions of such outcomes as feelings about self, other, topic discussed and communication satisfaction?
RQ5: What are Latino, Asian American, African American, and Anglo friends' individual and joint feelings about the friendship?

METHODOLOGY

Respondents

In this study, four ethnic groups (African Americans, Latinos, Asian Americans and Anglo Americans) were chosen for comparison. . . .

Information concerning individual impressions included data from 48 Latinos, 44 Asian Americans, 20 African Americans, and 46 Anglo Americans. Ethnicity was identified from the label respondents used in describing their ethnic/cultural background. All of the initial friends were U.S. citizens (although some of their close friends were not). Latinos described themselves as Hispanic, Mexican American, Latino, and Mexican. Asian Americans most commonly described themselves as Chinese, Asian, Japanese American, and Chinese American. African Americans described themselves as Black, Black American, or African American. Anglos most commonly described themselves as Caucasian, White, White American, and Anglo. Respondents ranged from second to fourth generation. The relatively low number of African Americans suggests that caution is necessary in interpreting their responses.

Ninety-eight respondents were female; 60 were male. The mean age was 25, which was consistent with the mean age of students on campus. Demographics for the joint questionnaires filled out by the paired friends were as follows. In the Latino sample, there were 15 Latino–Latino pairs of friends, 4 Latino–Anglo pairs, 3 Latino–Asian pairs, and 1 pair each of Latino–African and Latino–Middle Eastern. Of the total 24 pairs, 14 involved friendships between females, 5 were male–female, and 5 were male–male. In the Asian sample, there were 14 Asian–Asian pairs, 4 Asian–Anglo pairs, 3 Asian–Latino pairs, and 1 Asian–Middle Eastern pair. Of those 22 pairs, 8 involved friendships between females, 9 between males, and 5 between males and females. The African American sample consisted of 6 pairs of African American friends, 2 African–Anglo pairs, 1 African–Latino pair, and 1 African–French pair. Of the 10 paired friends, 6 friendships were between females, 1 was between males, and 3 were between males and females. The Anglo sample included 23 pairs total: 11 Anglo–Anglo pairs, 4 Anglo–Latino pairs, 5 Anglo–Asian pairs, 2 Anglo–African pairs, and 1 Anglo–Armenian pair. Of the 23 pairs, 11 were between females, 3 were between males, and 3 included females and males.

Procedures

Respondents were recruited from communication courses. Those who agreed to participate received a questionnaire packet. They were to choose a close friend they had at the current time with whom they could meet in the next several weeks. A close friend was defined as "someone you trust, someone who accepts you and you can go to for emotional support, someone who has positive regard for you" and was consistent with that used by Adelman, Parks, and Albrecht (1990) and La Gaipa (1977). They were to meet with their close friend, and each was, both individually and silently, to complete the first questionnaire concerning their impressions of the friendship. The questionnaire asked the respondents to think about the close friendship and to indicate both how long they had known the other person and how long they had been friends. They were also asked to describe how the friendship began and developed, as well as when they defined themselves as close friends. The specific questions addressed were as follows: "Think about the friendship that you have with the close friend with whom you are meeting. How did your friendship with this person begin and then develop? How long have you known this person? How long have you been close friends?"

Respondents then recalled a recent conversation with the close friend in which the friend behaved appropriately. Appropriate behavior was defined as "conduct that is acceptable and expected—what a close friend should do and say". . . .

Respondents described when, where, and what was discussed. They also identified what they perceived to be the relational rules and outcomes. For instance, they described what the other person said and did that was appropriate, how they felt about themselves and the other person and the friendship after the conversation, and how they felt about the topic after the conversation. Next, respondents described any rules of appropriate behavior that related directly to gender and culture in their friendship. The next questions required respondents to describe an incident in which they were not treated as they wanted to be treated as a male or female and an incident in which they did not treat the friend as he or she wanted to be treated in the friendship. In a similar fashion, respondents described any rules of appropriate behavior that related to ethnic/cultural identity in the friendship. Specifically, they referred to an incident in which the friend did not treat their ethnic identity appropriately, or they did not treat their friend's ethnic identity appropriately.

The questions were as follows: "When did the conversation take place? Where did the conversation take place? What was the main topic discussed? What did the other person say and do that was appropriate? As a result of the conversation, how did you feel about yourself? How did you feel about the other person? As a result of the conversation, how did you feel about the friendship? After the conversation, how did you feel about the topic(s) that you discussed? What are some words, phrases or labels which describe this particular close friendship for you? Describe any rules of appropriate behavior that relate directly to gender in your friendship. In other words, as males and females in your friendship, what is appropriate for you to do and say? If you can recall a situation in which YOU WERE NOT TREATED AS YOU WANTED TO BE TREATED as a male or female in the friendship, please describe where you both were, the topic, and what the other person said or did that was not appropriate. If you can recall a situation in which YOU DID NOT TREAT YOUR FRIEND AS SHE OR HE WANTED TO BE TREATED as a male or female in your friendship, please describe where you both were, the topic, and what you said or did that was not appropriate. Describe any rules of appropriate behavior that relate to both your ethnic/cultural identities in your friendship. In other words, what should be said or done appropriately for both your cultural/ethnic identities? If you can recall a situation in which YOUR FRIEND DID NOT TREAT YOUR CULTURAL/ETHNIC IDENTITY APPROPRIATELY, please describe where you both were, the topic, and what your friend said or did that was not appropriate. If you can recall a situation in which YOU

DID NOT TREAT YOUR FRIEND'S CULTURAL/ ETHNIC IDENTITY APPROPRIATELY, please describe where you both were, the topic, and what you said or did that was not appropriate."

After respondents completed the individual questionnaires, they moved to the joint questionnaire. The instructions indicated that they were to record responses on which they reached agreement. The directions read: "If you need to clarify and briefly discuss before coming to agreement or consensus, do so and then write down your joint answer. If you cannot agree after discussing each question for a few minutes, write down each person's answer." Pairs chose a recent conversation in which both friends behaved appropriately and described the time, place, and topic of the conversation. Then, they described the appropriate things that they said and did. Finally, participants described how they felt about the friendship after the conversation and how satisfied they were with the overall discussion, as well as with each other's behavior. They also described rules pertaining to gender and cultural/ethnic identity and words or phrases that described the friendship.

The questions in the joint questionnaire were as follows: "What did each of you say and do that was appropriate? How satisfied were both of you with your conduct in the conversation? As a result of the conversation, how did both of you feel about the friendship? Describe any rules of appropriate behavior that relate directly to gender in your friendship. In other words, as males and females in your friendship, what is appropriate for both of you to do and say? Describe any rules of appropriate behavior that relate to your ethnic/ cultural identities in your friendship. In other words, what should be said or done appropriately for both your cultural/ethnic identities? What words, phrases or labels can you together agree describe this particular close friendship?"

Coder Training

Four research assistants served as coders for the study. Each identified with one of the ethnic groups being given attention. Three were female, and one was male. . . . The unit of analysis was the utterance in which a speech act or resulting feeling or perception was expressed. Coders read responses to each questionnaire item silently and recorded each speech act or resulting consequence on a separate slip of paper. For example, the respondents' descriptions of appropriate behavior recorded included, "She was grateful for my time," or "He listened until I was finished." Outcomes included such statement as, "After a whole night of talking I decided to dump the other friend!" or "The

friendship was strengthened," or "I felt like I could really finish my degree."

After each coder had recorded the acts and outcomes on the slips of paper, the four coders and the project director discussed them to ensure consistency in what was being recorded by each coder. When all four coders agreed on what to record, the training proceeded.

Each coder individually sorted the speech acts and outcomes for each respective questionnaire item into categories based on similarity of responses. The coders created categories by sorting what they thought were similar items into piles. They tried to identify no more than 10 categories of acts or outcomes for each questionnaire item; however, there was no specific restriction on the number. For example, rule categories that emerged included "Courtesy" and "Showing Respect," while outcome categories included "Understanding" and "Relational Support."

After each coder listed his or her categories of acts and outcomes on a summary sheet, he or she discussed the categories and examples for each questionnaire item with the other coders. Discussion continued until consensus (100% agreement) was reached by the four coders and project director. A label was then chosen and agreed upon for each category identified. For example, the rule category of "Politeness" was selected as the best descriptor of what each of the four individual coders originally labeled as "Courtesy," "Politeness," "Being Polite," and "Good Manners."

Actual Coding

The actual coding proceeded in the same manner as described above. Because many friendships studied involved partners from different ethnic groups, coders were assigned in a specific way. First, a coder from the respondent's ethnic group recorded speech acts and outcomes on slips of paper. Next, the coder sorted them into categories of rules and outcomes. Results were recorded on a summary sheet. Then a second coder from a different ethnic group sorted the same slips of paper and recorded the sort on a summary sheet. Finally, the coders discussed their independent sorts until they reached consensus. The same procedure was used for the joint questionnaires. . . .

RESULTS AND INTERPRETATIONS

The majority of the respondents noted that they had 2 to 4 close friends. Half of the respondents said that most of their close friends were of their own sex, and half said most of their close friends were of the opposite sex. Sixty-four respondents (41%) noted that most of their close friends were from their own culture, 15 (9%) said that most of their close friends were from a different culture, and 79 (50%) remarked that they had friends from their own culture and other culture groups. Latinos, Asian Americans, and African Americans felt that it took, on average, about a year to develop a close friendship. Anglos felt that it took, on average, a few months.

Friendship Identity Norms

The first research question examined individual and joint conversational rules for the friendship. General friendship conversational rules agreed upon by both friends were somewhat different from those described individually. In general, the joint rules included more references to relational support, whereas the individual impressions included more references to content issues, such as advice or exchanging ideas. Latinos and Asian Americans differed from the other two groups in perceived joint rules. In particular, they listed many more appropriate behaviors that were relationally based, such as respect, listening, supportiveness, and caring. The joint descriptions of appropriate behavior provided by African Americans and Anglos evidenced such relationally based behaviors as showing understanding, support, and respect, but also included as many individual behaviors, such as sincerity, honesty, openness, and keeping perspective.

The individual rules described by Latinos emphasized relational support. They mentioned positive feedback frequently, for instance, "She told me I was a good friend" and "She said I was helpful to her." A number of respondents mentioned sharing, listening, and disclosing as appropriate, and a few described behaviors characterized by the coders as caring, acceptance, and understanding. Joint rules described by Latinos reflected the same theme of relational support, but emphasis was on respect. For example, one pair noted, "We never put the other person down." Listening, openness, and support also emerged in the joint discussions.

The rules described by Asian Americans individually revealed themes of exchanging ideas and helping one another. The coders labeled the most frequently mentioned rule category "appropriate exchange of ideas." For instance, respondents noted that the partner "gave constructive criticism" and "asked me what to do." Relational support was a secondary theme evidenced by acceptance and encouragement, as well as concern. "She told me she had gotten a bad grade too and told me I could still pass my class" is an example. Listening

and nonverbal support were also mentioned, as in, "He listened to my story without interrupting once."

The joint rules described by Asian Americans suggested a theme of relational support. The most frequently agreed upon rule category was "appropriate caring." Several instances of categories of courtesy and listening, for example, "We always listen to anything and everything, and show we care," were also mentioned. Honesty was also a common theme in the Asian American joint conversations.

African Americans' descriptions of the individual rules were characterized by a somewhat unique overall issue—that of demonstrating respect or consideration for the individual. For instance, the coders identified consideration as a frequent theme, as well as sharing ideas while demonstrating respect. One respondent described discussing politics and said, "Respect. He respects who I am." Another example reflected disclosure and problem solving: "I can tell him anything and he'll help me work it out." Common interests were described in such statements as, "We both like to eat," and "We like the same people." Understanding was the most often cited theme in the jointly agreed upon rules for African Americans. Also frequently mentioned were sincerity, honesty, respect, and support. "When she tells me she understands, there's no doubt of it" is a case in point, as well as, "I trust him to tell me the truth and it strengthens our friendship."

Anglo American rules described by individuals exhibited a high frequency of personalized information and content issues. Rule categories most frequently mentioned were disclosure and advice, while talking about common interests also emerged. "We talk about personal stuff, about our families and relationships," "I can depend on him for advice," and "Her opinion is always valuable to me" are illustrative. Listening and understanding were also viewed as important.

Joint impressions were a bit different. An issue of trust and knowing where the other person stood emerged in the way of comments about honesty, openness, and confidentiality. "We know we can be honest and open with one another, so we respect opinions more" illustrates the point. Also, a theme of helping the other person figure out what to do was reflected in statements relating to keeping one's perspective, for instance, "We rely on each other to give objective feedback," and putting in required effort, "We are willing to be there for each other no matter if it is 3:00 A.M."

In summary, some similarities and some differences emerged in joint and individual perceptions of norms. Overall, Latinos most frequently referred to relationally supportive conduct, Asian Americans focused on exchanging ideas, African Americans were concerned with showing respect and consideration for the individual, and Anglos tended to deal with honest disclosure and advice.

Gender Identity Norms

The second research question addressed gender identity norms in the close friendship. Four items on the questionnaire related to gender rules, with one requesting individual's impressions, two requesting description of rule violations by the other person and the self, and one requesting joint impressions of gender rules.

It is interesting that the most common comments from individual respondents regarding their perceptions of gender identity rules in their friendship were "There are no rules" or "Not applicable!" Most often they said that there were no rule violations in their friendship. However, this response was nonexistent or lessened in frequency in the joint description of gender rules for all but the Anglo group.

Even though Latinos most frequently indicated that there were no gender rules, some also gave specific descriptions of what should not be done. Several of these descriptions involved females describing male conduct and recommending that males should not "try to get romantic" and "If we go together to a party, we leave together." Rule violations, when described, revealed insensitivity or rudeness. The joint impressions of gender rules specified mutual respect for needs.

Asian Americans most frequently mentioned being able to discuss anything with the other as a gender rule, for instance, "I can ask his opinion on the bathing suit" or "She will talk to me about how women are." The next most frequent response was that there were no rules, followed by courtesy and general behaviors showing respect for both genders. Although over half the respondents failed to identify any specific rule violation by self or other, a third mentioned being inconsiderate themselves, or experiencing the other being inconsiderate to their gender identity. The joint impressions of the gender rules emphasized respect and consideration for gender differences and reflected an emphasis on respecting females, in particular. "We show respect for one another" and "He shows that he respects my being a woman" are examples.

African Americans most frequently responded that there were no rules pertaining to different genders and secondarily listed specific behaviors implying respect for gender needs. Over half declined to mention any rule violation by self, but those who did described being inconsiderate, as in, "I forgot to call her and let her know I would be late." Over half said they could not recall any rule violation by their friend, but of the third who could, they described lack of consideration of gender identity needs. "He kept assuming that I wanted to talk about politics and his kind of music" is one such instance. Joint impressions reflected higher frequencies of women describing gender based norms and themes relating to respect for the female role in friendship. "He understands what it's like to be single at my age" is illustrative.

Anglo American individual impressions of the gender rules included a wide array of examples of appropriate conduct. "He doesn't treat me like I am brainless" and "She brought me some new clothes" are representative. Openness in discussing gender issues was also important. "We talk about our relationship openly. Because it involves both sexes, it gets complicated" is a case in point. Similar to other ethnic groups, a little more than a third could recall a rule violation by the other person, which took the form of what the coders labeled "being inconsiderate" in respect to gender identity needs.

A third of the Anglos said they had not violated any rules. For those who did admit to rule violations, they mentioned the most diverse rule violations by self, including nonsupport, lack of respect, being offensive, and showing anger. Examples were "She needed to talk about a guy's behavior at work, and I didn't want to hear about it" and "I told him to quite whining, that he'd get another job." Jointly, Anglos said that either there were no gender rules, or they described specific behaviors, such as "Sharing decision making instead of him planning the whole picnic and then telling me afterward" and "She doesn't talk about clothes and shopping when she's around me." Overall, respect for both persons' gender needs as defined by each individual was described as appropriate.

Ethnic Identity Norms

Ethnic identity norms formed the theme of the third research question. In all ethnic groups, the most common response was that no rules pertaining to ethnic identity applied to the relationship. However, respect and appreciation of cultural differences were two other themes that crossed all groups. Again, joint impressions were different from individual impressions. Latino, Asian American, and Anglo American respondents individually noted no particular ethnic identity rules for the friendship, but joint descriptions of ethnic identity rules in these three groups increased dramatically after discussion. Only African American responses included low frequencies of no ethnic rules in both individual and joint impressions.

Latinos who mentioned ethnic identity rules described respect, exchanging ideas, and learning more about the other person's cultural background, for instance, "I go to his house and get to hear his family talk about their country." Morality also appeared in the talk, especially in comments concerning not taking advantage of the other person's lack of language proficiency or upbringing. "I never put him down because he was raised without an education, or his parents don't speak with good grammar" and "It is important to him to be a good Catholic and honor the church" are good examples. Rule violations, such as unfair stereotyping, surfaced in a few cases. The majority of Latinos could not recall a rule violation of self or other concerning their ethnic identity.

Asian Americans mentioned similar themes in both the individual and joint impressions of ethnic rules. Many listed specific behaviors that were similar to the following examples: "Respect the family" and "Help each other to do well in school." Although "no rule violations" was the most frequent response, a few Asian Americans did point to self and other rule violations. Specially detailed were instances of behaving in the wrong way and being impolite, or not greeting the other friend's family member appropriately.

African Americans most commonly described understanding and appreciating culture as appropriate. Rule violations were extremely rare. Appreciation and identification with ethnic background and "pride in our roots" as well as "we show respect for our history" characterized the joint impressions for African Americans. Comments from two respondents illustrate the point: "Improving the status of blacks in the community by getting a good job" and "being proud of being who we are."

Anglo Americans' descriptions of cultural rules focused on showing respect for other cultures are reflected in such responses as, "We don't relate to each other on the basis of background; we're friends." However, a high percentage of the respondents left the answer blank on the joint impressions question. The few who gave examples of joint impressions of cultural rules offered such observation as, "We are open to learn about everyone's culture." About a third of the Anglos indicated no rule violations, but a small number noted stereotyping and criticism by self and other. Unearned privilege and assumptions about others adapting to Anglo norms may be evident in such comments of the Anglos as, "Culture doesn't even enter in here at all."

Individual Impressions of Outcomes

The fourth research question dealt with individual impressions of such outcomes as feelings about self, other, topic, and satisfaction with the communication

in the discussion. In general, the outcomes described were positive with regard to self and other. Respondents also described positive feelings about the topic of the recalled discussion. Asian Americans and Anglos were the only groups to mention any negative feelings whatsoever. All groups reported feeling satisfied with the discussion; however, Anglos provided the most detailed responses.

Latinos mentioned more positive feelings about self that were directly related to the friendship, such as, "happy that I was worthy of her friendship." All groups frequently described feeling good, feeling better, and other positive emotions, such as more confident. "I felt befriended, trusted" and "I felt like I was ready to face my boss" were offered by two Latinos. Asian Americans, in addition to describing feeling positive and feeling better and more confident, added descriptions of feeling reassured. African Americans also felt more motivated and comforted as a result of conversations with friends. Anglo Americans additionally talked about feeling needed, knowledgeable, helpful, and relieved. Asian Americans (and Anglos) were the only groups to mention that they felt badly about themselves as a result of the recalled conversation. A few in each group summarized these feelings as simply feeling bad about self. One Anglo noted, "I felt badly about my rude behavior."

Feelings about the other person were predominantly positive in all groups. Descriptions ranged from appreciative, noted specially by Latinos and Asian Armenians, to generally "good!" by Asian Americans and Anglos to listing the friend's positive characteristics, such as "She is like family" or "He is always fun to be around" by African Americans. Latino respondents frequently focused on relational behaviors in that they often depicted the other as a caring person, one to be trusted and respected. African Americans were the only group in which "grateful to the other" emerged as a category.

Feelings about the topic were also predominantly "good" or "better than before." Asian Americans mentioned feeling "good that the problem was solved." Asian, African and Anglo Americans did mention some negative emotions, for instance, "unsure" and "frustrated," and described problems that "remained unresolved," such as "Neither one of us will give an inch." Latinos and Anglos both noted that the topic continued to be an important one after the conversation was concluded.

A majority of friends in all groups reported feeling satisfied with their own and their friends' conduct in the recalled conversations. Asian Americans and Anglos were the only groups with persons who described feelings of dissatisfaction, feelings of "kind of in-between satisfaction and dissatisfaction" as one Asian American put it, and Anglos were the only group to note their dissatisfaction in the form of unresolved issues and anger about issues.

Individual and Joint Feelings about the Friendship

The fifth research question addressed individual and joint feelings about the friendship as a result of the recalled conversation. The results indicated that, for the most part, all groups felt similarly and positively about the friendship in the individual as well as joint descriptions.

Individuals from Latino and Anglo cultures reported feeling even stronger about the friendship after the conversation. Asians most frequently reported feeling "positive overall" and closer, whereas African Americans gave the most diverse descriptions of feelings about the friendship. These ranged from "supported completely" and "bonded, like we talk about in our communication classes" to "accepted" and "unsure," as well as "OK, no particular change." Anglos were the only group to mention feeling "like we are special and unique."

Joint feelings about the friendship also reflected a positive evaluative theme. Asians and Anglos were the only groups in which a few friends described feeling differently (one felt positively and one felt negatively about the friendship as a result of the recalled conversation).

DISCUSSION

Several caveats are necessary in interpreting the data. First, caution is required when drawing conclusions because of the relatively small sample sizes, in general, and the limited number of respondents in the African American sample, in particular. There may be a bias in the individual descriptions of the friendships because although the friends completed the questionnaires privately, they did so in the presence of the other friend. However, the frequency with which differences in descriptions emerged suggests that this kind of bias was minimal. It is also important to compare the results of this study with those of other current research to provide a larger context for interpretation and to guard against "overinterpretation" of the data. Taken together with the results in a continuing program of research, the findings are noteworthy. . . .

Given the results of the current study and the continuing program of research of which it is an outgrowth,

tentative overall themes in the norms and outcomes for each ethnic group can be posited. For instance, Latino friendships were characterized by rules of relational support and mutual respect for gender needs. Latinos emphasized affirming common values and showing respect for differences in their joint impressions of the rules. This result is consistent with that in previous research by Collier, Ribeau, and Hecht (1986), who found that Latino acquaintances were less likely to alter their conduct, regardless of whether they were talking with another Latino or an Anglo. In the present study, Latinos linked their positive feelings about the self and other directly to the relationship, felt better about the topic after the recalled conversation, felt satisfied with the communication, and felt stronger and closer about the friendship after the recalled conversation.

For Latino friendship communication, a theme of relational support and bonding can be proposed. This theme is consistent with previous research by Collier (1989), in which a core symbol of bondedness was advanced for Latino friends. Also, in a study of unequal status relationships between advisors and advisees in college, Collier (1988b) concluded that Latinos preferred establishing relational trust and confirmation prior to attention to task.

In this study, Asian American friendships were characterized by helping one another to achieve goals as well as by relational support. Gender rules were discussed in terms of the need for care and courtesy and the demonstration of the parties' respect for each other's gender identities, particularly among females. It was appropriate to show respect for any cultural differences. If Asian Americans, like Asians, are relatively high on the power distance dimension (Hofstede, 1980), as well as high context (Hall, 1976), then descriptions of such rule violations as impoliteness and improper greetings would be viewed as having negative consequences. Overall, the outcomes experienced from following such rules resulted in feeling positively about self, the other, the topic, and the communication in the recalled conversation. Individual and joint feelings about the friendship were also generally positive.

Asian Americans have been shown to prefer "face-saving" and nonconfrontive behaviors to protect image (Doi, 1973; Nomura & Barnlund, 1983). Asian friendships were characterized by courtesy, as well as restraint, in a previous study by Collier (1989). Collier (1988b) also found that in relationships with Anglo advisors, Asians preferred moderate self-disclosure, formality, and non-confrontation. Asian Americans reported taking a year to develop their friendships. Collier and Shimizu (1993) and Barnlund (1988) found that the Japanese in their samples took much longer to develop friendships but maintained them longer than European Americans. Demeanor was proposed as a core symbol for Asian American friends in a previous study (Collier, 1989). A caring, positive exchange of ideas was a theme for Asian American friendship communication in this study.

African American descriptions of friendship competencies reflected respect for the individual as a member of the ethnic group. Notable categories included respect, understanding (from similar experiences for instance) and appreciating culture. Problem-solving and gender identity rules were also emphasized. Respect for women was viewed as necessary and appropriate. African Americans described a variety of positive outcomes from following the rules in the friendship, including positive feelings about self, other, and the topic. They also provided diverse descriptions of feelings about the friendship.

These results are consistent with a previous study of African American friendships in which a core symbol of respect for the individual was posited by Collier (1989). Such rules of preferred conduct and outcomes are also consistent with the core symbols of sharing, uniqueness, positivity, realism, and assertiveness that, according to Hecht, Collier, and Ribeau (1993), characterize African American communication. Further, the competencies identified here are also related to issues that have been previously identified as salient for African Americans, such as authenticity, goal attainment, acceptance, and understanding (Hecht, Larkey, & Johnson, 1992). Finally, the results of this study are consistent with previous research indicating that African Americans expect mutual participation in improving interethnic conversations that are dissatisfying. The overall themes characterizing friendship communication in this study were respect and acceptance.

Anglo American friendships revealed themes consistent with those emerging in past research. Anglos described attention to content and task issues as appropriate for friends. Specific examples included advice giving, sharing information, and commonality of interest in activities. They viewed as appropriate depending on a friend for help. Further, sincerity was a theme illustrated by comments concerning honesty, openness, and confidentiality. This theme reflects the U.S. American preference for being genuine and authentic (Barnlund, 1988). U.S. Americans have also been described as relatively individualistic (Hofstede, 1980) and more "doing" than "being" oriented (Stewart, 1972). In short, close friends were expected to help each other achieve goals and develop as individuals.

Anglo respondents described the appropriateness of respecting both friends' gender identity needs and also noted that it was appropriate to be able to discuss issues about gender in their friendship openly. This

may indicate that Anglos are willing to talk explicitly about a relationship, which fits with the existing description of Anglo Americans' placing emphasis in verbal messages as the locus of meaning or being low context according to Hall (1976).

Respect for other cultures was mentioned occasionally along with comments indicating that ethnic or cultural identity was not relevant to friendships in general. Since Collier (1988a, 1988b) has shown that Anglos identify themselves as unique individuals, and intercultural friendships are based on managing the tension between individuality and group identification, this finding could be an example of the paradox inherent in personal and social identity negotiation processes. Anglos felt positively about themselves, the other, and the topic of the recalled conversation.

Anglos also described feelings of dissatisfaction, and some friends expressed different perceptions about their friendship, which is further evidence of individualistic definitions of what is acceptable in a friendship. Power and implicit, unearned privilege may be evident in Anglo Americans describing themselves as spoken to learn about everyone's culture, on the one hand, and culture as not being relevant on the other. These types of responses may demonstrate that it is easiest for the group with the most socioeconomic and sociocultural power to ignore the rules, assume they have the power as individuals to change the rules, or assume that no rules exist, since others are adapting to them rather than vice versa. Given the responses of the Anglos in this study, the theme for Anglo friendships was recognition of individual needs. . . .

REFERENCES

Adams, R. G., & Blieszner, R. (1994). An integrative conceptual framework for friendship research. *Journal of Social and Personal Relationships, 11,* 163–184.

Adelman, M. B., Parks, M. R., & Albrecht, T. (1990). The nature of friendship and its development. In J. Stewart (Ed.), *Bridges not walls* (5th ed., pp. 283–292). New York: McGraw-Hill.

Argyle, M., & Henderson, M. (1984). The rules of friendship. *Journal of Personal and Social Relationships, 1,* 211–212.

Banks, J. A. (1987). *Teaching strategies for ethnic studies* (4th ed.). Boston: Allyn and Bacon.

Barnlund, D.C. (1988). *Communicative styles of Japanese and Americans.* Belmont CA: Wadsworth.

Collier, M. J. (1988a). A comparison of conversations among and between domestic culture groups: How intra- and intercultural competencies vary. *Communication Quarterly, 36,* 122–124.

Collier, M. J. (1988b). Competent communication in intercultural advisement contexts. *Howard Journal of Communications, 1,* 3–21.

Collier, M. J. (1989, February). *Ethnic background, core symbols and themes in ethnic friendships.* Paper presented at the Western Speech Communication Association Conference, Spokane, WA.

Collier, M. J. (1991). Conflict competence within African, Mexican, and Anglo American friendships. In S. Ting-Toomey & F. Korzenny (Eds.), *Cross-cultural interpersonal communication* (pp. 132–154). Newbury Park, CA: Sage.

Collier, M. J., Ribeau, S., & Hecht, M. L. (1986). Intracultural communication rules and outcomes within three domestic cultures. *International Journal of Intercultural Relations, 10,* 439–458.

Collier, M. J., & Shimizu, M. (1993, May). *Close friendships: A cross-cultural comparison of males and females in Japan and the United States.* Paper presented at the International Communication Association Conference, Washington, DC.

Collier, M. J., & Thomas, M. (1988). Identity in intercultural communication: An interpretive perspective. In Y. Kim & W. Gudykunst (Eds.), *Theories of intercultural communication* (pp. 99–120). Newbury Park, CA: Sage.

Cooper, J. M. (1980). Aristotle on friendship. In A. S. Rorty (Ed.), *Essays on Aristotle's ethics* (pp. 301–340). Berkeley, CA: University of California Press.

Doi, R. (1973). *The anatomy of dependence.* Tokyo: Kodansha International.

Duck, S. W. (1990). Relationships as unfinished business: Out of the frying pan and into the 1990's. *Journal of Social and Personal Relationships, 7,* 5–28.

Geertz, C. (1973). *The interpretation of cultures.* New York: Basic Books.

Giles, H., Bourhis, R. Y., & Taylor, D. (1977). Towards a theory of language in ethnic group relations. In H. Giles & R. St. Clair (Eds.), *Language, ethnicity and intergroup relations* (pp. 307–408). London: Academic Press.

Goffman, E. (1959). *The presentation of self in everyday life.* Garden City, NY: Doubleday.

Graham, H. (1983). Caring: A labour of love. In J. Finch & D. Groves (Eds.), *A labor of love: Women, work and caring* (pp. 13–30). London: Routledge & Kegan Paul.

Gudykunst, W., & Nishida, T. (1986). The influence of cultural variability on perceptions of communication behavior associated with relationship terms. *Human Communication Research, 13,* 147–166.

Hall, E. T. (1976). *Beyond culture.* Garden City, NY: Anchor Books.

Hays, R. B. (1989). The day-to-day functioning of close versus casual friendships. *Journal of Social and Personal Relationships, 6,* 21–37.

Hecht, M. L. (1984). Ethnic communication: A comparative analysis of satisfying communication. *International Journal of Intercultural Relations, 8,* 135–151.

Hecht, M. L., Collier, M. J., & Ribeau, S. (1993). Ethnic identity. In *African American communication* (pp. 59–81, 114–158). Newbury Park, CA: Sage.

Hecht, M. L., Larkey, L. K., & Johnson, J. N. (1992). African American and European American perceptions

of problematic issues in interethnic communication effectiveness. *Human Communication Research, 19,* 209–236.

Hecht, M. L., & Ribeau, S. (1984). Ethnic communication: A comparative analysis of satisfying communication. *International Journal of Intercultural Relations, 8,* 135–151.

Helgeson, V. S., Shaver, P., & Dyer, M. (1987). Prototypes of intimacy and distance in same-sex and opposite-sex relationships. *Journal of Social and Personal Relationships, 4,* 195–233.

Hilliard, C. R. (1994). *Multi-ethnic women's identity and perceptions of competent communication.* Unpublished master's thesis, Oregon State University, Corvallis, OR.

Hofstede, G. (1980). *Culture's consequences.* Newbury Park, CA: Sage.

Hooks, B. (1995). *Killing rage: Ending racism.* New York: H. Holt & Co.

Hymes, D. (1962). The ethnography of speaking. In T. Gladwin & W. C. Sturtevant (Eds.), *Anthropology and human behavior* (pp. 13–53). Washington, DC: Anthropological Society of Washington.

Jones, D.C. (1991). Friendship satisfaction and gender: An examination of sex differences in contributors to friendship satisfaction. *Journal of Social and Personal Relationship, 8,* 167–185.

Kim, Y. Y. (1991). Intercultural communication competence. In S. Ting-Toomey & F. Korzenny (Eds.), *Cross-cultural interpersonal communication* (pp. 299–321). Newbury Park, CA: Sage.

La Gaipa, J. J. (1977). Testing a multidimensional approach to friendship. In S. Duck (Ed.), *Theory and practice in interpersonal attraction* (pp. 250–270). London: Academic Press.

Martin, J. N. (1986). Training issues in cross-cultural orientation. *International Journal of Intercultural Relations, 10,* 103–116.

Nomura, N., & Barnlund, D. (1983). Patterns of interpersonal criticism in Japan and United States. *International Journal of Intercultural Relations, 7,* 1–18.

Pearce, W. B., & Cronen, V. (1980). *Communication, action and meaning,* New York: Praeger.

Philipsen, G. (1989). Speech and the communal function in four cultures. In S. Ting-Toomey & F. Korzenny (Eds.), *Language, communication and culture: Current directions* (pp. 79–92). Newbury Park, CA: Sage.

Schneider, D. (1976). Notes toward a theory of culture. In K. Basso & H. Selby (Eds.), *Meaning in anthropology* (pp. 197–220). Albuquerque, NM: University of New Mexico Press.

Spitzberg, B., & Cupach, W. (1984). *Interpersonal communication competence.* Beverly Hills, CA: Sage.

Stewart, E. (1972). *American cultural patterns: A cross-cultural perspective.* Pittsburgh, PA: Regional Council for International Education.

Tajfel, H. (1978). Interindividual and intergroup behavior. In H. Tajfel (Ed.), *Differentiation between social groups* (pp. 27–60). London: Academic Press.

Taylor, D., & Altman, I. (1987). Communication in interpersonal relationships: Social penetration processes. In
M. Roloff & G. Miller (Eds.), *Interpersonal processes:
New directions in communication research* (pp. 257–
277). Newbury Park, CA: Sage.

Taylor, D. A., & Belgrave, F. Z. (1986). The effects of perceived intimacy and valence on self-disclosure reciprocity. *Personality and Social Psychology Bulletin,
12,* 247–255.

Ting-Toomey, S. (1988). Intercultural conflict styles: A face
negotiation theory. In Y. Kim & W. Gudykunst (Eds.),
Theories in intercultural communication (pp. 213–238).
Newbury Park, CA: Sage.

CHECK YOUR UNDERSTANDING

1. Define friendship.
2. What are the similarities among Latinos, Asian Americans, African Americans, and Anglos in terms of how they view friendship? What are the differences?
3. How do you define a competent friend in terms of communication? What do you believe friends should not do? What is the most important thing friends do for one another? How do your answers to these questions compare with the results of Collier's study?
4. If you have a friend from another culture, describe your friendship. What activities do you do together? What do you talk about?

CHAPTER ACTIVITIES

Case Studies/Narratives

Case Study 1

Yoko is a Japanese student at an Eastern university. Her fiance, also Japanese, lives in Japan. Although Yoko is delighted about her approaching marriage, she is troubled because she would like to retain her maiden name. In Japan, it is legally established that the wife must take the husband's last name. Yoko knows that parliament is scheduled to discuss changes in the law soon; however, the change will not occur before her wedding date.

Assume that Yoko is asking your advice as a friend. What would you say to her?

Case Study 2

Mary Jo and her roommate were walking home on Railroad Street in Bernice, Louisiana, and were stopped by a young East Indian man (around 18 years old) carrying incense sticks. He walked up to Mary Jo and her roommate and asked them to smell the incense sticks. In response, Mary Jo said, "I have a cold and cannot smell much of anything," and her roommate said, "No, thank you." The young man, much to the surprise of Mary Jo and her friend, became very angry, and began to shout at them. Later, Mary Jo felt devastated by the East Indian's response and wondered why he had felt they "owed him a conversation." Discuss the interpersonal implications of "owing" others a conversation. Was Mary Jo obligated to respond to the young East Indian's request? What might have accounted for his anger?

Case Study 3

Soo Kim works in a gift shop in a southern town. One day a Middle Eastern male entered the shop to buy a small gift, which cost a little over 20 dollars. As he was writing a check for the purchase, Kim told him he would have to make it payable to the shop, and that she would require a piece of identification. Kim's request to see identification, however, infuriated the Middle Eastern male. What do you think accounted for the man's behavior?

INDEX

Abstractions, 106–107
Accent, 84
Accommodation, 116, 127
Accountability reasoning, 308–309
Achievement, 35
Acquired immune deficiency syndrome
    (AIDS), 98, 239, 261
Active listening, 49–50
Adams, R. G., 321
Adelman, M. B., 324
Advertisements, 269, 278
Affective dimension, 299
Affective style, 111
Affiliation, 125
African American Language (AAL), 84
African Americans
    communication among women, 113–119,
        247–248
    ebonics and, 116
    and popular culture, 271
    portrayal in the media, 273, 275
    spirituality of, 247–248
    traditions of, 236
African cultures, 89–96, 108, 217, 231–236,
        305, 308
    dilemma tales in, 266
Akan people, 234, 235
Akst, Daniel, 86
Alba, Richard, 76, 86, 90
Alberts, J. K., 114, 117, 118
Albrecht, T., 324
Ali, Monica, 81
Allen, M., 199
Allport, G., 52
Alphabets, 106
Alternative dispute resolution, 230
Altman, I., 165
American culture
    friendship in, 313–314
    perceptions of, 254–256, 288–289
    stereotypes of, 51–52
Analogic style, 218
Andersen, P. A., 133, 134
Anderson, J., 199
Angelucci, P., 240
Angier, Natalie, 272
Anten, Todd, 283–289
Arab cultures, 6, 21, 25, 246, 303
Arbitration, 230
Arendt, Hannah, 94
Argyle, M., 134, 322
Aristotle, 89, 93, 320
Armstrong, G. B., 284
Artifacts, 139
Asante, M., 77
Ascription, 273

Asian cultures, 164, 303
    concept of contracts in, 228–229
    listening in, 158–159
    teaching in, 196
Asian Indians, in America, 172–179
Assimilation, 206–207
Association behaviors, 164
Assumptions, 33, 35
    and culture, 33
    of similarities, 312–315
Astrow, A. B., 247
Attribution error, 48, 49
Attributions, 43, 46
    bias in, 48
    making accurate, 49–50
    of motive, 61
Attribution theory, 47
Authoritarian culture, 28
Authority, cultural views of, 224–225
Avoidance, 127
Ayim, M., 111

Balinese culture, 19, 139
Ball-Rokeach, S. J., 284
Barker, P., 260
Barlow, W., 77, 274
Barna, LaRay M., 305, 310, 312–319
Barnlund, D., 7
Baxter, L. A., 170
Beall, Melissa, 155–161
"Because of" thinking, 308–309
Becker, Ernest, 315
Bedouin culture, 132–133
Behavior, attribution theories of, 47
Behavioral dimension, 299
Being culture, 34, 133
Being-in-becoming, 34
Beliefs, 20–21
Bell, Alan P., 99
Bennett, M., 134, 137, 294, 315
Bennett, W. L., 262
Benson, H., 259
Berlin, Isaiah, 300
Bethell, T., 82
Bettelheim, B., 260
Bhatt, Archana J., 172–179
Biconstruals, 128
Binary opposition, 308
Bin Ladin, Carmen, 74
Biomedical belief system, 240
Birdwhistell, R., 133
Blake, C., 232
Blieszner, R., 321
Body language, 135
Bond, Michael, 21, 29–31, 48, 138
Bonding, 165

Book of Changes, The (I Ching), 165
Bourdieu, P., 82, 85
Bowman, B., 194
Brazilian culture, 227
Brentar, J. E., 284
Brislin, R., 48, 53, 208
Bristow, T., 259, 261
Brod, H., 101
Brody, J., 246
Brooks, John, 274
Brown, K., 280
Brownell, J., 150–151, 152
Browning, F., 100
Bruner, J., 258
Bureaucratic power, 82
Burke, J., 245
Burke, K., 53, 270
Bush, G. W., 304
Business
    anticipating cultural differences, 223–224
    cultural values in, 26–32
    intercultural negotiations, 216–219
    international, questions for, 218–219
    language in, 228–229
    listening skills in, 151, 156
    persuasive style in, 217–218
    reasoning in, 217–218
    relationships in, 216–217, 298
    women in, 226

Cakim, Idil, 283–289
Calloway-Thomas, Carolyn, 89–96
Canadian culture, 206
Cantril, Hadley, 58
Cargile, A. C., 83, 85, 258
Caring, in language, 118
Caste, 175–176
Categorizing, 308. See also Stereotypes
Category width, 49
Catholicism, 188–189
Celebratory response, 117–118
Cell phones, in remote areas, 268
Chan, J., 248, 249
Change
    adjusting to, 214–215
    inevitability of, 213
Chan-Herur, K. C., 156
Chen, G. M., 152, 165–167, 292, 293
Chen, T., 170
Chesebro, James W., 97–101
Chinese culture, 268
    beliefs in, 251
    communication in, 48, 142–143
    conducting business in, 218, 226–227
    customs in, 139
    education in, 193

333

Chinese culture *(continued)*
  face in, 123–124
  family in, 7, 143, 168
  footbinding in, 143–147
  language in, 140, 164
  nonverbal communication in, 142–143
  practice of law in, 221–230
  women in, 77, 139, 143–147
  Yin and Yang in, 148–149
Chism, N., 200
Christianity, 79
Chronemics, 136
Chua, Amy, 82, 303
Class
  and cultural identity, 80–85
  defined, 81
  dimensions of, 81–82
  grammar and, 83–85
  in the media, 273
  property and, 82
Class achievement, 273
Classroom, intercultural, 199–201
Classroom culture, 194–195
Clinard, H., 156
Closed couples, 99
Clothing
  and class, 85
  of other cultures, 139
  on television, 285
Cluckhorn, Clyde, 6
Coakley, C., 151, 156
Coetzee, J. M., 89–96
Cognition, 37, 233
  complexity of, 46
Cognitive bias, 52
Cognitive dimension, 299
Cognitive dissonance, 57
Cognitive styles, 197
  field dependent versus field
    independent, 198
Cognitive system, mind as, 57
Coherence, 9–10
Collaboration, 127
Collectivist cultures, 27, 46, 124, 136,
    195, 218
Collectivist families, 167–168
Collier, Mary Jane, 310, 320–330
Collins, P. H., 118
Combs, A., 3
Commitment, in ethnic identity, 76–77
Common ground, seeking, 309–310
Communication
  content component of, 6
  continuous, 4
  cultural identity and, 71
  culture and, 1–9, 226
  defined, 3–6
  eight properties of, 3–4
  empathic, 300
  ethnocentrism and, 44
  of feelings, 186–187
  focusing on the process of, 51
  health and, 239
  indirect forms of, 48
  intercultural. *See* Intercultural
    communication
  intercultural conflict, 126–129
  interracial, 113–119
  irreversible and unrepeatable, 5
  learning about, 204

narrative approach to, 7–10
  in personal relationships, 64–68
  relationship component of, 6
  rules and norms, 272, 294, 306–307
  symbolic, 3–4
  systemic, 6
  transaction model of, 5
Communication patterns
  ethnicity and, 182
  transmission of, 181–191
Communication styles, 16
  direct versus indirect, 110
  elaborate versus succinct, 110
  insight into, 301
  instrumental versus affective, 111
  personal versus contextual, 110–111
  verbal, 109–111
Competency Practices (Hoel), 298
Competent intercultural communication. *See*
    Intercultural competence
Competitive-cooperative dimension, 125
Complexity of our cognitions, 46
Compromise, 127
Concrete behavior, 33
Condon, J., 194, 199, 302
Conflict emotional expressions, 129
Conflict episodes, 121–122
Conflict facework behaviors, 128–129
Conflict goal assessments, 125–126
Conflict grid, 127
Conflict intensity, 126
Conflict interaction styles, 126–127
Conflict negotiation, 121
Conflict norms, 123
Conflict resolution
  depersonalization in, 233
  peacemaking traditions and, 231–236
  Western approach to, 232
Conflict resources, 126
Conflict styles, 127–128
Confucian dynamism, 30–31
Confucianism, 31, 79, 80, 167, 243
Confucius, 30–31
Congenial expectation, 211
Connotative meaning, 106
Conquergood, Dwight, 255
Constitutive rules, 107, 108
Content conflict goals, 125
Contextual style, 110–111
Contracts, differing concepts of, 228–229
Control, 125
Cook, D., 80
Cooper, E., 199
Cooper, Laura Elizabeth Pearson, 163
Cooper, Pamela, 44, 143–147, 151, 153, 199
Coordinated management of meaning
    (CMM), 107
Cotter, Michael, 260–261, 263
Cottle, S., 275
Covariance theory, 47
Coward, H., 251
Creeden, S., 263
Cremations, 19
Criticism, 209
Croll, E., 147
Crossen, C., 82
Cultural assumptions, 38–39
Cultural attributions, 48
Cultural background, 320
Cultural community, 279

Cultural competence, 322–323
Cultural conflict, 121–129
  model for, 121–129
  peacemaking and, 231–236
Cultural display rules, 129
Cultural forms, 33
Cultural identity, 70, 320–321
  characteristics of, 72–83
  class and, 80–85
  defined, 71–72
  ethnicity and, 78
  formation of, 72
  language and, 83–85
  and nonverbal markers, 85–86
  patriarchy and gender and, 73–74
  personal identity and, 70, 86
  regional factors in, 78–79
  religion and, 79–80
  role in communication, 71
  unexamined, 72
Cultural identity achievement, 72
Cultural identity search, 72
Cultural metaphors, 11–18
Cultural norms, 129
  ethnic and dominant, 116
Cultural patterns, 19–32, 33–34, 218
  approaches to studying, 21–32
  Balinese, 19
  beliefs, values, and norms, 20–21
  defined, 20
Cultural rationales, 241
Cultural relativism, 20, 44
Cultural transmission, 276–277
Cultural values, 33–41, 121
  in business, 26–32
  patterns of, 122–123
Cultural variability perspective, 121
Culture(s)
  assimilation of, 206–207
  communication and, 1–9, 6
  complexity of, 308
  on the continuum, 22
  cooperative versus competitive, 198
  defined, 6–7
  dimensions of, 82, 245
  gender and, 74
  global, 70–71, 270
  information-based versus
    agricultural, 212
  interrelatedness of, 307
  language and, 104, 108–109, 113–119
  levels of, 33–41
  perception and, 43–44
  politics and, 304
  popular, 268–271
  power dimension of, 245–246
Culture's Core (Lustig), 1
Culture shock, 205, 317–318
Cupach, W., 323
Cushner, K., 48

Dance, F., 4
Daniel, J., 21
Danielian, Jack, 33–41
Darwin, Charles, 312
Dates, J., 77, 274
Dating, 107
Death, communication about, 187–188
Death Anxiety Scale, 261

Decision making
    global revolution and, 215–216
    modes of, 34
Denotive meaning, 106
Dependency theory, 284
Depersonalization, 35
Detweiler, R., 49
DeVito, J. A., 204
Dialectical tensions, 170
Direct style, 110
Disassociation behaviors, 164
Discrimination, 53
Disease, conceptions of, 241–242
Disgrace (Coetzee), 89–96
Disrespect, 222
Distancing, 184
Distractions, to listening, 153
Doctor-patient power dynamics, 245–246
Doing culture, 34, 133
Domhoff, G., 273
Donohue, S. L., 184
Donohue, W., 232
Dress codes, gender and, 74
Drucker, J., 280
DuBois, W. E. B., 232
Duck, S. W., 321
Dunn,R., 197
Durham, M. G., 139
Dye, T., 273
Dyer, M., 322

Eames, E., 173
Ear lobes, 139
East African ethnic groups, 77
East Asian culture, 167
Ebonics, 116
Economics
    changing community of, 213
    diversity in workplace, 211–213
    effect on communications, 210
    ethnic conflict and, 303
    global dynamics and, 303–304
    global transformations in, 210–211
    influence of, 303
    intercultural difficulties and, 303
    uncertainty reduction, 213–215
Educated class, 81
Education, 193. *See also* Teaching
    cognitive styles and, 197
    cultural background and, 194–195
    cultural dimensions of, 194–197
    functions of schools, 194–195
    intercultural classrooms and, 199–201
    learning styles and, 197
    understanding cultural differences, 199
Egan, K., 258
Egocentric bias, 49
Egyptian culture, 80
Ekman, P., 134, 312
Elaborate style, 110
Emotional display
    cultural variations in, 134
Emotional expression, norms of, 129
Empathy, 300
Engholm, C., 216
Epston, D., 260
Equality, 34
Erickson, Milton, 260
Erikson, Erick, 76
Ervin-Tripp, Susan, 115

Essed, Philomena, 116
Essence and energy, 37
Ethical communication, credo for, 294
Ethical conflict, 82, 303
    building on, 296–297
Ethical rules, 31
Ethic of care, 118
Ethics, 291
    defined, 291–292
    gift-giving as bribery, 291
    in health care, 250–252
    in intercultural communication, 293–295
    moral reasoning, 292–293
Ethnic cleansing, 74
Ethnic friendships, 320–330
Ethnic group, 75
Ethnic identity, 75–77
Ethnicity, 74–78, 321
    communication and, 182
    conceptions of, 75
    ethnic identity and, 75–76
    social allocation and, 75
    social solidarity and, 75
Ethnocentrism, 20, 43–44, 121, 137
Evaluating, 151
    tendency of, 316
Evasive responses, 115–116
Ewe, 234, 235
Expectation, 43
Experimenting, 165
Eye contact, 136, 137

Face, 168
    concept of, 123–124
    dimensions of, 124
Face concerns, 123–124
Face-negotiation theory, 127–128
Face orientations, 128
Facework, 128–129
Facial expressions, 133–134
Fackler, M., 139
Factual distraction, 153
Fadiman, Anne, 254–256
Fairness, 293
Familism, 244
Family of orientation, 242
Family of procreation, 242
Family(s), 167–169
    collectivist, 167–168
    conception of, 302
    in Confucianism, 31
    cultural differences in, 7, 19, 167, 169
    defined, 302
    and health care, 242–244
    interactional style in, 302
    in other cultures, 191, 243
    portrayed on television, 287–288
    role of, 167
    structure of, 167
Far East culture, 138
Fassihi, F., 74
Feedback, 49, 50
Feelings
    communication of, 186–187
    expression of, 129, 134
    in friendship, 328–329
Feldman, M. S., 262
Feminine cultures, 28–29, 226
Feminine identity, 73
Field dependent, 198

Field independent, 198
Fisher, Glen, 20, 53, 56–63
Fisher, W. R., 8–9, 257, 258, 262
Flores, G., 244
Footbinding, 143–147
Foregrounding, 234
Foreign accent, 85
Foreign Corrupt Practices Act (FCPA), 296
Foreigners, 106
Foreign jurisdiction, 221–230
Foreign language, 106, 107
Forney, Matt, 142–143
Foster, George M., 37
Foster, Robert J., 33–41
Fowles, J., 271
Frankel, Charles, 314, 315
French culture, 140, 210–211
Frey, L. R., 259
Fridlund, A., 134
Friends
    in American culture, 35
    in the workplace, 212
Friendship
    characterizing, 321–322
    cultural differences in, 322
    and culture, 169–170, 321–322
    defined, 320
    ethnic identity norms in, 320–330
    feelings in, 328–329
    gender identity norms in, 327
    results of research on, 323–330
    rules and norms of, 322–323, 326–327
    sex differences in, 322
Friendship maintenance, 322
Friesen, W., 134
Fudong, Han, 239
Fukuyama, Francis, 96
Fussell, P., 83, 85, 274

Gabler, Neal, 270
Galanti, Geri-Ann, 242, 245
Galvin, Kathleen, 181–191
Gardner, R. A., 260
Gates, Anita, 268
Gay masculinity, 98–101
Gay pornography, 100
Gayspeak, 98, 99
Geertz, C., 174
Gender, 73–74
    business and, 226
    culture and, 74
    and health care, 244–245
    media and, 272–276
Gender formation, 73–74
Gender identity, gay men and, 97–101
Gender roles, common, 73, 226
George, M., 241, 248, 249
Gestures, 135
Gibb, Jack, 317
Gilroy, Paul, 71, 72, 79, 90
Giordano, J., 181
Global advertising, 278
Global culture, 70–71, 270
Global economic community, dynamics
    of, 213
Global health, 239
*Globalization and Its Discontent*s
    (Stiglitz), 303
Global transformations, 210–211
Global village, 279

Gold, J. B., 258
Golden Rule, 31
Gonzalez, A., 136
Gonzalez, J., 279
Grammar, 105
  and class, 83–85
Gray, J. J., 139
Greek culture, 76
Greeley, A., 186
Greenberg, B. S., 284
Group bias, 48
Group think, 62
Gudykunst, W. B., 44, 49–50, 64, 109, 124, 138, 218, 321

Haapanen, L. W., 20
Hahn, R. A., 242
Hall, Alice, 283–289
Hall, Edward T., 7, 21, 25, 48, 136, 137, 156–157, 212, 330
Hall, J., 134
Hall, M. R., 25
Hall, Stuart, 273
Hamilton, D., 50–51
Handshake, 43
Hannerz, U., 78, 281, 307
Haptics, 138
Harper, R., 135
Harris, Jean, 154
Harris, M., 144
Harrison, Roger, 319
Hartmann, P., 284
Hawaiians, identity of, 280
Hayes, Joseph J., 98–99
Hays, R. B., 321
Healing. See Health
Health, 238
  belief systems and, 240
  global, 239
  hot-cold theories of, 248–250
Health care
  barriers to effective, 240–252
  cultural differences in, 238
  ethical issues in, 250–252
  family and, 242–244
  gender and, 244–245
  knowledge-based approach to, 241
  in other cultures, 254–256
  power relationships in, 245–246
  religion and spirituality and, 246–250
  storytelling as healing, 256–266
  U.S., 262
Health communication, 239, 241
Hearing, 150
Hecht, M. L., 114, 117, 118, 321, 322, 323, 329, 330
Hegemony, 276–277
Heider, F., 47
Helgeson, V. S., 322
Henderson, M., 322
Henley, N., 114
Hierarchical power structures, 27–28
High anxiety, 317
High-certainty avoidance culture, 28
High-context cultures, 25–26, 46, 110, 156, 212
Hill, L., 279
Hilliard, C. R., 322
Hinduism, 79, 80

Hindus, 133
Hip-hop culture, 86
Hispanic culture, 199
Hmong culture, 240, 242, 254–256
Hodgkinson, Harold, 195, 241, 278
Hoel, J. Richard, Jr., 221–230, 296–297, 298
Hoel, Rick, 209
Hoffmaster, B., 251
Hofstede, Geert H., 21, 26–29, 30, 31, 81, 82, 164, 195, 204, 207, 213–214, 218, 245
Hoijer, J., 109
Homosexual relationships, 97–101
Honesty, 293
Hope, loss of, 211
Horgan, E. S., 188
Horizontal individualism, 27
Hoskin, J., 140
Hospice, 262
Houston, Marsha, 111, 113–119
Hsu, F., 48
Hu, H. C., 123
Hudson, R. A., 84, 301
Hui, Edwin, 243
Human-heartedness, 30
Humility, 223
Humor, 185–186
Hunter, J. D., 270
Huntington, Samuel P., 70–71, 79
HURIER model, 150
Husband, G., 284
Huygens, Christiaan, 136
Hymes, D., 306

Identity, culture and, 7. See also Cultural identity
Identity-based goals, 126
Igbo culture, peacemaking in, 235–236, 305
Illness
  cultural practices to ward off, 248–249
  folk beliefs about, 250
Imaginative participation, 300
Immigrants, 76, 172, 182, 214
Independent-self individuals, 123
Indexing, 107
Indian cultures, 302, 305
Indirect style, 110
Individual, perception of, 36–37
Individual-centered language, 110–111
Individualism, 14, 36–37
Individualism/collectivism dimension, 26–27, 123, 195, 218
Individualistic cultures, 26–27, 136
Information processing, institutionalized, 61–62
Informative story condition, 260
Ingroup-outgroup perceptual boundaries, 124–125
Initiating, 165
"In spite of" thinking, 308–309
Instrumental style, 111
Integration, 30
Intensifying, 165
Interaction constructs, 45
Intercultural communication. See Communication
  business and, 216–218
  competency in. See Intercultural competence

conflict and, 126–129
context and, 7
defined, 7
economics and, 209–219
need for, 3
nonverbal, 132–141
principles and rules of, 293
stumbling blocks to, 305, 312–319
verbal, 103–112
Intercultural competence, 298–310
  competency practices, 298
  developing, 298–310
  factors influencing, 300–307
  framing an approach to, 307–310
  goal of, 319
  individual abilities and, 299–300
  local and global dimensions of, 307
  problems with ethnic friendships and, 320–330
Intercultural conflict. See Cultural conflict
Intercultural effectives, basic rules of, 310
Interdependent-self individuals, 123
International Listening Association, 160
Internet, 278–280
Interpersonal relationships, 233
Interpersonal relationship systems, 97–101
Interpreting, 151
Interracial communication, 113–119
Iranian culture, 74, 245
  personal communication in, 64–68
Irish-American families, 181–191
Ishii, S., 80
Islamic cultures, 79, 80
Isomorphic attributions, 48
Israeli culture, 11–18
Iwata, Y., 138

Jackson, Ronald, 90
James, William, 300
Jandt, F. E., 134
Janis, Irving, 62
Japanese culture, 138, 313, 316
  communication in, 46
  family in, 302
  friendship in, 322
  listening in, 149–150
  marriage in, 168–169
  social face in, 124
  values in, 21
Jensen, A., 45
Jhally, Sut, 277
Johansson, P., 273
Johnson, Ben, 83
Johnson, S., 214
Jones, D. C., 321
Jory, P., 278, 281
Justice, storytelling and, 262–263

Kammen, M., 269
Karmi, G., 299
Karmi, Ghada, G., 78
Kaufman, M., 101
Kelley, H. H., 45, 47
Kennedy, Paul, 210
Kennelly, Brendan, 185
Kerbo, H., 81, 273
Kilbourne, J., 272, 277
Kilko, B., 279

Kim, M. S., 138
Kim, Young Yun, 44, 211, 299, 317, 319
Kinesics, 135–136
King, Larry, 274
King, Martin Luther, Jr., 234
Kipling, Rudyard, 42
Kirkwood, W. G., 258, 262
Kitayama, S., 123
Kleinfield, J., 198
Klopf, D., 80
Kluckhohn, C., 34, 164
Kluckhohn, Florence R., 21, 22, 25, 33
Knapp, M., 134, 164–165
Ko, Dorothy, 144, 145
Kochman, A. T., 111
Koester, J., 134, 138
Kohlberg, L., 292–293
Kohls, L. R., 51–52
Korean culture, 48, 135, 212
Kramarae, C., 114
Kroeber, Alfred, 6
Kunta, Q., 51
Kurz, David, 11–18

La Gaipa, J. J., 324
Langer, Ellen, 51
Language
    in business, 216228–229
    communication differences in, 184–185
    and cultural identity, 83–85
    and culture, 6, 104, 108–109, 113–119
    and cyberspace, 279–280
    defined, 104–105
    effective use of, 104
    foreign, 106, 107
    individual-centered, 110–111
    knowledge of relationships in, 109
    linguistic codes in, 83
    linguistic prejudice and, 111–112
    power relationships in, 111
    pragmatics and, 107–108
    role-centered, 110–111
    role of, in cyberspace, 279–280
    semantics and, 106–107
    social context of, 306–307
    structure of, 105–106
    in translation, 104
    triangle of meaning, 104–105
    verbal and nonverbal, 6
Language differences, 315
Larsen, Chris, 280
Larson, D., 4
Latino culture, 249
Law, cultural practice of, 221–230
Learning styles, 197–198
Levy, Howard, 143
Lewis, B., 74
Lewis, R., 105, 108, 152
Lifestyle patterns, values and, 215
Limited good, image of, 37
Limits, concept of, 37
Linden, Eugene, 239
Linguistic determinism, 108
Linguistic prejudice, 84, 111–112
Linguistic relativity, 108
Lipman, D., 259
Lippi-Green, Rosina, 116
Listening, 149. *See also* Storylistening
    across cultures, 153–154

active, 151
barriers to effective, 153
cultural differences in, 225
defined, 150
effect of specific behaviors on, 157
HURIER model of, 150, 151
impact of culture on, 156, 158
intercultural, 154, 155–161
levels of, 152–153
and success in business, 151
Littlejohn, S., 48
Livo, N., 257
Long-term orientation, 31
Looking-glass theory, 76
Losing face, 168
Low-context cultures, 25, 26, 110,
    156, 212
Low intensity conflict, 126
Low-power distance cultures, 28
Luken, J., 44
Lull, J., 269, 276
Lustig, Myron W., 134, 138

McCombie, Susan, 242
McCourt, Frank, 184
McDonald, M., 251, 252
McGoldrick, M., 181, 182, 184, 187, 188
MacLennan, Janet, 203–207
McLuhan, Marshall, 279
McNamara, Robert, 60
Mandela, Nelson, 79
Maori culture, 79
Marcus, H. R., 123
Markers, 85–86
Marriage, traditional, 172–179
Martin, J. N., 320, 323
Marx, David, 270–271
Masculine culture, 28–29, 226
Masculine identity, 73
Masculinities, 98, 101
Masculinity
    factors determining, 97–101
    gay men and, 97–101
Masculinity/femininity dimension, 28–29,
    196–197, 218
Mate selection, Asian Indian, 172–179
Matrilineal societies, 168
Matrimonial advertisements, 172–179
Matsumoto, Y., 218
May, Jim, 263
Mbuti people, 232, 235
Mead, Margaret, 314
Meade, E. H., 259
Media
    advertising and, 277–278
    class in, 273
    cultural transmission and, 275–276
    gender messages in, 272–276
    movies, 270
    newspapers, 276
    norms and, 272
    popular culture, 268–271
    power and, 276–277
    race in, 274–276
    television, 270, 274, 276, 281, 283–289
Mediterranean cultures, 138
Mehrabian, A., 133
Mental distraction, 153
Merkerson, S. Epatha, 275

Merritt, B., 275
Mexican American culture, 244
Mexican culture, 250–251
Microcultures, 7
Middle-class people, 83, 85
Middle Eastern cultures, 6, 246
Mindfulness, 51
Mindlessness, 51
Mindsets, 56, 59
Moderation, 31
Monochronic time, 129, 137, 199
Montgomery, B., 170
Moore, Roy, 79, 80
Moral development, 292
Moral discipline, 30
Moral reasoning, 292–293
Morisaki, S., 124
Morris, D., 309
Morrison, Toni, 77
Motivation, 35
Movies, 270
Multicultural classroom, 199–201
Multicultural perspective, 30
Murdock, G., 309
Murdock, Rupert, 276
Muslim culture, 20, 217
Mutual-face, 124
Mutuality, 293

Narrative. *See* Storytelling
    as communication, 7–10
    in criminal defense, 263
    logic of good reasons and, 10
    and popular culture, 271
    as a therapeutic tool, 260
    truthfulness or reliability of, 9–10
Narrative logic, 257
Narrative rationality, 9–10
Narrative Therapy, 260
National Hospice Organization, 262
National Storytelling Network, 262
Native American cultures, 195, 199,
    243–244, 272, 306
Naturalistic system, 240
Nayar culture (India), 302
Near East culture, 138
Nebergall, R., 316
Negative coding, 115, 116
Negativity, 49
Negotiations
    intercultural, 218–219
    international, 228
Nelson, A., 280
Neuendorf, K. A., 284
Neuliep, J., 4, 7
Newlin, K., 248
Newspapers, 276
Nishida, T., 64, 321
Nonjudgmentalism, 293
Nonverbal communication
    categories of, 135
    characteristics of, 134
    codes of, 135–140
    functions of, 134–135
    importance of, 133
    universality of, 133–134
Nonverbal intercultural communication,
    103–112
Nonverbal misinterpretations, 315

Norms, 21, 306, 317, 323
    cultural patterns and, 20
    media and, 272
North American culture, 83, 138

Occupational class, 81
O'Connor, R., 188
Oetzel, John, 121–129
Okabe, R., 46, 110
Omae, K., 281
Open-mindedness, 293
Opoku, K., 232
Optical illusions, 58
Optimism, 36
Oral tradition, 234
Ornstein, R., 245
Ostermeier, T., 156, 157
Other-face, 124
Othus, J., 258
Outsourcing, 280

Paralanguage, 140
Paraphrasing, 49–50
Park, M., 111
Parks, M. R., 324
Passive-aggressive response, 127
Patel, K. A., 139
Paton, Alan, 93
Patriarchal societies, 73, 77, 168
Patriarchy, 73–74, 244
Patton, George S., 85–86
Pauses, 110
Peacemaking traditions, African, 231–236
Pearce, J., 187, 188
Peasant societies, 37
Pedersen, P., 212
Penfield, Joyce, 233, 235
Perception, 42
    of abstract subjects, 59
    components of, 43
    culture and, 6, 43–44
    effect of television on, 283–289
    language differences and, 62–63
    locked-in, 59
    nature of the stimulus and, 60
    personality factor in, 49
    prejudice, discrimination, and racism and, 52–53
    process of, 42–43
    and reasoning, 56–63
    of self, 36–37, 46
    social cognition and, 45–50
    stereotypes and, 50–52
    of the United States, 224
    visual, 58
    world, differences in, 35–36
Perception checking, 49, 50
Personal attributes, 47
Personal constructs, 45
Personal identity, 70, 86–87
Personalistic system, 240
Personality error, 48
Personal relationships, communication in, 64–68
Personal space, 136
    value system and, 137
    violation of, 138

Personal style, 110–111
Philipsen, G., 321
Physical characteristics, perception of, 139
Physical constructs, 45
Physiological reactions, to communication response, 318
Plain talk, 185
Plato, 223
Plurals, 106
Politics, culture and, 304
Pollack, A., 302
Polychronic time, 129, 136, 137, 199
Popular culture, 268–271
    storytelling in, 271–272
Pornography, gay, 100
Porter, R., 156, 240
Powell, R., 199
Power
    bureaucratic, 82
    hegemonic, 276
Power dimension, 164
Power distance, 27–28, 123, 128, 195, 218, 245–246
Power relationships
    in health care, 245–246
    in language, 111
Preconceptions, 315–316. *See also* Stereotypes
Prejudice, 52–53
    linguistic, 84, 111–112
    stereotypes and, 305
Premature closure, 49
Presentational style, 217–218
Prestige, 234
Privacy, 137, 183, 302
Progress, concept of, 35–36
Projection theory, 60–61
Property, and class, 82
Propriety, 183
Proverb, in West Africa, 233–234
Proxemics, 136–138
Psychological constructs, 45

Quasilogical style, 217

Racial identity, 90
Racism, 53
Rahim, M. A., 127
Ramsey, S., 135
Rape, 91
Ratanakul, P., 251
Rawlins, W. K., 170
Reasoning, perception and, 56–63
Redundancy, feelings of, 211
Regulative rules, 108
Relational conflict goals, 125–126
Relationship management, 230
Relationships
    basic, 31
    business, 216–218
    cultivating, 298
    cultivating foreign, 222–223
    defined, 163–164
    developmental models of, 164–167
    development of, 164–167
    dialectical tensions in, 170

documenting, 298
    families, 167–169
    friends, 169–170
    homosexual, 97–101
    interpersonal, 233
    labeling, 46
    parameters in, 125
    personal, 64–68
    universal dimensions of, 164
Religion, 79–80
    defined, 79
    diversity of, 305–306
    and health care, 246–250
    and identity, 188
    impact on health, 247
Religious fundamentalism, 214
Remembering, 150
Respect, 294
Responding, 151
Rheingold, Harold, 279
Ribeau, S., 114, 117, 118, 321, 322, 329, 330
Rietz, S., 257
Role-centered language, 110–111
Role constructs, 45
Rootedness, 302
Ross, M., 232
Rowland, D., 216
Rozhon, Tracie, 86
Rules, 272
    principles and, 294
Ryali, R., 173

Sadri, Golnaz, 53, 64–68
Salience, 76–77
Samovar, L., 156, 194, 240
Sapir, Edward, 108
Sapir-Whorf hypothesis, 6, 63, 108, 109
Saran, P., 173
Saudia Arabian culture, 74
Schultz, W., 163
Seagrave, Sterling, 145
Self
    knowledge of, 300–301
    perception of, 36–37, 123
    value of, 27
Self-construals, 128
Self-disclosure, 163–164
Self-expression, 34
Self-face, 124, 128
Self-fulfilling prophecy, 45–46, 50
Self-image, 76
Self-monitoring, 46
Self-perception, 46
Selye, H., 318
Selznick, P., 301
Semantic distractions, 153
Sentence order, 105
Severe Acute respiratory syndrome (SARS), 239
Sex, communication about, 187–188
Shahar, Lucy, 11–18
Shamanism, 255
Shaver, P., 322
Sherif, C. W., 316
Sherif, W., 316
Sherman-Williams, B., 51

Shimizu, M., 322
Shioiri, T., 134
Short, J. A., 49
Short-term orientation, 31
Shuter, Rober, 295
Shweder, R. A., 305
Silences, in conversation, 110, 306
Simonds, C. J., 151, 153, 199
Singer, M., 42
Sitaram, K. S., 20
Smiles, 135
Smith, C. S., 303
Smith, H., 79
Smitherman, Geneva, 21, 117
Social class. *See* Class
Social cognition, perception and, 45–50
Social construction, 73
Social conventions, 34–35
Social relationships, 34–35
Sociocultural roots, 302
Song, Young-Bae, 281
Sorensen, Gail, 200
Sorrentino, R. M., 49
South African culture, 89–96
Southeast Asian culture, 138, 249
Space
    aspects of, 37
    cultural rules for use of, 137
    personal, 136–138
Spaces in Between, The (Cooper), 163
Speaking perspectives, 114
Spector, R. E., 247
Speech acts, 107
Speicher, B. L., 152
Speight, George, 82
Spender, D., 111
Spiritual Caregivers Association, 262
Spirituality
    concept of, 247
    and health, 246–250
Spitzberg, B., 323
Stallings, F., 259
Starosta, W. J., 152, 292, 293
Stereotypes, 50–52
    individual and social, 50
    of other cultures, 315–316
    and prejudices, 305
    as self-fulfilling prophecies, 50
Stewart, Edward C., 33–41, 134, 137, 315
Stiglitz, Joseph E., 82, 303
Stone, Richard, 261
Story consultation, 263
Story listener, 263–264
Storylistening
    communication effects of, 257–263
    health benefits of, 260
    in hospice work, 261
Storytellers, 9
Storytelling
    as communication, 256–266
    in the courts, 262–263
    healing powers of, 256–266
    oral, 257, 258–259
    in popular culture, 271–272
    search for community in, 258–259
    theoretical explanation for effects
        of, 258

Stress, 317, 318
    workplace, 211
Strodtbeck, F., 21, 22, 25, 164
Subordinate behaviors, 164
Succinct style, 110
Summer, W. G., 43
Sunwolf, 256–266
Superordination-subordination behaviors,
    164
Swarns, R. L., 94
Syntax, 105
Systems, characteristics of, 6

Tano, D. V., 86
Taylor, Charles, 76, 77, 90
Taylor, D., 165
Taylor, S. E., 260
Teaching
    in another culture, 193, 203–207, 209
    universal enjoyment of, 207
    variety of methods of, 200
Technology, 139
    culture and the internet, 278–280
    flow of information and, 280–281
    international dimensions of, 280–281
    in remote areas, 268
Television, 270, 274–275, 281
    audience reliance on, 283–289
    effect on viewer perceptions, 283–289
    as information source, 283–289
    people and class and, 274
    typicality of, 283–289
Terminally ill people, 260–261
Territorialism, 37, 136
Thai culture, 20, 138, 140, 247
Thomas, B., 147
Thomas, Jack E., 89–96
Thomlison, T. D., 156
Thompson, Leonard, 92, 95
Thurow, Lester C., 214
Time
    concepts of, 36–37, 129, 225
    view of, 21
Ting-Toomey, Stella, 109, 121–129, 138
Toffler, Alvin, 210
Touching behavior, 138
Tran, H. T., 258
Trenholm, S., 45
Triandis, H. C., 27, 48, 123, 124, 129, 164
Triangle of meaning, 104–105
Trompenaars, Fons, 218
Trudgill, P., 83, 84
Trujillo, Mary Adams, 231–236
Trust/distrust dimension, 125
Tsujimura, A., 46
Tuan, Y.-F., 78–79, 304

Uncertainty avoidance, 28, 196, 214, 218
Uncertainty reduction, 213–215
Understanding, 150
Understatement, 110
Universalism/particularism dimension, 218
Universalistic cultures, 218
Ursin, H., 318

Values
    and culture, 20, 21, 33

level of, 33
and lifestyle patterns, 215
threatened, 214
van Dijk, T. A., 52, 53, 111, 275
Van Doren, C., 72
Vangelisti, A., 164–165
Verbal communication styles, 109–111
Verbal intercultural communication, 103
    frustration of, 103–104, 112
Vertical individualism, 27
Viadero, Debra, 194
Vickers, J., 147
Vietnamese culture, 228
Virtue, expressions of, 211
Visual perception, 58
Vocal characteristics, 140
Vocal qualifiers, 140
von Franz, M.-L., 260

Walker-Moffat, Wendy, 255
Warschauer, Mark, 279–280
We and They (Kipling), 42
Webster, L. G., 263
Weimann, G., 284
Weinberg, Martin S., 99
West African culture, 231–236
Western canon, 77
Western culture, 111, 135, 313
White, M., 260
Whorf, Benjamin Lee, 63, 108
Whorfian hypothesis. *See* Sapri-Whorf
    hypothesis
Willem, Jean-Pierre, 255
Williamson, Judith, 277
Witherell, C. S., 258
Wolvin, A. D., 151, 156
Women
    African American, 113–119
    clothing of, 139
    communication among, 113–119
    equal rights for, 217
    in other cultures, 74, 139, 226, 245
    in the United States, 77
Wood, J. T., 73
Word meaning, 106
Work, team-based model of, 216
Workforce, multicultural, 212
Working class, 81
Workplace, 211
    diversity in, 211–213
Worldview, 218, 305

Xi, Changsheng, 164

Yeh, C.-H., 247
Yin and Yang concept, 248–249
Yoon, Y., 64
Yoruba people, 235
Yousef, F., 302
Yugoslavia, 74
Yum, J. O., 48, 167

Zandpour, Fred, 53, 64–68
Zarembo, A., 136
Zimbardo, P., 136
Zulus, 108, 308